D0916157

"an outstanding piece of work."
—Charles Dallara, The Institute of International Finance

"absolutely remarkable, well-informed and documented, balanced and extremely clear in its findings."
—Jacques de Larosière, European Bank for Reconstruction and Development

"It is truly amazing how Cline has managed to digest and explain clearly a vast amount of material."
—W. Max Corden, Johns Hopkins University

"This book will be the definitive work on the debt crisis."
—Paul Volcker, former Chairman, Federal Reserve Board

WILLIAM R. CLINE

International Debt
Reexamined

Institute for International Economics
Washington, DC
February 1995

William R. Cline, *Senior Fellow*, was formerly a Senior Fellow at the Brookings Institution (1973–81); Deputy Director for Development and Trade Research at the US Treasury (1971–73); Ford Foundation Visiting Professor in Brazil (1970–71) and Assistant Professor at Princeton University (1967–70). He is the author of 20 books including *The Economics of Global Warming* (1992), *The Future of World Trade in Textiles and Apparel* (revised edition 1990), *United States External Adjustment and the World Economy* (1989), *International Debt: Systemic Risk and Policy Response* (1984), *Trade Policy in the 1980s* (1984), *World Inflation and the Developing Countries* (1981), and *Trade Negotiations in the Tokyo Round* (1978).

INSTITUTE FOR INTERNATIONAL ECONOMICS
11 Dupont Circle, NW
Washington, DC 20036–1207
(202) 328–9000 FAX: (202) 328–0900

C. Fred Bergsten, *Director*
Christine F. Lowry, Director of Publications

Typesetting by BG Composition
Printing by Automated Graphic Systems

Printed in the United States of America
97 96 95   5 4 3 2 1

Library of Congress Cataloging-in-Publication Data

Cline, William R.
  International debt reexamined / William R. Cline.
    p. cm.
  Includes bibliographical references and index.

  1. Debts, External—Developing countries. 2. Debt relief—Developing countries. I. Title. II. Series.
HJ8899.C55   1994
336.3′435′091724—dc20   93-2926
                                               CIP

ISBN 0-88132-083-8

Marketed and Distributed outside the USA and Canada by Longman Group UK Limited, London

The views expressed in this publication are those of the author. This publication is part of the overall program of the Institute, as endorsed by its Board of Directors, but does not necessarily reflect the views of individual members of the Board or the Advisory Committee.

Contents

Preface   **xi**

Acknowledgments   **xv**

1 Overview   **1**

Lessons from the Debt Crisis   1
Trends in the Debt Burden   4
Debt Forecasts in Retrospect   7
Debt Theory   10
The International Debt Strategy   14
Latin American Experience   21
Russia and Eastern Europe   26
Capital Markets in the 1990s   29
Institutional Change   34

2 Vital Signs for the Debt Strategy   **39**

Debt Indicators   39
Economic Growth and Inflation   57
Key Debtors   60
Trends for Other Country Groups   68
Bank Vulnerability   70
Overview   77

3 A Decomposition Analysis of Debt Forecasts in the 1980s   **89**

Introduction   89
The Model   89
The Emerging Debate   91
Decomposition Method   101
Actual versus Expected International Environment   101
Scenario Error   104

Model Error 109
Alternative Reviews of the Forecasts 122
Overview and Policy Implications 124
Annex 3A Decomposition of Forecast Error 127
Annex 3B The Impact of World Disinflation on
     Creditworthiness 133

4 Debt Theory: A Critical Review of Literature 139
The Theory of Sovereign Lending 139
Debt Capacity Projection Models 147
The Internal Transfer Problem 152
The Economics of Debt Forgiveness 157
Evidence on Investment Disincentives 182
An Alternative View: Risk-Compensated Forgiveness 183
The Buyback Controversy 187
Historical Lessons 193
Conclusion 201

5 Evolution and Evaluation of the Debt Strategy 203
Evolution of the Strategy 205
Intellectual Evolution 222
Brady Agreements, 1990–94 231
Evaluating Brady Plan Results 243
Catalytic Debt Relief: A Political-Economic Model 250
The Debt Strategy Overall 253
Implications for Future Policy 268

6 Economic Adjustment and Debt Strategy in Latin America 275
Introduction 275
Colombia 277
Chile 284
Mexico 292
Venezuela 302
Argentina 309
Brazil 319
Peru 329
Lessons from the Latin American Experience 335
Conclusion 343

**7 Debt Problems in the 1990s: Russia, Eastern Europe, and
  Sub-Saharan Africa 345**
Russia 346
Eastern Europe 360
Sub-Saharan Africa 367
Annex 7A Reestimating Russia's Exports 402
Annex 7B A Debt Simulation Model for Africa 407

8 Capital Markets in the 1990s   **423**

Introduction   423
The Capital Market Resurgence   424
Changing Composition of Capital Flows   430
Repatriation of Flight Capital   438
Institutional Investors   448
International Bond Market   449
Sustainability   457
An Embarrassment of Riches? Moderating Inflows   465
Geographical Concentration   470
A Future Debt Crisis?   472
New Institutions?   482
Conclusion   485
Annex 8A   Costs of an International Bondholders
            Insurance Corporation   488

9 Epilogue: The Mexican Peso Crisis of December 1994   **495**

References   **507**

Index   **523**

Tables

2.1   Gross external debt, 1982–93   40
2.2   Gross external debt—deflated, 1982–93   44
2.3   Net external debt/exports of goods and services, 1982–93   46
2.4   Net external debt/GNP, 1982–93   48
2.5   Net interest payments/exports of goods and services, 1982–93   52
2.6   Central government fiscal balances, 1982–92   56
2.7   Real GDP growth rate, 1982–93   58
2.8   Commercial bank claims on developing countries, 1982–93   61
2.9   Total long-term claims of commercial banks, 1982–92   62
2.10   Exposure of US banks relative to capital, 1982–92   72
2.11   Exposure of nine largest US banks relative to capital, 1982–92   74
2.12   Exposure of UK banks relative to capital, 1982–91   78
2.13   Exposure of German banks relative to capital, 1982–92   80
2.14   Exposure of French banks relative to capital, 1982–92   82
2.15   Commercial debt of big four debtors, 1982–91   84
3.1   Debt forecasts versus actual outcomes: oil importers and
      exporters, 1983–87   97
3.2   Debt forecasts versus actual outcomes: Argentina, Brazil, Mexico,
      Venezuela, 1983–87   99
3.3   Variable assumptions and outcomes, 1983–87   102

3.4	Projection accuracy as of 1987	106
3.5	Estimated capital flight, 1984–87	112
3.6	Actual versus backcast dollar export price changes	115
3.7	Trade price regression estimates	117
3.8	Alternative export elasticities	121
3.9	Net direct investment, 1984–87	124
3b.1	Illustrative impact of lower inflation and interest rates	136
5.1	Long-term debt of Baker-17 countries to commercial banks and official lenders, 1970 and 1982–88	211
5.2	Non-oil commodity exports of Baker-17 countries, 1979–81 and 1987–89	231
5.3	Brady Plan agreements, 1989–94	234
5.4	Severely indebted middle-income countries without Brady agreements	242
5.5	Bond market reentry after 1930s defaults	254
5.6	Selected Brady Plan enhancements	264
6.1	Economic indicators for Columbia, 1982–93	278
6.2	Economic indicators for Chile, 1982–93	285
6.3	Economic indicators for Mexico, 1982–93	293
6.4	Economic indicators for Venezuela, 1982–93	303
6.5	Economic indicators for Argentina, 1982–93	310
6.6	Economic indicators for Brazil, 1982–93	320
6.7	Economic indicators for Peru, 1982–93	330
6.8	Debt strategy and economic performance in Latin America	337
7.1	FSU exports to non-FSU markets	347
7.2	Russia: alternative debt strategies	356
7.3	Debt indicators for Eastern Europe, 1992	364
7.4	Debt indicators for sub-Saharan Africa	370
7.5	Indicators of debt dynamics in Latin America and sub-Saharan Africa	378
7.6	Baseline run: sub-Saharan Africa	381
7.7	Impact of alternative policies on African debt, 1993 and 1997	386
7a.1	FSU exports according to IMF, 1986–92	403
7b.1	Africa debt projection model parameters	410
7b.2	Baseline run: Sudasombis, 1992–97	411
7b.3	Baseline run: Mozagascaire, 1992–97	413
7b.4	Baseline run: Congethivoire, 1992–97	415
7b.5	Baseline run: Nigeria, 1992–97	417
7b.6	Baseline run: Kentzamgola, 1992–97	419
7b.7	Baseline run: Senguinali, 1992–97	421
8.1	Current accounts and capital flows: developing countries, 1980–93	425
8.2	Private capital flows to Latin America and Asia: selected categories, 1989–93	431

8.3	Composition of net capital flows to seven Latin American countries, 1981–92	434
8.4	Stock of flight capital abroad, 1977–91	442
8.5	Private foreign and domestic assets, 1992	445
8.6	Predicted repatriation of flight capital	447
8.7	Capital inflows and fiscal deficits in Argentina, Brazil, Mexico, and Venezuela, 1980–92	452
8.8	International bond issues by major debtor countries, 1989–93	454
8.9	Developing country bond spreads: regression estimates	456
8.10	Exposure of debtor countries to interest fluctuation	474
8a.1	Cumulative sinking fund value of an International Bondholders Insurance Corporation	491

Figures

2.1	17 heavily indebted countries, 1982–93	51
2.2	Secondary market value, 1989(Q4)–1994(Q2)	55
2.3	Argentina: debt indicators, 1982–93	64
2.4	Brazil: debt indicators, 1982–93	65
2.5	Mexico: debt indicators, 1982–93	66
2.6	Venezuela: debt indicators, 1982–93	67
2.7	Low income countries: debt indicators, 1982–93	69
2.8	Middle income countries: debt indicators, 1982–93	70
2.9	Eastern Europe: debt indicators, 1982–93	71
2.10	Debt breakdown of 33 countries by net debt/exports, 1982–93	86
2.11	Debt breakdown of 33 countries by net debt/GNP, 1982–93	87
2.12	Debt breakdown of 33 countries by net interest payments/exports, 1982–93	88
4.1	The debt-relief Laffer curve	163
4.2	Debt and investment incentive	169
4.3	Market-oriented debt reduction	184
4.4	Expected value and face value of debt by bank group	186
4.5	Impact of buybacks	190
5.1	Alternative estimates of private bank and official-sector debt of Baker-15	229
5.2	Brady agreements and net capital flows	249
5.3	Country policy, luck, and need for debt forgiveness	257
6.1	Real per capita GDP, four largest debtors	276
6.2	Real per capita GDP, three intermediate debtors	277
6.3	Consumer price path, intermediate inflation countries	279
6.4	Consumer price path, high inflation countries	280
6.5	Mexico: average rates on 3–month Treasury bills	299
6.6	Mexico: nonoil trade and real exchange rates	301
6.7	Brazil: monthly inflation, July 1985–January 1993	321
6.8	Primary fiscal balances, 1981–91	336
8.1	Capital inflows, Latin America and Asia	427

8.2	Stockmarket nominal dollar index	428
8.3	Current account, Latin America and Asia	429
8.4	Capital flow decomposition, Western Hemisphere	432
8.5	Capital flow decomposition, Asia	433
8.6	Current account/XGNFS, four Latin American countries	458
8.7	Fiscal deficit and capital inflow, four Latin American countries	460
8.8	CA/XGS five-year moving average, five OECD countries	462
8.9	CA/XGS five-year moving average, four Asian countries	462

Preface

The Third World debt crisis was one of the most dramatic and significant global economic events in history. It threatened the stability of the world financial system and plunged most of Latin America, and some other parts of the world, into a "lost decade" for economic growth. Its long-term ramifications, including on economic policy in the debtor countries and on the proclivity of banks to lend abroad, will be profound.

Scores if not hundreds of interpretations of the crisis are thus bound to appear over the decades ahead. This volume attempts the first complete analysis of that type. It does so in full recognition of the risk of drawing lessons from such a tumultuous period so soon, but also in the view that an early appraisal—while memories of the events are still fresh—could be uniquely valuable.

No one is more qualified to prepare such a review and appraisal than William R. Cline. Dr. Cline's initial studies of the crisis, published by the Institute in 1983–85, were the first comprehensive analyses of the problem with accompanying recommendations for policy responses by all the key parties. Professor Paul Krugman characterized Cline's pioneering work as "a remarkable achievement, and the best single thing written on the debt crisis" (*Journal of International Economics*, May 1986). The Institute is thus delighted to publish Dr. Cline's review of the entire period and the lessons that he believes it offers for the future.

The Institute for International Economics is a private nonprofit institution for the study and discussion of international economic policy. Its purpose is to analyze important issues in that area and to develop and communicate practical new approaches for dealing with them. The Institute is completely nonpartisan.

The Institute is funded largely by philanthropic foundations. Major institutional grants are now being received from the German Marshall Fund of the United States, which created the Institute with a generous commitment of funds in 1981, and from the Ford Foundation, the William M. Keck, Jr. Foundation, the Korea Foundation, the C. V. Starr Foundation, and the United States–Japan Foundation. A number of other foundations and private corporations also contribute to the highly diversified financial resources of the Institute. About 12 percent of the Institute's resources in our latest fiscal year were provided by contributors outside the United States, including about 5 percent from Japan. This project was partly supported under a program grant from the Andrew Mellon Foundation.

The Board of Directors bears overall responsibility for the Institute and gives general guidance and approval to its research program—including identification of topics that are likely to become important to international economic policymakers over the medium run (generally, one to three years), and which thus should be addressed by the Institute. The Director, working closely with the staff and outside Advisory Committee, is responsible for the development of particular projects and makes the final decision to publish an individual study.

The Institute hopes that its studies and other activities will contribute to building a stronger foundation for international economic policy around the world. We invite readers of these publications to let us know how they think we can best accomplish this objective.

C. FRED BERGSTEN
Director
January 1995

Acknowledgments

I am grateful to the following people for comments on all or parts of an earlier draft of this book: C. Fred Bergsten, Lawrence J. Brainard, Mary Chaves, Richard N. Cooper, W. Max Corden, Charles H. Dallara, Jacques de Larosière, Rudiger Dornbusch, Barry Eichengreen, Jeffrey A. Frankel, Morris Goldstein, Mitchell Hedstrom, Ronald Johannes, Paul McGonagle, David C. Mulford, Ognian Pishev, William R. Rhodes, Sergei Shatalov, Ernest Stern, Brian C. Stuart, Edwin M. Truman, Paul A. Volcker, and John Williamson; as well as participants in study group meetings in Washington on 15 June 1994 and 8 November 1993. None of these individuals should be held responsible for remaining limitations of the study. This book would have been impossible without the massive, inspired, and painstaking research assistance of Chang-Tai Hsieh and Albert Y. Kim.

1

Overview

This study of the debt crisis of the 1980s and early 1990s has two objectives. The first is to provide a comprehensive analytical account of one of the most traumatic international financial disturbances of this century. The second is to derive lessons for international debt policy and development strategy in the rest of the 1990s and beyond. This chapter summarizes the principal findings.[1]

Lessons from the Debt Crisis

More than a dozen years after the outbreak of the Latin American debt crisis, at least a dozen salient policy lessons have emerged from the experience, as developed in this study.

Contingent, Evolutionary, and Informed International Policymaking Succeeded

This study judges the overall international debt strategy a success. Each of the distinct phases of the strategy represented a sensible approach in view of the circumstances at the time. The strategy successfully avoided an international financial collapse despite initial vulnerability of the banking system. Most debtors had regained access to capital markets within a decade, whereas this process had required 40 years after the

---

1. As this study went to press, Mexico entered an exchange rate crisis, discussed in the epilogue to this book. Despite casting a temporary shadow on emerging markets, the crisis seemed unlikely to alter the central findings of this study.

defaults of the 1930s (and some 25 years even if time out is taken for World War II and its aftermath). Critiques contending that the collapse in debtor country growth could have been averted by an earlier shift to the Brady Plan's emphasis on debt forgiveness are questionable. Overall, the experience suggests that contingent international policy strategy, informed by the best possible analytical work at each stage and subject to fundamental change based on evolving experience and new information, can contribute vitally to systemic stability and long-term functioning of capital markets.

Solvency Begins at Home

Although global shocks (such as high interest rates and world recession in the early 1980s) can precipitate an international crisis, sound domestic economic policies can minimize a country's susceptibility to, and are the only sure basis for a country's emergence from, such crises. Achieving proper policies may require structural reform. Sweeping structural change in such areas as trade liberalization and privatization characterized the eventually successful responses within Latin America to the debt crisis.

Fiscal Balance Is Paramount

Domestic fiscal balance is the single most important policy requirement for minimizing the risk of external debt difficulties. Large fiscal deficits contribute to a resource gap that translates into an external deficit and debt buildup in the absence of unusually high domestic saving rates. Fiscal deficits intensify a debt crisis by adding an internal transfer problem (mobilizing resources from the private sector for transfer to the public sector) to the external transfer problem (raising export revenue to service foreign debt). Fiscal imbalance contributes to inflation, and with chronically high inflation or even hyperinflation, the climate is hostile for investment and growth. Without growth, the political sustainability of external debt servicing is eroded.

Pursue an Open Economic Model and Realistic Exchange Rates for Export Growth

The countries (including several in Asia) that most successfully avoided the ravages of the international debt crisis were those that maintained persistent growth in exports, the economic base for servicing external debt. Two factors are central for sustained export growth: an open or outward-oriented economy and a realistic exchange rate. Inward orientation behind high protection discourages exports by instilling a bias for production for the domestic market rather than the world market. Over-valued exchange rates penalize exports and subsidize imports.

Cooperative, Market-Oriented Solutions Work Best

When debt workouts are necessary, the greatest possible adherence to market orientation and at least quasi-voluntary rather than mandatory design is important in facilitating subsequent access to capital markets, even though the principal sources of capital in the aftermath may be different from those in the crisis. Unilateral defaults, debtor cartels, and other confrontational strategies can be counterproductive for debtors.

Do Not Socialize Private Debt

Governments of borrowing countries should make it clear to private-sector nationals and foreign creditors that the government will not assume responsibility for the real domestic burden of private debt. Where governments took over the burden of private debt, they tended to add an internal transfer problem to the external transfer problem.

Avoid Capital Flight

The record shows far more severe difficulties with external debt in Latin America than would have been expected based solely on current account gaps. A deep layer of additional debt burdens came from private capital flight, involving the conversion of domestic currency into foreign exchange financed by rising government external debt. Realistic domestic interest rates and exchange rates and political stability are the best assurances against capital flight.

Keep External Deficits Moderate Regardless of Source

Governments of developing countries should have clear objectives for prudent levels of external deficits. Where these deficits stem primarily from financing fiscal deficits, these ceiling levels should be lower. Even where fiscal accounts are in balance, however, policy should seek to limit external current account deficits to levels consistent with medium-term sustainability. That the external finance is going to private rather than public uses is no guarantee against wrenching disruptions if there is an abrupt cutoff in capital inflows.

Politics and Psychology Frequently Dominate Economics

Developed-country governments and private-sector creditors should keep in mind that potential debt conflicts inescapably involve political as well as technical economic dimensions. Creditors should take this fact into account when lending to countries with populist domestic political conditions. The psychological and political influences also mean that the benefits of a negotiated workout along Brady Plan lines can be larger than might be expected based solely on the size of debt forgiveness.

Adjust to Reality but Avoid Self-fulfilling Prophecy of Defeat

Creditors should recognize that when objective circumstances change sharply (e.g., because of a collapse in the price of oil), revision of the original terms of the credit may be necessary, including possible reduction of its net present value. They should build this possibility into their lending spread, before such an event, and be prepared to cooperate with other creditors in joint action to deal with such an eventuality if it occurs. Additionally or alternatively, they should pursue instruments that incorporate risk sharing with the debtor. At the same time, it would be incorrect to conclude from the experience of the 1980s that the initial phases of the debt strategy, premised on relending rather than debt forgiveness, were naively overoptimistic. Thus, with the benefit of hindsight it would have been a historical mistake to assume in 1983 that such countries as South Korea, Colombia, and Chile would need to have a significant portion of their debt forgiven.

Intellectual Debate Matters

The intense analytical debate within academic and policy circles played a major role in shaping the evolving debt strategy.

Responsible Policies in Industrial Countries Matter for Developing-Country Debt

Historically high real interest rates were a hallmark of the outbreak and early phases of the debt crisis, as were other distortions such as an overvalued dollar. Policy disequilibria in industrial countries (and in particular, the unusual US policy mix of tight money and loose fiscal policy under Reaganomics in the early 1980s) contributed to these international economic pressures and helped cause and prolong the debt crisis.

Trends in the Debt Burden

These lessons derive from the interpretation of the debt crisis set forth in the chapters that follow. The point of departure for this analysis is an empirical review in chapter 2 of trends in debt indicators.

Already by 1992, one decade after the onset of the crisis with Mexico's temporary suspension of principal payments in August 1982, the dominant emerging view was that the debt crisis was over. The debt burden data reviewed in chapter 2, and even more dramatically the capital inflow data considered in chapter 8, suggest that at least for the countries (primarily in Latin America) that were at the center of the 1980s crisis, this view was correct. The analysis of chapter 2 focuses on 17 highly indebted countries (designated HD17) identified under the 1985 Baker Plan, as illustrative of the outcome for the countries considered to be at the core of the 1980s crisis.

The ideal pattern for resolution of the problem would have been slow growth in nominal debt, even slower growth or actual decline in interest obligations, and rapid growth in GDP and exports, with the consequence of a steadily declining relative debt burden. Instead, in a first phase from 1982 to 1987 the debt of the HD17 rose by 35 percent in nominal dollar terms, while the dollar value of exports rose by only 2 percent (chapter 2, table 2.1; IMF 1992a). The ratio of net debt to exports of goods and nonfactor services rose from 290 percent in 1982 to a peak of 384 percent in 1986, to an important degree as the consequence of the collapse in oil prices and the export base of key debtors such as Mexico and Venezuela. The rise in the debt/exports ratio ran counter to the initial strategy of growing out of the problem, although more consistently with that strategy the drop in world interest rates permitted a decline in the interest/exports ratio from 30 percent in 1982 to a plateau of 25 percent by the mid-1980s.

In a second phase, in 1988–89, debt fell, and it then rose modestly to stand only about 9 percent above the 1987 level by 1993. By implication, for the full period 1982–93 new borrowing covered about one-third of interest due on the original debt, not far from the fraction originally envisioned in the approach of concerted lending of new money. Because there was some new borrowing by the early 1990s and because eligible long-term bank debt was only about half of total debt, Brady Plan reductions primarily served to arrest the growth of debt rather than lower it substantially. Market-based debt reduction through debt-equity conversion and buybacks also helped limit debt buildup after 1987.

On the strength of a 70 percent increase in exports from their 1986 trough, by 1993 the debt/exports ratio for the HD17 group was down to 225 percent, nearing the threshold of 200 percent for gross debt/exports often considered indicative of creditworthiness. There were corresponding but even wider swings in the ratio of net debt to GNP, with changes in real exchange rates amplifying the underlying shifts in the debt/exports ratio. Net debt relative to GNP peaked at 67 percent in 1987 and by 1993 had fallen to 42 percent.

Conceptually the best measure of the debt burden is the ratio of net interest (on an accrual basis) to exports of goods and services, which fell to 11 percent by 1992–93, or less than two-fifths its level at the outset of the crisis. Secondary market prices for bank debt provide another gauge of creditworthiness. They fell sharply from 1986 to 1987–88 following the 1987 Brazilian moratorium and the setting aside of large loan-loss reserves by the banks (chapter 5), but they were up again strongly by 1990 for Mexico and Venezuela and by 1991 for Argentina and Brazil.

In sum, by 1993 the debt indicators uniformly showed marked improvement to more normal, sustainable levels for the HD17, and most of the improvement was already in place by 1991. For a wider sample of 33 developing countries representing six-sevenths of all LDC debt, there was similar improvement. Applying a threshold of 15 percent for the ratio of net interest to exports of goods and services, countries accounting for 60 percent of total external debt of this group were in debt difficulty in 1982–88, but the fraction was down to 27 percent by 1991 and 17 percent by 1993.

Indicators of domestic economic performance similarly showed deterioration in the mid-1980s but major improvement by the early 1990s. For Latin America, the primary locus of the debt crisis, real economic growth fell from an average of 6.2 percent in 1967–81 to −2 percent in 1982–83. After an interim recovery to 3.5 percent growth in 1984–87, the rate fell again to 0.6 percent in 1988–90, a relapse that contributed to the change in the international strategy to debt reduction under the 1989 Brady Plan. By 1991–93, growth had rebounded to 3.3 percent. Similarly, average inflation reached crisis levels of 800 to 1,200 percent for Latin America in 1988–90, but fell dramatically (if Brazil is excluded) to 22 percent in 1991, 19 percent in 1992, and even lower in 1993.[2]

By the early 1990s the principal locus of the debt problem had shifted to Africa and the economies in transition. Trends in these regions are reviewed briefly in chapter 2, and more complete analysis is presented in chapter 7 (summarized below).

At the outset of the debt crisis, the international banking and financial systems were in real jeopardy because of the high exposure of leading banks to countries caught up in the crisis. For the nine largest US banks, exposure to the HD17 countries stood at 194 percent of capital and reserves in 1982, so that definitive default on this debt could have provoked bankruptcy at the heart of the industrial country banking system. By 1992 this ratio was down to 51 percent, as the consequence of a more than doubling in the bank's capital base (partly attributable to the setting aside of large loan-loss reserves by 1987 and after), some charging off of claims, and buybacks and debt-equity conversions. In contrast, as late as 1986 a forgiveness of half of claims on the HD17 would have eliminated two-thirds of the capital of the nine largest US banks, casting

---

2. IMF 1993f, 139; 1990b, 112; ECLAC 1993.

doubt on the feasibility of much earlier and deeper debt forgiveness than that which eventuated in the debt strategy.

Debt Forecasts in Retrospect

Early in the debt crisis, projections in Cline (1983, 1984) suggested that it should be possible for debtor countries to grow their way out of the debt crisis by increasing exports. The projections were reportedly influential at the time (e.g., see Krugman 1994). Although they proved qualitatively correct for a number of the countries included (such as Chile, South Korea, and Turkey), the projections turned out to be too optimistic for the large Latin American debtors. Chapter 3 attempts to see where the forecasts went wrong, and where they went right.

The point of departure of the early analysis was that the debt crisis had occurred in exceptionally unfavorable world economic conditions, during the worst global recession since the 1930s and in the face of extremely high interest rates. It was reasonable to expect that a return to a more normal world economic environment might provide the right conditions for problem debtor countries to return to creditworthiness.

The analysis used to test this hypothesis was a set of projections of the trade and debt of 19 major debtors considered vulnerable to the debt crisis at the time. The projection model related the volume of each debtor country's exports to industrial country growth (demand volume) and the debtor's real exchange rate (price incentive). Import volumes were a function of domestic growth and the real exchange rate. Dollar prices of traded goods depended on world inflation and the strength of the dollar (weaker dollar, higher dollar price to maintain real values). Export prices also incorporated a cyclical response of commodity prices to industrial country recovery. Oil imports and exports depended on hypothesized oil prices, and although the analysis expected no major change, it warned that a large reduction in oil prices could undermine debt recovery because of the greater dependence of oil-exporting debtors on oil exports than of oil-importing debtors on oil imports.

The central projection indicated that over the period 1983 to 1987, the debt/exports ratio should decline from about 200 percent to about 140 percent for the 19 countries, with the greatest decline being shown by the oil-importing countries. This projection formed the basis for judging the debt crisis to be one of illiquidity requiring transitional lending, rather than insolvency requiring bankruptcy-like forgiveness. The former strategy seemed to hold the promise of much earlier reentry of debtors into world capital markets, and far less risk for the banking system.

Subsequent projections at the International Monetary Fund (IMF) and elsewhere reached similar conclusions, and the solvency diagnosis remained the paradigm of the debt strategy until the Brady Plan for debt reduction in 1989. One important lesson of this process is that there was a systematic and informed attempt of the international financial community to apply rigorous analysis to develop the proper policy response to this historic crisis, an encouraging fact whether or not the resulting interim diagnosis proved ultimately valid.

Several contemporary critics judged the projections' assumptions about the world economy to be too optimistic, but global recovery actually performed as assumed. Closer to the mark were skepticism that commodity prices would rebound as projected, the somewhat later critique that the internal fiscal transfer problem to service debt could be more of a problem than the external transfer problem examined using balance of payments projections, and the critique that restored capacity to service debt might not necessarily translate into restored willingness to do so.

Chapter 3 compares actual outcomes with the original projections for the period 1984–87. The nominal dollar values of both exports and imports were much lower than forecast. A central reason was that world inflation in the period averaged less than 1 percent annually (wholesale prices), whereas the forecast had anticipated rates of nearly 6 percent. One result was that the dollar export base of the debt/exports ratio was much lower than expected. Another was that, because interest rates did not fall as much as inflation, the rise in the real interest rate left the debt burden higher than predicted.

The analysis in chapter 3 distinguishes between scenario error, which regards assumptions about such variables as industrial country growth, world inflation, international interest rates, and oil prices, and model error, which refers to "elasticities" and other equation parameters as well as outright omission of some important variables. Application of the original model to the actual data for industrial country growth and other exogenous variables permits the estimation of a "backcast." Divergence of the backcast from the actual outcome measures the extent of scenario error. The remaining error is model error.

The decomposition of forecast error shows that some things went right. With respect to scenarios, world growth and the eventual depreciation of the dollar turned out as favorably as forecast. The decline in world interest rates was even greater than predicted, contributing to the improvement in the interest/exports ratio reviewed above. The model's trade elasticities also performed adequately.

Several things went wrong. On the scenario side, the single largest blow to the projections (and the strategy) was the collapse of oil prices to $16 per barrel in 1986, compared with a forecast of $35. The sharp deceleration in world inflation was also important, with its implications for a lower-than-expected nominal export base and higher real interest rate. Debtor country growth was below scenario levels, helping to keep external deficits low but undermining political sustainability of the strategy.

On the model side, a major error was failure to incorporate capital flight in the projection model. Whereas the current account projections substantially overstated cumulative deficits, the debt projections nonetheless proved close to the mark. The reason was that there was large ongoing capital flight (alternatively estimated at about $100 billion and $135 billion for the 19 countries during 1984–87) that caused debt to build up by much more than cumulative current account deficits.

In addition, the increased dollar valuation of debt denominated in deutsche marks, yen, and other nondollar currencies, as a consequence of the dollar's decline in 1985 and after, caused a major rise in the nominal dollar stock of debt (by $86 billion for these countries over this period). The model had omitted this effect, on the view that nondollar debt was limited. In retrospect the principle of interest rate–exchange rate parity was confirmed, with the lesson that it could be deceptive to borrow in nondollar currencies in pursuit of low interest rates. This strategy meant that the debtor enjoyed the temporary illusion of low rates but only at the expense of later exchange-rate valuation losses. Together, the model errors of omitting capital flight and exchange rate valuation effects accounted for more than the total forecast error understating debt buildup, meaning that the net effect of other scenario and model errors was to overstate the buildup.

Model performance on commodity price response to world recovery is more ambiguous; whereas there was overprediction through 1987, by 1989 commodity prices had rebounded closer to projected levels (and new statistical tests confirm sensitivity to the industrial country business cycle as well as the strength of the dollar). Finally, the model made no allowance for an internal transfer problem related to the government's ability to raise resources from the public to service the debt; yet fiscal problems played a major role in some countries such as Brazil where performance on trade surpluses was strong.

An important aspect of the commodity price outcome is the question of whether the initial debt strategy sowed the seeds of its own destruction by relying on export expansion as the way for debtors to grow out of the problem, thereby dooming them collectively to a collapse in terms of trade for commodity exports. Analysis in chapter 5 (table 5.2) rejects this hypothesis by showing that the heavily indebted Baker-17 countries actually experienced a modest reduction in their share of world commodity exports from 1979–81 to 1987–89, whereas a substantial increase would have been required to provide evidence consistent with the thesis of the self-destructing debt strategy.

The decomposition analysis of chapter 3 suggests that formulation of the debt strategy in 1983–84 was not unduly optimistic about the prospective improvement in the international economic environment. For debtors not exporting oil, the conditions were broadly sufficient for recovery following the basic strategy, so long as domestic policies were sound and as a result fiscal problems were not severe and capital flight was limited. Chile and Colombia are examples. In contrast, for oil exporters such as Mexico, the 1986 collapse in oil prices provided an objective basis for a subsequent shift in the international strategy.

Debt Theory

The debt crisis spawned a mushrooming of theoretical economic literature seeking to explain what had happened and to lay a firm basis for policy response; chapter 4 attempts to provide a connoisseur's tour. For readers more interested in or comfortable with the policy implications than the formal analysis in this literature, chapter 5 revisits its salient entries from the standpoint of how the evolving theoretical debate shaped the changing debt strategy.

Seminal work by Eaton and Gersovitz (1981) asked why anyone would lend to a foreign country, considering there is no tangible collateral as in domestic loans. As a substitute, their model cites the country's own self-interest in preserving its credit reputation because of the welfare gains obtainable through the use of foreign borrowing for "consumption smoothing" across good and bad years. It also suggests a credit ceiling: the lenders' evaluation of the country's point of indifference between retaining future access to consumption smoothing and the windfall gain from repudiating existing debt. This ceiling is higher if creditors know they can impose greater penalties; gunboats are the borrowers' best friend. Eaton, Gersovitz, and Stiglitz (1986) add the paradox that lending should not take place for developmental reasons, because the time profile would involve solely lending at first and repayment subsequently, and there would be no incentive to keep paying in the second phase. That countries nonetheless have done so suggests that there is something missing from this approach, which might be called the model of the optimizing deadbeat. One candidate is an element of country honor or pride; another is borrower expectation of lower risk premiums and wider market opportunities through full commitment to integration into the international financial system.

Cooper and Sachs (1985) model the distinctions between a liquidity crisis, insolvency, and repudiation. Their judgment that panics resulting from individual bank responses in a bad year can cause illiquidity even when the country is solvent (present value of potential future trade surpluses exceeds debt) was consistent with the emphasis on this distinction early in the debt strategy. Bulow and Rogoff (1989a) develop a model of sovereign lending that relies on asset seizure, export blockage, and loss of terms-of-trade gains as the sovereign incentive that replaces tangible collateral. Their earlier (1988b) dismissal of Eaton-Gersovitz consumption smoothing, on grounds that, essentially, a country can accomplish that objective by defaulting and using the proceeds to buy an insurance contract with Lloyds of London, is highly unrealistic. The result is that their subsequent model may appropriately be seen as an additive reason for sovereign lending.

Numerous authors developed projection models in the early 1980s similar to that of Cline (1983), including the notable entries of Morgan Guaranty (1983), Enders and Mattione (1984), and Dornbusch and Fischer (1984). There was similar modeling work at the Council of Economic Advisers (Krugman 1985) and Federal Reserve (Dooley, Helkie, Tryon, and Underwood 1986). As the conclusion of such models was usually that debtors could grow out of the problem, it is not surprising that the official view in the early 1980s was that the problem was not one of fundamental insolvency. Even so, the Cline (1983) projections had evoked a "firestorm of criticism" (Eaton and Taylor 1986) and intense debate about parameters and scenario assumptions. One critique of the whole class of projection models was that they did not address debtor incentive to pay (Eaton, Gersovitz, and Stiglitz 1986). However, the transfer capacity examined in the projection models was surely a necessary if not sufficient condition for eventual full honoring of the debt.

Whereas the projection models focused on export capacity to carry out the external transfer, by the late 1980s there was increasing emphasis on the importance of the internal transfer problem: the government had to mobilize resources from the private sector to service external public debt. Wiesner (1985) was an early advocate of the view that the debt crisis stemmed primarily from domestic fiscal imbalances. Work at the OECD by Reisen and Van Trotsenburg (1988) documented the swing in net financial transfers and its impact on government investment. Dornbusch (1988) emphasized the budgetary problems and inflationary consequences of the debt-servicing burden, stressing the interaction with the external transfer problem: devaluation to spur exports raised the domestic currency price and thus GDP share of external debt service.

As chapter 4 notes, however, typically analysts did not follow through the implicit logic that a fiscal transfer problem more likely required refinancing rather than forgiveness, nor the point that plausible forgiveness on foreign debt would provide fiscal adjustment comparable to only modest reduction in total domestic spending. Bacha (1989b) more explicitly recognized that external debt relief without domestic fiscal reform is unlikely to avoid inflationary pressures.

By the late 1980s, the dominant theme of the debt literature had turned to debt forgiveness, and more explicitly, to the conditions under which it could benefit not only the debtor but also the creditor. Krugman (1988) challenged the earlier paradigm of illiquidity versus insolvency on grounds that it is impossible to know for sure whether the country is insolvent. However, this emphasis on uncertainty seems less than illuminating. A classic role of central banks is to lend if borrowers are illiquid but not insolvent (Bagehot 1873), and central bankers have always been paid to tell the difference.

The principal emerging proposition justifying debt reduction mutually beneficial to debtor and creditor was the notion of a debt overhang that acted like a tax to depress investment and thus future debt payment capacity (e.g., Sachs 1989g). The most crystalizing expression of this concept was Krugman's (1989a) "debt Laffer curve." It showed creditors' expected value on the vertical axis and debt face value on the horizontal. Shaped like an inverted U lying increasingly below the 45° line and turning downward after a peak, the curve suggested that the debt overhang could be so large that forgiving debt (to the right of the curve's peak) would increase creditors' expected claims.

Subsequent literature has not been kind to the debt overhang argument. Cline (1989c), Claessens (1990), and Cohen (1990) use data on secondary market prices to show that very few countries are to the right of the peak of the debt Laffer curve. Diwan and Rodrik (1992) argue persuasively that the size of external debt servicing is too small relative to GDP to place a major taxlike disincentive on investment. Warner (1991) applies statistical tests and finds no special explanatory role for a debt overhang in determining investment in debtor countries; Cohen (1993) finds the same empirical result using different methodology.

The debt Laffer curve turns out to be a more productive concept if attention is limited to its more plausible upward-sloping portion and if forgiveness is conceived of as risk-compensated debt reduction that holds expected creditor value constant by reducing face value while increasing security through third-party collateral (Williamson 1988; Cline 1991; and chapter 4 in this volume). Risk-compensated, voluntary, market-oriented debt reduction provides the best analytical framework for understanding the Brady Plan. A parallel interpretation is that debt payments are the minimum of capacity to pay and willingness to pay, and that modest forgiveness-cum-collateralization can shift willingness upward by improving perceived equity in burden sharing (as suggested in the model developed in chapter 5 of this volume).

Nonetheless, debt overhang and the debt Laffer curve were dominant concepts on the eve of the Brady Plan. Other analytical statements of mutually beneficial debt reduction were developed by Corden (1989), who showed that a country close to subsistence could be pushed into endogenous debt forgiveness unless given relief; and Helpman (1989), who showed that with mobile international capital modest reduction in the debt overhang tax could generate a large increase in investment. Both authors also noted, however, that from standard theory, debt forgiveness could reduce rather than increase investment by reducing future debt payments, increasing future consumption, reducing future marginal utility of consumption, and thereby reducing the return to abstaining from current consumption.

Dooley (1989b) provided the principal alternative concept of debt overhang: the idea that with large secondary market discounts, investors placing new resources into a country would suddenly see their value collapse to comparable discount prices. However, this notion was not consistent with the observed insulation of other classes of investment (direct, portfolio, bond) from the tainted bank debt market, and this imperfect substitutability was especially evident by the early 1990s with large new inflows of capital other than syndicated long-term bank lending.

Diwan and Rodrik (1992) developed a model incorporating international financial institution (IFI) conditionality as the missing ingredient for market-based debt reduction. As set forth in chapter 4, the overall sense of their approach is on the mark but some components are not (such as the view that the IFIs must face losses comparable proportionately to those of the banks).

Bulow and Rogoff (1988a) sought to demonstrate that buybacks are detrimental to debtors. Their core assumption was that the face value of the debt is meaningless whereas the secondary market value is the proper measure of its value and burden. They argued that because buybacks can push up the secondary market price by enough to offset the volume of debt retired, they are undesirable. From the vantage point of 1994, this reasoning looks like an expensive miscalculation (for example, to any Mexican state firm that could have retired debt at less than 40 cents on the dollar in the late 1980s). Alternative theoretical work by Froot (1989) found instead that buybacks can usually benefit the debtor, except when the country must use its own resources and its reserves are already severely depleted.

A final strand of the debt literature is that of historical analysis. This part of the literature in the late 1980s had the flavor that the crisis had been mismanaged because today's policymakers were woefully ignorant of historical experience; but often this judgment fails to take account of the different circumstances. Thus, Eichengreen and Portes (1989) seemed to extol the felicitous growth results of the heavy defaulters in the 1930s without considering the change in Latin America's economic structure by the 1980s. Movement toward autarky was relatively easy in the 1930s when import substitution had barely begun, but would have been much more costly in the 1980s when inward-looking growth had already reached inefficient extremes.

Fishlow (1986) distinguished between developmental defaults (e.g., Australia and Canada in the 1890s) and public revenue defaults (e.g., Russia in 1913, Germany in the interwar period). He suggested that the debt crisis of the 1980s was in the latter category because of the unusual and to some extent politically motivated lending of the 1970s, and thus it was likely to be an episode of insolvency. The outcome by the 1990s suggested at the least that both types of default were present. Several major countries (especially outside Latin America) did not ultimately need forgiveness; and those that did received amounts that were relatively small compared to total (though not bank) external debt.

The International Debt Strategy

Chapter 5 reviews the evolution of the debt strategy and evaluates its performance. There were three goals to the strategy: avoiding collapse of the international banking and financial systems, minimizing the economic dislocation of the debtor countries, and restoring their capital market access. Overall the strategy succeeded brilliantly on the first and third objectives. Superficially the results were much more disappointing on the second. However, even on the goal of domestic growth the strategy achieved important success by encouraging domestic economic policy reforms that, after a time lag, brought stability and renewed growth. In several important cases poor growth in the 1980s reflected distortions of domestic policy and economic structure that eventually would have to have been addressed even without the debt crisis, and indeed the crisis played a role in forcing the needed reforms.

There were three distinct phases to the strategy: initial emergency lending to Mexico and subsequent coordinated lending to other individual countries (1982–85); the indicative Baker Plan which set targets for bank and official lending and called for structural reform in debtor economies (1986–88); and the Brady Plan, emphasizing debt reduction agreements (1989–94).

The first phase amounted to involuntary lending by banks, orchestrated primarily by the IMF, which played the role of overcoming the free-rider incentive of banks acting individually (Cline 1983). The central premise was that the debt problem was not one of insolvency, so that further lending was appropriate. By 1984, with the advent of multiyear rescheduling agreements (MYRAs), strong global recovery, and interim recovery in Latin America, the initial debt strategy was at its high-water mark. By 1985, however, it became apparent that voluntary lending was not returning. Imports had been compressed severely. The devastating earthquake in Mexico and the return to civilian politics in Argentina and Brazil escalated the political component of debt policy.

In late 1985, a new US secretary of Treasury, James Baker, announced an indicative plan whereby the banks would lend $20 billion to 15 major problem debtors (later extended to 17) over three years and the multilateral banks would increase their total lending by $10 billion (to a gross level of $20 billion over the period, matching the bank target) in return for debtor government policy reforms improving fiscal balances, liberalizing imports and direct investment, and privatizing state firms. The popular image of the Baker Plan is that it failed because the banks did not lend their promised amounts. However, their new-money packages amounted to at least two-thirds of the target, even though their exposures rose by less because of buybacks and debt-equity conversions (which were part of the solution, not part of the problem). Multilateral lenders increased net lending by a considerably smaller share of their target, but in both cases country policy disarray and absence of IMF agreements contributed to the shortfall.

The latter part of this period was one of experimentation with market-based debt reduction, including substantial programs of conversion of debt into equity as well as the Mexico–Morgan Guaranty conversion bond and the Brazilian exit bond in 1988. However, several key factors spelled the ultimate eclipse of the Baker Plan.

First, and perhaps the most important, the collapse of oil prices in 1986 changed the objective prospects for key debtors such as Mexico and Venezuela from solvency to potential insolvency.

Second, by 1987 and after there was widespread provisioning by banks against possible losses on their loans to developing countries. Partly as a consequence, secondary market prices fell from a range of 70 cents on the dollar to about 35 cents by 1989. The combination of these two developments provided a natural opportunity to implement financial workouts that involved a trade of some portion of the face value of bank claims in exchange for increased security through officially aided collateralization.

Third, and related, there was a rising incidence of interest arrears, led by Brazil's moratorium in early 1987. That act, which had primarily been a political response to distract attention from the failed Cruzado Plan, played an important role in bringing about the watershed change of bank provisioning.

Fourth, the growing divergence of interests among the banks, and the increasing reluctance of European, Japanese, and regional US banks to lend new money, gave the impression by late 1987 that the new money strategy was no longer viable. As an attempt to deal with these divergences, already by 1988 the strategy emphasized the menu approach, whereby some banks would exit by converting claims to concessional bonds, while others would continue the new-money strategy with the aid of such devices as new-money bonds (seen as partially senior to normal loans).

Fifth, domestic and international political pressures were mounting for a wider conversion to debt relief. US congressional critics emphasized the drop in US exports to Latin America and the threat to new democracies in the region, and they proposed international facilities to buy up the debt at low secondary market prices and convey some relief to the debtors. Policy leaders abroad, such as Japanese Prime Minister Kiichi Miyazawa, French President François Mitterand, and German banker Alfred Herrhausen, joined the call for a shift in the strategy toward debt forgiveness. Mexico—always in the avant-garde of the evolving debt strategy—got a new president who was not only pledged to debt reduction but also close to the new US president, George Bush.

Sixth, there was growing frustration among US policymakers that the public-sector share of debt was rising and that of the banks was falling, even though the trend was a return to patterns predating the unusual petrodollar recycling of the 1970s and still left bank exposure far higher than that of the public sector. Seventh, in terms of the conceptual framework, "the academics' drumbeat of criticism of the Baker strategy during 1987 and 1988 helped keep up the pressure for change . . ." (Fischer 1989b, v). Analytical work at the IMF and World Bank reflected the changing dominant paradigm of the problem from illiquidity to insolvency.

In the final months of 1988, US policymakers conducted an intensive review of the debt strategy, in part because the original time horizon for the Baker Plan was ending. The change at Treasury from Secretary Baker to Secretary Brady brought a new viewpoint more oriented toward securitized workout. President-elect George Bush was inclined to the view that fairness required some greater sacrifice on the part of the banks. By the end of 1988, key US policymakers had agreed to shift the debt strategy toward debt reduction. In early 1989, hundreds of deaths in Caracas riots protesting new austerity measures provided a flashpoint that, in the broader public perception, seemed to heighten the need for a change in the international strategy.

In March 1989 new US Treasury Secretary Nicholas Brady announced the next phase of the debt strategy, which was to emphasize debt (or debt-service) reduction. The Brady Plan sought to introduce public-sector collateral as the catalyst to convince banks to reduce their existing claims on debtor countries. Treasury spokespersons suggested that nearly 40 countries could be eligible, and debt could be reduced by $70 billion. The plan also gave at least lip service to additional lending of new money by those banks that preferred this option. To the carrot of official enhancements for conversion bonds, the new strategy added the stick of IMF "lending into arrears," a reversal of past policy whereby the agency had refused to lend to a country until it had reached an agreement with the banks.

Crucially, the Brady Plan was quasi-voluntary (at least as much so as the previous strategy of concerted lending) because it incorporated the alternative of new money; and it was market-oriented, in that the depth of cut typically negotiated was commensurate with the existing secondary market price on the one hand and the extent of collateralization of the replacement claims on the other. Forcing forgiveness all the way down to the secondary market price (e.g., to about 40 cents on the dollar for Mexico, instead of the 65 cents Mexican negotiators accepted) without prompt cash payment would have transformed the plan into a more mandatory regime.[3] The result probably would have been to precipitate lengthy legal challenges by the banks and to cast a pall over capital markets instead of restoring confidence.

Also crucial was the plan's case-by-case, policy-conditional nature. The alternative of a global agency to purchase and partially forgive debt could easily have slid toward less emphasis on policy reform and greater moral hazard, inducing countries to expect automatic relief.

By May 1994, five years after its inauguration, there were Brady Plan agreements in place or tentatively agreed upon for 18 countries representing about $190 billion in long-term bank claims (table 5.3), or about 80 percent of the total debt originally considered eligible; the amount forgiven was about $60 billion, close to the original Brady target. Among the severely indebted middle-income countries, there were few plausible remaining candidates other than Panama, Peru, and Côte d'Ivoire. Others such as Algeria, Jamaica, Morocco, and Hungary had stated their intention to avoid forgiveness or primarily owed debt to official rather than bank creditors.

The agreements had typically provided for forgiveness of 30 to 35 percent (but higher for small, lower-income countries), usually in the form of discount bonds that cut face value or else par bonds that retained full nominal value but cut interest rates to 6 percent or less. Enhancements typically amounted to about 40 percent of the amount forgiven, suggesting an immediate rate of return of 150 percent on the enhancement funds if gauged against the original face obligation. For the agreements to date (including those in principle), the IMF, World Bank, and Japanese Export-Import Bank will have provided some $25 billion or less in enhancements, about two-thirds the amount originally anticipated in the Brady Plan.

Some packages included new money or buybacks, or both. Overall, however, new money was limited, totaling only about 2 percent of original exposure. The effect was an exodus of the banks from long-term lending to Brady countries, at least temporarily. However, other forms of new capital flows surged.

As late as 1991–92, numerous critics argued that the Brady Plan was too little relief too late. By 1994, in contrast, there was growing evidence that the plan had succeeded. The most rigorous retrospective research was that on Mexico by Claessens, Oks, and van Wijnbergen (1993, 1), who pronounced the deal a "spectacular success." Their econometric analysis found that the principal reason was that the agreement removed uncertainty associated with "high and volatile external transfers" (5), thereby providing confidence about sustainability of the

---

3. Ironically, as noted in chapter 5, at the height of the Mexican negotiations the managing director of the International Monetary Fund seemed to be insisting on deep cuts down to the existing secondary market value (Camdessus 1989).

exchange rate regime and permitting a steep decline in the domestic interest rate. A consequence was a rebound in the growth rate of domestic real investment from only 1 percent in 1982–88 to 11 percent in 1989–91. Their tests rejected statistical significance of the level (as opposed to prospective volatility) of the transfer, thereby rejecting the debt overhang thesis.

The authors do not explicitly recognize a crucial implication of their findings: on economic criteria alone, a MYRA might have been sufficient for Mexico. Moreover, if oil prices had not collapsed, Mexico would not have needed Brady forgiveness on economic grounds, because the former cost the country about $8 billion annually whereas the latter saved it only about $1½ billion annually.

Other evidence of the success of the Brady Plan includes the dramatic resurgence of capital to Latin America. Net capital inflows to the region, which had fallen from over $40 billion in 1981 to a plateau of about $10 billion annually in 1983–89, rebounded to nearly $60 billion by 1992 (chapter 8, figure 8.1, and the cover of this book). Typically the largest increase was in the year of the announcement of the Brady agreement in principle (1989 for Mexico, 1990 for Venezuela, and 1992 for Argentina and Brazil); in most cases, the rebound of secondary market prices was to levels consistent with the expectation of nearly full honoring of what remained of the debt. In addition, by 1992–93 growth and price stability in Latin America were greatly improved, as noted above.

The size of Brady relief was relatively small. The central reason was that long-term bank claims typically were no more than half of total debt (with much of the rest owed to bilateral and multilateral creditors), so that forgiveness of one-third meant removal of only about one-sixth of the country's total debt burden. The corresponding forgiveness on interest obligations amounted to 1 percent of GDP or less, and some 3 percent of exports or less. It is something of a paradox that forgiveness this modest could have had such a strong favorable impact.

Chapter 5 develops a political-economic model that helps resolve this paradox. The expected debt servicing fraction is postulated to be the minimum of two concepts: capacity to pay and willingness to pay. Capacity to pay is related to the normal economic variables, such as the debt/exports ratio. However, willingness to pay is related to such variables as recent economic hardship, the degree of political populism in the country, and the degree of equity perceived in the sharing of the burden of adjustment between banks and the country. Moderate debt relief increases capacity to pay modestly, but by sharply changing perceived equity, it may substantially increase willingness to pay. If so, then the binding constraint can switch from the willingness variable to the capacity variable, a shift that explains a revival of the country's perceived creditworthiness and secondary market price despite limited reduction in the debt burden.

A case can be made that psychological factors were nearly as important on the side of capital market perceptions. Repatriation of capital by nationals and new portfolio investments by international investors may have been influenced as much by general market psychology as by any close examination of underlying debt burden and creditworthiness indicators. In financial markets, it is useful to recall Keynes's analogy to guessing the outcome of a beauty contest: what matters is not what one thinks about the candidates' relative beauty (i.e., a close analysis of the changes in debt burden), but what one thinks the judges will think (i.e., generalized public impressions influenced by a signal event such as Brady forgiveness). In part the two sides interact, because it is rational for the foreign investors to stay out so long as they think the country remains in the mode constrained by willingness to pay, regardless of the economic fundamentals.

The strong positive results of the Brady Plan despite the modest amount of its relief also reflects the key role that Secretary Brady attributed to prospective capital repatriation once the air was cleared on the debt problem. By the conventional IMF balance of payments projections the deals often were either precarious or simply insufficient to close the financing gap in the absence of a revival of private capital inflows.

Chapter 5 reaches the following overall evaluation of the debt strategy to date. In historical terms, the strategy has been resoundingly successful in restoring capital market access. After the previous debt crisis in the 1930s, defaulting LDCs were locked out of capital markets for four decades (table 5.5). One reason for the better outcome this time is the existence of international financial institutions absent in the interwar period. Another reason for the impressive return of capital flows in the early 1990s was the adoption of a quasi-voluntary, market-oriented approach to debt forgiveness. The overall strategy also succeeded unequivocally in safeguarding the international banking and financial systems.

The sequential phases of the strategy represented adaptive, contingent policymaking that evolved in the face of changing evidence. The initial premise of the strategy, that most debtors were fundamentally solvent, was not far wide of the mark. Even after Brady forgiveness, only about 6 percent of total debt of the middle-income countries had to be forgiven. Moreover, in the absence of the oil price collapse in 1986, forgiveness would not have been necessary on economic grounds for important debtors such as Mexico, Venezuela, Ecuador, and Nigeria.

More broadly, as suggested by figure 5.3, countries that had sound domestic economic policies (especially fiscal) and adequate international luck turned out not to need forgiveness (South Korea, Colombia, Chile). Countries with good domestic policies but bad luck (Mexico with respect to oil) did wind up needing forgiveness. Some countries with adequate or even favorable luck but poor domestic economic policies (such as

Brazil) eventually received forgiveness more as a matter of market opportunity (with low secondary market prices) than as an unavoidable outcome. Under the premise that initial international strategy should not be designed to accommodate bad domestic policy nor to assume a severe international shock, it was arguably appropriate to initiate the debt strategy on the premise of solvency even for the countries that in the end received forgiveness.

The principal critique of the overall strategy has been that forgiveness came too late and was too limited. However, it would have been inappropriate to shift to debt forgiveness as the main strategy before the collapse of oil prices in 1986. As noted, before that event the objective conditions of the oil-exporting debtors were much more consistent with a diagnosis of solvency. In contrast, the oil-importing debtor countries obtained savings from the price decline that were too small to have been a driving force in determining the debt outcome; and among this group, the ultimate need for debt forgiveness turned primarily on domestic economic policy rather than external conditions (as shown, for example, in the contrast between Chile and Brazil).[4]

It would have been risky to the banking system to shift to debt forgiveness before the banks set aside large loan-loss provisions beginning in 1987, so that the debt strategy's objective of international financial stability would have been compromised.[5] Moreover, the Brady Plan was leveraged on low secondary market prices. Because these prices were still relatively high in 1986 and early 1987, much less relief might have been secured if the plan had been adopted before those prices had fallen to their lows of 1988–89.

Most fundamentally, governments of several debtor countries might not have been prepared to adopt the necessary domestic economic reforms if debt forgiveness had been the main strategy earlier. Forgiveness might have been seen as an easy, alternative solution. Yet without the reforms, any forgiveness would likely have proven to be insufficient to reestablish the grounds for a return to growth and price stability. Finally, the record shows that the March 1989 inaugural date for the Brady Plan was not the binding constraint for most countries, for it was not until 1992 and after that such countries as Argentina and Brazil reached agreements in principle.

Chapter 5 also suggests that the prospective public cost of Brady enhancements is extremely small. Debtors typically honored obligations

---

4. Because of high relative debt, the Argentine case may be an exception, although there too domestic fiscal imbalance was a dominant force determining debt difficulty.

5. As discussed in chapter 5, the timing and amount of bank loss reserves were of course not exogenous to the policy climate, but any generalized creditor government mandates for larger and earlier reserves would have been inconsistent with objective prospects before the oil price collapse.

to the IFIs even at the depths of the debt crisis, and these privileged creditors seem unlikely to experience losses on the enhancement loans.

In sum, the judgment in chapter 5 is that the international debt strategy has been broadly successful and has shown the flexibility to respond to new circumstances. Success was greatest in preserving the stability of the international financial system and in restoring capital market access. The poorer outcome with respect to domestic economic growth and inflation in the debtor countries seems unlikely to have been remediable to a very great degree through the alternative of having moved to deeper and earlier forgiveness. Finally, chapter 5 considers in its conclusion the implications of this experience for future policy.

Latin American Experience

Chapter 6 reviews the experience of adjustment to the debt crisis in the seven largest Latin American countries. In all cases to at least some degree, by the early 1990s there had been a transformation of economic policy away from import-substituting industrialization with a large role of the state in the economy toward trade liberalization, privatization of state firms, and liberalization of foreign investment. Most observers would agree that the traumatic challenge to the old economic model posed by the debt crisis played a major role in this sweeping change.

Colombia managed to avoid not only debt forgiveness but even formal debt rescheduling (with the help of successive "Jumbo" coordinated loans of $1 billion to $1½ billion each). The central reason was that its fiscal conservatism had kept the country from overborrowing in the 1970s. Urrutia (1991) attributes fiscal prudence to a clientelistic polity based on regional barons who traditionally select as presidential candidates technocrats who will not be a threat. Even so, contagion from the Latin American neighborhood effect did cause frustratingly slow return of voluntary lending. After temporary balance of payments problems in 1982–83, the government implemented an exchange rate correction through accelerating the crawl while tightening fiscal policy, with laudable results in avoiding induced inflation.

Colombia's very success meant less pressure for structural reform, but by the early 1990s the growing political power of exporters and their concern about continued access to major world markets, combined with the need for anti-inflationary innovations, led to trade liberalization, enrolling the country in the "Washington consensus" policy profile (Williamson 1990) that by then dominated most of the region. Overall, Colombia's good results reflected good domestic policy. Chapter 6 considers and rejects the alternative hypothesis that drug money was the secret to the country's success.

Chile too avoided Brady forgiveness, but it required formal rescheduling in the 1980s. Despite fiscal balance, by 1981 the economy had high external private debt as the consequence of an overvalued exchange rate. The strong peso had resulted from pursuit of a questionable theory whereby a fixed rate would force Chilean inflation quickly to world levels despite domestic wage indexing. Higher oil prices and a collapse in copper prices also contributed. Although the banks forced the Chilean government to assume responsibility for the debt after the outbreak of the debt crisis, the government did so in a way that retained the bulk of real value claims on private debtors, thereby avoiding the severe worsening of the internal transfer problem that occurred in Argentina from a similar takeover of the debt.

Chile astutely used debt-equity swaps and capital repatriation mechanisms to reduce its debt by about one-third of the initial stock. The country also achieved rapid export growth. The result was successful application of the strategy of growing out of the debt crisis, even though Chile was one of the most heavily indebted countries at the outset of the crisis. Despite massive recession in 1982, by the late 1980s per capita GDP stood higher above the 1979–81 base than in any other major Latin American country except Colombia; and although real wages had fallen, they had done so from an abnormally high 1980–82 base. Critics often dismiss the relevance of Chile's success on grounds of the authoritarian control of the Pinochet regime, but increasingly the country's successful policies attracted attention and inspired emulation elsewhere in the region.

Mexico began adjustment under the de la Madrid regime in 1983. It faced one of the largest challenges in the region, because of the shock of lower oil prices in 1986 and after. Fiscal correction was the centerpiece of Mexico's adjustment. The primary fiscal deficit (excluding interest) had reached 8 percent of GDP in 1981; by 1988 there was a primary surplus of 8 percent of GDP despite the loss of about 5 percent of GDP in fiscal revenue from lower oil prices. Adjustment centered on spending cuts, which took a heavy toll on government investment and left the private sector the challenge of leading investment reactivation. By the late 1980s a virtuous circle of lower deficits and resultingly lower interest on domestic debt did leave room for increased, but targeted, social spending.

In 1986 Mexico joined the General Agreement on Tariffs and Trade (GATT). By the early 1990s it had sold off the state telephone and airline companies and, healing bitter private-sector wounds, reprivatized the banks. Inflation remained high in 1987 despite fiscal adjustment, and the government implemented the Solidarity Pact to break inertial inflation. An exchange rate anchor rapidly reduced inflation but may have left a legacy of overvaluation, as current account deficits were on the order of 50 percent of exports of goods and services by the early 1990s.

As noted above, Mexico played a leading role in the evolving international debt strategy, and its Brady deal had major positive effects from improved expectations. The Salinas regime achieved an additional positive confidence shock from successful negotiation of the North American Free Trade Agreement (NAFTA). By end-1994, however, the combination of political shocks and the large current-account deficit had led to a collapse of the peso, as examined in the epilogue.

Venezuela pursued an inward-oriented economic model with heavy state intervention, and after the oil bonanza of the 1970s the economy entered a prolonged decline. When oil prices fell in the 1980s the government drew down international reserves rather than take corrective fiscal and exchange measures. In early 1989 President Carlos Andrés Pérez adopted the "Great Turnaround," an orthodox reform package that unified and devalued the exchange rate, eliminated price controls, and liberalized imports and direct investment. After recession and high inflation the first year, there was strong growth and acceptable inflation in 1990–92.

In 1989–90 fiscal balances moved from a deficit of 9 percent of GDP to a surplus of 1 percent, largely with the help of the peculiar structure whereby dollar revenue was state-owned (oil exports) so devaluation strengthened bolivar fiscal accounts (but depressed the economy). Permanent fiscal reform proved more evasive, and the Venezuelan congress repeatedly refused to adopt the value-added tax that was to be the key to supplementing uncertain oil revenue.

Venezuela began the 1980s with relatively low debt, but the combination of massive capital flight and a collapse in oil prices catapulted its debt/exports ratio to nearly 300 percent by the late 1980s even as reserves disappeared. The country's timing was favorable to benefit from the Brady Plan. By 1993–94, however, political unraveling that saw the president deposed for corruption and a possible turn toward populist politics under a new president meant that the Venezuelan outcome from the debt crisis stood in doubt. The central reason was that the public still harkened back to the days of high subsidies and a strong bolivar, even though the fundamentals were radically different because per capita public revenue from oil had fallen from $1,700 in 1981 to $382 by 1992.

In *Argentina*, by contrast, hyperinflation so traumatized the public that it was ready for a complete rejection of the economic model of the past. In that model, high protection, state firm losses, and chronic fiscal deficits had contributed to a decline in per capita income by 20 percent from 1980 to 1989, even though by the late 1980s Argentina was not servicing its external debt. The Austral Plan of 1985 and its successors repeatedly collapsed because temporary measures such as export taxes and forced saving were not replaced with permanent tax revenue. Hyperinflation erupted in mid-1989.

The new regime of Carlos Menem adopted radical reform that reduced protection, massively privatized state firms, and deregulated the economy. As in Mexico, fiscal reform was the keystone. Revenue of the value-added tax rose from 3 percent of GDP to 8 percent, and the nominal fiscal deficit fell from 20 percent of GDP in 1987 to a surplus of 1 percent in 1992. The 1991 Convertibility Plan set a fixed parity against the dollar into law and established a currency-board structure whereby the domestic money base had to be backed by international reserves. After recession in 1988–89, GDP grew at almost 9 percent annually in 1991–92. As in Mexico, the principal question by 1993–94 was whether the exchange rate anchor against inflation would be an Achilles' heel, as the current account deficit reached uncomfortably high levels.

Argentina had a legacy of high external debt, and in 1982 the government effectively assumed private external debt with compensation at only a fraction of real value, causing an internal transfer problem as well. Debt rose rapidly in the early 1980s from new money and in the late 1980s from arrears that resulted when a collapsed IMF program brought suspension of bank lending packages. Argentina's Brady deal helped resolve its debt problem, but the watershed change toward sound domestic policies was the fundamental remedy.

By early 1994 *Brazil* was still groping its way toward such policies. A decade earlier the country seemed to be sustaining growth while the rest of Latin America collapsed around it, but prolonged recession began by the second half of the 1980s. Like Argentina, Brazil experienced a series of heterodox plans that successively collapsed for lack of fundamental fiscal adjustment. Indexation made inertial inflation the most resilient in the region and perhaps the world.

In 1990 the new regime of Fernando Collor de Mello sought structural and emacroeconomic reform. A massive, ill-advised asset freeze paralyzed activity, yet inflation soon revived as funds were subsequently released. The real (operational) fiscal balance did improve markedly, but primarily as the consequence of temporary measures such as a 25 percent tax on stock market holdings and repressed real earnings on frozen government bonds. By mid-1991 inflation was back in the range of 20 to 30 percent per month.

The government fared better in structural reform. It cut tariffs sharply, phased out nontariff barriers, and privatized some steel and other state firms. Macroeconomic adjustment, in contrast, required reform of the populist constitution of 1988, especially provisions such as the massive transfer of federal revenue to the states without corresponding reassignment of responsibilities.

By mid-1994, Brazil had embarked on a new stabilization plan involving replacement of the currency by the *real*, initially set at parity with the dollar, and prohibiting indexed contracts for intervals shorter than one year. The plan enjoyed impressive initial success, and in the October elections its author, former finance minister Fernando Henrique Cardoso, won the presidency despite an earlier lead by the leftist candidate ''Lula.'' However, permanent fiscal reform to underpin the plan remained unfinished business for the prospective new government.

As noted above, Brazil's 1987 debt moratorium played an important role in the evolution of the debt strategy. Prolonged arrears later in the decade amounted to default by default rather than by design, because of the syndrome of failed IMF packages and thus bank lending suspensions (for example, after the promising 1988 agreement based on the menu approach). Even so, Brazil reached Brady agreement by 1992 and finalized the agreement in early 1994 with the help of a bank waiver that permitted the country to use part of its own by then large reserves in lieu of IMF approval.

For most of the past decade, *Peru* stood at the unfavorable end of the spectrum of economic policy and performance among major Latin American countries. Alan García's populist policies in the mid-1980s brought a classical cycle of unsustainable boom followed by recession. By the late 1980s real per capita income had fallen by 28 percent and hyperinflation erupted.

García set a 10 percent of exports limit on debt servicing and more generally engaged in a confrontational debt policy that served as an illuminating test case of the theory that countries could painlessly default (e.g., Kaletsky 1985). Lago (1991) concludes that the policy failed even to achieve limiting payments to the ceiling, caused cutoffs in trade credit and in relations with the IFIs, and contributed to macroeconomic failure. Yet Peru's debt burden had actually been lower than that of Chile and Argentina, so its turbulent debt experience was more the consequence of domestic policy choices than external factors.

In 1990 the new Fujimori government imposed a shock treatment stabilization program that put government spending on a cash basis, cut tariffs to a uniform 15 percent, and allowed the exchange rate to float. By 1993, inflation, which had reached nearly 8,000 percent in 1990, was down to 40 percent, and the economy was recovering. Fujimori cleared arrears with the IFIs and entered Brady negotiations with the banks, and the price of Peruvian debt rose from a low of 3 cents on the dollar in 1989 to 43 cents by late 1993.

Chapter 6 emphasizes the central pattern of fiscal adjustment as the single most important factor in achieving domestic stabilization and resolution of the debt problem. Moreover, it presents a rank correlation test that shows an almost perfect fit between country economic performance on growth and inflation, on the one hand, and the degree of cooperativeness with foreign creditors in working out the debt problem on the other, suggesting that confrontation is costly domestically rather than being a painless solution. The chapter concludes by noting that the principal challenges for the future are maintaining the political underpinnings of the economic reform programs and dealing with the specific issue of the trade-off between inflationary expectations and possibly excessive external deficits associated with a fixed exchange rate.

Russia and Eastern Europe

As the Latin American debt crisis receded by the early 1990s, new regional debt problems took its place. The tumultuous transition from Communism in the former Soviet Union (FSU) and Eastern Europe brought new debt difficulties or aggravated old ones; and the international community increasingly focused its attention on the long-standing problem of African debt. In both regions external debt is much more heavily owed to bilateral or multilateral donors, and less heavily to private banks, than was the case for Latin America, making the debt issue inherently more political and less a question of market considerations.

The largest single external debt in these regions is the $80 billion owed by *Russia*. Under the country's zero-option agreements with other FSU states, Russia assumed all former Soviet external debt and external assets. By the end of 1992, the country had arrears of about $12 billion, necessitating Paris Club reschedulings in 1993 and again in 1994. The Soviet Union had not been considered heavily indebted, but the Russian case is less clear. World Bank data show a collapse in the export base from FSU exports of over $80 billion in 1990 to Russian exports of $40 billion in 1992, suggesting severe erosion. However, as shown in annex 7A, this collapse is a statistical illusion caused by Russian data that overvalue ruble-based exports. Trade data from partners instead show FSU exports were in the range of $45 billion to $50 billion, so there has been no implosion of Russian exports (although the central government's control over hard-currency earnings has eroded and state firms have engaged in capital flight).

Chapter 7 suggests that a proper measure of the Russian debt/exports ratio in 1992 is about 200 percent, close to the threshold typically associated with creditworthiness. Moreover, the hard-currency value of Russia's external assets (e.g., state firm assets abroad and loans to developing countries) is at least on the order of some $25 billion. The extent of indebtedness is thus not so severe as to indicate a need for significant forgiveness. Instead, the problem is domestic macroeconomic chaos. Orderly debt servicing cannot be expected until domestic conditions are stabilized, in the first instance through the reduction of massive fiscal deficits and central bank credit expansion.

The analysis of chapter 7 includes illustrative simulations exploring the merits of a debt forgiveness as opposed to market-oriented rollover for Russia. Under assumptions of larger future borrowing possibilities and lower spreads above international interest rates, a rollover approach appears capable of generating benefits comparable to or greater than those of a forgiveness approach. Moreover, Russia's debt burden is considerably lighter than was that of the principal relevant comparator, Poland, and so far Russian authorities have not sought forgiveness. However, the simulations also suggest that if new lending were greater than some $10 billion to $15 billion annually, the debt burden could build up precariously. The implication is that if the West believes that resource flows beyond this range are essential to a politically sustainable transition of the Russian economy, some degree of concessionality may be necessary, even though Russia's per capita income level is sufficiently high that the country would not meet the usual international standards for concessional assistance.

In *Eastern Europe*, there have been two basic debt models: the Polish-Bulgarian and the Czech-Hungarian. As reviewed in chapter 7, both Poland and Bulgaria borrowed heavily in the 1970s to sustain ambitious investment programs and consumption, whereas Czechoslovakia and Hungary pursued more prudent internal and external policies. In Poland the imposition of martial law in 1981 caused a chill on the capital market. After numerous reschedulings in the 1980s, by early 1990 the new democratic government sought "radical debt reduction" from Western governments, which held two-thirds of its debt, in support of the "pioneering role of Poland in the political transition" (Balcerowicz 1994, 160). The Paris Club effectively granted a 50 percent forgiveness of debt in the spring of 1991. After lengthy negotiations, the banks agreed to reduce debt by 45 percent in March 1994.

Bulgaria similarly sought debt relief. Its exports were perhaps the hardest hit in Eastern Europe, because of collapse of exports to Gulf states, unusually high dependence on the Soviet market (which collapsed), and geographical blockage of routes to the European market as a result of civil war in Yugoslavia. Private banks accounted for the bulk of Bulgarian debt, and by November 1993 they agreed in principle to debt reduction equivalent to 50 percent of claims (chapter 7).

Czechoslovakia and Hungary, in contrast, never accumulated as much debt. In 1991 the Institute of International Finance commended the fact that "Hungary has painstakingly serviced its external debt and maintained market access" (Schulmann 1991). Whereas Polish debt sold on the secondary market for 35 cents on the dollar, the price for Hungary was 65 cents. Czechoslovakia enjoyed an investment-grade rating by the private agencies, and Hungary, near-investment grade. Their debt burdens are sufficiently low (an interest/exports ratio of 13 percent, for Hungary) that continued adherence to the same strategy makes sense, in view of the investment already made in maintaining a strong credit record.

The popular image of *sub-Saharan Africa* (SSA) is one of a subcontinent uniformly mired in hopelessly excessive debt. The analysis in chapter 7 suggests, however, that the debt problem is much more sharply differentiated between some countries with heavy debt burdens and others only lightly indebted. For the latter countries, debt management and assured rollover of principal are more important than forgiveness.

SSA external debt rose from $84 billion in 1980 to $194 billion by 1992, whereas the nominal value of exports stagnated because of falling prices for oil (Nigeria) and other commodities. The economic value of the total debt is considerably lower, because much of it is from official donors at concessional rates. Of 45 SSA countries, the World Bank considers 27 "severely indebted," and these account for 88 percent of external debt. However, the World Bank criterion employs present value of debt service relative to exports. That concept counts amortization as a real burden, whereas in meaningful economic terms it is merely a reshuffling of the balance sheet (reduction of both assets and liabilities). This intermixture is particularly misleading when interest rates are concessional.

The more meaningful measure is the interest/exports ratio. Surprisingly, in 1992 only 13 of the 45 SSA countries had an interest/exports ratio in excess of 15 percent, a relatively comfortable threshold characteristic of post-Brady Latin America. Half of the SSA countries have interest/exports ratios under 10 percent. In contrast, in 1988 the ratio for Latin America stood at 36 percent.

Chapter 7 develops debt simulations for the 45 SSA countries, clustered into six alternative groupings arrayed by severity of the interest/exports ratio. The most indebted group includes Sudan and Somalia, hopelessly overindebted with an interest/exports ratio of almost 200 percent. The next includes Mozambique, Madagascar, and Zaire; the next, a cluster including Côte d'Ivoire, Ethiopia, and Congo; next, Nigeria. There are 14 countries in "Kentzamgola" (including Kenya, Tanzania, Zambia, and Angola), with interest/exports ratios of 10 to 15 percent; and finally, 19 countries in "Senguinali" (including Senegal, Guinea, and Mali), with interest/exports ratios below 10 percent.

The model assumes modest export growth, 2 percent real and 2 percent in price increases. The rise in commodity prices in early 1994 is consistent with the expectation of an upturn in the long commodity cycle. Average interest rates by class of debt are based on cross-country regressions of past patterns. Grants received are assumed to rise at 4 percent in nominal terms, and in some sense may be considered part of a reliable quasi-export base.

The policy simulations calculate the impact of enhanced Toronto terms, which would cut official debt service by 50 percent over a two-year consolidation period and then cut the remaining stock of official debt by 50 percent; Trinidad terms, with similar but deeper (two-thirds) cuts; and Brady relief for bank claims. The projections show the following results (table 7.7).

None of these schemes is sufficient for Sudan-Somalia, where some $14 billion in claims may have to be forgiven primarily as a matter of truth in lending.[6] For Mozambique-Madagascar-Zaire, Trinidad terms cut the interest/exports ratio from a high 32 percent in 1997 to a reason-

---

6. Needless to say, debt forgiveness is less important than an end to civil war as a precondition for stable growth.

able 14 percent. For Côte d'Ivoire and Congo, combined Trinidad/Brady terms leave the ratio at 18 percent by that year. For the Kentzamgola group, enhanced Toronto terms cut the 1997 interest/exports ratio from 16 percent to 13 percent; and for Senguinali, the baseline ratio is already as low as 6 percent—although some relief along Toronto lines might seem necessary on political grounds. This differentiated package provides present values of forgiveness broadly proportionate to population shares, except for Sudan-Somalia (much higher) and the 13 countries in Kentzamgola and 19 in Senguinali (windfall relief share at about half of population share). Appropriately, however, the groups with the lowest share in relief have the highest per capita incomes.

More fundamentally, forgiveness relief is not necessarily desirable if the country has a relatively low debt burden. The economics of charity (Schmidt 1964) provide that for constant donor cost, grants are appropriate where recipients have low domestic return, but loans are more efficient where the domestic return is high. Domestic returns should be high if proper policies are followed, given the sparse capital endowment. Many African countries with relatively low debt burdens would do better to receive larger volumes of loans in the future rather than the likely smaller volume of grants that would be the only appropriate follow-on of deep forgiveness.

A key issue is whether to exempt the IFIs from debt forgiveness. The answer is probably yes, but their shareholders—primarily the Group of Seven (G-7) industrial countries—should stand ready to provide correspondingly larger bilateral relief where necessary. Another central issue is the degree of policy conditionality. All observers agree that economic and governance conditionality is important. Lancaster (1991) suggests a "shortleash" approach of debt relief on two-year installments. However, that approach may sacrifice a considerable portion of the favorable expectations shock that was shown to be so important by the disproportionately favorable response of Mexican Brady relief. Where countries have demonstrated adherence to Structural Adjustment Facility (SAF) and other conditional programs in the past, more definitive relief (e.g., Trinidad or the second phase of enhanced Toronto) would seem more appropriate.

In sum, the surprising conclusion for sub-Saharan Africa is that many countries require only light debt forgiveness, and for them the more important question is to assure the certainty associated with multiyear rollover (of the Latin American MYRA type). Correspondingly, it would mislead many of these countries to convey the impression that the forgiveness of their debt would provide much economic stimulus.

Capital Markets in the 1990s

Chapter 8 examines the prospects for capital markets in the post–debt crisis phase. The resurgence of capital inflows to Latin America by 1991 and especially 1992 reflected macroeconomic and structural reform and positive confidence effects of Brady agreements. However, external factors were at work as well. There is an uncanny similarity between the time path of net capital inflows to Latin America and those to Asian developing countries, where the debt crisis was largely avoided (figure 8.1). The push of funds from low US interest rates and the pull of capital from larger Asian current account deficits in the face of recession in industrial country markets were influences. So was the process of institutional substitution from syndicated bank lending, seriously arrested by the mid-1980s, to bond and other securities by the early 1990s. Even the vocabulary changed: developing countries were now "emerging markets," and a "haircut" became the particular style of a financial instrument rather than the anticipated loss of bankers on their claims.[7]

Calvo, Leiderman, and Reinhart (1993) provide statistical tests showing the influence of US financial conditions on capital flows to Latin America. However, it is highly unlikely that the capital market resurgence would have occurred in the absence of policy reform and debt normalization.

Chapter 8 documents the historic shift in the composition of capital flows from commercial bank lending to direct investment, bonds, and other portfolio flows. Banks accounted for two-thirds of positive inflows to Latin America in 1981–82, but only 10 percent in 1990–91, while direct investment rose from 14 percent to 32 percent. The largest new source was a residual difficult to document statistically, but primarily equities and short-term capital.[8] One question is whether this is hot or merely lukewarm money. Equity capital is not necessarily easy to withdraw, because a stock market run levies its own exit tax. In any event, few analysts had predicted the extent to which other private-sector capital would replace bank lending in the postcrisis phase.

One important dynamic may have been market perception that bonds enjoy seniority, as they typically were honored during the debt crisis. Estimates in chapter 8 show that after completion of the Brady Plan, outstanding bonds (including Brady conversion bonds) in Latin America will have risen from $18 billion in 1986 to about $125 billion, whereas long-term bank claims will have fallen from $97 billion to about $30 billion. With bonds then accounting for about 80 percent of the combined total, it will no longer be feasible for them to hold effective seniority. The capital markets may not yet have recognized this shift.

Chapter 8 develops a portfolio-share model of Latin American capital flight repatriation. The calculations first estimate the outstanding stock

---

7. Many of the traders in emerging market equities are too young to have been involved in the financial markets at the depths of the Latin American debt crisis.

8. As for the debt crisis interim in this historical shift, by the late 1980s interest arrears were a major source of financing for Argentina, Brazil, and Peru.

of capital flight, based on World Bank annual flows enhanced by probable reinvested earnings abroad. The stock estimates are high, particularly for Argentina and Mexico (where by 1990 the stocks stood at about $75 billion and $90 billion, respectively). The model postulates that the watershed shift from debt crisis conditions to normality should be expected to cut by half the desired share for foreign assets in the portfolios of Latin American nationals. Data on domestic capital markets suggest that the share of foreign assets in portfolios was especially high in Argentina and Venezuela, and relatively low in Chile where the domestic capital market is robust.

Assuming a stock adjustment path, the model calculates remarkably high initial levels of expected capital repatriation for Argentina and Mexico: about $8 billion each in 1992. However, because the portfolio share reconfiguration eventually stabilizes, this expected reflow declines over time, to about $3 billion for each of these two countries by 1996. The paths are more moderate for other major countries.

The capital repatriation analysis provides both reassurance and a warning. The reassurance is that the seemingly excessive current account deficits of Argentina and Mexico were financed to an important degree with non-debt-creating capital repatriation. The warning, however, is that the downward glide path for repatriation means the countries will need to narrow deficits in the future, or undertake other types of financing that involve a future servicing burden. Thus, for the six largest Latin American countries the capital repatriation analysis predicts a decline of reflows from $25 billion in 1992 to $8 billion by 1996 (table 8.6).

Although there is no allowance for changes in desired portfolio composition as the result of a rise in US interest rates, this influence should be far smaller than that of the regime shift from debt crisis to normality. At the same time, there are indications that by 1993 and after there was a forceful entry of new institutional investors (such as mutual and pension funds) into the capital market flows to debtor countries. As a result, completion of the portfolio adjustment phase for flight capital of nationals would not need to imply a sharp reduction in availability of inflows, but rather a shift in their composition toward more burdensome flows bearing foreign interest and remittances of dividends.

Statistical tests in chapter 8 suggest that the bond market has been discriminating rather than promiscuous in its upsurge in the 1990s. The tests relate the issue spreads above government bonds in source countries to the logarithm of inflation (a proxy for policy instability), per capita income, real growth of exports and GDP, private versus public borrower, and whether the country asked for Brady debt reduction. The results are broadly significant and have the right signs. A country with inflation of 1,100 percent pays 300 basis points higher spread than one with 3 percent inflation. The penalty for Brady reduction is 75 basis points. More broadly, the data on bond markets, which provided $80 billion to 25 developing countries in 1989–93 (and about $20 billion to Mexico alone), suggest widespread capital market access and major promise for this vehicle.

To examine sustainability of the renewed capital flows, chapter 8 first examines the role of fiscal deficits. The analysis shows a sharp historic break: before 1987, there was a close correlation between capital inflows to the four largest Latin American countries and the size of their real fiscal deficits. After 1987, the two were no longer related, and the large inflows of the early 1990s were not to finance large fiscal deficits. This fact provides considerable grounds for comfort that the inflows of the 1990s are more sustainable than those of the late 1970s and early 1980s, even if one does not fully subscribe to the Nigel Lawson (UK Treasury) theory that current account deficits pose no problem if they do not stem from fiscal deficits.

An alternative gauge to sustainability is historical experience. Data in chapter 8 show that among five high-borrowing industrial countries, the highest current account deficits have been on the order of 30 percent of exports of goods and services (Spain, Denmark); and the same ceiling holds for three of four high-borrowing Asian countries. Only South Korea reached current account deficits as high as 50 percent of exports of goods and services, and then only for a brief period in the late 1960s. History thus suggests that the current account deficits of Argentina and Mexico, about 50 percent of exports of goods and services in 1992–93, are too large to be sustained over a long period. These large deficits arose more because of dramatic increases in imports (associated with trade liberalization as well as the exchange-rate anchor strategy to fight inflation) than from poor export performance, suggesting that if export growth can be maintained the deficits should narrow as import growth returns to more normal levels.

The capital market resurgence in the 1990s largely removed the problems of the Latin American debt crisis, but brought new if smaller problems. One was pressure on domestic monetary aggregates and thus inflation. Another was upward pressure on real exchange rates, and thus erosion of trade competitiveness purchased at considerable cost in the 1980s. Chapter 8 provides a brief review of the various efforts of countries to moderate capital inflows, and of the emerging literature addressing this problem. There would seem to be some merit to the view of Schadler, Carkovic, Bennett, and Kahn (1993) that where the inflows are in response to improved domestic policies and institutions the flows should be considered as "equilibrating," and that conversely inflows induced by high interest rates will be self-correcting if the government does not sterilize and thus permits interest rates to moderate. The authors favor fiscal tightening as the principal way to deal with excessive inflows and argue that alternatives such as high bank reserve requirements on foreign deposits have only temporary effects.

The art of dealing with the embarrassment of riches is far from well-established, however, and fiscal tightening is less than a panacea—as suggested by the Mexican case, where by 1993 the growth rate was down to 1 percent partly because of this response. However, this issue area may prove transitory if the tightening of international credit markets in 1994 (when US bond rates rose by 200 basis points) dampens the pressure of capital flows to developing countries. A dip in Brady bond prices in early 1994 was one indication of this possibility.

Capital market observers have lamented the exclusion of Eastern Europe and Africa from the resurgence of the early 1990s. However, Africa was never prominent in market borrowing. The bigger surprise was for Eastern Europe, considering that early in the decade many thought the region would preempt so much capital for the transition to capitalism that Latin America and other areas would be deprived. Instead, and remarkably, for 1992 capital inflows to Eastern Europe, Russia, and the Ukraine amounted to only $2\frac{1}{2}$ billion. In addition to macroeconomic transition problems, Eastern Europe so far has offered less opportunity for private equity inflows, because of infant stock markets and because of the more restrictive nature of privatizations in comparison with those of Latin America.

Once Eastern Europe (and Africa) do develop greater appeal for international capital, there should be little problem of crowding out other developing regions. The stock of financial assets in the industrial countries is on the order of $20 trillion, whereas capital flows to developing countries are in the range of $120 billion. Merely the reallocation of one-half of one percent of global portfolios to these countries annually could double these flows, and there is evidence that insurance companies and other institutional investors are prepared to increase portfolio shares held in emerging market assets.

Chapter 8 examines whether there is likely to be a new debt crisis in the next decade or so. The discussion suggests that the extent of borrowing today, and especially its use to finance fiscal deficits, is much less troublesome than it was in the 1970s and early 1980s. Debt indicators are much improved, as discussed above. For the late 1990s, economic recovery in Europe and Japan, plus Uruguay Round trade liberalization, should spur developing country exports.

The analysis examines vulnerability to a rise in world interest rates. The Baker-17 countries have reduced their variable interest external debt from 200 percent of exports in 1982 to about 135 percent (including allowance for Brady discount bonds). If the London interbank offer rate (LIBOR) were to rise from $3\frac{1}{2}$ percent in 1992–93 to 6 percent, the additional debt service burden would amount to only $3\frac{1}{2}$ percent of export earnings, which for their part would probably be strengthening because of the likely joint rise in industrial country growth and interest rates. Nor is there much vulnerability left from possible further declines in oil prices.

For its part, the international banking system is no longer vulnerable to LDC debt. Moreover, as Goldstein and Folkerts-Landau (1993) point out, the shift of capital markets from bank lending to securities provides not only greater flexibility but also a market mechanism for signaling difficulties as they arise. The correction of Latin American stock markets in the second half of 1992 already played some role in this direction, moderating inflows in 1993. As discussed above, however, one possible area for concern is excessive exuberance of the bond markets, in part because of the possible misperception of preferred-risk status.

Broadly, the response to the query about a new debt crisis is in the negative.[9] The world financial system is not at risk, and it seems likely that for at least the next decade the debtor countries that pursue sound domestic economic policies will continue to have access to capital markets, albeit at a possibly rising going interest rate.

Institutional Change

Chapter 8 concludes with consideration of institutional changes in the international credit market. Williamson (1992) has proposed the creation of an international entity to administer bankruptcy workouts, analogously to domestic US chapter 21 arrangements. Fukao (1992) has criticized the proposal on grounds that the impossibility of placing creditors on the board of directors of a borrowing country causes the analogy with domestic bankruptcy to break down. However, there is no reason why a given class of bonds or loans could not explicitly contain a clause providing for third-party arbitration and renegotiation of terms in the event of external shocks. Creditors entering into such contracts would presumably decide whether there should be a corresponding risk premium. Cautious borrowing countries might refrain from entering into loans that did not contain such a clause.

It would seem undesirable, however, to interpret such arrangements as applicable across the board to all credits despite the absence of pre-agreement on such procedures. Indeed, if the IMF had been in charge of a generalized bankruptcy agency in June 1989, the depth of debt forgiveness might have been set deeper than in the Brady framework to the detriment of market reentry, as discussed in chapter 5. Vulnerability to such arbitration should thus be consciously entered into and agreed in advance by the creditor.

A specific potential problem for the future capital market is that flows in the 1990s are developing primarily in the form of bonds and other securities rather than in syndicated bank loans, and thus could be much more difficult to orchestrate into coordinated measures in a future debt

9. This conclusion still holds after the Mexican peso crisis of December 1994 (see epilogue).

crisis than in that of the 1980s. The concentration of bank loans in large banks, and the centralization through advisory committees, greatly facilitated the orchestration of involuntary or concerted lending in the initial phase and through the Baker Plan, as well as the negotiations of reductions in the Brady Plan. Widely dispersed bonds in the 1990s would return the structure of lending to that of the 1930s, making corresponding organized response to a crisis difficult. More favorably, the prospect of major losses of dispersed bondholders would not have the same potential for systemic financial crisis that was present in the case of bank loans at the outbreak of the debt crisis.

The shift in the composition of flows suggests that special approaches should be considered for the international bond market in particular. Chapter 8 suggests that at some point, industrial country governments should communicate in some fashion that bond investors will be on their own in a future debt crisis—at least if there seems to be a trend toward excessive bond lending.

It would be worthwhile to go further and consider the creation of an International Bondholders Insurance Corporation (IBIC). Its purpose would be to secure a steadier and more sustainable flow of bond lending and greater chances of sound economic policies in borrowing countries.

The IBIC could be housed (for example) in the World Bank. It could essentially do for bonds what the Multilateral Investment Guarantee Agency (MIGA) does for direct investment, but hopefully on a much larger scale. Each year the IBIC board would evaluate the economic policies of borrowing countries. Countries with sound policies would qualify for coinsurance rates of, say, 60 to 80 percent of any future shortfall from scheduled interest payments on bonds issued in the year in question. Countries with weaker policies would be eligible only for lower coinsurance rates, perhaps as low as 20 percent. With a standard premium of, say, 50 basis points per year on covered bonds, the variable coinsurance rate would be an incentive to investors to purchase insured bonds of countries with strong policies but eschew those of countries with poor policies.

The agency would reinvest all premium receipts in safe international securities. In the event of country suspension of interest payment on the bond, the agency would pay to the insured party the coinsurance portion of the shortfall in interest due.

An important function of this arrangement would be to provide to the international official sector a vehicle through which signals could be sent regarding the soundness of economic policies in the borrowing country. One of the problems in the run-up to the debt crisis in the 1980s was that the ease of borrowing from the banks enabled Latin American and other middle-income countries to stay away from the International Monetary Fund, and there was no institutional arrangement for policy evaluation. Although the private credit-rating agencies (primarily Moody's and

Standard and Poor's) play this role for developing country bonds, there is some inherent risk that rating agencies become captives of client countries. Another role for the IBIC would be to act as the coordinating agent in the event that a country did go into arrears on its bonds.

Just as IBIC downgrading could send a signal to investors to hold back when country policy began to go awry, the agency's insurance could encourage bond capital flows when country policies were sound and the country's new bonds were eligible for the more favorable coinsurance rates. One possible effect would be to tip borderline cases toward investment-grade ratings by the National Association of Insurance Companies (in the United States, and its counterparts elsewhere), thereby markedly widening the potential supply of investment funds in view of the large portfolios of insurance and pension funds. At the same time, it would be appropriate for a participating country to reserve the right to remove itself from the insurance coverage during a period in which it was concerned about excessive capital inflows. New bonds issued by residents of that country would not be eligible for coverage until the country requested to be included again.

Any insurance scheme must address a start-up phase when accumulated premiums are small relative to potential exposure. Even so, the actuarial arithmetic of the arrangement would seem manageable. Chapter 8 and annex 8A set forth Monte Carlo random experiments to track the profit-loss trajectory of a hypothetical IBIC insuring bonds of the 20 largest middle-income countries over a 10-year period. The calculations suggest that under the great majority of cases, such an agency would make a profit. Indeed, it might be structured to have joint public-private stock participation. The estimates suggest that initial capital on the order of $100 million to $300 million would be ample.

In the absence of, or in addition to, the IBIC, the World Bank and/or IMF could play a signaling role through timely publication of summary country policy evaluations for perhaps 10 or 20 major countries active in the international bond market. The World Bank already publishes, with some lag, somewhat less detailed policy reviews (e.g., World Bank 1993e). The full internal country reviews of the agencies would not need to be made public, however.[10]

More immediately, the international community will need to decide soon whether the Brady Plan is a permanent fixture of the financial system, or should be declared a success and terminated. The Brady Plan was designed specifically to deal with the aftermath of the debt crisis of the 1980s, in other words with preexisting debt. There is a significant element of moral hazard if such a mechanism extends to debt contracted after its creation. That is, if creditors in the mid-1990s and beyond take

---

10. The traditional case for confidentiality of these reports turns on the difficulty of obtaining sensitive information from governments otherwise.

undue comfort that their losses will be minimized by Brady arrangements with official collateral, they might be less cautious than otherwise in evaluating borrowing countries. Similarly, if debtors consider that under the new conditions of the game debt forgiveness is more the rule than the exception, they could be insufficiently cautious in undertaking new debt.

As suggested in chapter 5, this potential for moral hazard, together with the fact that the Brady Plan is now in its final mopping-up stages, suggests that it is appropriate to consider announcing an ending date of, say, mid-1996 for the arrangement. After that date, countries could not expect IMF and World Bank set-asides for collateral on debt reduction instruments. This deadline could have the salutary effect of expediting agreement between banks and debtors on the few remaining unresolved cases, as well as shortening the gap between agreement in principle and implementation. Alternatively, the agencies could at least declare that these funds would only be available to support conversion instruments replacing debt originally contracted before a specified cutoff date, such as 1992.

Finally, chapter 5 suggests that additional regulatory guidelines for country limits on exposure of banks and securities firms would be helpful to guard against a repetition of the excessive lending of the 1970s. However, a possible chill on the emerging markets following the end-1994 Mexican peso crisis (epilogue) could warrant postponement of such measures until buoyancy returns to these markets.

2

Vital Signs for the Debt Strategy

More than a decade after the first major suspension of payments on Latin American debt, there is by now a broad perception that the debt crisis is over. This chapter examines the principal economic indicators for debt, developing country growth, and vulnerability of the international banking system to consider whether this perception is warranted.

Debt Indicators

In 1985 the "Baker Plan" identified 15 major debtor countries (later extended to 17) as a target group for measures within the international debt strategy. Although this group was not meant to be exclusive, it serves as an important benchmark for the countries considered to have been at the forefront of the debt crisis in the mid-1980s. Table 2.1 reports trends in total external debt for the 17 highly indebted countries (referred to below as HD17), as well as for three other country groupings. The data are from the World Bank's debt database (World Bank 1989b, 1990, 1992a, 1993b, 1995). In all, the data cover the 33 largest debtors among the developing countries. These nations accounted for 85 percent of the debt of all developing countries in 1982.[1] The discussion of this chapter focuses on trends through 1993, the most recent year for which debt data are available. It should be kept in mind, however, that in many cases the definitive improvement in debt indicators had already been achieved by 1992 or even earlier.

---

1. Note, however, that the trends for these relatively large debtors may not be the same as for numerous smaller debtor countries.

Table 2.1 Gross external debt, 1982-93 (millions of dollars)

Country	1982	1983	1984	1985	1986	1987	1988	1989	1990	1991	1992	1993
17 heavily indebted countries												
Argentina	43,634	45,919	48,858	50,946	52,450	58,458	58,741	65,257	62,234	65,397	67,770	74,473
Bolivia	3,328	4,069	4,317	4,805	5,575	5,836	4,902	4,136	4,278	4,076	4,220	4,212
Brazil	92,961	98,341	105,419	106,121	113,705	123,837	115,712	111,373	116,417	117,350	121,063	132,749
Chile	17,315	17,928	19,737	20,384	21,144	21,489	19,582	18,032	19,227	17,947	19,134	20,637
Colombia	10,306	11,412	12,039	14,245	15,362	17,008	16,994	16,878	17,231	17,337	17,197	17,173
Costa Rica	3,646	4,188	3,992	4,401	4,576	4,721	4,545	4,603	3,772	4,049	3,965	3,872
Côte d'Ivoire	8,945	8,843	8,565	9,638	10,548	12,575	12,574	14,056	16,622	17,559	17,988	19,145
Ecuador	7,705	7,595	8,305	8,702	9,334	10,474	10,746	11,317	12,109	12,468	12,280	14,110
Jamaica	2,846	3,445	3,585	4,089	4,216	4,733	4,569	4,573	4,663	4,516	4,393	4,279
Mexico	86,081	92,974	94,830	96,867	100,889	109,469	99,213	93,838	106,026	115,362	113,423	118,028
Morocco	12,535	13,399	14,219	16,526	17,907	20,796	21,026	21,639	23,531	21,567	21,599	21,430
Nigeria	12,954	18,540	18,536	19,550	23,403	30,655	31,246	31,997	34,537	34,436	30,998	32,531
Peru	10,712	11,343	12,157	12,884	14,888	17,491	18,245	18,583	20,069	20,719	20,293	20,328
Philippines	24,412	24,211	24,357	26,639	28,206	29,784	29,009	28,719	30,612	32,454	32,101	35,269
Uruguay	2,647	3,292	3,271	3,919	3,906	4,299	3,821	5,246	5,850	6,149	6,659	7,259
Venezuela	32,158	38,303	36,886	35,334	34,340	34,569	34,738	32,377	33,170	34,122	37,774	37,464
Yugoslavia	19,900	20,477	19,644	22,251	21,501	22,470	21,176	19,072	17,837	16,471	16,294	11,314[a]
SUBTOTAL	392,085	424,279	438,717	457,301	481,950	528,664	506,839	501,696	528,185	541,979	547,151	574,273

Other low income												
India	27,438	32,004	33,826	40,971	48,278	55,727	58,443	73,393	81,994	83,952	90,131	91,781
Indonesia	25,133	30,230	32,020	36,709	42,922	52,500	54,095	56,169	68,835	76,838	81,396	89,095
Pakistan	11,638	11,937	12,139	13,370	14,868	16,670	16,913	18,259	20,567	22,936	24,097	26,050
Sudan	7,218	7,601	8,612	9,128	9,870	11,562	11,934	13,844	15,303	15,834	16,085	16,560
Zaire	5,079	5,336	5,290	6,171	7,190	8,758	8,562	9,239	10,271	10,826	10,968	11,279
Zambia	3,689	3,782	3,804	4,576	5,745	6,625	6,840	6,710	7,242	7,286	6,943	6,788
SUBTOTAL	80,195	90,890	95,691	110,925	128,873	151,842	156,787	177,614	204,212	217,672	229,620	241,553
Other middle income												
Algeria	17,641	16,369	15,892	18,260	22,651	24,410	26,043	27,096	27,857	28,199	26,813	25,757
Egypt	29,526	32,636	35,692	42,140	46,346	52,198	52,677	51,714	40,455	41,019	40,517	40,626
South Korea	37,330	40,419	42,099	47,133	46,724	39,808	35,716	32,799	34,987	39,734	46,157	49,203
Malaysia	13,354	17,550	18,733	20,269	21,880	22,839	18,567	16,278	16,079	17,811	19,959	23,335
Syria	6,187	8,637	8,579	10,863	12,795	15,690	16,561	17,389	17,068	18,942	19,016	19,975
Thailand	12,238	13,902	15,013	17,552	18,505	20,305	21,673	23,452	28,264	35,954	39,612	45,819
Turkey	19,716	20,324	21,606	25,996	32,847	40,797	40,811	41,302	49,066	50,085	55,604	67,861
SUBTOTAL	135,992	149,837	157,614	182,213	201,748	216,047	212,048	210,030	213,776	231,744	247,678	272,576
Other Eastern Europe												
Hungary	10,196	10,735	10,993	13,956	16,908	19,585	19,609	20,397	21,276	22,624	21,975	24,771
Poland	18,738	20,149	21,132	33,307	36,641	42,603	42,103	43,096	49,367	53,603	48,695	45,305
Romania	10,003	9,128	7,758	7,008	6,983	6,580	2,960	1,087	1,173	2,152	3,533	4,456
SUBTOTAL	38,937	40,012	39,883	54,271	60,532	68,768	64,672	64,580	71,816	78,379	74,203	74,532
TOTAL, 33 countries	647,209	705,018	731,905	804,710	873,103	965,321	940,346	953,920	1,017,989	1,069,774	1,098,652	1,162,934

a. 1993 Yugoslavia figure excludes Croatia, Macedonia, and Slovenia.

Source: World Bank, *World Debt Tables* (*WDT*), various years.

Before considering the trends, it is useful to ask what would have been the ideal pattern. In the mid-1980s it was common for commentators to state two contradictory critiques of the debt strategy: first, alarm that total debt was rising, thereby indicating that the debt problem was not solved; and second, frustration that banks were not lending new money to the debtor countries, implying that the banks were not doing their part to solve the problem. Of course, the more the banks lent, the more the debt totals would rise, so rising debt could be considered either a favorable or unfavorable sign. The raw data can further be misleading because debt reductions from debt-equity conversion, discounted buybacks, or debt forgiveness can be a source of improvement rather than an indication of difficulty from lack of access to new borrowing.

The ideal pattern for debt trends would have been a moderate nominal increase at a pace well below the export growth rate and, probably, the interest rate as well as a stabilization or absolute decline of nominal debt when and where debt-equity conversions and other debt reductions became substantial. The export growth rate is relevant because exports provide the base out of which foreign exchange earnings must be drawn for debt servicing. The interest rate is relevant because in a phase of consolidation, debt should be growing more slowly than implied by complete rollover of interest on past debt.

In the event, the growth of debt of heavily indebted countries from 1982 through 1993 was positive but moderate, at rates below both the growth of exports and the interest rate. There were two distinct phases. From 1982 to 1987, *nominal external debt* of the HD17 in dollar terms rose by a cumulative 34.8 percent (table 2.1). Over the same period, cumulative interest on the debt, estimated on the basis of LIBOR (London interbank offer rate) plus a spread of 1 percent, amounted to 57.5 percent. New borrowing thus covered about three-fifths of interest obligations on the original debt.

In contrast, after 1987 debt either fell absolutely (1988–89) or grew at moderate rates and was offset by rising external reserves (discussed below). Nominal dollar debt for the HD17 fell by 5 percent from 1987 to 1989, and then rose by about 14 percent from 1989 to 1993, for a net increase of only 8.6 percent over the six-year period. By 1993, cumulative interest on the original 1982 debt stood at 141 percent (again based on LIBOR plus 1 percent), whereas the actual debt outstanding was only 46.5 percent above the 1982 base. For the full period, new borrowing thus covered only one-third of interest due on the original debt. The decline in debt during 1988–89 reflected debt-equity conversions and discounted buybacks. Similarly, the relatively slow growth in 1990–93 in part reflected the influence of debt reduction under the Brady Plan.

By 1993 the stock of debt was somewhat exaggerated in comparison with its economic value, because by then there were substantial amounts of Brady "par bonds" that had kept the face value of bank debt but cut interest rates. Argentina, Mexico, and Venezuela had a combined total of $45 billion in par bonds, with economic value only worth about two-thirds that amount because of the reduced interest rates (see chapters 5 and 6). For the three countries, total gross debt overstated economic value by about 7 percent as a result.

Two other considerations reinforce the diagnosis of only moderate debt buildup after 1989. First, reserves rose by more than debt. Second, the increased debt in this period went mainly to the private sector, so that there were lesser implications of a public sector "internal transfer burden" from this increased debt than from the bulk of the debt in the 1980s.

For the HD17 countries, from 1989 to 1993 gross debt rose from $501.7 billion to $574.3 billion, or by $72.6 billion. During the same period, their nongold reserves rose from $37.4 billion to $114.5 billion, or by $77.1 billion. Net debt thus declined in absolute nominal terms, and fell even further in real terms and relative to the export base (as discussed below). Despite the revival of the capital markets in the early 1990s, the HD17 were not getting overindebted once again—their nominal net debt was not even rising.

Real external debt of the HD17, after taking account of world inflation, rose substantially less than nominal debt (table 2.2). If the US wholesale price index is used to deflate the dollar value of debt, real external debt of the group rose by 23.1 percent over the period 1982–93, or by 1.9 percent annually. If the unit value of exports of industrial countries is applied as the deflator, real debt was only about 1 percent higher in 1993 than in 1982, after first rising by about 25 percent from 1982 to 1985 as the dollar rose against European currencies and the yen, and then falling back again as the dollar depreciated.

The absolute level of debt by 1993 as compared with 1988, the last year before the Brady Plan, provides a gauge of the extent to which the shift toward debt reduction as the official strategy accomplished a lowering of the debt burden. For the HD17, the nominal value of external debt was 13.3 percent higher at the end of 1993 than at the end of 1988 (table 2.1). It is evident, then, that there was no massive reduction in overall debt as the consequence of the Brady Plan. Brady Plan reductions played a crucial psychological role in selected countries, but hardly amounted to a deep and widespread alleviation of debt.

Yet the aggregates did show major improvement in the level of debt as normalized by the economic base of exports and GNP, especially as measured against the most unfavorable years, 1986–87. Table 2.3 reports trends in the *ratio of net external debt* (gross debt minus reserves) *to exports of goods and nonfactor services.*[2] For the HD17 countries, this ratio rose

---

2. Gold is excluded from reserves in the data set here. The series slightly overstates net external debt as a result, by about 3 percent for Latin American debtor countries.

Table 2.2 Gross external debt—deflated, 1982-93

	1982	1983	1984	1985	1986	1987	1988	1989	1990	1991	1992	1993
Deflated by US wholesale prices, constant 1982 prices												
HD-17	392,085	419,089	423,002	443,125	480,957	513,817	473,604	446,823	454,136	465,171	466,716	482,668
Other low income	80,195	89,778	92,263	107,486	128,608	147,578	146,506	158,187	175,582	186,824	195,864	203,022
Other middle income	135,992	148,004	151,968	176,564	201,332	209,979	198,143	187,058	183,806	198,902	211,268	229,096
Other Eastern Europe	38,937	39,523	38,454	52,589	60,407	66,837	60,431	57,517	61,748	67,271	63,295	62,643
Total	647,209	696,394	705,688	779,764	871,305	938,211	878,684	849,585	875,272	918,167	937,142	977,429
Deflated by industrial country export prices, constant 1982 prices												
HD-17	392,085	438,190	466,137	489,769	448,452	439,596	395,933	390,776	376,622	389,570	381,093	395,032
Other low income	80,195	93,870	101,672	118,801	119,916	126,260	122,479	138,345	145,613	156,461	159,931	166,160
Other middle income	135,992	154,750	167,465	195,150	187,726	179,648	165,648	163,594	152,433	166,576	172,509	187,500
Other Eastern Europe	38,937	41,324	42,376	58,124	56,325	57,182	50,521	50,302	51,208	56,338	51,683	51,269
Total	647,209	728,133	777,649	861,844	812,418	802,685	734,581	743,017	725,876	768,945	765,215	799,961

Sources: Gross external debt, see table 2.1. US wholesale prices, and industrial country export prices, from IMF, *International Financial Statistics (IFS)* and *World Economic Outlook*.

from 290 percent in 1982 to a peak of 384 percent in 1986, and then declined to 225 percent by 1993.[3] The large jump in 1986 was driven for the oil exporters by the fall in oil prices and in Argentina and Brazil by the erosion of exports associated with domestic price stabilization programs. In short, during the decade of the debt crisis the debt/exports ratio first deteriorated, rising by about one-fourth; and then improved, to a level about one-fourth below its 1982 base.

For the HD17, in 1986 the dollar value of exports stood 6 percent lower than in 1982, at $122.9 billion versus $130.9 billion (IMF 1994a). Four oil countries alone (Ecuador, Mexico, Nigeria, and Venezuela) more than accounted for this decline, as their combined exports fell by almost $20 billion as a consequence of the oil price collapse. By 1993, in contrast, exports of the HD17 had surged to $208.3 billion, an increase of 70 percent from the 1986 trough (IMF 1994a).

In broad terms, then, it was a brisk recovery of export earnings combined with a buildup in reserves that fully offset any rise in debt, rather than a massive write-down in debt, that caused debt indicators for the highly indebted countries to improve so much in the period 1989–93. The end result was to leave net debt/exports ratios in 1993 far below their 1986 peak, and substantially below their starting point in 1982 as well. As interest rates had fallen sharply from the 1982 levels, overall improvement was even greater, as discussed below.

Table 2.4 shows an alternative measure of the debt burden, the *ratio of net external debt to gross national product*. The GNP figures are World Bank estimates that use the current exchange rate to convert domestic currency GNP into dollar values. On this measure, for the HD17 there was a jump of about one-fourth in the relative debt burden from 1982 to 1983 (that is, from 41 percent to 52 percent), a plateau for four years, and another large rise to a 67 percent peak in 1987. Moderate reduction in 1988–89 and brisk improvement in 1990–93 brought the ratio back down to 42 percent by the end of the period.

These swings were more pronounced than for the real value of debt. Major changes in real exchange rates contributed to the difference. For example, the dramatic drop of the debt/GNP ratio for Argentina from a peak of 118 percent in 1989 to 41 percent in 1992 reflected a reversal of a severely undervalued exchange rate in 1989. For the group as a whole, the debt/GNP ratio by 1993 was much lower than for the bulk of the

---

3. For group averages, 1982 GNP shares are applied as weights. Base-period economic size would seem to be the most relevant weighting criterion. Current debt would bias the average toward a rising debt burden, as the countries with rapidly growing debt would obtain an increasing weight. Base-period debt could be an appropriate alternative weighting system if the focus were primarily on aggregate debt, for example from the perspective of creditors. Note that weighting by base-period GNP tends to emphasize larger countries, especially because they are less open and tend to have larger GNP relative to external variables including debt.

Table 2.3 Net external debt/exports of goods and services, 1982-93 (percentage)

Country	1982	1983	1984	1985	1986	1987	1988	1989	1990	1991	1992	1993
17 heavily indebted countries												
Argentina	447.8	481.8	495.6	474.9	589.7	698.3	497.0	542.5	389.2	409.3	390.9	384.0
Bolivia	348.6	455.5	496.9	639.5	811.9	882.7	715.0	453.5	420.9	432.7	522.4	500.0
Brazil	405.3	398.1	324.5	344.7	446.6	416.1	294.9	272.2	314.4	318.1	246.3	238.1
Chile	333.9	343.4	404.1	398.9	359.1	300.9	198.7	149.8	129.6	97.5	79.6	92.9
Colombia	145.7	251.4	206.6	282.6	197.0	204.3	204.0	181.5	148.4	121.3	106.5	99.3
Costa Rica	306.3	342.3	281.1	319.1	290.6	291.6	239.2	209.7	166.7	143.8	114.5	95.1
Côte d'Ivoire	319.6	354.1	285.8	304.9	287.8	360.5	386.9	428.2	462.1	535.5	524.4	583.5
Ecuador	273.3	261.0	264.2	241.8	330.4	408.3	391.4	375.3	346.4	338.7	315.0	357.9
Jamaica	219.9	277.3	276.0	335.1	311.0	299.8	267.8	235.9	204.1	198.1	153.8	164.2
Mexico	328.0	328.3	291.4	335.5	435.3	351.3	323.3	266.3	250.8	246.4	228.4	207.4
Morocco	422.0	455.4	472.6	523.0	497.3	488.4	380.2	425.5	344.3	305.3	285.7	293.3
Nigeria	89.6	163.4	139.0	133.1	357.4	379.5	421.4	359.0	209.5	228.3	233.8	235.8
Peru	229.1	267.8	275.8	291.2	400.4	469.0	481.1	405.9	468.5	438.8	418.8	388.5
Philippines	344.7	344.4	337.8	379.1	343.8	357.3	295.2	247.2	259.8	233.8	190.2	190.6
Uruguay	79.7	148.2	180.6	230.5	160.4	157.1	124.1	185.2	205.6	285.3	284.8	274.1
Venezuela	145.7	193.5	166.9	164.2	294.0	250.3	286.3	201.5	132.0	144.3	182.6	181.0
Yugoslavia	126.9	149.5	139.7	152.7	131.9	138.4	107.9	78.6	59.8	84.8	119.8	119.8[b]
AVERAGE[a]	290.4	311.8	278.4	298.8	384.4	368.1	312.8	276.1	252.1	255.0	231.8	225.3
Other low income												
India	190.2	207.3	208.5	268.9	310.8	324.0	309.5	342.8	324.1	330.3	325.6	302.7
Indonesia	108.6	137.8	127.8	163.8	255.1	256.7	234.9	204.1	209.5	197.4	184.2	191.5
Pakistan	339.8	273.3	339.5	359.7	352.5	329.6	314.2	296.7	298.0	285.0	280.2	300.3

Sudan	823.5	968.1	1,105.4	1,113.7	1,792.7	2,644.3	2,025.1	1,692.5	3,064.5	4,170.3	4,359.4	4,225.3
Zaire	292.7	283.5	246.3	294.8	337.0	428.2	352.0	383.1	436.2	471.7	477.9	589.3
Zambia	332.0	356.7	387.3	505.8	767.7	723.8	537.4	462.2	505.1	625.4	553.2	520.1
AVERAGE[a]	201.3	215.7	221.5	270.5	337.6	365.1	330.9	332.8	356.3	382.0	378.9	371.4
excluding Sudan	187.5	199.1	201.9	251.9	305.4	314.7	293.5	302.7	296.5	298.3	290.9	286.2
Other middle income												
Algeria	108.4	108.0	107.7	113.8	243.7	237.3	310.8	261.7	201.5	210.0	199.3	194.3
Egypt	422.8	466.8	510.0	602.7	759.9	753.8	716.3	685.8	381.9	326.2	261.3	242.3
South Korea	125.3	128.3	120.0	138.2	106.4	65.8	33.7	24.5	27.2	31.8	33.1	29.6
Malaysia	70.2	89.2	81.3	89.4	101.4	76.4	51.5	30.7	19.2	18.0	6.0	-7.6
Syria	241.0	346.4	354.3	429.2	800.4	790.4	812.3	449.0	335.3	416.2	429.5	425.2
Thailand	125.1	150.8	140.8	168.8	141.4	111.1	76.3	55.1	51.2	51.9	48.1	49.4
Turkey	238.7	242.7	213.0	229.4	305.8	281.9	224.9	207.4	213.3	210.7	211.8	245.2
AVERAGE[a]	171.9	188.1	182.2	208.0	266.8	242.6	225.8	185.4	142.5	143.8	135.8	137.5
Other Eastern Europe												
Hungary	81.6	99.3	97.4	128.3	147.1	164.0	164.4	162.5	168.6	153.2	125.5	165.3
Poland	135.3	142.5	146.5	248.6	257.8	288.6	245.4	253.8	235.7	276.4	238.5	231.8
Romania	77.1	70.3	52.3	62.4	61.3	46.0	17.8	-6.8	12.5	34.9	53.9	60.8
AVERAGE	105.1	108.9	103.9	160.5	167.6	179.3	148.9	143.6	143.2	167.8	152.3	158.4
AVERAGE[a], 33 countries	237.3	254.9	236.4	266.6	337.4	331.1	288.6	261.8	246.4	255.4	239.5	235.2

a. Average based on 1982 GNP weights.
b. Yugoslavia 1993 repeats previous year figure.

Sources: Gross external debt, see table 2.1. Nongold reserves and exports of goods and services from IFS. Exports is sum of merchandise f.o.b and service credits in IFS.

Table 2.4 Net external debt/GNP, 1982-93 (percentage)

Country	1982	1983	1984	1985	1986	1987	1988	1989	1990	1991	1992	1993
17 heavily indebted countries												
Argentina	79.0	75.3	65.8	78.8	66.9	74.6	62.4	118.0	58.0	45.4	40.6	40.3
Bolivia	101.4	141.9	167.6	169.3	151.4	141.7	115.2	92.3	96.6	83.1	79.5	76.1
Brazil	34.6	48.3	47.1	45.2	42.1	41.4	33.7	23.6	23.6	27.7	25.5	25.1
Chile	68.7	87.6	100.6	126.1	125.9	110.1	81.4	61.4	50.6	34.0	25.4	26.4
Colombia	16.8	25.1	28.6	37.8	37.9	40.2	36.6	35.5	34.2	28.3	20.9	19.5
Costa Rica	157.1	137.8	107.0	106.9	98.0	100.1	91.3	80.2	59.5	57.1	46.9	42.8
Côte d'Ivoire	126.7	140.8	140.5	152.4	121.3	132.6	133.2	168.4	195.9	217.1	206.9	222.7
Ecuador	64.2	70.9	82.6	71.0	83.9	101.8	111.0	118.5	114.9	106.0	94.9	104.1
Jamaica	97.6	110.3	160.4	226.8	195.3	181.0	145.7	127.3	128.8	146.7	153.0	136.2
Mexico	52.0	63.8	52.9	52.4	78.2	73.0	57.2	44.5	41.2	34.9	29.3	28.7
Morocco	83.4	99.9	116.5	135.6	108.5	113.4	96.8	97.5	85.9	69.6	65.4	64.4
Nigeria	12.4	19.8	18.6	22.9	57.7	121.2	105.1	105.8	95.3	94.6	107.3	108.1
Peru	37.8	52.4	52.9	73.1	60.2	64.9	101.7	64.8	57.4	37.8	35.8	32.4
Philippines	59.9	68.8	75.2	87.1	90.5	88.0	74.3	64.9	67.0	63.8	51.6	56.0
Uruguay	27.9	60.8	64.2	85.7	61.6	53.5	45.2	62.1	66.7	60.6	54.6	57.0
Venezuela	32.9	38.8	48.4	41.9	47.3	61.3	54.1	68.9	52.1	44.8	47.4	47.9
Yugoslavia	30.3	41.7	41.8	45.8	31.0	33.5	31.5	19.4	14.2	15.8	22.3	22.3[b]
AVERAGE[a]	41.5	52.2	51.5	54.6	59.7	66.9	57.6	54.4	46.9	43.9	42.4	42.5
Other low income												
India	12.6	13.6	14.5	16.3	18.5	19.4	19.8	26.0	27.6	32.7	35.4	32.9
Indonesia	24.4	31.7	33.1	37.9	50.6	64.9	61.2	56.4	60.4	60.9	56.7	58.4
Pakistan	35.1	35.2	36.2	38.0	41.8	46.3	41.7	43.1	49.4	47.8	46.3	48.1

Sudan	101.1	82.5	76.9	93.0	73.9	73.4	120.5	133.2	175.1	220.5	224.1	217.2
Zaire	36.1	47.8	75.9	89.5	89.8	116.3	97.4	105.9	140.1	161.2	177.6	221.8
Zambia	99.9	121.4	152.9	216.4	412.1	371.1	207.7	166.0	215.9	218.5	266.5	250.1
AVERAGE[a]	21.8	24.7	27.1	31.2	38.0	43.5	40.7	43.2	48.6	53.4	54.9	55.7
excluding Sudan	20.0	23.4	26.0	29.8	37.3	42.9	38.9	41.2	45.9	49.7	51.2	52.1
Other middle income												
Algeria	34.7	30.4	28.6	27.3	34.1	36.2	44.0	49.0	47.0	65.7	58.7	57.3
Egypt	121.1	121.3	122.3	131.7	141.9	158.6	182.0	161.2	119.4	117.1	85.9	79.1
South Korea	48.4	47.9	45.2	49.3	42.2	28.1	13.5	8.3	8.3	9.3	9.9	9.2
Malaysia	37.5	49.5	47.4	53.0	61.2	52.0	36.8	24.1	15.5	15.4	5.0	-6.6
Syria	43.6	49.2	47.7	66.1	97.5	141.5	162.7	172.3	130.7	115.7	107.5	105.2
Thailand	30.5	31.3	32.2	41.9	38.5	34.1	26.6	20.4	18.6	20.1	18.7	19.2
Turkey	36.2	38.3	42.2	48.4	55.5	58.9	55.9	47.2	40.4	42.4	45.7	53.1
AVERAGE[a]	46.6	47.7	47.4	53.1	56.6	56.1	53.7	48.0	39.3	42.3	37.5	36.8
Other Eastern Europe												
Hungary	35.1	46.2	47.7	59.7	64.2	71.6	65.5	68.6	64.2	61.8	49.8	54.2
Poland	29.0	26.6	27.4	47.4	50.5	67.4	60.8	51.6	76.2	65.2	50.0	44.6
Romania	19.7	20.5	15.4	13.1	11.7	13.7	5.4	-1.9	2.1	6.3	12.2	13.8
AVERAGE[a]	26.6	27.7	26.5	37.0	38.7	48.6	41.5	35.0	47.2	43.2	36.2	35.0
AVERAGE[a], 33 countries	37.1	43.8	43.7	48.1	53.0	58.8	52.2	49.5	46.0	45.5	43.6	43.6

a. Average based on 1982 GNP weights.
b. Yugoslavia 1993 repeats previous year figure.

Sources: Gross external debt, see table 2.1. Nongold reserves and exports of goods and services from *IFS*.

decade of the 1980s. Nonetheless, it was little different from the ratio at the outset of the debt crisis in 1982. However, real exchange rates were often at unsustainably strong levels on the eve of the debt crisis, so the debt/GNP ratios at that time were misleadingly low.

A final measure of the relative debt burden is provided by the *ratio of net interest payments to exports of goods and nonfactor services*. The appropriate accounting concept for this measure (and the definition used in the data shown in table 2.5) is accrual rather than cash. Otherwise, a country's measured debt burden would suddenly disappear if it stopped paying interest, even though interest arrears were accumulating.[4]

The interest/exports ratio is perhaps the best indicator of the relative debt burden, as it captures not only the stock of debt but also its price—the interest rate. This price fell substantially during the course of the 1980s. Thus, LIBOR fell from an average of 11.2 percent in 1982–84 to 7.9 percent in 1985–90, 5.9 percent in 1991, 3.8 percent in 1992, and 3.25 percent in 1993 (IMF 1992a, 1994a). Similarly, the interest/exports ratio is superior to the more conventional "debt service ratio," which includes principal payments. Repayment of principal is not an economic burden as it is merely an exchange of one asset (resources) for another—a reduction in liability. Nor was principal repayment a cash-flow burden for most of the major troubled debtor countries in the 1980s, as the norm was full rollover of principal in debt reschedulings.

Although not all debt is at variable interest, there was enough responsiveness in the falling interest-rate price of debt that for the HD17 countries the ratio of net interest to exports of goods and services fell from 30 percent in 1982 to a plateau of 25 percent in 1984–88 and about 11 percent by 1992–93. For this crucial ratio, then, there was a reduction by more than one-half from the beginning of the debt crisis to 1993. In contrast, the simple net debt/exports ratio only fell by about one-fourth (table 2.3). Moreover, there was consistent progress on the interest/exports ratio, whereas the debt/exports ratio showed a substantial worsening from the outbreak of the crisis to the period 1986–87.

It is worth noting that even on the more appropriate measure, interest/exports, the debt strategy was "stuck" at a plateau at the eve of the policy shift toward forgiveness under the Brady Plan (1988), although it was well below the 1982 level. In contrast, the debt/exports ratio was close to its high and still well above the 1982 level. Those who focused on debt relative to exports—rather than on the cost of debt incorporating the influence of falling interest rates—could easily have

---

4. The interest data used for table 2.5 are as follows. Cash interest payments reported by the World Bank (1993b) are augmented by any increment in interest arrears to obtain accrual interest for the year in question. (The data for 1993 are estimated based on total capital service debits reported in IMF, 1994a, and the ratio of interest to total capital service debits in recent years.) Interest earnings on official reserves, imputed at the US Treasury bill rate, are deducted to obtain net interest.

Figure 2.1 17 heavily indebted countries, 1982-93

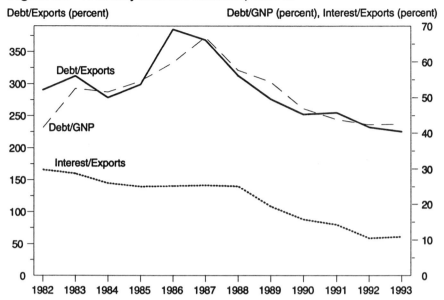

reached the overly pessimistic conclusion of a steady deterioration rather than slowdown in improvement.

Figure 2.1 summarizes the trends for the external debt burden of the HD17 countries. Under all three measures there was major improvement by 1990–93 as compared to the mid-1980s. Over the period 1982–93, the improvement was the greatest when measured by the criterion incorporating both the cost and amount of debt (interest/exports).

The International Monetary Fund provides estimates of more recent and prospective debt trends. The institution estimates that for the (original) Baker 15 countries—almost identical in economic size to the expanded group of 17 considered here—the ratio of debt to GNP fell from 35.8 percent in 1993 to 31.7 percent in 1994 and a projected 29.7 percent for 1995, but that the interest/exports ratio rose from 14.7 percent in 1993 to 18.6 percent in 1994 and an expected 17.5 percent in 1995 (IMF 1994b, 179–80).

The IMF estimates of the interest/exports ratio indicate that by 1994 the HD17 debt burden was back up to its 1989 level (18.5 percent; IMF 1994b, 180). Although the rise in LIBOR in 1994 no doubt caused some rise in this ratio, the IMF estimates would seem misleading. First, the gross interest/exports ratio does not take account of interest earnings on reserves, which were rising rapidly as discussed above. Second, the whole IMF series is somewhat higher than the corresponding World Bank data (which place the 1993 gross interest/exports ratio for Latin America at only 12.3 percent; World Bank 1993b, 1: 186).

Table 2.5 Net interest payments[a]/exports of goods and services, 1982-93 (percentage)

Country	1982	1983	1984	1985	1986	1987	1988	1989	1990	1991	1992	1993
17 heavily indebted countries												
Argentina	33.3	62.8	55.6	48.0	46.8	47.1	41.9	44.8	26.5	36.2	16.3	13.4
Bolivia	10.5	38.5	52.4	40.1	22.5	20.8	15.7	12.0	14.3	13.6	17.3	16.8
Brazil	47.1	38.7	28.5	28.5	29.1	35.8	34.7	20.2	19.5	13.3	6.8	8.8
Chile	40.5	32.9	46.7	38.8	27.9	23.5	13.1	14.5	17.5	13.9	10.8	7.5
Colombia	12.5	18.8	16.0	25.5	22.7	17.0	16.8	19.5	13.6	11.5	9.1	10.7
Costa Rica	28.9	45.4	21.9	25.9	20.6	20.2	15.5	9.1	4.7	6.4	6.1	7.2
Côte d'Ivoire	24.7	27.6	23.3	23.8	24.1	18.7	25.9	26.3	20.3	22.7	24.1	27.0
Ecuador	34.9	21.5	28.8	24.4	28.6	33.1	26.6	25.9	27.4	24.8	14.9	14.7
Jamaica	14.6	16.6	23.9	23.9	22.7	18.2	16.0	14.9	11.1	10.6	7.6	7.2
Mexico	37.8	32.1	30.7	30.6	31.6	23.3	21.4	20.4	12.5	13.8	12.4	13.0
Morocco	25.9	25.4	26.6	24.1	25.2	23.3	22.6	21.3	19.1	19.3	15.8	16.8
Nigeria	8.3	12.3	15.8	12.5	12.0	16.5	23.9	16.7	16.8	17.2	13.2	17.1
Peru[b]	22.2	20.1	30.9	27.6	30.6	30.0	33.8	30.0	40.5	34.5	29.9	31.3
Philippines	32.7	25.3	22.9	20.7	18.1	18.5	19.0	16.4	12.4	11.2	11.2	7.9
Uruguay	4.8	15.0	20.5	22.6	17.0	16.0	13.4	7.5	7.5	2.1	3.8	2.2
Venezuela	5.5	9.6	4.6	9.1	14.0	11.3	14.0	11.7	4.3	3.5	9.5	4.6
Yugoslavia	11.0	12.5	18.4	11.7	12.3	10.9	9.7	5.3	4.4	5.0	3.7	3.7[c]
AVERAGE[d]	29.8	28.7	26.0	25.0	25.2	25.4	25.1	19.4	15.8	14.3	10.5	10.9
Other low income												
India	0.3	7.5	9.3	11.2	13.5	14.9	15.8	15.2	15.2	14.9	12.0	11.1
Indonesia	7.0	8.1	7.6	8.4	12.9	13.1	13.7	12.1	11.4	11.0	9.1	10.3
Pakistan	9.2	9.0	9.6	11.1	11.9	10.2	10.6	10.0	10.6	11.0	10.8	12.2
Sudan	43.5	24.0	41.2	48.9	76.3	138.9	92.9	166.9	153.9	113.9	97.3	89.2

Zaire	21.0	7.4	12.4	13.4	9.3	8.8	15.8	5.9	11.0	21.5	25.8	24.3
Zambia	17.0	14.1	11.2	21.4	19.6	29.8	19.0	21.3	7.6	26.1	13.1	14.7
AVERAGE[d]	4.9	8.2	9.7	11.4	14.4	16.6	16.4	16.8	16.5	16.0	13.5	13.3
excluding Sudan	4.1	7.8	9.0	10.6	13.1	13.9	14.7	13.5	13.4	13.9	11.7	11.6
Other middle income												
Algeria	9.2	9.1	10.0	9.9	16.6	16.0	23.7	19.1	15.1	16.0	16.4	16.9
Egypt	15.1	19.4	18.6	22.3	39.2	6.9	18.9	18.2	-1.5	-2.2	9.3	3.1
South Korea	12.8	10.7	10.3	10.9	7.6	4.5	3.0	1.8	0.4	0.3	0.5	0.2
Malaysia	2.2	3.8	5.1	6.3	6.8	4.7	3.2	1.3	-1.1	0.0	-0.5	0.7
Syria	4.9	6.0	6.4	5.9	10.8	9.6	11.7	5.9	7.8	5.0	4.8	6.2
Thailand	10.2	11.6	10.8	12.3	9.9	7.3	5.8	3.9	3.2	4.0	4.1	5.6
Turkey	19.7	21.8	17.6	15.3	16.9	15.1	16.4	13.6	12.2	11.1	11.8	12.2
AVERAGE[d]	12.0	12.6	11.8	12.1	14.1	9.3	11.3	8.9	5.6	5.5	6.7	6.6
Other Eastern Europe												
Hungary	10.0	9.1	9.9	8.5	10.0	9.4	9.7	11.7	11.9	11.1	10.6	14.9
Poland[e]	22.0	20.1	18.6	18.7	18.4	19.8	17.5	19.2	17.5	16.0	21.7	21.5
Romania	5.2	4.6	3.8	5.3	5.3	4.4	1.7	-0.7	-2.6	-0.2	2.9	2.6
AVERAGE[d]	13.9	12.6	11.8	12.1	12.2	12.4	10.4	10.7	9.2	9.3	13.0	13.5
AVERAGE[d], 33 countries	20.5	20.5	19.1	19.0	20.1	19.9	19.8	16.4	13.7	12.8	10.7	10.9

a. Interest payments, calculated on accrual basis.
b. Peru net interest payments from central bank.
c. Yugoslavia 1993 repeats previous year figure.
d. Average based on 1982 GNP weights.
e. Poland net interest payments from BOP Statistics Yearbook.

Sources: Gross external debt, see table 2.1. Nongold reserves and exports of goods and services from IFS. Interest payments from WDT, receipts from BOP Statistics Yearbook.

In sum, although there may have been a rise in the interest/exports ratio in 1994 as a consequence of rising dollar interest rates, a proper evaluation including the influence of interest earned on reserves would be likely to show that even in 1994 the net interest/exports ratio remained well below the 1989 level for the HD17, and even further below the 1982 level. Chapter 8 examines the issue of vulnerability of the major debtors to increased interest rates in the mid-1990s.

A supplementary measure of debt health is the secondary market price for bank claims (percent of face value). Figure 2.2 shows strong upward trends in these prices by 1990 for Mexico and Venezuela and by 1991 for Argentina and Brazil. Moreover, the price range of 65 to 70 cents on the dollar by late 1991 and early 1992 for Mexican and Venezuelan debt effectively meant close to 100 cents for each dollar of converted obligation under the Brady Plan agreements, implying that the "bad-credit" risk premium had largely disappeared. The prices reported here are for the "par bond" after conversion, and these bonds were set at fixed interest rates calibrated to provide a 35 percent debt reduction in the case of Mexico and 30 percent in the Venezuelan case.[5]

By the first half of 1994, however, there had been an abrupt reduction on the order of one-fourth from the peaks. The shift of the US Federal Reserve toward higher interest rates in February 1994 triggered the drop, but there were also effects of political uncertainty (assassination of the leading presidential candidate in Mexico, rising risk of a leftist presidential victory in Brazil). The largest drop was in Venezuela, where the new government adopted interventionist policies, and where a domestic banking crisis emerged in early 1994. By August 1994 there had been significant price recoveries for Mexican and Brazilian debt associated with improved expectations for presidential elections. As this review suggests, the secondary market price is a far more volatile indicator of debt prospects than the traditional debt ratios. Despite its fluctuations in 1994, the overall trend for secondary market prices in the period after the adoption of the Brady Plan remained positive (figure 2.2).

So far the review of this chapter has considered indicators of debt burden viewed from the perspective of the external transfer problem. However, as stressed in the debt literature (chapter 4) and in the country studies of debt recovery in Latin America (chapter 6), the internal transfer problem of mobilizing resources from the private sector to service public debt can be equally or more important. Thus, in the late 1980s Argentina and Brazil experienced large external surpluses but went into arrears on external debt largely because the governments were experi-

---

5. Note, however, that the par bond price also contains an element of interest rate gain, as international rates had fallen by early 1992 to levels below those prevailing at the time of the two countries' respective debt reduction agreements.

Figure 2.2 Secondary market value, 1989 (Q4)-1994 (Q2)

cents per dollar

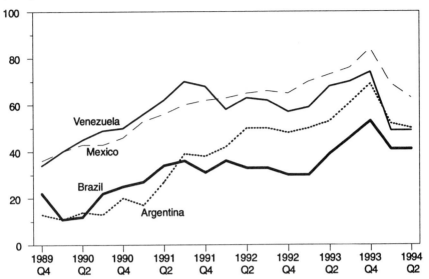

Source: World Bank, *Financial Flows to Developing Countries*, various issues.

encing severe fiscal deficits and foreign debt service was not their highest priority use for their scarce revenues.

Table 2.6 reports the trends for fiscal deficits for the 17 heavily indebted countries. It cannot be emphasized too strongly that these standardized data, from the International Monetary Fund's international tables (IMF 1994c), are shaky. Fiscal data are notoriously difficult to compile, and different countries report different concepts. Particularly where inflation is high, the "real" deficit may be much smaller than the nominal deficit. However, with the caveat that the data in table 2.6 should be viewed only as illustrative, they do show a favorable trend toward reduction of fiscal deficits from high levels in the early and mid-1980s to much lower levels by 1990–92.

More reliable fiscal data from major Latin American countries (typically on bases different from the standardized presentation in table 2.6) are presented in chapter 6. The analysis there confirms the sharp improvement in fiscal performance in the cases of Argentina, Mexico, and (at least through 1991) Venezuela, and emphasizes the crucial role of this adjustment in making possible the resolution of the debt problem.

In sum, for the large, heavily indebted countries, several major indicators showed that, by 1991–92 and after, the relative burden of external debt had declined and creditworthiness had improved substantially.

Table 2.6 Central government fiscal balances, 1982-92 (percentage of GDP)

Country	1982	1983	1984	1985	1986	1987	1988	1989	1990	1991	1992
17 heavily indebted countries											
Argentina	-5.03	-7.95	-3.38	-5.51	-1.97	-2.86	-1.88	-0.38	..	..	..
Bolivia	..	..	..	..	-0.06	0.66	-0.64	-1.24	-1.49	-0.06	..
Brazil	-2.62	-4.21	-5.09	-11.12	-13.30	-12.04	-15.24	-16.07	-5.64	-0.92	..
Chile	-0.98	-2.63	-2.97	-2.29	-0.92	0.44	-0.21	1.80	0.84	1.55	2.29
Colombia	-4.73	-4.19	-4.32	-2.71	-0.86	-0.69	-1.33	-1.90	..	..	..
Costa Rica	-0.88	-2.01	-0.74	-1.25	-4.48	-2.91	..	-2.13	-3.14	-1.33	..
Côte d'Ivoire	..	..	..	..	..	..	..	..	..	..	..
Ecuador	-4.45	-2.51	-0.83	1.98	-2.24	-2.28	-0.05	1.88	0.19	..	..
Jamaica	-14.53	-18.33	-5.57	-8.20	..	..	..	..	..	..	..
Mexico	-14.84	-7.62	-7.11	-8.40	-13.14	-13.57	-10.33	-5.22	-0.74	..	..
Morocco	-11.44	-7.75	-6.02	-7.28	-7.67	-4.48	-3.22	-5.13	-2.22	..	..
Nigeria	..	..	-4.41	-2.76	-3.38	-8.22	..	..	..	..	..
Peru	-3.22	-7.52	-4.45	-2.42	-4.10	-6.23	-3.60	-5.66	-3.73	-1.40	-1.64
Philippines	-4.54	-2.02	-1.90	-1.95	-5.03	-2.44	-2.90	-2.11	-3.48	-2.12	-1.19
Uruguay	-9.06	-4.15	-5.65	-2.43	-0.70	-0.85	-1.67	-3.33	0.37	0.93	..
Venezuela	-4.35	-1.51	3.34	5.26	-2.02	-5.85	-7.73	-1.61	1.11	4.41	-3.17
Yugoslavia	..	..	..	..	..	..	..	..	..	..	..
AVERAGE[a]	-6.30	-5.01	-4.18	-5.93	-8.23	-8.72	-9.29	-7.65	-2.77	0.07	-1.72
AVERAGE[a] without Brazil	-8.36	-5.45	-3.76	-3.51	-5.86	-7.17	-5.94	-2.94	-0.77	1.48	-1.72

.. = not available

a. Averages are weighted with 1982 GDP.

Source: IFS, government deficit table.

Economic Growth and Inflation

From the standpoint of commercial creditors, debt and creditworthiness measures are of the most relevance in evaluating progress on the debt problem. However, from the viewpoint of the debtor countries, external debt is primarily of importance because of its influence on domestic economic performance, especially on economic growth and inflation. Table 2.7 shows the pervasive recession in the heavily indebted countries in the first two years of the debt crisis. Although there was then an interim period of favorable growth in 1984–87 (averaging almost 3 percent annually for the HD17), growth weakened in 1988–90, with serious recessions in such countries as Argentina, Brazil, Peru, and Venezuela. In 1991 the group returned to average growth of over 3 percent (excluding Yugoslavia). This recovery reflected the fruits of successful adjustment programs in Argentina, Mexico, and Venezuela, and renewed positive if sluggish growth in Brazil. In 1992 growth moderated (to 2.5 percent without Yugoslavia), but in 1993 the rate was back up to an estimated 3.2 percent (for the 13 countries with data available) as heavily weighted Brazil recovered from recession.

The downward slide of average growth after 1985–86 undoubtedly played a role in the eventual move toward a debt reduction strategy by 1989. Mexico had been a key country for international debt policy from the outset, and that nation experienced severe recession already in 1986 with the collapse in oil prices. The oil shock also hit Ecuador (recession in 1987) and, after a period of delay and the running down of reserves, Venezuela (where output fell by almost 8 percent in 1989).

The late 1980s were also a period of hyperinflation and severe recession in some nonoil countries: Argentina, Peru, and Brazil (with recession in 1988 and again in 1990). Overall, the pattern was one of unsatisfactory growth in the key debtor countries by the second half of the decade. Although both external and domestic influences were at fault, unfavorable growth contributed to the sense that the existing debt strategy was not working.

In addition, high inflation aggravated the climate of economic crisis. For Latin America the average rate of inflation was on the order of 200 percent in 1984–85, fell to 65 percent in 1986 with transitory price freeze programs in Argentina and Brazil, and then surged to some 800 percent in 1987 and over 1,000 percent annually in 1988–89 (ECLAC 1991, 36). The relationship of high inflation to external debt policy was ambiguous, but typically it was argued in terms of two influences. First, debt service placed a burden on domestic government budgets. Second, the sharp devaluations needed to stimulate export growth imposed cost-push inflationary pressure.

If mediocre or worse growth and deteriorating inflation contributed to the atmosphere that led to the Brady Plan in 1989, by 1991 there was a

Table 2.7 Real GDP growth rate, 1982-93 (percentage)

Country	1982	1983	1984	1985	1986	1987	1988	1989	1990	1991	1992	1993
17 heavily indebted countries												
Argentina	-5.0	2.9	2.5	-4.4	5.6	2.5	-2.5	-4.5	0.4	8.5	8.7	6.0
Bolivia	-4.4	-4.5	-0.6	-1.0	-2.5	2.6	3.0	2.8	2.6	4.1	3.4	3.0
Brazil	0.6	-3.4	5.3	7.9	7.6	3.6	-0.1	3.3	-4.1	0.9	-0.9	4.5
Chile	-14.1	-0.7	6.4	2.5	5.6	5.7	7.4	10.0	2.1	6.0	10.4	6.0
Colombia	0.9	1.6	3.4	3.1	5.8	5.4	4.1	3.4	4.1	2.3	3.5	4.5
Costa Rica	-7.3	2.9	8.0	0.7	5.5	4.8	3.4	5.6	3.6	1.3	7.3	6.1
Côte d'Ivoire	-10.8	-11.2	-2.8	4.9	3.4	-1.6	-2.0	-1.1	-2.1	-0.8	7.5	..
Ecuador	1.2	-2.8	4.2	4.3	3.1	-6.0	10.5	0.6	2.4	3.8	3.5	1.5
Jamaica	1.2	2.3	-0.9	-4.6	1.7	6.2	1.5	4.6	3.8	2.0	0.8	2.0
Mexico	-0.6	-5.3	3.7	2.7	-3.7	1.8	1.4	3.1	3.9	3.6	2.6	1.0
Morocco	9.6	-0.6	4.3	6.3	8.4	-2.6	10.4	2.2	3.7	5.1	-3.0	..
Nigeria	-0.3	-5.4	-5.1	9.4	3.1	-0.5	9.9	7.4	8.2	4.5	4.1	..
Peru	-0.2	-12.6	5.8	2.1	9.3	8.3	-8.2	-11.8	-4.3	2.6	-2.8	6.4
Philippines	3.6	1.9	-7.6	-7.4	3.4	4.8	6.3	6.0	2.4	-1.0	0.6	1.7
Uruguay	-9.4	-5.9	-1.1	1.5	8.9	7.9	-0.2	0.5	0.9	1.9	7.4	1.5
Venezuela	0.7	-5.6	-1.4	1.4	6.3	4.5	6.2	-7.8	6.9	10.4	7.3	0.0
Yugoslavia	0.5	-1.0	2.0	0.5	3.6	-1.0	-2.0	0.8	-7.5	-17.0	-34.0	..
AVERAGE[a]	-0.4	-3.4	2.1	3.8	4.1	2.6	2.3	2.0	0.9	2.3	0.1	..
excluding Yugoslavia	-0.4	-3.5	2.1	4.1	4.2	2.9	2.6	1.9	1.5	3.5	2.5	3.2[b]
Other low income												
India	3.8	7.4	3.7	5.5	4.5	4.9	9.7	6.2	5.5	2.3	3.3	..
Indonesia	2.2	4.2	7.0	2.5	5.9	10.5	0.5	8.7	7.4	6.6	5.8	..
Pakistan	6.5	6.8	5.1	7.6	5.5	6.5	7.6	5.0	5.3	7.7	3.0	2.6

Sudan	-5.6	0.0	21.5	-1.8	3.9	1.4	1.6	1.6	-0.3	6.0	8.9	..
Zaire	-0.4	1.3	4.9	1.1	4.7	2.6	2.5	0.6	0.6	-6.0	-8.0	..
Zambia	-2.8	-2.0	-0.4	1.6	0.6	2.8	1.9	1.0	0.7	-2.0	-2.8	..
AVERAGE[a]	3.2	5.9	5.1	4.5	4.9	6.4	6.5	6.5	5.7	3.7	3.6	..
Other middle income												
Algeria	1.9	8.4	5.5	5.6	-0.2	-0.7	-1.9	4.9	-1.4	0.2	2.8	..
Egypt	9.5	10.3	8.8	7.4	4.8	8.7	3.5	2.2	2.3	1.2	0.4	..
South Korea	7.3	11.8	9.4	6.9	12.4	12.0	11.5	6.2	9.2	8.4	4.8	5.5
Malaysia	5.9	6.3	7.8	-1.0	1.0	5.4	8.9	8.7	9.8	8.6	8.0	8.0
Syria	2.1	1.4	-4.1	6.1	-4.9	1.9	13.3	-10.0	12.6	8.2	8.0	..
Thailand	4.1	7.3	7.1	3.5	4.9	9.5	13.2	12.0	10.0	8.0	7.5	..
Turkey	4.6	3.3	6.0	5.1	8.1	7.4	3.8	1.9	9.1	0.7	5.3	..
AVERAGE[a]	5.3	7.8	6.9	5.1	5.8	7.2	7.1	5.0	7.1	4.9	5.0	..
Other Eastern Europe												
Hungary	2.8	0.7	2.6	-0.3	2.4	3.8	2.7	3.8	-4.0	-11.9	-8.5	..
Poland	-4.8	5.6	5.6	3.6	4.2	2.0	4.4	0.2	-12.0	-7.6	1.0	..
Romania	4.0	6.1	5.9	-0.1	2.3	0.8	-0.5	-5.8	-7.4	-15.1	-15.4	..
AVERAGE[a]	-0.3	5.0	5.2	1.6	3.2	1.9	2.3	-1.4	-9.0	-11.1	-6.6	..
AVERAGE[a], 33 countries	1.3	1.1	3.8	4.0	4.5	4.1	3.9	3.0	2.0	1.8	0.9	..
excluding Yugoslavia	1.3	1.2	3.8	4.1	4.5	4.3	4.2	3.1	2.4	2.5	2.4	..

.. = not available
a. Average based on 1982 GNP weights from WDT.
b. 13 countries.

Sources: IFS, WDT, World Economic Outlook.

contrary pattern of much improved domestic economic conditions in the HD17 countries. Average inflation in Latin America was back down to 200 percent. If Brazil is excluded, Latin American inflation fell to 49 percent in 1991 and 22 percent by 1992, and economic growth stood at 5 percent and 4.3 percent in these two years, respectively (ECLAC 1992, 2–3). Performance on these criteria was thus consistent with the pattern of improvement on the measures more directly related to external debt. More fundamentally, improved growth and price stability reflected the results of domestic policy reforms, and these reforms were preconditions for sustainable resolution of the debt problem. No amount of financial engineering could substitute for underlying policy reform, and indeed both the Baker and Brady plans had stressed domestic reform as the quid pro quo for debt restructuring and relief.

Key Debtors

External debt of developing countries is highly concentrated. Among the 17 heavily indebted countries, the five largest debtors—Brazil, Mexico, Argentina, Venezuela, and the Philippines—accounted for 71 percent of total debt in 1982 and 68 percent in 1992. The principal change among major debtors over the decade was the emergence of Nigeria, which was at the median point of the group by size of debt in 1982 but surpassed the Philippines as the fifth largest debtor in the period 1987–91 (table 2.1).

For bank claims, concentration was even greater. Among the 17 highly indebted countries, just four accounted for 73 percent of debt to commercial banks in 1982: Brazil, Mexico, Argentina, and Venezuela. By 1993, the same four countries represented 79 percent of bank claims on the HD17 (table 2.8).

Outside of the HD17 country grouping, only one country had debt as large as that of the big four in 1982: South Korea, whose debt was slightly above that of Venezuela. By 1990, however, five other countries had joined the ranks of the superdebtors: India, Indonesia, Egypt, Turkey, and Poland. By then each of these countries had external debt in the range of $40 billion to $70 billion (table 2.1). However, the rise of debt in these countries primarily reflected official rather than private lending. Thus, even by 1990–91 none of these five countries had debt to banks on the scale of the Latin American big four debtors (table 2.9).

At least from the standpoint of the private financial system, then, the core of the debt problem resided in just the four large Latin American debtor countries. A major reason that pronouncements of the end to the debt crisis already by mid-1992 seemed plausible was simply the fact that of these four countries, Brady Plan debt reduction programs had been completed for two (Mexico and Venezuela) and tentatively agreed upon

Table 2.8 Commercial bank claims on developing countries, 1982-93 (millions of dollars)

Country	1982	1983	1984	1985	1986	1987	1988	1989	1990	1991	1992	1993
17 heavily indebted countries												
Argentina	22,168	23,244	25,941	28,937	32,408	35,253	35,112	32,369	30,766	31,282	33,569	30,351
Bolivia	659	542	642	620	627	726	533	341	284	260	302	411
Brazil	56,082	57,389	75,747	76,890	81,071	81,002	75,871	70,849	66,997	61,428	64,132	68,957
Chile	10,433	10,877	13,627	14,335	14,050	12,869	10,827	9,061	8,867	8,038	10,121	9,967
Colombia	5,541	5,886	6,942	6,461	6,542	6,647	6,955	6,629	6,801	6,610	7,260	7,626
Costa Rica	695	681	835	836	870	1,387	1,266	1,091	828	740	834	1,217
Côte d'Ivoire	2,905	2,656	2,587	2,939	3,310	3,667	3,354	3,259	3,266	2,765	2,475	2,227
Ecuador	4,099	4,151	4,771	5,172	5,282	5,061	4,882	4,582	4,081	3,919	3,601	3,246
Jamaica	511	496	610	673	517	533	578	692	624	421	485	497
Mexico	58,978	62,819	72,769	74,520	74,229	75,846	69,387	70,147	55,944	65,064	67,785	68,966
Morocco	3,557	3,554	4,483	4,846	5,198	5,649	5,081	5,170	5,310	5,416	5,239	4,952
Nigeria	6,980	8,088	8,130	9,104	9,980	10,690	8,869	7,441	6,990	5,808	4,563	4,133
Peru	5,216	4,909	5,776	5,608	5,282	5,050	4,556	4,066	3,851	3,644	3,388	3,157
Philippines	8,329	8,049	13,666	13,414	14,114	14,351	12,269	9,641	9,559	8,751	7,433	6,603
Uruguay	1,235	1,537	1,971	1,953	1,960	2,116	2,019	2,036	2,141	1,918	2,525	2,699
Venezuela	22,657	21,955	26,173	25,827	25,056	25,021	25,770	24,122	17,910	18,276	18,580	17,365
Yugoslavia	9,329	9,148	9,647	10,487	10,259	10,099	9,013	7,588	7,281	5,791	4,691	3,935
SUBTOTAL	219,374	225,981	274,317	282,622	290,755	295,967	276,342	259,084	231,500	230,131	236,983	236,309

Source: Bank for International Settlements, *International Banking and Financial Market Developments*, various years.

Table 2.9 Total long-term claims of commercial banks, 1982-92 (millions of dollars)

Country	1982	1983	1984	1985	1986	1987	1988	1989	1990	1991	1992
17 heavily indebted countries											
Argentina	18,104	23,478	24,781	25,291	27,331	30,626	29,742	32,564	24,541	23,108	23,661
Bolivia	910	1,213	1,243	1,457	1,450	1,120	592	434	390	362	314
Brazil	57,605	62,684	69,953	67,283	68,641	70,274	67,348	55,957	52,856	51,694	56,839
Chile	12,100	12,763	14,801	14,743	14,443	13,240	10,787	8,603	8,941	8,904	9,146
Colombia	3,758	4,171	4,695	4,974	5,869	5,503	5,795	5,418	5,331	5,262	4,950
Costa Rica	1,190	1,664	1,598	1,832	1,820	1,710	1,629	1,566	345	321	345
Côte d'Ivoire	3,487	3,467	3,963	4,772	5,362	5,947	6,244	6,663	7,083	7,421	5,106
Ecuador	3,600	4,485	4,937	5,115	5,349	5,352	4,961	5,005	5,048	5,050	4,863
Jamaica	467	443	461	462	451	436	409	364	331	314	291
Mexico	46,666	65,036	70,267	71,442	70,262	73,995	59,990	53,422	14,153	15,916	18,781
Morocco	2,744	2,591	2,621	2,691	2,725	2,882	3,397	3,390	3,379	3,368	3,447
Nigeria	5,531	6,074	5,534	4,921	3,545	7,082	6,775	6,428	6,105	5,933	331
Peru	3,061	4,525	5,072	3,437	3,438	3,475	3,382	3,482	3,515	3,426	3,402
Philippines	6,786	7,166	6,856	7,116	10,717	11,168	9,978	9,201	7,804	7,162	3,426
Uruguay	1,243	2,013	1,988	1,944	1,993	2,136	1,877	1,783	1,682	643	740
Venezuela	14,800	20,581	24,699	23,347	29,794	27,450	25,256	24,298	4,013	3,798	3,920
Yugoslavia	12,004	12,836	12,003	13,595	11,610	10,989	11,956	10,163	9,185	8,966	8,803
SUBTOTAL	194,056	235,190	255,472	254,422	264,800	273,385	250,118	228,741	154,702	151,648	148,365

Other low income											
India	1,800	2,306	2,888	3,693	4,672	6,421	7,237	7,985	8,428	8,612	8,375
Indonesia	6,848	8,272	8,712	9,005	9,910	11,551	12,249	12,893	15,715	17,699	20,230
Pakistan	624	446	600	447	491	691	572	619	542	430	307
Sudan	1,276	1,094	1,229	1,328	1,567	2,045	1,800	1,884	2,147	2,075	1,968
Zaire	531	509	540	544	541	538	518	520	524	519	516
Zambia	132	110	93	70	70	70	70	70	72	77	87
SUBTOTAL	11,211	12,737	14,062	15,087	17,251	21,316	22,446	23,971	27,428	29,412	31,483
Other middle income											
Algeria	4,439	4,328	3,941	4,258	5,867	7,037	7,668	6,874	6,184	5,591	6,572
Egypt	923	906	819	1,125	1,320	1,480	1,599	1,615	1,683	1,724	1,292
South Korea	11,346	14,022	16,153	19,338	17,806	11,377	9,844	8,509	7,848	9,782	11,408
Malaysia	7,589	8,690	9,751	7,552	7,845	7,491	5,889	4,163	3,775	3,929	4,909
Syria	0	0	0	20	26	23	17	9	0	0	0
Thailand	4,216	4,494	5,121	6,055	6,039	6,551	6,792	8,065	9,627	12,597	14,423
Turkey	4,873	5,033	5,665	6,509	8,943	12,086	11,920	12,501	14,192	13,686	14,969
SUBTOTAL	33,386	37,473	41,450	44,857	47,846	46,045	43,729	41,736	43,309	47,309	53,573
Other Eastern Europe											
Hungary	5,112	4,325	4,974	6,446	8,217	10,665	9,912	10,249	9,647	8,400	6,982
Poland	..	..	..	7,700	8,778	9,862	9,160	8,984	9,963	10,032	9,406
Romania	4,086	3,735	3,153	2,620	1,942	1,721	326	0	0	0	0
SUBTOTAL	9,198	8,060	8,127	16,766	18,937	22,248	19,398	19,233	19,610	18,432	16,388
TOTAL, 33 countries	247,851	293,460	319,111	331,132	348,834	362,994	335,691	313,681	245,049	246,801	249,809

.. = not available

Source: World Bank, *World Debt Tables*, various years.

Figure 2.3 Argentina: debt indicators, 1982-93

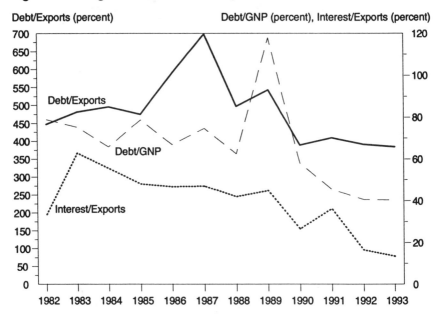

for the other two (Argentina and Brazil); in three of the four countries, economic growth and more moderate inflation had been restored.

Figures 2.3 to 2.6 show the trends for the principal measures of debt burden for the four large Latin American debtors. *Argentina* (figure 2.3) has shown the most dramatic reduction in the ratio of net external debt to exports of goods and services, from nearly 700 percent in 1987 to slightly below 400 percent in 1990–92 (even before Brady Plan cuts). The further improvement by 1993 was modest despite the Brady cuts, in part because the par bonds exaggerated the value of remaining debt. By 1987, exports were about 19 percent below their 1985 level, largely because of falling world prices for agricultural goods (with declines on the order of 50 percent for wheat and maize from 1982–83 highs). At the same time debt mounted rapidly with large new-money agreements under the Baker Plan and borrowing from the international financial institutions.

The debt/exports ratio had fallen sharply again by 1990, primarily as the consequence of a doubling of export earnings from their 1987 low. Recovering world commodity prices helped, but there was also a large expansion in manufactured exports (including processed foods) in response to real devaluation in 1987–89. On the other hand, the extreme devaluation of 1989 associated with hyperinflation led by exchange rate collapse meant that the debt/GNP ratio reached a high of nearly 120 percent. That is, domestic GNP evaluated in dollars was shrinking rapidly as the exchange rate depreciated. The real exchange rate then reversed and

Figure 2.4 Brazil: debt indicators, 1982-93

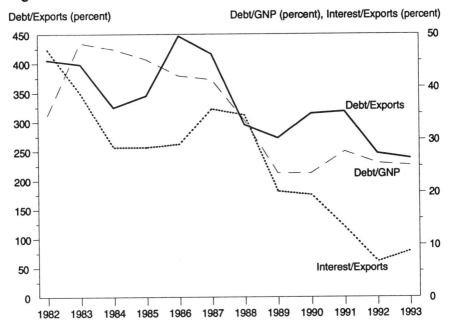

appreciated in 1990–92, and the debt/GNP ratio fell to much more moderate levels consistent with the improvement shown on other measures.

By 1992 Argentina's debt indicators were much closer to manageable levels, and by 1993 there was more improvement from the Brady Plan debt reduction. The ratio of net interest to exports of goods and services fell to 13.4 percent by 1993. What the indicators do not reveal is the corresponding cycle in the internal transfer problem. In the period 1988–90 there was a severe fiscal constraint that led the government to build up interest arrears on external debt despite the presence of a large trade surplus and improving external debt indicators. In contrast, by 1991 and after, major fiscal correction had provided the basis for mobilizing the internal transfer necessary for external debt service.

Brazil (figure 2.4) has also shown major improvement on the principal debt indicators. Net interest payments have fallen from nearly 50 percent of exports of goods and services in 1982 to under 20 percent by 1990 and only 8.8 percent by 1993 (table 2.5). The net debt/exports ratio has declined from a peak of nearly 450 percent in 1986 to only 238 percent in 1993. A temporary upward reversion of the debt/exports ratio in 1990–91 reflected a decline in exports, which fell by some 8 percent whereas debt continued to rise through mounting interest arrears. Export stagnation reflected an appreciation in the real exchange rate by about 20 percent from 1988 to 1991. By 1992, export earnings had rebounded briskly (by 16 percent; IMF 1993a, 126).

Figure 2.5 Mexico: debt indicators, 1982-93

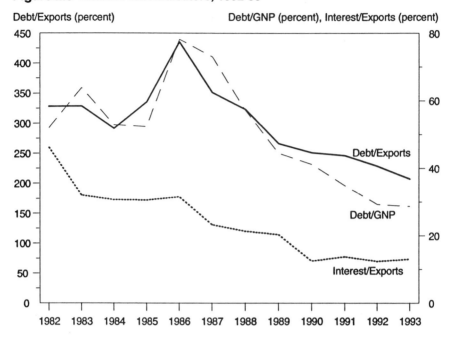

Debt/Exports (percent)　　　　　　　　　Debt/GNP (percent), Interest/Exports (percent)

Real appreciation of the Brazilian currency held the debt/GNP ratio relatively low despite rising debt and domestic recession in 1990–91. As was the case earlier in Argentina, however, by the early 1990s the principal problem for debt policy in Brazil was the domestic fiscal deficit and macroeconomic instability associated with monthly inflation rates on the order of 20 percent or more. Improvement on the external indicators was sufficient to enable Brazilian negotiators to reach a tentative Brady Plan agreement with banks in mid-1992, but decisive implementation of domestic stabilization seemed likely to be an eventual requirement if any such agreement was to stand the test of time.

The debt indicators for *Mexico* (figure 2.5) show steady improvement since 1986, when the debt/exports ratio peaked at 435 percent with the collapse in oil prices and export earnings. If oil prices had not fallen, Mexico's debt indicators would probably have shown a smooth improvement for the whole period since 1982–83, and indeed the key measure of net interest payments relative to exports of goods and services has shown a steady improvement barely interrupted by the 1986 oil shock. By 1993, in part with the help of the Brady Plan reduction, Mexico's debt indicators were at levels usually associated with creditworthiness. Net interest payments were only 13 percent of exports of goods and services, net debt was only 207 percent of exports, and net debt was about 29 percent of GNP. Mexico's fiscal performance was strong, so there was no remaining inter-

Figure 2.6 Venezuela: debt indicators, 1982-93

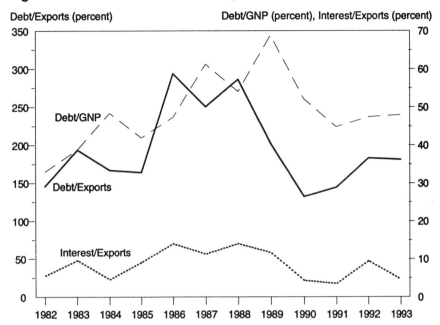

Debt/Exports (percent)   Debt/GNP (percent), Interest/Exports (percent)

nal transfer problem. The government took the position that the debt problem had been overcome, so in the psychological dimension the atmosphere was also favorable.

For *Venezuela* (figure 2.6), the debt indicators essentially tell three stories. First, the country was relatively less indebted than the other major debtors through most of the 1980s. Thus, net interest payments hovered in the range of only 10 percent of exports of goods and services, a relatively low level. Second, the debt-export ratio only surged to high levels with the collapse of oil prices in 1986, and even then remained well below the levels reached in the mid-1980s by other major Latin American debtors. The sensitivity of the debt-export ratio to oil stemmed from the high share of oil in exports, totaling some 80 percent or more. Third, for Venezuela by 1990–93 the one indicator that remained relatively high was the debt/GNP ratio. The reason was a large real devaluation in 1989, which had reduced the dollar value of GNP. The devaluation was crucial to reestablishing fiscal balance (as the government owns oil export earnings and its revenue rises in terms of bolivars when the bolivar devalues against the dollar) and stimulating nonoil exports, but it did mean that debt relative to GNP showed less improvement by 1990–92 than the debt/exports ratio. Even so, the measures taken together indicated that by 1991–92 Venezuela too was back to what would normally be considered well within the bounds of creditworthiness.

Overall, for the four key Latin American debtors the debt indicators have shown major improvement since 1986–87. Because the normal debt indicators do not report the state of the fiscal balances (the internal transfer) nor difficulties with inflation, they do not reveal the principal problem case that remained among the four big debtors as of 1992–93: that of Brazil. Even there, by mid-1994 a new stabilization plan offered hope for dealing with inflation (chapter 6).

Trends for Other Country Groups

Figure 2.7 shows a rising trend in relative indebtedness for the principal low-income countries not already included in the HD17. However, for India and Pakistan this trend may be interpreted as a reflection of increased integration into world capital markets and access to official credit. The Indonesian case reflects greater borrowing after the oil price collapse, yet Indonesia has been notable for its success in avoiding debt rescheduling. Moreover, for this group of countries the ratio of net interest to exports of goods and services has remained relatively low (well below 15 percent), although it has risen in the past decade. Because much of debt is on a concessional basis, the interest/exports ratio is more meaningful than the debt/exports ratio—which by itself might imply indebtedness above comfortable levels.

Within this group, Zaire and especially Zambia represent the debt problems of many sub-Saharan African countries. In Zambia, external debt has been in a high range of some 200 percent of GNP, placing the interest/exports ratio at typically over 20 percent of exports despite concessional interest rates (tables 2.4 and 2.5).[6] Civil war meant a collapse of exports in Sudan and extraordinarily high debt burden ratios (tables 2.3 to 2.5), and the country is excluded from the low-income group shown in figure 2.7.

As discussed in chapter 7, at least two central problems characterize the debt of many sub-Saharan countries. First, they have a relatively large accumulation of official loans that probably should have been extended on a basis of grants in the first place. Second, they continue to run substantial trade deficits financed by additional concessional lending. As a result, rather than generating trade surpluses that can pay much of the interest on past debt, as has been the case in recent years in Latin America, they remain in a phase of incurring relatively more additional debt to finance not only interest but also inward resource transfers. The debt problem of the region is distinct from that in Latin America, and the indicators reported here do not show the same systematic trend toward improvement that may be identified for most of the major Latin American debtor countries. As emphasized in chapter 7, however, there is a sharp

---

6. The drop in the interest/exports ratio for Zambia in 1990 reflects official rescheduling and understates normal accrual-based obligations.

Figure 2.7 Low-income countries:[a] debt indicators, 1982-93

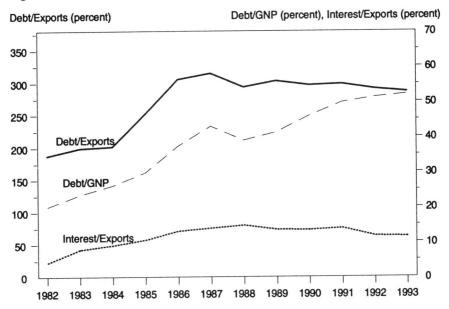

a. India, Indonesia, Pakistan, Zaire, and Zambia (weighted by 1982 GNP).

differentiation among countries within Africa, with some extremely heavily indebted but a surprising number of others relatively lightly burdened by debt.

Middle-income countries outside the HD17 have shown a pattern of debt trends not unlike that in Latin America, with deterioration in the debt/ exports and debt/GNP ratios in 1985–86 but major improvement since then, and flat or improving trends for the interest/exports ratio (figure 2.8). This group includes the strong countries of South Korea, Malaysia, Thailand, and Turkey. The deterioration in 1986 reflects the presence of major oil exporters (Algeria and Egypt). For the group as a whole, the interest burden has remained relatively low (10 percent of exports or less). These countries escaped the largely Latin American debt crisis of the 1980s, in part because they began the decade with much less debt but also because of energetic policies to increase exports and reduce debt (in South Korea in particular).

Eastern Europe was the locus of the debt crisis before it hit Latin America. The summary trends in Hungary, Poland, and Romania (figure 2.9) show an increase in the debt burden from 1982 to 1990 as measured by debt relative to exports or GNP, but a flat or gradually declining burden as measured by the interest/exports ratio. The aggregate masks a radical decline in debt in Romania, where the government adopted draconian measures to repay debt. Debt has been much higher in Poland and, to a

Figure 2.8 Middle-income countries:[a] debt indicators, 1982-93

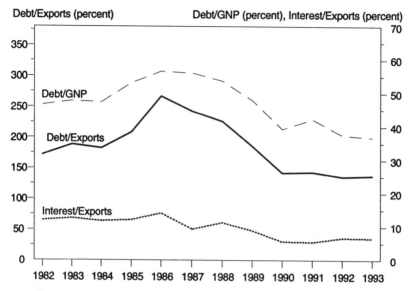

Debt/Exports (percent)

Debt/GNP (percent), Interest/Exports (percent)

a. Algeria, Egypt, South Korea, Malaysia, Syria, Thailand, and Turkey (weighted by 1982 GNP).

lesser extent, Hungary. Chapter 7 examines debt policies and experience in Eastern Europe and Russia, as well as sub-Saharan Africa.

Bank Vulnerability

By the late 1980s it was already a stylized fact that whereas the developing countries still remained in severe debt difficulties, the banks were no longer in the serious jeopardy that they faced at the outset of the debt crisis. The negative view of this trend was that the banks had failed to provide enough new lending to the debtor countries. The positive interpretation was that the banks had taken prudential measures to set aside loan-loss reserves and otherwise rebuild capital more generally and had sold back debt at a discount or converted it into equity. There was some truth in both views, but the latter was the more accurate.[7]

As indicated in tables 2.8 and 2.9, the outstanding stock of bank loans to the HD17 rose substantially from 1982 through 1987, and then declined. The more comprehensive data of table 2.8 (which include short-term loans and bank holdings of Brady conversion bonds) show that for

---

7. For an evaluation of the banks' performance under Baker Plan commitments to new lending, see Cline (1989a). Broadly, the banks met about two-thirds of the targeted lending under that phase of the debt strategy.

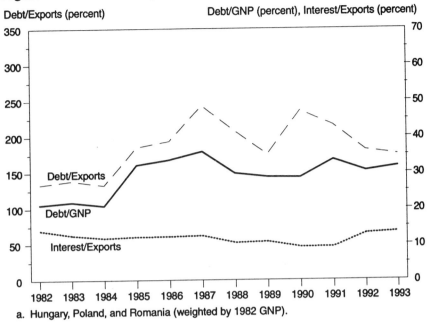

Figure 2.9 Eastern Europe:[a] debt indicators, 1982-93

Debt/Exports (percent)
Debt/GNP (percent), Interest/Exports (percent)

Debt/Exports

Debt/GNP

Interest/Exports

a. Hungary, Poland, and Romania (weighted by 1982 GNP).

these countries, claims by international banks rose by 35 percent from 1982 to their peak of $296 billion in 1987, and then fell by 22 percent to $230 billion by 1991. By then, the nominal dollar amount was only 5 percent above the level at the beginning of this nine-year period.

Importantly, in 1992 nominal bank claims rose again for the first time in four years. The amount held approximately constant in 1993. Furthermore, this time the increased exposure was voluntary, rather than the consequence of "concerted" packages. Bank claims on Mexico alone rose by $13 billion from 1990 to 1993, marking a new, post-Brady phase of reengagement by the banks on a commercial basis.

During the 1980s the banks had built up capital, including loan-loss reserves, and in addition had written down some value-impaired debt and engaged in market-based debt reduction and conversion. As a result, their relative exposure to the LDC debt problem was much reduced. As indicated in tables 2.10 and 2.11, exposure to the HD17 countries fell from 130 percent of capital and reserves in 1982 to only 27 percent by 1992 for all US banks, and from 194 percent to 51 percent for the nine largest banks. The decline represented four influences: a buildup in capital base, the setting aside of loan-loss reserves, the charging off of claims (usually upon the event of sale of the loan to the secondary market at a loss), and the reduction of debt through discounted buybacks or debt-equity conversion. Tables 2.10 and 2.11 show that capital rose from 1982 to 1992 by 158 percent for all US banks and by the same proportion for the nine largest.

Table 2.10 Exposure of US banks relative to capital,[a] 1982-92 (percentages)

Country	1982	1983	1984	1985	1986	1987	1988	1989	1990	1991	1992
17 heavily indebted countries											
Argentina	11.7	10.7	8.6	8.0	7.3	6.8	5.8	3.1	2.3	2.4	3.2
Bolivia	0.5	0.4	0.2	0.1	0.1	0.1	0.0	0.0	0.0	0.0	0.0
Brazil	28.9	26.0	25.9	21.6	19.3	16.5	14.3	11.2	7.5	4.4	4.0
Chile	8.6	7.8	7.3	6.2	5.6	4.6	3.7	2.7	2.0	1.7	1.7
Colombia	4.5	4.2	3.2	2.5	1.9	1.6	1.6	1.3	1.2	1.1	1.1
Costa Rica	0.7	0.6	0.5	0.4	0.4	0.3	0.2	0.1	0.1	0.1	0.1
Côte d'Ivoire	0.9	0.7	0.5	0.3	0.3	0.3	0.2	0.1	0.0	0.0	0.0
Ecuador	2.9	2.6	2.3	2.0	1.9	1.5	1.1	0.7	0.5	0.3	0.3
Jamaica	0.4	0.4	0.4	0.2	0.2	0.1	0.1	0.1	0.1	0.1	0.1
Mexico	34.5	33.2	28.8	23.7	20.4	17.6	13.2	11.1	9.9	10.6	9.5
Morocco	1.1	1.1	1.0	0.9	0.8	0.6	0.5	0.4	0.4	0.4	0.3
Nigeria	2.6	2.6	1.7	1.1	0.8	0.7	0.6	0.5	0.3	0.3	0.2
Peru	3.6	3.1	2.6	1.6	1.2	0.7	0.4	0.1	0.1	0.1	0.1
Philippines	8.1	7.6	5.9	5.1	4.4	3.6	2.9	2.2	2.1	1.9	1.6
Uruguay	1.3	1.3	1.2	0.9	0.8	0.7	0.7	0.6	0.5	0.6	0.6
Venezuela	16.4	14.2	11.7	9.6	7.8	6.4	5.9	4.9	4.2	4.4	3.7
Yugoslavia	3.3	3.1	2.6	2.3	1.8	1.5	1.4	1.1	0.8	0.6	0.3
SUBTOTAL	130.1	119.8	104.3	86.6	74.8	63.6	52.7	40.4	32.0	28.9	26.7
Other low income											
India	1.2	0.9	0.8	0.9	0.9	0.8	0.6	0.6	0.4	0.2	0.3
Indonesia	4.2	4.5	3.7	2.6	1.9	1.2	0.8	0.7	0.9	1.0	1.1
Pakistan	0.3	0.4	0.3	0.2	0.2	0.1	0.1	0.1	0.0	0.1	0.1

Sudan	0.3	0.2	0.1	0.1	0.0	0.0	0.0	0.0	0.0	0.0	0.0
Zaire	0.2	0.1	0.0	0.0	0.0	0.0	0.0	0.0	0.0	0.0	0.0
Zambia	0.3	0.2	0.1	0.1	0.1	0.1	0.0	0.0	0.0	0.0	0.0
SUBTOTAL	6.5	6.2	5.0	3.9	3.0	2.1	1.5	1.4	1.4	1.3	1.5
Other middle income											
Algeria	1.8	1.5	1.1	0.8	0.7	0.6	0.5	0.4	0.4	0.3	0.3
Egypt	1.7	2.0	1.4	0.9	0.6	0.3	0.2	0.1	0.1	0.1	0.1
South Korea	15.6	14.5	10.8	8.7	5.2	3.0	2.8	2.7	2.8	2.4	2.2
Malaysia	2.0	2.3	1.9	1.0	0.6	0.4	0.3	0.2	0.2	0.3	0.4
Syria	0.0	0.1	0.0	0.0	0.0	0.0	0.0	0.0	0.0	0.0	0.0
Thailand	2.5	2.7	2.4	1.8	1.0	0.6	0.7	0.7	0.9	1.0	1.0
Turkey	2.1	2.2	2.2	2.0	1.8	1.6	1.1	0.8	1.0	0.9	0.7
SUBTOTAL	25.7	25.1	19.8	15.3	9.9	6.6	5.7	5.0	5.4	5.1	4.7
Other Eastern Europe											
Hungary	1.3	1.1	0.8	0.6	0.3	0.3	0.2	0.2	0.1	0.2	0.1
Poland	2.1	1.3	0.8	0.5	0.4	0.3	0.2	0.2	0.2	0.2	0.1
Romania	0.4	0.3	0.2	0.2	0.1	0.1	0.0	0.0	0.0	0.0	0.0
SUBTOTAL	3.9	2.8	1.8	1.2	0.8	0.7	0.5	0.4	0.3	0.4	0.2
TOTAL, 33 countries	166.2	153.9	130.9	107.0	88.5	73.0	60.4	47.2	39.2	35.7	33.1
Memo:											
Subtotal of claims HD17 ($mn)	91,844	95,034	96,169	91,237	86,795	82,193	71,450	58,698	48,985	45,247	48,560
Total, 33 countries ($mn)	117,325	122,062	120,668	112,788	102,695	94,361	81,933	68,575	59,873	55,843	60,219
Capital (billion of dollars)	71	79	92	105	116	129	136	145	153	156	182

a. Figures for all years are end of year.

Source: Federal Financial Institutions Examination Council, Country Exposure Lending Survey.

Table 2.11 Exposure of nine largest US banks relative to capital,[a] 1982-92 (percentage)

Country	1982	1983	1984	1985	1986	1987	1988	1989	1990	1991	1992
17 heavily indebted countries											
Argentina	17.7	17.0	13.9	13.9	12.7	12.2	10.8	6.1	4.6	4.8	5.5
Bolivia	0.8	0.6	0.3	0.1	0.1	0.1	0.1	0.0	0.0	0.0	0.0
Brazil	45.8	42.2	43.1	36.8	32.9	29.1	26.8	23.3	16.9	10.6	7.9
Chile	11.5	10.9	10.4	9.6	8.9	7.8	6.5	5.5	4.1	3.9	3.3
Colombia	7.7	7.1	5.9	4.5	3.3	2.7	2.5	2.4	2.4	2.5	2.1
Costa Rica	0.8	0.7	0.6	0.5	0.5	0.3	0.2	0.2	0.1	0.1	0.1
Côte d'Ivoire	1.7	1.3	0.9	0.6	0.6	0.6	0.5	0.3	0.1	0.1	0.0
Ecuador	4.0	3.9	3.6	3.2	2.9	2.4	2.0	1.4	0.9	0.8	0.5
Jamaica	0.8	0.8	0.7	0.5	0.4	0.3	0.2	0.2	0.2	0.2	0.1
Mexico	44.4	44.8	40.0	33.3	28.6	25.9	21.1	20.2	19.1	22.3	17.9
Morocco	2.0	2.4	1.9	1.6	1.5	1.3	1.1	0.9	0.8	0.8	0.5
Nigeria	5.0	4.9	7.5	2.1	1.4	1.4	1.2	1.0	0.7	0.7	0.3
Peru	4.7	4.3	3.5	2.3	1.8	0.9	0.6	0.2	0.1	0.1	0.1
Philippines	13.4	12.4	10.2	9.0	7.9	6.4	5.2	4.4	4.5	4.3	3.3
Uruguay	2.1	2.4	2.2	1.7	1.5	1.4	1.2	1.1	1.0	1.1	1.0
Venezuela	26.9	24.2	20.3	16.9	13.9	11.3	10.1	10.0	9.5	10.2	7.3
Yugoslavia	5.0	4.9	4.1	3.6	2.8	2.4	2.3	2.1	1.5	1.1	0.5
SUBTOTAL	194.2	185.1	169.3	140.1	121.6	106.6	92.5	79.6	66.7	63.5	50.6
Other low income											
India	2.1	1.9	1.5	1.7	1.8	1.4	0.9	0.7	0.8	0.3	0.5
Indonesia	8.6	9.6	7.5	5.4	3.8	2.4	1.6	1.5	1.6	2.3	2.2
Pakistan	0.7	0.8	0.6	0.6	0.4	0.2	0.2	0.2	0.1	0.2	0.2

Sudan	0.6	0.3	0.2	0.1	0.1	0.0	0.0	0.0	0.0	0.0	0.0
Zaire	0.4	0.2	0.1	0.1	0.0	0.0	0.0	0.0	0.0	0.0	0.0
Zambia	0.5	0.3	0.3	0.2	0.2	0.1	0.1	0.0	0.0	0.0	0.0
SUBTOTAL	12.9	13.2	10.2	8.2	6.2	4.2	2.8	2.5	2.6	2.8	2.9
Other middle income											
Algeria	3.1	2.6	1.9	1.4	1.3	1.1	0.7	0.5	0.5	0.5	0.4
Egypt	3.1	3.3	2.3	1.5	0.8	0.4	0.2	0.1	0.2	0.1	0.1
South Korea	24.6	21.1	15.3	12.0	7.5	5.2	4.1	4.5	4.8	4.4	3.3
Malaysia	3.9	4.4	3.6	2.1	1.3	0.7	0.6	0.5	0.5	0.8	0.8
Syria	0.1	0.1	0.1	0.0	0.0	0.0	0.0	0.0	0.0	0.0	0.0
Thailand	4.0	4.4	4.0	2.8	1.2	0.7	0.7	0.8	1.2	1.6	1.4
Turkey	3.2	3.7	3.7	3.5	3.1	2.6	1.7	1.4	1.8	1.7	1.3
SUBTOTAL	42.0	39.6	28.9	23.4	15.2	10.8	8.1	7.8	9.0	9.2	7.4
Other Eastern Europe											
Hungary	1.9	1.8	1.3	0.9	0.4	0.5	0.4	0.3	0.3	0.6	0.3
Poland	3.3	2.2	1.3	1.0	0.8	0.6	0.4	0.4	0.4	0.4	0.3
Romania	0.8	0.5	0.5	0.3	0.2	0.2	0.1	0.0	0.0	0.0	0.0
SUBTOTAL	6.0	4.5	3.1	2.2	1.5	1.3	0.9	0.8	0.7	1.0	0.5
TOTAL, 33 countries	255.0	242.3	211.5	174.0	144.5	122.9	104.2	90.6	78.9	76.5	61.4
Memo:											
Subtotal of claims HD17 ($mn)	56,325	58,297	62,115	59,281	56,768	54,877	51,591	45,349	39,539	36,449	37,903
Total claims ($mn)	73,958	76,339	77,602	73,583	67,475	63,279	58,137	51,634	46,813	43,923	46,010
Capital (billions of dollars)	29	32	37	42	47	52	56	57	59	57	75

a. Figures for all years are end of year.

Source: Federal Financial Institutions Examination Council, *Country Exposure Lending Survey.*

Voluntary loan-loss reserves did not reduce reported claims of US banks. However, these provisions did augment their capital and reserve base, and thereby contributed to a decline in the ratio of exposure to capital and reserves (tables 2.10 and 2.11). In contrast, the US bank data do exclude those reserves mandatorily set aside because of regulator classification of a country as subject to Allocated Transfer Risk Reserve (ATRR). The sharp reductions in reported claims on Argentina and Brazil in particular in the period from 1988 to 1991 reflect ATRR set-asides of 50 percent or more. The high mandatory reserves for these countries stemmed from their accumulation of large arrears on interest payments.

There were similar trends toward higher capital and lower exposure/capital ratios for banks of other industrial countries, despite the fact that their typical practice is to include in reported debt all claims rather than to exclude allocated loan-loss reserves. From 1982 to 1991, exposure of UK banks to the HD17 countries fell from 85 percent of capital to 12 percent (table 2.12). From 1982 to 1992, this ratio fell from 31 percent to 19 percent for German banks, and from 135 percent (in 1984) to 23 percent for French banks (tables 2.13 and 2.14). The overall effect was to disarm the threat of the debt bomb to the international financial system.

It is noteworthy that the reduction in relative exposure reflected not only rising capital and reserves but also a falling absolute level of exposure. Returning to table 2.10, it is evident that there was a large reduction of claims after 1987. US banks had about $92 billion in claims on the HD17 countries in 1982, and still held $82 billion in 1987. By 1991, these claims had fallen to $45 billion, a reduction of 45 percent over four years. The most dramatic decline occurred for Brazil, where US bank claims by 1991 were 68 percent below their 1987 level. As noted, this decline was exaggerated by reporting on a basis exclusive of mandatory country reserves. Nonetheless, even for other major debtors where reserves were not mandated (because interest had not gone into arrears and economic policies appeared more sound), such as Chile, Mexico, and Venezuela, there were also substantial reductions in bank claims.

The basic dynamic in this process was not so much Brady Plan debt reduction (although by 1990–91 that was important in Mexico and Venezuela) as market adjustment to the debt problem. After banks had set aside major reserves beginning in 1987, led by Citibank's Brazil-inspired reserves against LDC loans that year, they were increasingly in a position to absorb losses associated with debt-equity conversions and market-based buybacks.[8]

---

8. For example, in Brazil in 1988 alone an estimated $6.7 billion of external debt was extinguished through "informal" debt buybacks by private and state firms. In this process, the enterprise would pay local currency to the creditor at some discount. The creditor would then convert the payment into dollars at an additional discount (typically on the order of 30 percent) in the parallel, or black, market (*Gazeta Mercantil*, 13 November 1989).

The time path of reduced relative bank exposure sheds light on the policy question of whether the Brady Plan might have been inaugurated earlier. The plan emerged only in 1989. Suppose its emphasis on debt reduction had instead been adopted in 1986. The divergence between these two years for the exposure/capital ratio (for the HD17) was 122 percent versus 80 percent for the nine largest US banks, 52 percent versus 21 percent for UK banks, 39 percent versus 28 percent for German banks, and 79 percent versus 52 percent for French banks. On this basis, there was still relatively high vulnerability in the large US banks as of 1986, and to some extent in the French banks.

Whereas adoption of Brady Plan debt reduction as early as 1986 might have placed strain on the financial system, the extent of vulnerability remaining by 1991 may be considered by asking what impact would occur from debt reduction applied to all HD17 countries. The norm of Brady Plan cuts has been 35 percent (the effective reduction for Mexico for long-term bank debt). An across-the-board forgiveness of this amount for these countries would have cost the nine largest US banks 22 percent of capital in 1991—a substantial but quite manageable impact. The same outcome would have cut capital by about 10 percent or less for all US banks and those in France and Germany, and by only 4 percent for UK banks.

Another consideration is that at the height of the debt crisis there were calls for debt reductions that considerably exceeded the 35 percent benchmark, reaching the range of 50 to 60 percent. As countries made underlying progress it became evident that more moderate reductions were manageable. Forgiveness of 55 percent of bank claims on HD17 countries in 1986 would have eliminated 67 percent of the capital of the nine largest US banks, 41 percent for all US banks, 29 percent for those in the United Kingdom, 21 percent for German banks, and 43 percent of capital for French banks. Whether or not at the cost of undue economic dislocation in debtor countries, the delay in recourse to debt forgiveness thus at least purchased a considerable reduction in the extent of the possible shock to the international banking system.

Overview

Figures 2.10 through 2.12 provide a summary view of the trends for all 33 countries, which again represent about six-sevenths of all LDC debt. These figures report the fraction of total debt owed by countries that exceed specified creditworthiness thresholds. In each case there are two thresholds, one more rigorous and the other easier to meet but still representing moderately acceptable creditworthiness. Figure 2.10 shows a sharp improvement since 1987 on the debt/exports ratio if the moderate threshold of 250 percent is applied. In 1987, 81.6 percent of debt was owed by countries with debt/exports ratios above this limit. This share

Table 2.12 Exposure of UK banks relative to capital, 1982-91 (percentage)

Country	1982	1983	1984	1985	1986	1987	1988	1989	1990	1991
17 heavily indebted countries										
Argentina	9.2	8.3	7.8	7.0	5.8	4.9	3.8	2.5	1.6	1.5
Bolivia	0.4	0.4	0.3	0.2	0.1	0.1	0.0	0.0	0.0	0.0
Brazil	18.9	20.0	21.4	17.5	13.5	11.2	7.0	5.3	3.2	2.8
Chile	4.6	4.2	4.8	4.2	3.0	2.0	1.2	0.5	0.4	0.3
Colombia	1.6	1.9	1.8	1.4	1.1	0.8	0.7	0.6	0.4	0.4
Costa Rica	0.5	0.4	0.4	0.4	0.3	0.2	0.2	0.1	0.0	0.0
Côte d'Ivoire	1.0	0.9	0.8	0.6	0.5	0.4	0.3	0.2	0.2	0.1
Ecuador	2.0	1.8	1.7	1.5	1.1	1.0	0.7	0.6	0.4	0.4
Jamaica	0.1	0.1	0.1	0.1	0.1	0.0	0.0	0.1	0.0	0.0
Mexico	22.4	20.3	20.0	16.6	12.3	10.1	7.7	5.7	3.4	3.5
Morocco	0.8	0.8	0.8	0.7	0.6	0.5	0.3	0.3	0.3	0.2
Nigeria	3.8	5.0	5.5	4.8	4.0	3.4	2.3	1.3	0.7	0.5
Peru	1.9	1.8	1.6	1.2	0.9	0.8	0.5	0.4	0.2	0.2
Philippines	4.1	4.6	0.0	2.9	2.3	1.7	1.3	0.7	0.5	0.5
Uruguay	0.9	0.9	0.9	0.7	0.5	0.4	0.3	0.2	0.2	0.1
Venezuela	8.1	7.0	6.3	5.2	3.7	3.0	2.4	1.7	1.5	1.4
Yugoslavia	4.6	4.1	3.9	3.5	2.4	1.6	1.3	0.8	0.5	0.4
SUBTOTAL	85.0	82.5	78.2	68.6	52.4	42.4	30.3	21.0	13.6	12.2

Other middle income										
Malaysia	4.1	4.4	4.4	2.8	2.0	1.1	0.4	0.3	0.3	0.3
South Korea	7.8	7.2	6.7	5.2	3.5	2.4	1.3	1.0	0.8	1.0
Thailand	1.5	1.4	1.1	0.8	0.3	0.2	0.1	0.1	0.2	0.2
Egypt	2.3	2.1	1.7	1.4	0.9	0.8	0.7	0.5	0.4	0.4
SUBTOTAL	15.6	15.0	13.9	10.1	6.6	4.5	2.5	1.9	1.8	2.0
Other Eastern Europe										
East Germany	4.0	2.9	2.6	1.8	1.3	1.0	0.9	1.0	0.8	n.a.
Hungary	2.2	1.8	1.9	1.3	0.8	0.7	0.5	0.4	0.3	0.2
Poland	4.8	4.0	2.6	2.2	1.6	1.5	1.1	0.9	0.8	0.7
USSR	7.6	5.2	5.6	4.8	4.6	3.7	3.1	2.8	2.7	1.9
SUBTOTAL	18.7	13.9	12.7	10.1	8.3	6.9	5.6	5.0	4.7	2.9
TOTAL, 25 countries	119.3	111.4	104.7	88.8	67.4	53.7	38.4	27.9	20.0	17.1
Memo:										
Total claims ($mn)	45,451	46,103	45,710	46,353	47,496	46,449	41,378	36,622	29,168	25,760
Capital (millions pounds Sterling)										
in pounds Sterling	19,133	23,160	25,635	28,192	32,595	36,496	40,914	55,447	61,307	64,001
in other currency	2,634	4,118	7,028	12,060	15,432	16,275	19,519	24,565	20,264	21,310
Total (mn pounds Sterling)	21,767	27,278	32,663	40,252	48,027	52,771	60,433	80,012	81,571	85,311
Total ($ mn)	38,103	41,381	43,648	52,179	70,456	86,486	107,655	131,196	145,580	150,949
US$/Pound	1.7505	1.517	1.3363	1.2963	1.467	1.6389	1.7814	1.6397	1.7847	1.7694

Source: Bank of England, *Quarterly Bulletin* (several issues). US$/Pound exchange rate from *IFS*.

Table 2.13 Exposure of German banks relative to capital, 1982-92 (percentage)

Country	1982	1983	1984	1985	1986	1987	1988	1989	1990	1991	1992
17 heavily indebted countries											
Argentina	3.6	3.9	5.8	6.9	5.5	5.2	5.1	5.1	4.3	4.0	4.0
Bolivia	0.2	0.3	0.2	0.2	0.2	0.2	0.1	0.2	0.2	0.2	0.2
Brazil	6.9	7.4	11.6	13.8	10.9	10.0	8.4	8.7	6.6	6.1	5.7
Chile	1.4	1.5	2.0	2.3	1.5	1.2	1.0	1.1	1.0	0.7	0.9
Colombia	0.8	0.7	0.8	1.0	0.9	0.9	0.9	1.0	0.7	0.6	0.6
Costa Rica	0.2	0.1	0.1	0.2	0.1	0.1	0.1	0.1	0.1	0.2	0.0
Côte d'Ivoire	0.4	0.4	0.4	0.4	0.3	0.3	0.3	0.3	0.2	0.2	0.2
Ecuador	0.4	0.4	0.7	0.7	0.6	0.5	0.5	0.5	0.5	0.4	0.3
Jamaica	0.0	0.0	0.0	0.0	0.0	0.0	0.0	0.0	0.0	0.0	0.0
Mexico	4.7	5.3	8.4	8.6	5.9	4.8	4.0	3.5	2.3	2.4	2.4
Morocco	0.8	0.8	1.0	1.3	1.1	1.0	0.9	1.0	0.8	0.7	0.6
Nigeria	2.7	3.1	3.4	3.6	2.7	2.1	1.4	1.1	0.9	0.7	0.4
Peru	0.7	0.7	0.8	1.0	0.9	0.8	0.7	0.8	0.6	0.6	0.5
Philippines	0.7	0.8	1.1	1.2	0.9	0.7	0.5	0.5	0.3	0.3	0.3
Uruguay	0.2	0.2	0.2	0.2	0.2	0.1	0.1	0.1	0.1	0.2	0.1
Venezuela	4.2	3.6	4.6	4.8	3.2	2.6	2.5	2.4	1.5	1.4	1.4
Yugoslavia	3.7	3.4	3.8	4.4	3.6	3.0	2.4	1.8	1.7	1.3	1.0
SUBTOTAL	31.4	32.6	45.1	50.7	38.5	33.5	29.0	28.0	21.8	19.9	18.5

Other middle income											
Malaysia			0.5	1.2	1.3	1.0	0.9	0.7	0.7	0.5	0.6
South Korea			1.5	1.9	2.5	2.0	1.4	1.3	1.6	2.0	2.0
Thailand			0.9	1.0	0.9	0.9	0.9	0.8	1.0	1.3	1.4
Egypt			2.3	2.6	2.3	2.7	2.7	2.3	2.6	1.9	1.4
SUBTOTAL			5.2	6.6	7.0	6.6	5.8	5.1	5.9	5.8	5.4
Other Eastern Europe											
Hungary			1.6	1.6	2.6	2.5	3.0	2.7	3.3	2.4	2.0
Poland			6.9	5.4	5.5	5.6	5.0	4.1	4.0	3.5	3.0
Soviet Union			4.3	5.8	8.5	6.6	5.5	6.4	7.3	15.4	16.5
SUBTOTAL			12.8	12.7	16.7	14.7	13.6	13.1	14.6	21.3	21.5
TOTAL			49.5	51.9	68.8	59.9	52.9	47.2	48.6	47.0	45.4
Memo:											
Total claims ($ millions)	19,961	21,376	28,675	33,658	39,821	45,594	43,505	45,545	58,390	76,218	87,368
Capital (millions DM)											
Resident banks	89,671	96,173	104,389	114,759	127,967	137,432	145,343	160,981	198,712	217,990	245,221
Loan loss prov.	6,503	6,785	7,242	7,739	7,990	8,257	6,034	3,129	18,134	34,758	38,839
Foreign branches	1,766	2,177	2,289	2,629	2,608	2,840	3,315	3,859	4,713	5,271	3,944
Foreign subsidiaries	..	..	4,771	5,201	5,915	6,330	7,200	8,380	9,836	11,349	12,565
Total (DM millions)	97,940	105,135	118,691	130,328	144,480	154,859	161,892	176,349	231,395	269,368	300,569
Total ($ millions)	40,361	41,176	41,706	44,269	66,535	86,157	92,183	93,803	143,217	162,319	192,463
DM/US$	2.4266	2.5533	2.8459	2.944	2.1715	1.7974	1.7562	1.88	1.6157	1.6595	1.5617

Note: Claims for 1984–92 include claims of resident German banks, foreign branches of German banks, and foreign subsidiaries of German banks. Claims for 1982 and 1983 only include claims of resident German banks and foreign branches of German banks.

Sources: Claims from Deutsche Bundesbank, Statistiche Beihefte zu den Monatsberichten der Deutschen Bundesbanken Reihe 3. Capital from Monthly Report of Deutsche Bundesbank. DM/US$ exchange rate from IFS.

Table 2.14 Exposure of French banks relative to capital, 1982-92 (percentage)

Country	1982	1983	1984	1985	1986	1987	1988	1989	1990	1991	1992
17 heavily indebted countries											
Argentina	..	..	8.8	8.5	5.4	4.4	4.2	4.0	3.2	3.2	2.3
Bolivia	..	..	0.0	0.0	0.0	0.0	0.1	0.0	0.0	0.0	0.0
Brazil	..	..	39.6	36.7	23.4	18.5	15.8	15.1	12.5	11.1	7.5
Chile	..	..	2.2	0.0	0.0	0.0	0.7	1.0	0.9	0.7	0.5
Colombia	..	..	0.0	0.0	0.0	0.0	0.8	0.7	0.7	0.7	0.6
Costa Rica	..	..	0.0	0.0	0.0	0.0	0.1	0.1	0.0	0.0	0.0
Côte d'Ivoire	..	..	7.5	7.5	5.3	4.7	3.7	3.6	3.0	2.5	1.9
Ecuador	..	..	0.0	0.0	0.0	0.0	0.3	0.3	0.3	0.3	0.2
Jamaica	..	..	0.0	0.0	0.0	0.0	0.1	0.1	0.0	0.0	0.0
Mexico	..	..	26.3	24.3	15.0	11.5	8.4	8.9	3.5	3.4	2.7
Morocco	..	..	9.0	9.8	6.2	5.2	3.7	3.7	3.4	2.8	2.1
Nigeria	..	..	11.5	11.5	7.6	6.2	4.6	3.6	2.7	2.3	1.2
Peru	..	..	3.1	3.0	0.0	0.0	1.2	1.2	1.0	1.0	0.6
Philippines	..	..	6.0	6.1	4.2	2.7	1.6	2.0	1.7	2.3	0.9
Uruguay	..	..	0.4	0.4	0.2	0.2	0.2	0.2	0.0	0.0	0.2
Venezuela	..	..	12.3	10.8	7.0	5.8	5.1	5.0	2.4	2.1	1.3
Yugoslavia	..	..	8.3	8.0	4.6	3.5	2.3	2.1	1.5	1.0	0.7
SUBTOTAL	..	..	135.0	126.6	78.9	62.8	52.8	51.7	37.1	33.5	22.7

Other middle income										
Malaysia	..	..	4.6	4.3	2.4	0.0	1.1	0.8	0.6	0.6	0.5
South Korea	..	..	8.2	12.2	14.9	6.8	6.5	7.7	6.7	6.5	4.7
Thailand	..	..	0.0	0.7	0.4	0.0	0.9	1.4	1.6	1.4	1.5
Egypt	..	..	11.1	11.0	7.1	6.2	4.9	5.0	4.1	3.6	2.3
SUBTOTAL	..	..	23.9	28.2	24.8	13.0	13.4	14.8	13.1	12.1	8.9
Other Eastern Europe										
Hungary	..	..	3.5	2.7	1.7	1.3	1.3	1.3	0.7	0.4	0.2
Poland	..	..	8.2	7.9	4.5	3.7	2.6	2.5	2.0	1.6	1.4
USSR	..	..	0.0	18.0	15.0	13.0	11.2	15.6	11.0	7.5	4.5
SUBTOTAL	..	..	11.8	28.6	21.2	18.0	15.1	19.4	13.7	9.5	6.0
TOTAL, 25 countries	..	..	170.6	183.4	125.0	93.8	81.4	85.8	63.9	55.1	37.7
Memo:										
Total claims ($ millions)	..	..	33,425	40,419	46,181	45,261	44,048	48,182	43,211	38,373	37,794
Capital										
billion francs	124	145	171	198	256	290	323	358	368	393	531
million US$	18,913	19,078	19,590	22,036	36,947	48,231	54,139	56,128	67,636	69,655	100,363
Francs/US$	6.5721	7.6213	8.7391	8.9852	6.9261	6.0107	5.9569	6.3801	5.4453	5.6421	5.2938

.. = not available

Sources: Claims from Banque de France, *Bulletin Trimestriel.* Capital from Banque de France, *Statistique Monetaires Definitives.* Franc/US$ exchange rate from *IFS.*

Table 2.15 Commercial debt of big four debtors, 1982-91 (millions of dollars)

Country	1982[a]	1983[a]	1984	1985	1986	1987	1988	1989	1990	1991
Argentina										
US banks	8,231	8,504	7,975	8,411	8,524	8,812	7,879	4,500	3,497	3,813
UK banks	3,517	3,419	3,394	3,677	4,110	4,206	4,108	3,343	2,352	2,244
German banks	1,434	1,588	2,425	3,056	3,682	4,476	4,716	4,767	6,099	6,422
French banks	..	..	1,728	1,877	2,005	2,136	2,299	2,265	2,169	2,255
TOTAL	13,182	13,511	15,522	17,021	18,321	19,630	19,002	14,875	14,117	14,734
WDT	18,104	23,478	24,781	25,291	27,331	30,626	29,742	32,564	24,541	23,108
BIS	22,168	23,244	25,941	28,937	32,408	35,253	35,112	32,369	30,766	31,282
Brazil										
US banks	20,438	20,653	23,869	22,796	22,404	21,275	19,391	16,284	11,444	6,897
UK banks	7,216	8,296	9,344	9,140	9,515	9,673	7,585	6,890	4,694	4,226
German banks	2,777	3,061	4,850	6,099	7,257	8,574	7,705	8,138	9,505	9,842
French banks	..	..	7,760	8,081	8,655	8,917	8,579	8,463	8,466	7,704
TOTAL	30,431	32,010	45,823	46,116	47,831	48,439	43,260	39,775	34,109	28,669
WDT	54,624	62,684	69,953	67,283	68,641	70,274	67,348	55,957	52,856	51,694
BIS	56,082	57,389	75,747	76,890	81,071	81,002	75,871	70,849	66,997	61,428

Mexico										
US banks	24,377	26,338	26,525	24,934	23,654	22,722	17,887	16,060	15,212	16,516
UK banks	8,539	8,394	8,746	8,669	8,674	8,773	8,291	7,500	4,909	5,270
German banks	1,913	2,202	3,515	3,818	3,909	4,145	3,725	3,256	3,353	3,882
French banks	..	..	5,145	5,346	5,528	5,535	4,559	4,995	2,400	2,367
TOTAL	34,828	36,933	43,931	42,767	41,765	41,175	34,462	31,811	25,874	28,035
WDT	46,642	65,036	70,267	71,442	70,262	73,995	59,990	53,422	14,153	15,916
BIS	58,978	62,819	72,769	74,520	74,229	75,846	69,387	70,147	55,944	65,064
Venezuela										
US banks	11,575	11,257	10,813	10,091	9,112	8,320	8,001	7,149	6,440	6,806
UK banks	2,320	2,432	2,379	2,398	2,065	1,915	1,871	1,655	1,186	873
German banks	1,694	1,464	1,927	2,117	2,123	2,254	2,318	2,262	2,188	2,319
French banks	..	..	2,406	2,387	2,602	2,806	2,779	2,810	1,644	1,458
TOTAL	15,589	15,153	17,525	16,993	15,902	15,295	14,969	13,876	11,458	11,456
WDT	14,957	20,444	24,568	23,347	29,794	27,450	25,256	24,298	4,013	3,798
BIS	22,657	21,955	26,173	25,827	25,056	25,021	25,770	24,122	17,910	18,276

.. = not available

a. Totals exclude France.

Sources: Bank claims: US from *Country Exposure Lending Survey*, UK from Bank of England *Quarterly Series*, France from Banque de France, *Bulletin Trimestriel*, Germany from *Statistiches Beihefte zu den Monatsberichten der Deutschen Bundesbanken* Reihe 3. WDT from *World Debt Tables*, BIS from *International Banking and Financial Markets Development*.

Figure 2.10 Debt breakdown of 33 countries by net debt/exports, 1982-93

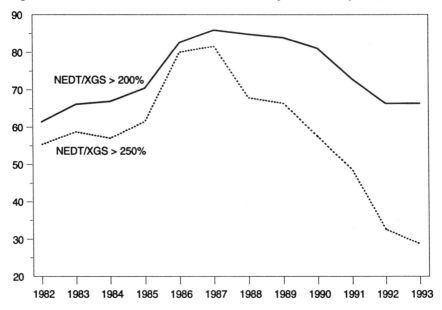

was down to only 28.7 percent by 1993. Imposition of a more stringent test, a debt/exports ratio of 200 percent or less, finds less of an improvement since 1987, but the trend with the 250 percent screen is probably the more meaningful.

Trends are more uniformly favorable using the debt/GNP criterion (figure 2.11). In 1986, 85 percent of debt was owed by countries with debt over 40 percent of GNP; by 1993, this share was down to 54 percent of debt. By a less stringent test, 50 percent of GNP, the share of total debt held by countries with above-threshold debt burdens, has fallen from two-thirds in 1987 to 37.9 percent in 1993.

Finally, on the criterion most meaningful in economic terms—net interest as a fraction of exports of goods and services—the fraction of debt owed by countries exceeding a stringent test (15 percent ratio) has fallen from a plateau of about 60 percent in 1982–88 to 17 percent by 1993 (figure 2.12). With a somewhat less stringent test of a 20 percent net interest/exports ratio, the improvement has also been dramatic. About 50 percent of debt was owed by countries with interest burdens exceeding this limit in 1982–86; but by 1993, only 9.7 percent of total debt was owed by countries exceeding this limit.

On this basis, it may be said that whereas one-half to three-fourths of debt of developing countries was in jeopardy by traditional creditworthiness rules of thumb in 1982–87, by 1992 only about one-fourth to one-third of debt remained so. Moreover, for the countries that were at the epicenter of the debt crisis, debt trends have been unambiguously favor-

Figure 2.11   Debt breakdown of 33 countries by net debt/GNP, 1982-93

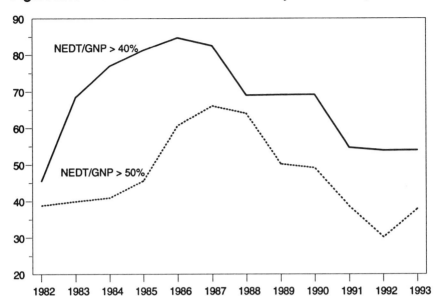

able in recent years, as the analysis of the four large Latin American debtors indicates.

The broad implication is that the debt strategy is working. There is no basis in the overall trends for a major shift in global debt policy toward much deeper forgiveness beyond existing Brady Plan norms. Of course, improvement in the trends could stall out, or the indicators could turn worse again, if the world economy entered into prolonged recession or experienced a shock of sustained high interest rates. Nonetheless, as examined in chapter 8, by 1994 the vulnerability of major debtors to such shocks as a rise in international interest rates was much more limited than in the early 1980s.

Whether the debt crisis was already over by 1992–94, or the debt problem resolved, was less clear than that there had been major progress in the period 1989–94. The largest debtor of all, Brazil, had yet to resolve the domestic economic policy difficulties that were a precondition to sustainable resolution of its debt problem—although the Real Plan of mid-1994 offered new promise. From the standpoint of vulnerability of the banking system, the debt crisis was already over by about 1989. For sub-Saharan Africa, the debt problem remains severe for many countries, as examined in chapter 7. Moreover, the new task of dealing with the debt of the former Soviet Union has shifted the geographical locus of the debt problem.

Despite the remaining problem areas, however, by 1992–93 the debt crisis was over as a major threat to industrial country financial systems

**Figure 2.12   Debt breakdown of 33 countries by net interest payments/
exports, 1982-93**

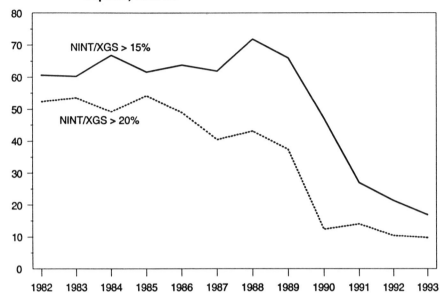

and as the principal cause of recession in Latin America. The systemwide
debt crisis by then had become a closed chapter in international economic
history, concentrated in the mid-1980s and overcome in part by international strategy (examined in chapter 5) but most importantly by economic
policy reform within individual debtor countries (examined in chapter 6
for the major Latin American debtors).

3

A Decomposition Analysis of Debt Forecasts in the 1980s

Introduction

Early in the debt crisis, Cline (1983, 1984) presented projections of trade and external debt indicators for the major debtor countries. Some observers have indicated that the projections were influential in policy formation at the time (Sachs 1988b, 171; Bailey 1990; Krugman 1994, 692). The main thrust of this early analysis was that with world recovery from the severe global recession, it should prove possible for major debtor countries to increase exports and gradually return to credit-worthiness. For most Latin American debtors, the estimates proved to be too optimistic, and the debt problem more intransigent, than the analysis had suggested. This chapter seeks to analyze what went wrong with the projections, and what went right. The objective is to facilitate a proper understanding of the evolution of the debt crisis and to provide a basis for lessons for future policy.

The Model[1]

The debt crisis erupted in 1982 during the worst world recession since the 1930s. Extremely high interest rates had been a driving force of both the recession and the breakdown in debt servicing. It was reasonable to expect that as the world economy returned to growth and interest rates

---

1. The reader interested only in the summary results is invited to proceed to the final section of this chapter.

returned to more normal levels, debtor country exports would rise, debt-service burdens would moderate, creditworthiness indicators would return to more favorable levels, and debtor countries might be able to export and grow their way out of the debt crisis rather than being forced into permanent default. Cyclical recovery in industrial countries also seemed likely to boost real prices of commodities exported by developing countries. As the dollar was unusually strong in 1983–84, there was the added prospect of dollar depreciation. Dollar depreciation in turn seemed likely to spur world trade prices in dollar terms; otherwise trade prices in deutsche marks, yen, and other major currencies would have to fall by the amount of the dollar depreciation, an unlikely outcome. As debt was largely denominated in dollars, a rise in dollar prices of goods would strengthen the trade base relative to the debt burden.

The projections applied a single model with some standardized and some country-specific parameters to data for the 19 largest debtor countries. The estimates used a "consistency" balance of payments model, comprising conventional trade equations and accounting equations linking external deficits to the buildup of debt and consequential debt servicing.

The model is of the following form.[2] The volume of nonoil exports depends on two central variables: the level of economic activity in industrial countries (Y_{DC}), to represent the income component of demand; and the level of the real exchange rate (ER^*) in the exporting country (with a lag spread over two years), to represent the influence of relative price.

$$X_q^{no} = f(Y_{DC}, ER^*) \tag{3.1}$$

Change in the dollar price of exports ($\dot{p}_x$) depends on world inflation (i_w) and the extent of dollar depreciation (d). A 1 percent trade-weighted depreciation of the dollar raises dollar prices of traded goods by 0.8 percent.[3] In addition, primarily because of the behavior of commodity prices, export prices depend on the cyclical status of the world economy as measured by the change in the industrial country growth rate (Δg_{DC}).[4] Thus:

---

2. For full model details, see Cline (1984, appendix B).

3. The notion is that dollar export prices should change little for US exporters, but by almost the full extent of the dollar depreciation for exporters in other currencies. As US exports are only about 12 percent of the world total (IMF 1991c, 121), a price-impact coefficient of 0.8 makes some allowance for unchanged dollar prices for exports of other dollar-area countries as well.

4. These "terms-of-trade" relationships of real export prices to the global business cycle were estimated individually by major debtor, to take account of differing degrees of importance of commodities in exports, and of cyclical price sensitivity across different commodities.

$$\dot{p}_x = f(i_w, d, \Delta g_{DC}). \tag{3.2}$$

Change in the dollar value of nonoil exports is the combined effect of change in volume and change in price.

The volume of nonoil imports depends on the level of economic activity in the country in question (Y_d), the real exchange rate (again lagged over two years), and the cyclical status of the domestic economy (Δg_d):

$$M_q^{no} = f(Y_d, ER^*, \Delta g_d) \tag{3.3}$$

Change in the dollar price of nonoil imports depends on world inflation and dollar depreciation:

$$\dot{p}_m = f(i_w, d) \tag{3.4}$$

For its part, oil trade is treated extremely simply in the model. The volume of oil exports or imports is set at the base year level, and the oil price is assumed exogenously. This treatment makes no allowance for response of oil trade to domestic growth or oil price change.

Exports and imports of nonfactor services are set at a constant (base-year) fraction of nonoil merchandise exports and imports, respectively. Interest payments depend on external debt at the end of the previous year, the level of international interest rates (London interbank offer rate [LIBOR]), and an average fixed rate for the portion of debt at fixed rates. Interest receipts on reserves depend on the level of nongold reserves at the end of the previous year and the US Treasury bill interest rate. Real transfers grow at 3 percent, and their dollar prices rise along with world inflation, taking into account dollar depreciation (i.e., equation 3.4). The current account balance equals the sum of the trade balance plus the balance on services and transfers.

Direct foreign investment grows at 3 percent in real terms and in dollar terms incorporates the influence of world inflation and dollar depreciation. Reserves rise by 20 percent of the increase in imports. Net new borrowing equals the current account deficit, plus the change in reserves, minus capital inflows in the form of direct investment. Debt at the end of the year equals the level at the beginning of the year plus the amount of net borrowing required during the year.

The Emerging Debate

The central finding of the model as applied in the Cline (1983, 1984) projections was that there should be considerable improvement in creditworthiness for the major debtor countries over the medium term. Thus, for the 19 largest debtor countries the projections called for a decline of the ratio of net debt (total minus reserves) to exports of goods and nonfactor services from 196 percent in 1983 to 144 percent by 1987. The expected decline was greater for oil-importing countries (from 205 percent to 132 percent), but the projections also called for some improvement for oil exporters (from 184 percent to 167 percent).

At the same time, however, alternative simulations of the model showed that this progress would depend on the key international variables: industrial country growth, world interest rates, and oil prices. The study specifically warned that any large decline in oil prices would make the debtor countries as a group much worse off. This result reflected the fact that the share of oil in exports is much larger for the oil-exporting debtors (e.g., Venezuela and Mexico) than is the share of oil in imports of the oil-importing debtors (e.g., Brazil and Chile).

Illiquidity Versus Insolvency

Because the central finding was one of expected improvement, Cline (1983, 1984) suggested that the international debt problem should primarily be seen as one of "illiquidity" rather than "insolvency" requiring major debt write-downs. This heuristic distinction was to some extent misleading, because it was evident that extra liquidity alone was likely to be insufficient and that important policy reforms were necessary. Nonetheless, it provided a conceptual underpinning for the initial strategy of concerted lending rather than debt forgiveness (or, in a confrontational instead of cooperative mode, repudiation). This framework persisted until 1989, when the Brady Plan shifted emphasis from new lending to debt forgiveness, and thus implicitly to a diagnosis of fundamental insolvency. Even then, however, the provision of official "enhancements" as compensation through lower risk kept the strategy in a market-oriented rather than command-and-control mode.

The analogy of the original distinction between illiquidity and insolvency is to central banking. There the tradition is that the central bank should stand ready to lend to illiquid commercial banks (those whose total assets exceed liabilities but whose liquid assets do not cover current liabilities) but should refuse to lend to insolvent banks (those whose total assets are less than total liabilities). The classic statement of this principle is from Bagehot (1873), the late-19th-century English financial commentator:

> In opposition to what might be at first sight supposed, the best way for the bank or banks who have the custody of the bank reserve to deal with a drain arising from internal discredit, is to lend freely . . . . A panic, in a word, is a species of neuralgia, and according to the rules of science you must not starve it. The holders of the cash reserve must be ready . . . to lend to merchants, to minor bankers, to "this man and that man," *whenever the security is good*. (48, 51; emphasis added)

The central bank analogy thus implied that if the international policy community could mobilize additional lending, from the banks as well as official sources, countries with "good security" (i.e., solvency) could be tided over until the financial panic in developing country debt subsided. Projection models of debt-servicing capacity provided a formal basis for judging whether the country's security was good.

In addition, there was a perception that if the problem could be managed without forced debt forgiveness, the debtor countries would have a better chance of retaining a favorable credit reputation in the future, and thus of achieving early reentry into world capital markets on a voluntary basis. A key implication was that it would be better for the debtor country itself, especially over the longer term, if debt could be managed rather than forced into default and forgiveness.

For several of the major debtor countries covered in the Cline (1983, 1984) projections, the diagnosis of fundamental solvency and lack of need for debt forgiveness turned out to be accurate. These countries included Chile, South Korea, Indonesia, Turkey, Yugoslavia, Algeria, Portugal, Thailand, Hungary, and Romania. Several of these nations largely escaped the debt crisis, despite great concern at the outset of the crisis about the debt of a number of them (e.g., South Korea). It is no coincidence that most of these countries were geographically outside of Latin America, as the psychological "neighborhood" or "contagion" effect was important in the developing crisis. Even for the countries that eventually received debt reductions under the Brady Plan (including Mexico, Venezuela, the Philippines, Argentina, and Brazil), the depth of this reduction was relatively limited (typically about 15 percent of total external debt, although about twice that deep for long-term debt owed to banks).

Contemporary Critiques

At the time, several authors criticized the projections in Cline (1983, 1984) as too optimistic. Klein (1984) and Fishlow (1985a) argued that industrial country growth would not be as high as projected; in the event, growth was even higher than assumed in the projections (as reviewed below). Dornbusch and Fischer (1984, 41) argued that the assumptions on interest rates and dollar depreciation were too optimistic; in the event, the historical outcome on these variables was even more favorable than projected (see below).

With respect to the model's parameters, a frequent critique was that the elasticity of debtor country exports with respect to industrial country growth was too high (Dornbusch and Fischer 1984, 39; Fishlow 1984, 1985b). As discussed below, however, this criticism typically missed the distinction between the specific formulation of the export equation and more conventional formulations.

More telling critiques, as it turned out, were that the model overstated prospective export price increases. Fishlow (1984, 31–58; 1985b, 114–22) argued that a decline in the dollar was unlikely to raise the dollar price of exports. Dornbusch and Fischer argued that the "pass-through" of dollar depreciation to higher dollar trade prices was more likely to be only about 0.5 rather than 0.8 (Dornbusch and Fischer 1984, 39). Dornbusch and Fischer (1984, 39) also argued that the model's estimated terms of trade response to industrial country recovery was too large. Fishlow (1985b, 117) provided an estimate of 1.4 for the elasticity of commodity terms of trade with respect to changes in OECD growth rates, smaller than the typical estimates in Cline (1984).

There were three other, more fundamental critiques. First, Fishlow (1985b) argued that the level of outward resource transfers implied by the projections was politically unsustainable. Second, and later, Cardoso and Dornbusch (1989) and Sachs (1989a) emphasized that the model ignored the domestic economic consequences of the debt strategy. The model stressed trade flows but did not address the "internal transfer" of resources from the public to the state to provide external servicing of government debt to replace previous external financing. This transfer imposed inflationary pressure and caused cutbacks in government investment as a means of fiscal adjustment as well as rising real interest rates in response to increased domestic government borrowing. Moreover, there was an interaction between the external and internal transfers, as the devaluation required to achieve the former caused the external interest payments to rise as a fraction of GDP expressed in domestic currency—thereby aggravating the latter (Cardoso and Dornbusch 1989).

There were clearly elements of truth in both of these lines of criticism, especially the concept of a dominant internal rather than external transfer problem. Even so, the experience of the past decade has demonstrated that countries with good domestic policies were able to overcome the resource constraint and internal transfer problems. Moreover, fiscal difficulties in such countries as Argentina and Brazil had at least as much to do with domestic developments (including patronage politics and excessive government employment after a return to democracy) as with the task of mobilizing the internal transfer to carry out the external transfer.

Third, Gersovitz (1986) argued that the projections failed to incorporate analytical modeling of the country's decision-making process with regard to whether or not to make payments on external debt. A country that decided it could gain by failing to pay would take measures that would tend to alter the prospective trade outlook (e.g., reduce exports and increase imports from baseline). This view may be called the "optimizing deadbeat" model of debtor behavior (chapter 4 below). In contrast, the implicit assumption in the 1983–84 projections was that countries that could meet external payments with the help of refinancing while achieving reasonable domestic growth would do so, and that none would engage in "beggar-thy-creditor" behavior, if only for fear of long-term repercussions in world capital markets.

Chapter 5 below proposes a political-economic model that seeks to explain why there was so much improvement from so little debt reduction in the Brady Plan. The model there suggests that market valuation of the debt is the minimum of two concepts: ability to pay and willingness to pay. That model suggests that for several countries, the latter variable jumped to a much higher, nonconstraining level as a consequence of improved perceived equity resulting from Brady relief, despite its modest magnitude. There is an element of Gersovitz (optimizing deadbeat) behavior in this reformulation, but only an element. The heuristic model in chapter 5 does suggest that the 1983–84 modeling of debt payment capacity was only a part of the analytical task, and that diagnosing political perception of equity was an important missing ingredient.

Contemporary Projections

The International Monetary Fund's annual issues of its *World Economic Outlook* provide perhaps the best guide to evolving mainstream policy thinking on international economic problems, including debt. The May 1983 issue contained no medium-term projections, but it did note that expected world economic recovery in 1983–84 should increase export volumes and commodity prices for debtor countries (IMF 1983, 71). By April 1984, the IMF began to include medium-term projections. Its assumptions were similar to those in the Cline (1983, 1984) projections.[5] The IMF projected that for major borrowing countries, the ratio of external debt to exports of goods and services would fall from 194 percent in 1983 to 165 percent by 1987 and 150 percent by 1990 (IMF 1984, 219). In qualitative terms this outlook was comparable to the projections in Cline (1983, 1984).[6]

---

5. The IMF projected US inflation in 1985–90 at 4.1 percent; a decline in interest rates by 1988–90 to 3 percentage points below the 1983 level; a modest improvement in terms of trade of developing countries by 1984–85; and international oil prices "unchanged in nominal terms in 1984–85, and that thereafter rise in step with prices of manufactured goods" (IMF 1984, 21). The corresponding exogenous variable assumptions in Cline (1983, 1984) were mostly similar, as reviewed below.

6. By 1984 these projections were thus part of the establishment view, although when first issued in 1983 they had been highly controversial (*Wall Street Journal*, 26 May 1983). Note also that parallel projections at the US Federal Reserve Board anticipated that the banks could gradually work down their uncomfortably high exposure/capital ratios while providing a reasonable share of new money under the baseline scenario (Terrell 1984).

The Outcome

Table 3.1 reports the actual debt trends in 1983–87 for the 19 major debtor countries divided into two groups: oil importers and oil exporters.[7] For comparison, the table also shows the forecasts in Cline (1984). It should be kept in mind that the 19 countries included several "success" cases (e.g., South Korea) as well as the more problematic (primarily Latin American) debtors.

A striking feature of these results is that the nominal dollar value levels of both exports and imports turned out to be far below the projections. Thus, by 1987 actual export earnings were 25 percent below projection for oil importers and 42 percent below projection for oil exporters. Import values were 28 percent below the projected level for oil importers and 51 percent below projection for oil exporters. Nominal trade levels below expectation meant that the denominator for the debt ratios—the dollar value of exports—was unexpectedly low, working against the anticipated improvement for the ratios.

The outcome on current account was ironically much "better" than projected. For the oil importers, the cumulative current account deficit in 1984–87 was only $10 billion, compared to a projected $74 billion. For oil exporters, the cumulative deficit was also only $10 billion, whereas the projected deficit had amounted to $78 billion. This outcome was even more surprising, given the collapse in oil prices. In both cases, lack of external finance was a major factor driving the low current account deficit. However, it is also the case that countries adopted austerity programs and exchange rate devaluations that caused reversals on current account that often exceeded what was necessary in view of external debt refinancing.[8]

The actual trends for debt were about the same as projected. The absolute debt level by 1987 stood at $732 billion for the 19 countries, compared with $676 billion projected. However, $52 billion of the $56 billion difference was attributable to "discovered debt," the difference between actual debt in the base year (1983) and the estimated value available at the time of the projections (see table 3.1). In contrast, the

---

7. Oil importers: Argentina, Brazil, Chile, Hungary, Israel, South Korea, Philippines, Portugal, Romania, Thailand, Turkey, and Yugoslavia. Oil exporters: Algeria, Ecuador, Egypt, Indonesia, Mexico, Peru, and Venezuela. Note that the analysis of this chapter is based on the published World Bank debt data available through the issue: World Bank (1993b). The slightly revised debt series of World Bank (1995), available only as this study went to press, are reported in chapter 2, table 2.1.

8. Nor is the better-than-expected current account performance explained by trends in the successful countries outside Latin America. For Argentina, Brazil, Mexico, and Venezuela, the cumulative current account deficit for 1984–87 was only $5.7 billion, compared with a projection of $27.1 billion (table 3.2).

Table 3.1 Debt forecasts versus actual outcomes: oil importers and exporters, 1983-87 (billions of dollars and percentages)

		1983	1984	1985	1986	1987
Oil importers						
Exports	Forecast	117.0	136.8	164.0	193.8	217.4
	Actual	115.3	128.6	126.0	133.6	162.1
Imports	Forecast	119.8	134.7	156.8	189.6	210.0
	Actual	118.7	120.0	114.8	123.5	150.6
Current Account	Forecast	−24.0	−21.2	−19.4	−20.0	−13.6
	Actual	−22.0	−10.4	−2.8	−1.0	4.0
Debt	Forecast	322.0	344.0	365.0	388.0	401.0
	Actual	344.9	359.6	383.9	406.1	433.0
Net debt/XGS (percent)	Forecast	205.0	186.0	163.0	145.0	132.0
	Actual	231.8	214.9	230.9	229.3	201.9
NIP[a]/XGS (percent)	Forecast	20.5	19.6	19.3	15.8	13.5
	Actual	26.9	24.1	22.9	20.2	18.3
Oil exporters						
Exports	Forecast	76.5	81.1	87.0	102.5	111.3
	Actual	77.4	83.3	77.2	54.4	65.1
Imports	Forecast	57.3	69.5	83.1	99.3	109.6
	Actual	55.5	57.6	55.7	51.9	54.0
Current Account	Forecast	1.4	−9.8	−20.7	−22.9	−24.3
	Actual	2.1	4.6	1.6	−13.5	−2.2
Debt	Forecast	199.2	209.2	229.8	252.4	275.0
	Actual	228.1	234.9	248.6	268.7	298.7
Net debt/XGS (percent)	Forecast	184.0	178.0	178.0	167.0	167.0
	Actual	228.4	215.8	243.1	360.8	331.4
NIP[a]/XGS (percent)	Forecast	15.5	16.4	17.3	14.7	13.2
	Actual	20.3	19.2	20.7	28.8	21.3

a. Net interest payments (NIP) on accrual basis.

Source: Exports, imports, current account, and reserves from *IFS*. Gross debt and interest payments from *WDT*. Interest received from BOP, *IFS*.

increase in debt was extremely close to the projection. During 1984–87, external debt of the 19 countries rose by $159 billion, compared to a rise of $155 billion in the projections (table 3.1).

This close adherence was a paradox in view of the fact that cumulative current account deficits were far smaller than projected ($20 billion actual instead of the $152 billion projected). Most of the unexplained rise in debt (after adjusting for data discovery) was attributable to ongoing capital flight over this period, and, to a lesser extent, to a ballooning of the dollar valuation of the stock of debt denominated in other hard currencies as the dollar depreciated. Neither phenomenon had been included in the projection model. In short, the model's projections for trends in the level of debt were right but for the wrong reasons.

Primarily because of the lower-than-expected nominal value of exports (but also because of discovered debt), the ratio of net debt to exports of goods and nonfactor services showed much less improvement over the period than projected. For the oil-importing group, this ratio fell only from 232 percent to 202 percent from 1983 to 1987, instead of declining from 205 percent to 132 percent.[9] The outcome was far worse for the oil-exporting countries. Their net debt-exports ratio *rose* from 228 percent to 331 percent, rather than declining from 184 percent to 167 percent as projected. Of course, the driving force in this deterioration was the collapse in oil prices in 1986 and after, as discussed below.

The outcome for creditworthiness improvement was considerably closer to that projected on the other key indicator, the ratio of net interest payments to exports of goods and services. This ratio is conceptually more appropriate than the debt/exports ratio, because it takes account of the *price* of debt—the interest rate—as well as the volume of debt. Here again, the problem of discovered debt meant that the 1983-base actual ratio was higher than in the original projections. After allowing for this shift, however, the trendline in the actual interest/exports ratio for oil importers was almost identical to the projected trend. From 1983 to 1987, both series fell by about one-third. For the oil importers, the larger-than-expected drop in world interest rates broadly compensated for the smaller-than-expected rise in the nominal value of exports. The outcome was also broadly consistent with the projections for the oil-exporting countries through 1985, but by 1986–87 the debt burden was substantially above the expected level even on this measure (again because of the collapse in oil prices).

The fact that many oil-importing countries experienced ongoing debt difficulties even though their debt burdens moderated as measured by the interest/exports ratio raises important questions. This paradox could imply that the original strategy was in error, that even successful reduction of the indebtedness indicators would not have resolved the problem. Nor does the paradox disappear if the focus is shifted to the main problem countries. As indicated in table 3.2, the interest/exports ratio behaved close to the model projections for Brazil, Mexico, and Venezuela, despite the problems with trade prices and especially oil prices.[10]

The explanation of this paradox is at least threefold. First, creditors may have paid more attention to the simple debt/exports ratio than to the more appropriate interest/exports ratio. Second, banks that had been shocked

---

9. The divergence in the base year 1983 is attributable to "discovered" debt.

10. The actual outcome for this indicator was also close to the forecast trend for Argentina through 1986, although the divergence was substantial by 1987.

Table 3.2 Debt forecasts versus actual outcomes: Argentina, Brazil, Mexico, Venezuela, 1983-87 (billions of dollars and percentages)

		1983	1984	1985	1986	1987
Argentina						
Exports	Forecast	7.7	8.5	10.4	12.6	14.1
	Actual	7.8	8.1	8.4	6.9	6.4
Imports	Forecast	4.6	5.2	6.5	7.8	8.7
	Actual	4.1	4.1	3.5	4.4	5.3
Current account	Forecast	−2.6	−2.6	−3.4	−2.4	−1.4
	Actual	−2.4	−2.5	−1.0	−2.9	−4.2
Debt	Forecast	44.0	46.6	50.0	52.5	53.9
	Actual	45.9	48.9	50.9	52.5	58.5
Net debt[a]/XGS (percent)	Forecast	486.0	465.0	408.0	352.0	321.0
	Actual	481.8	495.6	474.9	589.7	698.3
NIP[b]/XGS (percent)	Forecast	56.5	52.4	52.2	41.7	34.4
	Actual	62.8	55.6	48.0	46.8	47.1
Growth rate	Forecast	2.0	3.5	5.0	5.0	5.0
	Actual	2.9	2.5	−4.4	5.6	2.5
Brazil						
Exports	Forecast	21.9	25.7	29.5	35.0	39.3
	Actual	21.9	27.0	25.6	22.3	26.2
Imports	Forecast	15.4	16.2	18.2	22.7	24.9
	Actual	15.4	13.9	13.2	14.0	15.1
Current account	Forecast	−6.5	−4.5	−5.1	−4.4	−1.7
	Actual	−6.8	0.0	−0.3	−5.3	−1.5
Debt	Forecast	91.9	96.0	100.5	104.3	104.7
	Actual	98.3	105.3	106.1	113.7	123.9
Net debt/XGS (percent)	Forecast	366.0	322.0	294.0	255.0	227.0
	Actual	397.8	324.0	344.1	446.0	415.5
NIP[b]/XGS (percent)	Forecast	40.7	39.1	40.5	32.5	26.8
	Actual	38.7	28.5	28.5	29.1	35.8
Growth rate	Forecast	−3.3	1.5	3.0	6.0	6.0
	Actual	−3.4	5.3	7.9	7.5	3.6

(table continued on next page)

by payments suspension were not prepared to renew voluntary lending even where creditworthiness indicators had improved substantially. Third, domestic political dynamics meant that several countries were inclined to enter arrears or seek debt relief even when on external creditworthiness indicators they might not need to do so.[11]

---

11. The contrast between Chile and Venezuela is telling in this regard. Chile did not seek Brady Plan debt reduction; Venezuela did. Yet for most of the second half of the 1980s, Chile's interest/exports ratio was considerably higher than that of Venezuela.

Table 3.2 (continued)

		1983	1984	1985	1986	1987
Mexico						
Exports	Forecast	21.4	22.6	23.6	27.8	30.0
	Actual	22.3	24.2	21.7	16.0	20.6
Imports	Forecast	7.7	11.4	13.5	16.2	18.0
	Actual	8.6	11.3	13.2	11.4	12.2
Current account	Forecast	5.5	0.6	−2.0	−0.4	0.9
	Actual	5.4	4.2	1.1	−1.7	4.0
Debt	Forecast	87.6	87.2	88.9	88.9	87.1
	Actual	93.0	94.8	96.9	100.9	109.5
Net debt[a]/XGS (percent)	Forecast	308.0	284.0	271.0	230.0	206.0
	Actual	325.0	288.9	332.7	430.7	346.9
NIP[b]/XGS (percent)	Forecast	32.8	33.2	34.9	27.7	22.7
	Actual	32.1	30.7	30.6	31.6	23.3
Growth rate	Forecast	−4.7	2.0	4.0	6.0	6.0
	Actual	−4.2	3.7	2.7	−3.9	1.7
Venezuela						
Exports	Forecast	14.7	14.9	15.2	18.1	19.3
	Actual	14.6	15.9	14.3	8.5	10.4
Imports	Forecast	5.3	7.4	9.4	11.3	12.5
	Actual	6.4	7.2	7.5	7.9	8.9
Current account	Forecast	5.1	1.8	−0.9	−0.7	−0.9
	Actual	4.4	4.7	3.3	−2.2	−1.4
Debt	Forecast	34.0	32.5	33.7	34.6	35.6
	Actual	38.3	36.9	35.3	34.3	34.7
Net debt/XGS (percent)	Forecast	146.0	132.0	133.0	115.0	111.0
	Actual	165.9	145.8	139.7	246.8	202.8
NIP[b]/XGS (percent)	Forecast	5.1	10.8	11.9	9.0	7.1
	Actual	9.6	4.6	9.1	14.0	11.3
Growth rate	Forecast	−2.0	2.5	4.5	4.5	4.5
	Actual	−5.6	−1.4	1.4	6.3	4.5

a. Deducts reserves including gold.
b. Net interest payments (NIP) on accrual basis.

Sources: Exports, imports, current account, and reserves from *IFS*.

Poor performance on domestic growth helps explain the paradox of a severe debt problem despite major progress on the interest/exports ratio. Although growth was close to the forecast for the broad country groupings, it fell considerably short for the large problem debtor countries. Thus, actual domestic growth in 1984–87 averaged 3.8 percent versus the projected 4.7 percent for oil importers, and 3.0 percent versus 4.3 percent for oil exporters. However, the averages mask overperformance by some (e.g., Asian) countries and underperformance by major Latin American debtors. Thus, growth over this period averaged only

1.1 percent in Argentina, 1.1 percent in Mexico, and 2.7 percent in Venezuela, well below the forecasts.[12]

Decomposition Method

Annex 3A presents the methodology used here to decompose the difference between forecast and actual outcome into its component parts. At a broad level, there are two sources of error: mistakes in assumed future values for exogenous variables, and mistakes in the projection model. Because a set of assumptions about future values of exogenous variables is commonly called a "scenario," the former type of error may be designated "scenario error," and is also what may be called "variable assumption error."

For its part, model error may include an incorrect value for a "parameter" in the model (such as the elasticity of exports with respect to OECD growth). It may also reflect improper specification of the variable (e.g., linear rather than nonlinear; contemporaneous rather than lagged). Model error also includes failure to incorporate a variable that should be taken into account.

Total forecast error is the difference between the forecasted variable (e.g., exports) and its actual level. The component attributable to scenario error may be calculated by conducting what may be called a "backcast." The backcast reproduces the estimates using the original model but applying the actual historical values of the exogenous variables, rather than the values that were assumed at the time of the forecast.

The backcast tells what the model would have predicted with perfect foresight about the exogenous variables. It should therefore track the actual outcome insofar as the model is correct. The remaining difference between the "backcast" and the actual outcome is thus attributable to model error. This error is more serious than scenario error in one sense: it means the model is unlikely to be accurate for future projections, even if the forecaster is lucky enough to be on target for the assumptions about exogenous variable values.

Actual versus Expected International Environment

Table 3.3 reports the forecasted values for the key international variables in the Cline (1984) projections, along with the corresponding actual values for the period 1984–87. The important variable of industrial country growth turned out to be more favorable than projected. Thus, for

---

12. Brazil's average growth of 6.1 percent was above the forecast average of 4.1 percent for 1984–87. However, the country's growth fell precipitously in later years.

Table 3.3 Variable assumptions and outcomes, 1983-87
(percentages except where noted)

	1983	1984	1985	1986	1987
OECD growth					
Forecast	1.5	4.2	2.7	2.4	3.0
Actual	2.6	4.8	3.4	2.7	3.3
LIBOR					
Forecast	10	10.5	12.5	11	9.4
Actual	9.6	10.8	8.3	6.8	7.1
Oil price ($/bbl)					
Forecast	29	29	29	34	36
Actual	29	28	27	14	18
Dollar depreciation					
Forecast	−5.8	0.0	10.0	10.0	0.0
Actual	−3.2	−7.9	−3.3	19.8	12.3
World inflation					
Forecast	5.0	5.0	5.8	6.2	6.0
Actual	5.0	3.7	1.5	−3.1	0.9
Debtor country growth					
Oil importers					
Forecast	1.3	3.4	4.5	5.4	5.4
Actual	0.7	1.7	3.9	3.0	6.5
Oil exporters					
Forecast	−1.2	2.7	4.3	5.1	5.1
Actual	−1.9	3.9	3.2	1.4	3.4

this period average actual growth was almost ¹/₂ percentage point higher than assumed in the projections, with the largest difference in 1985. The high-growth phase of world recovery was longer than expected, and the plateau of growth after recovery higher.

World interest rates were also more favorable than projected. On average, in 1984–87 LIBOR was 2.6 percentage points (260 basis points) lower than assumed in the 1984 projections, at an average of 8.25 percent instead of the expected 10.85 percent. This large difference played the dominant role in the improvement of the interest/exports ratio along a path close to that predicted despite the below-expectation performance of exports, as discussed above.

There was an even larger reduction of world inflation from anticipated levels. In 1984–87, wholesale price inflation averaged only 0.75 percent annually instead of 5.75 percent as expected (table 3.3).[13] This reduction in average inflation by 5 percentage points from the expected average was about twice the decline in interest rates and meant an increase of 2.4

---

13. The inflation rate refers to average wholesale price inflation (in domestic currencies) for the industrial countries (IMF 1991b, 115).

percentage points in average real interest rates from baseline expectations for the period. As examined below, the net effect of interest rate and inflation changes was favorable from the standpoint of cash flow, but unfavorable from the standpoint of long-term debt burden. Dollar depreciation was approximately the same as projected for 1984–87 (about 20 percent), although its timing was much different. The dollar *appreciated* by 11 percent in 1984–85, but then it depreciated by 34.5 percent in 1986–87. The result was that by 1987 the dollar stood 19.8 percent below its 1983 base, versus a projected decline of 21 percent for the period.[14]

On the other major international variable, the price of oil, the outcome was a major deterioration from the trends anticipated. In 1986–87, world oil prices averaged $16 per barrel, whereas the projections had called for an average of $35 per barrel. A collapse in oil prices did occur, with the adverse consequences that the original analysis had warned about but had not expected as the base case.

Two of the international variables—interest rates and world inflation—are closely interconnected, and their interplay has subtle effects on the debt burden. Annex 3B analyzes the impact of world disinflation on the debt problem. It is demonstrated there that if there is instantaneous adjustment of expectations and interest rates fall simultaneously with and by the same amount as world inflation, there will be *no* change in the debt/exports ratio or long-term debt burden, but there will still be cash-flow relief from a lower interest-exports ratio. Specifically, for each percentage point of joint reduction in inflation and the interest rate, there is a reduction of the interest/exports ratio by about k percentage points, where k is the debt/exports ratio.

Average inflation fell by about 5 percentage points annually in 1983–87 from the expected baseline, whereas LIBOR fell by only 2.6 percentage points. However, the interest rate change has a leveraged impact on the interest/exports ratio. With LIBOR plus spread initially at about 11 percent, the 2.6 percentage point drop amounted to a reduction of interest payments by almost one-fourth, far more than the initial decline of the nominal export base by 5 percent from baseline from the reduction in inflation.

Nominal interest rate relief in the mid-1980s thus helped reduce the proximate cash-flow problem, even though real interest rates were considerably higher than had been anticipated. Another way of looking at the nominal versus real interest rate impact is to recall that in the early 1980s, it was common to note that high world inflation and high nominal interest rates had caused a cash-flow problem for debtor countries by effectively causing a premature amortization. That is, the originally intended timetable for interest and principal payments had essentially

---

14. The dollar index used here is the IMF's nominal effective exchange rate index, based on weights for trade in manufactured goods for 17 industrial countries (IMF 1990a, 729).

been reconfigured to shift real payments to the early part of the period and compensate through inflationary erosion of the real principal payments due late in the period—cold comfort to countries that could not meet current payments. Falling nominal interest rates and falling inflation in the mid-1980s represented a reversal of this cash-flow problem.

Overall, the international economic environment was broadly as favorable as Cline (1983, 1984) had predicted for oil-importing countries, but much more hostile for oil-exporting countries. The model may be used to calculate the effect of "scenario error" resulting from differences between the predicted and actual outcome on these international economic environment variables.

Scenario Error

Table 3.4 presents the central results of the decomposition analysis and its identification of scenario and model error.[15] The table first shows actual, forecast, and "backcast" values for trade, the current account, and the debt indicators. The backcast applies the actual rather than originally assumed values of the exogenous variables, such as industrial country growth. As noted above (and discussed in annex 3A), the difference between the backcast and the forecast is the amount of scenario error (variable assumption error) for all exogenous variables taken together. This error is reported in absolute terms in the second panel of the table. The third panel reports this error as a percentage of actual outcome.

Again in the upper panel, the table also shows a series of alternative backcasts, in each of which all exogenous variables are set at actual levels except the variable under scrutiny—for which the originally assumed values are applied. The difference between each such "partial backcast" and the full backcast, reported in the table's second panel, shows the amount of error attributable to mistaken assumption for the variable in question. These individual differences thus provide the basis for decomposing scenario error into the contribution from each exogenous variable individually. The third panel of the table presents these individual variable assumption errors as a percentage of the overall backcast estimate for each of the projection concepts.

Because the model has nonlinearities,[16] there are interactions that keep the sum of individual variable assumption errors from being

---

15. Note that an alternative basis for estimating scenario error is to apply the impact parameters identified in Cline (1984, 53–60) to the divergences of exogenous variables from their predicted paths. The results of that exercise, not reported here, are broadly in accord with the more formal decomposition analysis discussed here.

16. For example, the price and exchange rate variables are *multiplied* by the trade volumes rather than being simply additive.

exactly equal to the total combined variable assumption error (scenario error). For example, for oil importers the forecast for exports is $217.4 billion; the backcast is $199.6 billion; so the scenario error is the difference, $17.8 billion (center panel). However, the sum of individually estimated variable assumption errors (center panel, same row) is $23.5 billion, close to the joint backcast error but not equal to it. This divergence must be kept in mind in ascribing relative importance to the individual variable assumption errors reported in the second panel of table 3.4.

For trade performance, table 3.4 shows that export earnings by 1987 were overpredicted by 34 percent for oil importers (panel 3). Of this total error, 23 percent was attributable to model error and 11 percent to scenario error. Model error, discussed below, was driven by overestimation of the price-increasing impact of dollar depreciation (at least as of 1987) and, to a much lesser degree, of terms of trade response to global recovery. For its part, total scenario error was more than accounted for by the overestimation of world inflation, partially offset by underprediction of industrial country growth and debtor country real depreciation.

The projections overestimated 1987 import levels of oil-importing countries by 39 percent, and by 47 percent for scenario error alone. Overprediction of world inflation accounted for about half of the latter, with the remainder attributable to overstatement of oil import prices, overprediction of debtor country growth, and understatement of their real exchange rate depreciation.

Export earnings of oil exporters by 1987 were overestimated by 71 percent, with the bulk of the error stemming understandably from scenario error on oil prices. More surprising, import values were overstated by an even larger proportion. Scenario error accounted for about half of this overstatement, driven by overestimation of world inflation and underestimation of country depreciation. The other half of the error stemmed from the model, as discussed below.

For the current account, if industrial country growth had been at the modestly lower projected level the current account of oil importers would have been worse by an estimated $12 billion annually by 1987 (table 3.4, middle panel, right-hand side). If LIBOR had been higher as projected, this balance would have been worse by about $6 billion. However, lower-than-expected world inflation made the nominal value of the group's trade surplus unexpectedly low, increasing the deficit by about $22 billion. The net influence of these international variables was thus approximately neutral.

The decomposition analysis shows a significant favorable effect of the oil price reduction for the oil importers. Lower-than-expected oil prices improved their current account balance by some $20 billion by 1987 (table 3.4). However, it is also evident that divergences on the domestic variables were as important as those on international variables. For the

Table 3.4 Projection accuracy as of 1987 (billions of dollars except where noted)

Backcasts	Actual	Forecast	Backcast	Backcast with assumed values for only:						
				GW	IW	Poll	$	LIBOR	Gd	ER*
Oil importers										
Exports	162.1	217.4	199.6	191.1	241.5	200.3	199.9	199.6	199.6	188.7
Imports	150.6	210.1	139.2	139.2	166.2	156.3	139.5	139.2	147.5	149.0
Current account	4.0	−13.6	61.6	49.3	83.3	41.8	63.8	55.7	47.3	33.9
Debt	433.0	401.3	235.0	265.3	202.7	282.7	209.4	259.2	288.0	273.3
Net debt/XGS (percent)	201.9	132.4	82.5	98.4	55.8	99.6	72.1	91.7	103.2	102.4
Oil exporters										
Exports	65.1	111.3	77.5	75.3	87.3	109.5	77.9	77.5	77.5	75.0
Imports	54.0	109.6	81.5	81.5	98.8	81.5	80.8	81.5	84.3	87.4
Current account	−2.2	−24.4	−19.3	−22.8	−28.9	15.8	−21.5	−27.2	−23.9	−27.0
Debt	298.7	275.0	293.8	302.2	318.3	216.8	315.4	314.8	296.2	294.5
Net debt/XGS (percent)	331.0	166.8	249.8	265.8	235.2	135.2	270.1	269.9	253.0	253.6

Error breakdown	Forecast error	Model error	Scenario error	Partial contribution to scenario error:							
				GW	IW	Poll	$	LIBOR	Gd	ER*	TOTAL
Oil importers											
Exports	55.3	37.5	17.8	−8.5	41.9	0.7	0.3	0.0	0.0	−10.9	23.5
Imports	59.5	−11.4	70.9	0.0	27.0	17.1	0.3	0.0	8.3	9.8	62.5
Current account	−17.6	57.6	−75.2	−12.3	21.7	−19.8	2.2	−5.9	−14.3	−27.7	−56.1
Debt	−31.7	−198.0	166.3	30.3	−32.3	47.7	−25.6	24.2	53.0	38.3	135.6
Net debt/XGS (percent)	−69.5	−119.4	49.9	15.9	−26.7	17.1	−10.4	9.2	20.7	19.9	45.7

Oil exporters											
Exports	46.2	12.4	33.8	-2.2	9.8	32.0	0.4	0.0	0.0	-2.5	37.5
Imports	55.6	27.5	28.1	0.0	17.3	0.0	-0.7	0.0	2.8	5.9	25.3
Current account	-22.2	-17.1	-5.1	-3.5	-9.6	35.1	-2.2	-7.9	-4.6	-7.7	-0.4
Debt	-23.7	-4.9	-18.8	8.4	24.5	-77.0	21.6	21.0	2.4	0.7	1.6
Net debt/XGS (percent)	-164.2	-81.2	-83.0	16.0	-14.6	-114.6	20.3	20.1	3.2	3.8	-65.8
Percentage error (percent)											
Oil importers,											
Exports	34.1	23.1	11.0	-4.3	21.0	0.4	0.2	0.0	0.0	-5.5	
Imports	39.5	-7.6	47.1	0.0	19.4	12.3	0.2	0.0	6.0	7.0	
Current account	-440.0	1,440.0	-1,880.0	-20.0	35.2	-32.1	3.6	-9.6	-23.2	-45.0	
Debt	-7.3	-45.7	38.4	12.9	-13.7	20.3	-10.9	10.3	22.6	16.3	
Net debt/XGS (percent)	-34.4	-59.1	24.7	19.3	-32.4	20.7	-12.6	11.2	25.1	24.1	
Oil exporters											
Exports	71.0	19.0	51.9	-2.8	12.6	41.3	0.5	0.0	0.0	-3.2	
Imports	103.0	50.9	52.0	0.0	21.2	0.0	-0.9	0.0	3.4	7.2	
Current account	1,009.1	777.3	231.8	18.1	49.7	-181.9	11.4	40.9	23.8	39.9	
Debt	-7.9	-1.6	-6.3	2.9	8.3	-26.2	7.4	7.1	0.8	0.2	
Net debt/XGS (percent)	-49.6	-24.5	-25.1	6.4	-5.8	-45.9	8.1	8.0	1.3	1.5	

GW = world growth; iW = world inflation; Poil = oil price; $ = dollar depreciation; Gd = domestic growth; ER* = real exchange rate.

Note: Partial errors do not equal model error due to nonlinearities in model.

oil importers, lower-than-expected domestic growth (and thus imports) and greater-than-expected real exchange rate depreciation caused the current account by 1987 to be more favorable than expected in the baseline (by $14 billion and $28 billion, respectively).

Altogether, there was a large scenario error that understated current account performance for the oil-importing countries (i.e., overstated their deficits). However, as indicated in table 3.4, this unexpectedly favorable outcome on the exogenous variables was largely offset by unfavorable divergences associated with model error. That is, given the actual exogenous variable values, the outcome predicted by the model was considerably too favorable ("model error," discussed below). Moreover, lower-than-expected domestic growth and greater-than-expected real exchange rate depreciation were "favorable" for the current account but not necessarily for the political sustainability of the debt strategy, given the resulting pressure on income levels and domestic inflation.

For the oil exporters, the composition of scenario error shows patterns similar to those for the oil importers. Oil prices are extremely important, and without their collapse in 1986 the current account of the oil exporters would have been stronger in 1987 by about $35 billion (table 3.4, middle). The deviation from industrial country growth has the right sign (but is relatively small, given the absence of impact of growth on oil exports in the model). As in the case of oil importers (but to a lesser degree), deviation of domestic growth and the real exchange rate from the baseline made a positive contribution to the current account (i.e., caused negative scenario error on the size of the deficit).

A seeming anomaly for the oil exporters is that lower-than-expected world inflation benefited rather than damaged the current account (i.e., negative variable assumption error on the size of the deficit). The explanation is that nominal oil exports are fixed in the model, so that lower world inflation provides a gain from lower import prices that is not offset by a loss in lower export prices.

For external debt, table 3.4 shows that the forecast was close to the actual outcome for oil importers, but for the wrong reasons. There was a large overstatement of debt from the standpoint of exogenous variable assumptions (as the variables turned out to be more favorable than expected), but an even larger understatement caused by the specification of the model (which was too optimistic). Similarly, for oil exporters the debt forecast was close to the actual value, but only because unexpected favorable effects associated with world inflation, interest rates, and dollar depreciation approximately compensated for the unexpected oil price collapse. Even though debt was close to the forecast, the debt/exports ratio turned out much worse than expected because of the decline in oil export earnings.

In summary, for oil importers the net effect of mistaken assumptions about the baseline values of exogenous variables, or scenario error, was approximately neutral overall. Actual developments were more favorable than expected for world growth, interest rates, and oil import prices; neutral for the dollar; but less favorable than expected for world inflationary erosion of the debt burden relative to the export base. In contrast to this benign overall external environment for the oil importers, the collapse in oil prices meant that for the oil exporters the external circumstances were much less favorable than had been projected. As the baseline international economic assumptions had led to the prognosis of broad general improvement on debt in the face of a friendly international economic environment, the actual outcomes reinforced this outlook for oil importers but sharply reversed it for oil exporters.

To the extent that the model itself was accurate, the implication of this conclusion is that those oil-importing countries that had worse-than-expected outcomes did so primarily for domestic reasons rather than as the consequence of adverse external events, whereas for oil exporters the external shock of lower oil prices can easily explain the shortfall in outcome from expected debt performance. As capital flight is largely a matter of domestic policy, unexpected capital flight adds to this qualitative conclusion of domestic rather than external derailment. However, as analyzed below, there were at least two important errors in the model associated with dollar depreciation (timing of change in traded goods prices and debt stock valuation effects) that meant even the oil importers were not necessarily in as favorable an international environment as had been expected.

Model Error

As indicated in table 3.4, by 1987 the misspecification of the projection model was responsible for an overstatement of 23 percent for export values and an understatement of about 8 percent for import values, for the oil importing countries. As a result, model error caused a large overstatement of the current account position (by about $58 billion for 1987). The cumulative effect was that the model itself led to an understatement of external debt by almost $200 billion (largely offset, however, by the overstatement of debt from the side of mistaken exogenous variable assumptions).

For the oil exporters, there was a similar model error of about 20 percent overstatement on the export side and an even larger overstatement of imports. The net result was model understatement of the current account outcome (overstatement of current account deficit). Nonetheless, additional model influences meant that the model error for debt buildup was in the direction of understatement (though by a small amount relative to the debt baseline).

There are at least four promising places to look for the origins of the model errors: capital flight, valuation of nondollar debt, calculation of export prices, and parameters assumed for trade elasticities.

Capital Flight and Exchange Rate Valuation

The 1984 model essentially ruled out subsequent capital flight. The principal reason was that countries such as Venezuela and Mexico that had already been severely affected by capital flight caused by distorted domestic policies (overvalued exchange rates, unduly low domestic interest rates) seemed unlikely to return to these policies. This view was reinforced by the simple fact that these countries had nearly exhausted reserves and were in no position to continue turning over foreign exchange on demand to individuals and firms that wished to convert domestic currency into dollars.

How important was the omission of capital flight from the model? The answer may be obtained by calculating actual capital flight during the projection period. The initial set of estimates here applies the conventional "current account residuals" approach. This method compares debt buildup plus net direct investment inflow, on the financial sources side, against the accumulated current account deficits and increases in reserves, on the uses side. Any excess of sources over uses is attributed to capital flight.

For the oil importers, the increase in debt from the end of 1983 to the end of 1987 amounted to $88.1 billion (table 3.1). Reserves rose by $13.8 billion (against a forecast of $18.1 billion). The cumulative current account deficit was only $10.3 billion. Net direct investment summed to $10.8 billion (table 3.9 below). Capital flight was thus $74.8 billion.[17] This influence was thus a relatively large source of model error for oil importers—approximately 35 percent of the total reported in table 3.4.

For the oil exporters, the same calculations are as follows. Debt rose by $70.6 billion; cumulative current account deficits amounted to $9.6 billion; reserves rose by $9.8 billion (versus a forecast of $8.4 billion); and cumulative net direct investment was $8.8 billion. Capital flight was thus an estimated $60 billion, again constituting a major source of model error by its exclusion. Indeed, as total model error only contributed $4.9 billion to understatement of oil-exporter debt accumulation, there were substantial model errors working in the other direction that offset the great bulk of the capital flight omission.

---

17. $F = \Delta D + CA + I - \Delta R$, where F is capital flight, D is external debt, CA is cumulative current account, I is cumulative net direct investment inflow, R is reserves, and Δ represents change. Note that the debt buildup in the calculation is against actual ex post debt, and does not include the "discovered debt" difference between (understated) forecast and actual debt even in the base year—caused by inadequate coverage in debt data at the time of the forecast.

For the 19 countries together, capital flight during 1984–87 contributed $134.8 billion to increased debt, based on the summary "residuals" calculations just presented. Total debt rose over the period by $158.7 billion (from $573 billion to $731.7 billion, table 3.1). On this basis, five-sixths of the observed buildup in debt went to finance capital flight. The implication is that debt performance would have been far superior if capital flight had been avoided, even taking account of the disappointing growth of the export base. Thus, in the absence of capital flight, for oil importers the ratio of net debt to exports of goods and services would have fallen from 232 percent in 1983 to 164 percent by 1987 (instead of just to 202 percent, table 3.1); and for oil exporters over the same period the increase in this ratio would have been only from 228 percent to 255 percent, rather than to 331 percent.

Table 3.5 shows alternative estimates of capital flight by the World Bank for these debtor countries, using essentially the same method just described.[18] Large capital flight is evident in Mexico, Brazil, Turkey, and Egypt. Total capital flight for the 19 countries during 1984–87 amounts to $101.9 billion, in the World Bank estimates (compared to $135 billion in the simple summary estimates above). On this alternative basis, capital flight accounted for two-thirds of the rise in external debt for these countries over this period.

Relatively large capital flight in 1986–87 for Brazil and 1987 for Argentina was related to fiscal difficulties. In each country in the late 1980s, the government's fiscal weakness increasingly kept it from being in a position to purchase the large surpluses earned in the private sector's external trade account. The effect was a sort of "forced capital flight" that coexisted with growing arrears on official external debt.

The World Bank's capital flight database reveals another, related source of model error: exchange rate valuation effects. The stock of debt denominated in deutsche marks, yen, and other nondollar currencies diminished in nominal dollar terms when the dollar strengthened in 1983–84, but then rose sharply in dollar value when the dollar fell in 1985–87. Thus, for the 19 countries considered here, dollar valuation effects reduced the nominal dollar value of the stock of debt by $5.2

---

18. Claessens and Naude 1993. Note that the concept applied in table 3.5 includes private nonguaranteed debt. Note further that unlike the estimates in chapter 8 below, there is no adjustment here to remove private earnings on capital held abroad. Typically these earnings are in the accrual data for balance of payments, but do not actually reenter the country. Their inclusion tends to overstate capital flight by reporting capital services exports that are not really available to the country's cash flow. However, these earnings were part of services exports in the database used for the model projections, so the proper capital flight concept for comparison must include them. Technically this procedure attributes to capital flight as model error one component that more properly is another type of model error: misspecification of the goods and services export variable (inclusive rather than exclusive of private capital earnings retained abroad), with the result of an underestimate in the projected buildup of debt.

Table 3.5 Estimated capital flight,[a] 1984–87 (millions of dollars)

Country	1984	1985	1986	1987	Cumulative 1984–87
Venezuela	1,595	−32	618	261	2,442
Mexico	4,439	3,954	3,957	10,587	22,937
Argentina	790	−14	−810	3,166	3,132
Brazil	3,627	−1,963	4,650	6,213	12,527
Yugoslavia	−397	2,321	−715	1,862	3,071
Algeria	113	−76	3,385	1,759	5,181
South Korea	100	2,022	3,876	278	6,276
Indonesia	−1,271	−1,781	2,044	5,646	4,638
Chile	−311	−539	617	1,024	791
Israel	−143	532	1,997	−711	1,675[b]
Turkey	−60	877	4,514	5,720	11,051
Philippines	−1,351	1,132	1,157	1,049	1,987
Egypt	2,075	3,254	3,414	5,171	13,914
Peru	288	−350	1,050	1,344	2,332
Ecuador	584	374	248	153	1,359
Portugal	89	443	1,115	359	2,006
Hungary	317	1,338	906	1,722	4,283
Romania	1,595	−32	618	261	2,442
Thailand	−929	−108	307	568	−162
Oil exporters	7,823	5,343	14,716	24,921	52,803
Oil importers	3,327	6,009	18,232	21,512	49,079

a. Capital flight is the World Bank residual plus private nonguaranteed debt.
b. Israel computed from other sources.

Source: World Bank Capital Flight Database.

billion in 1983 and $7.6 billion in 1984, but then raised the dollar debt value by $22.8 billion in 1985, $29.6 billion in 1986, and $41.6 billion in 1987. The cumulative total over 1984–87 was $86.4 billion. This amount represented an increment of 12.8 percent above the baseline total debt stock projected for the 19 countries for 1987 (table 3.1). Yet whereas the model took account of dollar devaluation effects on trade prices, it omitted any dollar valuation effects on debt stock, largely because it had seemed at the time that the share of nondollar debt in the total stock was too small to make a substantial difference.[19]

---

19. An important component of the exchange valuation effect was for debt owed to the multilateral development banks. Truman (1989, 731) estimates that in 1986-87, dollar depreciation raised the dollar value of repayments from the Baker countries to the MDBs by almost $10 billion, and as a result cut the net disbursements from MDBs to these countries by about half from levels that otherwise would have been reached.

In retrospect, the burden of exchange rate valuation effects represented the concept of interest rate–exchange rate parity. According to this principle, the interest differential between assets denominated in two different currencies is equal to the expected rate of depreciation of the higher-interest-rate currency against the lower-interest-rate one. Investors consider total return, and when dollar interest rates were abnormally high in the early 1980s, the implication was that an eventual decline in the dollar would be required to make the cumulative total return on interest plus exchange rate valuation comparable with returns on deutsche mark or yen assets bearing lower nominal interest rates. For borrowers, the lesson is that borrowing in the harder currency at lower interest rates can be deceptive. It provides only initial and illusory benefits, as the low interest costs up-front are enjoyed only at the expense of exchange valuation costs farther in the horizon.

The large impact of capital flight (defined to exclude dollar valuation effects) has implications for evaluation of the debt strategy. It was largely within the power of debtor countries to limit capital flight by adopting appropriate domestic policies on interest rates, the exchange rate, capital account convertibility, and fiscal balances. That there was so much capital flight leakage indicates a serious breakdown in these domestic policies. At the same time, the valuation effects of the falling dollar on the debt stock were beyond the control of the borrowers.

The World Bank capital flight database indicates that for the 19 countries originally examined in Cline (1984), a total of $188 billion in increased debt over the period 1984–87 can be explained by the combined influences of capital flight (55 percent of this amount) and exchange rate valuation effects (45 percent). These two influences alone can thus account for about three-fourths of the understatement of debt buildup attributable to model error (table 3.4), and they more than account for the total observed buildup in debt.

Trade Prices

Another possible source of model error is the treatment of prices of traded goods. The overstatement of these prices generally by overestimation of world inflation has been discussed above as an important source of scenario error. However, the model itself further influences trade prices as follows. First, export prices recover based on an elasticity with respect to cyclical recovery in the industrial country economies, a terms-of-trade effect reflecting the sensitivity of commodity prices to the world business cycle (equation 3.2 above). Second, prices of both exports and imports respond to depreciation of the dollar.

Table 3.4 indicates that model error caused overstatement of 1987 exports of oil-importing countries by 23 percent. Export prices weaker than expected, even given actual international inflation trends, account for most of this shortfall. Cumulative dollar depreciation over 1984–87 was about 20 percent. With the model's assumption that dollar trade prices rise by 0.8 times dollar depreciation, export and import prices should have risen by 16 percent from this source. Actual industrial country inflation was a cumulative 2.9 percent. From these two influences combined, debtor country nonoil export prices should have risen by 19.6 percent.

In addition, there was a large cyclical recovery in industrial country growth, which rose from −0.2 percent in 1982 to 4.8 percent by 1984, before returning to a plateau of about 3 percent (table 3.3). The median "cyclical elasticity" estimated for the 19 countries was 1.15 for current change in OECD growth, 1.78 for growth change in the previous year (Cline 1984, 247). Applying these estimates to the actual path of OECD growth in 1984–87, by 1987 cyclical recovery should have increased export prices by 5.8 percent. Taking into account actual trade shares and country-specific elasticities the effect is lower, and the model predicts only a 2.2 percent export price increase for the oil importers from global cyclical recovery.[20] This influence thus turns out to have been only a minor source of predicted price increase, incapable of contributing a large share of total model error.

The resulting backcast for export prices for oil-importing countries is an increase of 22.5 percent from 1983 to 1987, far below the corresponding forecast of 48.4 percent. But even the backcast, which applies actual international values for world inflation, dollar depreciation, and OECD growth, turned out far too optimistic. Thus, the IMF has estimated that export prices of non-fuel-exporting developing countries rose by only 2.9 percent over the period 1984–87 (IMF 1991a, 158).

As indicated in table 3.6, for 11 oil-importing countries considered here (excluding Romania, for which data are not available), export prices rose by only 5.8 percent from 1983 to 1987 (weighted by 1984 exports). In contrast, the "backcast" indicates that the model would have predicted an increase of 22.2 percent for these countries over this period. For the oil-importing countries the failure of export prices to rise by as much as expected in view of the actual decline of the dollar, world inflation, and OECD recovery thus accounts for three-fourths of the shortfall in export earnings attributable to underlying model error (i.e., [22.2–5.8]/22.5).[21]

---

20. For example, South Korea has a large trade weight and has a zero cyclical elasticity of export prices, primarily because the country exports manufactures rather than commodities.

21. It is more difficult to make comparable estimates for the oil-exporting countries, because reliable indexes do not exist for prices of their nonoil exports, which in any case tend to be a limited share of their total exports.

Table 3.6 Actual versus backcast dollar export price changes
(percentage change from 1983)

	1987		1989	
Country	Actual	Predicted[a]	Actual	Predicted[a]
Argentina	−7.6	21.5	11.8	32.5
Brazil	2.1	25.8	20.4	41.5
Chile	4.5	29.8	51.0	47.1
Hungary	2.0	22.2	−0.1	35.0
Israel	7.0	23.1	29.3	35.9
Philippines	−5.4	21.3	2.4	31.9
Portugal	33.2	20.4	39.3	31.1
South Korea	12.0	19.6	39.6	30.4
Thailand	0.1	21.1	11.8	31.8
Turkey	12.0	20.7	73.3	31.4
Yugoslavia	5.5	20.1	32.1	30.9
Weighted average	5.8	22.2	27.9	34.6

a. "Predicted" applies model to actual values of exogenous variables.

Commodity price weakness played an important role in the model's overprediction of export prices. For the five commodity-exporting countries among the 11 oil importers considered here, from 1983 to 1987 export prices actually declined by a range of 5 to 8 percent for two (Argentina and the Philippines), and rose by a range of only 0 to 5 percent for the other three (Brazil, Chile, and Thailand; table 3.6). Similarly, the IMF's index of nonfuel commodity prices fell by 7.2 percent from 1983 to 1987 (although it then surged by 23 percent in 1988; IMF 1990a, 183).

In retrospect there may be something to the hypothesis that commodity prices in the 1980s continued a long-term decline in real terms, and that their increase in the 1970s had been only a temporary interruption of this trend.[22] The implication would be that the model might appropriately have included a term for long-term trend decline in real commodity prices. Note, however, that the analysis in chapter 5 below rejects the hypothesis that it was the export-oriented debt strategy itself that caused falling commodity prices during the 1980s.

---

22. Ardeni and Wright (1992) have presented statistical estimates in support of the Singer-Prebisch hypothesis of declining terms of trade for commodity exporters (nonoil). Data compiled by Nordhaus (1992) show striking and systematic declines in "real" prices for numerous commodities over the past century, with the exception of the 1970s. However, he uses manufacturing wages as the deflator, thereby intermixing real income growth and commodity price decline.

Moreover, much of the problem in predicting export prices may have been in the time lags rather than in concept. Table 3.6 reports the actual and "backcast" export price increases for the 11 oil-importing countries not only from 1983 to 1987 but also to 1989. It turns out that the addition of just two years to the horizon very substantially closes the gap between actual and predicted price increases. By 1989, export prices should have risen by a weighted average of 34.6 percent for these countries (backcast). Instead, they rose by 27.9 percent, or by four-fifths of the expected amount. This belated catch-up suggests that the price-boosting effect of dollar depreciation eventually occurred but only with a lag. The last year of major dollar depreciation was 1987. It is plausible that less-than-immediate pass-through to trade prices meant the full effect did not show up until 1989.

Table 3.7 sheds further light on the trade price issue. The upper panel reports statistical regression results relating commodity prices to the change in industrial country growth (dGDC), the same variable lagged one year (dGDCl), the average rate of industrial country wholesale price inflation in domestic currency (WINFL), and the effective (trade-weighted) nominal value of the dollar (DOLLAR). Standard errors are in parentheses.

The equations are estimated over the period 1970–91. They show a strong procyclical behavior of commodity prices. The coefficients on change in OECD growth sum to about eight, meaning that a sustained increase of 1 percentage point in the OECD growth rate would raise commodity prices by 8 percent over two years. Moreover, movements in commodity price inflation are larger than (and correlated with) those of OECD wholesale price inflation. Commodity prices have an observed "elasticity" of about 2 with respect to industrial country wholesale prices, as an increase (decrease) of 1 percentage point in the latter is associated with an increase (decrease) of 2.3 percentage points in the former (four-commodity average).[23]

One interpretation of this result is that, above some threshold for inflation, where the negative intercept for commodity price inflation neutralizes the multiplicative response to industrial country inflation and leaves the two rates about equal, commodity inflation responds more than proportionately to either an increase or decrease in OECD inflation. Moreover, because the negative intercept is large (−8 percent annual average), the overall effect is that commodity prices tend to drift

---

23. However, the direction of causation is ambiguous in the absence of further analysis. As commodities are part of the wholesale price index, there is simultaneity involved, and to some extent the greater-than-unity relationship is just what one would expect for the behavior of one component of a broader aggregate if other components are random. There are other forces that influence both sets of prices, although the equation in principle removes the influence of changes in OECD growth.

Table 3.7 Trade price regression estimates (percent per year 1970-91)

	Constant	dGDC	dGDCI	WINFL	Dollar	R-square
I. Commodities						
Beverages	−3.6	6.52	6.11	1.87	−0.08	0.39
	(24.4)	(2.8)	(2.7)	(1.2)	(0.7)	
Food	−12.4	3.36	2.84	2.88	−1.31	0.56
	(15.3)	(1.8)	(1.7)	(0.8)	(0.4)	
Agricultural raw materials	−6.7	5.14	2.58	2.27	−1.36	0.67
	(11.6)	(1.4)	(1.3)	(0.6)	(0.3)	
Metals	−8.7	1.68	3.14	2.2	−1.11	0.55
	(13.2)	(1.5)	(1.5)	(0.6)	(0.4)	
Average	−7.9	4.18	3.67	2.31	−0.97	0.54
II. Countries						
A. Exports						
Argentina	−6.2	1.76	0.7	1.84	−0.69	0.60
	(8.1)	(1.0)	(0.9)	(0.4)	(0.2)	
Brazil	−4.8	1.27	2.83	1.73	−0.58	0.67
	(7.7)	(0.9)	(0.8)	(0.4)	(0.2)	
Chile	−12.5	4.00	4.30	2.72	−1.50	0.59
	(15.9)	(1.9)	(1.7)	(0.8)	(0.5)	
Colombia	−3.5	2.87	3.77	1.66	−0.4	0.28
	(19.4)	(2.3)	(2.1)	(1.0)	(0.6)	

(table continued on next page)

downward in real terms in "normal" years, surge in boom years, and collapse in years of stagnation or recession.[24]

The commodity price equations tend to confirm the expected influence of the dollar for the period 1970–91. On average, a 1 percent change in the nominal value of the (trade-weighted) dollar causes a change by 1 percent in the opposite direction for commodity prices (although this relationship is absent for beverage commodities).

---

24. For the averages of 1981–91, dGDC = −.02 percent and WINFL = 2.83 percent. Omitting the influence of the dollar, the average "normal" commodity price trend was thus −7.9 + (4.18 + 3.67)(−.02) + 2.31(2.83) = −1.5 percent annually, implying average real decline in commodity prices by 4.3 percent annually. In contrast, if dGDC = dGDCl = 1 percent and WINFL = 5 percent, the predicted commodity price increase reaches 11.5 percent (about 6 percent real). If dGDC = dGDCl = −1 percent and WINFL = 0 (i.e., a recessionary period), commodity prices fall by 15.8 percent. Note that although the intercept is not statistically significant, it is systematically of the same order of magnitude for the four separate commodity equations.

Table 3.7 (continued)

	Constant	dGDC	dGDCI	WINFL	Dollar	R-square
Mexico[a]	−5.8	1.24	0.94	1.86	−0.38	0.51
	(9.8)	(1.2)	(1.1)	(0.5)	(0.3)	
Philippines	−15.1	0.48	2.95	3.10	−0.90	0.65
	(13.4)	(1.6)	(1.5)	(0.7)	(0.4)	
Average	−8.0	1.94	2.58	2.15	−0.74	0.55
B. Imports						
Argentina	3.2	...	...	0.61	−0.67	0.31
	(8.6)	...	...	(0.4)	(0.2)	
Brazil	−4.2	...	...	1.35	−0.54	0.47
	(7.7)	...	...	(0.4)	(0.2)	
Chile	−6.1	...	...	2.17	−0.87	0.69
	(8.0)	...	...	(0.4)	(0.2)	
Colombia	−4.3	...	...	1.51	−0.22	0.86
	(3.2)	...	...	(0.1)	(0.1)	
Mexico	−3.0	...	...	1.68	−0.77	0.73
	(5.7)	...	...	(0.3)	(0.2)	
Philippines	−7.9	...	...	2.21	−0.34	0.60
	(9.4)	...	...	(0.4)	(0.3)	
Venezuela	−1.3	...	...	1.22	−0.77	0.89
	(2.7)	...	...	(0.1)	(0.1)	
Average	−3.4	...	...	1.54	−0.60	0.65

... = not applicable

note: Standard error in parentheses below each regression coefficient.

a. Nonoil.

The rest of the table shows similar statistical equations for export and import price inflation for several individual debtor countries. These equations find approximately the same cyclical elasticities for export price response to OECD growth as in the 1984 study.[25] As in the commodity price equations, the country export equations show large negative intercepts but high elasticities with respect to OECD wholesale prices. For the six countries examined, the elasticity of export prices with respect to the nominal trade-weighted exchange rate of the dollar is −0.74, close to the parameter of −0.8 used in the earlier study. The table shows similar results on the import price side (but with no influence estimated for OECD growth change).

The regression results of table 3.7 tend to confirm the trade price parameter and specification assumptions used in the 1984 debt model.

---

25. Thus, the sums of the coefficients on current and lagged change in OECD growth in the 1984 and present studies are, respectively, 4.36 and 4.1 for Brazil; 9.98 and 8.3 for Chile; and 2.42 and 3.43 for the Philippines (table 3.7 and Cline 1984, 247).

In conjunction with the data shown in table 3.6, these results suggest that model error attributable to specification of trade prices, and in particular their relationship to the strength of the dollar, is exaggerated when the horizon of the analysis is cut off at 1987 rather than later (when the dollar's decline had more time to feed through to trade prices). That is, the projection model performed better than is revealed by backcasts extending only through 1987.

There is economic policy content in these observations. Matters looked worse in 1987, the second full year of the Baker Plan, than they turned out by 1989—the year the move to debt reduction under the latter plan was adopted. The improvement was evident in the nominal value of exports. For the oil-importing major debtor countries considered here, the dollar value of exports rose by 15 percent annually in 1988–89, versus 10 percent in 1984–87 (calculated from IMF 1991c). For all oil-importing countries in Latin America, the dollar value of exports grew at 9 percent in the latter period, versus 4.4 percent annually in the earlier period (calculated from ECLAC 1991 and other issues). This increased pace of aggregate dollar export earnings is consistent with the analysis of table 3.6 showing the catch-up of export prices closer to model-based levels (backcast, though not forecast because of lower world inflation) by 1989.

In terms of the key debt indicators, the improvement in the export base by 1989 was reflected in a major decline in the ratio of net debt to exports of goods and services, from its peak of about 385 percent in 1986–87 to a level of about 275 percent by 1989, for the 17 "heavily indebted countries" (chapter 2, table 2.3). The broad implication is that there was considerable prospective improvement in the debt problem already in the pipeline even without the 1989 shift in debt policy toward debt reduction.

Chapter 5 suggests that the beneficial effects of Brady Plan forgiveness were disproportionately large in view of the modest extent of forgiveness. The fact that there was substantial improvement in the underlying external payments situation by 1989 even without that relief can help explain this paradox. The implication is that by then, there was a gap between the psychological perception of the severity of the debt problem and its actual, improved status. In such circumstances, the psychological boost given by the Brady Plan could be particularly effective. A corresponding implication is that without the underlying improvements in the debt burden by 1989, the Brady Plan might have been inadequate.

Trade Elasticities

With the bulk of model error for exports of oil-importing debtors accounted for by overstatement of trade prices (as of 1987), there is little error left to attribute to elasticities relating export volume to industrial country growth and debtor country real exchange rates. Nonetheless, as noted above, this part of the model was the subject of criticism; so a summary examination is warranted. Essentially, in the Cline (1984) specification, there was a *marginal* elasticity of 3.0, which appeared high; but it had the same effect as a more conventional *average* elasticity of 2 because of the presence of a negative intercept for export growth.[26]

The projection model applied a negative intercept of 3 percent export volume decline when OECD growth is zero, and a marginal elasticity of 3.0 for OECD growth. Application of these parameters to actual industrial country growth in 1984–87 (table 3.3) yields the result that the volume of exports from nonoil debtor countries should have risen by 34 percent over this period, other things being equal. The actual increase of export volume for non-fuel-exporting developing countries amounted to 42 percent (IMF 1991a, 156). If some allowance is made for the impact of real exchange rate devaluations as countries sought to adjust to the debt crisis, the increase in export volume accords well with what would have been expected given the model's trade elasticities. The model's export elasticities thus do not appear to have been a major source of error.[27]

Table 3.8 reports a comparison of the export elasticities of the Cline (1984) model with those of other, subsequent studies. As indicated above, the "average" income elasticity for exports in the 1984 model was equivalent to 2.0 for "normal" OECD growth of 3 percent. This is the same elasticity as used by Dooley, Helkie, Tryon, and Underwood (1986) and Helkie and Howard (1991). The more detailed studies by Marquez and McNeilly (1988) and Dittus and O'Brien (1991) tended to yield elasticities on the order of 1.5 to 2. Where these various studies estimated price elasticities, they tended to be higher than in the 1984 model (e.g., in the range of 1 to 2, rather than 0.5).

On the import side, model error was relatively small for oil-importing countries (table 3.4). However, there was large model error for imports

---

26. The central export equation provided for volume growth equal to −3 percent plus 3 × OECD growth. At typical industrial country growth of 3 percent, this relationship yielded LDC export growth of 6 percent. The corresponding "average" elasticity was 6 percent export growth/3 percent OECD growth = 2. See Cline (1985b).

27. Note, however, that a simple regression relating the export volume growth and OECD growth data cited here (both in percentage terms) yields the following results for the period 1981–91:

$$g_x = 4.0 + 1.42\, g_{oecd}; R^2 = 0.28 \qquad (3.5)$$
$$(3.6)\ (0.75)$$

where standard error is shown in parentheses. Although the positive intercept of exogenous growth at 4 percent is not statistically significant, it is sufficiently large that it suggests there should be an element of positive autonomous growth in estimating these exports. Correspondingly, the elasticity of industrial country growth, at 1.4, is even smaller than a typical "average" value of 2. The trend toward relatively high autonomous growth was evident in 1991 in particular, when the volume of these exports grew by 9.5 percent but industrial country growth was only 0.6 percent (IMF 1992b, 93, 118).

Table 3.8 Alternative export elasticities

Author	Exporter	Elasticity on:	
		(1) OECD income	(2) Price
Cline (1984)	Nonoil LDCs	3.00[a]	−0.50
Dooley, Helkie, Tryon, Underwood (1986)	8 countries	2.00	−1.00
Helkie and Howard (1991)	8 countries	2.00	−1.00
Marquez and McNeilly (1988)	Nonoil LDCs	1.37 to 1.94	−0.62 to −1.33
	SITC 0+1	−0.14 to 0.51	0.08 to −0.61
	SITC 2+4	−0.78 to −0.36	0.04 to −0.42
	SITC 5 to 9	2.36 to 2.99	−1.03 to −1.85
Dittus and O'Brien (1991)			
Argentina	Manufactures	0.28	−2.70
Brazil	Manufactures	1.51	−1.39
Mexico	Manufactures	2.20	..
Other Latin America	Manufactures	0.31	..
Argentina	Raw materials	1.59	..
Brazil	Raw materials	1.02	−0.43
Chile	Raw materials	2.36	..
Mexico	Raw materials	1.39	..
Argentina	Nonfactor svcs	2.31	..
Brazil	Nonfactor svcs	1.56	..
Chile	Nonfactor svcs	2.44	..
Mexico	Nonfactor svcs	1.05	..

a. Marginal elasticity. Total effect with negative intercept and normal OECD growth = 2.00.

SITC 0+1 = agricultural commodities; 2+4 = nonenergy raw materials; 5 to 9 = manufactures.

.. = not available.

of oil-exporting countries by 1987. The projections had estimated imports for the countries in question at $110 billion in that year, whereas the actual level was only $54 billion. Of the difference, $28 billion was attributable to model error (rather than scenario error).

The most likely source of this error was the imposition of import controls in oil-exporting debtor countries as the consequence of the payments squeeze associated with the double effect of lower oil prices and the seizing-up of capital markets because of the debt crisis. As indicated in table 3.2, actual imports are close to the projected levels for Mexico and Venezuela through 1985, but they are only about two-thirds the projected levels by 1987.[28]

---

28. Conversely, a shift in trade policy in the other direction, toward opening, accounted for a surge in Mexico's imports in subsequent years to levels above what the model would have predicted.

Overall, the trade elasticities in the Cline (1984) model do not appear to have caused a major bias in model results. However, on the export side, the simple regression estimate noted above for the 1980s as a whole (n. 27 above) suggests the presence of a positive rather than negative intercept (i.e., autonomous LDC export growth even when OECD growth is zero), and correspondingly the appropriateness of a lower marginal elasticity than used in the original model. This pattern provides support for using a marginal elasticity of 2, as in most other studies.

Alternative Reviews of the Forecasts

In late 1987, Cardoso and Dornbusch (1989) reviewed the Cline (1984) projections for the Brazilian case to determine "what went wrong with muddling through" (303). They note that whereas Brazil's current account had been approximately as predicted, the debt/exports ratio was much worse because the nominal value of exports had only risen 10 percent, rather than doubling as the projections had anticipated, and because large capital outflows (absent in the projections) had added to external debt. These divergences are consistent with the principal findings above (e.g., low export prices and large capital flight).

Cardoso and Dornbusch note that the problem had not been with failure of industrial country growth to meet expectations, citing four major factors that diverged from the earlier outlook. First, real interest rates were expected to decline much more than they did. Second, real commodity prices kept falling, rather than recovering from what had been thought to be a cyclical low. Third, there had been inflationary consequences of the internal transfer problem (as discussed above), unanticipated in the original debt strategy. Fourth, there had been creditor cartel fatigue that had undermined concerted (or "involuntary") lending, especially through divisions between smaller and larger banks (304–06). The only favorable factor (for Brazil) had been the collapse in oil prices.

This diagnosis accords in most regards with the analysis presented here. One important difference, however, is that Cardoso and Dornbusch attribute a strictly negative impact to the behavior of real interest rates. On the contrary, as analyzed above and more fully in annex 3B below, the decline in nominal rates beyond expectation provided important cash-flow relief, despite the even larger decline in inflation and thus the rise in real interest rates from baseline.

In 1991, researchers at the OECD provided a more comprehensive review of debt projections and examination of what had gone wrong (or right) with them. Dittus, O'Brien, and Blommestein (1991) provide modeling calculations for Latin America that find results similar to those indicated here. They note that OECD growth and interest rates had met the Cline (1983) forecast expectations,[29] but that nonoil export prices had declined by 11 percent from 1983 to 1986 rather than rising by 39 percent as in that study's base case. They cite the collapse in oil prices and the presence of large capital flight as sources of divergence from the original forecasts. The authors concur that if international and domestic variables had turned out as predicted, the strategy of exporting and growing along a "Narrow Path out of the crisis may not only have appeared feasible, but even likely" (143). They reach this conclusion based on simulations of their model, which has the benefit of hindsight for parameter estimation.

The OECD authors then examine what went wrong with the Narrow Path forecast for the period 1983–85.[30] For Brazil, they find that the largest adverse impact was from the failure of international inflation and traded goods prices to rise as expected, an outcome that not only weakened the export value denominator of the debt/exports ratio but also reduced the nominal value of the trade surplus. The trade price effect increased the debt/exports ratio by an estimated 111 percent from baseline. The second most important influence was the "domestic" policy weakness that led to capital flight as well as lower-than-expected direct investment inflow, contributing 42 percentage points to the deterioration in the debt/exports ratio.

For Mexico, the authors find the domestic factors dominant through 1985, as the combined influence of capital flight and low direct investment raised the debt/exports ratio by about 100 percentage points above baseline (although by 1986 the collapse in oil prices was more important, adding 140 percentage points to the ratio). Emphasis on capital flight for both countries accords with the analysis here.[31]

---

29. They examine the 1983 projections, which had a more favorable baseline for interest rates than the 1984 estimates.

30. Note that the OECD study also provides an intriguing analysis of the implications of fiscal imbalance and low private saving in the United States for the Latin American debt problem in the period 1981–86. The simulations indicate that in the absence of these two US distortions, international interest rates would have been sufficiently lower to reduce the debt/exports ratio by almost 70 percentage points by 1986 (from a baseline level of some 300 percent) and, even more dramatically, to cut the interest/exports ratio by nearly half (from a baseline level of 20 percent; Dittus, O'Brien, and Blommestein 1991, 157).

31. Dittus, O'Brien, and Blommestein also judge that, in light of the more representative nature of Brazil's trade structure than that of Mexico for Latin America as a whole, "the high value of the dollar and related lower than expected world trade prices were major, and possibly the most important, factors explaining the unexpectedly small progress in credit-worthiness of Latin America during the first four years after 1982" (1991, 149). Although the results in the present study for 1987 cast doubt on the importance of the dollar, as trade prices were still weak by that year despite large dollar depreciation, the commodity and export price regressions tend to confirm the importance of dollar strength; and extending the horizon past 1987 substantially reduces overprediction of the impact of dollar depreciation on trade prices (tables 3.6 and 3.7 above).

Table 3.9 Net direct investment, 1984-87 (millions of dollars)

Country	1984	1985	1986	1987	Cumulative 1984–87
Venezuela	–3	57	–444	–16	–406
Mexico	390	491	1,160	1,796	3,837
Argentina	268	919	574	–19	1,742
Brazil	1,556	1,267	177	1,087	4,087
Yugoslavia	0	0	0	0	0
Algeria	–14	–2	11	–11	–16
South Korea	73	200	325	418	1,016
Indonesia	222	310	258	385	1,175
Chile	78	114	116	230	538
Israel	29	48	58	191	326
Turkey	113	99	125	106	443
Philippines	9	12	127	307	455
Egypt	713	1,175	1,211	929	4,028
Peru	–89	1	22	32	–34
Ecuador	50	62	70	75	257
Portugal	187	252	238	476	1,153
Hungary	0	0	0	0	0
Romania	0	0	0	0	0
Thailand	400	162	261	182	1,005
Oil exporters	1,269	2,094	2,288	3,190	8,841
Oil importers	2,713	3,073	2,001	2,978	10,765

Note: Balance of payments basis; positive figures indicate net cash inflow.

Source: IMF 1992a.

Overview and Policy Implications

The preceding analysis provides a basis for answering the question of what went wrong and what went right with the 1983–84 prognosis that debtor countries could export and grow their way out of the debt crisis.

What Went Right

- International growth, interest rates, and dollar correction were all at least as favorable as in the baseline forecast.

- Lower interest rates meant that the interest/exports ratio continued to show improvement close to the projected path, despite a shortfall in exports.

- Current account deficits were actually smaller than forecast.

- The trade elasticities in the model performed adequately, despite contemporary criticism that they were too optimistic.

What Went Wrong

- The single most severe blow to the debt strategy was the collapse of oil prices in 1986. Its strong negative effect for the oil-exporting debtors and only moderate favorable effect for oil importers had been highlighted in the 1984 projections, but the base case scenario had called for modestly rising nominal oil prices rather than a decline by half.

- From the debtors' standpoint, the sharp deceleration in world inflation (at the wholesale price level) was also unfavorable, because it left the nominal value of their export base smaller than had been expected, working against the expected decline in the debt/exports ratio. Even if interest rates had fallen immediately by the same amount as the decline in inflation, the result would still have been adverse because of the lesser real erosion of inherited fixed-interest debt.[32]

- The fact that international interest rates declined by less than world inflation meant a rise in the real interest rate and a corresponding increase in the debt/exports ratio and the long-term burden of debt—even though the decline in nominal interest rates and the interest/exports ratio was still sufficient to provide cash-flow relief.

- Capital flight was very large, and accounted for two-thirds to five-sixths of the debt buildup. The projection model made no allowance for this financial leakage, because of the mistaken premise that by 1983 countries had already learned to clamp down on it.

- There was a substantial rise in the dollar value of the debt stock because of the change in valuation of the debt denominated in deutsche marks, yen, and other nondollar currencies, an effect omitted from the model.

- Debtor country growth was below the projected level, helping keep current account deficits down but eroding the political sustainability of the debt strategy.

- The projection model made no allowance for an "internal transfer problem," the difficulty of mobilizing fiscal revenue from the private sector to pay interest on the government's external debt, yet this influence was important in some countries such as Argentina and Brazil.

---

32. As noted in annex 3B, however, for variable-interest debt there is no change in the debt/exports ratio as a consequence of a simultaneous reduction in world inflation and world interest rates by equal magnitudes.

- Through 1987, the response of export (and import) prices to depreciation of the dollar was far below model expectations, contributing to the shortfall of export earnings from expected levels. However, the expected price effect was much more fully realized by 1989.

- Commodity prices were nonetheless somewhat weaker than could be explained by the expected influences, suggesting a long-term trend of erosion that had been only temporarily interrupted by experience in the 1970s.

Overall, the analysis here suggests that the international debt strategy as of 1983–84 was not unduly optimistic about prospective improvement of the international economic environment; indeed, actual developments in industrial country growth and interest rates turned out better than expected. Weak trade prices neutralized these gains, but still left oil-importing countries in a broadly favorable position to adhere to the strategy of exporting out of the crisis. The 1986 oil price collapse meant the environment was much worse than expected for oil exporters, however.

As developed more fully in chapters 5 and 6, for countries with strong domestic policies and favorable fiscal performance, especially Chile but also several other countries that were considered in danger at the outset (including South Korea), the international economic environment and pre-Brady debt strategy proved adequate. For the oil-importing countries that were unable to avoid Brady Plan debt reduction, the principal reason was difficulty from the internal transfer problem rather than the external transfer. Weak fiscal performance meant a breakdown in debt servicing under the original strategy even though trade and current account deficits were actually smaller than had been expected. Large capital flight aggravated the problem, by leading to larger debt buildup than required by current account balances. Changes in dollar valuation of debt as the dollar fell did add an exogenously imposed burden, however.

For oil exporters (e.g., Mexico and Venezuela), the analysis here confirms the obvious: the collapse in oil prices in 1986 imposed a severe unanticipated burden on recovery from the debt crisis. Evolution of the debt strategy to include collateralized conversion to reduced-payment bonds was especially appropriate for oil-exporting countries that had pursued favorable domestic policies but faced this new external shock.

Annex 3A

Decomposition of Forecast Error

''Economists are people who tell you what will happen and then explain why it didn't.'' What follows is a simple technique for carrying out the second of these two tasks.

Model Error versus Scenario Assumption Error

Economic projections can only go wrong for two reasons. First, the model is wrong. Second, the assumed values applied to the exogenous variables in the model in the projection scenario turn out to be wrong. Accordingly, all projection errors can be decomposed into model error and scenario assumption error. The first is the more fundamental, because it means that the projection inherently could not be correct except by pure chance. Like venial rather than cardinal sins, the mistakes arising from the second category (variable values assumed in the projection scenario) are lesser and more remediable. For example, if it is found that error is primarily from exogenous variable assumptions rather than the model itself, the same model may appropriately be used for future forecasts, with wishes of ''better luck next time'' in the secondary dimension of assumed variable values. Moreover, the forecaster ideally will have warned the user that the variable assumptions are ''judgmental,'' whereas the quantitative relationships that determine their impact on the dependent variable are ''analytical.''

A ''model'' is an equation or set of equations, each of which has parameters applied to variables specified in particular ways. Model error is thus essentially error in parameter values, specification (e.g., linear vs. logarithmic), and variable inclusion (i.e., omission of an important variable). Similarly, as the assumptions made to implement the projection are applied to exogenous variables, the second type of error is ''variable assumption'' or ''scenario'' error.

Model Error as Backcast versus Actual

Model parameter error is all error that would have occurred in the projection even if the analyst had enjoyed perfect foresight in assigning assumed future values to the exogenous variables. We may designate as a ''backcast'' the predictions that would have been made under these circumstances. The backcast is the set of projections for the same (now historical) periods as in the original forecast, but estimated by applying the same model to the *actual* values of the exogenous variables that in fact attained, rather than their originally anticipated values.

Let y_t be the actual value of the dependent variable being projected for year t. Let an asterisk designate a projected (as opposed to actual) value. Let superscript f designate forecast. Then the error of the forecast equals

$$e_t = y_t^{*f} - y_t \qquad (3A.1)$$

Let superscript b refer to backcast. Then model error (designated by superscript m) may be estimated as

$$e_t^m = y_t^{*b} - y_t \qquad (3A.2)$$

That is, because y_t^{*b} tells what the predicted dependent variable would have been when applying the values of the exogenous variables that actually attained, the only possible remaining difference between this estimate and the actually observed dependent variable y_t is error that arises from incorrect model parameter values. In short, model error equals the difference between backcast and actual values for the dependent variable.

Total error equals model error plus variable assumption error (designated by superscript v):

$$e_t = e_t^m + e_t^v \qquad (3A.3)$$

For its part, variable assumption or scenario error may be identified by comparing the projected dependent variable using the original forecast assumptions and the projected result when using the actual backcast variable values:

$$e_t^v = y_t^{*f} - y_t^{*b} \qquad (3A.4)$$

This direct estimate of variable assumption error is consistent with the indirect estimate by residual from consideration of total error and model error, as we have from equations 3A.1 and 3A.2:

$$e_t^v = e_t - e_t^m = [y_t^{*f} - y_t] - [y_t^{*b} - y_t] = y_t^{*f} - y_t^{*b} \qquad (3A.5)$$

Decomposing Variable Assumption Error

Suppose that the model uses n exogenous variables to explain the dependent variable. Then we may decompose variable assumption error, e_t, into component parts, each of which states the contribution of mistaken assumption on the individual exogenous variable in question. For this purpose, a hybrid projection may be considered, in which the originally assumed variable value is applied for the specific variable of interest, and the actual (backcast) variable values are applied for all other variables. The difference between this hybrid projection and the pure backcast projection will tell the extent to which error in the assumed value of the particular variable in question caused the overall forecast to diverge from the backcast. Thus,

$$e_{i,t}^v = y_t^{*fi,bni} - y_t^{*b} \tag{3A.6}$$

where $e_{i,t}^v$ is the error contributed by mistaken assumption on variable i; as before, $y*$ signifies projection estimate of the dependent variable; superscript fi refers to forecast assumption for exogenous variable i; and superscript bni refers to actual (backcast) value for all other ("non-i") exogenous variables.

In a simple linear model of the form $y_t^* = \alpha + \Sigma_{i=1}^n \beta_i x_{i,t}$, where $x_{i,t}$ is the value of exogenous variable i in year t, we have[1]

$$e_{i,t}^v = \beta_i[x_{i,t}^f - x_{i,t}^b] \tag{3A.6'}$$

By definition of decomposition into parts, it should be the case that the sum of the individual variable mistaken-assumption error contributions equals total variable assumption error, or:

$$\Sigma_i e_{i,t}^v = e_t^v \tag{3A.7}$$

In the linear case just considered, this summation will hold valid. In nonlinear models, it will not, except by chance.[2] In the nonlinear case, if the contributions to variable assumption error from each and every exogenous variable are of uniform sign, these individual contributions may be scaled up or down so that their summation equals total variable assumption error, or

$$e_{i,t}^{v'} = [e_{i,t}^v][e_t^v/\Sigma_i e_{i,t}^v] \tag{3A.8}$$

---

1. The example here is contemporaneous, but the exogenous variable may also be specified with a lag.

2. Consider two alternative models: $y = \beta_1 x_1 + \beta_2 x_2$ (linear), and $y = x_1^{\beta 1} x_2^{\beta 2}$ (nonlinear). Suppose the forecast assumption was that $x_1 = x_2 = 1$, whereas the actual record was that $x_1 = 1.1$ and $x_2 = 0.9$. Suppose that in both models, $\beta_1 = \beta_2 = 0.5$. In the linear model, we have individual error contributions of: $e^{x1} = -0.05$; $e^{x2} = +0.05$. The sum of components is: $e^v = e^{x1} + e^{x2} = 0$. In contrast, in the nonlinear model: $e^{x1} = 0.9^{0.5}[1.0^{0.5} - 1.1^{0.5}] = -0.046$; $e^{x2} = 1.1^{0.5}[1.0^{0.5} - 0.9^{0.5}] = +0.054$; $e^{x1} + e^{x2} = .008$. In this case, the sum of the two component variable assumption errors considerably exceeds the total variable assumption error estimated directly: $e^v = [1.0^{0.5} \times 1.0^{0.5}] - [1.1^{0.5} \times 0.9^{0.5}] = 0.005$. The divergence arises from interaction between the exogenous variables in the nonlinear model, in contrast to their independence in the linear model. It may be shown that when interaction is not a problem—e.g., because only one of the assumed variable values diverges from the actual realized value—the linear and nonlinear models both give total variable assumption error equal to the sum of the estimated components.

However, in the nonlinear case where some exogenous variables have a positive variable assumption error contribution and others have a negative contribution, it will not in general be meaningful to make this scaling correction, and decomposition for variable assumption error will remain imprecise.

To recapitulate, so far we have established a method for decomposing forecast error into (a) model error and (b) variable assumption or scenario error. In addition, we have identified a means of further decomposing variable assumption error into the contribution from each exogenous variable, although this attribution is only approximate when the model is nonlinear.

Diagnosing Individual Parameter Error

It is more difficult to decompose the model error into contributions from the individual parameters assigned to each of the respective exogenous variables. The most appropriate means for this purpose is to reestimate the model using statistical (e.g., regression) techniques and the new, longer series of actual data, which now includes as historical observations the periods that were only future projections in the original analysis. Thus, in the linear model, the contribution to model error from the original parameter estimate β_i for variable i may be estimated as

$$e_{i,t}^m = [\beta_i - \beta_i']x_{i,t}^b \qquad (3A.9)$$

where β_i' is the new estimate of the model parameter for variable i. The new β_i' differs from the original estimate of β_i either because the addition of the new observations in the data series changes the parameter estimate or because some alternative method other than the statistical regression technique now being applied was used in establishing the initially used value of the parameter (including the case of simple parameter assumption).

This method will only succeed in identifying the contribution of each variable parameter to total model error insofar as the ex post reestimation of the model provides an accurate estimation of dependent variable behavior. In terms of the coefficient of determination of the regression (R^2), or the proportion of the variance of the dependent variable explained by the model, a low R^2 will mean that the potential amount of individually identified parameter error in the forecast is also low, and that much of the model error must remain unidentified.

Where regression or other statistical techniques are unsatisfactory (for example, because of insufficient observations even with the extended series), some progress toward decomposition of model parameter error may nonetheless be made through the use of "Bayesian prior" values for the parameters.[3] If the substitution of all original parameter estimates by their respective Bayesian prior values improves adherence of the backcast to the actual outcome, then these priors may be considered a superior set of parameters for the forecasting task at hand. Model parameter error may then be decomposed into the contributions by specific parameters by applying equation 3A.8, this time using the Bayesian prior rather than a new statistical estimation for the value of β'_i.

Interaction of Model and Variable Assumption Error

Suppose that a completely accurate model has been identified, so that in terms of the linear example above,

$$e'_t = y_t - [\alpha + \Sigma_i \beta'_i x_{i,t}] = 0 \qquad (3A.10)$$

It is evident that the new, completely accurate set of model parameters will change the estimate of variable assumption error. The contribution of variable assumptions to total forecast error should now be evaluated as before using the difference between forecast and backcast (equation 3A.4 above), but this time using the more accurate model parameters (β'_i) rather than the original parameters (β_i). The final and precise (or, where the revised parameters are still not perfectly accurate, "improved") estimate for variable assumption error will then be

$$e^{v'}_t = y^{*f'}_t - y^{*b'}_t \qquad (3A.11)$$

where all elements are as before except that the prime refers to application of the revised model parameters rather than the original parameter estimates.

Overview

The method suggested here should provide a relatively accurate gauge of the role of variable assumptions (the "scenario") in causing forecast error, a good sense of the decomposition of this error by individual variable, a relatively accurate attribution of the share of total forecast error to model parameter error, and at least some impression (but with considerable less accuracy) of the role of each parameter in model error. Decomposition along these lines should provide insight into the economics of the problem at hand. Where forecast error is primarily from variable assumption, the straightforward interpretation is that the broad causal variables simply turned out to be different from expectation, and

---

3. For example, the Bayesian prior for a price elasticity of imports might be -1.0, based on numerous international examples.

analysis may pursue the question of whether there is any systematic reason that may fruitfully be kept in mind in making future assumptions about these variables. Where the error stems mainly from the model, the decomposition techniques suggested here should provide a basis for improving the forecasting model. Comparison of the original and revised model should also reveal information about the responsiveness of the economy in question to the normal causal variables. In some cases it may be possible to glean policy conclusions from the divergences of observed behavior from the original model assumptions.[4]

---

4. Suppose, for example, that model reestimation reveals an unusually low responsiveness of exports to the real exchange rate. This finding may point to structural obstacles, such as import barriers abroad or domestic protection, that bias firms in favor of sale to the home market.

Annex 3B

The Impact of World Disinflation on Creditworthiness

Historically, inflation has benefited debtors and damaged creditors by eroding the real value of debt obligations. By the early 1980s, however, it was widely considered that developing country debtors could no longer benefit from world inflation, because capital markets had become too sophisticated to lend at fixed rates. Indeed, the advent of syndicated bank lending at variable interest rates in the 1970s was a crucial institutional change that had facilitated the large buildup of debt in developing countries after the first oil shock.

By the mid-1980s, the world economy had entered a phase of disinflation. Wholesale price inflation in industrial countries fell from a peak of 13.7 percent in 1980 to 3.3 percent by 1983 and fell further to a remarkable -3.6 percent in 1986, thanks to the collapse of oil prices in that year. Most forecasts did not anticipate this implosion of world inflation. It is useful to consider what they might have expected regarding the debt problem if they had successfully anticipated the disinflation.

In the first instance, if all debt is at variable interest rates, and if world disinflation is instantaneously accompanied by corresponding reductions in world interest rates, there might appropriately have been the expectation of neutral effects for LDC debtors.[1] After all, if further inflation could not help debtors because of variable rates, disinflation should not harm them.

As it turned out, world disinflation was associated with a substantial lag of interest rate declines behind reductions in inflation. This pattern was understandable in terms of the slowness of expectations to adjust to the new environment. The results were mixed for debtors. The temporary rise in real interest rates caused by the interest rate lag imposed a rise in the real burden of the debt obligation from a long-term perspective. However, the reduction in nominal interest rates provided cash-flow relief even though rates fell by less than inflation. In terms of the debt indicators, the cash-flow gains showed up in a decline in the interest/exports ratio even as the debt/exports ratio showed further deterioration (for 1984 through 1987).

These influences may be formalized by considering a simple accounting model of debt accumulation. Suppose exports (X) and imports (M) both grow at the same real rate, g. Suppose world inflation is rate i. Then nominal trade values grow at $g + i$. Suppose there is instan-

---

1. Note that as of 1984, almost four-fifths of long-term debt owed by Latin America was at variable interest rates (World Bank 1991, 138).

taneous adjustment of interest rates to inflation, so that the nominal interest rate r is always equal to $r^* + i$, where r^* is a constant real interest rate. Suppose there is no buildup in reserves and no capital inflow other than from debt accumulation. Then we may write the debt/exports ratio in year t as

$$y_t \equiv D_t/X_t = \frac{D_{t-1}(1 + r^* + i) - X_{t-1}(1 + g + i) + M_{t-1}(1 + g + i)}{X_{t-1}(1 + g + i)} \quad (3B.1)$$

The first term in the numerator on the right hand side indicates that debt grows by inheritance at the rate of the nominal interest rate, which equals the constant real rate plus world inflation. The second term indicates that export receipts reduce debt; the third term, that import outlays increase debt. The two trade values equal previous year levels as augmented by real growth (g) and inflation (i). The denominator repeats the export measure.

Now consider the behavior of the debt/exports ratio in response to a change in world inflation. First, we may rewrite equation 3B.1 as

$$y_t = \frac{k_{t-1}(1 + r^* + i)}{(1 + g + i)} - 1 + \beta \quad (3B.2)$$

where k is the debt/exports ratio in the base year and β is the ratio of imports to exports. This formulation already provides an important result: because the final two terms "$-1 + \beta$" are constant and unaffected by inflation, *whether the trade balance is in surplus or deficit does not alter the impact of a change in inflation on the debt/exports ratio.*

This result is somewhat counterintuitive, because lower inflation means a smaller absolute trade surplus (for unchanged real volumes of exports and imports). However, this effect is neutralized by the correspondingly smaller nominal value of the denominator, export earnings.

Differentiating 3B.2 with respect to world inflation (i), we have:[2]

$$\frac{dy_t}{di} = k_{t-1} \frac{[1 - (1 + r^* + i)/(1 + g + i)]}{1 + g + i} \quad (3B.3)$$

If the real interest rate (r^*) is approximately the same magnitude as the real growth of trade (g), the numerator on the right-hand side approximates zero. Thus, it turns out that this derivative is approximately zero, so that *the debt/exports ratio is invariant with respect to world inflation.* At the intuitive level, the basic reason why lower inflation matched by a lower interest rate leaves the debt/exports ratio un-

---

2. The differential may be found by applying $d(u/v) = [vdu - udv]/v^2$.

changed is that vegetative growth of debt from the interest rate falls by just the same amount as passive growth in the nominal export base from lower world inflation.

The other debt indicator, the interest/exports ratio, may be written as

$$z_t \equiv I_t/X_t = \frac{(r^* + i)D_{t-1}}{X_{t-1}(1 + g + i)} = \frac{k_{t-1}(r^* + i)}{(1 + g + i)} \tag{3B.4}$$

Again differentiating with respect to world inflation, we have:

$$\frac{dz_t}{di} = k_{t-1}\frac{[1 - (r^* + i)/(1 + g + i)]}{1 + g + i} \tag{3B.5}$$

Again using the fact that the real interest rate and the trade growth rate are of approximately the same size, we may set $r^* = g$ so that the right hand side becomes merely $k_{t-1}/(1 + g + i)^2$.

Suppose as a rough approximation $r^* = g = 0.04$, $i = .06$, and $k_{t-1} = 4.0$ (real interest rate and trade growth both at 4 percent, nominal inflation of 6 percent, and an initial debt/exports ratio of 400 percent). Then the derivative of the interest/exports ratio with respect to the inflation rate is $4/(1.1)^2 \approx 3.3$. Applied to a 1 percentage point change in the inflation rate (change in i by 0.01), this impact is 0.033. This result means that *for each percentage point reduction in world inflation, the interest/exports ratio will decline by somewhat less than* k *percentage points, where* k *is the initial debt/exports ratio.*

These results indicate that whereas a reduction in world inflation exactly matched by a reduction in world interest rates has no impact on the debt/exports ratio, it provides a substantial reduction in the interest/exports ratio. In the example just given, the initial interest/exports ratio is 36 percent.[3] The reduction of world interest rates by 1 percentage point reduces this ratio to 33 percent, a reduction by one-tenth.

The intuitive reason for the drop in the interest/exports ratio is that there is a strong "leveraging" of interest effects. A 1 percentage-point drop in the interest rate will be a decline of 10 percent or so in the interest bill, if the original interest rate was on the order of 10 percent, but an associated drop of world inflation by 1 percentage point will reduce the nominal value of the export base by only 1 percent.[4] The

---

3. That is: with the initial debt/exports ratio at 400 percent and nominal interest at 10 percent, interest in the subsequent year will be the fraction 40/110 of exports, allowing for nominal export growth.

4. Actually the export value reduction may be larger, if the elasticity of about 2 (estimated below) for the price change of debtor country exports in response to change in industrial country wholesale prices is valid. Even so, the export value change will be proportionately much smaller than the reduction in interest payments.

Table 3b.1 Illustrative impact of lower inflation and interest rates

year:	0	1	2	3	4	5
Base						
X	100	112	125	140	157	176
M	75	84	94	105	118	132
TB	25	28	31	35	39	44
INT		40	41	42	43	43
CA		−12	−10	−7	−4	1
D	400	412	422	429	432	432
INT/X		0.36	0.33	0.30	0.27	0.25
D/X		3.68	3.36	3.05	2.75	2.45
Case A						
X	100	111	123	137	152	169
M	75	83	92	103	114	126
TB	25	28	31	34	38	42
INT		36	37	37	38	38
CA		−8	−6	−3	0	5
D	400	408	414	417	417	412
INT/X		0.32	0.30	0.27	0.25	0.22
D/X		3.68	3.36	3.05	2.75	2.45
Case B						
X	100	107	114	123	131	140
M	75	80	86	92	98	105
TB	25	27	29	31	33	35
INT		30	30	31	31	31
CA		−3	−2	0	2	4
D	400	405	409	411	411	409
INT/X		0.28	0.27	0.25	0.23	0.22
D/X		3.79	3.57	3.35	3.13	2.92

X = exports; M = imports; TB = trade balance; INT = interest paid; CA = current account balance; D = external debt.

Case A: interest rate and inflation rate lower by 1 percent.
Case B: interest rate lower by 2.5 percent; inflation lower by 5 percent.

lower the initial interest rate, the larger the leverage, because a 1 percentage-point drop in the interest rate will be a larger proportion of the initial interest rate and thus bring a larger proportionate reduction in interest payments. Of course, this leverage can work to the debtor's disadvantage in a period of rising world inflation and interest rates (as in the late 1970s and early 1980s).

Table 3B.1 reports a simple simulation that verifies these results with a numerical illustration. The profile is that of a Latin American country in the mid-1980s with a high debt/exports ratio and a substantial trade surplus. Exports begin at $100 million, imports at $75 million, and debt at $400 million. In the baseline, world inflation is 6 percent, the nominal interest rate is 10 percent, and real trade volumes grow at 6 percent. In this simple economy the current account merely equals the trade surplus minus interest paid, and interest is based on the interest rate applied to debt at the end of the previous year.

In case A, the projection is shocked by reducing world inflation and interest rates both by 1 percent. As indicated in the table, the resulting change in the debt/exports ratio is so small that it is not noticeable to two decimal points, and the baseline path for this ratio remains unchanged. Thus, the result of invariance of the debt/exports ratio with respect to joint change in world inflation and the interest rate is confirmed.

Again in case A, the reduction of the interest rate by 1 percent causes an immediate drop of the interest/exports ratio by about 4 percentage points (from 36 percent to 32 percent), confirming the second result above—that the interest/exports ratio should fall by about k percentage points for each percentage point drop in the interest rate, where k is the initial debt/exports ratio. After the first-year fall, the new time path for the interest/exports ratio parallels the baseline at a level lower by approximately this constant amount.

In case B, world inflation falls by 5 percent and is a constant 1 percent per year over the five-year period instead of 6 percent. However, the interest rate falls by only 2.5 percent. The result is a *rise* in the debt/exports ratio (which is 292 percent at the end of the period instead of 245 percent) but a sharp *decline* in the interest/exports ratio. Because of the cumulative effect of the higher real interest rate, the large improvement in the interest/exports ratio in the first year (from 36 percent to 28 percent) is considerably narrowed by the end of the period (25 percent in baseline versus 22 percent in case B).

This exercise confirms that when disinflation involves a lag in expectations and thus a lag in the decline of interest rates behind that in inflation, there will be an adverse impact on the debt/exports ratio and the long-term debt burden, but there can nonetheless be an improvement in the interest/exports ratio and thus the country's cash-flow situation. This is precisely what happened to the debtor countries in the mid-1980s, when the drop in average world inflation was about 5 percentage points but the decline in LIBOR was only about $2^{1}/_{2}$ percentage points, as discussed above.

The analysis here does yield a paradox: disinflation is good for debtors if expectations adjust instantaneously. Under that condition, disinflation reduces the cash-flow problem (lower interest/exports ratio) without worsening the long-term debt burden (or affecting the debt/exports ratio). This paradox in turn forces out an implicit assumption behind the usual notion that inflation is the debtor's friend and disinflation his or her enemy: the assumption—a realistic one—that expectations do not adjust instantaneously, so the interest rate lags behind inflation changes (in the extreme case, by being fixed rather than variable in the debt contract).

4

Debt Theory: A Critical Review of the Literature

The debt crisis of the 1980s elicited an outpouring of economic literature analyzing sovereign lending, the circumstances of default, prospective outlooks for recovery, and the issue of debt forgiveness. Lessons derived from earlier historical episodes of default also featured prominently in the emerging literature. This chapter reviews the leading contributions, with an emphasis on theoretical analyses and in particular on the question of debt relief. In addition, there is a large literature on country adjustment experience, considered in chapter 6 for Latin America.

The Theory of Sovereign Lending

Eaton and Gersovitz (1981) provided a seminal contribution dealing with the central problem of why anyone would lend to a sovereign nation free from the domestic debtor's vulnerability to seizure of collateral. Their analysis was inspired in part by the resumption of sovereign lending to developing countries after the oil shock of the mid-1970s, in contrast to the long absence of such lending after the defaults of the 1930s.

Rather than appealing to foreign creditors' scope for seizing vessels in foreign ports and the like, the authors invoke the concept of preserving the nation's reputation for creditworthiness so that the country could borrow in the future. They specify a model in which the country has alternating bad and good years (e.g., a predictable crop cycle). The country borrows in a bad year and repays with interest in the following good year. The model amounts to the smoothing of consumption under a utility function with declining marginal utility, such that the present discounted value of consumption is maximized by being able to supplement domestic output with borrowed consumption in the bad years and forgoing some extra consumption in the good years. In this model, default carries its own "endogenous penalty": the denial of future access to credit. In their words: "The government chooses to repay because it knows that at some time in the future it may face another shock during which it will again desire to borrow."

The Eaton-Gersovitz model does have a credit ceiling: creditors will lend no more than the amount that just makes the country indifferent between sacrificing all future borrowing for consumption-smoothing purposes and enjoying the windfall gain of shedding its outstanding debt. This ceiling varies positively with the size of the annual production fluctuations (standard deviation of income)—because the penalty of forgoing consumption-smoothing borrowing is more severe if fluctuations are larger, and the point of indifference will be at a larger outstanding debt. Larger fluctuation of income also raises the country's desired level of borrowing, because consumption smoothing is more important. Actual borrowing in a given year is the minimum of the credit ceiling, on the one hand, and the amount that maximizes discounted country utility, on the other (which depends in part on the international interest rate).

The amount the country desires to borrow rises with the growth rate, both because absolute future fluctuations are thus larger and because future marginal utility at the time of repayment is smaller. The credit ceiling also rises with the growth rate, unless there is an unusually large rate of dropoff in marginal utility in the utility function (in which case creditors must worry about the country's lesser pain from forgoing future consumption smoothing). The credit ceiling also rises if there is a larger exogenous penalty that can be imposed, because then it will take a larger windfall gain from repudiation to compensate for the additional loss of the exogenous penalty. Gunboats are the borrower's best friend.

The authors find that introduction of uncertainty clouds or reverses some of the conclusions. With stochastic income variations, two bad years can occur back to back, pushing the country toward high marginal utility of consumption and endangering repayment. Under these conditions, larger-than-expected fluctuation can reduce rather than increase the credit ceiling.

The Eaton-Gersovitz model resonates with much of the underlying policy strategy during the debt crisis, as it subscribes to the notion that debtor countries have an interest in honoring their debt because of their stake in future market access. In a subsequent survey article, Eaton, Gersovitz, and Stiglitz (1986) point out that the model requires an infinite horizon. If there is a terminal period of repayment, the country will always find it advantageous to default in that period. Knowing this, lenders will not lend. Fortunately, countries are infinite-lived. The three authors also appeal to game theory to identify another reason for sovereign lending with repudiation risk. They note that in an infinitely repeatable game in which identities of players are remembered, "reputation as cooperative players can succeed in enforcing some degree of cooperation" (493).

However, Eaton, Gersovitz, and Stiglitz (1986) also argue that lending cannot occur for economic development purposes, as opposed to consumption smoothing. A country with a low capital endowment that is strictly a borrower in the first part of the horizon and strictly a repayer later will be an unsuitable risk to creditors, because they will perceive that in the second phase "the debtor will lose nothing by being denied access to credit markets" (491). Yet this proposition flies in the face of the central neoclassical view of international capital markets: capital is reallocated from developed countries, where it is relatively abundant and its return is lower, to developing countries, where capital is more scarce and its return is higher. Nor does it accord with the postwar history of successful "graduates" from development lending, such as Italy, Spain, Greece, and Finland.[1]

One way to resolve this paradox is to recognize that there is an important element of "honor" or national pride in the commitment to international rules of the game on the part of many debtor country governments.[2] The absence of this element in penalty-based models of sovereign debt leaves them with a flavor of "optimizing deadbeat" behavior on the part of debtors that is difficult to harmonize with the observed performance not only of full development-borrowing graduates but also newly industrialized countries such as South Korea and Chile. After all, South Korea had high external debt at the beginning of the 1980s and chose an aggressive program of repayment rather than default, a choice difficult to explain within the Eaton-Gersovitz-Stiglitz framework. A similar but alternative explanation is that implicitly the "penalties" of default far exceed the legally limited recourse to asset and shipments seizures (see Kaletsky 1985) and the stake in consumption smoothing. Instead, the penalties include effective denial of full entry into advanced nation status, with the low risk premiums and full integration into international goods and capital markets associated with that

---

1. These four countries received a total of $1.3 billion in World Bank lending in the early postwar period, equivalent to about $6 billion at today's prices (World Bank 1974, 112).

2. Note that Aaron (1994) has stressed the importance of such non-Benthamite-utilitarian values as self-respect and respect by others, as well as altruism, as elements typically omitted in economic models, to the detriment of their ability to explain behavior. In terms of the simple summary equation suggested by Eaton, Gersovitz, and Stiglitz (1986), whereby $L \leq P/(1 + i)$, with L the amount lent in the first period, P the maximum penalty that can be extracted for nonpayment in the second period, and i the international interest rate, we would have $L \leq P/(1 + i) + H$, where H is the value the borrowing country places on its "honor."

status.[3] Perhaps the best illustration of these benefits of "normalcy" is the sharp decline on the Mexican treasury bill rate that followed its normalization of relations with creditors after its Brady Plan debt agreement, discussed in chapters 5 and 6.

Cooper and Sachs (1985) examine optimal borrowing from the debtor country's standpoint. They first distinguish among three types of risk: *insolvency, illiquidity,* and *repudiation.* Their solvency constraint on borrowing states that debt cannot exceed the present discounted value of the country's potential future trade surpluses, discounting at the international interest rate. Illiquidity may arise even if the country is solvent by this definition, because in a bad year individual banks may fear that others will seek to exit and "a panic may ensue" (25). Although in principle a single large bank cognizant of continued solvency could extend finance to cover the cash-flow problem, capital requirements and regulatory constraints are likely to preclude this possibility, so that each bank has an incentive to stop lending once others do so.

As for repudiation risk, the authors assume that creditors can impose sanctions against default amounting to θW, where W is the "wealth" of the country (the present discounted value of its future income), of which one component is the collections they achieve through foreign asset seizures amounting to γW. Repudiation of outstanding debt D yields a gain of $(D - \theta W)$ to the debtor and a loss of $D(1 - \gamma)$ to the creditors.[4] Creditors set a credit ceiling in the light of their prospective losses from repudiation. The ceiling is higher if their ability to impose sanctions (θ) is greater.[5] The difference between θ and γ provides space for the negotiation of a side payment to settle a default, whereby if the country wholly extracts the rent the banks receive only γW, whereas if the banks capture the full rent in dispute they receive a side-payment of $(\theta - \gamma)W$ from the country. This observation may be seen as having foreshadowed the bargaining in the later Brady Plan workouts.[6]

---

3. In this alternative, the term "H" in the previous note becomes a proxy for these benefits of first-class rather than second-class international economic citizenship.

4. The authors apparently assume the country is "lent up" to its solvency point, so that $D = W$; otherwise the final term in the parentheses should be $\gamma W/D$.

5. Note, however, that the authors recognize a trade-off for the country: greater sanction potential increases borrowing potential but also exposes the country to greater penalty if something goes wrong. They surmise that the country benefits the most from an intermediate value of θ (Cooper and Sachs 1985, 41).

6. Note that Eaton, Gersovitz, and Stiglitz (1986) dismiss the Cooper-Sachs formulation of the penalty as fraction θ of country wealth on grounds that setting such a penalty is "clearly not a plausible one in the same way as an exclusion from future borrowing or trade transactions" (492). However, the effect of this formulation is not much different from that of the growth factor in the Eaton-Gersovitz model; both essentially provide a scaling factor that relates the credit ceiling to the size of the debtor economy.

Cooper and Sachs then demonstrate the familiar result that, if solvency is the only constraint, the country's optimal borrowing path smooths consumption over time. It does so such that at all points in time marginal utility of consumption, discounted by the net of the time preference rate and the international borrowing rate, is a constant, which in turn equals the marginal utility of wealth (28). Because transitory shocks have little impact on this long-term marginal utility of wealth whereas permanent shocks reduce wealth and raise its marginal utility, the optimal borrowing path confirms the admonition to "finance a temporary shock, adjust to a permanent shock" (where "adjustment" means reducing consumption and thus raising its marginal utility).

The two authors then introduce government external borrowing to foster domestic development and demonstrate that this strategy requires a rising tax rate over time (to shift consumption to the present, paid for by higher output and taxes in the future). If there is a ceiling on the tax rate, optimal borrowing will be *below* the amount indicated simply by the equation of marginal product of capital with world borrowing costs. This finding hints at the fiscal "internal transfer" problem that features prominently in later debt literature. The analysis then introduces the liquidity constraint by incorporating a probability that in the second period banks will panic and cut off credit. The positive relationship of this probability to the debt level (and the failure of private decisions to incorporate this negative externality) provides another reason for the government to limit borrowing from abroad. Yet another reason arises from the behavioral tendency of foreign creditors to assume that private-sector external debt will be assumed by the government in a crisis.

Cooper and Sachs suggest that repudiation risk can be partly tempered by precommitment to use of borrowing for investment rather than consumption, because the resulting second-period output will be higher and so will the creditor's credit rationing ceiling (which they specify as $D < \theta Q/(1 + r)$, where Q is second-period output and r is the international lending rate). They stress that both liquidity risk and the repudiation risk are likely to limit indebtedness to levels far below potential solvency levels.

The Cooper-Sachs formulation is consistent with the initial phases of management of the international debt crisis, when there was an emphasis on the distinction between the appropriateness of lending to countries experiencing a liquidity crisis as opposed to the inappropriateness of additional lending if the problem were one of fundamental insolvency (Cline 1983). Their recognition of liquidity constraints seems far more realistic than the subsequent judgment by Ahmed and Summers (1992) that "the entire liquidity-solvency dichotomy is somewhat misconceived. There would be no reason for a borrower to encounter a liquidity problem if its solvency was not in doubt" (17). Surely the Cooper-Sachs recognition of creditor panics is closer to what happened in the early 1980s; consider that even Chile faced a collapse in voluntary lending and for some time needed concerted lending packages, though it did not eventually require debt forgiveness.

At the same time, Cooper and Sachs recognized that there was a solvency constraint involving prospective capacity to generate trade surpluses. In this regard they would seem to have come closer to the mark than Eaton, Gersovitz, and Stiglitz (1986), who consider the concern of Diaz-Alejandro (1984) about the external transfer problem as misplaced because small countries cannot depress their terms of trade (501).[7] The potential for insolvency in turn was the justification for projection analyses that investigated whether debtor countries could achieve sufficient export growth to grow their way out of the debt problem (e.g., Cline 1983, 1984; Morgan Guaranty 1983; Enders and Mattione 1984, as discussed below).

Bulow and Rogoff (1989a) construct an alternative model of sovereign debt. As discussed below, they first dismiss the Eaton-Gersovitz concept of a default penalty from the sacrifice of future access to borrowing for consumption smoothing. Instead, they identify gains from trade as the origin of the potential penalty required to provide creditors with the counterpart of physical collateral otherwise missing in sovereign lending.

The authors apply a game-theoretic bargaining approach, in which the (Nash) equilibrium for the maximum annual payment creditors can extract, expressed as a fraction of the country's GDP, is

$$q = \min \frac{\gamma + \delta}{2\gamma + \delta + r}, \frac{P - 1}{P}, \beta \qquad (4.1)$$

Here, γ is the rate of depreciation of stocks (e.g., bananas rotting on the docks), δ is the country's time preference rate, r is the international interest rate, P is the price at which domestic output can be exchanged for foreign goods, and β is the largest proportion by which banks can reduce the country's exports through legal harassment and other retaliatory measures in the event of a default.

Bulow and Rogoff call the first of these three criteria the "bargaining" zone. When this expression is the minimum of the three measures, banks can extract the fraction $(\gamma + \delta)/(2\gamma + \delta + r)$ of the value of the country's annual GDP valued at its world market price (Py). Given that $\delta > r$, in this region banks will always be able to claim more than half of a country's GDP annually. Although the authors do not explicitly say so, this result is so far in excess of observed debt levels (implying debt service exceeding half of GDP and thus debt over, say, 5 times GDP) that it is unlikely to be the relevant equilibrium region.

---

7. Although both Cooper-Sachs and Eaton-Gersovitz-Stiglitz consider the solvency constraint to be binding under normal circumstances.

The second of the three criteria is the gain from trade; a solution in this region involves autarky. If the trade gain is low ($P \to 1$), the country can cease trading with minimal loss, and the banks' threat to disrupt exports is empty. The banks will achieve only a minimal repayment.

The third region, where β is the minimum of the three criteria, is a "punishment-constrained" zone. Here the best the banks can do is to offer to accept βPy in annual payments (i.e., fraction β of annual GDP evaluated at the price it commands when sold on the world export market), leaving the country $(1 - \beta)Py$.

Knowing the ceiling on what they can extract annually (qPy), banks will set a corresponding credit ceiling equal to their present discounted value of this annual stream:

$$\Re = \frac{Pyq}{r} \tag{4.2}$$

The authors then examine the impact of adding uncertainty in a stochastic rather than deterministic formulation. One result is that an unanticipated rise in world interest rates can *help* a loaned-up debtor, which cannot pay more but now faces creditors more impatient to get back some portion of their money for investment elsewhere. In another extension of the analysis, although without formal modeling, the authors suggest that if gains from trade with the debtor country are important to the governments of the creditor countries, these governments may be forced to make side payments to the debtor (if bank lending is competitive) or the banks (if it is monopolistic) to resolve a default. The authors conclude with the reasonable judgment that rather than from irrational lenders, the debt crisis originated primarily from unanticipated increases in the interest rate, decreases in terms of trade, and bank anticipation that government side payments would be forthcoming in the event of trouble.

The Bulow-Rogoff trade-gains model of sovereign debt is intuitively appealing, although less than operational in realistic terms. It makes no distinction between tradeable and nontradeable goods in the economy. Of its three regions, the bargaining zone gives a high measure (>0.5, as discussed above), and is unlikely to set q (equation 4.1). Gains from trade are also likely to be relatively high, especially for small countries.[8] A plausible value for P might be in the range of 1.4, implying $(P - 1)/P \approx 0.3$.

The binding region would seem most likely to be the punishment zone, as it is difficult to envision bank blockage of country exports by more than, say, 30 to 40 percent, with corresponding GDP losses of no

---

8. Thus, Latin American countries typically had to impose tariffs in the 50–100 percent range in the 1950s and 1960s to move significantly in the direction of autarky.

more than, say, 15 to 20 percent (i.e., $\beta = 0.15$).[9] Even with this binding measure, the model would seem to potentially overstate the debt ceiling substantially. For consistency with observed ceilings of debt stocks in the vicinity of 100 percent of GDP (and more typically 30 to 50 percent, for larger countries), β would have to be no more than about 0.03.[10]

Perhaps in part because their trade-gains disruption model already generates embarrassingly high debt ceilings (although the authors themselves do not place values on their parameters), Bulow and Rogoff (1988c) dispense with the Eaton-Gersovitz consumption-smoothing source of creditor security. They argue that at any point in time a country can default and use the money saved to purchase insurance contracts that achieve the same future consumption-smoothing function at less cost. However, the notion that Brazil (for example) could approach Lloyds of London with the money saved by not paying Citibank and purchase a contract to hedge all future export fluctuations into perpetuity is so far-fetched that the argument amounts to little more than a curiosity.

This judgment would leave consumption smoothing as *additive* to export blockage as a further element providing the counterpart of domestic physical collateral in the sphere of international sovereign lending. What is remarkable is that the combined effect of the (Eaton-Gersovitz) consumption-smoothing and (Bulow-Rogoff) trade-gains approaches is to suggest relatively high debt ceilings (as discussed above just for the latter approach). The implication is that sovereign lending may not be as difficult to mobilize as the absence of collateral would suggest. Another implication is that the repudiation risk may not be so binding after all, so that attention may appropriately be paid to payment capacity—a major concern in the actual evolution of the debt crisis and policy response to it.[11]

From the vantage point of the early 1990s, it would seem that as the debt crisis evolved there was relatively little manifestation of punitive behavior, and there was substantial country honoring of debt under circumstances that the theoretical literature might have suggested would yield a deep(er) forced forgiveness. Peru and Brazil experienced some trade credit difficulties because of arrears, but Brazil managed

---

9. Suppose exports are 25 percent of GDP (small-country case), the shadow price of foreign exchange is 2, and bank retaliation reduces exports by one-third. Then GDP loss is $16^{1/2}$ percent ($= 0.25 \times 2 \times 0.33$).

10. Thus, with $\beta = q = 0.15$ and taking account of country growth rate at g, the debt ceiling would be $0.15Py/(r - g)$, or approximately $5^{1/2}$ times GDP if $r = 0.08$, $g = 0.04$, and $P = 1.4$. With these parameters, a debt/GDP ceiling of 100 percent would require $\beta \leq 0.029$.

11. Correspondingly, the unrealistically high debt ceiling that derives from export-blockage potential alone (β), as outlined above, is one reason why those who dismiss the payments capacity constraint may be understating its importance relative to the repudiation constraint.

nonetheless to achieve large, chronic trade surpluses. There have been no major episodes of seizure of assets abroad or of export shipments. This experience suggests modest limits on the extent of the export disruption threat.

But if creditors have been less aggressive than the theory suggests, debtors also seem to have been less inclined to exercise their repudiation potential than the theory assumes. Chile and Colombia illustrate the point best. Certainly Chile and probably Colombia could have pleaded successfully for debt forgiveness under the Brady Plan. Neither did so. Their behavior suggests an important weight attached to the concept suggested above: a mixture of "honor," on the one hand, and value attributed to being a full-fledged member of the international financial system, on the other. These two countries, along with others such as South Korea and Indonesia, illustrate behavior based on paying full (albeit rescheduled) obligation subject to a *capacity* constraint, rather than optimizing deadbeat behavior whereby the country seeks to wriggle out of its debt obligation to the full extent possible given the creditors' sanction potential. As discussed in chapter 8, by 1992–93 there were tangible rewards from this strategy for Chile, in the form of reinstatement of formal investment-grade rating by the major rating agencies and correspondingly lower borrowing spreads.[12]

Debt Capacity Projection Models

Because the behavior of many debtor countries has been closer to the honoring of full debt subject to payment capacity, rather than optimal wriggling out of obligations subject to penalties, the studies in the mid-1980s that attempted to assess the future evolution of debt-servicing capacity were of substantial relevance. Chapter 3 provides a detailed analysis of one set of these projections (Cline 1983, 1984), examining with the benefit of hindsight whether the parameters and assumptions for exogenous variables were consistent with what actually occurred subsequently. Other models of this genre included Morgan Guaranty (1983); Council of Economic Advisers (1984); Enders and Mattione (1984); Dornbusch and Fischer (1985); Filatov and Mattione (1985); Feldstein (1986); Dooley, Helkie, Tryon, and Underwood (1986); Helkie and Howard (1991); and Dittus, O'Brien, and Blommestein (1991).

Typically the projection models focused on the "external transfer" and examined whether prospective export growth would be sufficient to permit a reduction in the key debt ratios (debt relative to exports, interest obligation relative to exports) to more "normal" levels within a

---

12. In contrast, in the late 1980s Peru, and to a lesser extent Brazil (and even Argentina before 1990), revealed behavior more in keeping with the model of paying the minimum possible.

reasonable period of time. The models typically linked LDC export growth to GDP growth in the industrial countries, and import growth to growth of GDP in the debtor country. The country's real exchange rate influenced both exports and imports. Real commodity prices depended on world interest rates (negatively) and industrial country growth (positively); and increases in nominal dollar prices of traded goods depended on world inflation (positively) as well as prospective depreciation of the dollar against other currencies (positively).

The projections in Cline (1983) had suggested that international economic recovery and adjustment of the overvalued dollar would permit major improvement in the debt indicators for major debtors. That study thus judged that the debt crisis was primarily one of illiquidity rather than insolvency, and accordingly that refinancing rather than debt forgiveness was the appropriate policy response (as discussed in chapter 3). Krugman (1985, 97) judged that these projections were reasonable, and noted that the Council of Economic Advisers (1984) had reached similar conclusions with "back of the envelope" calculations.

Others at the time were more harsh. Eaton and Taylor (1986) noted that the Cline (1983, 1984) projections had provoked a "firestorm of criticism" (77). Their survey recounts the critiques as including "a likely slowdown in the US in 1985–86," an excessive OECD income elasticity for LDC exports, increased protection, and slow LDC growth as the price for achieving external transfer. However, as examined in chapter 3, international growth turned out even more robust than projected; the export elasticity was comparable to that in most studies when its specific formulation was taken into account; and several countries did achieve growth despite the external transfer.

The Eaton-Taylor review did usefully make the point that the economic interrelationship between the industrial and developing countries was more complex than could be captured with a trade elasticity, and moreover that projections with such models were highly sensitive to assumptions. Specifying income elasticities of 2.0 for LDC imports, 2.2 for OECD imports from LDCs, and a terms-of-trade elasticity of -0.5 with respect to dollar strength, the authors noted that debtor country growth rates consistent with an unchanged current account deficit could range all the way from $+7.6$ percent under optimistic assumptions (OECD growth of 3 percent, dollar devaluation of 10 percent, interest rate reduction by 1 percent) to -1.5 percent under pessimistic assumptions (1.2 percent, 5 percent *appreciation*, and $+1$ percent, respectively).[13]

---

13. For their own part, Eaton and Taylor (1986) inclined toward the pessimistic scenarios and inferred that debtors could find it attractive to move toward closed trade. They stated: "in a decade of likely loan revulsion, an outward-oriented growth strategy—at least vis a vis the North—is not likely to pay off grandly. . . . If the Panglossian vision of miraculous disappearance of the debt crisis does not materialize, the poor economies would do well to

Practitioners of these projections were well aware of their sensitivity. However, the suite of macrovariables in question had been so unfavorable in the 1980–82 period that there was every reason to believe that some reversion toward normalcy and recovery was the more likely constellation of macroeconomic assumptions. For policy purposes, a judgment was necessary about the more likely outcome, and it would have been a mistake to base policy on the possibility that all would turn out wrong. As indicated in chapter 3, this bet was essentially validated, except for the temporary delay in commodity price response and the singularly important collapse in the price of oil in 1986. As noted in chapter 3, the policy guidance given by the projection models with moderately optimistic assumptions was broadly right for the nonoil debtors, certainly with respect to the external economic environment (as opposed to the internal issues of fiscal adjustment and capital flight).

In late 1984, Filatov and Mattione (1985) conducted experiments comparing the projection models of Cline (1983, 1984), Dornbusch and Fischer (1984), and their Morgan Guaranty Trust (MGT) model. Their model provided (modest) sectoral detail for export elasticities and endogenous determination of country growth in response to trade and capital flows. They simulated the three alternative models under identical assumptions about external macroeconomic variables and domestic growth for Brazil, Chile, and Mexico. One finding was that the base year (1983 versus 1984) made a major difference, in particular because trade projections reflected the absolute levels of exports and imports in the base year.

Under fairly standard global macro assumptions (including a constant nominal price of oil), the Filatov-Mattione version of the Dornbusch-Fischer model projected a massive current-account surplus by 1990 for the three countries together ($34 billion), and their version of the Cline model, a substantial surplus ($12 billion); but their own MGT model projected a small deficit ($2 billion). The irony was that the Dornbusch-Fischer model showed such a bullish outcome, in view of the pessimism of those authors based on their own shorter-run projections.

Filatov and Mattione examined sensitivity and in particular focused on the relative impact of changes in OECD growth and international interest rates. The issue was important and controversial at the time, because the world economy was entering recovery but interest rates were also heading back up. Cline (1984, 60) had found that a 1 percent rise in OECD growth had as much favorable effect for the debtors as a 7-percentage-point cut in the London interbank offer rate (LIBOR), whereas Dornbusch and Fischer (35–36) had placed the relative impact

---

heed the example of Candide and friends, and tend to their own gardens . . . [through] changes in commercial and industrial policy" (260). As it turned out, the debtor countries did change these policies, but toward open trade instead.

lower at only about two to one. Filatov and Mattione's simulations tended to support the lower estimate for "the short run" (the second year), but a range of 3 to 5 for the longer run (the sixth year), averaging over the three countries and three models.[14] The interest effects were immediate but did not cumulate rapidly, whereas sustained higher OECD growth had a rapidly cumulating effect on debtor external balances. Appropriately, the authors stressed that the trade-off question depended importantly on the context. Whereas world recession caused by high interest rates would be devastating, in contrast "strong [world] recovery can coexist with high real interest rates . . . [and the] net effect would be beneficial to the borrowing countries."[15]

Also in 1984, Dooley, Helkie, Tryon, and Underwood (1986) carried out similar projections for the major developing countries. They reached conclusions similar to Cline (1983, 1984) and Morgan Guaranty (1983). However, they emphasized the "amortization adjusted interest payments" as the key indicator of the debt burden. This measure removed "inflationary amortization"—that is, the erosion of the real stock of debt caused by world inflation and the corresponding transferal of principal payment into the inflationary premium in the interest rate—to calculate an adjusted interest/exports ratio. They noted that despite similar results to the previous models, their estimates gave relatively greater weight to the importance of lower real interest rates and to exchange rates, and relatively less weight to industrial country growth. Like those in the earlier studies, their oil price projections did not anticipate the 1986 collapse. As the authors were based at the Federal Reserve, it is likely that their results, along with those of the Council of Economic Advisers staff (noted above), tended to contribute to the coalescence of official views around the diagnoses and prognoses of the earlier projection models.[16]

---

14. Although Filatov and Mattione did not explicitly so state, one reason for the higher short-run effect of growth in the Cline (1984) model is the specification of a negative export growth intercept with a relatively high marginal (but "typical" average) elasticity of exports with respect to OECD growth. See chapter 3.

15. As the authors recognized, this conclusion referred to the ease of mobilizing the external transfer, not to country welfare (given that increased exports required resources whereas lower interest rates would provide a windfall gain). Note also that on another issue, the favorable impact of prospective dollar depreciation, the MGT model indicated that the Cline (1993) results were overstated and the Dornbusch-Fischer (1984) estimates understated.

16. In another study in this period, Enders and Mattione (1984) projected relatively similar external sector results, but anticipated far less satisfactory domestic growth for the Latin American debtors. They expected the seven large debtors to grow at an average rate of only 1.1 percent annually in 1983–87. As it turned out, Latin American growth in the period was higher at an average of 2.2 percent (ECLAC 1991), though still lower than in the Cline (1983) projections. The period of severe recession came later, as the region's

The Federal Reserve team subsequently reexamined the debt outlook, this time for the 1990s (Helkie and Howard 1991). Their new projections showed favorable (falling) baseline trends for debt/exports ratios in Chile and Venezuela; rising trends that could comfortably be turned around to declining trends with a 10 percent real depreciation in Brazil and Mexico; but prospectively more intransigent problems of high debt/exports levels for Argentina, Peru, and the Philippines.

In short, numerous projection exercises by policy analysts in the 1980s tended to find that it was feasible for most of the debtor countries to grow and export their way out of the debt problem (except for the special case of oil-exporting countries after 1986), although the projections were not without their critics. Eaton, Gersovitz, and Stiglitz (1986) had a much more fundamental critique of the projection models than any concern about macroeconomic or parameter assumptions. They dismissed such projections as providing no information about whether countries were willing to service their debt; for this purpose, they argued, a debt theory such as that in Eaton and Gersovitz (1981) was necessary. If a country found it advantageous to default, its policies would change so that its imports were higher and its exports lower than in the baselines forecast by the projection models. While obviously true in principle, this cavalier attitude toward evaluation of debt-servicing capacity would appear to have been in error on two grounds. First, whereas external transfer capacity may not have been a *sufficient* condition for servicing the debt, it was certainly a *necessary* condition. In other words, payments capacity and the solvency constraint (e.g., in the Cooper-Sachs classification) were not as redundant and therefore irrelevant as Eaton-Gersovitz (1981) and Bulow-Rogoff (1988b) assumed. Second, the behavior of countries such as Chile seemed to reveal a tendency among some, and perhaps the majority, of countries to honor their debt if they had the "capacity" to do so, even though narrowly measured benefits and costs might suggest they should default instead.

As indicated in chapter 2, the key debt ratios had shown major improvement for most debtor countries by 1991–92, with the help of lower international interest rates, country adjustment measures, and in some cases Brady Plan debt reductions. Given enough time, the outcome seemed broadly to conform more closely to the more favorable external sector projections than to the pessimistic ones. However, moderate debt forgiveness became the policy rule rather than the exception under the Brady Plan. One reason was that the collapse of oil prices in

---

growth slowed to an average of 0.7 percent annually in 1988–90, before recovering to 3 percent in 1991–92 (ECLAC 1992). Although the oil price collapse contributed to this slowdown, severe difficulty with domestic inflation (including hyperinflation) was the primary cause. As discussed in chapter 6, the debt problem contributed to, but was not the primary cause of, these inflationary problems.

1986 did inflict a major blow to external transfer capacity for such oil-exporting countries as Mexico and Venezuela. For the oil-importing countries, however, another influence seems to have been at work. Debt-servicing capacity was constrained not so much by trade possibilities for external transfer as by fiscal limits to the "internal transfer" associated with the servicing of government debt.

The Internal Transfer Problem

Although much of the initial analysis of the debt crisis focused on the influence of international shocks, especially the rise of international interest rates to extremely high levels in the early 1980s, Wiesner (1985) was an early advocate of the view that the problem was primarily fiscal. Previously a finance minister of Colombia, which skirted the debt crisis largely because of fiscal prudence in the 1970s, he argued:

> No other set of factors explains more of the debt crisis than the fiscal deficits incurred by most of the major countries in Latin America. . . . I have no doubt that the main problem was excessive public (and private) spending that was financed by both easy domestic credit policies and by ample resources from abroad. The world recession and high real rates of interest in international markets aggravated the crisis, but . . . previous domestic macroeconomic policies had made economies more vulnerable to exogenous factors. (191)

Wiesner pointed out that from 1979 to 1982, three of the four largest debtors (Argentina, Brazil, and Mexico) had more than doubled their fiscal deficits from about 6 percent of GDP to 15 percent. He suggested that the fiscal disequilibrium underlying the debt crisis was "ultimately . . . an unresolved political struggle between competing groups that wanted to have a larger share of the income" (191).

At the time, Wiesner's overwhelming emphasis on domestic fiscal causes of the debt crisis seemed dubious. After all, if the principal origin of the problem was internal, why did so many countries suddenly get into trouble at the same time? Moreover, there were important counterexamples: Chile in particular fell into the debt crisis along with other Latin American countries, even though its fiscal performance was stellar.

In retrospect, the fiscal argument looks better. Countries did not all suddenly start running large fiscal deficits after August 1982, but they did all suddenly face a drying up of external financing for the fiscal deficits they had become accustomed to by then. Even the exceptions seemed to be of the type that proved the rule. Thus, in Chile the government wound up "socializing" the private external debt problem, partly because of pressure from external banks (Díaz-Alejandro 1984) and partly because of the need to avoid a collapse of the domestic banking system.[17] In Argentina, in part to compensate for generalized conditions of near bankruptcy, the government provided foreign exchange for the servicing of private external debt on terms that turned out to be highly subsidized, thereby enlarging the internal transfer component of the debt problem (chapter 6). Thus, whatever the extent of the domestic fiscal origins of the debt problem on the eve of the debt crisis, the internal transfer problem was often intensified after its eruption.

By the end of the 1980s it was increasingly clear that the countries that were overcoming the debt problem were those that were dealing effectively with their domestic fiscal problems. In Chile, Mexico, and to a lesser extent Venezuela, fiscal reform closed the previously large deficits, and debt servicing and renegotiation proceeded apace. Where populism was stronger and political structures were weaker—in Peru, Brazil, and to a lesser extent Argentina—serious fiscal imbalances persisted and countries entered into extended arrears on external debt. It was no accident that in Argentina, after the outbreak of hyperinflation in 1989 had traumatized the public and discredited the politics of populism, a new phase of fiscal reform facilitated debt normalization. Through the early 1990s, Brazilian ingenuity with indexation avoided outright hyperinflation, but it was unclear for how long.

As the debt crisis lingered on in the late 1980s, analysts increasingly turned to the fiscal "internal transfer problem" as the explanation. In a study for the OECD Development Center, Reisen and Van Trotsenburg (1988) emphasized this problem as the reason that earlier projection studies' calculations of prospective return to creditworthiness (including Cline 1983, but also similar estimates by the IMF and World Bank) had not been realized in fact despite achievement of the projected improvements in industrial country market growth and reductions in LIBOR.[18]

The authors focused on eight large debtor countries. Usefully, their sample included not only the large Latin American countries (Argentina, Brazil, Mexico, and Venezuela), but also major Asian debtors (Indonesia, South Korea, and the Philippines). They first argued that the debt crisis had caused net financial transfers (NFT)—defined as net capital flow plus net factor payments—to deteriorate to negative magnitudes large by historical standards. Thus, for the seven countries, the unweighted average NFT fell from +2.8 percent of GDP in 1980–81 to −3.7 percent of GDP in 1983–85 (and as much as −6.8 percent in Argentina). By comparison, interwar transfers by Germany had been 2.5 percent of GDP, and French transfers in the early 1870s associated with reparations for the Franco-Prussian War had reached 5.6 percent of

---

17. Note, however, that the perception of the burden of Chile's socialization of the debt has probably been exaggerated, as discussed in chapter 6.

18. For further discussion, see the review of projection analyses above and in chapter 3.

GDP. However, their historical data also show that outward US net financial transfers averaged 3 percent of GDP from 1949 to 1961—hardly a period when the United States suffered a severe growth-reducing burden from its external financial relationships.

The authors then argued that the bulk of the NFT fell upon the public sector. Thus, private debt accounted for only 17 percent of long-term external debt as of 1985 (seven countries, unweighted average). As a result, the public sector had to carry out the bulk of the financial transfer. In turn, this transfer was large relative to government revenue. Debt service payable on external public and publicly guaranteed debt was an unweighted average of 28.8 percent of public-sector revenue in 1984 for the seven countries (up from 20 percent in 1981). Indeed, the authors suggest that the ratio of the public net financial transfer abroad to total government revenue is a key indicator of the debt burden that had heretofore been neglected.

Governments could service external debt only within the confines of the following budget equation:

$$G + \alpha NFT = \Delta M + \Delta D + \Delta D^* + T \qquad (4.3)$$

where α is the fraction of net financial transfers for which the government is responsible, G is other government spending, ΔM is monetization of budget deficits, D and D^* are domestic and foreign debt respectively, and T is fiscal revenue.

Reisen and Van Trotsenberg (1988) found that the principal form of fiscal adjustment was a cutback in noninterest spending, typically focused on government investment. Thus, from 1981 to 1984, noninterest government spending as a share of GDP fell by about one-fifth in Indonesia and South Korea, nearly one-third in Mexico and the Philippines, and nearly one-half in Venezuela (where state oil firm investments collapsed). Moderate cuts in deficits of state enterprises helped in this process.[19] Argentina was an important exception, as it carried out only minimal cuts despite high initial government spending as a share of GDP.[20] Fiscal adjustment was typically minimal on the revenue side, as five out of six countries with available data showed government revenue no higher in 1984 than in 1981 (Mexico was the sole exception; 36–37).

The authors then argue that the need in several countries to resort to monetization and the "inflation tax" aggravated the internal transfer problem. Under these circumstances, saving and investment declined, capital flight increased, and exchange rate devaluations typically exceeded amounts that would hold the real exchange rate constant. The

---

19. These deficits were an unweighted average of 4.8 percent of GDP in 1981, falling to 2.8 percent of GDP in 1984 (38).

20. Lack of data clouded the outcome in Brazil.

result was that foreign debt service obligations grew further as a fraction of GDP, because of the larger real domestic currency equivalent. Thus, the authors calculate that real depreciation enlarged the burden of external debt service in the initial years of the debt crisis by about 2 percent of GDP in Brazil, Mexico, and the Philippines, and even more in Argentina (61).[21]

The central thrust of the Reisen-Van Trotsenburg study was thus to argue that the weakness of domestic fiscal adjustment was a major reason why the debtor countries had not regained creditworthiness despite global economic recovery. Other analysts concurred (e.g., Sachs 1987, 307–9). Dornbusch (1988a) emphasized the budgetary problem imposed by the government's sudden need to mobilize 3 or 4 percent of GDP for debt service that previously was covered by new lending (or by the private sector prior to government assumption of private debt). Enumerating the difficulties of doing so by raising taxes, cutting subsidies, firing government workers, or freezing their wages, he observes that the typical response was to issue new domestic debt or print money. It was thus "no accident that Argentina and Brazil experienced extraordinary inflation rates in the aftermath of the debt crisis" (175).

Dornbusch (1988a) too stressed the interaction of devaluation and the budgetary problem. The need to devalue to gain competitiveness increases the value of debt service in home currency, "produces a larger peso deficit, and hence gives rise to the need for increased inflationary finance" (176). He adds that in the classical hyperinflations, large devaluations were often the precursor to uncontrolled inflation. Krugman (1990, 96) agreed, noting that one reason the early projections of debt recovery had gone wrong was that ". . . just about everyone failed to take into account the fact that devaluation in the debtor countries, intended to help them service their debt, would immediately reduce the dollar value of their GNPs and hence raise the apparent size of the burden."

Analysts who emphasized the internal transfer problem rarely carried through their analysis to the implications for the appropriate amount, if any, of debt forgiveness. Indeed, the logic of the internal transfer problem leads not to forgiveness, but to some form of assured recycling of debt-service payments (such as Williamson's [1988] favored interest capitalization, if concerted new-money packages cannot be mobilized). After all, the problem is that suddenly the government must cover its spending either by domestic taxes or the domestic inflation tax, rather

---

21. Note, however, that the authors' calculation of a similar effect for Venezuela is suspect, because the country's revenue—which is almost wholly dependent on dollar earnings of the state oil firm—rises in terms of bolivar equivalent when the bolivar depreciates, and by much more than any induced increase in the government's domestic bolivar spending on salaries and other noninterest categories.

than by foreign borrowing. If foreign borrowing were still an option, the internal transfer problem would disappear.

Moreover, even if the diagnosis is that the government is bankrupt domestically as well as internationally, and that some part of its debt (domestic and/or foreign) must be forgiven, there is no presumption that the country will be best off in the future if it concentrates the reduction solely on foreign claims. In proper perspective these claims are too small for a plausible extent of forgiveness to make a massive difference to the fiscal situation.

Thus, whereas the Reisen-Van Trotsenburg data depict foreign debt service as preempting about 30 percent of government revenue, the bulk of this outlay is cash flow for principal and the inflationary component of interest, rather than for the real component of interest. With long-term claims of foreign banks typically no more than 50 percent of GDP, and real interest rates no more than 4 percent, the real cost of servicing the debt is only about 2 percent of GDP. With government revenue on the order of 25 to 30 percent of GDP, even the complete elimination of external long-term bank claims provides fiscal relief comparable only to the alternative of an increase in revenue by about 6 to 8 percent. More plausible forgiveness (on the order of one-third, as in Brady Plan experience) means even more limited fiscal relief from foreign debt relief. The real cost (as opposed to cash-flow) drain on the fiscal accounts from external bank debt is thus too small to represent much of a solution to the fiscal problem.

Bacha (1989b) recognizes that the underlying resolution of the fiscal problem has to come from curtailment of noninvestment government spending. He develops a "three-gap" model that adds a "fiscal gap" to the traditional savings and foreign exchange gaps in the two-gap model of growth. The gap approach essentially asks which constraint is binding. In the early development models, growth stemmed from capital accumulation, and the binding constraint was the level of saving for new investment. The subsequent two-gap (Chenery-Bruno) model proposed that if investment required imported equipment, and if export levels were rigidly predetermined (e.g., because of commodity supply or demand restrictions), realized investment and saving could fall short of the level potentially attainable with actual and unrealized domestic saving. Under these circumstances, foreign aid could have a high payoff.

Bacha suggests that a third constraint may be binding: a fiscal constraint. His premise is the idea popular in the 1950s development literature (and once again in the 1980s new economic growth theory) that government investment (e.g., in infrastructure) generates externalities that induce private investment. Because government and private investment are complements, a reduction in government investment reduces private investment and growth.

Under these conditions, Bacha introduces an investment Laffer curve, with investment on the vertical axis and the rate of inflation on the horizontal axis. The fiscal gap is depicted by a dome-shaped curve. In the initial phase of the curve, investment rises as the government mobilizes more resources through the inflation tax. Eventually, however, the curve turns down. Higher inflation begins to reduce the real revenue of the inflation tax, and the country heads toward hyperinflation. Toward the top of the dome, investment that could be mobilized from the standpoint of the government's fiscal role exceeds the amount feasible from the standpoint of the savings and foreign exchange constraints, and the fiscal constraint is not binding. However, at the pathological side of the fiscal Laffer curve, the fiscal gap is the one that is binding.

Importantly, Bacha (1989b) does not see simple debt forgiveness as the solution to the fiscal constraint. He envisions domestic fiscal reform as the centerpiece, because of the need to raise revenue directly (rather than by the inflationary tax) and to cut noninvestment government spending. External debt forgiveness enters only as a potential carrot that might shift the domestic political balance from its existing impasse blocking fiscal reform: "conditional external debt relief might provide the necessary incentive for such fiscal austerity" (13). If debt is forgiven with no link to domestic fiscal reform, the result is likely to be simply a buildup of external reserves and increased inflationary pressure.[22]

The Economics of Debt Forgiveness

Several key debtors were able to cope with the internal as well as external transfer problem without eventually seeking debt forgiveness. These countries included South Korea, Indonesia, and other Asian countries, as well as Chile and Colombia in Latin America. Arguably, the internal transfer problem would have been overcome without debt forgiveness in Mexico and Venezuela as well in the absence of the 1986 collapse in oil prices and the corresponding fall in government revenue.

However, by the late 1980s the debt literature was not focusing on the political or cultural differences that explained why some countries overcame the external and internal transfer problems whereas others did not. Instead, there was an increasing concentration on the potential for debt forgiveness as a solution to the problem, and especially negotiated reduction in debt that could benefit creditors as well as debtors. In a sense this next phase in the literature accepted as a point of departure

---

22. Thus: "Countries facing a fiscal constraint—but not a foreign exchange constraint, neither a savings constraint—thus find themselves in a difficult position to argue for debt relief. They would either lack absorptive capacity, and increase foreign reserves without limit, or would have to resume an inflationary course of growth." (Bacha 1989b, 11)

that either the external transfer problem, or the internal transfer problem, or both, encumbered the country with a "debt overhang" that was detrimental to investment and efficiency.

The common theme in much of the debt-forgiveness literature was the search for analytical demonstration that it could benefit the *creditors* as well as the debtor to forgive some of the debt. Intellectually such analysis was more intriguing than the consideration of simple zero-sum games in which an unrequited transfer to the debtor had to be argued on political or humanitarian grounds. No doubt many analysts also saw a greater chance for a movement of the debt strategy toward forgiveness if banks could be convinced that such a strategy was in their own interest.

At the outset, it is important to clarify terminology. Three different terms have variously been used interchangeably: debt relief, debt reduction, and debt forgiveness. The formal concept in question is the agreement by creditors to reduce the present discounted value of the claim, either by selling it back to the debtor for cash at a discount (buyback), by reducing the principal of the claim (what came to be called the discount bond), or by reducing the interest obligation while maintaining principal intact (par bond).

The official community has adopted "debt and debt-service reduction" as the phrase to identify this concept. Unfortunately, this terminology is inaccurate for the measurement of windfall benefit conferred on the debtor by the creditor through change in the obligation. The reason is that typically there is some element of new money in a Brady deal (or other debt workout). The phrase "debt reduction" leads to the erroneous deduction of any such new money from the other components of the package to arrive at a net debt reduction figure (see the discussion of the World Bank's Debt Reduction Equivalent measure in chapter 5 below). Yet for purposes of estimating the windfall transfer from creditor to debtor, it is the gross reduction (i.e., excluding debt buildup from new money) that is relevant. New money raises both debt and assets, and it is a wash with respect to real burden.

For its part, "debt relief" is a term that became too general to carry a precise meaning of present-value reduction of the burden. In the mid-1980s the term frequently meant no more than rescheduling, and indeed the same practice now characterizes discussions of Russian debt arrangements.

That leaves "forgiveness." For some, this term carries a politically charged overtone because it seems to imply that creditors act out of generosity, whereas instead they should carry some of the blame for the initial lending mistake. Nonetheless, forgiveness is the only technically accurate term to describe the agreement of the creditor in the legal reduction of the present value of the stream of the debtor's obligation. Accordingly, it is the term primarily used in this study for that concept, and as used here it includes forgiveness both of principal and of interest.

The use here should not be interpreted to carry any moral judgment one way or another.[23]

Krugman (1988) examines the conditions under which it is to the creditors' interest to forgive a portion of a country's debt rather than refinance it. By refinancing, the banks essentially purchase an option to retain full face value if the country does well. The trade-off with forgiveness stems from the fact that "the burden of debt distorts the country's incentives, since the benefits of good performance go largely to creditors rather than itself" (253).

It is useful to underscore at the outset that this disincentive effect is central to the Krugman (1988) and Sachs (1986) analyses of debt forgiveness. However, the strength of the disincentive is questionable. Diwan and Rodrik (1992) rightly point out two reasons to doubt the force of the disincentive. First, individual investors do not face a marginal "tax" for the country's debt payment even if the government in some sense does. Second, the size of the transfer, on the order of 2 to 5 percent of GDP, is too small to constitute a serious disincentive (i.e., a marginal income tax of 2 to 5 percent).

Krugman (1988) merely accepts the notion of the disincentive effect, but he might have argued that for a country with debt payment constrained by a fiscal problem, even 2 percent of GDP may seem large. This amount could be the entire fiscal gap, in which case it could indeed be true technically that all of the benefits of the fiscal adjustment go to the creditors. Even this formulation tends to overstate the disincentive case, however. As tax revenue is typically on the order of 30 percent of GDP and expenditure the same, freeing up 2 percent of GDP to pay creditors constitutes a drain of only one-thirtieth on each side of the accounts (i.e., reducing spending by $1/30$ and raising tax revenue by $1/30$). Viewed in this way, once again the marginal disincentive from the debt seems too small to distort country behavior.

Krugman (1988, 254) defines a situation of debt "overhang" as the "presence of an existing 'inherited' debt sufficiently large that creditors do not expect with confidence to be fully repaid." He notes that Krugman (1985) and Sachs (1984) showed that under these circumstances creditors have an incentive to lend even at an expected loss to protect their existing claims, a point already noted in Cline (1983, 74–75)—where it is described as "involuntary lending." Krugman (1988) makes the simplifying assumption that the country's "maximum resource trans-

---

23. In this regard, it is illuminating that the term sometimes used in Spanish America for this concept is *sinceramiento*, or making the debt honest (sincere) by recognizing that only a part of it can be paid. Another term used in the region has been *quita*, release from a debt. It is a matter for linguistic philosophers to consider why Spanish has such a term and English does not. One person's forgiveness is another's *sinceramiento* or *quita*. Each may have part of the truth.

fers are given." Debt overhang then exists if existing debt D exceeds these maximum repayments.

In a two-period model with no uncertainty, existing debt D, maximum repayment x_1 in the present (first) period and x_2 in the next (final) period, and creditor opportunity cost i, the creditors provide new lending of $D - x_1$ in the first period (refinance) only if

$$(1 + i)(D - x_1) < x_2 \qquad (4.4)$$

Otherwise, banks would have to forgive the excess of the left-hand side over the right.

Adding uncertainty, Krugman changes the maximum transfer in the second period to a random variable: x_G in a good state and x_B in a bad state. The probability of the good state is p. The expected present value of repayment in period 2 is

$$\frac{[px_G + (1 - p)x_B]}{(1 + i)} \qquad (4.5)$$

If this amount exceeds outstanding debt less the repayment in the first period $(D - x_1)$, Krugman avers that there will be no liquidity problem so long as the country pays a high enough interest rate. This interest rate is set by the lenders at rate r such that it totally exhausts the payment in the "good" state when applied to the amount lent in the present period

$$L(1 + r) = x_G, \text{ where } L = D - x_1 \qquad (4.6)$$

New lenders would not enter, because the expected value of the lending is only

$$\frac{[px_G + (1 - p)x_B]}{(1 + i)} < L \qquad (4.7)$$

Existing creditors provide "defensive" lending, however, because it "insures that they receive the full present value of the country's potential resource transfer" (258).

From this analysis Krugman concludes that the distinction between illiquidity and insolvency, which featured prominently in the early handling of the debt crisis (and is emphasized in Cline 1983), is "not useful." "If we knew the country could repay the full present value of its debt—or even if the expected value of potential payments were large enough—the country could attract voluntary lending by offering a sufficiently high interest premium" (258).

Krugman's dismissal of the illiquidity-insolvency distinction is easy to misinterpret as implying that there *is* no difference, because solvent borrowers can always raise capital (as seems to be the view of Ahmed and Summers 1992). Instead, Krugman (1988) says whether a country is solvent is "not a well-defined question" because "it is simply unknown whether the country can earn enough to repay its debt" (256–57). But surely the tradition of central bank lending to an illiquid, but not to an insolvent, borrower (Bagehot 1873) never stood on the assumption that the central bank "knows" for sure that the borrower can repay. Judgment calls are what central bankers are paid for. In the LDC debt context, classification of a country as "illiquid" or "insolvent," through such means as debt-service projections, was within this central banking tradition of making a best-judgment call.

Nor does the distinction between illiquid and insolvent disappear by virtue of the country's paying a high enough interest premium to attract lenders, the device Krugman proposes. Indeed, a classic feature of credit rationing is that creditors are scared off by a borrower that signals its desperation by being willing to pay exorbitant rates (Stiglitz and Weiss 1981). Another reason for a meaningful distinction between illiquidity and insolvency is the influence of "many lenders" and the consequential free-rider problem (noted as well by Krugman). In short, there would seem little in the way of a rigorous demonstration in Krugman (1988) or elsewhere that there is no difference between illiquidity and insolvency; instead, the proper qualification is that we (and the International Monetary Fund) cannot know for sure which class the country belongs in. But again, that is why the public pays central bankers and IMF experts: to make such judgments. Nor is the issue purely semantic: Krugman seeks to dispel the illiquid-insolvent dichotomy as a basis for financing versus forgiving, so that he can instead provide an alternative basis—the comparison of the creditors' option value (relending) against distortions caused by the disincentive effect.

Krugman formalizes his argument with a model of debt overhang. In a two-period model, the maximum repayment capacity in the second period is $x_2 = s + z$, where s is a random variable and z reflects the amount of adjustment effort undertaken. Creditors (re)lend outstanding debt less what was repaid in the first period, or $L = D - x_1$, at interest rate r. The debtor maximizes expected utility, which varies positively with $(s + z)$, negatively with repayment ($L[1 + r]$), and negatively with a function $v(z)$ capturing "the dislike of the country for making adjustments that enlarge its future ability to pay creditors" (261)—a curious formulation that presumably means cost of adjustment, barring xenophobia.

The debtor's optimal adjustment is negatively related to the interest rate, as more of the benefits of adjustment leak abroad. The creditors' optimal interest rate depends positively on the fraction of the probability distribution that places second-period payment capacity in a zone sufficiently high to repay the loan fully, and it varies negatively with the adverse effect of the interest rate on country adjustment as weighted by the fraction of the probability distribution covering second-period outcomes less favorable. The model thus formalizes the following intuition: banks strike a balance between relending, to preserve the option of repayment in favorable states, and forgiving (in this case, in the form of a below-market interest rate), to reduce the disincentive effects of repayment and encourage adjustment. The analysis then goes on to demonstrate that, whereas such proposals as conversion of debt to equity shares in exports do not remove the disincentive effect, conversion to purely state-contingent instruments would do so. However, the latter are impractical because the state of nature is difficult to specify.

In his best-known formulation of the debt-forgiveness issue, Krugman (1989a) postulates the existence of a "debt Laffer curve." Shown in figure 4.1, the curve shows expected repayment on the ordinate ("value"), and the face amount of debt on the abscissa. The curve follows the 45° line in an initial phase where debt is low. At point C, a debt overhang begins: the expected repayment begins to fall short of the face value of debt. At a point such as L, the slope of the ray from the origin—which tells the secondary market price of the debt—is less than unity. At some point R the curve actually begins to turn down again, as additional face value of debt imposes such large disincentive effects that the expected total repayment falls rather than rising as the consequence of further lending.

The ideal case for market-based debt reduction is where a country is beyond this turning point (e.g., at a point such as D_0), because reduction of the debt obligation (to D_1) will benefit both the debtor and the creditors. As Krugman puts it, "arguments that debt relief is in everyone's interest are, in effect, arguments that countries are on the wrong side of the debt relief Laffer curve." He judges that whereas many could agree that "hugely indebted" countries such as Bolivia are on the wrong side, "for the major debtors the question is anybody's guess" (265).

Despite its intuitive appeal, in practice the debt Laffer curve provided little justification for debt forgiveness mutually beneficial to creditors and debtors, precisely because few countries *were* on the wrong side of the curve. Implicit or explicit empirical estimates based on the use of the secondary market price as the measure of expected value of repayment have tended to find few debtors in this position. A major reason was simply that creditors had tended to lend the most to the most promising countries rather than the least.

In one well-known call for debt reduction, Sachs and Huizinga (1987) argued that forgiving debt would make both the banks and the debtors better off, because of the disincentive effects of high debt. Yet the Sachs-Huizinga regression equation for secondary market price actually implied that few countries would be on the wrong side of the debt Laffer

Figure 4.1   The debt-relief Laffer curve

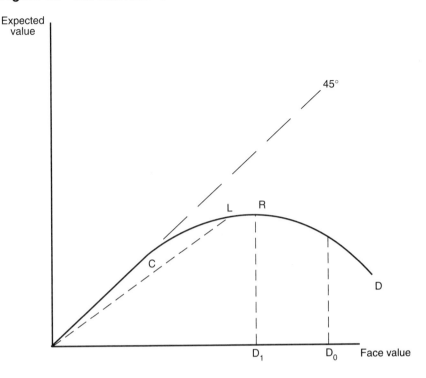

curve.[24] Further empirical analysis tended to confirm explicitly that few major debtors were on the wrong side of the debt Laffer curve. Claessens (1990) estimated secondary market price in the period 1986–88 for 29 highly indebted countries, as a function of the debt/exports ratio

---

24. As shown in Cline (1989c). Thus, Sachs and Huizinga estimated the equation $p_c = 77.2 - 9.6A - 17.2S - 0.15[D/Y \%] + 2.2[g \%]$, where p_c is the secondary market price in cents per dollar, A and S are dummy variables for adverse regulator classification and unilateral suspension, respectively, $D/Y \%$ is external debt as a percentage of GDP, and $g \%$ is GNP growth in percentage points.

If the debt/GDP and growth variables are redefined as ratios (D/Y, g) and the secondary market price is expressed as a fraction p, then the total market value of the debt (V) equals, $V = pD = 0.772D - 0.096AD - 0.172SD - 0.15D^2/Y + 0.022gD$. Assuming average growth of $g = .02$, we have $V = kD - 0.15D^2/Y$, where $k = 0.816$ for nonclassified, nonspending countries and 0.518 for classified, suspending countries.

The debt Laffer curve turns down where the derivative of market value of debt with respect to total face value turns negative. This point occurs where $dV/dD = k - 0.3D/Y$. This critical debt/GDP ratio occurs at $D/Y = 2.72$ for the favorable case of $k = 0.816$, and at 1.83 for the unfavorable case of $k = 0.548$. So even in unfavorable conditions, the debt/ GDP ratio is on the order of 200 percent at the turning point on the debt Laffer curve. For the major debtors such as Argentina, Brazil, Mexico, and Venezuela, the debt/GDP ratio is typically in the range of 30 to 50 percent, far below the critical level. Note that the test in Cline (1989c) was inspired by an early version of Claessens (1990).

and the export growth rate. He then calculated the point where the derivative of market value of debt with respect to face value of debt ($d[pV]/dD$) turned negative. Taking into account differing export growth rates, this turning point tended to be in the range of 700 to 900 percent for the debt/exports ratio. Claessens found that of the 29 countries, only five were on the wrong side of the Laffer curve (Bolivia, Sudan, Peru, Zambia, and Nicaragua). Using a similar approach based on secondary market prices and debt indicators, D. Cohen (1990) found no statistical support for the presence of debtors in a position where reducing the nominal value of debt would increase its market value, even when restricting the sample to highly indebted countries.

The paucity of countries on the wrong side of the Laffer curve might seem to have condemned "voluntary" debt reduction to oblivion; yet under the Brady Plan this approach became the central strategy. Indeed, Krugman (1989a) explicitly argues that for countries located on the (normal) upward-sloping flank of the debt Laffer curve, "market-based" debt reduction schemes could not provide mutual benefit for creditors and debtors any more than unilateral forgiveness could. He maintains that the conditions for mutual gains were the same for unilateral forgiveness as for such schemes as buybacks and debt-equity swaps.

In terms of Krugman's own analysis, there would appear to have been a debatable key assumption.[25] His numerical example specifies a two-period case in which the country owes $100 billion. In the bad state, it earns only $20 billion in foreign exchange in the second period. It has $5 billion in reserves, so it can pay $25 billion in that state. In the good state, its export earnings are $110 billion, and it can repay the full $100 billion (ignoring interest). The probability of the bad state is 2/3 and that of the good state 1/3. Creditors thus expect payment of (2/3)(25) + (1/3)(100) = 50, and the secondary market price is 50/100 = 0.5.

If the country uses its reserves for buybacks reducing debt by $10 billion, the banks that sell receive $5 billion regardless of the second-period state. Those that do not sell receive $20 billion in the bad state and the remaining $90 billion in the good state. The banks that do not sell thus have an expected value of their claim of 20(2/3) + 90(1/3) = $43.33 billion, implying a secondary market price of only 43.33/90 = 0.481. The buyback has *reduced* the secondary market price and moreover made banks worse off (i.e., without the buyback their expected total receipts were $50 billion; with the buyback the expected pool falls to $48.33 billion, or the $5 billion reserves received plus the expected value of remaining claims). Krugman thus concludes that buybacks cannot benefit the creditors—unless there is a disincentive effect of the debt that causes a sufficient rise in the probability of the good state to more than compensate for the loss just illustrated.

---

25. The analytics of buybacks are discussed in greater detail below.

As with many numerical examples, however, this one is subject to reversal by small changes in assumptions. Krugman's conclusion reverses if one makes the reasonable assumption that the country would hold on to its reserves in the second period in the bad state, rather than handing them over along with the $20 billion in export earnings. In this case, the buyback *increases* the secondary market price, and creditors as a group are better off from the buyback.[26] Importantly, by far the bulk of the literature on buybacks expects that they drive *up* the secondary market price rather than reduce it (and indeed many criticize this instrument for this reason, an issue discussed below). As Krugman's debt-equity conclusion is derivative from his buyback demonstration, it too no longer holds.

More fundamentally, however, there are two reasons why market-based debt reduction can provide mutual benefits to creditors and debtors that Krugman's analysis misses.[27] First, there is a potential for collateral ("enhancements") provided by a third, official party to induce the creditors to exchange part of their claim in return for greater certainty (holding expected repayment constant). Importantly, this mechanism need not simply shift the expected loss to the third party if (a) it has inherently senior status, as is arguably the case with the IMF and World Bank, or (b) it has an independent and superior evaluation of the probability distribution of the bad and good states in the second period that is more optimistic than that of the banks. The second reason is that the banks themselves are divided into two groups, one with pessimistic expectations for the second period and the other with optimistic expectations. Both of these influences have been at work in the functioning of the Brady Plan.

One of the most influential advocates of debt relief, Jeffrey Sachs, provided another analysis seeking to demonstrate that relief could benefit both the debtor and its creditors (Sachs 1989g). Unlike Krugman's agnostic position on the empirical relevance of the debt-relief Laffer curve, Sach's view was that the mutual benefits of relief were likely to be more pervasive, and that the debt strategy had relied too much on new lending and too little on "selective use of debt forgiveness" (81).[28]

---

26. The comparison then becomes as follows. Without the buyback, expected payments are $(2/3)(20) + (1/3)(100) = \$46.67$ billion, with secondary market price 0.467. With the buyback, the selling banks receive $5 billion, nominal debt falls by $10.7 billion, and remaining banks have an expected claim of $(2/3)(20) + (1/3)(\$89.3) = \$43.1$ billion. The secondary market price *rises* to $49.1/89.3 = 0.483$.

27. As set forth in Cline (1991) and discussed below in the present study.

28. Even so, he supported case-by-case treatment. Thus: "Certainly, there is no reason to consider writing off the debt of the South Korean economy, nor would the South Koreans choose to risk their international reputation by seeking debt forgiveness. Similarly, Brazil has demonstrated over the past decade the capacity to maintain high growth in the presence of high levels of indebtedness" (81). Ironically, by mid-1993 Brazil was the only major debtor still in large arrears, and the country did not finalize its Brady Plan debt reduction until early 1994.

Like Krugman, Sachs relies on a disincentive effect of existing debt to reach the conclusion of mutually beneficial forgiveness: "since debt forgiveness overcomes economic inefficiencies that hamper the growth of the debtor, it is not surprising that debt forgiveness can be designed in such a way as to improve the position of both the creditors and the debtors" (91).

Sachs applies a two-period model in which bargaining between the debtor and creditors is such that the debtor agrees to repay at most the fraction z of second-period gross domestic product (Q_2). The economy's output is a function F of capital (K), which in the second period depends on first-period capital stock (K_1) plus investment during the first period (I_1). Creditors may collectively decide to forgive a portion of the initial debt stock D, down to the reduced level R. New one-period loans attracted in the first period will not exceed the maximum the country is prepared to repay in the second period, taking account of interest and the existing (reduced) obligations to the original creditors. Thus,

$$D_1(1 + r) < zQ_2 - R = zQ_2[K_1 + I_1(D_1, R)] - R \qquad (4.8)$$

where the bracketed right-hand-side expression indicates that Q_2 is a function of first-period capital plus first-period investment, and the latter in turn is a positive function of the amount of new borrowing in period 1 (D_1) and a negative function of the (reduced) level of original claims. Sachs indicates that there is a maximum value of R^* such that if $R > R^*$, $D_1 = 0$.

The original creditors seek to maximize their ultimate repayment. In period 2 the country pays S, which equals the lesser of full legal claim T and country repayment ceiling zQ_2. The original creditors thus select R so as to maximize $S - (1 + r)D_1$, as this is the amount of period 2 debt service paid less the component going to the new lenders from period 1.

For its part, the country can invest $I_1 = Q_1 + D_1 - C_1$, or resource availability from output and new borrowing less domestic consumption. The country's utility maximization is achieved by max $U(C_1) + bU(C_2)$ subject to $C_1 = Q_1 - I_1$; $C_2 = Q_2 - S = (1 - z)F(K_1 + I_1)$. Note that the term "$b$" captures the time preference discount rate. This maximum occurs where:

$$U'(C_1) = (1 - z)F'(K_1 + I_1)bU'(C_2) \qquad (4.9)$$

Sachs then argues that if the original creditors forgive enough debt so that the remainder will be repaid, the term zQ_2 will no longer be a binding ceiling on payments in period 2. That is, the full (revised) legal obligation will be low enough to be paid without bumping up against this ceiling. As a result, the optimum solution given by equation 4.9 will now be obtained by the same expression but without the initial term

$(1 - z)$ on the right-hand side. With a larger right-hand side, there is a larger left-hand side $U'(C_1)$, and a larger value of first-period marginal utility means lower consumption and higher investment in the first period. What has happened is that the debt forgiveness has removed the marginal tax z on second-period output, thereby encouraging higher investment in the first period.[29] This change, Sachs argues, means that the creditors can receive just as much net as before (i.e., their full legal but revised claim equals what their partial repayment would have been), while the country can be better off than before—achieving higher investment and second-period output and consumption.

The principal shortcoming of the model is that Sachs does not consider plausible levels of z, and therefore fails to recognize that the marginal tax argument is likely to be de minimis—as Diwan and Rodrik (1992) rightly note. Few countries have bank obligations in excess of say 60 percent of GDP. With LIBOR at world inflation plus say 3 percent plus another 1 percent spread, the real interest rate obligation is only about $2\frac{1}{2}$ percent of GDP. That means that z is only 0.025. Surely this is too low a marginal tax rate to affect behavior.

Moreover, as Corden (1989) notes, there is an income effect that works in the opposite direction. Reduction of the fraction of GDP that must be paid to service debt has both a "substitution" and an "income" effect, as do all price changes. Sachs considers only the substitution effect, the distortion shifting incentives toward current consumption and away from investment. Corden notes that the income effect of debt relief would be to make the country richer, thereby raising rather than lowering its current consumption. In addition, in his comment on Sachs, Perry (1989) noted the moral-hazard problem of adopting debt relief based on the existing secondary market price. A country can drive its secondary market price down by issuing confrontational statements, so the secondary market price reflects not only ability but also willingness to pay.

Corden (1989) sets forth an alternative approach to demonstrate the theoretical possibility that debt forgiveness may be mutually beneficial to a debtor and its creditors. His construct requires invocation of the notion that without relief, the debtor could be forced to consumption below minimum subsistence levels. As this condition is extreme and unlikely to apply outside of sub-Saharan Africa, Corden is appropriately (and understatedly) cautious in recognizing that "the conditions required . . . cannot be automatically assumed" (257). Moreover, in the course of his demonstration, Corden actually shows that debt forgiveness may have a *dis*incentive effect on investment.

---

29. As Sachs puts it: "by writing down the debt to a level that will actually be paid, the debt becomes a lump-sum burden, rather than a marginal tax. It thus becomes profitable to invest more" (94).

Figure 4.2 illustrates the Corden analysis. The country has acquired a debt in period 1. In figure 4.2A, output, consumption, and investment are shown on the horizontal axis for period 2. Output and consumption are shown on the vertical axis for period 3, a terminal period collapsing all future periods (therefore requiring no further investment). Production in period 2 is OA'. The country decides how much to consume and how much to invest. Minimum subsistence consumption is OB'.

The consequence of consuming the entire period-2 output OA' is that production in period 3 is low, at only $A'A$. At the other extreme, investing $B'A'$—the maximum amount compatible with minimum consumption requirements—builds up productive capacity for the final period to output level $B'B$. Curve AB is thus a production possibility curve for period 3 in relation to the amount of investment undertaken in period 2.

The country chooses its optimal investment point at the tangency between the "intertemporal utility" curve and the production possibility curve, at point R. At this point, the marginal trade-off between consumption in periods 2 and 3 equals that between investment in period 2 and additional output in period 3.[30]

Now suppose the country's debt service obligation in period 3 from its old period-1 loans amounts to the vertical distance BC. Then its consumption possibility curve in period 3 is now everywhere lower than curve AB by the distance BC. It will consume as little as $A'C'$ in period 3 if it undertakes no investment, or as much as $B'C$ if it invests all period-2 output except enough for subsistence.

Corden then makes his first key point. The presence of the debt payment obligation in period 3 has the effect of reducing consumption potential, thereby raising marginal utility of consumption in period 3. With higher marginal utility, the optimum level of investment in period 2 will be higher—because it will now be socially profitable to transfer some consumption from period 2 to period 3. The result is that the tangency of the consumption possibility curve $C'C$ with the field of intertemporal utility curves will be at a *higher* level of investment—point S with period 2 investment of $S'A'$ rather than $R'A'$—than in the absence of the debt burden. Corden (1989) thus finds that, in the absence of other special considerations,

> debt service obligations in the future would increase investment now, and this can be interpreted to mean that current "adjustment effort" increased. . . . It follows that debt relief would reduce investment and adjustment effort . . . This is the *disincentive effect* of debt relief. (245)

Corden next goes on to introduce a special circumstance that can reverse this conclusion. The special condition is that "there is a mini-

---

30. Corden expresses period 3 values in magnitudes that already take account of any time preference discounting.

Figure 4.2 Debt and investment incentive

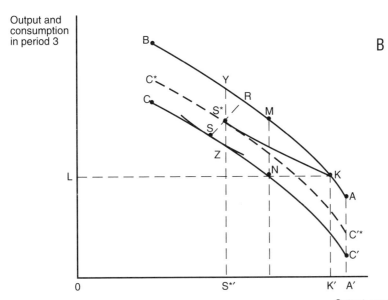

Output and
consumption
in period 3

A

B

C

R

S

A

C′

0   B′   S′   R′   A′

Output, consumption,
and investment
in period 2

Output and
consumption
in period 3

B

C*

C

Y

R

S*

M

S

Z

L

N

K

A

C′*

C′

0   S*′   K′ A′

Output, consumption,
and investment
in period 2

mum consumption level in period 3 and creditors will feel obliged to grant debt relief if it is needed for the country to attain this minimum level" (246). Corden calls such relief "endogenous debt relief." In figure 4.2B, consumption must be at least at a minimum level of OL in period 3. The country's capacity to pay in period 3 is the difference between the output curve AB and the minimum consumption level OL. The consumption possibility frontier in period 3 now becomes $CNKA$, rather than CC'. The range CN involves full debt service. To the right of this point, investment in period 2 is so low, and output in period 3 so low, that there is not enough period-3 output to cover both minimum consumption OL and full debt service OC. At point K, there is complete endogenous debt relief—no debt payment in period 3.

Corden then introduces the possibility of Sachs-type pro-incentive debt forgiveness by noting that under these conditions, the country's highest utility possibility may be at point K.[31] If so, then the country will do best to invest a minimal amount $K'A'$ so it can consume a lot in period 2, achieve minimum subsistence consumption in period 3, and enjoy complete endogenous debt relief. In this situation, creditors will find it attractive to forgive some debt, granting exogenous or intentional relief rather than being forced later to accept endogenous relief.

Exogenous relief may be portrayed as an upward movement of the CC' curve until it coincides with the curve AB at zero repayment obligation in period 3. Along one such debt relief curve $C*C'*$, the country's period-3 utility curve that passes through point K will just be tangent to the relief-adjusted consumption possibility curve, at point $S*$. The country will be indifferent between making minimal investment $K'A'$ and receiving endogenous debt relief, on the one hand, and undertaking far more investment $S*'A'$ in order to boost period-3 consumption from $K'K$ to $S*'S*$, on the other. (The latter choice provides more consumption in period 3 but less in period 2.) Creditors receive payment of $S*Y$, which is less than the full debt obligation ZY. However, if they do not grant this exogenous debt relief, they stand to receive nothing—because complete endogenous relief at point K is the alternative.

As the figure shows, this is a rather extreme binary or knife-edge situation, in which there is either large investment with exogenous relief or minimal investment with endogenous relief. Although the construct succeeds in the task of finding a theoretical situation in which creditors as well as debtors could benefit from planned debt forgiveness, its conditions seem sufficiently contrived that they cast doubt on the relevance of the case (not unlike the practical unlikelihood of a country's being on the wrong side of the debt Laffer curve). In particular, the country must be close enough to a meaningful minimum subsistence level of con-

---

31. However, he also is careful to emphasize that point S may still place the country on a higher utility curve.

sumption that the magnitude of debt repayment is enough to push it below this level.

For Latin American countries with per capita incomes on the order of $2,000 and annual real interest obligations on the order of $2^{1/2}$ percent of GDP, this case is implausible. It is difficult to believe that the difference between disposable per capita income of $2,000 and $1,950 is the difference that will push the country's populace below subsistence income (recall that many African countries have per capita incomes of $300 or less), and moreover that this difference will be perceived by creditors as such a cutoff point. In short, Corden first establishes that as a rule, debt relief will reduce investment incentives rather than increase them. He then goes on to prove that an exception exists. However, it is one of those exceptions that, because of its restrictiveness, is useful primarily in proving the rule.[32]

Helpman (1989a) uses a state-contingent model to examine whether debt forgiveness can benefit both the creditors and the debtor. He implicitly assumes that the internal transfer problem dominates: "A debt problem prevails in the sense that states exist in which the highest possible tax revenue is insufficient to cover debt service payments" (282). Using the operator θ to designate a random productivity shock (implicitly with $\theta > 1$ designating favorable shocks and $\theta < 1$ unfavorable shocks), and defining $E(I)$ as future period output as a function of present investment, t as the tax rate, D as debt, and R as unity plus the interest rate, his two-period model identifies a critical state θ_c as

$$\theta_c(D,I) = \frac{RD}{tE(I)} \tag{4.10}$$

For states of nature $\theta > \theta_c$, full debt service is paid in the second (terminal) period. Otherwise, the country pays only the maximum amount $tE(I)$. The effective tax rate τ for debt service is thus $\tau = t$ for $\theta \leq \theta_c$, and $\tau = RD/\theta E(I)$ for $\theta \geq \theta_c$.

Helpman then considers two cases: with and without international capital mobility. In the first, international capital markets value the "country" as they value the constellation of its firms: on the basis of the present discounted value of their net-earnings streams. In this abstraction, country output $E(I)$ becomes the "number of real equities," each of which is priced at

---

32. Corden (1988a) does seek to generalize the notion of "minimum consumption" beyond African subsistence levels by noting that it is a "simplification for heuristic purposes" denoting "a limit to the ability of a government to transfer resources" and noting that "the perceived minimum may well rise" along with per capita income (634). However, blurring the concept of minimum consumption in this way makes the approach transform into something closer to a model of political willingness to pay (such as that developed in chapter 5 below).

$$q(D,I) \equiv \frac{1}{R} \int_0^\infty [1 - \tau(\theta; D, I)]\theta \, dG(\theta) \qquad (4.11)$$

where $G(\theta)$ is the probability distribution function over the states.

The crucial point in equation 4.11 is that the price of the country's representative equity "declines in debt and increases in investment. It declines in debt because the larger the debt level the higher the tax rates in states with full repayment and the lower the after-tax return on equity" (1989, 288). Helpman then suggests that there can be multiple equilibria.

> When a single financial investor calculates the benefits of an additional unit of equity holding, he takes as given the tax structure and therefore the expected net return on equity. If he expects lower tax rates he is willing to pay a higher price for equity. Higher equity prices lead to higher investment. Higher investment, in turn, reduces tax rates in states of full repayment, thereby justifying the expected high return on equity. This mechanism is responsible for the multiplicity of equilibria. (290)

The result of this situation is that there can be "sharp investment responses to small changes in debt." The Sachs-type investment stimulus from debt forgiveness is thus present.

Helpman also shows, however, that if the economy is cut off from the world capital market and can only invest its domestic saving, and if the country is risk-averse, a Corden-type result occurs: debt forgiveness *reduces* investment. Lower debt means higher consumption in the future, and therefore lower future marginal utility, so long as the utility function is "strictly concave" because "residents of the debtor country are risk averse." Thus:

> An increase in debt reduces the return to equity in every state with full employment. This generates an income effect and a rate of return effect. . . . The net effect on [saving and therefore investment] depends on whether the income effect dominates the rate of return effect or vice versa. If . . . the degree of relative risk aversion is larger than 1, then . . . debt reduction depresses investment [and] creditors do not benefit from debt reduction. (293, 300)

Considering that declining marginal utility (risk aversion) is the standard assumption, this would seem the relevant case for the financially autarkic country. Moreover, because of the general divorce from capital markets during a debt crisis, the case of financial autarky would seem more relevant than the case of internationally mobile capital.

In short, Helpman's answer to the question of whether debt forgiveness can benefit the creditors is: it all depends. If, as suggested here, the capital cutoff case with risk aversion is the most relevant, then his analysis says the answer is in the negative. Even in his "multiple equilibria" case with mobile capital, where a bit of debt reduction prompts a surge in investment, the finding of creditor benefit from forgiveness seems suspect. The reason is that, like Sachs, Helpman does not consider the plausible magnitude for the tax disincentive effect. As noted, the driving force of the multiple equilibria and beneficial effects of debt relief is the effective tax rate τ in equation 4.11. Yet the highest marginal tax rate on GDP that foreign investors could expect as the tribute to be paid for the debt overhang is on the order of, say, 3 to 5 percent—implausibly low to have major disincentive effects.

Dooley (1989b) presents a succinct, intuitive argument as to why an external debt overhang can depress domestic investment. Although he does not explicitly say so, the implication is that creditors could benefit by forgiving some of the debt, because of the resulting rise in domestic investment and improved prospects that the country can service the remaining debt. Dooley bases his case on a single, clear, but questionable assumption: that domestic and foreign investors expect any investments they undertake to incur a loss of value similar to that already present for external debt as measured by the discount in secondary market prices. He argues:

> Since a new credit cannot be convincingly differentiated from existing credits, potential investors must assume that the market value of their new claims will immediately become identical to the value of existing claims. . . . Thus, the fact that claims on new capital will trade at roughly the same discount as existing claims has the result of restraining real investment. (75)

This view would appear to have been flawed in principle and, with the benefit of hindsight, in practice. In principle, it was evident even in the mid-1980s that new direct investment was not a perfect substitute for existing syndicated loan claims. Even new loans were not perfect substitutes for the old, tainted debt; there were numerous examples (including some formal components of reschedulings) where "new money" had shorter terms, higher interest rates, and implicitly some degree of seniority over preexisting long-term bank debt. Bonds typically enjoyed de facto seniority and in most cases were fully serviced even at the depths of the debt crisis. Investments in local stock markets generated equity holdings that were dispersed in ownership and were unlikely candidates for invitation to a creditor's forgiveness pledging campaign. Although Dooley also appealed to the argument of fear of future taxation to spread the losses to new investors, he did not address the mechanisms that could conceivably place tax rates at levels that would suddenly reduce the net values of these assets to the low ranges observed on secondary market prices of debt. Thus, it was never very plausible that a new limited bond issue by Venezuela's oil company, let alone an investment by General Motors in plant expansion in Brazil or an American depository receipt purchased in New York on equities traded in the

São Paulo stock exchange, would "immediately become identical to the value of existing claims" (Dooley 1989b, 75).

Hindsight has confirmed what could have been expected in principle. Thus, in 1990–92, net capital inflows into Brazil amounted to $16 billion (ECLAC 1992). In the same period, the secondary market price of Brazil's external debt to banks averaged 30 cents on the dollar (World Bank 1993a, 43). A significant portion of this capital went into a booming domestic stock market. This record is simply inconsistent with the hypothesis that investors expected any dollar placed in Brazil to fall immediately in value to only 30 cents. In sum, although the Dooley premise offered a breathtaking shortcut to the logical conclusion that debt forgiveness would spur investment, it was questionable from the outset and would seem to have been refuted by investor behavior by the early 1990s.

Kenen (1989) proposes another analytical basis on which forgiveness of debt might benefit both the creditor and the debtor. Appealing to the Eaton-Gersovitz (1981) approach in which a debtor repudiates when costs of servicing exceed expected benefits, Kenen identifies the possibility of mutually beneficial debt forgiveness when "it induces the debtor to postpone or renounce the repudiation of its remaining debt."

In Kenen's model, the debtor plans to repudiate in year k. The country holds reserve assets that pay the same interest rate r as its debt but in addition provide another effective component of return u reflecting benefits of import smoothing and exchange rate stabilization. At the date of debt repudiation, creditors are able to seize fraction α of these reserves. In addition, there is a terms-of-trade loss from repudiation (because of creditor harassment of trade), but this loss is smaller the later the date of repudiation. Finally, the model incorporates "income-reducing fiscal effects" along the lines of the Sachs-type investment depressant, and these negative effects rise with the size of debt-service payments.

The essence of the model is that, in view of the balance between the cost of debt service and the efficiency (fiscal) costs of the debt burden, on the one hand, and the benefits of retaining full claim to reserves and avoiding terms of trade loss on the other, there is an optimal year k for the country to default. Creditors can calculate this optimal year as well, and they can increase the expected value of claims by forgiving some debt such that the country's optimal repudiation date is postponed to $k + m$ (permitting m additional years of debt service to be received by the banks). Because k will tend to be earlier in cases in which the country can default with minimal penalty, Kenen concludes that "debt forgiveness will be mutually beneficial when the debt is large compared to the penalties for repudiation."

This conclusion essentially says that creditors will recognize that half a loaf is better than none. However, the analysis raises several questions.

The foremost is that it is in the "optimizing deadbeat" strand of the literature, an approach that is incapable of explaining the behavior of countries such as Chile and South Korea that have fully serviced their debt rather than seeking to escape responsibility for it. Even within the context of this optimal repudiation school, it is unclear whether there would be a very large group of countries that have large debt relative to penalties for repudiation. Ironically, within the Eaton-Gersovitz framework adopted by Kenen, this group should be a null set, because creditors would not have lent the money in the first place in view of the limited penalty potential.

Williamson (1988, 1989) provided perhaps the most practical and well-conceived formulation of voluntary debt reduction as well as the formulation closest in spirit to the Brady Plan actually adopted several months later.[33] Williamson first reviewed the difficulties in implementing a comprehensive scheme in which official entities would buy back debt from creditors at a discount and pass along the savings to the debtors. He noted the problems of inducing banks to participate (free-rider problem), determining country eligibility and repurchase price (with the risk of penalizing countries that had made major efforts to service debt), allocating public funds to countries not necessarily the most in need from a poverty/equity standpoint, and introducing moral hazard (incentive for a country to modify its action to depress the price of its debt).

Williamson suggested that these difficulties implied there could be more practical potential in voluntary debt reduction mechanisms rather than in comprehensive schemes. He identified two basic reasons for voluntary debt reduction. The first was a variant of the debt Laffer curve, wherein the marginal tax disincentive was not of the Sachs-Krugman type (investment depressing) but instead was an effective "tax" on foreign-exchange availability by virtue of the practice of estimating successive "new-money package" needs in light of observed export performance. That is, if a country succeeded in raising its exports, its only reward might be that it would be extended a smaller amount of "concerted lending" in the next new-money package. However, this effect is an argument for coordinated relending under different principles, not an argument for forgiveness. Williamson did cite the argument by Ize and Ortiz (1987) as a further variant on the debt Laffer curve: only with formal debt relief would the debtor country's citizens have enough confidence that the situation had stabilized to be willing to repatriate their flight capital. Once again, however, Ize and Ortiz do not necessarily call for forgiveness, and the alternative of assured refinancing would presumably provide much of the desired stabilization of

---

33. Precursors of the voluntary forgiveness approach emphasizing buybacks and exit bonds appear in Cline (1988a), Cline (1987), and Bergsten, Cline, and Williamson (1985).

expectations.[34] Indeed, as noted in chapter 5, statistical analysis of the Mexican Brady deal by Claessens, Oks, and van Wijnbergen (1993) implies that multiyear rescheduling would have done just as well as debt forgiveness in restoring confidence.

Williamson's second argument for voluntary debt reduction was the same one noted above (and set forth in detail in the discussion of figure 4.4 below): there are different classes of banks with different perceptions of the value of their claims. In a buyback operation, "the country has bought out the pessimists at a price which the optimists (and presumably the country) believe to be unrealistically low, thereby leaving those who remain better off" (1988, 18).[35] With a framework established for the logic of voluntary debt forgiveness, Williamson then considered the modalities. He favored the facilitation of buybacks (e.g., suspension of bank "sharing" clauses) and a program of exit bonds with World Bank guarantees. In reply to the critique that the latter (a close approximation of the Brady Plan)[36] is a public bailout of the banks, Williamson correctly argued the essence of what may be called "risk-compensated forgiveness" (discussed below): "this operation is designed to leave the welfare of the banks largely unchanged: acceptance of risk by the public sector persuades banks to exchange a high-risk, high-return asset for a low-risk, low-return asset" (38). Williamson also stressed the importance of making publicly supported debt reduction contingent on favorable policy performance, including that already accomplished by a growing list of Latin American countries (xii–xiii).

In addition, Williamson proposed the use of interest capitalization as a means of going beyond debt reduction, given that a mere reduction in the balance sheet obligation would contribute only modestly to a reduction in the outward transfer of resources. As it turned out, however, the return to large inflows of capital to Latin America in the early 1990s meant that the resource transfer problem largely disappeared or even became a problem of excessive *inward* transfer of resources. Brady Plan debt reductions were important in contributing the confidence neces-

---

34. The crux of the Ize-Ortiz argument is that citizens may fear it is easier for the government to "default" on its domestic debt by "a discrete devaluation which, by raising the price level, erodes the real value of domestic debt" than to default on its foreign debt (1987, 312). However, this is a curious concept of default, and it is not even valid where domestic interest rates are uncontrolled and can incorporate a risk premium against devaluation. The authors do not draw Williamson's inference of advisability of external debt reduction but rather seek to explain the coexistence of inflows of loans to the public sector and outflows of private capital.

35. The controversial issue of buybacks is discussed in detail below.

36. The Brady Plan involved World Bank and IMF loans specifically dedicated to collateralization of principal and of interest on a limited-term, rolling basis, rather than a full guarantee undertaken by the international institution itself.

sary to this reversal in some cases (especially Mexico), but not in all.[37] As discussed in chapter 8, the capital inflows in the early 1990s turned out to be from vehicles strictly different from the creditor banks (portfolio inflows, bonds, direct investment), obviating any need for interest capitalization.

Diwan and Rodrik (1992) have provided a theoretical analysis of debt forgiveness with conditional official support that is perhaps the most comprehensive attempt to formalize the analytics of a Brady Plan deal. Yet some of the key elements in their treatment are questionable. The central elements of their analysis include the following. Countries need new money to warrant undertaking the short-term costs of adjustment. Banks need the comfort of IFI (international financial institution) conditionality for assurance of country adjustment to be willing to provide either more new money or confer greater forgiveness than they would extend on their own. For their part, IFIs can extend new money without being fleeced by the banks so long as the banks in exchange reduce their claims on the country, thereby improving the market value of the IFI's own portfolio of claims on the country.

Diwan and Rodrik first convincingly criticize the standard assumption of most of the debt-forgiveness literature: that the debt overhang depresses investment through a disincentive effect. They argue:

> There is no compelling conceptual reason to believe that an aggregate ''tax,'' if it exists, will be internalized in private investment behavior: from the perspective of an individual investor, the aggregate transfer to creditors is an exogenous constant and is thus unaffected by the investor's decisions. . . . Furthermore, the importance of the overhang ''tax'' on investment is much in doubt empirically. From all indications, both the average and marginal tax rates implied by debt service are small. Net transfers to creditors rarely exceed 4 to 5 percent of gross national product (GNP). . . . We find that, on average, less than two cents of any dollar increase in income is actually captured by creditors. (6)

The authors instead see the influence of the debt overhang on investment as working through the liquidity problem: lack of access to international capital markets reduces investment below normal levels. They do not say so explicitly, but the implication is that the overall investment depressing effect is relatively limited—as the bulk of investment is primarily from domestic rather than foreign saving.

With little or no Sachs-Krugman ''tax'' disincentive from a debt overhang, Diwan and Rodrik must search elsewhere for the mechanics of debt forgiveness mutually beneficial to creditors and the debtor. The lever they need comes in the form of IFI conditionality. They first cite

---

37. Thus, capital reflows were also large to Brazil, which was slow in negotiating a Brady Plan. However, the inflows were at higher, ''junk-bond'' rates of return; and even in the Brazilian case, the largest increase in reflows coincided with announcement in principle of the Brady agreement.

World Bank studies of adjustment lending to the effect that in the first two years of a typical IMF adjustment program, country growth falls 5 percentage points below trend, as evidence of a "cost of adjustment."[38] Their analysis then focuses on the conditions under which the debtor will undertake adjustment.

In their model, if the country adjusts, its income rises from Y in the first period to $Y(1 + \theta)$ in the second (final) period. The cost of adjustment is K. Creditors have initial claims of D. They confer debt reduction of B and new loans of L. If the country defaults, the creditors can exact a penalty equal to fraction ϕ of the country's income. The world interest rate plus unity equals R. With IFI conditionality, the government's decision problem is:

$$\text{Max } W = U(C_1) + \beta C_2, \text{ subject to:}$$
$$C_1 = Y + L - K, \text{ if adjust; } Y, \text{ otherwise;} \qquad (4.12)$$
$$C_2 = \max \left[Y(1 + \theta) - R(D - B + L), (1 - \phi)Y(1 + \theta) \right] \text{ if adjust;}$$
$$\qquad \max \left[Y - R(D - B), (1 - \phi)Y \right] \text{ otherwise}$$

Thus, in the first period the country can consume income plus new borrowing minus the adjustment cost, if it adjusts; or income alone if it does not. If the country adjusts, in the second period it can consume income higher by proportion θ, less its repayment obligations of $R(D - B + L)$; or else it can default and consume all of the (enhanced) second-period income except for the fraction creditors can seize (ϕ). If the country does not adjust, then its second-period consumption is limited to income without the increased production potential from adjustment, deducting debt repayments if it pays or the default penalty if it does not.

Without the help of IFI conditionality, banks make (smaller amounts of) new loans that are not contingent on adjustment. The country's decision is the same except that its first-period consumption can be as high as $Y + L$ even *without* adjustment (rather than just Y), whereas its second-period consumption under conditions of repayment will then be $[Y - R(D - B + L)]$. In contrast, IFI conditionality means that new loans L are not forthcoming without adjustment.

Diwan and Rodrik define the presence of a debt overhang as a situation in which the country will choose not to repay the debt in full in the absence of adjustment and/or debt reduction, because the cost of repayment exceeds the penalty of default: $RD > \phi Y$. However, the rate of return to investment in adjustment exceeds the international interest rate, so the country will adjust if the amount of new lending L is large enough. Alternatively, the country can also be induced to adjust if the creditors extend debt reduction B, because second-period output will be

---

38. By comparison, the shortfall from trend is an average of 2.8 percent in the two years before the adjustment program and 2.1 percent in the third and fourth years of a program (Diwan and Rodrik 1992, 9).

larger as a consequence of the reduced implicit investment tax. The catalytic power of IFI conditionality is that it makes new lending conditional on adjustment. As a result:

> Conditionality enlarges the set of (B,L) combinations under which the debtor government finds it advantageous to adjust. . . . [It] alters the cost-benefit calculus of the government, which has now to compare the cost of adjustment against the cost of having to give up external financing. When the choice is between adjusting with new money and not adjusting without new money, it will take a lower amount of external financing to purchase adjustment. (Diwan and Rodrik 1992, 15)

Although the authors do not explicitly say so, their conditionality model amounts to a stick rather than a carrot. Without conditionality, the country can take the money (enjoying consumption $Y + L$ in period 1) and run (at a loss of ϕY in the second period). With conditionality, the country cannot take the money L unless it adjusts—because the creditors, marshaled to concerted action by the IFI, will not lend otherwise.

In the model, there is a role for both new money and forgiveness. New money alleviates the short-term adjustment cost, but "renders overhang more likely down the line" (14). Debt reduction "works against the overhang but has uncertain effects on the incentive to adjust" (14).[39]

With their analytical construct in place, Diwan and Rodrik (1992) then examine the potential for creditor-debtor deals. They assume that the maximum debt service the country will pay is fraction α of income. For a given bank package offering debt reduction B and new money L in return for adjustment, bank payoff amounts to

$$\pi(B,L) = \alpha Y(1 + \theta) - RL, \text{ so long as } L \geq L^* \qquad (4.13)$$

where L^* is the minimum new lending necessary to induce adjustment. The first right-hand term is the ceiling share of second-period income allocated to debt service; the second is principal and interest on the new money repayable in the second period.

It is at this point that the Diwan-Rodrik analysis seems to go awry. The authors seek empirical implementation of their model. They argue that θ is "in the range of 10 to 40 percentage points" for the permanent increase in output from adjustment (19). This range makes sense only in terms of a two-period model. Obviously, output cannot rise by 40 percent in the first year after adjustment, so in a continuous annual (as

---

39. Note that in practice, however, it is difficult to envision why a single-actor bank would both forgive old debt and lend new money. The act of writing down the debt tends to be associated with disengagement from activity in the country. Coexistence of the two modes requires the banking community dichotomy examined below. Thus, in the Brady Plan arrangements to date, few banks have selected *both* types of options.

opposed to two-period) formulation such proportionate increases must refer to a present-value concept.

The authors "take R to be 1.1," presumably meaning a 10 percent interest rate for one period (19). They use their regression estimates of debt servicing by highly indebted countries in the period 1982–90 to estimate α at 2 percent. They conclude that adjustment packages between banks and the debtor alone are unlikely. Thus, "when α is 2 percent and adjustment provides a 20 percent permanent increase in the debtor's income, the largest increase in exposure banks are willing to accept during the whole adjustment period is 0.36 percent of the country's GDP" (Diwan and Rodrik 1992, 19), or only about one-fifth of that amount annually as the adjustment period is typically spread over five years. Such flows will be too small to induce adjustment.

It would appear that there is an important mistake in this analysis: the intermixture of empirically estimated parameters applicable to normal annual flows, on the one hand, and conceptual parameters designed for a simple two-period model in which all future years are collapsed into a single second period (i.e., a stock), on the other. Instead, if α^* is the empirical estimate based on annual data, the proper value of α for application to the two-period model should be $\alpha^*/(r - g)$ percent of one year's GDP, where r is the creditor's discount rate and g is the country's growth rate. The reason is that Y in the second period of the two-period model is the discounted present value of all future years of annual income Y^*.[40]

Suppose $r = 0.08$, $g = 0.04$, and $\alpha^* = 0.02$. Second-period "income" telescopes to $Y_0/(.08 - .04) = 25Y_0$, where Y_0 is the initial annual GDP. Without adjustment, the banks can obtain a ceiling of $.02 \times 25Y_0 = 0.5Y_0$ in terminal period repayment. If adjustment raises income by proportion $\theta = 0.2$, the banks' maximum repayments rise to $.02 \times 25Y_0 \times 1.2 = 0.6Y_0$. The increment of their potential claim is $0.1Y_0$, or about thirty times as large as the Diwan-Rodrik interpretation of the empirical estimate $(0.0036Y_0)$. Given that initial exposure will typically be no more than, say, $0.5Y_0$, the adjustment prospect is enough to make banks increase their exposure by 20 percent—a result that should be no surprise since the impact of adjustment is also to raise the economic base against which their claim is levied by 20 percent. In short, the Diwan-Rodrik analysis of why banks cannot lend enough new money to stimulate adjustment without IFI help would appear to have reached the wrong conclusion because of a treatment of flows as if they were stocks. As discussed below, Bulow and Rogoff (1988a) seem to have made the same slip in their analysis of buybacks.

---

40. If there were no growth, the present value of an infinite stream of income of Y^* annually would be Y^*/r. With growth at rate g, the "net" discount rate in the denominator becomes $r - g$.

IFI conditionality can still come to the rescue if the problem is not that banks cannot lend enough to induce adjustment, but that free-rider problems impede a new-money package without the organizing force of the IFI. Diwan and Rodrik thus probably reach the right conclusion about the need for IFI conditionality, but for the wrong reason in terms of formal analysis.

Their formal analysis also takes them in another questionable direction. They treat IFI claims on the country as just as shaky as bank claims. As a result, they conclude that after a (Brady) debt reduction deal, there must still be a debt overhang and the secondary market price must still be well below unity. The reason is simply that otherwise, the IFI will have fleeced the banks. That is, the banks forgive fraction B/D, whereas the IFI keeps its initial claims intact. The only way for the IFI to achieve symmetrical losses with the banks is for its losses on IFI new money proportionately to equal those experienced by the banks. Such a loss can only arise if (a) the postdeal secondary market price is still at a substantial discount, and (b) the IFI enjoys no seniority. Hopefully, however, neither of these conditions obtains.

Once again it would seem that the model's mathematics get in the way of reasonable institutional interpretation, this time with no redeeming extraneous influence to salvage the conclusion. The prospects are excellent that the IMF and World Bank will lose nothing on their loans to Mexico; most of the banks lost 35 percent. Essentially the IFIs do have senior creditor status. Indeed, because of this status, they can play the role of providing collateral at minimal expected cost, as suggested in the analysis shown in figure 4.4 below. The conclusion that the IFIs must lose from a debt reduction deal is thus dubious, as is its corollary that the country must still be in debt overhang after the deal.[41]

More fundamental issues in the Diwan-Rodrik analysis include its adoption of the "optimizing deadbeat" framework (as discussed above with respect to the Eaton-Gersovitz and Kenen analyses); its assumption that adjustment comes only with external help, whereas the experience of Latin America in the late 1980s would suggest that adjustment provides its own reward with or without external help; and formulation

---

41. The essential problem is to treat all capital flows, and in particular both IFI and commercial bank syndicated long-term loans made before the debt crisis, as perfect substitutes. This mistake is the same one made by Dooley (1989b), as discussed above. Note also that it is in the treatment of the secondary market price that the slip intermixing stocks and flows becomes most transparent. Thus, the authors set the secondary market price at $\alpha Y/RD$, or the ratio of second-period retrievable claim to second-period repayable debt. However, applying the empirically estimated $\alpha^* = 0.02$ would mean that, with $R = 1.08$, a country with face value of external debt of $0.5Y_0$ would have a secondary market price of .037 ($= .02Y_0/[1.08 \times .5Y_0]$). Yet not even Bolivia managed to drive its secondary market price to less than 4 cents on the dollar.

of the main analysis in a "single actor bank" mode whereas diverse actors are a key to the problem.

Evidence on Investment Disincentives

In the late 1980s, debt theorists were postulating that the debt overhang depressed investment in debtor countries, and thus that debt forgiveness could revive investment and potentially benefit the debtor as well as the creditors. By the early 1990s, analysts were beginning to test the investment-depression argument empirically.

Warner (1991) estimates econometric equations for investment as a share of GDP in 13 heavily indebted countries prior to 1981, with terms of trade, the world (US) real interest rate, and industrial output in advanced countries as the explanatory variables. He then uses the equation to predict investment ratios for the period 1982–89. A major shortfall of actual from predicted investment would be required to provide evidence for the argument that the debt overhang depresses investment. Warner finds, instead, that for the 13 countries as a group, investment in 1982–89 systematically exceeded the predicted level. For individual countries, only Argentina and Nigeria showed actual investment consistently lower than predicted. Warner concludes that the debt crisis did not cause the collapse of investment. Instead, he gives great weight to the decline in terms of trade and the rise in world interest rates in the 1980s.[42]

Similarly, despite his earlier (D. Cohen 1990) enthusiasm for a scheme in which banks would annually forgive a fraction of debt service based on the hypothetical equilibrium (but not observed) secondary market price, Cohen (1993) finds only a minimal role for the debt crisis as a cause of the collapse in investment in debtor countries in the 1980s.[43] He first estimates a cross-country regression for the investment/GDP ratio as a function of per capita income, population growth, primary school enrollment, the export/GDP ratio, and inflation. He then introduces alternative measures of the debt burden for the period 1982–87 and finds

---

42. As analyzed in chapter 5, although some argue that the decline in terms of trade in turn was caused by the debt crisis as debtors flooded markets with their commodity exports in an attempt to service debt, the statistical evidence does not support this thesis.

43. In the earlier article, Cohen statistically rejected the argument of location of debtors on the wrong side of the debt Laffer curve, but instead based his call for forgiveness squarely on the Dooley argument of inefficiency caused by the divergence between the secondary market price and face value—which in turn implied inefficiently low capital investment in the debtor country. Cohen proposed annual rather than once-for-all forgiveness as an incentive to adjustment. However, it is unlikely that this short-leash approach would have generated the positive psychological boost achievable by seeming to deal with the debt problem once and for all, an effect that seems to have been important in at least the Mexican case.

them all statistically insignificant. A large stock of debt fails to predict low investment in the 1980s.

Cohen then refines his tests by using pre-1982 equations to predict investment, consumption, and government spending and then obtaining the "surprise" residual of total spending over GDP (and thus the trade deficit). The surprise residual trade balance serves as an explanatory variable for the surprise residual in the investment equation. In this manner, and after dividing his sample to concentrate on highly indebted countries, Cohen (1993) finally estimates a "crowding-out" coefficient of 0.35 for rescheduling countries. That is, an extra dollar of transfer abroad by these countries reduced domestic investment by 35 cents. He concludes:

> This shows that a service of the debt equal to 3 percent of GNP (which is almost an upper bound to the adjustment which was experienced in the 1980s) would reduce investment by 1 percent of GNP below the financial-autarky level. If one trusts this analysis, one sees that writing down the debt would not foster investment very much (if it was not accompanied by a large inflow of foreign capital). (439)

The minimal size of the investment-depressant effect of debt overhang found by Warner (1991) and by Cohen (1993) is consistent with the critique of the concept by Diwan and Rodrik (1992) on grounds that the implicit tax is too small to affect investment behavior, as discussed above.

An Alternative View: Risk-Compensated Forgiveness

The empirical weakness of the investment disincentive hypothesis suggests that its case for mutually beneficial forgiveness was limited. Instead, as suggested above, there is a more plausible analytical basis for "risk-compensated" debt forgiveness in which the creditors receive collateral "enhancements" in return for reducing their nominal claims. This approach requires no special assumptions about reduction in any perceived marginal tax on new investment. It draws instead on the potential to redistribute the rent implicit in the difference between the secondary market price and a higher, more realistic long-term expected value of the debt. Importantly, the actual international strategy that developed—the Brady Plan—involved precisely the type of "risk-compensated" forgiveness outlined here. Indeed, it is a curiosity of the literature that, with the important exception of Williamson (1988, 1989) as reviewed above, it focuses almost entirely on unrequited forgiveness, whereas practical policy implementation adopted the risk-compensated approach instead.

Figure 4.3 Market-oriented debt reduction

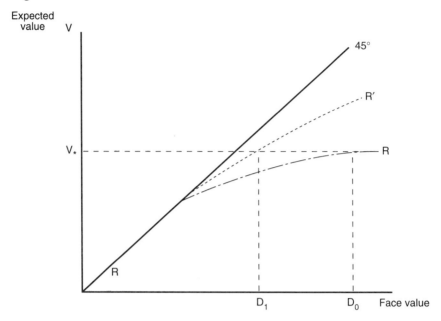

As suggested above, a positive-sum game from forgiveness arises if there is a third party with senior claim status that can provide collateral enhancements for reformulated debt, or if there is a dichotomy between one class of banks that is pessimistic about the country's future and another that is optimistic. Cline (1991) uses the diagram shown in figure 4.3 to show how the first of these two influences achieves collateralized debt reduction that makes the debtor better off without making the creditors' risk-adjusted position worse.

Banks hold claims with face value of D_0 and expected, or market, value of V^*, at a point on the upward-sloping flank of a debt Laffer curve. The IMF and World Bank provide resources that the country uses to purchase US Treasury zero-coupon bonds or other assets to provide partial collateral for conversion bonds. The banks accept conversion bonds with face value of D_1, conferring debt reduction of D_1D_0. Because of the presence of collateral, the debt Laffer curve shifts upward from RR to RR'. The banks are just indifferent between the previous situation and the debt reduction scheme so long as expected value holds constant at V^*. However, the composition of this expected value involves a higher probability of repayment and lower face value after the arrangement, because of the presence of the collateral (and, presumably, in part because the adjustment commitment and normalization associated with the package raise the probability of repayment). Debt reduction with enhancements thus provides gain to the debtor with no loss to the creditors, or with some gain to the creditors if they share in the potential rent and if debt reduction is slightly smaller than $D_1 D_0$ but the enhancements are the same. This analysis does require the assumption that banks are at least risk-neutral; highly risk-prone banks might not be interested in the exchange of claims for security. If banks are risk-averse, the scope for mutual gain is even greater.

The senior creditor status of the international agencies means that they do not face the same risk of holding claims on the country that the banks faced; or, alternatively, the international agencies have a "proper" diagnosis of future payment capacity of the country that is more sanguine than the banks' view (in part because their own participation and the consequential reaching of a deal can boost confidence and prospects). Thus the positive-sum game shown in figure 4.3 is not merely disguising a zero-sum game by hiding the transfer of losses to the third party.

The exchange of nominal claims for greater security depicted in figure 4.3 is only one reason for Brady Plan arrangements. Another reason is a dichotomy between pessimistic banks interested primarily in early exit and more optimistic banks intending to remain active in the country over the longer term (Bergsten, Cline, and Williamson 1985). Figure 4.4 illustrates the potential for debt reduction from this standpoint. Here, there are two classes of banks. Class A, holding claims of D^A_0, have a sharp dropoff in the slope of their perceived debt Laffer curve, R^A_0. (Note that this curve depends on the stock of claims of group B.) They are willing to sell on the secondary market at a price given by the slope of angle α_0. Banks in class B, holding claims of D^B_0, have a much steeper debt Laffer curve, R^B_0 (which in turn depends on the stock of class A claims). Internally they price the debt at the slope of β_0, where $\beta_0 > \alpha_0$.

Because of regulatory limits and concern about portfolio diversification, class B banks do not buy up debt from class A banks even though in their view its unit value (tan β_0) exceeds the secondary market price at which class A banks are willing to sell (tan α_0). However, a Brady Plan package can add enhancements such that the perceived debt Laffer curve shifts upward for the class A banks and they are held indifferent at V^*_A by a compensating reduction in nominal claims by the amount $D^A_1 D^A_0$, similarly to the same process in figure 4.3. For their part, the class B banks choose the new-money option in the package rather than debt reduction.[44] With the rise in the debt Laffer curve perceived by class B banks, caused by the reduction in the stock of class A bank claims, class B banks are able to hold their expected loss constant at x even though after lending new money they have a larger exposure than before, because the same vertical gap from the 45° line occurs further out along the nominal debt axis.

---

44. For example, in the Venezuelan case the new-money option attracted a substantial bloc of banks.

**Figure 4.4 Expected value (V) and face value (D) of debt
by bank group (A, B)**

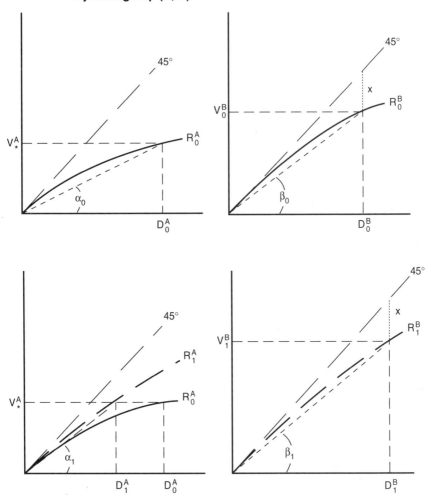

In the final equilibrium, the secondary market price is higher, at $\alpha_1 > \alpha_0$.[45] The package may or may not eliminate the wedge between the two classes' perceived secondary market price for uncollateralized debt ($\alpha_1 \leq \beta_1$).

In sum, consideration of participation by a (nearly) risk-exempt third party as guarantor, and/or of different risk perception among different classes of banks, provides a basis for a positive-sum game of (enhanced)

---

45. Note that the secondary market price for unconverted debt remains the slope of the ray to the original debt Laffer curve, not the (higher) curve for collateralized debt. Actually there should be some upward shift even in the uncollateralized curve, so long as debt reduction by class A banks exceeds increased exposure by class B banks (and as a further consequence of general confidence effects).

debt reduction along the Brady Plan lines. This conclusion contradicts the Krugman view that such arrangements cannot do any better than unilateral forgiveness and its zero-sum consequences except when the country is on the wrong side of the debt Laffer curve.

The Buyback Controversy

One of the most heatedly debated aspects of voluntary debt reduction has been whether debtor countries benefit from repurchases of their outstanding debt at low prices on the secondary market. In practice many countries have been keen to do so, as they consider the leveraged reduction of liabilities an attractive opportunity.[46]

Thus, if the secondary market price is 50 cents on the dollar and the claim has an interest rate of LIBOR plus 1 percent ($r + 0.01$), a dollar invested in repurchase has a return of $2r + 0.02$, so long as the alternative is eventually to pay the full obligation rather than ignore it. Indeed, the principal limitations on buybacks have been availability of cash and the institutional obstacle of sharing clauses in syndicated bank loans that pose a legal risk of intervention by third-party banks, rather than a lack of attractive return to the debtor.

Yet some analysts believe the debtors were seriously misguided to seek discounted buybacks. The underlying rationale of this line of reasoning seems to be that the debt is worthless anyway, so why pay even a low price to shed it. One manifestation of this argument is the fear that buybacks will drive up the secondary market price. Yet it is surely the case that if the country is ever to return to capital market normalcy, it is *desirable* for the secondary market price to return to par.

The mistaken assumption implicit in the critique is that the country somehow "possesses" the discount in the current market price as a permanent windfall gain of liability reduction, and that eroding this windfall involves an unnecessary sacrifice. However, because creditors retain legal claim to the full face value of the debt, the temporary windfall present in a deep secondary market discount cannot be evaluated without a more complete analysis of future scenarios. Specifically, permanently securing this windfall reduction of liabilities is likely to be achieved only at the expense of a costly isolation from the international economy, with the implication of net losses in the country's overall economic prospects.

Bulow and Rogoff (1988a) provide a formal statement of the critique of buybacks. They conclude that buybacks even at existing secondary mar-

---

46. Thus, as noted in chapter 2, Brazilian state firms eliminated nearly $7 billion of external debt in 1988 alone through discounted buybacks. Similarly, Mexican private external debt largely evaporated in the mid-1980s as firms took advantage of the opportunity to strengthen balance sheets through discounted buybacks.

ket prices (in their parlance, "average" debt value) are a costly mistake for the debtor, and that instead the country should be prepared to pay no more than the "marginal" value of its debt, which the authors argue is much lower.[47] Their model assumes that the country has investments that will generate income I; that banks have claims D that come due "as soon as I is realized"; but that "the most they can force the country to pay is qI, where $0 < q \leq 1$" (684). If the country defaults, creditors can collect only $qI < D$. The authors define $v(D)$ as the secondary market value of the debt with face value D. The marginal value of debt, $v'(D)$, or the amount by which market value of outstanding debt falls when a dollar is subtracted from the face value, is specified as $v'(D) = 1 - F(D)$, where $F(D)$ is the probability of default.

The key result of the Bulow-Rogoff model states that the buyback cost to the country exceeds the benefit if

$$1 - q[1 - v'(D)] > Dv'(D)/v(D) \qquad (4.14)$$

The right-hand side of equation 4.14 shows the benefit to the country from using one dollar to repurchase debt. The face value of the debt falls by $D/v(D)$ dollars (the inverse of the secondary market price). To many, that gain would be counted in full. However, Bulow and Rogoff allow only the fraction $v'(D)$ to be counted, as they consider the face value to have no "real" meaning. Thus, if the country's probability of default is 75 percent, it gains only 25 cents for each dollar of nominal face value of debt reduction.[48]

On the left-hand side, the cost of the buyback is the $1 disbursed, minus a term involving the fraction q of the outlay. The $1 is the cash paid for the buyback. The remaining expression subtracted takes account of the fact that "when a country defaults, which occurs with probability $F(D)$, creditors in effect pay for a fraction q of the repurchase. Since $F(D) = 1 - v'(D)$, creditors pay $q[1 - v'(D)]$" (1988a, 686).

Bulow and Rogoff then appear to commit the same analytical mistake as do Diwan and Rodrik (1992) in a subsequent study. Bulow and Rogoff estimate q by examining the level of annual net debt repayments in the highly indebted countries as a fraction of annual GDP. Net repayment is amortization plus interest less new borrowing. They find that the maximum range for this ratio is about 0.05 in the period 1980–86. They then use $q = 0.05$ as their principal estimate.

---

47. Thus, their critique does not depend on concern that the repurchase will drive up the secondary market price.

48. This approach is especially troublesome if the market price of the debt is low because of moral hazard behavior, or low "willingness" to pay as opposed to ability to pay. In the extreme, the country can keep driving down the secondary market price of its debt by making more confrontational statements, thereby yielding an even lower marginal value of debt and even lower "benefit" from bothering to repurchase it.

The problem (as in Diwan-Rodrik) is that this empirical estimate confuses a stock with a flow. The net annual debt service is a single year's installment on the stock of debt. Yet Bulow and Rogoff use it as the basis for setting the maximum plausible valuation of the entire outstanding stock of debt. The slip is transparent when the original definition of q is closely examined: $v(D) = qI$ where "bondholders have a claim of D that comes due as soon as I is realized" (684). But that is a simple two-period specification, with all principal and interest returned in the second period. The authors' empirical estimate for q is based on a single year's installment on a debt stock with multiyear maturity.

The authors note from equation 4.14, "Clearly, buybacks can work for debtor nations only if q has a sufficiently high value. We will argue . . . that q cannot possibly be large enough for any of today's debtors to make buybacks worth while" (686). It is not difficult to reach the opposite conclusion, however, once it is realized that observed net payments should be seen as a stream over time rather than a once-for-all payment. Suppose that the maximum annual net repayment is αY, where Y is the country's annual GDP. We may accept Bulow-Rogoff's estimate of 0.05 for α (but not for q). Suppose the creditor's real opportunity cost is at a discount rate of i. If the country's GDP is in steady state at Y_0, then the maximum value of the claim will be

$$v(D) = \int \alpha Y_0 e^{-it} = \alpha Y_0 / i \qquad (4.15)$$

If instead the country's GDP is growing at rate r, the net discount rate drops to $i - r$, and the maximum value of the claim is $v(D) = \alpha Y_0 / (i - r)$.

We may derive the proper measure of the Bulow-Rogoff q by considering plausible values. With $\alpha = 0.05$ (the proper interpretation of their data), $i = 0.08$, and $r = 0.04$, we have $v(D) = 0.05 Y_0 / (0.08 - 0.04) = 1.25 Y_0$. The plausible limit of the external claim is 125 percent of one year's GDP. The value for q as Bulow and Rogoff use it is then 125 percent, not 5 percent. The reason for the divergence is the confusion between stock and flow. Secondary market debt value is a stock and should be compared to the present value of a stream of the corresponding payments flow, not to just a single year's installment.

Williamson (1988) usefully notes that the essence of the Bulow-Rogoff argument may be captured by referring once again to the debt Laffer curve (figure 4.5). Suppose the country has nominal debt of k. The secondary market is priced as if the expected value of this stock of debt is only kc (far below the 45° line where expected value V equals face value D). The secondary market price is thus kc/Ok, or the slope of the ray from the origin to point c on the debt Laffer curve (labeled P_s). This is the Bulow-Rogoff "average price." At point c, the slope of the debt Laffer curve itself is much flatter, as shown by the tangent to the curve (labeled P').

Figure 4.5 Impact of buybacks

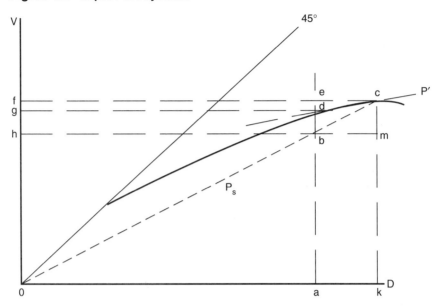

From the standpoint of the Brazilian state firms, buybacks seemed like a good deal, because they could erase liabilities of *ak* from their balance sheets at a cost of only *cm* in resource outlays, where $[cm] = P_s[ak]$. Bulow and Rogoff argue that this was a disservice to the country, because the firms used resources of *eb* ($= cm$) to achieve a reduction in the *market* value of the debt by only *ed*—the product of the reduction in the face value of the debt and the *marginal* price or slope of the debt Laffer curve (that is, $[ak]P'$).

Bulow and Rogoff would of course be right if all Brazil, and its state firms, would ever have to worry about paying off in the alternative scenario of avoiding this transaction were *ed*. However, Citibank's lawyers probably do not see matters that way. Nor does Williamson (1988), who argues:

> The distinction between the average and marginal cost of debt arises when the new money needed in "bad" states of the world amounts to a permanent partial forgiveness of interest, rather than its postponement. This is clearly a possible outcome, but those who do not regard it as a central expectation will conclude that the distinction between the average and marginal cost of debt is not of great import. . . . The marginal-average distinction does suggest that the return to buybacks may be less than implied by the formula (interest saving)÷(one minus discount) . . . However, it will not be drastically less except in the case of a country the nominal value of whose debt is of no consequence in determining its debt service obligation. (21)

The marginal-average distinction emphasized by Bulow and Rogoff has even stronger and perverse implications. Suppose in figure 4.5 that the country had been further to the right on the debt Laffer curve, beyond the peak of the curve. Then the slope of the curve is *negative*. The reduction of debt *increases* the market value. By the Bulow-Rogoff criterion, this reduction would cause welfare *losses* to the country, equal to the reduction in the face value of the debt multiplied by the negative slope of the debt Laffer curve (derivative of market value with respect to face value). Thus, the one case in which Krugman, Sachs, and virtually all other authors on the issue agree is an opportunity for Pareto-optimal debt forgiveness benefiting both the debtor and the creditors—when the country is on the wrong side of the debt Laffer curve—is precisely the case in which the Bulow-Rogoff criterion implies outright losses for the country from a buyback, a form of forgiveness.

In sharp contrast, Froot (1989), like Williamson, sees discounted buybacks as generally beneficial for the debtor. Froot's analysis focuses instead on how the benefits of buybacks depend on the source of the resources spent for the repurchase. There are four possible sources: (a) the creditors ("pure forgiveness"), (b) aid from a donor (as in the Bolivian buyback), (c) the debtor's future cash flow (uncollateralized exit bond), and (d) the country's present resources (reserves).

Under general assumptions, Froot (1989) demonstrates the following propositions. (1) Pure debt forgiveness benefits the debtor, but it benefits creditors only when the debtor is on the wrong side of the debt Laffer curve (investment disincentives of the debt overhang are dominant). (2) Buybacks using donor grants provide the same benefit to the debtor as pure debt forgiveness, but greater benefits to the creditors ("by the amount of the aid"). (3) Exit bonds (uncollateralized) provide the same benefits as pure debt forgiveness, to both the debtor and creditors. (4) For a given amount of debt relief, the incentive effects of a buyback out of present country resources are smaller than those from pure debt forgiveness, debtor welfare gains are lower and creditor gains are lower than under an equivalent buyback out of donor aid.

Froot notes that buybacks out of own resources (reserves) can reduce country welfare if reserves are low enough. The general argument is that present resources are optimally distributed between consumption and investment. The diversion of a portion of these resources reduces consumption, thereby raising the marginal utility of consumption at present relative to that in the future. Although the investment cutback also raises the return to investment, the net trade-off may shift the proportion of the remaining resources toward consumption. This shift may dominate the favorable investment incentive effects of reducing the debt overhang, so investment may fall.

In this connection, it is revealing that the most avid practitioners of buybacks in the Latin American context have been state firms and the private sector. One explanation might simply be that governments must more carefully observe legal "sharing" clauses. However, another explanation is consistent with Froot's focus on the scarcity of present resources. Where the effective transfer problem is internal (fiscal) rather than external (foreign exchange), the private sector and the state firms not under tight control by the central fiscal authority may consider "present resources" available for buybacks to be relatively abundant, whereas the central government considers them acutely scarce. This is especially the case when the debt problem involves large trade surpluses that translate into private capital flight rather than government repayment of external debt because the government does not have the revenue (or the domestic bond-floating credibility) to "purchase" the trade surplus.

Overall, the thrust of Froot's analysis is to show the broad equivalence of buybacks to pure forgiveness (a result similar to that in Krugman 1988), and to conclude that buybacks will generally benefit the debtor except under conditions of purchase out of extremely scarce present resources.

Nonetheless, there remains a "catch-22" type of syllogism that would seem superficially to recommend against buybacks. It goes as follows (consistent with the Bulow-Rogoff approach): (a) the debt is only "worth" what the secondary market price currently states; (b) buybacks will tend to push up the secondary market price; therefore, (c) buybacks involve repurchasing debt for more than it is "worth," causing a loss for the country. Bulow and Rogoff (1988a) cite the Bolivian experience as evidence. They note that in September 1986, Bolivia's bank debt with a face value of $670 million traded at only 6 cents in the secondary market, and so was "worth" only $40.2 million. After the March 1988 repurchase, the face value of the debt was reduced to $362 million, and repurchase resources amounted to $34 million. At book value the government thus expunged a $308 million debt for a donor-financed outlay of $34 million. Yet because the secondary market price rose to 11 cents, the remaining debt was now "worth" $39.8 million. In Bulow and Rogoff's opinion, the government thus reduced its effective debt by only $0.4 million, a pittance compared to the $34 million outlay.

Quite apart from the fact that the $34 million grant probably would not have been available for other uses, this critical diagnosis surely errs by identifying the current secondary market value of debt with its real long-term value and burden. It is well known that the secondary market is thin, and that the banks selling in the late 1980s were primarily regional banks with limited long-term interests in the countries in question but with an incentive to be able to tell shareholders that their books were clean of Latin American debt. Larger banks that had long-standing ties to the region and planned to be involved in it for decades to come typically were holding on to their claims and considered the secondary market prices derisory and unrepresentative. Although they considered the debt a bargain at the secondary market prices, they did not buy up even further blocs of it from the banks engaged in exodus because their own portfolios were already overextended in the paper. (The importance of divergent bank evaluations of the value of the debt has been stressed above.)

Thus, surely Williamson (1988) has it right when he says of Bulow and Rogoff's critique of the Bolivian buyback:[49]

> My interpretation is different: that the buyback eliminated the most pessimistic holders. Buying these out could be advantageous to Bolivia even if the result was to *increase* the total market value of its debt, which does not reflect (and still less determines) Bolivia's short-run payments, which are zero, but rather the date at which payments are expected to resume. By advancing that date and reducing the cost of resuming payment the buyback has benefited both the nonexiting banks and Bolivia. (21)

As it turned out, Bolivia's secondary market price remained at the 11 cent level throughout 1989–92. By mid-1993 it had risen to 16 cents on the dollar. In the central interpretation here, this change was a healthy sign. However, by the Bulow-Rogoff criterion, the change involved a welfare loss to the country. Since Bolivian authorities could probably drive the secondary market price back down by issuing a strong statement of repudiation, by implication Bulow and Rogoff would advocate that they do so. Most analysts would disagree.

Historical Lessons[50]

The final category of debt literature in recent years has been the endeavor to draw upon historical precedents for lessons about the 1980s debt crisis and appropriate policy to deal with it. The tendency in this literature has been to criticize the debt strategy of the mid-1980s as

---

49. Note that Rotemberg (1988) proposes another interpretation of why the deal was favorable to Bolivia despite the Bulow-Rogoff data on unchanged market value. He suggests that bargaining costs are larger for large debt and that creditors are more intransigent because more is at stake. As a result, lowering the magnitude of the debt through buybacks can reduce bargaining costs and facilitate settlement. Although this argument is plausible insofar as debtor country finance ministers are more free to allocate their scarce time to domestic growth rather than debt negotiations after a major buyback has temporarily "dealt" with the debt (as in the Bolivian case), its general importance would seem limited. One reason is that economy-of-scale considerations go in the other direction: if it takes 15 members of a bank advisory committee to deal with Brazil's debt just like that of Bolivia, the fixed costs are lower as a fraction of the debt at stake for the case with the higher debt magnitude.

50. The discussion here focuses primarily on just two of the most important studies: Fishlow (1986) and Eichengreen and Portes (1989). For a more comprehensive survey see Eichengreen (1991b). Also note the important compendium in Eichengreen and Lindert (1989).

insufficiently coming to terms with the need for a process of debt forgiveness and workout, based on historical precedent. However, one sometimes obtains the impression that the historical scholars turn Santayana's dictum upside down by inferring that, once aware of the past, the present is condemned to repeat it.

At the outset it is perhaps useful to recall the institutional environment of the 1970s and early 1980s. Primarily through the Bretton Woods institutions, the industrial countries had managed to assemble an international financial system far superior to that of the interwar period. The General Agreement on Tariffs and Trade (GATT) had successively opened trade, in contrast to the spiral toward closure in the 1930s. The IMF and World Bank had finished the task of postwar financial stabilization for Europe and Japan and had turned to concentration on the developing countries. The modern capital market seemingly had impressively met the challenge of the OPEC oil price increase by providing financial recycling to developing countries in the 1970s.

At the onset of the debt crisis in 1982, there was every reason to believe that this financial apparatus was a much more effective mechanism for dealing with problems of default than the nonsystem of the interwar period. There were thus grounds for the view that this time a debt crisis could be handled more efficiently than in previous historical episodes. In contrast, the burden of the historical studies has largely been to impose some humility on this postwar conceit: to undermine the notion that the system is much better prepared to cope today than in the past, to imply that the defaults and workouts of the 1930s and before are the historical norm, and to suggest that attempts to deny and delay this reality ignore historical experience. From the perspective of 1994, these critiques seem more valid than they did in say 1984, but less valid than they appeared in 1989 at the adoption of the Brady Plan and before the strong resurgence of capital flows to Latin America in the early 1990s.

Fishlow (1986) provides an early entry in this literature. He stresses the impressive success of the international capital markets before 1914, and their serious breakdown thereafter. International investment involved much larger fractions of creditor country (e.g., British) incomes, and much larger fractions of investment in borrowing countries (Australia, Canada, Argentina, Brazil) in the late 19th century than in the 1970s. Developmental finance dominated prior to 1914, particularly British lending for railroads in North America, Latin America, and Australia. Such investments tended to yield positive real returns consistently higher than domestic British consols. In contrast, more politicized French and German lending tended to concentrate on revenue bonds for Eastern European governments, culminating in large losses on Russian bonds after the revolution. This type of lending tended to go for the balancing of fiscal accounts rather than for infrastructure investment.

Fishlow (1986) distinguishes between two types of defaults before 1914: "developmental" and "public revenue." Developmental defaults occurred where there had been rapid investment in physical assets and temporary slowdowns in otherwise growing exports. For these, "the appropriate remedy was time" for exports to rise, and "investment bankers" provided that time with consolidated debt and brief periods of low or no interest (57). In contrast, revenue default was "a case of genuine insolvency" of "stagnating economies whose governments financed current outlays with loans that they were able to get by paying exorbitantly high interest rates." In these cases debt was "significantly written down." Importantly, then, Fishlow's reading of the pre-1914 period is that there were both cases of developmental "illiquidity" (including defaults in the 1890s by Australia, Canada, and Argentina) and fiscal "insolvency" (including the new Latin American republics in the 1820s; Turkey, Egypt, and Peru in the 1870s; and Russia in 1913). The historical record thus seems to confirm the utility of the distinction between sovereign illiquidity and insolvency.

After World War I, international lending shifted much more heavily to the revenue type. The United Kingdom and France owed large war debts to the United States, but in turn they held claims for German reparations. The Dawes Plan in 1924 set more reasonable German obligations and aided in the country's recovery after hyperinflation; but much of lending nonetheless remained a sort of Ponzi scheme covering war losses, in contrast to the lending for development of physical assets in the 1870–1913 period. In the mid-1920s, US banks aggressively and successfully marketed overseas bonds to the public; but by 1929 the even higher returns in the US stock market curtailed these flows, bursting the lending bubble.

Fishlow cites three systemic problems with international lending in the 1920s. First, unlike Britain before it, the United States as the new principal creditor was unprepared to ensure open trade markets (as signaled by the 1922 Fordney Act, which returned tariffs to their higher, pre-1913 levels). Finance could not permanently substitute for debtor export growth. Second, real interest rates were much higher than before the war.[51] Third, after the mid-1920s real commodity prices were in decline, so that Latin American lending in addition to politically based European loans were increasingly at risk.

With depression came default. By 1933, every South American country except Argentina was in default, largely because export earnings had typically fallen by more than 60 percent. Nonetheless, domestic stimulus and protection permitted "better performance by peripheral coun-

---

51. Real bond rates in the 1920s were over 6 percent. Lagging inflationary expectations after the inflationary outburst during World War I would seem likely to have been a reason. If so, this phenomenon was similar to what happened in the 1980s.

tries" than in the depressed economies of North America and Europe. The ascent of the National Socialist party to power in Germany stimulated capital flight, contributed to the collapse of the Austrian Creditanstalt, and led to default on the Dawes and Young loans by 1934.

Turning to the 1970s, Fishlow judges that the recycling of petrodollars was the driving force in debt accumulation through 1979. He notes that the borrowing was at low real interest rates and largely went to productive investments. However, the second oil shock of 1979 brought disaster. It directly affected oil importers, and in addition it provoked the combination of global recession and high interest rates that turned the debt burden onerous. Policy mistakes by Latin American countries in the late 1970s (overborrowing based on oil in Mexico, overvalued exchange rates to fight inflation in Argentina and Chile) added to the problem.

Noting, as of 1986, that "the strategy devised for dealing with the debt problem has thus far worked" (89), Fishlow issues warnings based on historical precedent. He argues that the 1970s lending boom was "an unnatural event . . . occasioned by disequilibrium in the global balance of payments," and thus more like the systemically plagued interwar problem than the "simple developmental defaults of the 19th century" (91–93). The 1980s policy response was tougher on debtors than the pattern in the pre-1913 developmental defaults, because this time there was "little willingness to consider such expedients as capitalization of interest," nor any promise of capital inflow. Moreover, the direct involvement of commercial banks meant that this time there was an objective of preserving bank solvency to prevent systemic distress, and "the means of doing so is forcing more of the real burden upon the debtor countries" (91). Yet especially the smaller debtors (as opposed to the newly industrialized countries [NICs]) were more likely to prove to be in positions equivalent to the historical revenue defaulters.

Fishlow emphasized that debtors had been locked out of the credit markets for 40 years after the Latin American revenue defaults in the 1820s, and for 40 years after the debacle of the 1930s. In retrospect, Fishlow was too pessimistic about the return of capital. The large reflow of capital to Latin America in 1991–94 suggests that the credit markets interpreted the 1980s experience as closer to a developmental default model than to revenue defaults. Nonetheless, Fishlow's diagnosis of an asymmetrical shouldering of the burden in the strategy through 1986 proved widely shared, as indicated by the shift to debt forgiveness as the new strategy in 1989.

In an influential historical study, Eichengreen and Portes (1986) apply econometric tests to examine leading hypotheses about historical debt experience. They first test the proposition that lending in the 1920s was indiscriminate and excessive because of bond pushing by issue houses. They find instead that risk premiums were statistically related to political-economic variables (trade surplus, budget surplus, geographic region), and that the bond markets of the 1920s were no less discriminating than the bank lending of the 1970s. Next they test the view (ascribed to Diaz-Alejandro 1984 and Fishlow 1986) that external commodity shock was the driving force in the defaults of the 1930s; instead, they find that other variables also played a major role (initial extent of indebtedness; domestic budget performance; and political aspects, e.g., Australia's ties to the United Kingdom).

The Eichengreen-Portes work was most sensational, however, for the following two findings. First, if countries are divided into "heavy" and "light" defaulters, "both GNP and industrial production expanded more quickly in the 'heavy defaulters' after 1931" (Eichengreen and Portes 1989, 74). Second, "there is scant evidence that defaulting debtors were differentially affected" in their subsequent access to capital markets (77). Despite the authors' numerous caveats, the policy message of these findings seemed to be that Latin American debtors in the 1980s were foolish to eschew default as a strategy.[52]

There are at least two major questions that must be raised about the econometric finding that "heavy defaulters" achieved better growth in the 1930s than light defaulters, at least with regard to implications for the 1980s. First and most important, it is highly unlikely that the shift to inward-looking growth through import substitution could have been repeated in the 1980s. In the 1930s, countries such as Brazil and Chile had a large array of labor-intensive industries where there was still limited domestic production and ample scope for easy import substitution. By the 1980s, import substitution had already gone far beyond the point of efficient utilization of domestic resources. Reinventing the option of the closed economy in the 1980s, the likely price of an outright default strategy, would have been far less successful than in the 1930s.

Second, an examination of the Eichengreen-Portes list of "heavies" and "lights" reveals that the latter group is dominated by countries presently in the OECD.[53] The fact that such countries as Canada, France, Italy, and Austria achieved relatively weaker recovery from the depression than "heavy defaulters" such as Brazil, Chile, Colombia, and Uruguay should surely be related to the closer integration of the former group into the economy of the "center." Thus, surely Canada was more likely to mimic the profound collapse of nominal GDP in the United States in the depression than was Brazil, regardless of Canadian debt policy. As Fishlow (1986) noted, the periphery did better in general

---

52. However, as noted below, the two authors now disclaim this interpretation.

53. In the Eichengreen-Portes groups, only three countries (Germany, Hungary, Poland) of the 12 in the "heavy defaulter" group are what might have been considered economies of the developed "center." Correspondingly, only 3 out of 16 "light defaulters" were from the periphery (Argentina, Nicaragua, and Venezuela).

than did the center. It is curious that the statistical tests excluded per capita income and geographical location, variables that might have netted out the center-periphery influence.

Importantly, the Eichengreen-Portes finding that there was "scant evidence" that defaulting debtors were "differentially affected" in subsequent access to capital markets can be rejected statistically using bond market data for their own country groupings. As shown in chapter 5 below, the initial year of reentry into the bond market was an average of 1972 for the "heavy" defaulters in the Eichengreen-Portes list, as compared to 1959 for the "light" defaulters. The 13-year difference in means is statistically significant at the 99 percent level.

In short, the Eichengreen-Portes stylized historical fact of the growth benefits of default warrants considerable skepticism, especially with respect to any extrapolation of this lesson to the debt crisis of the 1980s. Nor should debtor countries today be particularly comfortable with the notion that default carries no penalty for capital market access. Not only does a simple review of market reentry dates suggest that deeper default delays market access, but in addition, as elaborated below and examined in chapter 8, there are already major differences in risk premiums being charged to countries with differing behavior during the 1980s debt crisis.

Eichengreen and Portes argue that, for countries that have reentered capital markets, the statistical studies do not show adverse effects of default on borrowing prospects. The data refer variously to borrowing by 32 countries in the first postwar decade (Eichengreen 1989a); by six Latin American countries in the period 1950–64 (Jorgensen and Sachs 1989); and for international lending generally over 100 years (Lindert and Morton 1989). However, Ozler (1988) has shown, using the same default measure as Lindert and Morton, that in the 1970s, borrowers with a past record of default did in fact pay higher interest rate premiums. In response, Eichengreen (1991b) concedes only that "there is evidence for a short period in the 1970s that countries with prior records of default were charged larger spreads on new loans. But there is no evidence that they were rationed out of the market" (162). This statement would seem to be contradicted for at least bond market access, based on the analysis in chapter 5 below as just described.

When the historical data are in for the 1990s, it seems highly likely that differential spreads will once again be evident, and presumably the price of capital is relevant as well as its absolute access. In the early 1990s, large spread differentials were already present distinguishing the non-default countries from the quasi-default countries. Thus, by mid-1993, nondefaulters South Korea and Chile were paying spreads of only 70 and 150 basis points respectively above US Treasury bond rates, whereas countries that had exacted debt reductions were paying much higher spreads (Philippines, 600 basis points; Venezuela, 700; Brazil,

750).[54] Peru, in outright default, was not even in the market. Similarly, Chile enjoyed investment-grade ratings (Standard and Poor's BBB) whereas Brazil did not (Moody's B2; Salomon Brothers 1993a). More formal statistical analysis in chapter 8 below shows a significant differential in bond spreads for countries that had incurred debt forgiveness.

If Fishlow (1986) is right that the spread differentials decline or disappear once the country carries out a regime change, such adverse effects may diminish over time. However, it would be misleading to advertise painless, no-fault default to today's debtors on the basis of the historical tests cited by Eichengreen and Portes.

The Eichengreen-Portes historical analysis (1989) has four other important findings: industrial country governments had been soft on debtors in the 1930s but hard on them in the 1980s; investors in international lending had generally been compensated for greater losses by higher premiums, global debt resolution schemes had been tried and failed in the 1930s, and buybacks had played an important role in reducing the debt in the 1930s.

On government intervention, the authors conclude that "[w]hile US officials in the 1980s have made clear the priority they attach to maintaining debt service, in the 1930s and 1940s, when governments intervened, they might pressure both debtors and creditors to reach early agreement" (80). However, this conclusion is at odds with the authors' own instances of British pressure on behalf of private creditors of Argentina and Germany, as well as selected pressure through US Export-Import Bank cutoffs. The principal support for the assertion seems to be the perception of a higher priority assigned by Roosevelt to restoration of trade relations than to bondholders' problems, and the growing effort to reach solutions as World War II approached. The political assessment also fails to note the intense government pressure on banks to extend "new loans" after the outbreak of the 1980s debt crisis. Nonetheless, in the context of the pre–Brady Plan policy redefinitions in the late 1980s, the seeming historical asymmetry in government policy was a powerful message.

On returns to lending, Eichengreen and Portes (1989) estimate that for foreign loans issued between 1920 and 1929:

> The average nominal internal rate of return (weighted by issue value) was roughly 4 percent on dollar bonds and about 5 percent for sterling issues. Although dollar bondholders settled for approximately half of contractual interest and sterling bondholders for only slightly more, dollar bondholders did slightly worse than if they had held domestic Treasury bonds, and sterling

---

54. Based on author's discussion with Salomon Brothers experts. Note that Mexico's spread was slimmer, in the range of 210 basis points for Yankee bonds to 420 for stripped yields on Brady par bonds. However, the unique tie to the United States and the prospective North American Free Trade Agreement made Mexico a special case, and this would presumably have made its spreads considerably smaller than those for Chile in the absence of the experience of Brady Plan losses.

bondholders did slightly better. . . . Although some debtor countries received what can be interpreted as substantial relief, the defaults of the 1930s did not inflict unsupportable losses on creditors. (79)

The problem with this assessment is that it would seem misleading if applied to developing country debtors. As pointed out above, a long list of "light defaulters" included the more developed countries. Yet for the developing countries they specifically identify, the average rates of return were sharply negative (−7.4 percent for Brazil, −9.8 percent for Bolivia, and −14.76 percent for Hungary). Indeed, the stylized fact of "adequate returns" simply conflicts with the stylized fact of "painless default." Instead, what emerges from a closer reading is that returns were *not* compensatory for the class of mainly Latin American debtor countries that chose the option of deep default. It is thus not surprising that Ozler (1988) later found that these countries had to pay higher risk premiums in 1970s borrowing.

On historical precedents for global debt schemes, Eichengreen and Portes (1989) argue:

> Nearly every element of the global plans proposed in the 1980s—a special international lending facility, matched injections of private and public funds, conversion of existing assets into new ones featuring different contingencies—was first suggested in the 1930s. Ultimately, those global schemes foundered on the issues of who should fund and control their administration. (70)

Finally, Eichengreen and Portes find that market-based debt reduction through buybacks "made a useful contribution to resolving the debt crisis of the 1930s by reducing the debt overhang and eliminating marginal creditors" (70). They add:

> The argument that buybacks from reserves leave the debtor in worse shape (since reserves are sacrificed and the market price of remaining obligations simply rising [sic] to reflect the country's unchanged debt-servicing capacity) is difficult to reconcile with the actions of interwar governments, many of which used the option extensively, and with the market prices of the bonds repurchased at the time. [By] 1939 . . . a dozen countries in default had repatriated between 15 and 50 percent of their bonds since 1930. . . . Chile retired 18 percent at [an average price of] 59, Colombia 22 percent at 22, and Peru 31 percent at 21. (82)

Whereas bondholders' committees publicly opposed buybacks on grounds that the funds should go to paying interest, in private they were often more receptive. Eichengreen and Portes thus find historical support for buybacks as a beneficial way to reduce the debt obligation.[55]

---

55. Curiously, in a later survey Eichengreen (1991b) seems to give more credibility to the Bulow-Rogoff argument (reviewed above) by citing the possible outcome that buybacks

The broad message of the Eichengreen-Portes work in the late 1980s seemed to be that countries would be well-advised to repeat the defaults of the 1930s and at most make periodic repurchases of debt on the secondary market. That was the impression of the present author at the time of the conference presentation of Eichengreen and Portes (1989). This impression is also implicit in the comments of the discussant of that paper (Skiles 1989), who first noted that "one of the paper's main themes is that substantial similarities exist between the debt crisis of the 1930s and that of the 1980s," and then went on to enumerate why differences recommended a different response this time. From the standpoint of 1994, however, the two authors strongly dispute the notion that they had implied the desirability of a policy of default.[56] That the earlier misunderstanding could occur illustrates how highly charged the atmosphere of debt policy analysis was at the time.

Conclusion

A tour of the debt literature reveals an intellectually exhilarating flourishing of theory and empirical analysis in response to a historically significant international economic phenomenon. Even though some of the details, and even some of the principal concepts, in this literature seem questionable with the benefit of hindsight, the evolving analysis continually prodded policymakers into reconsidering the debt strategy. From this crucible, what emerged was a relatively well-informed and considered policy strategy that evolved over time, as set forth in chapter 5.

"will simply drive up the secondary market price of remaining debt, leaving the market value of the debt unchanged" (165). Eichengreen counters that prices typically did not rise enough to leave the debt unchanged. However, he fails to reject the underlying premise that the higher secondary market valuation of the debt represents a meaningful increase in the burden for the country, rather than a positive return to more normal capital market participation (as argued above).

56. Richard Portes, statement at conference on "Managing the World Economy of the Future: Lessons from the First Fifty Years after Bretton Woods." Washington (19–21 May 1994): Institute for International Economics; and Barry Eichengreen, 17 July 1994, personal communication with author.

5

Evolution and Evaluation of the Debt Strategy

[A] critical threshold for industrial country growth in 1984–86 is 3 percent annually. If this growth rate can be achieved, the debt problems of the developing countries should be manageable and should show considerable improvement. . . . The central result of this analysis is that the debt problem can be managed, and that it is essentially a problem of illiquidity, not insolvency.

—Cline (1983, 71)

[A]fter World War II . . . Mexico . . . settled at 20 cents on the dollar. . . . By historical standards, then, it is much too early to buy out the creditors. Ten years from now they may be eager to settle at 10–20 cents on the dollar.

—Dornbusch (1988b, 703)

The first of these two quotations depicts the conceptual framework that underlay the international debt strategy adopted in 1983–84. Albeit with a shift toward emphasis on longer-term structural reform, the same framework persisted through 1988. The second quotation reflects the depths of despair of many critics about the prospects of this strategy by the late 1980s, on the eve of the shift in the approach to debt forgiveness under the Brady Plan.

As noted in chapter 3, the dichotomy of illiquidity versus insolvency as the criterion for when additional lending rather than bankruptcy workout is appropriate dates back to central banking principles more than a century old (Bagehot 1873). Although its application to sovereign lending was always awkward, in part because the strictly short-term nature of the difficulty implicit in the term *illiquidity* was misleading, this criterion provided an important basis for the formulation of the debt strategy. In retrospect the initial diagnosis of illiquidity (or more appropriately, noninsolvency) was justifiable as a contingent strategy subject to change in the face of subsequent events. The alternative diagnosis of widespread fundamental insolvency would have been in error for many of the major debtors and would have precluded the eventual process of triage that separated the countries that needed debt forgiveness from those that did not.[1]

In the end the strategy of mobilizing additional lending rather than forgiving debt was successful for most Asian countries (including the major cases of South Korea and Indonesia) and for two important cases in Latin America (Chile and Colombia). For most of Latin America, however, the eventual remedy involved the forgiveness of about one-third of long-term claims held by banks.[2] The relinquished claims typically represented only about 15 percent of total external debt of the country. In contrast, domestic bankruptcy settlements usually involve losses of 70 percent or more on creditor claims (M. White 1984, 1989; Bradley and Rosenzweig 1992). Viewed against this benchmark, even the countries that received Brady Plan debt reductions were closer to being solvent than bankrupt, suggesting that the initial diagnosis of the international strategy was not too far off the mark.

Indeed, with reductions of only about 15 percent in overall debt burdens, the countries that received Brady debt reduction obtained relief that for strictly analytical purposes would have to be called marginal. The corresponding annual interest savings were on the order of only $1/2$ to 1 percent of GDP, or some 3 percent of export earnings. Yet the initial economic impact was highly positive in at least the Mexican case, and by 1993 the Latin American debt problem had practically vanished, as the key debtor countries experienced large new inflows of capital (chapter 8).

This chapter will suggest that the success of Brady Plan debt forgiveness despite its limited size was importantly related to market psychology and debtor country politics. For debtor governments, securing debt forgiveness was often a critical objective for domestic political purposes. Moreover, the ability of debtor country leaders to announce that the

---

1. Note that one particularly relevant central banker is skeptical of the illiquidity-insolvency dichotomy. Paul Volcker underscores the difficulty of telling whether a country is illiquid or insolvent. More fundamentally, he suggests that even with the benefit of hindsight it is questionable to categorize a country such as Mexico as having been insolvent, because its $15 billion-equivalent forgiven was small relative to its economic wealth. He considers that in cases where psychological and political factors ultimately determined a debt reduction outcome, the question beforehand was more one of how long the severe phase of adjustment and capital market cutoff would last and thus whether such relief would be necessary. At the same time, he stresses that there were much more obvious cases requiring bankruptcy treatment, such as those of Bolivia and Costa Rica, but that policymakers were stymied by the banks' fears of setting precedents affecting claims on larger countries if the banks gave large debt forgiveness in these more extreme small-country cases. Interview, 24 October 1994.

2. Much of Africa needs debt forgiveness as well (chapter 7), but African debt is largely to bilateral donors and was never a major part of the commercial bank debt crisis of the 1980s.

debt crisis had been overcome proved to be a tonic to domestic capital and exchange market expectations. To potential foreign lenders and nationals considering whether to repatriate capital, the market-oriented and quasi-voluntary nature of the Brady Plan provided important psychological assurance about the safety of new lending.

This chapter traces the evolution of the debt strategy from the initial rescue packages to the Baker Plan and then the Brady Plan, first in terms of policy measures and then in terms of the evolving intellectual debate. The chapter next reviews the Brady agreements, evaluates their outcomes to date, and considers the unfinished business that remains. The chapter then attempts to draw an overall evaluation of the debt strategy and to derive implications for future international policy toward external debt.

Evolution of the Strategy

Coordinated Balance of Payments Lending, 1982–85

There were three distinct phases of the debt strategy. The first began as an emergency response to Mexico's suspension of principal payments in August 1982. That event threatened the world financial system by placing the large international banks in jeopardy. The nine largest US banks had claims on Mexico alone amounting to 44 percent of their capital. The claims of these banks on all developing countries (including Eastern Europe but excluding high-income OPEC countries and offshore centers) amounted to $83 billion, or 285 percent of their capital (FFIEC 1982). Claims of other international banks were also high (chapter 2).

As Krugman (1994, 691) notes, the first Reagan administration had stressed international economic laissez-faire and had called for limiting the resources of the World Bank and International Monetary Fund on grounds that by providing a financial safety net, the institutions induced irresponsible private lending to developing countries. Yet faced with the risk of a 1930s-style international financial crisis, the administration promptly shifted to support an internationally coordinated response to the Mexican debt crisis.

In early August 1982, Mexico's Finance Minister Jesus Silva Herzog traveled to Washington to announce a debt moratorium. In the weeks that followed, the International Monetary Fund, the Federal Reserve, and the US Treasury worked closely together to launch a program of emergency refinancing. In October, IMF Managing Director Jacques de Larosière told bank representatives at a key meeting at the Federal Reserve in New York that the Fund would provide new lending for Mexico only if the banks did so as well. On the same day Federal Reserve Chairman Paul Volcker announced in a speech in Boston that banks that provided new loans to Mexico would not need to set aside loan-loss provisions on these loans, because they would be part of a coordinated package that would improve Mexico's creditworthiness.

The US government arranged $1 billion in commodity credits and $1 billion in prepayments for delivery of Mexican oil to the strategic petroleum reserve. The Bank for International Settlements (BIS) provided a $1.2 billion bridge loan. By November Mexico had signed an IMF Extended Fund Facility agreement worth $3.7 billion, and the banks had agreed to reschedule principal and committed $5 billion in new money (Cline 1984, 30–31). The inflow of private capital to Brazil dropped off abruptly following the Mexico crisis, and an emergency package of US Treasury and BIS bridge lending for Brazil was followed by an IMF agreement and $4.4 billion in new bank loans by the end of the year. Similar arrangements soon followed for Argentina and Yugoslavia (where formal debt rescheduling was avoided).

In these and subsequent coordinated lending packages, the IMF played the crucial role of coalescing the banks into joint action that otherwise would have been frustrated by the free-rider incentive for each bank to enjoy the benefits of increased lending by other banks but make no new loans of its own. The Fund's position that it would not lend unless there was a critical mass of banks committed to new lending was a change from its previous practice whereby an IMF loan was merely a green light for private lending. Conceivably the country advisory groups of 15 or so lead banks could have used peer pressure to achieve the same end, but the chances of mobilizing participation would have been considerably lower without the extra liquidity provided by the IMF, the prospect of Paris Club bilateral rescheduling (rigidly dependent on an IMF program), and the promise of better economic policies in the debtor country as the consequence of IMF conditionality. In short, the IMF became the enforcer of "involuntary lending" (Cline 1983, 74–79), or, in the subsequent and sanitized official language, concerted lending.

In the course of 1984–85, there followed a series of coordinated lending packages typically involving an IMF agreement, rescheduling of bank loans, and new money from the banks.[3] In addition to the original and follow-up packages for Mexico, Brazil, and Argentina, such programs were negotiated in Latin America for Chile, Costa Rica, Ecuador, Panama, Peru, and Uruguay (World Bank 1987). Colombia secured coordinated new money from the banks without formal rescheduling; Venezuela, loath to accept the IMF conditionality required for new money,

---

3. The term *new money* raises the hackles of some observers. Typically the new loans were insufficient to cover the full amount of interest coming due. Critics of involuntary or concerted lending tended to focus on the resulting negative net transfer and considered that there was no effective new money on a net basis.

obtained the opposite combination. Elsewhere, the banks agreed to similar programs for Côte d'Ivoire and the Philippines.

Initially these programs rescheduled debt coming due over only 18 months to 2 years; at relatively stiff terms, such as 2 percent over the US prime rate; and at intermediate maturities of 8 years or so. By the end of this period the terms were softening but still nonconcessional. The September 1984 agreement for Mexico established the benchmark for the Multiyear Rescheduling Agreement (MYRA). It cut the spread to about 1 percent; shifted the base from prime to London interbank offer rate (LIBOR), typically about 3/4 percent lower; stretched maturities to 14 years, and extended the coverage of principal coming due to 6 years (Bergsten, Cline, and Williamson 1985, 95–106).

The year 1984 was the high-water mark for the initial phase of the debt strategy. International economic recovery proved to be strong and the current accounts of key debtor countries shifted dramatically from deficits to surpluses—although disturbingly from a collapse in imports rather than an export boom. Economic growth in Latin America rebounded from an average of -1.9 percent in 1982–83 to 3.7 percent in 1984 (ECLAC 1988). For a time it appeared that the initial rounds of massive new-money packages plus the subsequent consolidations and maturity smoothings from MYRA reschedulings would suffice.

By 1985, however, the hopes for a definitive debt recovery began to fade. Economic growth in Latin America was once again strong (3.6 percent), and in such countries as Argentina and Mexico, inflation was moderating from high levels associated with sharp devaluations earlier in the debt crisis (ECLAC 1988, 17). Nonetheless, the initial round of large involuntary lending had been completed the year before, and there was no evidence that voluntary lending was returning to take its place. Thus, by IMF estimates, "concerted" lending to Latin America had amounted to $13.3 billion in 1983 and $15.5 billion in 1984, but fell to only $2.2 billion in 1985, while "spontaneous" lending virtually disappeared (falling from $1.9 billion in 1983 to $0.6 billion in 1984 and $0.2 billion in 1985; IMF 1990c, 89).

Import compression had been severe. Latin American imports had fallen from an exaggerated level of $124 billion in 1981 to a more normal level of $100 billion in 1982 and then to a depressed plateau of about $75 billion annually in 1983–85 (IMF 1992a, 115). It was increasingly difficult to foresee sustained growth if imports did not begin to grow again, and the environment of minimal voluntary lending dimmed prospects for import recovery.

By mid-1985 Mexican authorities were already speaking of a need for additional lending when in September a severe earthquake hit Mexico City, raising budgetary (but not import) costs by several billion dollars and further undermining the political viability of austerity in pursuit of external debt service. Moreover, the return from military to civilian government in Argentina in 1984 and Brazil in 1985 tended to escalate political as opposed to technical considerations in debt policy in those countries.

At the same time, a new team had taken over at the US Treasury. Secretary James Baker and Undersecretary Richard Darman were more inclined toward policy intervention than their predecessors, as shown most dramatically in the September 1985 Plaza Agreement on multilateral currency intervention to depreciate the overvalued dollar. They considered new alternatives, including a requirement that banks set aside loan-loss reserves without writing off debt, partly to redress the growing impression that the banks were not shouldering any of the adjustment burden. However, it quickly became clear that a shift in this direction could choke off new lending, and instead the Baker team concentrated its attention on mobilizing new lending under a more systematic program. At the annual meetings of the IMF and World Bank in Seoul, the Treasury team proposed the next phase of the debt strategy.

The Baker Plan, 1986–88[4]

The Baker proposal amounted to an indicative international plan for reinforcing the strategy of coordinated lending while at the same time shifting the focus of the debt strategy from short-term balance of payments adjustment toward long-term structural change. The plan set specific targets for lending. For a group of 15 heavily indebted countries (primarily the major Latin American debtors but also including the Philippines in Asia and Côte d'Ivoire, Morocco, and Nigeria in Africa) the plan set a goal of $20 billion in new lending by the private banks over the coming three years.[5] Total claims of the banks on this group of countries amounted to about $250 billion, so $20 billion in new money over three years represented approximately 3 percent of outstanding exposure annually. Considering that LIBOR stood at about 8 percent in 1985, this commitment represented the refinancing of about one-third of interest coming due on bank claims during this period.

During the same period, the multilateral development banks (mainly the World Bank and Inter-American Development Bank) were to provide $10 billion in additional lending to the same countries. This target represented an increase in net disbursements from $4 billion to $7 billion annually, thereby reaching approximate parity with the new lending target for the banks. At the same time, a tacit but important feature of the plan was that such lending would be needed to replace IMF lending,

---

4. For a more detailed review, see Cline (1989a).

5. The countries are listed in chapter 2, table 2.1. Note that two smaller but politically important countries were soon added to the list: Jamaica and Costa Rica.

because the repayment period was coming due on earlier IMF loans (which are shorter term). Conceptually it was also convenient to emphasize the role of the multilateral development banks rather than the IMF, because the plan stressed that it was time to shift the strategy from a focus of short-term adjustment to one of longer-term structural change.

The Baker Plan provided that for their part, the debtor countries were to strengthen the process of fiscal adjustment already begun and were in addition to undertake structural policy reform in three major areas: import liberalization, the liberalization of treatment of foreign investment, and privatization of state firms. At the time, the call for privatization seemed remarkably intrusive into internal matters; yet within a few years, the wave of privatization that swept Latin America went far beyond what might have been contemplated by the plan's architects.

Krugman (1994) notes the disappointment of many critics at the time of the Baker Plan that the new phase did not fundamentally shift from the premises of the initial debt strategy, and in particular did not move in the direction of debt forgiveness. He states that "the failure of the concerted lending strategy to deliver significant increases in commercial bank exposure was apparent by mid-1984" (703). Although it is true that flows of concerted lending fell in 1985 (as noted above), Krugman's interpretation is questionable. The reason for the decline was that the banks had not been asked for large additional involuntary lending for 1985. As noted, the idea as of 1984 had instead been that the only additional coordinated step necessary was the MYRA for stretching out maturities. The Baker Plan may be seen as a midcourse correction recognizing that because the resumption of voluntary lending was taking longer than expected, it was necessary to resort to a reinforcement of the concerted lending strategy on a more systematic basis.

The popular image of the Baker Plan is that it failed because "the commercial banks were unwilling to supply new money" (World Bank 1992a, 1: 51). However, this perception is contrary to the actual data. Cline (1989a, 181) showed that new-money packages extended to the Baker-17 countries in 1986–88 amounted to $12.8 billion, almost two-thirds of the target. More recent data reported by the World Bank show that the total of "new long-term money" from the commercial banks to these countries in the period September 1985 through December 1988 amounted to $18.1 billion and covered 10 of the 17 countries in the group (calculated from World Bank 1989b, 1: 62–73). For several of the other countries, such as Peru, new money was not forthcoming because of disarray in macroeconomic policies and the corresponding absence of IMF stabilization programs.

The perception that banks did not provide new lending stemmed in part from misleading data on bank exposure. As discussed in chapter 2, data based on creditor country reporting tended to show reductions in bank exposure that reflected loan-loss set-asides rather than repayment of principal. Moreover, debt-equity conversions, buybacks, and other market-based debt reductions had the effect of reducing exposure even though they were part of a solution to the debt problem rather than a manifestation that banks were not meeting their new lending objectives. Performance of bank lending based on exposure data accordingly understated the banks' efforts under the Baker Plan.

Thus, Cline (1990, 87) estimated that BIS data showed a reduction of bank claims on the Baker Plan countries by $9.7 billion from the end of 1985 to the end of 1988. In the same period, the banks converted $15.5 billion from debt to equity, $1 billion into exit bonds, eliminated $1 billion through buybacks, and cut debt by $8 billion in discounted restructurings (IIF 1989, 22). If this $26 billion total is offset against the decline of about $10 billion in BIS-reported claims, the net effect was an increase of about $16 billion, comparable to the two alternative estimates just described.[6]

In short, the banks delivered on perhaps some two-thirds or more of the new-money target set forth in the indicative Baker Plan. Ironically, strictly speaking the public sector had a poorer performance. As Cline (1989a, 180–81) shows, the multilateral development banks (MDBs) achieved an increase of only $300 million annually in their net lending to the Baker countries, or only one-tenth of the target. Moreover, net flows from the IMF shifted from a positive $1.7 billion in 1985 to a negative (i.e., net repayment) average of $900 million annually in 1986–88.

After taking account of the pre-Baker baseline for MDB lending ($4 billion annually) and bilateral lending (which averaged $1.9 billion annually, up from a trough of $700 million in 1985), overall public-sector net lending to the Baker countries was nonetheless larger than the total of new-money packages from the banks: a total of some $15.7 billion over three years versus $12.8 billion, respectively (Cline 1989a, 181). As Schilling (1989, 194) emphasized, the result was that the public sector/ commercial bank shares in net new lending were 55 percent/45 percent under the Baker Plan, despite the shortfall in additional MDB lending. This meant that the public-sector share was averaging upwards, from the 1985 shares of 27 percent public, 73 percent banks (table 5.1).

A major reason why both the MDBs and the banks lent less than prescribed by the plan was that debtor countries often did not have

---

6. Still another piece of evidence that the banks provided the bulk of the new money intended by the Baker Plan comes from the World Bank's data on debt stocks, which are from debtor reporting rather than creditor and thus omit any reductions attributable to loan-loss provisioning. These data show that for Latin America, long-term debt owed to commercial banks rose from $229 billion at the end of 1985 to $245 billion at the end of 1987, a $16 billion increase once again commensurate with the estimates here (World Bank 1990, 1: 142). By the end of 1988, however, the total fell to $222 billion, reflecting the large impact of the market-based debt reductions and conversions described here. It is no accident that this large reduction occurred only after the 1987 loan provisionings (described below).

Table 5.1 Long-term debt of Baker-17 countries[a] to commercial banks and official lenders, 1970 and 1982-88 (billions of dollars)

	1970	1982	1983	1984	1985	1986	1987	1988
Multi- and bilateral	9.6	48.0	54.9	60.4	76.4	102.0	129.5	130.2
IMF	0.2	6.6	12.6	15.0	18.6	20.4	22.0	19.3
Official total	9.8	54.6	67.5	75.4	95.0	122.4	151.6	149.5
Commercial bank debt	16.8	194.1	235.2	255.5	254.4	264.8	273.4	250.1
Interest arrears	0.0	0.4	1.3	2.8	2.1	2.1	6.6	6.3
Bank total unadjusted	16.8	194.4	236.5	258.3	256.5	266.9	280.0	256.4
Voluntary debt reduction cumulative (banks)	0.0	0.0	0.0	0.0	0.3	1.6	9.0	26.2
Bank total adjusted	16.8	194.4	236.5	258.3	256.8	268.5	289.0	282.6
TOTAL	26.6	249.1	304.0	333.7	351.8	391.0	440.5	432.1
Shares (percent):								
Total official	36.7	21.9	22.2	22.6	27.0	31.3	34.4	34.6
Total banks (adjusted)	63.3	78.1	77.8	77.4	73.0	68.7	65.6	65.4

a. For listing of countries, see table 2.1.

Sources: Calculated from World Bank 1992a, vol. 2; IIF 1989.

adequate macroeconomic adjustment programs and agreements in place with the IMF. However, it is also the case that the bank lending under the plan was heavily concentrated in the large debtor countries, suggesting that the plan had not taken into account the weak bargaining position of the smaller debtor countries.

Even for the larger countries the agreements tended to require protracted negotiations, which frequently broke down because of unstable macroeconomic policies. The large new-money packages of the Baker Plan were not implemented until March 1987 for Mexico, August of 1987 for Argentina, and November 1988 for Brazil (Cline 1989a). The delays for Argentina and Brazil in particular reflected extended periods in which the countries were not in compliance with IMF programs, and, in the case of Brazil, a phase in which the country consciously adopted a policy of going into arrears on interest.

Despite these difficulties, the Baker Plan not only mobilized the bulk of the new-money commitment of the banks, but it was also a period of experimentation that laid the groundwork for the subsequent Brady Plan. By 1987–88 there was increasing emphasis on the "menu approach" (Cline 1987) to mobilizing bank lending. This approach sought to address the divergent needs and objectives of the various classes of banks. One source of this divergence was different regulatory and accounting practices among the industrial countries. For example, the European banks were initially open to the idea of interest capitalization as a vehicle for mobilizing new money, but US banks viewed this option as anathema because US accounting conventions probably would have required setting aside loss provisions.[7]

Another fundamental distinction was between the banks that simply wanted to wipe their books clean of claims on troubled debtors (typically the regional US banks) and those that had long-term interests in remaining active in Latin America (the money center and other large international banks). In the later part of the Baker period, the "exit bond" was developed: a long-term bond with a below-market interest rate as a conversion instrument for banks that preferred not to increase their exposure by lending new money.[8] The Argentine package of 1987 was the first to include such an option. The Brazil package of 1988 was the most complete approach based on the menu concept, and included such

---

7. The more fundamental reason interest capitalization never caught on with the banks was that it seemed to invite a slide toward unilateralism wherein the debtor would simply announce the proportion of interest coming due to be capitalized.

8. Smaller banks tended to object that they had no obligation to participate in new-money packages in the first place, so they should not be expected to convert claims into exit bonds. However, peer pressure and perhaps the implicit sanctions in correspondent bank relationships with larger banks meant that participation through exit bonds was substantial in at least the 1988 Brazilian package.

instruments as new-money bonds; these were premised on the notion that because countries had tended not to reschedule bonds, this vehicle could convey an implicit seniority and thereby more easily mobilize new money.

Market-based debt reduction was also increasingly active in this period. Chile used debt-equity conversions extensively to reduce its external debt. After substantial debt-equity programs initially in Mexico, Argentina, and Brazil, these countries tended to suspend this instrument because of its impact on monetary expansion (a problem Chile could more easily deal with through compensating monetary measures because of its strong fiscal position and use of debt-equity in privatization). There were also discounted buybacks. In Brazil, several billion dollars worth of debt was retired in 1988 through "informal" buybacks, often by the state firms (see chapter 2, n. 8).

Two developments in the Baker Plan period were perhaps primarily responsible for the ultimate eclipse of the plan by its successor: the collapse of oil prices and the shift to major loan-loss provisioning by banks beginning in 1987. As analyzed in chapter 3, it was the fall of oil prices by half in 1986 that more than any other single factor derailed the strategy whereby debtor countries were earlier thought to be capable of growing and exporting their way out of the debt crisis.[9] That development meant that the capacity of Mexico, Venezuela, Ecuador, and Nigeria to service their debt was considerably below earlier expectations.[10]

The provisioning of debt, for its part, had the effect of sending a loud signal that the banks no longer considered their claims to be worth 100 cents on the dollar. As discussed in chapter 6, in early 1987 the Sarney government in Brazil adopted a moratorium, in considerable part as a political step to regain popularity after the collapse of the anti-inflationary Cruzado Plan. The moratorium failed to gain domestic political favor (Bresser Pereira 1994, 340). However, it did succeed in achieving the electrifying effect of prompting Citibank to set aside some $3 billion in reserves against its claims on developing countries, or about one-fourth of its sovereign debt. This action appears to have stemmed in part from the bank's negotiating strategy, in that it wanted to send a signal that despite Brazil's huge debt, the country could not intimidate the banks. Citibank's formal reasons for the move specifically cited the "decision to restructure our current exposure through debt/equity swaps, sales, and other measures," and more generally, the bank's

---

9. Truman (1989) also singles out the collapse of oil prices as a key reason why the Baker Plan turned out to be insufficient.

10. Note that the inclusion (partly on the recommendation of the IMF) of a provision in the 1986 new-money package for Mexico linking the amount of new bank lending to the price of oil provided an important psychological boost at a particularly dangerous time for the debt strategy.

intention to play a "constructive" role in the resolution of the debt problem (Reed 1987).[11]

Soon after, the other money center banks set aside comparable provisions. By December 1987, the Bank of Boston launched a second round of provisioning by the regional banks by raising its loan-loss reserves to 54 percent. Abroad, in the first quarter of 1988, Canadian authorities required that their banks increase provisioning against LDC loans from 15 percent to the range of 30–40 percent (Treasury 1989a). Although some major individual banks in Europe had reserved earlier, in general loan-loss provisioning in other countries (including Japan) followed rather than preceded the wave of set-asides begun by Citibank in early 1987.

The broad move to provisioning initiated two dynamics that would eventually contribute to the shift in the strategy from new lending to debt reduction. The first, as suggested by the public announcement by Citibank, was that higher reserves gave banks greater flexibility to undertake such debt reduction operations as debt-equity conversions and discounted cash buybacks.[12] The second was almost certainly unintended: the psychological impact of the wave of provisionings helped drive secondary market prices of debt of the Baker countries from a weighted average of 67 cents on the dollar at the beginning of the year to a range of 45–50 cents by the middle of 1987, and the prices eventually fell to a low of 32 cents (weighted average) in late 1989 (IMF 1990c, 37).

Without the low secondary market prices, the market-oriented debt conversion of the Brady Plan would have been impossible. Without the wave of bank provisioning, the secondary market prices would have been unlikely to fall as far as they did, and the secondary market would have been less well-developed. Brazil's 1987 moratorium thus indirectly set the stage for the Brady Plan.[13] It may be added that the shift in Brazil reflected primarily a downgrading of political willingness to pay, rather than any change in the underlying capacity to service external debt. The critical role of willingness to pay and its impact on market expectations is argued below to have been an important factor once again, though operating in the other direction, in explaining the renaissance of the Latin American capital markets in the 1990s after the launching of the Brady Plan.

Other major factors that contributed to the change from the Baker Plan to the Brady Plan included the following. There was a growing

---

11. Some observers add that as a young new chairman, Reed was eager to make his mark by showing that Citibank could afford large set-asides even if other large banks could not; and to distinguish his regime from that of his predecessor Walter Wriston, who had been closely identified with lending to developing countries (Volcker 1994, 215).

12. Also see Rhodes (1994, 729).

13. On this basis it might be argued that the Brazilian moratorium was a case of a confrontational approach that ultimately benefited the debtor. However, there were also costs to Brazil from going into moratorium, as discussed below.

problem of divergent interests among the banks, and therefore of mobilizing concerted lending packages. Partly because of differences in tax and reserve treatment, European and Japanese banks were increasingly resistant to new lending. So were US regional banks with relatively limited exposure and a desire to be able to say their books were free of LDC debt.

There was a growing problem of country arrears on interest, widely interpreted as a sign of failure of the existing strategy but usually stemming from the lack of IMF-approved adjustment programs and, consequently, new-money agreements with the banks. Interest arrears owed by Latin American countries had jumped from $3.7 billion in 1986 to $8.6 billion in 1987 and $9.0 billion in 1988, by which date the list of the region's countries in arrears included Argentina, Brazil, Costa Rica, the Dominican Republic, Ecuador, and Peru (but notably did not include Chile, Colombia, Mexico, or Venezuela; World Bank 1993b).[14]

As discussed below, other factors contributing to the strategy shift included political pressure from Congress; the growing view within the US administration that the public sector was taking over the risk while banks were exiting from lending; and criticism from academics.

The exit bond experiments in 1987–88 were the precursors to Brady debt forgiveness. The Argentine option in 1987 had no takers because it was priced at too deep a discount. In February 1988 Mexico, with the assistance of Morgan Guaranty, conducted an auction of collateralized 20–year bonds intended to extinguish bank claims at a discount close to that in the secondary market. The exercise fell short of expectations, as the government had arranged to buy up to $10 billion in US Treasury zero-coupon bonds but only issued $2.7 billion in exchange for $3.7 billion of bank claims (Cline 1988b). Both the volume and the discount were less than hoped, most importantly because the instruments had no collateral to back interest (Rhodes 1994). Nonetheless, the Mexico-Morgan deal was a conspicuous precedent for the Brady instruments. Similarly, the 1988 Brazilian new-money package included the alternative of converting claims into a 25–year bond with below-market interest (6 percent). Some 100 banks subscribed $1.1 billion to the instrument, and the amount could have been far higher if Brazilian negotiators had not initially resisted the option (Rhodes 1994, 729).

The Brady Plan, 1989–94

The collapse of oil prices in 1986 meant that Mexico and other oil exporters had suffered an objective reduction in debt-servicing capacity

---

14. Interest arrears rose as high as $27.7 billion in 1991, of which $19.8 billion was owed by Argentina and Brazil alone.

that justified reevaluating the original diagnosis of solvency in the debt strategy. The decline of secondary market prices on debt to ranges of 30 to 40 cents on the dollar (and much lower for some countries) meant, moreover, that there was a ready-made market opportunity for extinguishing debt at a discount even for nonoil countries, where payments arrears by 1987 and after tended to be associated more with domestic macroeconomic disarray (especially fiscal deficits). Because of the discount, there was an inherent opportunity for approaches that offered some form of increased security (collateral or direct cash in the instance of buybacks) in exchange for reduction in face value (chapter 4, figure 4.3). Moreover, many began to interpret the low secondary market prices as the measure of what the debt was really worth and thus all that the country should be obliged to pay, even though this interpretation was obviously subject to moral hazard as the country could easily drive down the price by confrontational statements and actions.

In the US Congress, leaders increasingly criticized the debt strategy for defending the interests of the banks to the detriment of US manufacturing firms and their workers. US exports to Latin America had fallen from $42 billion in 1981 to $26 billion in 1983, and although they returned to $35 billion by 1987 and $44 billion in 1988 (IMF 1988; 1992d), numerous calculations inferred that the debt crisis had cost hundreds of thousands of US export jobs. The more relevant, but rarely asked, questions were whether the original levels of Latin American imports were sustainable, and whether somehow forcing a forgiveness of the debt would benefit or jeopardize Latin American economies in the future and therefore the future number of US export jobs. Leaders also worried that the debt crisis could stifle the nascent return of democracy in Argentina, Brazil, and elsewhere in the region. As noted below, proposals emerged within the US Congress to establish an international agency to buy up the debt and to pressure banks to sell it at a discount.[15]

As had been the case at each previous crossroads on debt policy, the US-Mexico political connection was influential. As discussed in chapter 6, in late 1988 president-elect Carlos Salinas de Gortari set reduction in the debt owed as a core condition of his debt policy. Krugman (1994, 717) judges that Salinas's government had "decided quite early on that it needed a debt reduction, as much or more for domestic political reasons as for strictly economic ones," and notes that in the fall of 1988 George Bush had met with Salinas and "essentially promised that something would be delivered." Similarly, Citibank's William Rhodes (1994, 734) notes that Salinas had met with Bush and emphasized the importance of debt reduction, and he judges that the Brady Plan consequently had the full backing of the president.

---

15. The prototype for such proposals was first suggested by Peter B. Kenen (*New York Times*, 6 March 1983).

In the fall of 1988, the US Treasury (as well as the Federal Reserve) conducted an intensive review of debt policy, in part because the Baker Plan period was coming to the end of its original three-year horizon. In September 1988, the new secretary of the Treasury, Nicholas J. Brady, had already rejected a Japanese proposal for a shift toward voluntary debt reduction. Nonetheless, there was intense policy debate within the US government. By December of 1988, President-elect George Bush stated in answer to a press-conference question about debt policy that

> I think we should take a whole new look at it . . . because we've got enormous problems, particularly in our hemisphere, on third world debt. . . . I think you have to be very careful of forgiveness of debt. . . . I think we've got to find a more versatile answer than simply compelling private institutions to write off the debt. (*New York Times*, 20 December 1988)

By late 1988 the US Treasury was taking a more dominant role than before, relative to the Federal Reserve (Krugman 1994, 718). A fundamental policy shift was presumably easier for a new secretary than it would have been for James Baker (who had resigned to run the presidential campaign), whose name was imprinted on the existing strategy. Brady's Wall Street background may have made him more inclined toward a workout that took into account secondary market prices of the debt. A key architect of the Brady Plan, Treasury Undersecretary David Mulford, subsequently wrote:

> The turning point came in the spring of 1989 when the US government, under the leadership of President Bush and Treasury Secretary Nicholas J. Brady, designed a plan . . . for restructuring and reducing debt with the support of official resources. . . . [I]nstrumental in moving from debt management to debt resolution . . . [was] a recognition by governments and banks that the outstanding debt wasn't worth its face value. This was essential to a financial workout and the basis for realistic negotiations between the debtor nations and commercial banks. (*Wall Street Journal*, 21 August 1992, A7)

Already in early 1988, Mulford had proposed to Secretary James Baker a shift toward collateralized debt reduction.[16] Mulford believed that by the end of 1987 the existing strategy was flagging, and that new money was no longer forthcoming. Secretary Baker rejected the shift as impractical in an election year, when it would invite demands for similar debt reduction in the United States for farmers, municipalities, schools, and other hard-pressed debtors (believed to account for some $150 billion in shaky domestic loans).

In September of 1988, the new Treasury secretary, Nicholas J. Brady, went to a Group of Seven (G-7) meeting in Berlin, where debt was on

---

16. The account that follows draws on an interview with David C. Mulford, former undersecretary of Treasury (8 November 1994).

the agenda. He returned convinced that the Baker Plan was dead and asked Mulford to write up the proposal Mulford had discussed with him earlier for an alternative strategy.[17] To preclude subsequent blockage on any of several opposing arguments, the Treasury team first prepared what became known as the "truth serum" paper for review by a high-level interagency committee.[18] The paper argued that debt and arrears were growing, the banks were gradually getting out, and the IMF and World Bank were lending more money. Eventually the situation would show no improvement for the debtors, but there would have been a large transfer of risk from the banks to the public sector. After agreeing on a description of the existing situation, the interagency group proceeded to consider how to change the strategy, and by early December had agreed on the main elements of the new approach.

Some advisers to President-elect George Bush remained concerned about the political repercussions for domestic debtors of any move toward publicly collateralized debt forgiveness. At the same time, Bush felt that the banks should share some of the pain of adjustment to address the debt problem, and he decided to adopt the new approach. Mulford was authorized to present the draft plan to his foreign counterparts at the next G-7 meeting in January.

In February of 1989 riots in Caracas, associated with the austerity plan of the new regime of Carlos Andrés Pérez, caused an estimated 300 deaths (chapter 6). The event seemed to provide additional evidence that the existing debt strategy was causing political upheaval and that a new strategy was urgent.

On 10 March 1989, US Treasury Secretary Nicholas J. Brady announced a new plan for international debt that would shift the strategy from coordinated lending to the reduction, or partial forgiveness, of existing debt. The Brady Plan was premised on a voluntary, market-oriented approach to debt reduction. It wisely rejected any type of mandatory reduction, which probably would have faced an aggressive legal challenge by the banks and in any event would have done damage to the eventual restoration of normal capital market conditions that the earlier debt strategy had worked so hard to assure.[19]

---

17. Brady had identified the international debt problem and domestic banking reform as the two key priorities he would seek to address in his term as Secretary.

18. Among others, the committee included Secretary Brady, Federal Reserve Chairman Alan Greenspan, James Baker, Office of Management and Budget Director Richard Darman, NSC head Brent Scowcroft, and Secretary of State George Shultz.

19. Citibank's William Rhodes (1994, 734) reports that prior to the release of the plan he told Mulford that the debt reduction should be "voluntary, not mandatory," because the latter would have been of "doubtful legality and would not induce the cooperation of the international banking community."

The key new ingredient for voluntary debt reduction was the provision of public-sector funding for use in collateralization of conversion bonds. This policy departure rejected the critique that the public sector would be bailing out the banks, and it could do so credibly because the counterpart was debt forgiveness by the banks.

In outlining the plan before Congress, Undersecretary Mulford suggested that the plan could reduce the $340 billion debt of 39 countries by some $70 billion, with proportionate cuts potentially larger for Mexico (*Washington Post*, 17 March 1989). By mid-1989, some $34 billion had been earmarked for official support for collateral "enhancements," comprising $12 billion each from the International Monetary Fund and World Bank and $10 billion from the Japanese Export Import Bank (Cline 1990, 93).

The plan supplemented the carrot of enhancements with a new stick to encourage bank cooperation. For the first time, the IMF would not insist that a country have an agreement with the banks before the institution extended stabilization lending. There could thus be "lending into arrears," removing the previous implicit IMF leverage pressuring the prompt resolution of arrears.[20] US Treasury officials began to take a more tolerant attitude toward country arrears on interest owed to the banks, and considered them a "message" to the banks that if they did not reach agreement, the value of their claims might sink still further.[21]

The plan called for both debt reduction and further new money. There was a logical rationale for the coexistence of these two separate tracks as exclusive alternatives for different types of banks, but public reports of the initial pronouncements tended to imply that all banks would be expected to do both. It was unlikely that a given bank would choose both options. If a bank thought the country's long-term prospects were sound, it would tend to choose new money rather than debt reduction. If it thought the best that could be expected was to recover some fraction of past lending, it could hardly in good conscience place still more of depositors' money at risk.

One reason for the mixed signals on new money versus forgiveness was that there were two different viewpoints. From the start, the Treasury team emphasized debt forgiveness. In contrast, the Federal

---

20. In its 1992 review of debt policy, the World Bank thus notes: "The new strategy also marked a departure from earlier official practice by providing lending to a debtor country in arrears on its bank debt, if the country were negotiating in good faith on the basis of a sound financing plan" (World Bank 1992a, 1: 52). O'Connell (1993) reports that in its negotiations Argentina relied heavily on this aspect of the new plan, which took away a major source of leverage for the banks. Rhodes (1994, 732) has criticized the policy of IMF lending into arrears, and notes that G-7 finance ministers expressed misgivings about this policy at their September 1990 meeting. The practical question is, when is the country negotiating in good faith, as opposed to stalling and building up arrears to force deeper forgiveness?

21. David C. Mulford, interview, 19 November 1994.

Reserve, and especially Gerald Corrigan of the New York Fed, had grave reservations about the shift to debt forgiveness, and insisted that the plan had to include the option of new money to preserve a greater market orientation. Treasury officials did not object to inclusion of a new money option but did not expect much from it.

In the end, the plan was "voluntary" and "market-oriented": voluntary, precisely because it did give a bank the choice between new money and forgiveness (although the element of involuntariness already present in the earlier strategy of concerted lending still remained); and market-oriented, because in practice the depth of the debt reductions bore a close relationship to the preagreement secondary market price on the one hand and the extent of the risk reduction by enhancement collateral on the other.[22]

It took four months of acrimonious negotiations from the announcement of the Brady Plan to the agreement in principle on a debt reduction program for Mexico in July 1989. The central issue was the depth of the reduction. The initial Mexican negotiating position called for a 55 percent forgiveness, about the same discount then prevailing in the secondary market (*New York Times*, 22 May 1989, D1). The banks' initial bargaining position was a reduction of only 15 percent, subsequently raised to 22 percent (*Washington Post*, 8 June 1989, E5).

Early in the negotiations the managing director of the International Monetary Fund gave a speech before a banking audience that strongly, if implicitly, supported the initial Mexican position and scolded the banks for offering less. Announcing that the International Monetary Fund would be prepared to set aside 25 percent of standby or extended arrangement lending to a country for purposes of debt stock reduction and to increase lending by another 40 percent of the country's IMF quota for purposes of interest reduction, Michel Camdessus called for the banks that chose debt reduction to do their part in return by forgiving claims down to the secondary market level:

> Let me be quite frank with you . . . if banks wish to disengage from sovereign lending, or wish to exchange their existing claims for more secure assets, this is legitimate. But such operations must be undertaken at around market values for those claims. (Camdessus 1989, 12; also see *Washington Post*, 1 June 1989, E1)

Camdessus's position reflected the new thinking in the IMF emphasizing debt forgiveness (discussed below). However, reduction of debt all the way down to the secondary market price would have turned the Brady

---

22. Krugman (1994, 702) argues that the plan in practice abandoned its advertised voluntary nature. He notes that the device of "novation," whereby the new agreement superseded previous sharing clauses, meant that "the only 'voluntary' aspect . . . was the choice among several options . . . [including debt reduction or] . . . new money." Krugman is too fastidious on this point. No one ever said that the Brady Plan was *more* voluntary than the Baker Plan.

Plan into a non-market-oriented arrangement. The reason was that only if there were to be immediate cash buyback at that price could it be argued that the expected value of the banks' claims had been maintained but reconfigured with lower face value and higher security. Instead, the amount of collateral being offered represented only partial guarantees on a 30-year instrument. Indeed, the Mexican plan ruled out cash buybacks.

Mexican negotiators were more practical and recognized that to risk breakdown in the negotiations by holding out for the 55 percent reduction could have caused a run on the peso and a crisis in the precarious internal Mexican money market, where interest rates were extremely high already (chapter 6).[23] The deal they eventually struck for Mexico's $48.5 billion eligible long-term bank debt involved a reduction of 35 percent in principal value, for the "discount bond" variant that cut face value but maintained market-related interest rates (LIBOR plus 13/16ths). Banks could also choose a "par bond," which maintained 100 cents on the dollar in principal face value but adopted a fixed interest rate of $6^{1}/4$ percent, well below then-prevailing rates (about 10 percent including spread). The third option was to retain the full claim but provide additional "new-money" lending of 25 percent of exposure over three years (with one-half in the first).

The conversion bonds had 30-year maturities, with US Treasury zero-coupon bond collateral on principal and a moving guarantee of 18 months' interest. The total of $7.1 billion in enhancements was financed as follows: $2 billion from the World Bank, $1.3 billion from the IMF, $1.4 billion from the Export-Import Bank of Japan, $1.1 billion from a bridge loan from the banks (of which $650 million was subsequently refinanced by Japan's EXIM bank), and $1.4 billion from Mexico's reserves (Gurria and Fadl 1991). The conversion bonds provided for a "claw-back" whereby after the first seven years, 30 percent of any increase of oil prices above $14 per barrel (in real terms at 1989 prices) would be distributed to the bondholders. Conversely, if oil prices fell below $10 per barrel, the banks and official lenders were to provide an additional $800 million in lending (Cline 1991, 33).

Even though the depth of forgiveness was smaller in the Mexican deal than had been advocated by the International Monetary Fund, the agreement came only after forceful pressure on the banks by the US Treasury.[24] This pressure left bitterness among the banks that may have

---

23. Various accounts suggest, moreover, that despite the high public profile of the IMF in calling for deep forgiveness, in the actual negotiations the institution did not press the banks. The Fund's apparent quiescence in the negotiations may have resulted from suggestions by Treasury that the institution stay out of them. For its part, Treasury was active in pressuring the negotiations, but primarily for movement on both sides to reach agreement rather than on behalf of one party or the other.

24. Based on an interview with Mulford, 19 November 1994.

contributed to temporary delay before the conclusion of other country agreements. Although the Treasury did not again intervene forcefully, the basic pattern for most subsequent deals had already been set by the Mexico agreement.

Mexico's Finance Minister Pedro Aspe has written that the three options in the Mexico deal were "buyback equivalent. This means that in each case the relief reduction would be the same as if the resources used to guarantee each option were used to buy Mexican debt directly in the market at going market prices at the time when the negotiation started" (Aspe 1993, 141). He places that price at 42 cents on the dollar.[25]

Aspe's analysis confirms the concept of risk-compensated debt reduction suggested in chapter 4 as the essence of the Brady Plan. However, he does not acknowledge the corresponding implication that Mexico's (and, apparently, the IMF's) initial demand of 55 percent face value reduction would have placed the value of the conversion bonds well below the risk-adjusted value then present in the secondary market. Notably, Aspe omits any mention of the initial demand, referring instead to the position finally agreed with the advisory banks.

Mexican negotiators believed the country suffered from a debt overhang and needed debt and interest reduction, not new money; but they recognized that without the new money option the banks would have felt they were under compulsion (Gurria 1990). The negotiators' implicit discouragement of this option presumably contributed to its limited adoption by only 12 percent of banks (weighted by share in the value base), compared with 47 percent for par bonds and 41 percent for discount bonds (Aspe 1993, 142).

The Mexico Brady deal set the pattern for the dozen or so agreements that have followed since, as discussed below. Before turning to a review of the status of the plan, it is important to consider another aspect of the evolution of the debt strategy: the corresponding evolution in the debate on the intellectual underpinnings of the strategy.

Intellectual Evolution

The review of theoretical literature in chapter 4 showed that an immense amount of analytical effort was devoted to showing the conditions under which it could be mutually beneficial for creditors and debtors to

---

25. Assuming a risk-free interest rate of 8.5 percent, and "Mexico risk discount" of 17 percent, he calculates that the debt reduction (discount) bond had 5.6 cents in present value from the zero-coupon collateral on principal, 10.3 cents present value of collateralized interest, and 25.7 cents of noncollateralized interest, for a total of 41.6 cents (Aspe 1993, 134). Note that the calculation is inherently arbitrary, because the proper evaluation of the Mexico risk discount is unknown. Aspe's placement of this risk at 17 percent is plausible or even high for postagreement risk, but the 42-cent secondary market price means that the preagreement country risk discount for Mexico was much higher.

forgive a portion of the debt. That notion, of course, was the essence of the Brady Plan. What is of relevance for the present chapter is the way in which the dominant analytical framework within policy circles shifted over time.

It is illuminating to compare two conference volumes published by the World Bank. The first (Smith and Cuddington 1985) was from a conference held in April 1984, just when the initial crisis seemed to be yielding nicely to the strategy of growing out of the debt problem with the assistance of coordinated lending. In that volume, Paul Krugman (1985) judged that although the illiquidity-insolvency dichotomy was inadequate because the essential problem was uncertainty about solvency, the existing strategy of coordinated lending with official-sector participation was nonetheless well-advised, with the principal exception being that so far the arrangements had been too short-term. In the same volume, Cooper and Sachs (1985) provided a theoretical analysis that, among other things, suggested that "actual levels of external borrowing by developing countries are considerably less than could in principle be serviced by productive investments" (80), such that debt was well below solvency limits and primarily constrained by liquidity restrictions. The Bank's chief economist argued in the volume that with OECD growth of 3.5 percent, debtor country exports could grow at 11–12 percent, so that debt could grow by 7–8 percent and still be consistent with a falling debt-service ratio (Krueger 1985, 337). In short, the dominant intellectual paradigm was that of growing out of the debt problem (as in the model proposed in Cline 1983 and revisited in chapter 3 of this study) rather than forgiving enough debt to make the remainder viable.[26]

In contrast, when the World Bank held a similar conference in January 1989 (Husain and Diwan 1989), there was a strong emphasis on such concepts as debt overhang and the need to forgive debt, based on the new literature that had been developed in the interim by such authors as Dooley (1987b), Sachs (1989g), Krugman (1988), and others reviewed in chapter 4 above. The principal debate by the time of the 1989 conference tended to be about the fine-tuning of debt forgiveness (Claessens and Diwan 1989; D. Cohen 1989) on such matters as conditionality, rather than on whether the right strategy was to pursue coordinated new lending or to begin forgiving debt. In his forward to the published volume, written later in the year, the successor chief economist of the World Bank wrote:

> It was clear to the participants in this conference at the beginning of 1989, as it had been clear to many much earlier, that growth in the debtor countries would

---

26. Thus, two subsequently vigorous advocates of debt forgiveness, Jeffrey Sachs and Rudiger Dornbusch, were contributing authors in the volume, yet neither one called for a policy shift to forgiveness in his paper for the 1984 conference (see Cooper and Sachs 1985; Dornbusch 1985).

not return without debt relief. But the official agencies operate on the basis of an agreed-upon strategy, and none of them could openly confront the existing strategy without having an alternative to put in place. . . . So long as the United States was not willing to move, the IFIs were not free to speak—though to be sure the repeated emphasis on debt reduction, with "voluntary, market-based" added sotto voce by the heads of the World Bank and IMF, was signaling their conclusion that it was time to move on. . . . [T]he academics' drumbeat of criticism of the Baker strategy during 1987 and 1988 helped keep up the pressure for change—especially the pressure from Congress on the US administration. (Fischer 1989b, v)

Perhaps no academic was more visible, eloquent, or effective in beating the drum for debt forgiveness than Harvard University's Jeffrey Sachs (e.g., 1989b).[27]

A similar change of paradigm was evident at the other key international financial institution, the International Monetary Fund. A volume published in 1989 by the IMF (Frenkel, Dooley, and Wickham 1989) provided a state-of-the-art compendium of analytical papers on the debt problem. The papers typically emphasized the problem of debt overhang and its supposed depressing effect on domestic investment (discussed in chapter 4).

The introduction to the volume (of which one of the authors, Jacob Frenkel, was chief economist of the IMF at the time) recounted how a key paper in the volume by Max Corden and Michael Dooley, then of the IMF staff, had served as the basis for discussion at a February 1988 seminar of the Fund's executive board. The paper reviewed the pros and cons of voluntary and forced debt forgiveness. A subsequent paper by Dooley (1989b) was the basis for one of the two main arguments for a debt overhang: that investors will be discouraged from making new investments so long as the secondary market price on existing debt is below par, because of the fear that without subordination of old debt, the new financial claims will also be priced at near the market discount (a view disputed in chapter 4 above). The three editors explicitly noted:

> Central to the paper and to others that follow in this volume is the notion that the aggregate market value of claims on a debtor country reflect the expected present value of transfers that will be made available over time by the country to creditors. (Frenkel, Dooley, and Wickham 1989, 4)

Secondary market prices, of course, had collapsed from the range of 70 cents on the dollar to the range of 30–40 cents on the dollar after the

---

27. The change in Sachs's position from the early 1980s (illustrated by Cooper and Sachs 1985) to the late 1980s was no doubt influenced by his experience participating in the design of Bolivia's debt policy in 1986. That policy involved an ongoing moratorium on interest to banks, coupled with a buyback at 11 cents on the dollar with the help of $34 million in concessional aid for this purpose. Sachs viewed the outcome as a resounding success "for all the parties concerned" (Morales and Sachs 1990, 255).

Brazilian moratorium and bank provisioning of 1987. At that time, the major banks had tended to argue that the secondary market was extremely thin and its prices were not very meaningful. However, by 1988–89 analysts at the World Bank (e.g., Diwan and Kletzer 1992) and IMF were treating the secondary market price as the measure of what the banks expected to recover. In this framework, it was easy to conclude that some arrangement that conveyed this amount to the banks and exonerated the debtor country of the difference from par would be a healthy solution to the debt crisis. A corresponding implication was that the banks would somehow enjoy an unjustifiable windfall gain if public intervention, for example in buybacks, wound up boosting the market price and conveying a larger value to the banks.

If the centers of financial orthodoxy were shifting from the 1983–85 model of growing out of the debt with the help of coordinated lending to the new model of forgiving debt on a more-or-less voluntary and more-or-less market-oriented basis, other influential sources of opinion were increasingly calling for debt forgiveness as well. In September 1988 a blue-ribbon panel of the United Nations Association of the United States concluded that

> heavy external debt servicing requirements may . . . make the adoption of fundamental reforms extremely difficult. . . . The panel believes that voluntary debt service reduction should be pursued as a serious alternative or complement to more lending. It may be the only alternative for many smaller debtors that have already been written off by the banks. . . . Despite the losses entailed, debt service–reduction transactions can have considerable benefits for creditor banks as well, if the asset transformation or exchange enhances the quality of their loan portfolio. (A. Solomon et al. 1988, 37–38)

Think tanks were also moving toward the new paradigm. A publication by the Council on Foreign Relations attacked the past strategy of "muddling through" and called for debt relief that would be case-by-case; that would be voluntary and market-oriented, relying on conversion of bank claims to long-term bonds with creditor government guarantees; and that would entirely remove banks from the business of making balance of payments loans to governments (Islam 1988). In the autumn of 1988 the Institute for International Economics published a monograph by my colleague John Williamson, calling for voluntary debt reduction. The concept was to take advantage of the division among banks between one group that was extremely pessimistic and would settle for something like the secondary market price, and another group, holding perhaps two-thirds of the debt, that recognized that "if they find the short and medium run tolerable, debtors will be capable of servicing their debt fully in the long run" (Williamson 1989, 39). His approach featured buybacks and exit bonds guaranteed by the World Bank (but no direct lending for enhancements by the international financial institutions [IFIs]). Williamson added that more rapid results might require an arrangement whereby the pessimistic banks were essentially bought out at a steep discount by the remaining banks, which in turn would then convert their claims to instruments with full expected present value but with debt service linked to export earnings (47).

Several members of the US Congress were prominent in demanding a shift of the debt strategy. Typically their approaches placed more emphasis on "debt reduction" and less emphasis on "voluntary" action. As early as 1986, Senator Bill Bradley (D-NJ) proposed that banks forgive 18 percent of debt over three years (see Cline 1987, 80–81). Soon after the Brazilian suspension of payments in early 1987, Representatives Bruce Morrison (D-CT) and John LaFalce (D-NY) proposed that a new international entity be set up in the World Bank or International Monetary Fund to purchase debt from the banks at a discount on the secondary market and forgive the debtors the difference from face value (*Wall Street Journal*, 12 March 1987). Together with Representative Charles Schumer (D-NY), the two representatives authored a clause of the omnibus trade bill passed by the House of Representatives in 1987 that would have required the administration to negotiate the creation of a multilateral financial institution that would purchase developing country debt at a discount (Pease 1988, 100).

The final version of the omnibus trade bill instructed the secretary of the Treasury to "initiate discussions" with other countries "with the intent to negotiate the establishment of the International Debt Management Authority" which would "purchase sovereign debt of less developed countries from private creditors at an appropriate discount" and "enter into negotiations with the debtor countries for the purpose of restructuring the debt" (Public Law 100–418, 23 August 1988, sec. 3111). However, the bill authorized the secretary of Treasury to desist from such negotiations if the secretary determined that such discussions would materially increase "the discount at which sovereign debt is sold," "the probability of default on such debt," or "the likelihood of debt service failure or disruption" (Public Law 100–418, 23 August 1988, sec. 3111).

The Treasury department subsequently reported to Congress that an International Debt Management Authority would not be helpful for resolving the debt problem (Treasury 1989a). By then Secretary Brady had announced his plan. The Treasury report noted that the International Debt Management Authority proposed in the omnibus trade act would "inherently shift the risk on developing country loans from commercial banks to the international financial institutions or creditor governments" (4). In contrast, the Brady Plan approach would "minimize" such a shift, "avoid mandatory prices for debt exchanges (with prices preset by the facility), and . . . maintain a market-oriented approach to debt restructurings" (7).

The Treasury language reflects the concern at the time that if the banks achieved exit without forgiving a significant portion of the debt, the International Monetary Fund and other official lenders would end up bearing unnecessarily high risk while financing bank exodus. A manifestation of this mind-set that there was a zero-sum game between the banks and the official lenders was the restriction that less than one-half of IMF enhancements could be applied to buybacks, as discussed below.

The report went on to judge that the congressional proposals had already elevated Latin American expectations of generalized debt relief, perhaps contributing to a decline in secondary market prices. The fundamental point, however, was that by March 1989 the Treasury had come up with an alternative of its own that superseded the congressional movement for an international debt authority. To support its new plan, Treasury recommended that "the World Bank and IMF could re-direct a portion of their policy-based loans for use to . . . collateralize debt-for-bond exchanges with a significant discount" (Treasury 1989b, 26).

The policy diagnosis was also shifting in other industrial countries. French President François Mitterrand and Japanese Finance Minister (and subsequently Prime Minister) Kiichi Miyazawa had made proposals for market-oriented debt reduction prior to the Brady Plan (World Bank 1992a, 1: 52), as had Alfred Herrhausen, managing director of Deutsche Bank (Herrhausen 1988).[28]

In sum, on the eve of the Brady Plan there had been a major shift in the debt paradigm away from concerted new lending toward market-oriented debt reduction. Just how large a shift depended on the analyst. Some, including myself (Cline 1988a) and Williamson (1988), saw voluntary debt reduction as an important new opportunity presented by secondary market developments, but primarily as an adjunct to continued new lending by a core of large international banks with plans to remain over the longer term in the debtor countries. Others, including many of the authors in the IFI conference volumes cited above, sought a more definitive shift, implicitly with a greater element of coercion on the banks. In the end the Brady Plan was launched with rhetoric that seemed to come down heavily on the side of debt reduction. Even so, in practice the plan was sometimes applied with more emphasis on new

---

28. At the Toronto economic summit meeting in July 1988, Miyazawa floated a proposal whereby debtor countries would place part of their reserves into an IMF account for use as collateral on the principal of securities resulting from debt converted by banks (Miyazawa 1988). The terms of the securities (e.g., any interest or principal reduction) would be negotiated with the banks. Participation would be voluntary, and debtors would be expected to enter medium-term IMF adjustment programs. The tone of the proposal was that of an addition to the menu approach, following the pattern of the Mexico-Morgan deal. As such, the approach was less heavily focused on debt reduction than the Brady Plan. This nuance was consistent with the subsequent resistance of Japanese officials toward the forgiveness of bilateral debt. However, Japan was highly supportive of Brady deals for banks, and the country was the only source of bilateral funding for enhancements in most of these agreements.

lending by banks that planned to remain (Venezuela, Philippines); whereas in other cases (Argentina) the emphasis was even more heavily on debt reduction than in the Mexico agreement.

Before leaving the intellectual evolution of the debt strategy, and at the risk of some repetition of the discussion in chapter 4, it is important to single out the salient arguments that drove the shift from the Baker Plan to the Brady Plan.

Lack of Progress

It was common to cite an absence of progress on the debt problem. A typical argument was that debt/exports ratios had not declined. However, as shown in chapter 2, the most relevant debt indicator—the ratio of net interest payments to exports of goods and services—had in fact declined, from 30 percent in 1982 to 25 percent in 1985–88 and 19 percent in 1989 (table 2.5).

Transfer of Resources

The World Bank (1992a, 1: 50) has calculated that for the middle-income highly indebted countries (HICs), the net transfer of resources shifted from an inflow of 2.8 percent of GDP in 1973–81 to an outflow of 2 percent of GDP in 1982–91. The swing of almost 5 percent of GDP was adjusted to by an increase of domestic saving by 1.8 percent of GDP and a reduction of domestic investment by 3.1 percent of GDP. By the late 1980s there was a growing critique that the Baker Plan was not doing enough to restore resource transfers to the debtor countries. However, as the case of Chile showed, export-led growth as a vehicle for emerging from the debt crisis tended to make satisfactory domestic growth compatible with a smaller inflow of foreign saving. Moreover, the inflow of resources in the earlier period had been excessive.

The resource transfer argument also became increasingly less relevant for some key debtors that had simply suspended debt servicing to the banks, most notably Brazil and Argentina in the late 1980s. As discussed in chapter 6, these countries experienced severe problems of inflation and recession, and did so despite the absence of realized debt service payments to the banks. The reason was that their domestic macroeconomic policies (especially fiscal) were in disarray.

Bailing Out the Banks

Krugman (1994, 700) emphasizes that in the months before the announcement of the Brady Plan, policymakers increasingly focused on the fact that for the Baker countries there had been an apparent realloca-

Figure 5.1 Alternative estimates of private bank and official sector debt of Baker-15 (1982 dollars)

millions of dollars

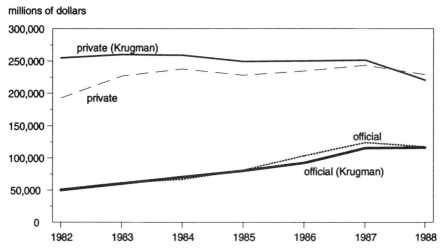

Sources: IMF, *International Financial Statistics;* World Bank, *World Debt Tables;* Krugman (1994).

tion of debt risk from the banks to the public sector. He notes, "A chart that looked something like [figure 5.1] . . . was the subject of alarmed discussion." At constant 1982 prices, the stock of official creditor loans to the Baker-15 countries had risen from $50 billion in 1982 to $120 billion by 1987 (and plateaued at that level through 1989), whereas the stock of bank loans had held approximately unchanged at $250 billion from 1982 through 1987 and then declined to $225 billion in 1988.

Figure 5.1 reproduces Krugman's chart in the solid lines. The figure also shows in broken lines the corresponding real debt stock figures based on World Bank data and adjusted to include interest arrears and adding back in voluntary debt reduction (from table 5.1, deflated by US consumer prices). The adjusted data show the same rise in public-sector claims. However, the adjusted estimates show a larger rise in bank debt from 1982 to 1987, and a considerably smaller decline in real bank debt from 1987 to 1988. Thus, if the chart that had been circulating had shown the appropriate data, it would have looked less like the banks were being bailed out.[29]

However, it is fair to say that those who feared a public bailout would still have been concerned by the rising share of public-sector debt, even with the adjusted data shown in the revised figure. The banks, of course, saw matters differently. The Institute of International Finance noted in January 1989, "The strong expansion of bank lending in the

29. It is unclear why Krugman's bank debt figures in the early 1980s are substantially above those now reported by the World Bank.

wake of the two sharp oil price hikes of the 1970s marked an aberration from historical trends and it could not be expected to continue'' (IIF 1989, 12). Bank representatives argued that the rising public-sector share was merely a restoration of more normal historical patterns. And indeed the data provide support: as shown in table 5.1, the decline in the bank share of bank plus public-sector debt stock owed by Baker countries from 78 percent in 1982 to 65 percent in 1988 brought this share back to almost exactly where it had stood in 1970.

In essence, it is a matter of value judgment whether the rising public-sector share over the 1980s represented bailing out the banks or restoring more balance to the lending shares after the inability and unwillingness of the public sector to undertake the petrodollar recycling required by the oil shocks had contributed to the mushrooming of the banks' share in the 1970s. Even after the relative rise of public-sector exposure after the debt crisis, the bank share by 1988 remained nearly twice as large as the public-sector share. Moreover, in retrospect it is notable that the Brady Plan brought substantial losses to the private banks but none to the official creditors (a sharp contrast to the publicly led debt reductions granted for Egypt and Poland).

Commodity Prices

Another important argument was that the initial strategy was not working because of the collapse in commodity prices. In fact, Kuczynski argued that the debtor response to the debt crisis had contributed importantly to driving down commodity prices, because the countries had increased exports to work their way out of the crisis (Kuczynski 1988, 140). If this were the case, it would be an important instance of an inherent external transfer problem stemming from falling terms of trade when the debtor seeks to carry out the transfer. The original debt strategy might then indeed have been internally inconsistent.

Table 5.2 suggests, however, that there is little or no evidence that the debt crisis was responsible for falling commodity prices. The table reports the aggregate share of the Baker-17 countries in world exports of ten commodity groups in 1979–81 and in 1987–89. In seven of the ten groups, the share of these highly indebted countries in commodity exports actually declined rather than increasing. The weighted average stood at 21.6 percent of world supply in 1979–81 and 19.3 percent in 1987–89. If the debtor countries had sharply increased their commodity exports because of the debt crisis, their world market share should have increased instead of eroding. Moreover, except for the cases of coffee and cocoa, the world market share of the debt-crisis countries was probably too small in the first place for even rapid export expansion to have driven down prices.

Table 5.2 Nonoil commodity exports of Baker-17 countries[a], 1979-81 and 1987-89

Commodity	Value (billions of dollars)		World share (percentages)	
	1979-81 average	1987-89 average	1979-81 average	1987-89 average
Meat	1.58	1.30	10.4	6.1
Maize	0.49	0.37	4.6	4.7
Fruit	1.95	2.86	18.7	18.5
Sugar	1.48	0.44	11.4	4.2
Coffee	5.92	5.28	50.2	45.8
Cocoa	2.16	1.87	46.7	41.2
Oil seeds	1.16	1.23	12.7	14.0
Cotton	0.45	0.18	7.3	3.2
Iron ore	2.06	2.31	31.9	38.7
Copper	2.46	2.64	21.7	16.5
TOTAL	19.68	18.48	20.0	17.2

a. For listing of countries, see table 2.1.

Source: Calculated from United Nations, *International Trade Statistics Yearbook*, 1982, 1990.

As analyzed in chapter 3, it is indeed the case that falling commodity prices accounted for some of the shortfall of progress on debt/exports ratios. The World Bank (1992a, 1: 42, 46) has calculated that whereas rising real export prices in the period 1973–81 meant that the debt/exports ratio stood at only 140 percent at the end of this period instead of the level of 220 percent it otherwise would have reached, the reverse happened in the 1980s. The debt/exports ratio for all developing countries rose from 140 percent in 1981 to a peak of 230 percent in 1986 before moderating to 175 percent in 1989; but if real export prices had remained constant instead of falling, the ratio would not have risen above 160 percent at its peak and by 1989 would have been down to 110 percent. That analysis is consistent with the findings in chapter 3. However, there is no evidence that it was increased exports forced by the debt crisis that caused the shift from rising real commodity prices in the 1970s to falling prices in the 1980s. Clearly the largest single change was in the trend of oil prices, which few would argue was driven by the debt crisis.

Brady Agreements, 1990–94

Status of the Plan

By October 1993, the International Monetary Fund (1993f, 72) was able to report that seven of the largest bank debtors, covering $116 billion in claims, had completed Brady deals for debt and debt-service reduction (DDSR); three others including Brazil had reached agreements with banks on another $50 billion; and five low-income countries had been able to extinguish their bank debt through buybacks at deep discounts with the help of the Debt Reduction Facility in the International Development Association (IDA). Altogether the IMF estimated that countries accounting for 80 percent of commercial banks' debt rescheduled in the 1980s had been involved in these restructurings; that the deals had reduced the net present value of the stream of debt service obligations by about $50 billion, or approximately one-third; and that the total cost of enhancements (collateral) for the operations had been $18 billion, of which $6$1/2$ billion came from international financial institutions.

By May 1994, fully five years after the inauguration of the Brady Plan, there had been deals completed or announced for 18 countries accounting for $191 billion in original bank claims (table 5.3). The set of countries overlapped heavily with the 17 countries identified earlier under the Baker Plan. Among the Latin American countries on the Baker list, all had received Brady deals by early 1994 except Chile, Colombia, Jamaica, and Peru. Chile, Colombia, and Jamaica did not request debt reduction, and bank negotiations with Peru were relatively well advanced.[30]

Financial Engineering

The three options in the Mexico plan served as the prototypes for the instruments applied in the other Brady deals, with variations. The only other major option added was the cash buyback, used in the first Philippines arrangement and especially in the small, low-income debtor deals financed by the special Debt Reduction Facility set up in the IDA.

Typically the menu included a discount bond with original claims reduced by 30 to 35 percent, interest at LIBOR plus 13/16ths, a "bullet" (single payment) maturity of 30 years, US Treasury zero-coupon bond collateral on principal, and a rolling guarantee on 12 to 18 months of interest; it also included a par bond retaining full face value but cutting interest to a fixed rate of 6 percent or so and providing similar maturity and collateralization. In addition, several cases provided for a buyback at a specified price, and/or the option of providing new money rather than reducing claims (for example, an increase of exposure by 25 percent over three years or so).

The Brazilian menu was the most complicated, with six options. The discount bond had the standard features. The par bond had a "step-

---

30. In the case of Jamaica, the banks provided MYRA reschedulings, and the government did not request forgiveness primarily because the amounts involved were so small. Thus, in 1985 long-term bank claims amounted to only 11 percent of Jamaica's total debt, and by 1992 this share was down to 7 percent (World Bank 1993b, 2: 218–19).

down, step-up" feature for interest rates (which dropped to 4 percent in the first year and rose gradually to 6 percent by the seventh year, and remained at 6 percent thereafter). A front-loaded interest reduction bond (FLIRB) similarly cut interest initially to 4 percent and then gradually raised the rate to LIBOR plus 13/16ths by the seventh year, and set the maturity at 15 years. The new-money option called for an increase of exposure by 18 percent at LIBOR plus 7/8ths, but was available only tied to parallel adoption of about six times as much money base placed into conversion bonds. A 20–year restructuring bond employed the step-down, step-up to LIBOR-plus for interest, but provided for gradual principal repayment after 10 years' grace. Finally, a 20-year FLIRB with capitalization (C-bond) set the interest at a fixed 8 percent but capitalized the difference between this rate and a step-down, step-up calendar (initially 4 percent, rising to 8 percent by year seven) (*Gazeta Mercantil*, 13 July 1992; World Bank 1993b, 1: 108).

The variations were designed to address economic and institutional differences among creditors and debtors. For Venezuela, which was relatively lightly indebted, a relatively large number of banks chose the new-money option.[31] Argentina had been relatively heavily indebted, and its negotiators did not include a new-money option. The cash buyback proved most relevant for small, low-income countries where the amount of bank debt was minimal and there was a financial angel to provide a grant for the buyback (either a consortium of bilateral donors as in Costa Rica and the first Bolivian deal preceding the Brady Plan; or the IDA facility). The discount bond was designed for banks primarily concerned about limiting interest fluctuation risk; the par bond, for banks in countries where regulatory and tax considerations made it preferable to retain full face value but accept a concessional interest rate. In the case of the Brazilian C-bond, the inclusion of interest capitalization reflected the differences between regulatory treatment in Europe (where there tended to be little difference from new money) and the United States (where capitalized interest typically would be provisioned against but new money would not be).

Grand Exodus

A striking feature of the summary shown in table 5.3 is that the amount of new money under the 18 Brady deals was minimal: only about 2 percent of exposure. In contrast, forgiveness was pervasive. Typically the face value reduction in the discount bond was 30 to 35 percent. The

---

31. Banks accounting for $6 billion of the $19 billion base selected the new-money option, which converted existing claims into 17-year bonds at LIBOR plus 1 percent (with no enhancements) and called for a 20 percent increase in exposure over two years (Cline and Conning 1991).

Table 5.3 Brady Plan agreements, 1989-94

Country	Date of agreement[a]	Eligible debt (billions of dollars)	Depth of cut[b] (percent)	Forgiveness: Equivalent[c] (billions of dollars)	Forgiveness: Fraction (percent)	New money (billions of dollars)	Buyback price (percent)
Mexico	9/15/89; 2/15/90	47.17	35	14.15	30.0	1.03	..
Philippines	1989; 1992	6.60	..	2.38	36.1	0.83	50
Costa Rica	11/16/89; 5/21/90	1.61	..	0.98	60.9	..	16
Venezuela	6/25/90; 12/17/90	19.01	30	3.76	19.8	1.17	45
Uruguay	11/2/90; 12/19/91	1.60	..	0.50	31.3	0.09	56
Niger[d]	3/8/91	0.11	..	0.09	82.0	..	18
Mozambique[d]	12/27/91	0.19	..	0.11	57.6	..	10
Nigeria	1/1992	5.34	..	2.60	48.7	..	40
Guyana[d]	11/24/92	0.07	..	0.06	86.0	..	14
Argentina	4/7/92; 4/7/93	29.34	35	8.43	28.7	..	..
Brazil	8/9/92; 4/15/94	50.00	35	14.00[e]	28.0	0.50[e]	..
Uganda[d]	2/26/93	0.17	..	0.13	78.3	..	12
Dominican Republic	5/3/93; pending	0.80	35	0.40[e]	50.0	..	25

Bolivia	5/19/93	0.18	..	0.14	79.0	..	16
Jordan	6/30/93; pending	0.80	35	0.26[e]	35.0	..	39
Bulgaria	11/25/93; pending	6.80[e]	50	3.40[e]	50.0	..	..
Poland	3/10/94; pending	14.00[e]	45	6.30[e]	45.0	..[f]	..[g]
Ecuador	5/2/94; pending	7.60	45	3.42[e]	45.0	..	..
TOTAL		191.40	..	61.12	31.9	3.62	..

.. = not available

a. The first date is agreement in principle; the second, final.
b. Discount bond basis.
c. Sum of reduction in face value of original debt and reduction in present value of interest reductions, less amount spent on buybacks.
d. IDA Debt Reduction Facility operations.
e. Estimate.
f. Outcome pending; limited to small amounts.
g. Pending.

Sources: World Bank 1990a, 1991a, 1992a, 1993a (all vol. 1); press reports.

aggregate forgiveness estimated in the table amounts to about 32 percent.[32] The implication is that for practical purposes the Brady Plan has been all forgiveness and no new money.

From the vantage point of 1994, the few banks that chose new money look prescient. Holders of original claims on Mexico can now expect eventual repayment at something close to full face value. The implication is that as a group, the banks were unduly pessimistic, or alternatively that they were intensively cajoled into the forgiveness options.[33] Indeed, by the time of the Brazilian deal the Brazilian negotiators set effective limits on the new-money option (and their Argentine counterparts ruled out the option completely), suggesting that by 1992 with the rebirth of the Latin American capital market many more banks might otherwise have opted for new money.

For at least the time being, the banks are now out of the long-term lending business to the Brady countries.[34] As noted in chapter 8, new long-term bank commitments in Latin America were less than $1 billion annually in 1991–92, in contrast to annual new commitments in the

---

32. As noted, the IMF (1993f, 72) reaches the same estimate for the forgiveness fraction. The calculation of table 5.3 estimates forgiveness as the reduction in face value (primarily the cut on discount bonds) plus present value of interest service reductions (from World Bank 1993b, 1: 37), minus resources spent on buybacks. For the small, low-income countries relying on buybacks, forgiveness is calculated as the difference between the buyback price and par, applied to the amount of debt repurchased.

Note that the World Bank (1993b, 37) reports a "total debt reduction equivalent" (TDRE) estimated as follows. DRE (debt reduction equivalent) = FNR − NM + PVIR + PPEC; TDRE = DRE − AOL, where FNR is the face value of debt reduction, NM is new money, PVIR is present value of interest reduction, PPEC is prepayment value of collateral (purchase price of the collateral), and AOL is additional official lending for the buybacks and enhancements. TDRE is a misleading concept if it is meant to convey a welfare effect, because it deducts new money without taking account of the fact that new money conveys an additional asset that offsets the additional liability. The appropriate measure for welfare purposes is instead the forgiveness equivalent, which tells the size of the windfall transfer from creditors to the debtor in comparison with the original terms. In practice, nonetheless, because new money was relatively small, and because PPEC tends to be canceled out by AOL, the World Bank's TDRE is a relatively close approximation of forgiveness. For the seven Brady cases the Bank considers (which exclude Brazil), TDRE amounts to $39 billion on a debt base of $110 billion, or 35 percent—close to the forgiveness fraction of one-third identified by the IMF and in the calculations of table 5.3.

33. Citibank's William Rhodes (1994, 734) has stated that "although the Treasury Department had pushed the banks to participate in the Mexico plan, most of them had been prepared to participate anyway."

34. An encouraging major exception was a syndicated loan for $500 million to Argentina in August 1994, led by Chemical Bank and Credit Suisse. The loan was for 18 months at 1½ percent above LIBOR. The Argentine government had decided to repackage its intended sale of remaining shares in a number of privatized gas transmission and distribution companies, and needed funds because of the delay. After considering loans collateralized by these prospective receipts, the government decided that bank interest was strong enough to borrow solely on the credit of the Argentine Republic.

range of $10 billion to $14 billion for Asian developing countries (see table 8.2). However, as also set forth in chapter 8, there has been a flood of alternative capital inflows into Latin America in the early 1990s.

What appeared to have happened by 1994 was the following. A debt strategy originally intended to orchestrate lending until countries could increase exports and restore creditworthiness (the Baker Plan) had given way to a forgiveness plan that had the predictable effect of cutting off new long-term lending from the banks (the Brady Plan). However, the broadly cooperative, market-oriented nature of the forgiveness plan contributed to an atmosphere of confidence for other categories of creditors, including bond lenders, so that renewed capital flows through other channels accomplished the return to the capital market. It seems highly likely that if instead more mandatory, below-market forgiveness had been forced (for example, by insisting that banks forgive down to the 1989 secondary market price without corresponding cash or fully collateralized payment), the return to the capital market would have been greatly delayed.

IDA Facility

In an atmosphere in which the official community had shifted to a strategy calling for bank forgiveness of debt owed by middle-income countries in return for collateral from international agencies, a natural policy spillover was the reexamination of debt policy toward low-income countries. One manifestation of this process was the move to enhanced Toronto terms for debt relief by bilateral donors (see chapter 7). Another was the creation of a special facility in the International Development Association. In 1989 the World Bank allocated $100 million to a new IDA Debt Reduction Facility (with additional allocations in subsequent years). Grants of up to $10 million per country were to be available for Brady-type cash buybacks or conversions of commercial bank debt, for countries that carried out adjustment programs and had parallel debt relief from bilateral creditors. The extremely deep discounts expected on these operations (table 5.3) tended to limit their number, in part because of bank concerns about precedent (World Bank 1990, 1: 27). Although the low-income countries owed relatively little debt to the banks, the new IDA window was a useful adjunct to and spinoff from the Brady Plan, and it would have been implausible without the new official blessing on reduction of bank debt accorded by the plan.

Tensions and Rigidities

The broad question of whether the Brady Plan was a success or failure is evaluated below. However, in completing the initial description of its implementation it is important to highlight some of the plan's operational problems.

One inherent tension in the plan has already been noted above: its ambivalence about whether banks were expected to provide new money or reduce their claims. This tension might have been resolved by a clearer emphasis on the division of bank response into new lending by banks planning to remain active in the country and forgiveness by the others. A greater emphasis on new lending by an important bloc of banks might have led to an earlier return of banks themselves to voluntary lending by the mid-1990s. Instead, except for the cases of the Philippines and Venezuela, the ambivalence was resolved by collapsing the new-money response to by far the lesser of the two vehicles. This asymmetrical allocation of the two basic options was accomplished either by debtor suasion (Mexico), outright preclusion of new money by the country negotiators (Argentina), or restrictive limits (Brazil). As discussed below, the disparate outcome was also undoubtedly influenced by the fact that far fewer of the banks turned out to really believe that the problem was not one of insolvency than had previously been apparent (including from the banks' own published analyses; IIF 1989). Just as herd instinct contributed to excessive bank lending in the 1970s, it seems to have contributed to excessive exodus in the Brady Plan.

Another tension was in the adequacy of enhancement funds in view of the mix of options chosen. As the plan progressed, US interest rates fell to the lowest levels in 30 years. The Mexico prototypes increasingly made the par bond, with a fixed interest rate of over 6 percent, look like a true bargain for the banks, in comparison to the discount bond. As banks increasingly opted for the par bond, which required more collateral because the principal to be collateralized retained full face value, country negotiators were forced to insist on rebalancing whereby banks had to shift some of their conversion bonds from par to discount. This iterative process was arguably sensible, under the circumstances, but delayed final agreements.

There were questionable rigidities in the allocation of IMF enhancement lending across alternative Brady debt reduction options. Enhancement funds were as follows. A fixed percent of the amount lent under an IMF standby or Extended Fund Facility (EFF) loan, usually 25 percent, was set aside for enhancement use. In addition, augmentation of resources up to 40 percent of quota was available. However, the set-asides were limited to use in operations that reduced principal (discount bonds and buybacks); and augmentation resources were limited to use in support of interest collateral on par or discount bonds.

For an EFF loan equal to 100 percent of quota, the rules meant potentially some 65 percent of quota in total enhancement resources. However, the restrictions meant that no more than 25 percent of quota could go to buybacks, which involved no interest collateralization and thus could not be supported by the augmentation resources. This constraint arbitrarily reduced the scope for buybacks, which otherwise might have been larger in such cases as that of Venezuela. At the same time, the earmarking of the set-aside resources for principal reduction meant that in cases where there was a general preference for par bonds (which reduced interest rather than principal), it was not possible to reallocate enhancement resources to accommodate this preference. The limitation of augmentation resources to interest support went in the same direction of favoring discount (principal-cutting) rather than par bonds, because par bonds required greater collateral for principal.

US officials in particular insisted on these limitations because they believed that the politics of the issue required visible reduction in the face value of the debt, even if in economic terms interest reduction would accomplish the same effect (and indeed could give the added benefit of a predictable interest stream, because par bonds paid a lower, fixed interest rate).[35] The broad concern seemed to be that par bonds retaining full face value might appear to be too sweet a deal for the banks, especially if interest rates were to fall so that the negotiated fixed rate no longer appeared as concessional. In retrospect these political considerations would seem questionable, and in fact the restrictions were subsequently liberalized.[36]

A more fundamental and on balance justifiable rigidity was that the IMF and World Bank enhancement funds, and thus generally the Brady Plan deals, were contingent on a satisfactory macroeconomic adjustment program, typically in the format of an IMF stabilization agreement. Critics saw this requirement as an internal contradiction, because the country could not achieve stability without the prior help of the debt relief. But the reality was that countries had the option of helping themselves to automatic refinancing of bank interest by unilaterally building up arrears (as both Argentina and Brazil did), so cash-flow pressure on both foreign exchange and budgetary outlays from the servicing of bank debt was not really the obstacle to stabilization. Because debt relief alone was almost certain to fail if domestic macroeconomic policies remained in disarray, there was good reason to insist on policy conditionality.

Brazil broke the straitjacket of IMF policy conditionality by obtaining a bank waiver and implementing its Brady deal without the help of IMF, World Bank, or other foreign official funding for enhancements. The country was able to do so because the wave of capital inflow that hit Latin America in 1991–93 (chapter 8) left Brazil with huge foreign

---

35. David C. Mulford, interview, 19 November 1994.

36. In 1992 the IMF extended the use of augmentation resources to include collateralization of principal on par bonds (a response to the rebalancing problem noted above), and in early 1994 it removed the restrictions completely. IMF staff, personal communication, 22 November 1994.

exchange reserves so that it could self-finance the enhancements for conversion bonds. Brazilian authorities even skirted the US Treasury's attempt to hold out for IMF approval by quietly buying up 30-year Treasury zero-coupon bonds for months ahead of the agreement rather than waiting for a special issue by Treasury itself (*Gazeta Mercantil*, 21 March 1994).

Purists might insist, as a result, that the Brazilian deal should not be considered part of the Brady Plan. For narrow purposes of judging the official sector's direct role in providing enhancements, this is of course correct. However, it is inconceivable that the Brazil deal would have been carried out in the absence of the watershed change in debt strategy marked by the Brady Plan. For all practical purposes of economic analysis, the agreement belongs firmly within the genus of that plan. Moreover, the Brazilian arrangement remained eligible for transit to full Brady status when and if the IMF approved the country's stabilization measures.

Unfinished Business

By the second quarter of 1994, the Brady Plan had progressed to the final mopping-up stage. The banks' signature of the Brazil deal on 15 April was the most conspicuous signal that not only was the debt crisis over but also the Brady Plan was largely complete. Bank agreements in rapid sequence at about the same time with Poland and Ecuador sent the same signal. Indeed, the Brazilian agreement provided grounds for anticipating an acceleration in completion of the remaining Brady deals. No longer would there be any large debtor country outstanding, so the stakes would be greatly reduced in any risk to the banks of an adverse demonstration effect from other, deeper forgiveness deals. Indeed, the first new agreement announced after the signing of the Brazilian deal, for Ecuador, provided for a significantly steeper forgiveness (45 percent on the discount bond, compared with 35 percent for Brazil; table 5.3).

In October 1993, the International Monetary Fund had stated that "[s]ome of the lower-middle-income countries . . . now actively negotiating debt packages . . . will require a greater degree of debt reduction than that provided in the Argentina or Mexico packages[,] . . . [possibly including] special treatment from official bilateral creditors . . ." (IMF 1993f, 73). About the same time another IMF document judged that "the group of middle- and lower-middle-income countries with debt problems still to come to terms with bank creditors on debt-reduction packages is now limited. Many of these remaining countries (including Bulgaria, Ecuador, Panama, Peru, and Poland) have already begun negotiations . . ." (Collyns et al. 1993, 3). By the second quarter of 1994, three of the five countries specifically mentioned had announced agreements in principle.

The Brady plan was designed primarily for severely indebted middle-income countries (SIMICs).[37] By the World Bank's criteria, in 1993 there were 19 countries that still warranted being placed on this list.[38] By early 1994, nine of these countries had negotiated Brady deals. The other ten SIMICs are listed in table 5.4, a possible inventory of Brady Plan candidates.

Only three Latin American nations remain on the SIMIC list without Brady deals: Jamaica, Panama, and Peru. As noted, Jamaica had eschewed requesting debt forgiveness, and Peru has been engaged with the banks in negotiations. If 10 percent of the country's total debt is set as a threshold below which bank debt is too small for Brady reduction to be of relevance, then the only SIMICs that remain as candidates are Algeria, Côte d' Ivoire, Morocco, Panama, and Peru (table 5.4).

Algeria has pursued a strategy of refinancing by a syndicate of international banks. Although its debt service ratio is high because of amortization (World Bank 1992c, 8–9), and the country could thus benefit from a MYRA, Algeria's interest/exports ratio at about 15 percent is relatively low, suggesting that debt forgiveness may not be necessary.[39]

Côte d'Ivoire experienced a severe decline of income and terms of trade in the early 1990s. The government adopted substantial fiscal adjustment and medium-term sectoral reforms but encountered difficulty in meeting IMF program targets (World Bank 1992c, 146–47). As suggested in chapter 7, the country would seem to be an appropriate candidate for both Brady Plan and Paris Club debt relief.

The World Bank (1992c, 369–71) gives Morocco exceptionally high marks for economic policy beginning in the second half of the 1980s. In 1990 and 1991, the country received large transfers from the Gulf states in connection with the Gulf War. In 1990, London Club bank creditors rescheduled the entire $3.2 billion in debt over 20 years and granted a waiver permitting the country to repurchase debt at secondary market prices. The Paris Club similarly rescheduled debt service due in 1991–92. The government expressed its intention that these would be the last reschedulings and sought to return to the capital markets by the mid-1990s. By late 1993, the secondary market price stood at 80 cents on the dollar (World Bank 1994b, 34). In view of the government's strategy

---

37. As discussed in chapter 7, because low-income African countries principally owe debt to official creditors, Paris Club debt relief by bilateral creditors according to Toronto terms (or subsequent reformulations) was the primary policy track envisioned for these countries.

38. Albania, Algeria, Angola, Argentina, Bolivia, Brazil, Bulgaria, Cameroon, Congo, Côte d' Ivoire, Ecuador, Jamaica, Jordan, Mexico, Morocco, Panama, Peru, Poland, and the Syrian Arab Republic (World Bank 1993b, 1: 165).

39. See chapter 7 for a critique of the World Bank's SIMIC criteria, which in many instances identify severe indebtedness even where the interest/exports ratio is low, because of a rapid amortization structure.

Table 5.4 Severely indebted middle-income countries without Brady agreements (May 1994)

Country	1992 total debt (millions of dollars)	1992 long-term bank debt	Bank share (percent)	Interest/XGS[a] (percent)
Albania	625	16	2.50	45.67
Algeria	26,349	6,572	24.94	14.66[b]
Angola	9,645	386	4.00	9.64
Cameroon	6,554	360	5.49	28.59
Congo	4,751	423	8.90	26.62
Côte d'Ivoire	17,997	5,106	28.37	31.88
Morocco	21,418	3,447	16.09	19.73
Panama	6,485	2,127	32.80	18.36
Peru	20,297	3,402	16.76	22.81
Syrian Arab Republic	16,513	0	0.00	27.71

a. Accrual basis; XGS = exports of goods and nonfactor services; interest estimated as total factor service debits less direct investment income debits.
b. Estimated from WDT interest payment figures.

Sources: World Bank, World Debt Tables, 1993a; IMF, International Financial Statistics, April 1994; IMF, Balance of Payments Statistics Yearbook, 1993g.

as well as the results realized in the secondary market, the case of Morocco seems more analogous to that of Chile and Colombia than to those of Latin American countries that have received debt reduction agreements, and Morocco may not be a likely candidate for Brady relief.

Both Panama and Peru still in debt discussions with bank creditors by late 1994. According to ECLAC (1993, 24), some observers expected that the Dominican Republic's Brady deal would serve as a model for these two countries.[40]

Status Summary

In sum, after five years the Brady Plan seems virtually complete. Among severely indebted middle-income countries, perhaps only three or four relevant candidates remain without agreements. Their total bank debt amounts to $20 billion or less. As noted, when US Treasury officials launched the Brady Plan in 1989, they spoke of its possible extension to 39 countries. These countries had a total of $279 billion in debt to foreign banks (Sachs 1989b, 93). As indicated in table 5.3, by May 1994 Brady

40. Possibly including the Dominican Republic's provision of a "corset" clause, whereby the banks' selection of options was to achieve a target of 50 percent debt forgiveness; and especially with respect to the negotiation of debt reduction for countries with high interest arrears.

deals had been agreed for 18 countries accounting for $191 billion in eligible bank debt. If another half-dozen countries receive agreements, accounting for some $20 billion, then two-thirds of the original Brady universe by number of countries and nearly 90 percent by value of eligible bank debt will have been covered under the plan.[41]

In terms of debt reduction, the original Treasury briefings had mentioned a figure of $70 billion. As shown in table 5.3, debt forgiveness under the plans already agreed by May 1994 amounted to about $60 billion, or 86 percent of the original target. Although there had been some increased debt corresponding to borrowing for the enhancements, it is a conceptual error to deduct this new debt from the forgiveness amount, because there is a corresponding new asset that the country owns (the zero-coupon bonds); thus the net effect on the country's balance sheet from borrowing for enhancements is a wash.

It is true that the Brady Plan got off to a slow start, and that the impressive coverage just reviewed came only by the end of five years rather than within three years as originally planned. As had been the case under the Baker Plan, problems of domestic macroeconomic policy imbalances tended to delay achievement of the indicative plan. Even so, the degree of performance on the plan's original targets can only be judged as remarkable, especially by the standards of most efforts at international economic coordination.

As for the rest of the original universe of Brady countries, which had included all developing countries that had engaged in debt rescheduling in the late 1980s, most of the omitted nations had opted out (as in the cases of Algeria, Jamaica, and Chile, which instead pursued maintenance of a creditworthiness record clear of forgiveness) or were likely to have their debt problems more directly addressed by Paris Club forgiveness (in the case of many African countries).

Evaluating Brady Plan Results

The International Monetary Fund probably spoke for the majority of analysts and policymakers when it judged, in October 1993, that

> Debt restructuring combined with improved policy implementation has allowed a number of countries to resolve their debt problems. Most of the middle income countries with mainly bank debt have been able to graduate from the process of rescheduling. . . . These countries' debt and debt-service ratios have been reduced substantially. . . . [They] have been able to achieve higher growth and lower inflation. This has been facilitated by the regaining of access to sponta-

---

41. The latter figure is based on the IMF's 80 percent estimate as of October 1993, noted above. Note that because only long-term bank claims are typically eligible for conversion, the total bank debt figure (which includes short-term claims) overstates the relevant universe for potential Brady deals.

neous private financing, particularly by Latin American countries, on a scale that had not been anticipated. (IMF 1993f, 72–73)

Early Critiques

At first there were much greater doubts about the potential of the Brady Plan. The central critique when the plan was announced was that it would not forgive sufficient debt, because its resources were too limited and/or because it took a voluntary rather than mandatory approach.

Thus, Sachs (1989b, 95) argued that "the Treasury has miscalculated the chances for significant debt reduction . . . because the negotiating framework gives too great an opening for each individual bank to hold out, hoping that somebody else (other banks, the IMF, Japan, etc.) will bear the inevitable losses." Sachs moreover described the new-money option as "just a disguised form of free-riding." He called for the IMF and World Bank to insist that banks holding at least 80 percent of claims accept debt reduction and that the IMF be prepared to lend to a country still in interest arrears to nonparticipating banks. Acknowledging that secondary market prices understated long-term debt servicing capacity, he suggested as a rule of thumb that debt be forgiven down to the secondary market price plus a premium of 20 percent (one-fifth, not 20 percentage *points*). For Mexico, Sachs specifically proposed that the "debt burden would be reduced to around 45 percent of the current face value" (99), consistent with his figure for the February 1989 secondary market price of 38 cents on the dollar plus a premium of one-fifth.

As noted above, however, the Mexico reduction was only 35 percent, not 55 percent. Not surprisingly, by September 1989, Sachs was extremely skeptical that the Brady Plan would succeed.[42] Others were equally dubious. Several months later Lustig (1990, 80) judged that the Mexico "agreement provides relatively little room for exogenous deviations or policy mistakes . . . [and that a]n agreement that gave Mexico more cash flow relief without increasing the debt output ratio would have been preferable." Later that year Islam (1990, 80) judged that the Brady Plan was being "implemented at a snail's pace with the debtors ultimately getting bread crumbs as relief."

Even as late as early 1992, after a year of remarkably high capital inflows into Latin America (chapter 8, figure 8.1), some analysts remained sharply critical of the Brady Plan. B. Cohen (1992, 167–71) wrote:

---

42. Thus: "It is already clear that at the very best, the current approach will not lead to sufficient debt reduction for any particular country to achieve a rapid restoration of creditworthiness. . . . [T]he market still believes that more than half of Mexico's debt will remain unpayable. [More generally] with voluntary debt reduction, the banks will always take too much of the "new money" option and too little of the debt reduction option . . . The official estimate is that 20 percent of exposure will accept the new money option. My guess is that the proportion will be quite a bit higher, at least 40 percent" (Sachs 1989h).

Not even the few direct beneficiaries of the Brady plan have had all that much to boast about. Commercial bank loans have been effectively reduced, but new liabilities were created to replace them. On a net basis, the shrinkage of nominal claims under the region's first four Brady agreements has amounted to less than $12 billion overall. In present value terms, the savings appear substantial, ranging from an estimated 23 percent of the face value of Venezuela's restructured bank debt to 31 percent for Mexico and to as much as 77 percent in the case of Costa Rica. But . . . cash flow savings vary from some 6 percent [of exports] for Mexico to no more than 2.5 percent for Venezuela. . . . It is clear that much of the region remains caught in the low-growth, high-debt-service trap. . . . If additional public money is to be provided to support Brady Plan negotiations, why not make it conditional on much more generous concessions than have been offered until now? And if banks continue to prove recalcitrant, why not threaten them with stiffer penalties for noncooperation?

Ironically, Cohen's country-expert coauthors in the same volume were much more upbeat (for example, Rubio 1992). Cohen's critique moreover misdiagnosed the arrival of new nonbank lending as a weakness rather than a strength that reflected success in returning to the capital market.

A central theme in all of the early critiques was that the size of forgiveness was too small to solve the debt problem. The analysis below develops a model of "catalytic debt relief" to explain how a modest amount of forgiveness could generate large positive results.

The early critiques came not just from academics. Economists at the World Bank and IMF also argued initially that the deals were "underfinanced."[43] Their expectation was that after partial debt forgiveness, flows of voluntary capital would not be forthcoming. US Treasury Secretary Brady and Undersecretary Mulford, both of whom had been active in private financial markets prior to office, maintained to the contrary that there would be renewed voluntary capital flows because of the favorable psychological impact of reaching agreement on a workout. These new inflows would close any financing gap left in the calculations done under the old assumptions of concerted lending. With the benefit of hindsight, we now know the Brady Plan architects were right. As reviewed in chapter 8, by 1991–93 capital inflows (and especially repatriation of flight capital) more than filled the financing gap and left much of Latin America awash in foreign exchange. As shown in chapter 8, the timing of these new inflows was closely linked to the announcements of Brady Plan deals.

Mexico Results

Enough time has elapsed for an evaluation of the impact of at least one Brady deal: that for Mexico. The analysts who have conducted the most

---

43. Based on interviews with former US Treasury officials.

rigorous examination of the Mexican Brady deal (Claessens, Oks, and van Wijnbergen 1993) conclude that in terms of restoration of growth and economic stability the agreement was a "spectacular success" (1).

Perhaps the first point to make about the Mexican case, however, is that on the basis of sheer arithmetic, debt forgiveness would not have been necessary if the price of oil had not collapsed in 1986. Cline (1991, 32) shows that whereas the decline in oil export earnings from 1984–85 to 1986–89 amounted to approximately $8 billion annually, the annual interest savings from the Brady Plan were only about $1.5 billion. This point is fundamental for the overall debt strategy, because it highlights the point that before the oil price collapse, the Baker Plan strategy should have been sufficient for at least Mexico, at least on strictly economic grounds. As developed below, however, politics and psychology are at least as important as economics in matters of creditworthiness and debt sustainability, and it would have required a positive endorsement of the Mexican political leadership to make MYRA rescheduling and moderate new lending under the Baker Plan sufficient even in an anti-monde in which oil prices had not collapsed.

Chapter 6 and Cline (1991) explain the success of the Mexican Brady deal primarily in terms of improved confidence and in particular the resolution of extreme uncertainty about exchange rate stability. As shown in figure 6.5, there was a sharp drop in the domestic interest rate in Mexico upon announcement of the Brady deal, and a further drop after its implementation.

Claessens, Oks, and van Wijnbergen (1993) share this diagnosis and confirm it econometrically. The authors first note that the cash-flow relief (interest and amortization) amounted to only about $4 billion annually, compared with a $200 billion economy, and that half of the relief could have been expected from rollover of amortization even without the deal. They explain the disproportionately favorable impact of the agreement as follows:

> High and volatile external transfers generated uncertainty about whether the future transfer burden could be met. This generated uncertainty about future exchange rate developments which, in turn, translated into high interest rates on domestic debt. "Ex post" real interest rates were almost 50% in the months before the debt accord was reached. With domestic public debt at approximately 20% of GDP in 1989, interest rates this high severely threatened the fiscal underpinnings of the stabilization program and led to a reduced level of private investment. (5)

Claessens, Oks, and van Wijnbergen draw on the literature on domestic debt and financial crisis to develop a model in which investors attach probabilities to two states: normal and crisis. The government is expected to pay for some portion of debt service by monetization. The higher this fraction, the more likely devaluation, and as a result, the higher the domestic currency interest rate. The higher interest rate in turn depresses the demand for money, reinforcing the crisis scenario.

The authors implement their model econometrically using the variance of the projected transfer to foreign creditors as the key variable for uncertainty. The value of this variable stood at 100 percent before the Brady agreement and had fallen to 45 percent by early 1990. Their regressions systematically show that this uncertainty variable is by far the most important in understanding the drop in interest rates, the revival of investment, and the reversal from capital flight to capital repatriation. Domestic investment, which had grown in real terms at a minimal 1 percent in 1982–88, grew at 11.2 percent annually in 1989–91 (6). The Claessens-Oks-van Wijnbergen regressions indicate a strong, statistically significant influence of the uncertainty variable on domestic investment growth, but statistical insignificance for the *level* of the net transfer on debt. The same result is found in explaining real domestic interest rates. When pure country risk is examined using the interest differential between dollar-denominated PAGAFEs issued by the Mexican government and US Treasury bill rates, the explanatory role of the variance of projected net transfers disappears, and the transfer level does become significant. However, the Brady deal change in transfer level only explains 4 percentage points out of the 20 percentage point drop in real interest rates. The finding is thus that "uncertainty about the future exchange rate" is the "dominant factor" in explaining the investment and growth response to debt relief.

There is a profound implication of this study that the authors do not explicitly recognize: the great bulk of the positive benefits of the Brady deal for Mexico could have been realized through a MYRA debt smoothing with no debt forgiveness. That is, it was the prospective severe bunching of amortization, not the level of the transfer, that generated the high uncertainty. Once again, however, it seems likely that lancing the political-psychological boil of perceived need for equity in passing along some of the burden of adjustment into bank losses was also a necessary ingredient, one not captured by the model.[44]

For debt theory, another important finding by the authors is explicit rejection of the popular "debt overhang theory" whereby excessive debt acts like a tax on domestic investment. At the informal level, they note that the $12 billion present-value debt relief of the Brady deal "would on a permanent basis allow at most a 1.5 percentage point cut in the corporate tax rate" (1). Their informal skepticism is virtually identical to that of Diwan and Rodrik (1992), who for similar reasons reject

---

44. In early 1991, the author asked one of Mexico's foremost financial experts (who had worked for years in both the Central Bank and Finance Ministry) how he explained the strongly favorable impact of the Brady deal despite the small size of its relief in the present value of total debt. His answer: "Prestidigitation."

the debt overhang thesis (as discussed in chapter 4). They go further and stress that in their equations for domestic investment the proxy variable for debt overhang (level of net transfer) is statistically insignificant and has the wrong sign (Claessens, Oks, and van Wijnbergen 1993, 14).

Other Evidence

For other major Brady deal countries, the interest rate uncertainty mechanism is less conspicuous than in the Mexican case. In Argentina, after announcement of the Brady deal in principle in April of 1992, the "country risk" spread between annual interest rates on domestic dollar-denominated government bonds (BONEX) and US Treasury bonds fell from 4.8 percent in 1992:1 to 3.9 percent in 1992:2. Although the spread rose in late 1992 because of a temporary drop in confidence about the country's stabilization plan, there was a second round of improvement after the Brady agreement was signed in April of 1993. The country risk spread fell from 6.5 percent in 1993:1 to 3.8 percent in 1993:2 (Cline 1995). In contrast, there was no apparent drop in the domestic interest rate in Venezuela after announcement of the Brady deal.[45] However, in these and other cases there were other signs of improvement. The most dramatic was typically in the capital account. As shown in figure 5.2, there were large shifts from capital outflows to capital inflows. The return to positive inflows typically did not occur until the year of the Brady agreement in principle (1989 for Mexico, 1990 for Venezuela, and 1992 for Argentina and Brazil).[46] If the capital flow reversal had been an undiscriminating phenomenon of world capital markets unrelated to the Brady Plan, there should have been no difference in the timing among the four countries.

Another measure of the positive impact of the Brady Plan was the rise in secondary market prices. Using monthly data on secondary market prices from 1986 through 1993, the World Bank (1993b, 1: 41) shows that "[f]or all countries, secondary-market prices rose quickly after the conclusion of debt-reduction operations." With the fourth quarter of 1989 as a base, by the fourth quarter of 1993 secondary market prices had risen by 128 percent for Mexico, 65 percent for the Philippines, 370 percent for Costa Rica, 109 percent for Venezuela, 60 percent for Uruguay, 408 percent for Argentina, and 109 percent for Brazil (calculated from World Bank 1994b, and September 1992 issue). By late 1993

---

45. The discount rate was constant at 33 percent in the first three quarters of 1990 despite the agreement in principle in June of that year, and the rate actually rose to 43 percent by the fourth quarter (IMF, *International Financial Statistics*, various issues).

46. On this basis the entry into positive inflows was a year late for Venezuela and a year early for Argentina. Even for Argentina the largest absolute increase was in the year of the agreement in principle.

Figure 5.2 Brady agreements and net capital flows

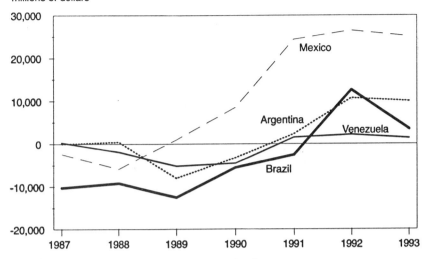

millions of dollars

Sources: IMF, *International Financial Statistics;* ECLAC 1993.

the prices were in a range of 80 to 82 cents on the dollar for Mexico, the Philippines, Costa Rica, and Uruguay; 71 cents for Venezuela; and 66 cents for Argentina.[47] As these prices were typically close to the face value of the discount bonds (and thus to 100 cents minus the debt-forgiveness fraction), the implication was that the market was applying little further country-risk discount to the converted debt. Brazil was the prime exception, as its secondary market price stood at only 46 cents (calculated from World Bank 1994b, and September 1992 issue).

Economic growth and price stability provided still further evidence of beneficial effects. In 1988–89, average economic growth for Mexico, Venezuela, and Argentina was −0.7 percent; by 1991–93, the average for these three large, relatively early Brady countries had risen to 5.3 percent (chapter 6).[48] For Mexico and Venezuela, inflation (year over year) averaged 62 percent in 1988–89, and the rate reached over 3,000 percent in Argentina in 1989. By 1992–93, the average rate for the three countries was down to 21.7 percent (and only 10 percent in Argentina and Mexico by 1993; chapter 6). Although factors other than the debt agreements contributed to the improvement, the change was consistent with a strong positive effect of the Brady Plan.

47. The prices are for par bonds, and thus they still refer to the market valuation of debt originally having a face value of 100 cents on the dollar. See chapter 8 for a discussion of the dip in prices in early 1994.

48. Note, however, that there was a disturbing slowdown in Mexico and Venezuela to 1 percent and 0 percent respectively in 1993.

Catalytic Debt Relief: A Political-Economic Model

A variety of indicators thus suggest that the Brady Plan had a major positive economic effect. Yet, as shown for the case of Mexico, the relative economic size of the debt forgiveness was modest. The fundamental reason was that bank claims were typically only about half of total debt, so that even reductions of about one-third on bank debt—painful enough for creditor banks—conveyed debt forgiveness equivalent to only about 15 percent of total debt. Claessens, Oks, and van Wijnbergen (1993) suggest one reason for large results from modest overall forgiveness: reduced exchange rate uncertainty. A broader approach emphasizing political behavior can similarly yield the result of disproportionately large favorable effects.

A key element in a political-economic model of debt relief is the notion of willingness to pay. J. Pierpont Morgan is said to have stated, "Willingness to pay is more important than ability to pay." As the difference between Nicolae Ceaușescu's Romania (chapter 7) and José Sarney's Brazil (chapter 6) illustrates, willingness is heavily determined by domestic politics. If a debt workout agreement provides the basis for a reversal in the domestic political position from "the debt must be reduced" to "our administration succeeded in putting the debt problem behind us," then it can switch the political willingness from unwilling to willing to pay. That switch can then enable a resumption of more normal capital market flows even if there has been little change in the economic magnitudes.

Let z be the fraction of full face value that either an existing or a prospective creditor (e.g., a bond purchaser) sets for expected repayment on new money lent to the country. Let C measure the economic capacity of the country to pay existing debt; W, the political willingness to pay. Both measures are admittedly amorphous, and neither will be found in any statistical series; but both are arguably meaningful.[49] Then,

$$z = Min(C, W) \tag{5.1}$$

Under normal circumstances, the country's economic capacity and political willingness to honor the debt are not in question, and z is 100 cents on the dollar. An economic shock (such as the collapse in the price of oil, for an oil exporter) can reduce C sharply, causing expected value of claims (z) to fall well below face value. Or a political shock (such as the failure of a domestic stabilization plan and need for some lightning rod

---

49. Numerous efforts have been made to develop statistical models of debt servicing capacity, essentially the "C" variable here. See for example Cline (1984, appendix A).

for political frustration) can cause W to fall substantially, with the result of reducing z even if there has been little change in C.

The familiar economic variables from the creditworthiness literature may be invoked to explain debt servicing capacity; for example,

$$C = f\left(\frac{D}{X}, g_x, \frac{D}{Y}, F, y, i_w\right) \qquad (5.2)$$

where D is external debt, X is exports, Y is GDP, g_x is export growth rate, F is fiscal deficit as a fraction of GDP, y is per capita income, and i_w is the world interest rate. The willingness to pay variable is

$$W = f(g_Y, \dot{p}, E, P, \rho_p) \qquad (5.3)$$

where g_Y is the recent growth rate of GDP, $\dot{p}$ is the inflation rate, E is a measure of perceived equity in the distribution of the burden of adjustment to the debt crisis between creditors and the debtor, P is a measure of the degree of populism in the country's current political structure and conjuncture, and ρ_p is the political discount rate.

The first two right-hand-side variables for equation 5.3 are clear enough, but the other three are loose and difficult to quantify though nonetheless meaningful. Populism essentially refers to the extent to which leaders pander to the less sophisticated but more numerous public by making simplistic promises that a narrower, more sophisticated group within the country (often including the leaders themselves) knows cannot be kept, as well as by placing blame on outside culprits (including external debt) for difficulties primarily caused by domestic mismanagement (see, for example, Dornbusch and Edwards 1991).

The political discount rate refers to the time horizon political leaders take into account for the consequences of their actions, and thus how heavily they discount more distant future effects. Abraham Lincoln had a low political discount rate, in that he was prepared to pursue a bloody civil war to secure a better long-term future for the United States; examples of a high political discount rate that permits leaders to seek short-term popularity despite the likelihood of disastrous longer-term consequences include Lyndon Johnson's refusal to raise taxes to finance the Vietnam War and Luis Echeverria's unfunded social-spending programs in Mexico in the 1970s. Preservation of a good credit reputation inherently involves trading off short-term pain for longer-term benefits of cheaper and more certain credit market access, and thus the political discount rate is one of the most important determinants of political willingness to honor debt.

For its part, perceived equity in the adjustment burden depends on how much the country has been forced to adjust by reducing its domestic growth rate and/or experiencing higher inflation, on the one hand,

and how much the creditor banks have assisted by providing new money (NM) or debt relief on principal (R_p) or interest (R_i), on the other:

$$E = f(\Delta g_Y, \Delta \dot{p}, NM, R_p, R_i) \qquad (5.4)$$

Populism is likely to depend on the strength of the country's democratic tradition (DT) and political party system, with more fragile traditions and institutions more vulnerable to populist pressures; the level of per capita income (y), with poorer countries often but not always more susceptible to populism; and the degree of inequality in the distribution of income (I_y), with more unequal societies more prone to unsustainable populist measures taken in the name of domestic equity. Thus:

$$P = f(DT, y, I_y) \qquad (5.5)$$

This political-economic system has joint (or general equilibrium) determination of the equations. Catalytic debt relief occurs when the initially binding constraint is willingness to pay, and the granting of debt relief has a major impact in raising willingness to pay so that after the relief the binding constraint on debt valuation is economic capacity to pay. Thus, suppose a specific package of debt relief R^* is administered, composed of R_p^* and R_i^*. From equation 5.4, the effect will be to raise perceived equity by $\Delta E = [\partial E / \partial R_p] R_p^* + [\partial E / \partial R_i] R_i^*$, where Δ refers to change and ∂ refers to the partial derivative. From equation 5.3, the consequential impact on willingness to pay will be: $\Delta W = [\partial W / \partial E] \Delta E = [\partial W / \partial E]\{[\partial E / \partial R_p] R_p^* + [\partial E / \partial R_i] R_i^*\}$.

The debt relief will also have an impact on capacity to pay. Let ΔD^* be the principal reduction and Δi^* be the interest reduction in the relief package. Then, from equation 5.2, the change in capacity to pay is $\Delta C = (1/X)(\partial C / \partial [D/X])(\Delta D^*) + (1/Y)(\partial C / \partial [D/Y])(\Delta D^*) + (\partial C / \partial i_w)(\Delta i^*)$.

Now suppose that the amount of debt relief is relatively small, so that the change in the capacity to pay (ΔC) is modest, and the new perceived capacity to pay is not much higher than the old: $C^* = C_0 + \Delta C$ (where the subscript 0 refers to before-relief conditions). Suppose, in contrast, that the relief operation permits a political about-face in which the country's leadership now expresses confidence that the debt problem is over rather than insisting on further debt forgiveness. The implication is that there is a large rise in willingness to pay, such that $\Delta W > \Delta C$. The result may be that whereas originally the willingness-to-pay variable was the lower of the two, and therefore was the binding constraint on market valuation, after the relief the capacity-to-pay variable is the lower of the two and is the new binding constraint. That is, $W_0 < C_0$; $\Delta W > \Delta C$; and $W^* > C^*$. As a result, market valuation rises abruptly and by considerably more than can be explained by the rise in capacity to pay: $z^* = C^* = C_0 + \Delta C > z_0 = W_0$; $z^* - z_0 = \Delta C + [C_0 - W_0]$.

The Debt Strategy Overall

The improvement in debtor economies by the early 1990s, the remarkable resurgence of capital inflows to Latin America (chapter 8), and the achievement of Brady Plan agreements for the bulk of the relevant debt and debtors by 1994 suggest that a dozen years after the outbreak of the debt crisis the international strategy to deal with the problem had finally yielded favorable results. This section considers the strategy as a whole for this period and asks what were its principal areas of success and failure.

Historical Perspective

Judged by comparison with capital market reentry after the last major international debt crisis, the widespread default on bonds by Latin American and some other countries in the 1930s, the debt strategy of the 1980s must be judged unambiguously a resounding success. Debtor countries were locked out of the capital markets for 40 years after the earlier episode; yet after less than a decade in the crisis of the 1980s, so much capital was reentering that countries had to devise measures to cope with an embarrassment of riches (chapter 8).

Table 5.5 presents data demonstrating the long delay for bond market reentry after the defaults of the 1930s. Countries classified by Eichengreen and Portes (1989) as "heavy" defaulters, such as Brazil, did not reenter the market until the early 1970s, a lag of about 40 years from the defaults of the 1930s. Even the "light" defaulters typically only reentered by the late 1950s. The placements of Australia and Canada show that there was once again an international bond market by the late 1940s, so only about 15 years of this delay was attributable to the collapse of the international market during the depression of the 1930s and World War II.

Moreover, the table clearly shows that the heavy defaulters reentered later (by 1972, on average) than the light defaulters (1959).[50] It was precisely the repetition of extremely lengthy delay of reentry shown by the heavy defaulters that the debt strategy of the 1980s sought to avoid.

In one sense it is not surprising that reentry was much faster after the debt crisis of the 1980s than after the episode a half-century earlier. In the 1980s there was a well-established system of international financial institutions that was capable of carrying out an integrated strategy. No such institutions existed in the 1930s, and the role of their absence in contributing to economic distress and ultimately to political conflict was the reason that the Allied powers invested so much effort in designing and subsequently maintaining the Bretton Woods institutions in the postwar period. Speedy and decisive action by the International Mone-

---

50. The 13-year difference in means is statistically significant at the 99 percent level.

Table 5.5 Bond market reentry after 1930s defaults

Light defaulters[a,b]		Heavy defaulters[a,c]	
Country	Year	Country	Year
Australia	1945	Germany	1965
Canada	1949	Hungary	1971
Belgium	1954	Costa Rica	1971
Norway	1955	Brazil	1972
Austria	1958	Greece	1972
Denmark	1959	Colombia	1973
France	1959	Chile	1974
Italy	1959	Poland	1976
Japan	1959	El Salvador	1978
New Zealand	1959		
Argentina	1961		
Finland	1963		
Venezuela	1965		
Spain	1967		
Nicaragua	1973		
Average	1959	Average	1972

a. Light and heavy categories as identified by Eichengreen and Portes (1989).
b. Light defaulters that had not reentered as of 1980: Czechoslovakia.
c. Heavy defaulters that had not reentered as of 1980: Bulgaria, Guatemala, Uruguay.

Sources: White Weld 1960, 1973; World Bank, *Annual Report*, various issues.

tary Fund and later the World Bank contributed importantly to the success of the debt strategy.

Equally or more important, in the debt crisis of the 1980s the US government took an active leadership role. As noted in chapter 4, Fishlow (1986) emphasizes that one of the reasons for the failure to deal successfully with international debt problems in the interwar period was that there was a vacuum of such leadership, as Britain could no longer provide it and the United States was not yet prepared to do so. This contrast too thus favored a more successful outcome for the debt crisis of the 1980s than that of the 1930s.

However, capital market revival would almost surely have been much less rapid if the wrong strategy had been adopted. The emphasis throughout on a cooperative, case-by-case, voluntary rather than mandatory, and market-oriented solution to the problem almost certainly was crucial to leaving a legacy of investor expectations that participation in these markets was relatively safe. As suggested above, the reasonable depth of cut in conversion bonds in relationship to the preexisting secondary market price on the one hand and the extent of collateral coverage on the other meant that the Brady Plan was market-oriented, and the inclusion of new-money options in most of the agreements preserved an element of voluntariness.

In contrast, judged by the alternative criterion of debtor country growth, the comparison with the 1930s superficially looks unfavorable. Indeed, as discussed in chapter 4, Eichengreen and Portes (1986) argue that the lesson of the 1930s was that defaulters did better on domestic growth than those countries that honored debt, with the implication (albeit not explicitly stated by the authors) that the debtors would have done better in the 1980s to repeat a default strategy. Krugman (1994, 737) also argues that because of relatively strong Latin American growth in the 1930s and very poor growth in the 1980s, it would be ''bizarre to argue that there had been a better outcome to the 1980s debt crisis.''

As argued in chapter 4, however, the growth comparison completely ignores the different developmental stages of the Latin American economies in the two periods. Burning bridges to the international financial community means committing to inward-oriented growth. Autarkic growth in the 1930s meant new opportunities to develop domestic light industry; by the 1980s it would have meant more severe distortions in the by-then-exhausted model of import-substituting industrialization, which even by the 1970s had already led to extreme departures from comparative advantage and entry into heavy industry. As revealed by the nearly unanimous turn toward outward-oriented growth as countries in the region adopted structural reform to deal with the 1980s crisis, most of the economic policymakers of the region agree with the diagnosis here rather than the view that another historic round of default and autarkic growth would have been preferable for the debtors.

Financial System Stability

There is virtually no disagreement that, taken as a whole, the debt strategy successfully preserved the stability of the international financial system under circumstances that had placed that system in extreme jeopardy. The strategy gave the banks time to build up capital and set aside loan-loss reserves so that their eventual losses on the debt were of manageable proportions rather than in amounts that could have turned the major banks insolvent (the risk at the outset of the crisis; see chapter 2). The most severe critics of the strategy argue instead that single-minded concentration on stability of the banking system through most of the 1980s caused a seriously unbalanced burden of adjustment that let the banks off lightly while punishing the debtor countries (e.g., B. Cohen 1992).

Adaptive, Contingent Policymaking

However, description of the debt strategy as an asymmetrical policy favoring the banks to the detriment of the debtors ignores both the critics' own recognition that initially the danger of international financial collapse had to be addressed and the fact that the banks in the end did experience losses of about one-third on their claims against the larger Latin American debtors.[51] A more balanced interpretation is that the debt strategy was a relatively successful case of adaptive policy evolution that at each stage established a contingent approach and, after further experience, adopted appropriate corrections. In this light, the principal debate centers not so much on the initial and ultimate formulations of the strategy but on whether policymakers took too long to make the midcourse corrections and thereby inflicted unnecessary suffering on the publics of debtor countries.

There is a good case that as a contingent strategy the initial phase premised on long-term solvency and interim lending was valid:

- In 1992 there were 76 middle-income countries with $1.16 trillion in external debt (World Bank 1993b, vol. 1). The Brady Plan has forgiven about $60 billion for 18 countries (table 5.3), and perhaps another $10 billion of forgiveness remains in the mopping-up stage. Thus, only about 6 percent of the total debt will have needed to be forgiven. Even on an ex post basis this outcome is far closer to validation of solvency than to confirmation of deep insolvency (as noted, in domestic bankruptcies creditors are fortunate to get even 30 cents on the dollar). With this ultimate outcome, it is all the more the case that at the outset there was a sound basis for accepting solvency as the initial working hypothesis.

- In the absence of the oil price collapse in 1986, there would not have been a need for forgiveness of debt for Mexico or Venezuela, at least on economic grounds. As noted, oil export losses far exceeded the eventual interest savings from debt forgiveness. Indeed, the most rigorous analysis to date (Claessens, Oks, and van Wijnbergen 1993) implies that even after the oil collapse Mexico could have secured the great bulk of the benefits of the Brady Plan through MYRA repayment smoothing without forgiveness—although the political-economic model just outlined suggests that what might have been feasible technically was not necessarily so politically.

- The midcourse correction of Baker Plan indicative targets for coordinated lending was a sensible adjustment to deal with increasing free-rider problems and to incorporate both public-sector lending and

---

51. Early entrants earned partially offsetting profits from spreads above LIBOR of 1 to $1\frac{1}{2}$ percent in the 1970s, and by 1982–83 rescheduling spreads temporarily reached over 2 percent (Bergsten, Cline, and Williamson 1985, 95). The cumulative offset was thus perhaps 15 percent on an early-vintage loan and less on average. On the other hand many banks incurred additional losses by the market decision to sell off Brady bonds at some further discount.

Figure 5.3 Country policy, luck, and need for debt forgiveness

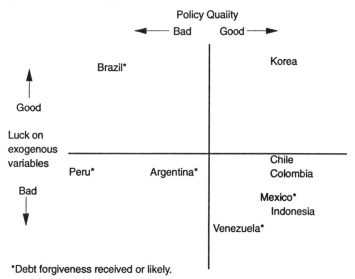

Policy Quality

◄──── Bad   Good ────►

Brazil*   Korea

Good

Luck on
exogenous
variables   Chile
Peru*   Argentina*   Colombia

Bad   Mexico*
                                   Indonesia
                          Venezuela*

*Debt forgiveness received or likely.

debtor structural reform more explicitly. The plan achieved a greater portion of its objectives than is commonly recognized, and might have achieved more if macroeconomic policies in some countries (such as Venezuela) had been such as to permit conclusion of IMF programs and new-lending packages.

- As portrayed in figure 5.3, countries that in the mid- and late 1980s had good domestic policies and adequate luck on external variables ultimately did not require debt reduction. South Korea quickly worked its way out of difficulty despite considerable international concern early in the crisis. Chile eventually did so as well, and Colombia even more fully escaped the crisis. Korea and Chile had the good luck of being oil importers in the face of lower oil prices, but weak commodity export prices for Chile and Colombia (and modest oil exports of the latter) meant that on balance those two countries had mildly bad (i.e., "adequate") luck. Because of good domestic policies Indonesia was able to avoid forgiveness despite the bad luck of lower oil prices. Mexico in contrast did not avoid debt reduction despite its good policies, in view of the oil shock. Venezuela was even more dependent on oil and had only marginally good domestic policies for most of the period, and so it also needed debt reduction.

Brazil is the clearest case where bad policy, primarily fiscal, placed the country ultimately in conditions for debt reduction, even though as an oil importer the country enjoyed the good luck of lower oil prices. Through most of the 1980s Argentine domestic policies were also in disarray (though somewhat less so), and the country had the bad luck of a major decline in commodity export prices (in part thanks to subsidized European grain exports). Peru too had moderately bad luck because of commodity prices (and its nascent oil exports), but it had the worst macroeconomic policies of all during most of the period (and thus Peru is located farthest to the left in the figure).

If the premise is accepted that countries with good domestic policies and adequate international luck did not need debt forgiveness, then the contingent strategy of beginning the international debt policy on a basis of a solvency diagnosis was appropriate. It would have been inappropriate to design a strategy that expected, and thereby perhaps contributed to, poor domestic policies. It would have been equally inappropriate to design a strategy premised on severe adverse developments (oil price collapse, interest rate surge). In the contingent strategy, those eventualities could be dealt with by changing course as they arose, essentially what was done.

Equitable Burden Sharing: Too Little Relief Too Late?

Many analysts could agree with most of what has been said so far about the strategy but would still condemn it overall on grounds that the sequence of midcourse corrections was too slow and systematically biased in favor of the banks and against the debtor countries. Indeed, a key architect of both the Baker and Brady Plans, US Treasury Undersecretary David Mulford, has stated: "In retrospect, Latin America could have suffered less had the international community been prepared earlier to recognize and work with the reality of the markets to resolve the debt crisis" (*Wall Street Journal*, 21 August 1992, A7). However, this debate really amounts to whether the Brady Plan should have been launched in 1987 or 1988 rather than early 1989.

- It would have made little sense to turn to debt forgiveness as the main strategy before the oil price collapse of 1986, which was the principal adverse development on objective economic grounds. As analyzed in chapter 3 (table 3.4), the collapse of oil prices below expected levels by 1987 had reduced exports of seven oil-exporting debtor countries by $32 billion from levels otherwise expected, or by 29 percent of their expected export base. In contrast, the collapse only reduced the import bill of 12 oil-importing debtor countries by $17.1 billion, or 8 percent of their predicted export base. The blow was definitive for the oil exporters, whereas the windfall gain was modest for the oil importers.

  Among oil importers that eventually received debt forgiveness, some such as Brazil arguably would not have needed it on purely economic grounds if domestic policies had been sound in the 1980s (although for other, more heavily indebted countries such as Argentina this case is less evident). For their part, the nonforgiveness cases of Chile and Colombia did not achieve that outcome primarily as a consequence of lower oil prices.[52]

- It would have been both infeasible in terms of bank preparedness and ineffective in terms of prospective depths of cut to launch debt forgiveness before 1987. The banks had not set aside large loan-loss reserves against LDC debt before the round of bank debt provisioning set off by Citibank in early 1987, so achievement of the goal of systemic risk containment could not have been assured if a policy of forgiveness had been adopted before then. Moreover, before this time secondary market prices for the larger debtors were in the range of 70 cents on the dollar, and market-related relief would not have generated cuts as deep as later occurred.

  It might be argued that as early as 1985 or 1986, creditor governments could have forced their banks to cut dividends and build up loan-loss reserves, with the result of making banks capable of sustaining losses earlier and driving down secondary market prices sooner. However, as analyzed in chapter 2, as of 1986 the exposure of the nine largest US banks to the Baker-17 countries still amounted to 122 percent of their capital. Implementation of a 35 percent forgiveness at that time would have reduced their capital by 43 percent, and by considerably more for some of them, which in view of other pressures on the banks then and later (including sour real estate loans) would potentially have jeopardized the objective of financial system stability. Nor is it clear which way mandated set-asides would have worked for bank strength, as sharply lower dividends and higher provisions might have made it more difficult to issue stock to raise capital.

  Crucially, monetary authorities also faced the dilemma that if they imposed reserve set-asides, the result would probably be to choke off the new lending that was the centerpiece of the Baker plan. They faced a second dilemma in that even for countries that seemed more obviously to require debt forgiveness, such as Bolivia and Costa Rica, policymakers confronted the problem that the banks were loath to forgive debt for fear of setting a precedent that would be taken up by larger debtors less in need of it.

- Even more fundamentally, there was a learning process not just for the designers of the international debt strategy but for debtor country policymakers. It took time for these policymakers to recognize the need for economic reform. For example, it was not until after the hyperinflation of 1989 that the Argentine public and policymakers were prepared to undertake the radical fiscal and structural reforms

---

52. Thus, Chile's savings on lower oil import costs by 1986 and after amounted to less than 10 percent of export earnings (calculated from IDB 1986, 444; IMF 1992a).

that generated the stability and growth achieved in the early 1990s. An early round of debt forgiveness would have sent the false message that there was an easy, externally provided solution to the economic crisis, whereas the great bulk of the solution could only come from domestic economic reform. That reform would probably have been postponed by the early granting of debt forgiveness and the corresponding illusion that external relief was the central remedy.[53]

- It also took time for some debtor countries to realize the costs of simply going into arrears. Brazil went into arrears in February–November 1987 and again in July 1989–December 1990, before it entered a program of partial (30 percent) payment of interest due in the latter instance. In the first suspension, trade credits dropped by an estimated $2 billion, and in the second, by $3 billion. Spreads on trade credit lines rose from 2–3 percent to 3–6 percent; maturities fell from 180–360 days to 30–45 days. Most importers were forced to operate on a cash basis. Capital flight accelerated, and foreign direct investment dwindled (World Bank 1991, 1: 37).

- In any event, domestic policy distortions delayed the completion of Brady deals past 1989 for all but three of the Brady countries (table 5.3). The timing of the plan's launching was thus not a binding constraint except perhaps for Mexico, the Philippines, and Costa Rica.[54] This fact alone largely turns moot the critique of excessive delay in transiting to the debt reduction strategy.

- If the Brady Plan might have been unlikely to have helped matters before 1987, would it not have been possible nonetheless to allocate a greater share of the debt adjustment burden to the banks and less to

---

53. Thus, Thomas Enders, a former US assistant secretary of state for Latin America, has stated that early in the crisis he had "been very worried that Latin America was a political tinderbox and . . . thought that the Treasury and the Federal Reserve should have taken a more lenient position. But, when the international institutions proposed a variety of sensible policy actions and made their loans conditional on policy performance . . . very little changed in the debtor nations. In the end, fundamental economic reform was instituted only when the people had become desperate. . . . [I]t would actually have been damaging . . . to have made large quantities of aid available through an early Brady Plan" (Enders 1994, 738–39). Similarly, Paul Volcker (Volcker and Gyohten 1992, 188) has stated, "What is not provable, but what I think seems evident to most experienced observers, is that the agony of the debt crisis provided the jolt necessary for Latin American leaders to rethink their old approaches and set off in fresh and much more promising directions." In contrast, my colleague John Williamson has argued that policy reform was an international trend in the late 1980s that would have swept Latin America even in the absence of the trauma of the debt crisis and even if Brady relief had occurred considerably earlier (debt study group, Washington, 8 November 1993).

54. Thus, for example, Venezuela's policy reforms did not come until the new Pérez government in 1989, so earlier availability of the Brady mechanism would not have helped.

the countries by insisting on much deeper cuts in bank claims (e.g., all the way down to the secondary market prices)? The answer to that question depends on the political discount rate. Perhaps on a time scale of three to five years the answer would be in the affirmative. However, over the longer term, the countries' creditworthiness would have been substantially compromised by a much more mandatory approach to debt relief, which would have been necessary to obtain far deeper cuts.

Moreover, it is unlikely that the remarkable resurgence of nonbank capital flows to Latin America by 1991–92 would have happened in a context of a mandatory deep-forgiveness plan. The vendors of Mexican bonds on the international markets, for example, would have had a much harder time persuading prospective customers that their paper was safe if there had been a deep, mandatory cut for the banks rather than a quasi-voluntary workout. One operational reason is simply that the banks would have fought such an outcome in the courts, and prolonged litigation could have cast a cloud over the Eurobond market for Latin America for years. The more fundamental reason is that the best evidence about how participants in a repeating game will play is from their past moves. Bond market expectations of future actions by industrial country governments and debtor countries would have had to factor in more negative prospects if there had been a mandatory Brady Plan with deep forgiveness. Similarly, expectations based on past debtor behavior undoubtedly contributed heavily to the inability of Latin America to borrow in world capital markets for decades after the defaults of the 1930s.

- On the issue of burden sharing more generally, many critics of the debt strategy (especially before the Brady Plan) tended to focus on assigning blame for past events rather than on the future consequences of policy action. There is no doubt that a goodly portion of the original responsibility for the debt crisis lay with overlending by the banks, as well as international shocks from high interest rates and global recession, just as there is no doubt that much of the responsibility lay with distorted country policies, especially fiscal (Cline 1983). But the relevant question for policy was never "whose fault" but instead always "where do the banks and the debtors go from here?" Much deeper (and more mandatory) forgiveness than in the Brady Plan could easily have made matters worse rather than better for the debtors in future years. In this sense, the usual discussion of equity tends to leave out an important dimension: equitable distribution of the adjustment as between the present in the debtor country and the future (for the same citizens and their children) in the same country.

Indeed, if the sole criterion for debt forgiveness were backward-looking "coresponsibility," then the proper amount to be forgiven might be calculated in the following way. Let Z be the fraction of the bank debt that was "excessive" as the result of imprudence by the borrower and the lender. Let D be total bank debt. Strict corresponsibility implies that the equitable amount to be forgiven is $\frac{1}{2}ZD$. In this way, the banks shoulder half of the burden of removing the excess debt, and the country shoulders the other half (by greater adjustment than would have been required in the absence of the excessive debt buildup). It is revealing to consider that this approach would validate the one-third Brady forgiveness as equitable on grounds of coresponsibility, so long as the amount of the excessive debt was no greater than two-thirds of bank debt ($Z \leq \frac{2}{3}$). It seems unlikely that more than two-thirds of the cumulative debt owed to banks was excessive.

A corresponding implication is that if total debt still seems excessive to some observers, backward-looking coresponsibility would tend to shift attention to other components of the debt, namely that borrowed from the public sector. It is sobering in this regard that a key architect of Colombia's debt policy has written that the burden sharing in the debt strategy was not equitable insofar as it omitted any forgiveness by the international financial institutions and little forgiveness by bilateral creditors (Garay 1993).

In any event, from the standpoint of 1992–93 the notion that forgiveness should have been deeper than in the Brady norm was increasingly inconsistent with the renewed abundance of capital inflows. The case for forgiveness on grounds that a shortage of external capital was suffocating debtor economies was becoming increasingly outdated.

Case-by-Case, Conditional Relief

Two important features of the Brady Plan were that it insisted on policy reform on the part of the beneficiary country and that it tailored each package to the special circumstances of the country. This approach minimized the moral hazard that debtor countries would simply take it for granted that a specified amount of relief should be forthcoming without necessarily adopting the domestic reforms that were the more important basis for any lasting solution.

Some earlier proposals had instead proposed global programs with greater uniformity and automaticity. Kenen (*New York Times*, 6 March 1983) proposed that a new International Debt Discount Corporation purchase LDC debt from banks at a discount of 10 percent and then grant a modest reduction in interest rates to the debtor countries and stretch out maturities.[55] Seemingly radical at the time, the proposal might seem like

---

55. The Kenen plan provided that although in principle treatment should be tailored by country, in practice there should be "standard terms." The lack of differentiation may

a bargain to the banks in retrospect. Ironically, the direct losses to the banks could have been comparable to those they ultimately experienced, but without the benefit of securing debtor-country policy reform in return.[56] Broadly the same may be said about the Bradley Plan of 1986.

The congressional proposals for an international debt authority (discussed above) might conceivably have been implemented in a policy-conditional, case-by-case manner. However, it seems more likely that that approach too would have been vulnerable to the moral hazard of automaticity. Debtor countries would have tended to perceive that the problem had been socialized by industrial country governments, and should therefore be approached on a primarily political level. In this context the incentive for meeting IMF-like policy conditions would have been weak. Correspondingly, in all of the schemes whereby the public sector would take over the debt at some initial discount, there was the risk that it would then be the public sector rather than the banks that would be in the position of having to undertake either new lending—as the bank incentive for involuntary lending would disappear (Cline 1983, 118)—or additional forgiveness.

What Cost to the Public?

Did the Brady Plan wind up bailing out the banks at the expense of the public sector? In the first instance, the answer is absolutely not. It was the banks, not the public sector, that granted debt forgiveness. The only question is whether public-sector lending for the enhancements will eventually be serviced or defaulted on by the debtor countries.

Table 5.6 reports the amounts and composition of public-sector lending for Brady bond enhancements in six of the country cases, accounting for about half of the Brady Plan total debt coverage. For these six countries, lending from the IMF, World Bank, Japanese Export Import Bank, IDB and bilateral sources provided $12 billion in enhancements to collat-

---

have reflected the plan's modest degree of forgiveness envisioned. Kenen also suggested that the plan should "probably" be limited to countries with an IMF seal of approval. However, it is unclear how that condition could have been operational, given that the plan would have to have begun with a big bang that definitively included or excluded each candidate debtor. Otherwise banks would not have been able to judge whether they would participate—as the plan required them to sell (a chosen fraction of) their loans at a discount to the IDDC either for all plan countries or for none. Comprehensive, simultaneous IMF adjustment programs for the full list of countries would have been nearly inconceivable.

56. If all middle-income countries had signed up, the 10 percent loss in 1983 would have amounted to $30 billion on the base of $300 billion outstanding loans (World Bank 1990, 1: 190). Cumulating at an opportunity cost of LIBOR plus 1 percent, this loss would have been equivalent to a loss of $73 billion in 1993. Thus, the eventual actual bank losses under the Brady Plan are broadly equivalent to what they would have been under the Kenen plan.

Table 5.6 Selected Brady Plan enhancements (millions of dollars)

Country	IMF	World Bank	Japan EXIM Bank	IDB	Other	Total	Debt forgiveness	Debt remainder equivalent	Enhance/ forgiveness (percent)	Enhance/ remainder (percent)
Mexico	1,697	2,010	2,050	0	0	5,757	14,150	33,020	40.7	17.4
Argentina	1,100	710	800	475	0	3,085	8,430	20,910	36.6	14.8
Venezuela	880	500	600	0	0	1,980	3,760	15,250	52.7	13.0
Philippines 1	120	200	300	0	0	620	2,380	4,220	47.1	26.5[a]
Philippines 2	200	100	200	0	0	500				
Costa Rica	0	0	0	0	183	183	980	630	18.7	29.0
Uruguay	35	65	0	30	0	130	500	1,100	26.0	11.8
TOTAL	4,032	3,585	3,950	505	183	12,255	30,200	75,130	40.6	16.3

a. Ratios for Philippines collapse both Brady deals into one.

Sources: World Bank, *World Debt Tables* vol. 2, various years; table 5.3.

eralize the equivalent of about $75 billion in remaining debt equivalent.[57] The corresponding forgiveness purchased amounted to about $30 billion. Thus, the ratio of public-sector enhancements to conveyed forgiveness was about 40 percent. One way to look at the enhancements, then, is that they were equivalent to an investment with an immediate return of 150 percent ($30 billion social profit to the debtor in exchange for an investment outlay of $12 billion).[58]

For the eventual total of Brady deals, the public-sector enhancements could reach close to twice as high (assuming Brazil's prospective currency reform qualifies the country for IMF enhancement lending). The resulting total of about $25 billion would be only about two-thirds as large as the original total expected (some $34 billion, as noted above). That the Brady Plan objectives may have nonetheless been largely fulfilled implies that the plan was more efficient than officially anticipated. Indeed, there was widespread concern at the outset that the program was underfunded in terms of public-sector funds available for enhancements.

In terms of public-sector cost, the relevant question is: what is the probability that the debtor countries will be unable to service or repay the enhancement funds lent to them? This probability should be extremely low. Even at the depths of the debt crisis, the major countries typically fully honored their debt to the IMF and World Bank, institutions that have enjoyed privileged creditor status. Especially after the Brady deal debt reductions, and in light of the great easing of access to capital markets for these countries in the early 1990s, there is even more reason to expect that these IFI claims will be fully honored in the future. Moreover, they are lent at rates that reflect at least opportunity cost of Treasury bonds of the United States and other industrial country members of the IMF, so that the public sector is not providing concessional financing. The short answer, then, is that the public-sector enhancements did not cost anything.[59]

Indeed, for precisely this reason, some representatives of the banking sector argue that if the question of equitable burden sharing is to be

---

57. The actual face value would be higher because par bonds at reduced interest overstate economic value.

58. This return is somewhat overstated because debtor countries also put up a modest amount of their own reserves in enhancements. Of course, the return is grossly misleading if one believes, as Bulow and Rogoff (1988a), that the true worth of the debt was no more than its initial secondary market price. The argument against that view is spelled out in chapter 4.

59. This view is diametrically opposed to that of Diwan and Rodrik (1992), who argue that the IMF and World Bank must have acquired enhancement claims that have a sufficiently high probability of default that their expected loss equals the actual loss imposed on the banks. Their underlying assumption is that the banks would not have gone into the deals without equal burden sharing by the IFIs. For a critique of that view, see chapter 4.

raised, it should incorporate the issue of intercreditor burden sharing. On this score, they argue, the public sector got off free in the Brady Plan, and the banks absorbed all of the losses. This view is of course the obverse of the public-sector concern that on the eve of the Brady Plan there was a process of shifting the debt risk from the banks to the public sector, as discussed above.

A more balanced view of burden sharing between the banks and the public sector must take account of the fact that elsewhere in the world, the bilateral creditors have granted substantial forgiveness: to Poland, Egypt, and to numerous African countries (as well as more modest forgiveness of US bilateral claims on Latin American countries under the Enterprise for the Americas Initiative).[60] The de facto pattern emerging was that where the dominant creditor was the banking sector, the banks took the main losses; where it was the bilateral creditors, they in their turn did so.[61] Another factor was that the official community was essentially exercising the new-money option: the IFIs and bilateral creditors typically did not forgive debt in the Brady deals, but they did extend new loans. If there were new-money options for the banks, why not for the public sector? Overall it is difficult to make the case that intercreditor burden sharing has been dramatically skewed either against or in favor of the banks as opposed to the public sector.

Will the Patients Relapse?

If Brady debt forgiveness was less than many analysts thought necessary, the implication is that the same analysts should be skeptical that the debt problem has been solved for the plan's graduates. A parallel concern might stem from the view that "the Greenspan plan was more important than the Brady Plan," and that the improvement for troubled debtors in the early 1990s was due more to the slack world capital market and low US interest rates than to Brady debt reform. That view would suggest concern that with the seeming shift toward a tighter world capital market and higher interest rates by early 1994 (following a strong US recovery in late 1993), the Brady graduates might enter into difficulty again.

As analyzed in chapters 6 and 8, there were reasons to be concerned that some of the graduates (Argentina and Mexico) had been running

---

60. By 1993, the United States had forgiven $875 million in Public Law 480 (food loan) and Agency for International Development debt owed by Argentina, Bolivia, Chile, Colombia, El Salvador, Jamaica, and Uruguay, or 54 percent of the original value of the claims involved (World Bank 1993b, 1: 36).

61. Although for Poland the banks' Brady deal gave almost the same depth of cut as the Paris Club's 50 percent.

excessive current-account deficits (see the epilogue on Mexico). However, as also suggested in chapter 8, the capital flows to the former problem-debtor countries have been sufficiently small compared to global capital markets that it is difficult to conceive of a collapse in capital market availability to Brady graduates as a group in the future, if they maintain well-balanced domestic macroeconomic policies. Even if the going interest rate for that capital rose somewhat because of general capital market tightening, the result should not be sufficiently burdensome to precipitate a reentry into the intensive-care ward for the Brady graduates. The vulnerability of these countries to increases in international interest rates is examined in chapter 8.

The greater risk of relapse comes not from the economic side but, once again, the political. By early 1994 there were signs of a slide back toward more populist policies in Venezuela, and the front-runner in the presidential elections in Brazil (Lula) was advocating renegotiation of the debt as well as social initiatives that would require considerable increases in public-sector resources. Although by the fourth quarter of 1994 political-economic trends were reverting to the center in both countries (and in Brazil centrist Fernando Henrique Cardoso had won the election on the strength of the Real Plan for economic stabilization), these swings illustrated persistent political vulnerability of the economic reforms.

Evaluation Summary

Taken as a whole, the international strategy to cope with the debt crisis was successful. There was complete success in avoiding international financial shock from a collapse of the commercial banking system, a risk that existed at the outset. The dramatic early return to international capital market access, in sharp contrast to the experience after defaults in the 1930s, must also be judged a success of the strategy, and was inherently linked to the market-oriented, quasi-voluntary nature of the plan. As for debtor country growth, it is implausible that the losses of the 1980s could have been much mitigated by an earlier shift in the debt strategy to forgiveness.

The strategy evolved over time, and at each stage the contingent approach adopted was consistent with plausible prospects in the international and domestic economies. Even before its final phase of debt forgiveness, the strategy proved sufficient to resolve the problems of countries that pursued sound domestic economic policies and did not face large adverse external shocks. After the oil shock of 1986, the underlying conditions turned more adverse. The bank provisioning of 1987 and the decline in secondary market prices set the stage for the final phase of the strategy, the Brady Plan.

Forgiveness under that plan had a disproportionately large favorable effect because of confidence restoration and because the lancing of the political boil of perceived inequity in the debt strategy reversed prior unwillingness to pay by some countries arguably in a position to pay on strictly economic grounds. Above all, it was the reform of domestic economic policies that provided the basis for any long-term success of the strategy. Some argue that these reforms would have been forthcoming even if concessional relief had occurred earlier, a proposition that is largely untestable but would seem inconsistent with the fact that typically it was delay in domestic economic reform rather than in the plan's starting date that proved to be the binding constraint.

Implications for Future Policy

As early as 1991 and certainly by 1992, Latin America entered into a new phase of capital market abundance and even excess. The overall handling of the debt crisis on a market-oriented basis almost certainly contributed to this outcome, as argued above, although there is no doubt validity in the notion that the Greenspan plan (low interest rates) importantly complemented the Brady Plan in bringing about the capital flow revival.

What are the lessons of the experience of international debt policy for capital markets in the remainder of the 1990s and beyond? The objectives of future policy should be to:

- prevent a repeat of the 1980s debt crisis;

- encourage sustainable capital inflows into productive investment in developing countries; and

- reinforce sound domestic economic policies and discourage weak ones.

Systemic Risk

Excessive syndicated bank lending to developing countries in the late 1970s placed the US and industrial country banking systems at risk upon the emergence of the debt crisis in 1982. The banks were badly burned and seem unlikely to repeat that experience; as noted, they have emigrated out of long-term lending to the countries that required Brady debt reduction.

The more relevant issue is whether the large renewed capital flows to Latin America could pose systemic risk through new channels. The vehicles of these flows are primarily international bonds, other portfolio flows by private investors into securities and even simply bank certificates of deposit, and direct investment. In principle, if a country defaults on these assets (or limits direct investment repatriations), it is the individual investors that lose; there is no threat to the financial system of the source countries.

In practice there might be some chance of systemic risk. It is not hard to envision the potential collapse of a large brokerage house because of a future default on LDC bonds. Political and possibly even monetary authorities might prefer to socialize the losses rather than inflict them on numerous account holders in the institution, thereby undermining confidence in securities houses more generally. Even so, it is difficult to imagine a situation in which the whole securities industry would be exposed to LDC bonds to the same extent that the banking sector was to LDC debt in the early 1980s. Some losses might or might not be socialized, but industrial country financial systems would not be placed at risk.

To be on the safe side, nonetheless, it might be desirable for bank regulators to limit the fraction of any bank's portfolio that can be placed in loans to a single country and to impose a parallel limit for total loans to a developing-country region.[62] Except for a few instances of holdover lending concentration, such limits would presumably not be binding for some years, but could prevent a renewed round of excessive lending later in the decade. Regulators of the securities industry could place similar limits on bonds held by securities houses for their own accounts. In light of the experience of the debt crisis, it would be appropriate to aggregate both private and sovereign obligations in this process.

Moral Hazard

The history of international lending is replete with swings between extremes. It remains to be seen whether the buoyancy of capital flows to Latin America in the early 1990s was the beginning of another extreme phase, a transitory phenomenon largely reflecting portfolio readjustment on flight capital (chapter 8) and temporarily low interest rates at the industrial country center, or a more sustainable trend.

Public policy can lean against excessive lending by ensuring that there is no moral hazard providing the expectation of private actors that their risks are limited because losses will be socialized. The aftermath of the Brady Plan may leave a modicum of such a moral hazard. Banks did suffer losses, but these losses were limited. Bondholders did not suffer

---

62. Before the debt crisis, US bank regulations did set a ceiling of 10 percent on the fraction of capital that a bank could lend to a single borrower. However, US authorities interpreted different official entities within a given country as different borrowers. The implication is the need for an additional layer of prudential limitation applying to all loans to a single country. This requirement could usefully be in two parts: one limit for loans to all government entities, and another that would also include loans to private borrowers.

losses, typically, with the result that there may be a false sense of security in the bond market. As analyzed in chapter 8, bonds (including the Brady conversion bonds) have gone from being a small minority of claims before the debt crisis to being a large majority after it, and they are thus no longer in a structural position to enjoy de facto seniority.

It may be appropriate for monetary authorities to send signals that the public sector will not bail out private investors if there is another round of the debt crisis. Admittedly, there is a delicate balance here, and any premature signal might choke off the revival of the capital flows.

Brady Sunset

One such signal would be to announce a termination date for official-sector support of new Brady debt reduction deals. The Brady Plan was designed to deal with the debt crisis of the 1980s. By 1994, almost all of the countries that had been swept up in that crisis had resolved their debt problems with the help of a Brady agreement (and in some cases, without one). There was never any conscious decision that Brady enhancements financed by the public should be available on a permanent basis to deal with new, future debt crises in totally different countries and regions.

So far, bonds have not been involved in the debt reduction conversions. However, bond purchasers might take undue comfort from the notion that, based on the experience of the early 1990s, in any future debt crisis there would be Brady-type arrangements to limit their losses.

It is worthwhile to consider announcing the end of Brady facilities as of, say, March 1996, the seventh anniversary of the plan. This decision would have the salutary effect of concentrating the minds of the banks and the country governments on the reaching of prompt agreement in the few remaining cases of unfinished Brady business. On the supply side, it would also remove a psychological security blanket from private investors that might otherwise serve as moral hazard inviting insufficient caution in bond, bank, or other capital flows to developing countries. Investors might then more closely scrutinize the economic policies of the country in question before investing. If so, countries with sound policies would not be adversely affected, while there would be increased discipline on other borrowing governments. On the demand side, phaseout of the Brady Plan would reestablish the principle that the central expectation for sovereign borrowing is that it will be repaid rather than forgiven, thereby raising the expected cost of borrowing and moderating country demand for it.

There is some risk that the preannounced sunset might stampede some countries into requesting Brady forgiveness when otherwise they might attempt to avoid this outcome. Russia is the most important case in point. To obviate this risk, the IFIs could seek to remove the moral hazard problem simply by announcing (immediately) that the cutoff date for debt eligible for conversion enhancements is 1992. In practice, however, this alternative is sufficiently technical and abstruse that it runs the risk of sending only a weak signal about the moral hazard problem.

Regulatory Practice

At present insurance companies and other institutional investors are subject to limits on the fraction of their assets they can place abroad, and moreover they are restricted to investment-grade assets (e.g., Standard and Poor's BBB and better). Consideration should be given to the addition of another regulatory screen: a country-risk examination by creditor country officials (for example, in the United States an interagency review team comprising Treasury, the Federal Reserve, and the Securities and Exchange Commission).

Such an additional screen could help guard against excessive debt buildup and the risk that the private rating agencies might be subject to undue influence by their clients (typically the country pays the agency to establish a rating). Conversely, the presence of a dual screen would mean that private ratings would also serve as a guard against undue politicization of the public-sector rating entity (e.g., the dominance of diplomatic over economic considerations). There could be a small degree of moral hazard in this arrangement in that investors might feel they had some claim to recompense from the government if they experienced losses from countries that had successfully passed the official credit screen, but on balance the arrangement would seem more likely to improve lending prudence than to provoke incautious lending.

Keep Private Risk Private

One of the important lessons of the debt crisis is that an internal transfer problem of inadequate fiscal capacity can occur as the result of de jure or de facto socialization of private debt, as occurred in Argentina (chapter 6). In such situations, private parties owing debt abroad succeed in shifting this debt to the domestic public sector without conveying domestic assets of equal value to the public sector. The effective increase in the net indebtedness of the government poses fiscal obstacles to debt servicing even if the private sector is generating a trade surplus that would suffice to deal with the external transfer problem.

It is obvious enough to state that in the future developing country governments should not assume such private debt, or at least not on terms of incomplete compensation with domestic assets. The problem is that domestic political situations generate such outcomes, and the political pressures (e.g., by politically influential business groups) cannot be lectured away. Unfortunately, there is no clear mechanism for discouraging lending that is made to private borrowers in the expectation of debtor country public-sector takeover in the event of a crisis. In practice the implication might be that the official creditworthiness screening entity referred to above should consider potential internal transfer (fiscal) problems even where the debt is primarily owed by the private sector.

A Powerless IMF?

In the late 1970s, the boom in private lending to debtor countries gave many the impression that the role of the IMF (and even the World Bank) had disappeared. The debt crisis rudely dismissed this impression, but there is a risk of a repetition of the marginalization of the Bretton Woods institutions as an effect of the private capital market boom in the 1990s.

The two organizations could nonetheless play a more active role in shaping private-sector perceptions of creditworthiness by issuing timely policy surveillance reviews on a basis available to the public, for at least the major borrowing countries. The detailed country reports would probably need to remain secret for the traditional reasons of country willingness to provide information (although countries confident of sound policies could be invited to authorize prompt public release of even these documents). But the World Bank already publishes somewhat out-of-date country synopses (e.g., World Bank 1993e); and the International Monetary Fund has increasingly made public its criticisms of industrial country policy errors (e.g., IMF 1992c, 26). A periodic publication by either institution or both reviewing the quality of economic policies in, say, the 10 largest developing countries borrowing on the international bond markets could go a long way both to maintain an important function for their expertise and to inject improved and more disinterested analysis into the capital markets.

Institutional Change

As developed in chapter 8 and annex 8A, there is a case for establishing a new entity (probably mixed public-private) to insure bonds issued by developing countries. Coinsurance rates would vary to reflect debtor policy quality and country risk. This arrangement could send a powerful signal to reinforce good policies. At the same time, the insurance function might substantially widen the capital market supply by facilitating the entry of such institutional investors as pension funds and insurance companies.

Chapter 8 also considers another institutional change: the creation of an international bankruptcy facility. As discussed there, so long as such an arrangement were limited to jurisdiction over obligations that clearly stated their eventual subjection to arbitration by the entity in the event of default, the proposal might have some merit. However, it is unclear that lenders and borrowers would find this vehicle to be attractive for conducting the bulk of their credit transactions.

6

Economic Adjustment and Debt Strategy in Latin America

Introduction

At the beginning of the debt crisis in 1982, the seven largest Latin American countries (Argentina, Brazil, Chile, Colombia, Mexico, Peru, and Venezuela) accounted for 39 percent of total external debt of developing countries. Six of the seven (omitting only Colombia) accounted for 74 percent of the external debt of the "severely indebted middle income countries" and for 82 percent of the long-term debt owed by these SIMICs to the commercial banks (World Bank 1989b). Just as the debt crisis was largely a Latin American phenomenon, its resolution depended primarily on policies (international and domestic) affecting these individual countries, which account for 82 percent of the region's population. This chapter thus examines the economic policies and debt strategies pursued by these principal debtor countries over the past decade. Because of the risk of premature evaluation of more recent events, the discussion concentrates on the period 1982–92. However, brief extensions of the analysis are included in cases in which important changes seemed to be under way subsequently.

Edwards (1993) has provided an extensive review of the process of policy reform in Latin America in the decade since the outbreak of the debt crisis. This experience is one of sweeping transformation of the dominant economic ideology in the region, from a model of heavy state intervention and closed-economy development of domestic industry to one of a market-oriented, open economy with limited participation of the government in production. This transformation and the economic

Figure 6.1   Real per capita GDP, four largest debtors (1979-81 = 100)

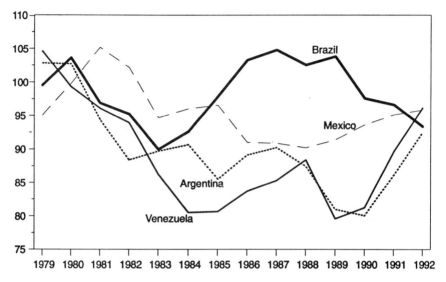

Source: IMF, International Financial Statistics (IFS).

reforms it generated provided the principal basis for recovery of the region from the debt crisis.[1]

As discussed in chapter 5, there is little doubt that the depth of the debt crisis was a primary factor in the change in policy regime for most of the major Latin American countries. Figures 6.1 through 6.4 depict the severity of this crisis in terms of the performance of domestic output and inflation during the past decade. For 1982-92 as a whole, real per capita income was lower than its 1979-81 base by 14.7 percent in Peru, 14.1 percent in Venezuela, 12.7 percent in Argentina, 5.7 percent in Mexico, and 2 percent in Brazil. The 1982-92 average was only 1.9 percent above the 1979-81 base in Chile, and a more favorable 8.4 percent above the base in Colombia.

Nor did the economic depression of the 1980s avoid massive inflation. Late in the decade Argentina and Peru entered into hyperinflation, Brazil experienced extremely high levels of inflation, and Mexico and Venezuela faced bouts of inflation far above their traditional levels (figures 6.3 and 6.4). However, the production and inflation trends shown in figure 6.1 through 6.4 also reveal hopeful patterns whereby economic performance on both measures was far more favorable by the early 1990s than in the mid-1980s (except in Brazil, where inflation remained

---

1. In this regard, it is telling that in Edwards's (1993) World Bank review, only 5 of 159 pages are devoted explicitly to external debt and the mechanisms for its management and reduction; the rest concern domestic economic reform.

Figure 6.2   Real per capita GDP, three intermediate debtors (1979-81 = 100)

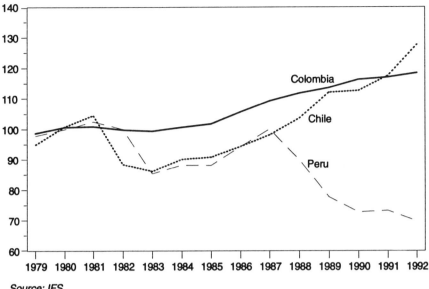

Source: IFS.

at extremely high levels, and in Peru, where production remained depressed).

The varying responses to this common challenge provide an important laboratory for testing the effectiveness of alternative macroeconomic and debt strategies. The regime change toward economic reform came earlier in Chile and Mexico, and later in Argentina, Venezuela, and Peru. Colombia consistently pursued stable fiscal policies and achieved low inflation but delayed structural reform until relatively late; Brazil had adopted structural reform by the early 1990s but failed to secure fiscal balance and moderate inflation. Debt strategies were the most consistently cooperative with international creditors in Chile and Colombia; somewhat more confrontational in Mexico and Venezuela; and substantially more so in Argentina, Brazil, and especially Peru.

Colombia

Colombia not only managed to avoid recourse to Brady Plan debt forgiveness but even circumvented formal rescheduling of its debt in the 1980s. The nation was able to do so because its domestic economic policies prior to the debt crisis had been more prudent than those of most Latin American countries. As a result, it had a lower relative level of external debt when the crisis occurred, and faced less extreme economic adjustments to respond.

Table 6.1 Economic indicators for Colombia, 1982-93 (percentages and billions of dollars)

Indicator	1982	1983	1984	1985	1986	1987	1988	1989	1990	1991	1992	1993
GDP growth (%)	0.9	1.6	3.4	3.1	5.8	5.4	4.1	3.4	4.1	2.3	3.5	4.5
Inflation (%)	24.5	19.8	16.1	24.0	18.9	23.3	28.1	25.8	29.1	30.4	27.0	..
Gross investment/GDP (%)	26.4	26.4	23.9	20.9	20.5	21.2	22.0	19.7	18.5	16.1	17.2	..
Fiscal balance/GDP (%) Cent	-2.0	-1.0	-4.3	-2.7	-1.3	-0.5	-1.4	-1.7	-0.1	-0.8	-1.5	..
Fiscal balance/GDP (%) NFPS	-7.9	-7.8	-6.9	-4.5	-0.1	-1.4	-2.2	-1.9	-0.3	-0.1	0.0	..
Real effective EXR (1985=100)	84.8	85.2	93.0	106.7	143.2	160.5	166.5	172.7	195.8	189.5	173.5	..
XGS (billions of dollars)	4.4	3.8	5.2	4.5	6.4	6.8	6.7	7.3	8.8	9.3	9.2	..
MGS (billions of dollars)	6.7	5.8	5.3	5.1	5.1	5.5	6.2	6.1	6.8	6.3	8.1	..
Current account balance (billions of dollars)	-3.1	-3.0	-1.4	-1.8	0.4	0.3	-0.2	-0.2	0.5	2.3	0.9	..
External debt (billions of dollars)	10.3	11.4	12.0	14.2	15.4	17.0	17.0	16.9	17.2	17.4	17.2	..
Reserves excl. gold (billions of dollars)	3.9	1.9	1.4	1.6	2.7	3.1	3.2	3.6	4.2	6.0	7.4	7.6

.. = data not available.

Inflation: consumer prices, year over year.
Fiscal balances: Cent = central government; NFPS = nonfinancial public sector.
XGS, MGS: exports and imports of goods and nonfactor services.

Sources: IMF 1992a, 1993h (growth, inflation, trade, current account, reserves); World Bank 1993b (debt); IDB 1991, 1993 (investment, fiscal balances, real exchange rate); ECLAC 1993 (fiscal balances).

Figure 6.3 Consumer price path, intermediate inflation countries

annual percentage change

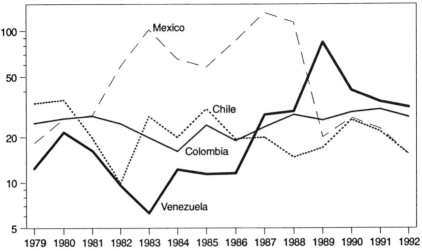

Source: IMF, *International Financial Statistics.*

Macroeconomic Policy

Fiscal conservatism and (for Latin America) relatively orthodox economic policies had characterized Colombian policy for decades. Urrutia (1991) argues that the underlying reason was a clientelistic rather than populist political system. A stable two-party system and democratic rule dated back more than a century. Rather than a powerful president, regional political barons dominated politics. Redistribution to their "clients," the populace committed in turn to support them at the polls, was local in nature rather than national in a rich versus poor framework. The regional politicians tended to select technocrats as presidential candidates, to avoid nourishing a rival power base. The system tended to generate public spending (e.g., in health and education) that was relatively strongly redistributive, contributing to legitimacy.

In Colombia, inflation has traditionally been politically unpopular. Thus, when inflation rose from less than 10 percent in 1967–71 to over 20 percent in 1973–74, the new Lopez administration tightened monetary and fiscal policy, even at the cost of a slowdown in growth (Ocampo 1989, 242). Exchange rate policy had been realistic since the adoption of the crawling peg in the late 1960s. Fiscal deficits averaged only 1 percent of GDP from 1975 through 1981 (Urrutia 1991, 373), in an era when deficits reached double digits in some other major Latin American countries.

Figure 6.4 Consumer price path, high inflation countries

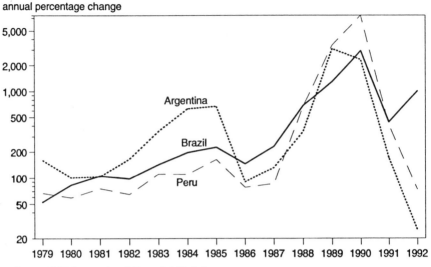

annual percentage change

Source: IMF, *International Financial Statistics*.

Debt Strategy

Fiscal conservatism domestically translated into caution in, and limited need for, borrowing abroad.[2] Whereas Brazil and Costa Rica used the coffee boom of the late 1970s as leverage for more borrowing abroad, and Mexico did the same with its newfound oil, Colombia used the coffee bonanza for fiscal consolidation. As a result, by the beginning of the debt crisis Colombia's net external debt stood at only 145 percent of exports of goods and services, compared with ratios typically at 300 percent or higher for other major debtors in the region (chapter 2, table 2.3). Debt would have been even lower if the Turbay administration (1978–82) had not relaxed some of the traditional economic prudence and increased government investment and wages in an attempt to regain faster growth (Ocampo 1989).

Despite low debt and a good policy record, Colombia encountered the adverse "neighborhood effect" of the Latin American debt crisis, and by 1983 and after the foreign banks were renewing loans only with great difficulty and orchestration. Efforts to revive growth, and overvaluation following the coffee boom, had led to a substantial current account deficit by 1982–83. With the added drain of amortization payments,

2. Urrutia (1991, 370–71) avers, "In the late 1970s, while foreign credit was inundating the region, Colombia, against the advice and pressure of international organizations and private bankers, actually decreased its foreign debt in order to facilitate monetary management during a period of high coffee prices."

reserves fell rapidly. The banks insisted that Colombia adopt an International Monetary Fund standby program (which would have been conditioned on faster trade liberalization), a move Colombian authorities found politically unacceptable.

After a "heterodox" phase of faster exchange rate crawl combined with higher import protection in 1982–83, and some softening up of the banks and international institutions through President Belisario Betancur's calling of the debtors' meeting of Latin American presidents at Cartagena in May 1984, Finance Minister Roberto Junguito implemented a forceful adjustment program comprising wider taxes, spending cuts, and a large acceleration of the exchange rate crawl. Fiscal tightening facilitated the hat trick of achieving a 30 percent real depreciation over the course of a year without accelerating inflation.

The new program and a loose IMF monitoring arrangement formed the basis for the "Jumbo" loan of $1 billion from the banks in 1985, followed by the $1 billion "Concorde" loan of 1987, the $1.5 billion "Challenger" loan in 1989, and the $1.6 billion "Hercules" loan in 1991. These amounted to involuntary refinancing of principal coming due without rescheduling. The political opposition called for outright rescheduling and lower interest spreads along the lines negotiated by other countries, but the government insisted that its strategy offered better prospects for a subsequent return to voluntary lending. By 1986 a temporary boom in coffee prices eased the pressure, and by 1987 exports from Colombia's newly developed oil sector provided an alternative major source of earnings (Hommes 1990). For the period 1986–90 Colombia was in current account surplus; and by then, with the help of the jumbo loans, it was out of the debt woods.

Even so, there was immense frustration that the banks had not treated Colombia more favorably and rewarded the country with more voluntary lending.[3] As late as 1988, a prominent Colombian economist warned that with the regional trend toward arrears, higher bank reserves, and greater latitude by international agencies, more "aggressive" solutions to the debt problem could emerge. He concluded:

> Under these conditions, the country could hardly choose any but the "heterodox" solutions, as a highly *uncertain* access to new commercial capital on a voluntary basis (the uncertainty of which would clearly increase with the generalized adoption of alternative debt strategies) can hardly be a substitute for a *certain* reduction in debt service obligations. (Ocampo 1989, 263)

As it turned out, a more heterodox solution did emerge. It was called the Brady Plan. Yet Colombia chose not to enroll, precisely because of the same dynamic that had determined its policy not to reschedule:

---

3. Ocampo's (1989) sharp critique in this regard is somewhat inconsistent with his own criticism of Colombian authorities' loss of prudence after 1978.

there was more to be gained over the long term through maintaining an impressive credit record than through savings that could be squeezed out from debt reduction.[4] Chilean authorities made the same decision. As noted in chapter 4, one tangible reward was investment-grade rating by the debt-rating agencies (by 1993, Standard and Poor's rated the two nations at BBB; Salomon Brothers 1993a). Being able to borrow at rates lower by some 200 basis points or more offered the prospect of longer-term compensation for Colombia's businesslike debt policy in the 1980s.

Structural Reform

Ironically, Colombia's success on external debt may have contributed to its tardy conversion to the wave of liberal policy reform that swept Latin America by the late 1980s. Thus, Williamson (1990b) excluded Colombia from his highest tier of countries ranked by policy reform, "because of its very limited implementation of microeconomic liberalization measures" (404). Less debt trauma seemed to mean consequentially less radical restructuring of the old order, including especially trade protection (in part because the leverage of international agencies was lesser).

As it subsequently turned out, however, by the early 1990s Colombia experienced major microeconomic reform of its own. The political power of nontraditional exporters had risen substantially, and there was a growing perception that export markets could suffer from foreign protection if Colombia's markets remained closed. Domestic industrialists increasingly recognized the high costs of inputs in a regime in which the full gamut of products was produced domestically at below-international scale. When it became apparent that the best means to confront inflation was through rapid import liberalization, the Gaviria regime was able to adopt it (Urrutia 1994). By 1992, the protective effect of tariffs and nontariff barriers had fallen from one of the highest levels in the region (83 percent in 1985) to one of the lowest (7 percent; Edwards 1993).

There is a final aspect of Colombian debt management that requires consideration: was debt easier to deal with because of drug money? This argument sometimes arises as a justification for why other Latin American countries could not have achieved the same results. The limited empirical analysis of this issue would seem to suggest that drug income played little role in moderating Colombia's debt problem.

One important consideration is that the "internal transfer problem" of government capacity to mobilize resources from the private sector

---

4. Garay (1993) adds another reason. A significant fraction of Colombia's external debt was owed to foreign branches of Colombian banks. Any government effort to secure forgiveness would have weakened these banks and run the risk that parts of their portfolios would have to be nationalized.

(chapter 4) would not have been affected by drug income, because it is not in the legal economy and escapes taxation. Another is that at least a cursory examination of Colombian balance of payments data does not reveal large amounts of unexplainable inflows of foreign exchange. One might expect any cornucopia of drug dollars to appear in errors and omissions, or else in the "services" exports (which tend to be easier to mask than goods exports). Neither category shows unusually high shares for Colombia.[5]

Two Colombian studies on the question come to purportedly differing conclusions, but on closer examination they are consistent with the view that drug money has not helped much even with the "external transfer problem." Urrutia (1990) cites estimates by Hernando José Gómez indicating that drug trade income in Colombia fell from an average of $2.8 billion annually in 1981–83 to $1.4 billion in 1984–86 and $807 million in 1987–88. These estimates would suggest that the income from drugs was falling just at the time Colombia was working its way out of the debt crisis and so could not have been a major part of the solution to the crisis. Moreover, Urrutia judges that "in each year, only a small fraction of these amounts enters Colombia in the form of foreign exchange" (117). By way of illustration, he notes that since 1980 expenditures on tourism abroad have exceeded earnings reported on tourism in Colombia, a category he suggests would have reflected repatriated drug earnings.

Arrieta et al. (1990) come to the opposite conclusion qualitatively, as they assert that "foreign exchange from drugs has contributed a certain abundance to the exchange balance, avoiding the large devaluations of other countries in Latin America and the reductions in real wages" (87). However, their central estimates (based on area planted in coca, estimates of imported coca paste from Bolivia and Peru, exports of cocaine, and US wholesale prices—which fell from $60,000 per kilogram in 1980–82 to $27,000 in 1986–88) indicate that Colombian cocaine exports were an annual average of $2.2 billion in 1981–83, $1.3 billion in 1984–86, and $1.3 billion in 1987–88. Their series thus also shows that drug exports were falling rather than rising during the crucial period for recovery from the debt problem.

The principal divergence in the two studies is that Arrieta et al. (1990) have a much higher estimate of the repatriation of drug export earnings into the Colombian economy. They construct price indexes that they suggest show imports are underinvoiced by 20 to 30 percent, and they argue that perhaps half of reported services exports are really drug income repatriation. They thus estimate foreign exchange receipts enter-

---

5. From 1982 through 1987, Colombia's errors and omissions were on average negative at about $100 million annually, rather than large and positive. In the same period, the ratio of nonfactor service exports to merchandise exports was 21 percent, just the same as for Chile (calculated from IMF 1992a).

ing the economy from drug trade at $900 million to $1.3 billion annually (84). This estimate implies that by the mid-1980s virtually the entire amount of drug export earnings entered the economy, rather than staying in investments abroad as suggested by Urrutia. Because unit value price indexes can be misleading, and because (as noted) reported service export earnings do not seem out of line with international experience, the Arrieta et al. estimates of repatriated foreign exchange earnings would seem exaggerated.

An estimate averaging of the two studies would place the contribution of drug money to Colombian foreign exchange availability in the vicinity of $500 million annually in the mid-1980s. If half of this amount entered in the form of underinvoicing imports and the other half in the form of overstated nonfactor services exports, then nondrug exports of goods and nonfactor services were about $250 million less than reported, or lower by about 5 percent. Colombia's reported ratio of net debt to exports of goods and services in this period was about 230 percent (chapter 2, table 2.3). Removing the drug portion of the export base, and cumulating an extra, say, $1.25 billion debt over five years to account for imports that otherwise would have had to be paid for by nondrug money, the debt/exports ratio might have reached about 15 percent higher without the help of drug money, or 265 percent rather than 230 percent.[6] This level would still have left Colombia in a relatively comfortable external transfer position, certainly in comparison to other major Latin American debtors.

In short, if other Latin American countries had followed the model of fiscal prudence and exchange rate realism that dominated Colombian policy before and during the debt crisis, they could likely have come much closer to replicating the Colombian success in managing external debt even without the help of drug money. Their initial debt stocks would have been lower, and like Colombia even without drug money, they would not have had an internal transfer problem.

Chile

Chile is widely regarded as perhaps the most successful Latin American country in carrying out economic adjustment and emerging from the debt crisis—or at least stands as *primus inter pares* along with Colombia and Mexico. Alone among the countries forced to reschedule debt, Chile has eschewed Brady Plan forgiveness as unnecessary. Skeptics tend to argue that Chile's case is exceptional because the country began its adjustment process in the 1970s well before the debt crisis, and because

---

6. With a 5 percent reduction in the export base and an increase of about 10 percent in the stock of debt.

Table 6.2 Economic indicators for Chile, 1982-93 (percentages and billions of dollars)

Indicator	1982	1983	1984	1985	1986	1987	1988	1989	1990	1991	1992	1993
GDP growth (%)	-14.1	-0.7	6.4	2.5	5.6	5.7	7.4	10.0	2.1	6.0	10.4	6.0
Inflation (%)	9.9	27.3	19.9	30.7	19.5	19.9	14.7	17.0	26.0	21.8	15.4	..
Gross investment/GDP (%)	30.3	12.2	19.8	16.1	17.1	19.8	20.1	23.6	22.5	21.6	25.0	..
Fiscal balance/GDP (%) Gen	-2.6	-3.7	-2.9	-1.8	-0.5	2.4	3.7	5.2	1.4	1.6	2.7	..
Real effective EXR (1985=100)	90.9	111.8	113.7	141.1	167.0	180.0	192.5	188.1	193.3	187.6	177.5	..
XGS (billions of dollars)	4.6	4.6	4.3	4.5	5.2	6.3	8.3	9.6	10.2	11.2	12.5	..
MGS (billions of dollars)	5.0	4.0	4.5	4.0	4.6	5.5	6.6	8.6	9.3	9.5	11.6	..
Current account balance (billions of dollars)	-2.3	-1.1	-2.1	-1.3	-1.1	-0.8	-0.2	-0.8	-0.6	0.1	-0.6	..
External debt (billions of dollars)	17.3	17.9	19.7	20.4	21.1	21.5	19.6	18.0	19.1	17.9	19.4	..
Reserves excl. gold (billions of dollars)	1.8	2.0	2.3	2.5	2.4	2.5	3.2	3.6	6.1	7.0	9.2	9.6

.. = data not available.

Inflation: consumer prices, year over year.
Fiscal balances: Gen = general government.
XGS, MGS: exports and imports of goods and nonfactor services.

Sources: IMF 1992a, 1993h (growth, inflation, trade, current account, reserves); World Bank 1993b (debt); IDB 1991, 1993 (investment, fiscal balances, real exchange rate); ECLAC 1993 (fiscal balances).

the Pinochet regime had the advantage of absolute power to enforce unpopular measures. Supporters have stressed that the collapse in Chile's terms of trade was more severe than for most other countries in the region. With respect to the debt problem itself, two features stand out: Chilean authorities consistently sought a market-oriented solution, and there was the major advantage that the domestic burden of the external debt remained primarily in the private sector rather than the responsibility of the public sector.

Macroeconomic Policy and Structural Change

Chile's structural reform did begin early. The populist measures of the Allende regime raised inflation from its traditional range of some 20 percent annually to nearly 400 percent by 1973, contributing to the military coup. By 1975 the Pinochet regime had indexed tax revenue, adopted a comprehensive 20 percent value-added tax, and undertaken cutbacks in government employment that reached nearly one-third by 1981, reducing the public payroll from 20 percent of GDP to 12 percent (Meller 1990, 77–78).

The military government eliminated import quotas and cut tariffs from their average of 105 percent in 1971 (and as high as 700 percent for some categories) to an average of 44 percent by 1975 and, by 1979, a uniform level of 10 percent (except for automobiles; Dornbusch and Edwards 1993). The government also reprivatized the array of firms and farms that had been socialized by the Allende regime, although the Pinochet government did not move to the phase of privatization of large "core" state enterprises (telecommunications, electricity) until the mid-1980s (Meller 1990, 80–81), and even then left the copper mines under state control. Overall, Chile adopted reforms conforming to the "Washington consensus" some 15 years before the invention of the term (Williamson 1990b) or the widespread implementation of its agenda elsewhere in the region.[7]

Why, then, did Chile get into trouble on its external debt in the early 1980s? Three reasons stand out. First and foremost, the policy error of selecting one particular variant of "Chicago School" economics—the adoption of a fixed exchange rate under the theory that the "law of one price" would force Chilean inflation down to world levels—led to severe overvaluation, external deficits, and debt buildup. Second, higher oil prices and lower copper prices meant that the terms of trade, which had already fallen from an index of 100 in 1965–74 to 50 in 1975–79, fell still

---

7. Piñera (1991) has argued that the existence of a large cadre of economists (mostly trained at the University of Chicago), and especially their ability to agree on the proper course of action in contrast to the divergent views of businessmen and interest groups, was a crucial ingredient to the adoption of these reforms.

further (to 40 by 1982). Third, the contagion effect of the Latin American debt problem precluded recourse to consumption smoothing through normal borrowing. Ironically, the most important source of the debt problem for most other debtors in the region, chronic fiscal imbalance, was absent in the Chilean case.

By 1979 the government had brought inflation down to approximately 30 percent, and it decided to fix the exchange rate to force inflation the rest of the way down to industrial country levels. Because domestic inflation lagged behind, from 1978 to 1981 the real effective exchange rate appreciated by 61 percent (calculated from IMF 1992a). The sharp strengthening of the peso, combined with falling copper prices, caused the trade deficit on goods and nonfactor services to balloon from $583 million in 1978 to $3.1 billion in 1981, or 62 percent of exports of goods and services (calculated from IMF 1992a).

Dornbusch and Edwards (1993) discuss two competing theories of the 1980–81 external-sector problem for Chile. The first is the exchange rate policy–error hypothesis just outlined ("indexation and inertia" in domestic inflation versus a fixed exchange rate, in the Dornbusch-Edwards formulation). The second is the view that there was such a large exogenous inflow of capital that Chilean authorities had no alternative to permitting the real exchange rate to appreciate and allowing the trade balance to move into large deficit. This second view is essentially the Nigel Lawson (UK Treasury) "consenting adults" view, whereby external current account deficits are of no concern to policymakers if the deficits arise from private-sector decisions rather than from fiscal imbalances.[8] The second view carries endorsement rather than reproach for policymakers. Surprisingly, Dornbusch and Edwards are unable to decide which theory is correct in the Chilean case. However, the simplest test is surely to examine the domestic real interest rate. If the problem was an exogenous inward flood of capital, domestic interest rates should have been low. Instead, the real interest rate on deposits reached 29 percent in 1981 (Dornbusch and Edwards 1993, 10).

Most analysts (including Corbo 1990; Meller 1990; and Fontaine 1989) agree with the "policy error" diagnosis of overvaluation in 1980–81, as discussed above. Corbo notes that the combined effect of overvaluation and excessive domestic demand brought the current account deficit to 14 percent of GDP in 1981. He also notes that wage indexation and the fixed, overvalued exchange rate caused the subsequent adjustment process to be "extremely costly in terms of unemployment." Thus, Chile's unemployment rate had already risen from 11 percent to 23 percent by June 1982, two months before the Latin American debt crisis began (97). Corbo further maintains that the internal disequilibrium provoked by the overvalued exchange rate was much more important

---

8. This view is examined in the discussion of Mexico below.

than external shocks in precipitating the 1982–83 crisis in the Chilean economy.

Chilean external adjustment first involved a massive recession in 1982–83 (figure 6.2), reducing excess demand. After experimentation with expansionary policies and renewed external-sector erosion in 1984, the government shifted to emphasis on exports as the source of growth. To this end it pursued progressive real depreciation of the exchange rate, which had shifted to a crawling peg regime by the end of 1981 after the collapse of the fixed rate experiment. From 1981 to 1986, real depreciation amounted to approximately 90 percent, which ''worked wonders in the promotion of exports and the substitution of imports'' (Fontaine 1989, 216). From 1984 to 1989 the dollar value of exports more than doubled (IMF 1992a).[9] The second half of the 1980s also saw the deepening of structural reform, with a move into the more massive phase of privatization and the transformation of the social security system from ''pay as you go'' to a regime with capitalized individual accounts.

Those who have evaluated the Chilean experience have turned in more mixed scores than might have been expected from the performance shown in figures 6.2 and 6.3. Two main critiques have emerged: first, that the adjustment was too costly in terms of forgone production; and second, that it was too inequitable in its toll on real wages (Meller 1990; Dornbusch and Edwards 1993). Meller (1990) divides the reduction in absorption (demand) into an unavoidable component for adjustment and an avoidable component caused by structural rigidities and policy overkill. By his method, fully half of the 30 percent of GDP absorption loss in 1982 was of the ''avoidable'' type, declining to zero only by 1986 (67). However, Corbo (1990) criticizes Meller's technique, noting that it treats any reduction in nontradeables output as ''avoidable'' whereas there must be a reallocation of resources and production from nontradeables to tradeables if external adjustment is to occur.

Dornbusch and Edwards (1993) reach the judgment of excessive output loss by comparing the actual trend of GDP against a ''potential'' trend. However, their potential GDP curve simply connects the successive peaks of 1971, 1980, and 1992 without asking whether output was unsustainably at above-full employment in 1980, as seems to have been the case. Moreover, if the two authors graded Chile on a curve, then it would surely emerge more favorably. As shown in figures 6.1 and 6.2, already by 1988 Chile's per capita GDP had risen higher above the 1979–81 base than in any of the other major Latin American countries except Colombia.[10] Indeed, as set forth below, an ''Economic Performance

---

9. Recovery in copper prices by 1988 helped, bringing the metal's share of exports back up to nearly 50 percent (IMF 1991c).

10. In view of the overwhelming lesson from Latin America in the 1980s on the centrality of fiscal adjustment, Dornbusch and Edwards (1993) would seem on especially doubtful

Index" that considers both per capita GDP growth and inflation ranks Chile first among the seven large Latin American countries for the decade ending in 1992.

As for the critique of falling real wages, Fontaine (1989) points out that real wages had reached abnormally high levels in 1980–82, and that although they did collapse in the 1983 recession, by 1986 they were back to within 5 percent of their 1980 level. Moreover, as occurred in Mexico, wage restraint facilitated employment expansion, so that unemployment fell from 20 percent in 1982 to $8\frac{1}{2}$ percent by 1986 even though the emergency public jobs programs fell from $9\frac{1}{2}$ percent of the labor force to $4\frac{1}{2}$ percent during the same period (215).

Debt Strategy

Chile's strategy on external debt during the past decade has been designed to maximize reliance on the market and minimize damage to the country's credit reputation. Chile was forced to reschedule principal, but otherwise punctually met its obligations. Unlike Brazil, Argentina, and Peru, the country did not enter into interest arrears. Unlike Mexico and Venezuela, Chile did not even seek debt reduction under the Brady Plan. Moreover, the market orientation of the strategy remained intact even after the shift from the military government to the new democratic regime of Patricio Aylwyn in 1990. Late in that year the government did agree with the banks to reschedule maturities on about $5 billion of debt, but that was the final chapter in Chile's debt problem. As discussed in chapter 8, soon thereafter the problem was too much foreign capital rather than too little.

Chile's debt performance is all the more remarkable considering that the country began the debt crisis with one of the highest debt/exports ratios in the region (chapter 2). The aggressive move toward a growth strategy based on export expansion, discussed above, dealt effectively with the "external transfer problem" by mobilizing foreign exchange to service the rescheduled debt. Chile's impressive performance on fiscal balance throughout the 1980s meant similarly that there was much less of an "internal transfer problem" than in most countries in the region.

However, there are two distinctive features of the Chilean debt problem that contributed importantly to its successful resolution. The first is that despite the fact that early in the debt crisis the foreign banks forced

---

ground in citing the "immense fiscal contraction reflected in the decline of the share of government spending" as a source of excessively costly adjustment (24). Indeed, the two authors themselves note that the growing demand from the external sector in the strategy of export-led growth more than offset the shrinkage of demand from public consumption (as exports rose from 20 percent of GDP in 1980 to 33 percent in 1992, whereas government consumption fell from 12 percent of GDP to 8.6 percent; 12).

the government to guarantee private debt (a phenomenon sharply criticized by Díaz-Alejandro 1984), the actual payment of the formerly private debt remained largely incumbent on the private debtors. Thus, on the eve of the debt crisis two-thirds of Chilean debt owed to foreign banks was owed by the private sector. The government guaranteed the rescheduled debt of the domestic financial system, and as the banks provided subsequent new-money packages to the government, it "recycled the foreign credits helping domestic debtors to meet their interest payments" (Fontaine 1989, 221). Moreover, the government did not even guarantee external debt of domestic nonfinancial corporations, which instead paid pesos to the government, which in turn assumed the external debt.

This arrangement was a sharp contrast to the cases of Brazil and Mexico, where the bulk of the debt was public in the first place, and the case of Argentina, where a highly subsidized government treatment of foreign exchange access for servicing private debt amounted to a shifting of the burden to the public sector. Chile thus had little internal transfer problem for two reasons: its strong underlying fiscal balance and the private- rather than public-sector shouldering of the servicing obligation.[11]

The second key feature of Chilean debt management was that it successfully used the discount available in the secondary market to induce repatriation and debt-equity transactions that had the effect of reducing the external debt well before the Brady Plan's alternative approach. This strategy consciously sought to use "balance sheet" adjustments (both in amount and composition) rather than the potentially more costly "flow" adjustments (trade surplus) to limit indebtedness. As a consequence, it was possible in the mid-1980s to refinance about half of interest coming due without causing a rise in the external debt stock. Moreover, the refinancing that occurred was only partly through involuntary lending by the banks. By 1985–87, more than one-third of the capital

---

11. It is difficult to discern this fact from the conventional debt data. Thus, the World Bank reports only the breakdown between private debt on the one hand and public and publicly guaranteed debt on the other. By this categorization, Chile might seem to have experienced socialization of the debt. Thus, the two respective debt totals were $8.1 billion and $6.6 billion in 1983, whereas by 1986 the mix had shifted to only $3.4 billion private and $14.7 billion public and publicly guaranteed (World Bank 1992a, 2: 70). Note also that the public sector did not fully escape socialization of the debt, because some large domestic banks holding foreign debt went bankrupt and had to be taken over by the central bank, and there was some subsidy element in central bank lending to the other banks (and hence contribution to the "quasi-fiscal deficit" of the central bank). Nonetheless, the bulk of servicing of the private external debt remained the responsibility of the private sector, as Fontaine (1989) suggests. Moreover, the banking crisis was largely independent of the external debt crisis, so central bank losses associated with the former should not be attributed to the latter.

account inflow was coming from voluntary lending: direct investment, suppliers credits in investment projects, trade credit, and repatriations (Fontaine 1989, 221–23).

One of Chile's former central bank presidents enunciated the strategy as follows.

> [T]hrough successful structural adjustment, GDP and export growth [might] be high enough to induce a gradual reduction in the relative debt burden. The problem with this approach is that it demands an unrealistically large dose of patience, especially when applied to an economy like Chile's that held, at the end of 1984, a foreign debt equivalent to 120 percent of its GDP and 4.6 times as large as its exports. By reducing the flow transfer to its creditors [through new borrowing], the Chilean strategy clearly ran the risk of aggravating the excess stock of debt problem. [To deal with this problem, the] object of . . . a financial restructuring would be to move from a situation in which the debt is maintained only by almost a unique class of creditors (commercial banks) . . . to a situation in which a plurality of creditors are involved and diverse risk-sharing provisions are used. . . . [D]ebt conversion mechanisms are exactly such a means of restructuring. From 1985 to date, these mechanisms have cut . . . some 20 percent of . . . debt with the international banks . . . thus rendering the *nominal* stock of debt roughly constant. (Fontaine 1989, 224–25)

Chile applied two main instruments for market-based debt reduction. Its "chapter 18" mechanism permitted private parties to purchase debt abroad at a discount, bring it to Chile, and negotiate its cancellation in pesos by the private debtors in question. This amounted to an incentive system for capital repatriation, as the central bank made no foreign exchange available for such repurchases. Auctioned limits of amounts permitted monthly under the mechanism helped limit the depth of the discount. The alternative "chapter 19" mechanism allowed foreigners to bring to Chile the external debt of a Chilean firm and negotiate discounted repayment in pesos for use in equity investment. Central bank approval was required for each case, capital could not be remitted abroad for 10 years, and profits had to be fully reinvested until the fifth year.

Larraín and Velasco (1990) estimate that from 1985 through 1988, the formal debt repurchases (chapter 18) reduced debt by $2.1 billion; debt-equity conversion (chapter 19), by $1.8 billion; and other mechanisms (including informal buybacks), by $2.3 billion, for a total of $6.2 billion or about one-third of the stock of Chile's external debt at the outset of the debt crisis (12).[12] They estimate that Chile received an average of 75 percent of the discount on the repurchases and 30 percent of the discount on the debt-equity conversions (41).

---

12. With the help of this reduction, the outstanding stock of debt was the same in 1989 ($18 billion) as in 1983, despite substantial voluntary and involuntary borrowing during the interim (World Bank 1992a, 2: 70).

Of these market-based reductions, fully two-thirds were of debt owed by the private sector. As a consequence, Chile experienced relatively little of the adverse side effects often cited for debt-equity conversion. Conversion of private debt requires neither money expansion (the pesos received by the investors are offset by those paid by the debtor) nor the issuance of domestic government debt. More generally, Chile's domestic fiscal balance meant the potential monetary problems from debt-equity conversion were limited, because sterilization at reasonable domestic interest rates was feasible.

Meller (1990, 83) and others have criticized the debt-equity scheme on grounds that it subsidized foreign investors by permitting them to purchase equity in privatized state enterprises at a discount of 30 to 40 percent on the secondary market. In retrospect, this critique does not hold. We now know that the Chilean government plans to honor its debt at 100 cents on the dollar; so if a foreign investor received par value for debt turned in to the government in exchange for equity investment in a privatized enterprise, the Chilean public merely honored the debt in one form (equity at par) rather than another (debt at par).

Overall, Chile's economic adjustment and debt management over the past decade can only be judged a success, as testified by the country's investment-grade ratings by the early 1990s (Salomon Brothers 1993a). Indeed, the adjustment was so successful that by 1991–93 the problem had become excessive capital inflow, with resulting pressure on money supply and real appreciation (as discussed in chapter 8).

Mexico[13]

Mexico's economic adjustment program began under President Miguel de la Madrid in 1983, and it was implemented by a strong economic team that included the next president, Carlos Salinas. The adjustment process was thus in place longer than in most other countries in the region (except for Colombia and Chile). However, the oil price collapse in 1986 meant that Mexico's adjustment task was also one of the most difficult. From 1982 through 1988 economic growth averaged virtually zero. Moreover, inflation reached as high as 160 percent in 1987 (December/December). In contrast, by 1989–92 economic growth was back up to an average rate of $3^{1}/_{2}$ percent, and inflation was down to the range of 15 to 25 percent annually. By 1993 inflation had fallen to 8.7 percent (December/December), although growth performance eroded to only 1 percent (table 6.3).

---

13. This section draws on Cline (1991). For discussion of the end-1994 peso crisis, see the epilogue.

Table 6.3 Economic indicators for Mexico, 1982-93 (percentages and billions of dollars)

Indicator	1982	1983	1984	1985	1986	1987	1988	1989	1990	1991	1992	1993
GDP growth (%)	-0.6	-5.3	3.7	2.7	-3.7	1.8	1.4	3.1	3.9	3.6	2.6	1.0
Inflation (%)	58.9	101.8	65.5	57.7	86.2	131.8	114.2	20.0	26.7	22.7	15.5	..
Gross investment/GDP (%)	35.5	20.2	20.7	22.2	18.3	18.8	21.2	21.6	22.8	23.6	25.0	..
Fiscal balance/GDP (%) PSBR	-16.9	-8.6	-8.5	-9.6	-16.0	-16.0	-13.0	-5.6	-3.9	-1.5	0.5	..
Fiscal balance/GDP (%) Prim	-7.3	4.2	4.8	3.4	1.6	4.7	8.0	7.9	7.8	5.3	5.6	..
Fiscal balance/GDP (%) Oper	-5.5	0.4	-0.3	-0.8	-2.4	1.8	-3.6	-1.7	2.2	3.3	3.6	..
Real EXR/G6 (1985=100)	117.6	121.4	100.7	100.0	133.1	134.2	109.5	104.8	102.7	92.1	84.7	78.9
XGS (billions of dollars)	26.0	27.1	30.0	27.4	21.9	27.6	29.1	32.9	38.4	39.6	41.4	..
MGS (billions of dollars)	20.1	12.8	16.2	18.4	16.3	17.2	24.9	31.1	41.2	48.7	59.7	..
Current account balance (billions of dollars)	-6.3	5.4	4.2	1.1	-1.7	4.0	-2.4	-4.0	-7.1	-13.8	-22.8	..
External debt (billions of dollars)	86.0	93.0	94.8	96.9	100.9	109.5	100.8	95.4	97.4	101.7	113.4	..
Reserves excl. gold (billions of dollars)	0.8	3.9	7.3	4.9	5.7	12.5	5.3	6.3	9.9	17.7	18.9	25.1

.. = data not available.

Inflation: consumer prices, year over year.

Fiscal balances: Oper = operational (real); PSBR = Public sector borrowing requirements; Prim = primary.

XGS, MGS: exports and imports of goods and nonfactor services.

Real EXR/G6: Real exchange rate against six large industrial countries, deflated by wholesale prices.

Sources: IMF 1992a, 1993h (growth, inflation, trade, current account, reserves); World Bank 1993b (debt); IDB 1991, 1993 (investment, fiscal balances, real exchange rate); ECLAC 1993 (fiscal balances); Banco de Mexico 1993 (fiscal balances).

Macroeconomic Policies

Fiscal correction was the centerpiece of Mexico's economic adjustment. The primary fiscal deficit had reached 8 percent of GDP in 1981.[14] The oil bonanza of the late 1970s had led to excessive government spending, much of it on populist programs, financed by borrowing against future oil exports. In part through sharp reductions of bloated expenditures, by 1983 the government had attained a primary fiscal surplus of 4 percent of GDP. Then in 1986 the fiscal balance deteriorated to a surplus of only 1.6 percent of GDP, as the collapse in oil prices cost the government approximately 5 percent of GDP in lost revenue.[15] A second round of belt tightening brought the primary fiscal surplus to a high plateau at about 8 percent of GDP by 1988 and after (Cline 1991). Mexico thus carried out a fiscal adjustment equal to 16 percent of GDP. This effort corresponded to five times the never-achieved Gramm-Rudman-Hollings target for US fiscal adjustment in the late 1980s.

Most of Mexico's fiscal adjustment came on the spending side. Excluding interest payments, government spending fell from 36 percent of GDP to 23 percent. The spending cutbacks took a heavy toll on government investment, which fell from 10 percent of GDP to 5 percent. This decline meant that if Mexico were to increase investment in the future, it would have to be largely through the efforts of the private sector because of the limits on the government's ability to expand capital expenditures.

By the late 1980s and especially after the Brady Plan deal, Mexico entered a fiscal virtuous circle. Reduction in noninterest deficits improved expectations, permitting a reduction in the high level of domestic interest rates, which in turn brought a further reduction in the overall government deficit through falling interest costs. By 1990–91 there had been enough dividends from this process to allow a major increase in social spending in the National Solidarity Program (PRO-NASOL). This program involved activities closely targeted on the poor, and thus it was much more efficient than the generalized food and other

---

14. There are three main concepts of fiscal balance: nominal, primary, and operational balance. The first includes all spending. The second excludes interest payments, on grounds that they are beyond the control of the government. Interest rates on external debt are determined by LIBOR. As for domestic debt, tight monetary policies designed to reduce inflation may increase government interest payments, thereby widening the nominal deficit and giving a false impression that policy is inflationary rather than anti-inflationary. The third concept is a measure of the "real" fiscal deficit. It excludes only the inflationary component of interest payments, which merely prevent the government's real debt stock from being eroded by inflation.

15. Note that there had also been modest fiscal relaxation in 1985 associated with midyear elections, and indeed after temporarily missing macroeconomic targets, Mexico only renewed its IMF program in the third quarter of 1986 (Cline 1991, 2–3).

subsidies that had been such a large fiscal drain at the beginning of the 1980s. The government also received large income from the privatization program, including some $8 billion from the sale of the telephone system alone.

Structural Change

In 1986, Mexico reversed its historical position and joined the General Agreement on Tariffs and Trade (GATT), thereby signaling a new open-trade strategy. The government cut the import coverage of quantitative restrictions from 100 percent in 1983 to 30 percent by 1985 and 14 percent by 1990 (Cline 1991, 21). Spurred by the need to fight inflation, in December 1987 it cut the maximum tariff from 100 percent to 20 percent. By 1990 the average tariff was only 10 percent on an unweighted basis, or 13 percent weighting by imports.

Privatization was the other main area of structural reform. By the early 1990s the government had sold off (or in some cases simply shut down) hundreds of state firms. Among the most important were the telephone company, the state airlines, and the banks. Nationalization of the banks in 1982 had caused lingering acrimony between the private sector and the government, and their reprivatization a decade later did much to heal this wound and revive the private sector's willingness to invest in Mexico's growth.

The politics of privatization proved surprisingly favorable more generally. President Salinas, a Harvard PhD in political economy, emphasized that the resources saved by selling off state firms would be reallocated to the social and infrastructure areas, the government's more fundamental obligation. He noted that in his frequent tours of rural towns, he never heard pleas for more jumbo jets for the state airline so residents could fly to Paris; he constantly heard requests for electricity and clean drinking water.

Incomes Policy and Exchange Rate Anchor

Fiscal adjustment was the centerpiece of the fight against inflation. However, it became evident that other instruments were needed as well. Thus, by 1987 the primary fiscal balance was favorable at a surplus of nearly 5 percent of GDP; but because of high inflation, the nominal interest payments on domestic debt ballooned the total (nominal) fiscal deficit to 16 percent of GDP. By that year, inflation had become dangerously locked in by the inertial impetus of quarterly adjustments of the minimum wage and ongoing crawling-peg adjustment of the peso against the dollar.

By late 1987, with inflation at 160 percent (December/December), it was clear that the government had to place its highest priority on reducing inflation. The government negotiated a "Solidarity Pact" with the labor unions and business. The pact placed a freeze on wages and prices. This heterodox shock thus resembled the Austral Plan in Argentina and the Cruzado Plan in Brazil (discussed below), but with a key difference: in Mexico the fiscal fundamentals were firmly in place, so the chances of sustainable reduction of inflation were far greater. Inflation did plummet, and by 1990–91 the government had been able to eliminate most controls on prices, even though it had successively renewed the Solidarity Pact's wage restraints.

With respect to the exchange rate, in the mid-1980s the government had used sharp devaluation of the peso to reduce imports and increase nonoil exports after the collapse of oil prices. Devaluation contributed to inflation however, directly through the rise in the peso price of imports and indirectly through the impact on public expectations about future peso weakness and inflation. At the end of 1987 the government shifted exchange rate policy from a regime of devaluation and crawling peg to one of a fixed exchange rate against the dollar, designed to stabilize inflationary expectations and serve as the "monetary anchor." Fixing the exchange rate was a key quid pro quo for the labor unions' acceptance of the wage freeze. By 1989 the new government of Carlos Salinas had shifted from a fixed rate to one with a gradual slide of one peso per day, or about 15 percent per year. Successive renewals of the Solidarity Pact cut the daily slide, so that by 1992 it amounted to only about 2 percent annually—for all practical purposes a fixed exchange rate.

The combined impact of the initial wage-price freeze and the stabilization in expectations from the exchange rate freeze brought an abrupt fall in inflation, from 160 percent in 1987 (December/December) to 50 percent in 1988, 20 percent by 1989, and 12 percent by 1992. Both devices would almost certainly have collapsed, however, if the fiscal performance had not been strong.

Debt Strategy

Throughout the Latin American debt crisis of the 1980s, Mexico was in the avant-garde of the changing international policy strategy. There were three main reasons. First, because of its common border with the United States, Mexico has tended to enjoy a higher priority in US policymaking circles than most other Latin American countries.[16] Second, Mexico's debt was one of the two largest in the region. Third, Mexican

---

16. The principal exception was in the dimension of East-West security, which during the Reagan administration focused heavily on Central America.

authorities tended to follow well-conceived domestic economic policies beginning in 1983, so that Mexico consistently qualified as an early candidate for improved terms at each stage of the evolving debt strategy.

Thus, in 1983 Mexico secured rescheduling of $23 billion in bank debt over 8 years at $1^7/_8$ percentage points spread above the London interbank offer rate (LIBOR). Under the multiyear rescheduling agreement (MYRA), in 1985 the country rescheduled $48 billion at 14-year maturities, and narrowed the spread to $1^1/_4$ percent. Then under the Baker Plan, in 1987 Mexico rescheduled $54 billion at 20-year maturities, seven years' grace, and 13/16 percent spread (World Bank 1992b, 1: 98; Bergsten, Cline, and Williamson 1985, 101–04). In each of these instances "Mexico terms" became the standard benchmark for other countries.

There was an important qualititative shift in Mexican debt strategy in 1986, after the Mexico City earthquake in late 1985 and the collapse of oil prices in 1986. Technical analysts within official circles began to emphasize the importance of debt reduction rather than new lending as the solution to the country's debt problem (Aspe 1993, 134; Cline and Roett 1986). The first important instance of the new approach was in Mexico's arrangement (implemented with Morgan Guaranty) to convert debt into 20-year bonds collateralized with US Treasury zero-coupon bonds. Although the "Mexico-Morgan" deal (March 1988) was small in magnitude ($3.7 billion converted at 70 cents on the dollar; Aspe 1993, 136), it provided a conceptual model that was subsequently important in designing the Brady Plan.

The real change in Mexican strategy arrived when the new president Carlos Salinas de Gortari took office in December 1988. Salinas called the existing transfers abroad "unacceptable and unsustainable." He enunciated four principles for his new administration's debt policy: the net transfer of resources should be reduced from its existing level of 5 percent of GDP by enough to permit a return to sustained growth, the value of existing debt should be reduced to closer to its secondary market price (then less than 50 cents on the dollar), Mexico should be assured of multiyear access to new loans without annual uncertainty, and the ratio of external debt to GNP should be reduced (Cline and Roett 1988; Aspe 1993, 138). The similarities between the Salinas agenda and the "Brady Plan" strategy announced four months later by the new US administration of George Bush were no coincidence; once again Mexico was helping set the pace for the changing debt strategy.

In 1989 and early 1990 Mexico negotiated a Brady Plan agreement that effectively cut its external debt by about $15 billion equivalent, against a total debt outstanding of nearly $100 billion. The reduction was 35 percent on long-term bank claims, which comprised about half of total external debt. The direct interest savings amounted to about $1.5 billion annually, or about two-thirds of one percent of GDP. From the narrow standpoint of direct impact on availability of "foreign saving," this transfer reduction had only limited effects on economic growth, perhaps on the order of one-fourth of one percentage point per year.[17] However, once indirect effects from more favorable expectations are taken into account, the growth impact was much larger.

In the Mexican case, the impact of the Brady Plan on domestic confidence turned out to be extremely important. Figure 6.5 shows the sharp decline in the interest rates the government had to pay on domestic Treasury bills after the Brady agreement. Before resolution of the debt problem, there was a large exchange rate risk premium associated with the possibility of a collapse in negotiations and a run on the peso. After the agreement this premium disappeared, providing the government with large savings on domestic interest payments and thus a large drop in the nominal fiscal deficit including interest.

Van Wijnbergen (1991) has estimated that the Brady deal accelerated Mexico's growth by 2 percentage points annually for the period 1989–94. Half of this amount was from the direct effect of external cash flow alleviation, and the other half was from the indirect effect of lower domestic interest rates and higher investment.[18] The economic impact of Mexico's Brady Plan debt reduction is discussed further in chapter 5.

Issues in the 1990s

By 1991–92 the Mexican economy was entering into a new phase. The debt problem had been resolved, inflation sharply reduced, and eco-

---

17. With savings on interest payments abroad equal to 0.61 percent of GDP ($1.5 billion relative to 1990 GDP), Mexico's annual net saving from abroad would rise by this amount. In the standard (Harrod-Domar) model of economic growth determined by capital availability, the growth rate equals the saving rate divided by the incremental capital output ratio (ICOR). With ICOR typically at 2 to 3, an increase in the saving rate by 0.6 percentage point would accelerate annual growth by 0.3 to 0.2 percentage points. If foreign exchange were the binding constraint rather than capital, the growth impact would be larger.

18. The van Wijnbergen (1991) estimate applies an econometric model that simulates the economy with and without the Brady deal. In the simulation, he calculates the cash-flow effect not only of the interest reduction but also of the rescheduling of principal. The combined total amounted to $4 billion annually, more than twice the impact of relief on interest obligations. This higher amount largely explains why his "direct" growth impact is larger than that suggested here based on a simple capital requirements model. (Divergence between the two estimates also reflects an implicit scarcity price on foreign exchange in the van Wijnbergen model.) Arguably, Mexico might have rescheduled principal without reducing the debt or interest obligation, so the van Wijnbergen calculation of the direct effect overstates the benefit from forgiveness. His indirect effect is calculated under the assumption that without the agreement, Mexico's domestic interest rate would have stayed at the high level of 30 percent in real terms. To the extent that credit markets demanded high real interest rates because of a perceived debt overhang, it may be more appropriate to ascribe the entire "indirect" effect to the debt reduction innovation of the Brady Plan.

Figure 6.5 Mexico: average rates on 3-month Treasury bills
(percent/year, uncompounded)

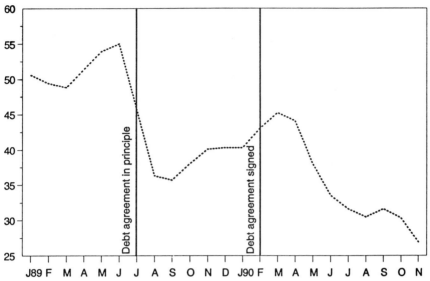

Source: Cline 1991.

nomic growth restored. The central focus of attention shifted to negotiation of the North American Free Trade Agreement. The NAFTA promised several years' worth of large direct investment inflows as multinational firms sought to locate production for the North American market in Mexico. It was widely seen as a vehicle for locking in the Mexican economic reforms, preserving them from possible future backsliding under a different government. And it offered assured access to the US market, a hedge against possible future US protectionism.

Two macroeconomic problems faced Mexican authorities by 1991–93: moderate but persistent inflation and an uncomfortably large external current account deficit. The rate of inflation had fallen to a range of 12 percent by 1992 and 10 percent from mid-1992 to mid-1993. However, Mexican authorities sought to bring the rate down to a level much closer to that of the United States. With the exchange rate slide at only about 2 percent annually in 1991–92 and about 4 percent annually after October 1992 (Banco de Mexico 1993, 94), persistence of inflation of 10 percent or higher would mean serious eventual overvaluation of the exchange rate.

The exchange rate, in turn, affected the external balance. By 1991 there were already signs that the pendulum had begun to swing too far in the use of the exchange rate as an anti-inflationary anchor rather than as the signal to trade performance. The external current account deficit reached $13 billion, or 5 percent of GDP. By 1992 the external deficit reached $22.8 billion, or 6.8 percent of GDP (IMF 1993a). The source of the rising deficit was primarily a rise in imports, from $12 billion in 1987 to $38 billion in 1991 and $48 billion by 1993. Trade liberalization had spurred imports, but they had also grown in response to both an appreciating real exchange rate after 1987 and recovering domestic growth. By 1992 the real exchange rate had appreciated by about 20 percent from its 1985 level against the dollar bilaterally, although the appreciation was less if measured against other major currencies or if wages rather than wholesale prices were used to compare competitiveness. As indicated in figure 6.6, there was a close correlation between the ratio of nonoil exports to imports, on the one hand, and the real exchange rate one year earlier on the other.[19]

The government's official view was that the external current account deficit was not a problem (Banco de Mexico 1993, 78–82). The rationale was the "consenting adults view," associated with former UK Chancellor Nigel Lawson. As noted above, this view held that so long as the government was not running a fiscal deficit, an external current account deficit was not a matter of concern. Instead, it was the consequence of private-sector capital inflows. With high capital inflows, the current account deficit had to be correspondingly high. If private firms decided to stop bringing in investment capital, the corresponding imports of capital goods would decline and so would the external current account deficit.

There was a grain of truth in this argument, as firms were bringing in more capital goods imports. However, a large part of the capital inflow of $24 billion in 1991 and $26 billion in 1992 was portfolio and other "footloose" money, and only one-fifth was in direct investment.[20] More broadly, the Lawson view assumed easy, instantaneous adjustment to small signals such as a modest real depreciation caused by capital outflow. In practice, trade tends to respond only with time lags of one or two years, and there can be exchange crises, recession, or both if an external crisis develops (as Mexico's experience of the 1980s so amply demonstrated). Although the Mexican government had built up a war chest of some $25 billion in reserves by early 1993 to deal with contingencies, there was a need for a fundamental assessment of what level of external deficit was prudent and sustainable.

One mitigating consideration was the return of flight capital. As developed in chapter 8, large capital reflows from this source seem to

---

19. The real exchange rate in the figure is the bilateral rate against the US dollar, deflating by wholesale prices for both countries. A rise in the index means more real pesos per real dollar, or real depreciation of the peso. The trade measure is the ratio of nonoil exports of goods and nonfactor services to imports of goods and nonfactor services.

20. The volatility of portfolio capital was illustrated by the abrupt swing from an outflow of $5 billion in 1990 to inflows of $9 billion in 1991 and $14 billion in 1992 (IMF 1993a).

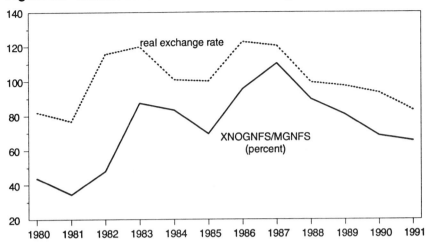

Figure 6.6 Mexico: nonoil trade and real exchange rates[a]

XNOGNFS = exports of nonoil goods and nonfactor services
MGNFS = import of goods and nonfactor services

a. Exchange rate is lagged by one year.
Source: Cline 1991.

have been present in the early 1990s. This form of finance does not build up external debt and is arguably consistent with incurring abnormally high external deficits at relatively low risk—so long as domestic policies are sufficiently stable and reform sufficiently well-consolidated that a future reversal to outflows of such funds is unlikely.

Over the medium term, it seems likely that the external deficit should be no more than 20 to 25 percent of exports of goods and services, or about $10 billion. If so, the government could increasingly face a dilemma of how to achieve a degree of external adjustment despite the straitjacket on the exchange rate imposed by its use as an anti-inflationary anchor. The related question is whether Mexican price expectations are still so sensitive that any decline in the exchange rate would simply be offset by equivalent increases in domestic peso prices, making it either impossible to obtain a real depreciation through a nominal one, or at least very costly to do so in terms of induced inflation.[21]

Overall, by 1992–94 the Mexican record looked extremely impressive in terms of structural reform and emergence from the debt crisis, and the

---

21. As an illustration of how deeply divided economists are on these issues, see the divergence of views between Dornbusch and Werner (1994), who by mid-1994 advocated a "final" maxidevaluation of 20 percent, and their discussant Guillermo Calvo, who feared the destabilization impact of such a measure on domestic inflation. Note that neither side addressed the point that capital flight reflows may have made outsized current account deficits in 1991–94 somewhat safer than they might otherwise appear.

NAFTA promised at least a decade of favorable growth. There were warning signals concerning the oversized external deficit, however. The government's initial response seemed to be to tighten fiscal policy further and dampen growth (in addition to a small step up in the peso's slide in 1992, to 4 percent annually). Whether that approach would work remained unclear, especially in view of the need to achieve sustained growth of 4 to 5 percent to make up for the lost decade of the 1980s.

Venezuela[22]

After a boom in the mid-1970s associated with the oil bonanza, Venezuela's per capita income declined by 25 percent from 1978 to 1989. An inward-oriented development model characterized by heavy state intervention had led to economic stagnation. Moreover, the economy was heavily dependent on oil, which accounted for 25 percent of GDP and 85 percent of exports. Inflation was moderate but in part because of repression through price controls, which by 1988 had led to severe shortages. By the late 1980s after oil prices fell, the government increasingly used up the large international reserves built up in the past rather than take corrective measures to reduce fiscal deficits and restore external equilibrium. A system of multiple exchange rates offered immense incentives for corruption in allocation of dollars at favorable rates.

Macroeconomic Policy

In early 1989 President Carlos Andrés Pérez took office. He immediately adopted a program of radical economic reform, called "the Great Turnaround." In his earlier term as president in the mid-1970s, he had presided over populist policies in the dispensing of the oil bonanza riches. It thus surprised many that his new program was a forceful call for orthodox, market-oriented reform. He recognized that Venezuela could no longer afford the subsidies and distortions of the oil boom era.

The reform package included unification and devaluation of the exchange rate, the elimination of price controls, sharp corrective price increases for public services, the freeing of interest rates, fiscal adjustment, and a wide range of structural reforms, especially privatization and import liberalization. By 1990–91 the program had achieved impressive macroeconomic results, but in the political dimension it failed for Pérez. After attempted coups in February and November 1992, by May 1993 the congress had ousted the president on charges of corruption and appointed an interim president until the elections scheduled for December.

---

22. This section draws on Cline and Conning (1991).

Table 6.4 Economic Indicators for Venezuela, 1982-93 (percentages and billions of dollars)

Indicator	1982	1983	1984	1985	1986	1987	1988	1989	1990	1991	1992	1993
GDP growth (%)	0.7	−5.6	−1.4	1.4	6.3	4.5	6.2	−7.8	6.9	10.4	7.3	0.0
Inflation (%)	9.6	6.3	12.2	11.4	11.5	28.1	29.5	84.2	40.8	34.2	31.4	..
Gross investment/GDP (%)	28.0	16.1	23.4	23.9	23.5	25.7	27.9	14.4	12.6	20.6	25.9	..
Fiscal balance/GDP (%) Cent	−2.1	−0.6	2.8	2.0	−0.4	−1.6	−7.4	−1.0	−2.1	2.8	−3.4	..
Fiscal balance/GDP (%) NFPS	..	..	2.2	0.0	−7.4	−6.0	−9.4	−1.1	1.2	0.6	−6.1	..
Real EXR/G6 (1985=100)	76.8	72.2	105.1	100.0	98.8	133.8	124.8	132.9	168.3	165.9	166.0	161.3
XGS (billions of dollars)	17.6	15.8	16.8	15.3	9.5	11.4	11.1	14.0	18.8	16.3	15.5	..
MGS (billions of dollars)	19.6	9.1	9.9	9.5	10.0	11.1	14.9	9.3	9.5	13.7	16.7	..
Current account balance (billions of dollars)	−4.2	4.4	4.7	3.3	−2.2	−1.4	−5.8	2.2	8.3	1.7	−3.4	..
External debt (billions of dollars)	32.2	38.3	36.9	35.3	34.3	34.7	34.8	32.5	33.3	34.4	37.2	..
Reserves excl. gold (billions of dollars)	6.6	7.6	8.9	10.3	6.4	6.0	3.1	4.1	8.3	10.7	9.6	9.2

.. = data not available.

Inflation: consumer prices, year over year.
Fiscal balances: Cent = central government; NFPS = nonfinancial public sector.
XGS, MGS: exports and imports of goods and nonfactor services.
Real EXR/G6: Real exchange rate against six large industrial countries, deflated by wholesale prices.

Sources: IMF 1992a, 1993h (growth, inflation, trade, current account, reserves); World Bank 1993b (debt); IDB 1991, 1993 (investment, fiscal balances, real exchange rate); ECLAC 1993 (fiscal balances).

The initial impact of the Pérez program was a severe recession, as GDP fell by 8 percent in 1989. One reason for the recession was that devaluation tends to be contractionary where exports are inelastic and largely owned by the public sector, as was the case for Venezuelan oil.[23] Another was that the private sector faced large losses on exchange guarantees for import letters of credit, undertaken by the previous regime but impossible for the new government to honor in full.

By 1990–92, however, there was a strong recovery. Economic growth reached 7 percent in 1990, 10 percent in 1991, and 7½ percent in 1992 (IMF 1993a). Economic performance was less favorable on price stabilization. Inflation, typically less than 30 percent in the mid-1980s (a rate that disguised additional but repressed inflation because of price controls), soared over 80 percent in 1989 with the large, one-time jump in prices associated with the large devaluation and freeing of prices (see table 6.4). By 1991–92 the rate was lower but still in the range of 30 percent.

In 1989–90, the government achieved a large fiscal improvement, from a deficit of 9 percent of GDP to a surplus of 1 percent. The great bulk of this improvement came from a structural peculiarity of the Venezuelan economy: the government is the owner of most export earnings because oil is in the public sector. As a result, the government enjoys a large rise in revenue expressed in the domestic currency when the bolivar devalues against the dollar. That is, the same dollar amount of oil exports and revenue translates into far more bolivars, helping eliminate the fiscal deficit because domestic bolivar expenses do not correspondingly rise.[24]

Permanent fiscal reform proved more evasive. Although the government did achieve a reform of the income tax structure involving lower marginal rates and a wider base, income tax revenue remained extremely low (1½ percent of GDP; Naim 1993, 77). Most importantly, for four years the congress refused to adopt the administration's central fiscal reform, a value-added tax that would reduce the heavy reliance of state finances on oil revenue. As of 1990, oil still accounted for 80 percent of central government revenue, posing the problems of fluctuation and secular decline. It was not until late 1993 under emergency authority granted by the congress that the interim regime of Ramón Velásquez was able to implement the (somewhat reduced) value-added tax.

---

23. In most economies, importers face a real income loss when there is a devaluation, but there is an expansionary offset from the gains experienced by exporters. The second half of this symmetrical relationship is largely absent in the Venezuelan private sector, because its exports are so small.

24. As noted, the same peculiarity of government ownership of exports meant a structural tendency toward recession as the consequence of devaluation.

Structural Change

Nonetheless, the Pérez administration achieved important permanent changes in the structure of the economy. The "Great Turnaround" program eliminated nontariff barriers on 94 percent of imports and cut average tariffs from 37 percent in early 1989 to 12 percent by 1992 (Naim 1993, 51). Maximum tariffs fell from 80 percent to 20 percent. The economic package unified exchange rates at close to the previous free-market rate, thereby effectively carrying out a large devaluation of the bolivar (by about 30 percent in real terms). The program adopted one of the most liberal regimes for foreign investment in Latin America.

The program also pursued sweeping privatization. By 1991 the government had privatized four banks, the national airline, the telephone company, the cellular telephone system, the ports, a shipyard, and several sugar mills and hotels (Naim 1993, 52). However, political uncertainty by 1992 brought a premature halt to the privatization agenda (which had included some portions of the electricity sector). Moreover, the government had not considered privatization of the state oil firm (considered to be an efficient company). Nor did the privatization program include the state aluminum and steel mills that had been built up after the mid-1970s as a way of "planting the oil," but which had at least questionable international competitiveness.

The Pérez administration eliminated generalized subsidies to food and housing, which had gone largely to the middle class, and replaced them with innovative antipoverty programs centered on payments to low-income families through the schools located in poor areas. Under a relatively broad definition used in Venezuela, the incidence of poverty had risen from 32 percent of households in 1982 to 54 percent by 1989. The government faced the problem that the mainline social agencies (education, health) had progressively lost the ability to deliver social services, as the consequence of budget cutbacks, extreme labor rigidities, and the use of these agencies for purposes of political patronage (Naim 1993, 80). The Pérez administration achieved only temporary success with the expedient of bypassing the mainline agencies by channeling funds through special new entities.

Debt Strategy

In the area of external debt, it was a paradox that Venezuela had an external debt problem at all. From 1971 to 1980, the country had experienced cumulative current account surpluses (of some $5 billion), whereas its external public-sector debt rose by $16 billion. Total external debt rose from $10 billion in 1977 to $37 billion by 1992, despite a cumulative current account deficit of only $4 billion over this period (Cline 1989d, 22, 44; IMF 1992a).

There were two reasons for the buildup in external debt. First, some parts of the public sector borrowed abroad even as other parts (the oil company and state investment company) accumulated foreign assets. Second, distorted incentives from domestic interest controls and an overvalued exchange rate caused a strong incentive for capital flight. Much of public-sector debt thus went to finance private capital flight, with regressive distributional implications in view of the high income of those placing assets abroad (M. Rodriguez 1987).

By 1982 with the outbreak of the Latin American debt crisis, Venezuela still had relatively low external debt. Net external debt was only about 145 percent of exports of goods and services (chapter 2, table 2.3). However, by 1986 the ratio of net debt to exports surged to close to 300 percent, as the consequence of a collapse in oil exports from $14.8 billion in 1984 to $7.2 billion in 1986 (IMF 1991c, 767). Nonetheless, through the late 1980s the government of President Jaime Lusinchi continued to draw down external reserves for the purpose of servicing debt, rather than submit to policy conditions of the International Monetary Fund as the prerequisite for a Baker Plan program of debt restructuring and coordinated new money.[25] It was the relentless and nearly complete exhaustion of reserves that brought the country to the brink of extreme economic crisis before the Pérez administration took office in early 1989.[26]

The new Pérez regime benefited from the timing of the Brady Plan for debt reduction. Indeed, the Caracas riots of February 1989, which claimed 300 lives (Naim 1993, 31), probably played a role in elevating the public perception of urgency of a shift in the debt strategy, then in the final stages of intense review and on the verge of moving from the Baker Plan's emphasis on new lending to the new Bush administration's Brady Plan strategy of debt reduction (chapter 5). The forceful economic reforms of the new Pérez administration made Venezuela a prime candidate for such an agreement. After arduous negotiations, which saw temporary interest arrears in late 1989 and early 1990, the government negotiated a reduction in bank claims only modestly smaller in relative terms than that obtained by Mexico, even though Venezuela's debt relative to exports and GNP had been considerably lower through most of the 1980s.

The debt reduction agreement converted $19.5 billion of commercial bank claims into par bonds at 6¼ percent interest (38 percent of the total claims), discount bonds with a 30 percent cut in principal (9 percent), and "step-down" par bonds with interest temporarily reduced (15 per-

---

25. Venezuela did negotiate a substantial lengthening of maturities, however.

26. Excluding gold, reserves and other public external assets stood at approximately $18 billion in 1980 (Cline 1989d, 44). By 1988, after the oil company's assets had been shifted into reserves, the nation's nongold reserves were down to only $3 billion (IMF 1992a).

cent). In addition, banks holding 31 percent of claims chose to extend "new money" equivalent to 20 percent of exposure. At the opposite extreme, banks holding 7 percent of claims chose cash buybacks at 45 cents on the dollar (Cline and Conning 1991).

The banks emerged from the agreement with a relatively favorable attitude toward Venezuela, in part because the country's negotiators had extensively involved representatives of the banks in the design of the package's options. The moderate depth of the cuts and the relatively large group of banks choosing the new-money option reflected the market-oriented nature of the agreement.

Issues in the 1990s

By 1992 there had been important fiscal erosion. High oil prices associated with the Gulf War had encouraged an excessive increase in the spending budget for 1991. By 1992, oil prices had fallen by enough to cost some 5 percent of GDP in revenue loss. Moreover, the political uncertainty of 1992 contributed to fiscal unraveling by forcing postponement of an increase in gasoline prices closer to world levels, deterring increases in prices of electricity and other state services, and further complicating congressional approval of the proposed value-added tax. As a result, from a surplus of 1.3 percent of GDP in 1991, the fiscal accounts shifted to a deficit of 6½ percent of GDP in 1992 (Naim 1993, 75–77).

In the face of incomplete fiscal correction, the government leaned on tight monetary policy as the temporary alternative to limit inflation. As a result, interest rates rose sharply. The discount rate increased from 43 percent in 1991 to 50 percent by the end of 1992 and nearly 70 percent by the second quarter of 1993 (IMF 1993a). The mix of loose fiscal and tight monetary policy was seen as a holding action while the country entered an interim regime, pending the elections of December 1993.

Venezuela faced important decisions of long-term strategy as well as short-term stabilization. A central issue was whether to diversify the economy or instead emphasize the country's comparative advantage in oil in future development. In this debate, it was not clear that full recognition was given to the potential price-spoiling impact of expanding Venezuelan oil output, nor that any risk premium was being assessed to take account of the vulnerability of extreme specialization. In 1990–91 the oil company developed a plan for massive investment in oil and other energy areas, amounting to $50 billion over six years. However, the weakening of oil prices again by 1992 brought a scaling back of these ambitious plans.

The market-oriented reforms of the Pérez administration evoked considerable political discontent. The public remained nostalgic about the populist programs and cheap dollar of the 1970s and early 1980s. Yet the hard reality was that, because of lower prices and lower export quotas within OPEC, public revenue from oil fell from $1,700 per capita in 1981 to only $382 in 1992 (Naim 1993, 37). Recognition of the decline in the oil rents available for distribution to the public in the form of entitlements had not sunk in, and there was a popular tendency to attribute scarcity in a land so wealthy as Venezuela to the corruption of officials.

Naim (1993) emphasizes that the Pérez administration failed to communicate adequately to the public the urgency of and rationale for its reforms. In addition, he stresses that the progressive breakdown in the provision of traditional public social services (because of the rigidities discussed above) contributed to the atmosphere that led to the two coup attempts in 1992 and President Pérez's ouster in 1993, despite the stellar performance on GDP growth and other macroeconomic variables by 1990–93. Moreover, he argues that the new government had no alternative to its "shock treatment," not only because the economy was in extreme crisis in 1988 but also because public administration had become so weak it lacked the skilled cadres that would have been necessary to implement a more nuanced, gradualist program.[27]

The 1994 Financial Crisis

Overall, the Venezuelan experience in the period 1989–93 was one of a fundamentally well-designed economic adjustment program relatively well implemented but in severe jeopardy of incomplete execution and partial reversal because of unrealistic public expectations and the resulting political unpopularity of the program. In 1994, however, the economic environment turned far worse. The new president, Rafael Caldera, took office in February. On the basis of his first term in office (1969–74) and his campaign, he was perceived as being in the populist, state interventionist mold, even though his cabinet included individuals committed to the deepening of privatization and other reforms. The new government rescinded the value-added tax and at least initially kept gasoline prices far below world levels. However, it imposed a sales tax, a luxury tax, and higher marginal tax rates, thereby arguably addressing the fiscal problem. But the collapse of the largest bank (Banco Latino) in January had already triggered a banking crisis, and the decline of oil prices in early 1994 aggravated matters. Soon the government suspended the constitution's guarantee of private-sector economic rights, a clause that had also been suspended for more than 30 years before its restitution in 1992 by President Pérez.

Under these circumstances there was a strong uncertainty motive for capital flight. To deal with the ensuing pressure on foreign exchange, in late June the government imposed controls on all foreign exchange

---

27. As an example, Naim cites an alternative of only partial rather than complete price decontrol.

transactions, adopted extensive price controls, and declared that to avoid hoarding, the government could seize property without compensation. Approvals of foreign exchange expenditures were negligible during the next two months, causing uncertainty about availability of manufacturing inputs and even food supply. The banking crisis widened, and by August 1994, 11 banks accounting for half of domestic deposits had failed (*New York Times,* 19 August 1994).

The international investment community's perception of Venezuelan credit risk fell sharply. The price of Brady par bonds fell from 75 cents in January to 45 cents in July, and spreads on new bond issues rose to the range of 900 to 1,000 basis points (Salomon Brothers 1994c). By the third quarter of 1994, it was too early to tell whether this market reaction was excessive. Much would depend on whether the Caldera government returned to market mechanisms and normal property rights, or instead intensified controls further. In its defense, the new government had inherited the banking crisis, which had stemmed from inadequate supervision arrangements, especially on offshore affiliates.

Even under an optimistic scenario in which the higher oil prices by mid-1994 and a staunching of the banking crisis by the third quarter permitted improved expectations, a relaxation of exchange controls, and a gradual rollback in the emergency measures, a severe recession seemed likely for 1994. Moreover, some medium-term damage to domestic and foreign investor confidence seemed unavoidable. This optimistic scenario would nonetheless perhaps permit a return to and consolidation of the structural reforms of the Pérez administration. Under a pessimistic scenario driven by populist-interventionist dynamics, much worse outcomes would be likely.

Argentina[28]

In the 1930s Argentines enjoyed a standard of living comparable to that in Italy or Finland (Balassa, Bueno, Kuczynski, and Simonsen 1986). In the following decades the country lagged behind international development, largely as the consequence of an economic model emphasizing high protection against imports, state intervention, and unsustainable populist measures. By the 1970s growth was low, and in the 1980s it turned negative. Per capita income in 1989 was 20 percent below the peak reached in 1980. In mid-1989 and again in early 1990, hyperinflation erupted and prices rose temporarily at rates of 100 to 200 percent per month.

By then external debt was not the main problem; indeed, Argentina paid no principal or interest on debt to foreign banks in 1989, yet suf-

---

28. This section draws on Cline (1992) and Cline (1993).

Table 6.5 Economic indicators for Argentina, 1982-93 (percentages and billions of dollars)

Indicator	1982	1983	1984	1985	1986	1987	1988	1989	1990	1991	1992	1993
GDP growth (%)	-5.0	2.9	2.5	-4.4	5.6	2.5	-2.5	-4.5	0.4	8.5	8.7	6.0
Inflation (%)	164.8	343.8	626.7	672.1	90.1	131.3	343.0	3,079.8	2,31	4.0	171.7	24.9
Gross investment/GDP (%)	21.5	18.6	17.6	15.5	16.7	18.7	18.6	15.0	13.5	15.5	18.7	..
Fiscal balance/GDP (%) Cent	-3.7	-10.1	-5.7	-3.1	-3.2	-5.7	-4.0	-2.7	-1.4	-1.1	-0.3	..
Fiscal balance/GDP (%) NFPS	..	-9.6	-7.0	-4.0	-3.1	-5.0	-6.0	-3.8	-2.8	-0.9	-0.1	..
Real EXR/G6 (1985=100)	106.3	92.6	86.1	100.0	111.7	126.8	113.7	135.6	115.6	102.9	105.2	100.5
XGS (billions of dollars)	9.2	9.3	12.1	10.0	8.4	8.1	11.1	11.8	14.8	14.4	14.7	15.7
MGS (billions of dollars)	6.5	5.8	6.0	5.3	6.5	7.6	7.3	6.3	6.4	11.1	18.2	20.5
Current account balance (billions of dollars)	-2.4	-2.4	-2.5	-1.0	-2.9	-4.2	-1.6	-1.3	4.6	-0.7	-6.7	-7.6
External debt (billions of dollars)	43.6	45.9	48.9	50.9	52.5	58.5	58.7	65.0	61.9	65.3	67.6	..
Reserves excl. gold (billions of dollars)	2.5	1.2	1.2	3.3	2.7	1.6	3.4	1.5	4.6	6.6	10.4	14.1

.. = data not available.

Inflation: consumer prices, year over year.
Fiscal balances: Cent = central government; NFPS = nonfinancial public sector.
XGS, MGS: exports and imports of goods and nonfactor services.
Real EXR/G6: Real exchange rate against six large industrial countries, deflated by wholesale prices.

Sources: IMF 1992a, 1993h (growth, inflation, trade, current account, reserves); World Bank 1993b (debt); IDB 1991, 1993 (investment, fiscal balances, real exchange rate); ECLAC 1993 (fiscal balances).

fered its worst inflation and depression on record that year. Instead, chronic fiscal deficits were the chief cause of persistent inflation, which in turn discouraged investment and led to stagnation. The budget deficit reached as high as 16 percent of gross domestic product in the worst years of the 1980s. Periodic stabilization programs, such as the "hetero-dox shock" Austral Plan of 1985, systematically came unraveled as Argentine authorities were unable to replace temporary measures such as export taxes and forced saving with permanent tax revenue. The government had to resort to a hidden "inflation tax" to appropriate resources it could not collect directly. Persistent losses by state firms (as much as one percent of GDP annually in the state railway alone) and featherbedding in provincial governments after the return to civilian rule in the mid-1980s aggravated the deficit problem.

Macroeconomic Policies

The administration of Carlos Menem, who took power in mid-1989, adopted a program of radical reform that achieved impressive results. Traumatized by hyperinflation, the Argentine public was ready for a complete rejection of the past economic model. Like Nixon in his open-ing to China, Menem as a Peronist could not be flanked politically in his essentially orthodox economic reforms.

These reforms amounted to an aggressive application of the "Wash-ington consensus" package of structural adjustment measures. They included fiscal restructuring, a sharp reduction in import protection, privatization of state firms, thoroughgoing deregulation of the economy, and price decontrol.

Even as the government persisted in its program of structural reform, there were macroeconomic mishaps. A burst of central bank lending to the provinces and social security system at the end of 1990 brought a new round of inflation in early 1991. Then a new minister of economy, Harvard-trained Domingo Cavallo, launched the "Convertibility Plan" in March 1991. The plan fixed the exchange rate at one peso to the dollar and wrote into law that the domestic money base could not exceed the amount of foreign exchange reserves. Mandatory dollar backing for the currency meant the government could no longer freely print money to cover deficits. Technically a "currency board" arrangement, the new regime was comparable in effect to adopting the gold standard. The convertibility law immediately provided strong credibility to the govern-ment's commitment to stopping inflation. Combined with the underly-ing fiscal reform already under way, the increased confidence brought a sudden drop in inflation.

By 1992–93 the record under the Convertibility Plan was the best for any Argentine stabilization program in recent history. Inflation, which reached 5,000 percent in 1989 (December/December), fell by 1992 to 17$\frac{1}{2}$

percent for consumer prices and only 3 percent for wholesale prices. Gross domestic product, which fell by a cumulative 7 percent in the recession of 1988–89, stabilized in 1990 and rose by 9 percent annually in 1991–92 and 6 percent in 1993. Real investment rose by 35 percent in 1991 and again in 1992, after having fallen by nearly 50 percent in the previous three years. By 1992, nominal interest rates on deposits were down to 12 percent annually (Ministerio de Economia 1993), far lower in real terms than during previous stabilization efforts. Even so, capital inflow from abroad was buoyant, reaching $2.3 billion in 1991 and $10.6 billion in 1992 (compared with exports of goods and services of $14.8 billion in 1992; IMF 1993a).

With lower interest rates and more stable inflationary expectations, the public rebuilt money holdings. Broad money (M4) returned to about 17 percent of GDP from a level below 7 percent in 1990. Although real wages fell by 25 percent in 1989 in the face of hyperinflation, by 1992 they had recovered to their 1988 level. Moreover, social indicators had begun to improve once again. Thus, the incidence of persons in poverty, which had risen from 10 percent in 1980 to approximately 30 percent by 1988, fell to 19 percent by 1992 (Morley 1992; Argentine Economic Cabinet 1993, 58).[29]

As in Mexico, the centerpiece of economic adjustment in Argentina was fiscal reform. The Menem government widened the coverage of the value-added tax (VAT) and greatly increased enforcement of its collection. Revenues from the VAT rose from an average of about 3 percent of GDP in 1983–88 (and as low as 1.6 percent in 1989) to 8 percent of GDP by 1992. As a result, the primary fiscal balance rose from a deficit of 6 percent of GDP in 1989 to a surplus of 3.4 percent of GDP in 1992 (2.2 percent excluding capital revenue from privatization). The sharp decline in inflation and nominal interest rates meant that improvement was even greater for the nominal fiscal balance, which went from a deficit of 20 percent of GDP in 1987 to a surplus of 1 percent in 1992.

Exchange Rate Policy

Whereas fiscal adjustment was the ultimate underpinning of the Convertibility Plan, the unique feature of an exchange rate fixed by law (and the currency-board limitation of domestic money to the amount backed by dollar reserves) was its proximate "anchor." This mechanism succeeded brilliantly in halting inflationary expectations. However, a crucial question was whether this anchor could become an Achilles' heel with respect to external-sector performance. Certainly the Southern Cone experience in the early 1980s had seen severe overvaluation of exchange

---

29. The poverty line is defined as twice the income required to purchase basic food requirements.

rates in both Chile and Argentina as the consequence of setting fixed rates that lagged far behind inflation, and the overvalued rates had precipitated external-sector crises.

By 1992–93, whether the Argentine peso had become overvalued as a consequence of the fixed exchange rate regime was a matter of fierce debate. Citing numerous measures, Conesa (1992, 333) argued that the equilibrium real exchange rate by 1992 was 1.4 to the dollar rather than the legal parity of unity. And indeed, on one measure—consumer prices—there appeared to be risk of overvaluation. Thus, from the beginning of the Convertibility Plan through the end of 1992, consumer prices had risen by 42 percent, but the exchange rate had remained unchanged. However, by another measure—wholesale prices—the rate looked much less overvalued. During the same period, wholesale prices had risen only 6 percent.

There are two ways to judge whether the exchange rate is overvalued: retrospective and prospective. The retrospective method examines the "real exchange rate" and asks whether it has appreciated substantially relative to levels associated with external equilibrium in the past. The prospective method asks whether at the existing real exchange rate, the current account balance is at a sustainable level or instead is headed toward dangerously large deficits. The Argentine case may be considered under each method in turn.

Under the retrospective method, it is necessary to choose deflators in the calculation of the real exchange rate. There has been ongoing controversy over the proper deflators (Edwards 1988, 53–56). The most direct line of reasoning points toward use of the wholesale price index in both the home and foreign countries to deflate, because wholesale prices refer primarily to goods actually traded. In contrast, consumer prices (or GDP deflators) are heavily influenced by prices of services and other nontradeables (Balassa 1964).[30]

However, there is an earlier tradition dating back to Keynes (1930) that argues the wholesale price index is too heavily influenced by international prices of traded goods and is thus biased toward understating any change in the relative prices of the country in question. To confuse matters further, a more recent concept of the real exchange rate does not even consider prices of the home country compared with those abroad but instead focuses on the *domestic* price of tradeables relative to the price of nontradeables, under the argument that it is this price signal that moves resources from one sector to the other (e.g., Black 1977, 13).

---

30. Balassa (1964) emphasized that if there were systematically higher productivity growth in tradeable goods than in nontradeables (as has been the case), purchasing power parity measures based on a broad price index (consumer prices or GDP deflator) would give a mistaken indication of a need for exchange rate depreciation.

Harberger (1986) recommends a hybrid measure that deflates using foreign wholesale and domestic consumer prices.[31]

In general and for the Argentine case, it would seem that wholesale prices are the proper deflator on both sides. It is the price of traded goods that matters to foreign purchasers. Japan can export automobiles on the basis of the price of Toyotas. To compute Japan's competitive ability on the basis of its hotel prices would give a highly misleading impression of overvaluation. Attempting to measure the relative price of tradeables and nontradeables domestically confuses causal forces affecting the future supply of exports with present demonstrated price competitiveness in international markets. It is better to address the forces affecting future export supply through the prospective analysis of trade balance trends rather than to intermix this concept with observed price performance.

Nor is it the case, for Argentina, that wholesale prices merely mirror world prices and are thus biased. Using a detailed examination of the composition of the Argentine wholesale price index, Cline (1992) demonstrates that the overall wholesale price index tracks extremely closely with the component for domestic manufactures, whereas it diverges considerably from the component for imports alone (which, for its part, tracks the nominal exchange rate as expected). More generally, the wide swings in wholesale price–deflated real exchange rates internationally (for example, for the United States in the 1980s) eloquently reject the "law of one price" thesis underlying the critique that wholesale prices are biased deflators.[32]

In short, the proper measure for retrospective analysis uses the real exchange rate deflating by wholesale prices on all sides. On this measure, by the fourth quarter of 1992 Argentina's real exchange rate (against six industrial country currencies) was at approximately the same level as its average during the period 1982–88. By the retrospective test, then, the convertibility plan had not led to overvaluation of the peso. This conclusion is reinforced by the fact that the Menem government eliminated taxes on agricultural exports that had reached the range of 25 percent, and otherwise reduced the "Argentine cost" through the deregulation of ports and other productivity-enhancing measures.

---

31. The Harberger approach has the inconvenient implication that, at least among industrial countries, virtually every country would be measured to have a secularly appreciating real exchange rate—which of course is impossible since real appreciation by some should mean real depreciation by others. The reason for this result is that secularly consumer prices have risen faster than wholesale prices. Thus, from 1962 to 1991 consumer prices multiplied by 4.5 times in the United States and wholesale prices only 3.7 times; the corresponding comparison in Japan was 4.6 versus 2.1 times, respectively (IMF 1992a). By the Harberger method, each country appreciated in real terms against the other.

32. If the "law of one price," that tradeable goods are homogeneous and everywhere have identical prices, were right, there would never be any variation in the real exchange rate deflated by wholesale prices.

By the prospective test, the evidence was less comforting. The large deterioration in the external accounts in 1991–92 was the main area of disappointing economic performance. Exports in 1992 were slightly below their level two years earlier, whereas imports rose by 265 percent over the same period. From a surplus of $8.6 billion in 1990, the trade balance fell to a deficit of $1.4 billion in 1992. The corresponding decline in the current account balance was from a surplus of $1.9 billion in 1990 to a deficit of $8.4 billion in 1992 (IMF 1993a). Some of this reduction was expected as the normal consequence of recovery of the economy and thus of imports from their depressed level in 1990. However, the process went far beyond official expectations. The central question for the exchange rate policy was thus whether the fixed rate was compatible with avoiding still further widening of the trade deficit, or preferably, reducing it to more sustainable levels.

One reason for the widening trade gap was the macroeconomic divergence between Argentina and Brazil, its principal partner in the nascent free trade area of MERCOSUL (which also includes Paraguay and Uruguay). From 1990 to 1992, Argentina's imports from Brazil rose by 360 percent, whereas its imports from other sources rose by 230 percent (Cline 1993). In this period Brazil was in serious recession and had a relatively devalued real exchange rate, whereas Argentina was entering recovery and moving to a more normal real exchange rate after extreme real devaluation in 1989 and early 1990. The MERCOSUL bode well for the economies of all four of its participants, but it faced initial difficulties from macroeconomic divergence between the largest partners.

As analyzed in chapter 8, much of the large capital inflow and corresponding external-sector deficit for Argentina in 1991–93 seems likely to have been financed by the repatriation of flight capital. To some extent this phenomenon justifies a temporarily high external deficit, as noted above for the Mexican case. Even so, the 1992–93 current account deficits of over 50 percent of exports of goods and services seemed potentially risky, regardless of their origins (including "consenting adult" private-capital market forces). Like that of the Mexican adjustment model, future success of the Argentine Convertibility Plan depended heavily on increased productivity from structural reform as the vehicle for achieving international competitiveness without nominal depreciation, in view of the key role of the fixed exchange rate anchor against inflation.

Structural Change

The Menem administration intensified the trade opening already begun by his predecessor, Raúl Alfonsín. From levels over 100 percent in some products, maximum tariffs had already fallen to 40 percent; the Menem regime cut the ceiling to 22 percent and the average to 10 percent.

In its first three years, the government privatized the state telephone and airline companies, sold exploration rights on state oil lands, sold important rail lines, and began privatization of electric utilities and most remaining state firms (including the national gas company and state steel plant). Capital revenue from privatizations in 1990–92 amounted to some $11 billion, or nearly 5 percent of 1992 GDP.[33] Despite some difficulties (for example, with meeting investment pledges in the privatized airline), this process of sweeping privatization promised better service to the public, a future source of tax revenue rather than budgetary drain, and the freeing-up of state resources to concentrate on its more fundamental obligations in social infrastructure. As just one example, in the past the state railway had chronically run deficits on the order of 1 percent of GDP annually.

Debt Strategy

An important part of Argentina's debt problem had stemmed from the effective transfer of private to public external debt without a commensurate transfer of private assets to the public sector. The mechanism was as follows. At the beginning of the 1980s, nearly half of external debt was private. The government had encouraged private debt rollover in 1981 by issuing exchange guarantees. Then, in 1982 there was a series of devaluations that cumulatively amounted to several hundred percent. In part because of the exchange guarantees, and in part because in the crisis economy after the South Atlantic war in early 1982 private firms were on the verge of bankruptcy, the government engaged in a series of operations amounting to subsidized provision of foreign exchange to private debtors. The private sector could obtain foreign exchange for debt service by paying domestic currency in cash in an amount equivalent to the dollars at the old exchange rate, while undertaking peso-denominated bond debt to the government for the remainder of the debt-service obligation (i.e., the peso increment corresponding to the change in the exchange rate). With interest on these peso obligations at rates far below subsequent inflation, the result was that the government turned over foreign exchange in return for domestic assets (cash and bonds) worth only a fraction as much in real terms.

In the meantime, the government borrowed abroad to obtain the dollars to carry out these operations. The overall result was the effective socialization of private external debt at much less than full value compensation to the government by the private debtors (Gonzalez Fraga 1989, 54–55; C. Rodriguez 1989, 85). This phenomenon imposed an internal (fiscal) transfer problem on top of the external transfer problem.

---

33. About half of the capital receipts were in cash; the remainder was in debt-equity conversions.

Indeed, it was the internal transfer problem that subsequently dominated Argentina's debt difficulties. Through most of the 1980s Argentina showed a capacity to generate large trade surpluses. However, especially by late in the decade, it was unable to mobilize the fiscal transfer to purchase this trade surplus from the private sector, with the effective result of private capital flight rather than the servicing of public external debt.

Argentine external debt built up more rapidly in the 1980s than in most countries in the region, rising by about 35 percent from 1983 to 1989. In the early part of this period the buildup was from coordinated new-money packages. However, by April 1988 the government ceased interest payments to foreign banks. After that date, relatively rapid debt buildup resulted from the accumulation of arrears (which had reached over $9 billion by the end of 1991, or one-seventh of total external debt; World Bank 1992a, vol. 2).

Argentina's debt arrears in 1988–91 were more the consequence of unintended delay than intentional default. Through most of 1988, negotiations were proceeding with banks for a new-money package that in turn would enable the government to become current on interest. However, the recurrent dynamic was that a pending IMF agreement would fail to materialize because of inadequate performance on domestic fiscal targets. The IMF agreements in turn were the prerequisite for a new-money package from the banks. There were successive phases of optimism (such as that associated with large adjustment lending from the World Bank in late 1988, despite the inability of Argentine negotiators and the IMF to come to agreement) and subsequent disillusionment (Cline and Roett 1988). In essence, what emerged was default by default, rather than default by design. The collapse of the economy into hyperinflation and the forced acceleration of the date for new elections meant that this dynamic simply intensified in 1989.

On the strength of the policy reforms and demonstrable results of the Convertibility Plan, by April 1992 the new Menem government successfully negotiated a Brady Plan debt reduction agreement with foreign banks. The agreement called for the conversion of $23 billion in long-term bank claims (out of Argentina's total external debt of approximately $65 billion) into "par bonds" with reduced interest rates (about two-thirds of the total) or "discount bonds" reducing face value by 35 percent. The banks effectively reduced their claims by about one-third in exchange for international collateral on principal and one-year's interest. In addition, debt-equity conversions in the massive privatizations further reduced external debt by about $6 billion.

Argentine negotiators did not include new money in their menu of debt options. The proximate reason was that it was much cheaper for Argentina to secure debt reduction than to take on new money. The underlying reason, however, was that by most measures (debt relative to exports, secondary market price), the Argentine debt burden had been relatively higher through most of the 1980s than that for Mexico and Venezuela. Correspondingly, debt reduction broadly on the Mexican terms already appeared a reasonable bargain for the banks; and indeed, it is unclear that many would have been prepared to extend new loans as an alternative (especially considering the slim response to this option even in the less severe Mexican case).

Like Mexico's similar agreement, the Brady Plan arrangement seemed likely to enable Argentina to put the debt problem behind it. Debt-equity conversions for privatization, lower world interest rates, and higher exports had already enabled the country to reduce its ratio of debt (net of reserves) to exports of goods and services from nearly 700 percent in 1987 (the highest among major Latin American debtors) to 390 percent by 1992 (chapter 2, table 2.3).

Allowing for an effective cut of about $9 billion from the Brady deal and taking into account the run-up in reserves, by the end of 1993 this ratio was down to about 285 percent. The burden of public-sector external debt fell even more dramatically, from a peak of 59.7 percent of GDP in 1989 to 19.9 percent in 1992 and 18 percent in 1993 (Argentine Economic Cabinet 1993, 22). The corresponding fiscal burden of government interest payments on foreign debt fell from 7 percent of GDP in 1989 to less than $1^{1}/_{2}$ percent for 1992 and after. In both cases the improvement occurred in considerable part because recovery of the exchange rate catapulted Argentina's GDP measured in dollars from only $77 billion in 1989 to $228 billion by 1992 (IMF 1993a, 82).

Issues in the 1990s

The Convertibility Plan achieved unaccustomed macroeconomic stability and renewed growth. However, by 1993 Argentina still faced a social deficit to be redressed. As noted, poverty incidence increased in the 1980s before moderating in the early 1990s. Economic growth would further reduce poverty problems, but as the central government shed its responsibilities in infrastructure (to the private sector) and even health and education (to the provinces), it made sense to concentrate more of its effort on programs focused on the poor. Reform of the social security system and provincial finances were other important challenges the government was beginning to address.

Higher investment was crucial for future growth. Investment fell from 24 percent of GDP in 1980–81 to 13 percent by 1990 (Argentine Economic Cabinet 1993, 81), but it was back up to 19 percent by 1992 (table 6.5). Sustained growth of 4 to 5 percent annually was likely to require a return of investment to the range of 20 percent of GDP. As suggested by the rebound by 1992, much of the financing for this increase seemed likely to be largely available from the reduced dissaving of the government (fiscal adjustment) and the lower payments abroad on external debt.

The international capital market gave the Menem administration and its Convertibility Plan a strong vote of confidence. Already by 1991 the government floated well over $500 million on the international bond markets, and private firms a comparable amount. Eurobond issues amounted to a total of $4.8 billion during 1992–93 (*Financial Times*, 10 November 1993). Spurred by privatizations, direct investment was up to $2.4 billion by 1991, three times the average for 1985–89. As analyzed in chapter 8 below, Argentine citizens appear to have repatriated some of the large cache of assets they hold abroad, and significant ongoing inflows might be expected from this source. The stock market has been the most dramatic indicator of confidence, as share prices in dollar terms quadrupled from the beginning of the Convertibility Plan through the mid-1992 (and, after a sharp correction, remained twice their pre-plan level by mid-1993; FIEL 1993).

Brazil[34]

As indicated in figure 6.1, for a time in the mid-1980s Brazil seemed to be more successful than most other Latin American countries in restoring economic growth after the initial shock of the debt crisis. The peak of this seeming success was early in the Cruzado Plan of 1986. However, without underlying fiscal adjustment, Brazil then entered a prolonged phase of recession and extremely high inflation.

As may be seen in figures 6.1 and 6.3, from 1987 through 1992 Brazil experienced prolonged recession and rising inflation. Cumulative real growth in 1988–92 was −1 percent, and per capita income fell by 11 percent. Failure to achieve sustained growth is no great surprise given the persistence of high inflation, which had been on the order of 1,000 percent or more annually in four of the five years of 1988–92 (figure 6.4). High inflation, in turn, stemmed primarily from persistent fiscal imbalance, and from the ''inertial'' force of pervasive indexation in the Brazilian economy.

Macroeconomic Policies

Figure 6.7 shows the cycle of temporary stabilization and eventual renewed outbreak of high inflation under a succession of heterodox ''plans'' over the past decade. Each plan involved an initial wage-price freeze. The Cruzado Plan of 1986 held the freeze so long that serious

---

34. An earlier version of this section appears in Cline (1993).

Table 6.6 Economic Indicators for Brazil, 1982-93 (percentages and billions of dollars)

Indicator	1982	1983	1984	1985	1986	1987	1988	1989	1990	1991	1992	1993
GDP growth (%)	0.6	-3.4	5.3	7.9	7.6	3.6	-0.1	3.3	-4.1	0.9	-0.9	4.5
Inflation (%)	97.8	142.1	197.0	226.9	145.2	229.7	682.3	1287.0	2937.8	440.9	1008.7	..
Gross investment/GDP (%)	27.7	20.5	20.2	24.6	25.0	23.8	22.7	22.3	21.4	20.4	20.5	..
Fiscal balance/GDP (%) NFPS	-16.6	-21.3	-24.3	-28.5	-11.2	-32.2	-52.8	-82.7	-29.3	-25.8	..	..
Fiscal balance/GDP (%) Oper	-7.3	-4.4	-2.7	-4.4	-3.6	-5.7	-4.8	-6.8	1.3	-1.3	-1.5	..
Real EXR/G6 (1985=100)	88.5	105.3	98.4	100.0	104.9	109.8	99.2	80.7	68.6	84.3	92.3	81.0
XGS (billions of dollars)	22.0	23.6	28.9	27.7	24.2	28.2	36.0	37.5	34.7	34.4	40.0	..
MGS (billions of dollars)	24.8	19.5	17.6	16.9	18.4	19.3	19.9	24.1	27.2	26.9	27.7	..
Current account balance (billions of dollars)	-16.3	-6.8	0.0	-0.3	-5.3	-1.5	4.2	1.0	-3.8	-1.4	6.3	..
External debt (billions of dollars)	92.8	98.3	105.5	106.1	113.7	123.9	115.7	111.4	116.4	116.5	121.1	..
Reserves excl. gold (billions of dollars)	3.9	4.4	11.5	10.6	5.8	6.7	9.4	9.3	7.4	8.0	22.5	30.6

.. = data not available.

Inflation: consumer prices, year over year.

Fiscal balances: Oper = operational (real); NFPS = nonfinancial public sector.

XGS, MGS: exports and imports of goods and nonfactor services.

Real EXR/G6: Real exchange rate against six large industrial countries, deflated by wholesale prices.

Sources: IMF 1992a, 1993h (growth, inflation, trade, current account, reserves); World Bank 1993b (debt); IDB 1991, 1993 (investment, fiscal balances, real exchange rate); ECLAC 1993 (fiscal balances).

Figure 6.7 Brazil: monthly inflation, July 1985–January 1993

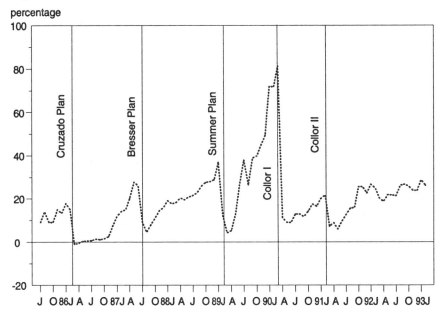

percentage

Source: IMF, *International Financial Statistics.*

shortages developed, and failure to obtain fiscal balance meant that repressed inflation erupted when prices were decontrolled. The same basic dynamic of inadequate fiscal adjustment to validate the ''hetero-dox shock'' of wage-price freeze was repeated in the Bresser Plan (named for Finance Minister Luiz Carlos Bresser Pereira) in 1987, and the Summer Plan of 1989. In each successive episode the resurgence of inflation was earlier and more extreme, and by early 1990 the country had entered hyperinflation (figure 6.7).

In March 1990, the new administration of Fernando Collor de Mello adopted a severe stabilization program based on an 18-month freeze of some $80 billion in bank accounts over $1,000 and holdings of govern-ment obligations. Despite a temporary price freeze, inflation fell no lower than 10 percent monthly. However, the asset freeze caused extreme liquidity problems for firms, paralyzing output and precipitat-ing deep recession. As a result, the government was soon freeing many of the blocked bank accounts. By June inflation was rising, and the government then turned to tight monetary policy and high real interest rates to limit inflation. Monthly inflation nonetheless crept steadily up to the 20 percent range by January 1991.

There was major fiscal improvement in 1990, as the operational bal-ance (which includes only the ''real'' component of interest payments) moved from a deficit of almost 7 percent of GDP to a surplus of 1.3 percent. However, the fiscal gains were largely transitory. They stemmed primarily from large one-time taxes on financial holdings (25 percent for the stock market, 8 percent on savings accounts) and from the forced compression of the real interest rate on frozen government obligations (to only 6 percent). The government also planned a reduction of nearly 200,000 government jobs but encountered obstacles from the constitution's guarantee of civil service tenure. By 1992, the operational deficit was back to 1.5 percent of GDP.

Inertial inflation from widespread de facto indexation was a major factor in the stubbornness of inflation in the face of the asset freeze and severe recession, even though the Collor government initially resisted demands for legally required wage indexation. In addition, there were adverse supply shocks in 1990 from a large crop decline and from higher oil prices associated with the Gulf War. More fundamentally, it seems likely that the public remained unpersuaded that stability was at hand, in view of the temporary nature of the fiscal adjustment and the prospect of the release of blocked cruzado accounts at the end of the 18-month freeze.

In January 1991 the Collor government sought to consolidate the stabilization program with a second phase (Collor II). The new plan set price controls, froze wages, and eliminated the formal indexation that remained by deindexing government bonds. However, inflation did not fall below the range of 6 to 8 percent monthly, reflecting widespread disregard of the freeze and the exhaustion of price controls as a credible instrument after so many previous failures. Minimum wages were reindexed by March. By May 1991 the economic portfolio passed to Marcilio-Marques Moreira (former ambassador to the United States), who ended the price controls and shifted to high real interest rates as the anti-inflationary strategy, pending fiscal reform.

By mid-1991 the administration was pursuing constitutional reform to higher range of about 20 to 25 percent monthly once again in the final quarter of the year, after a large devaluation of the cruzeiro (which had lagged behind inflation), substantial monetary pressure from the inflow of capital in response to high interest rates, and the impact of the release of blocked cruzado accounts. Nonetheless, the "orthodox" tight money policy this time held the inflation rate at a new high but stable plateau, a departure from the profile of the four previous "plan" episodes (figure 6.7). By mid-1992 the administration had proposed a major tax reform, but by then policymaking was increasingly hampered by the political crisis that led to impeachment of President Collor. Moreover, by May 1992 the congress had passed legislation reinstating legally required wage indexation for salaries up to three minimum wages, with correction every four months based on the consumer price index (and more frequently for low-end wages). By December wage indexation had been extended to salaries up to six times the minimum wage.

Analysts of the Brazilian experience have been divided in their diagnosis of the failure of the Collor program to reduce inflation. Tavares (1992) has argued that the problem cannot be blamed on the fiscal deficit, because of the fiscal adjustment achieved in 1990. She blames financial market speculation (which, however, is surely a consequence rather than cause of inflation) and excessive reliance on an active monetary and foreign exchange policy. The critique of monetary policy would seem to have some merit, as discussed below; but exchange policy merely managed to restore the real exchange rate after substantial real appreciation before the Collor government and in its initial period (when a floating-rate regime was combined with a domestic liquidity squeeze and the resulting inflow of capital bid up the real exchange rate).

The simplest answer to the Tavares skepticism on the fiscal deficit is that the adjustment of 1990 was perceived as neither permanent nor sufficient. The revenue measures were temporary and the reduction in government interest burden artificial from the asset freeze, as noted. Kiguel and Liviatan (1992) judge that Brazil's fiscal performance would have to have reached a sustainable primary surplus (i.e., excluding interest) of at least 4 percent of GDP to halt high inflation. However, their historical review of hyperinflation experiences also suggests to them that a more definitive demonstration of government commitment to stabilization would have been required as well. They cite as examples a more forceful privatization program, a definitive solution to the domestic debt problem, and an end to central bank financing of state deficits. Finally, the paradox is partly attributable to the fact that the data may be misleading. The deficit data do not include large losses of public banks (e.g., Caixa Economico) from deterioration of loan portfolio, debts to the social funds, and state firm deficits financed otherwise than by borrowing from the Treasury.[35] Moreover, calculation of the inflationary correction of domestic debt to arrive at the operational deficit can generate widely different results, depending on the method chosen, and by some methods the operational deficit remained large even by 1990–92.[36]

Fiscal adjustment is clearly a necessary condition for Brazilian stabilization, but it is unlikely to be a sufficient condition by itself. Without fiscal adjustment, the burden falls too heavily on monetary policy for any sustainable fight against inflation. The result is exorbitant real interest rates that far exceed the growth of the economy and thus cause a mushrooming of the domestic debt relative to the economy. Moreover, domestic debt has been held on an overnight basis and serves as a form

---

35. Personal communication with author, Persio Arida, 14 December 1992.

36. In particular, when a national accounts basis is applied; Eliana Cardoso, personal communication with author, 21 September 1994.

of quasi-money, so that high interest rates induce "loose" money if attention is shifted from the price of money (interest rate) to its volume (monetary aggregates including quasi-money). At the same time, beyond fiscal adjustment it is also necessary to break the inertial force of indexation. Past attempts to do so through price freezes have unfortunately discredited that option. Legally required full retroactive wage indexation is a particularly serious obstacle to breaking inertial inflation. As discussed briefly below, the Real Plan of mid-1994 sought to address these various requirements for stabilization.

Structural Change

Despite its failure to secure stabilization and growth, the Collor administration implemented important structural reforms that should eventually bear fruit. It adopted a radical reversal of Brazil's past tradition of high protection, reducing the maximum tariff from 105 percent in 1990 to 40 percent by 1994 and lowering average tariffs from 32 percent to 14 percent over the same period. Liberalization included the phasing out of the program of "market reserve" for small computers.

The Collor government embraced privatization, initially calling for the sale of a dozen state firms in the areas of steel, petrochemicals, and fertilizer, worth some $20 billion. After a slow start in the face of political opposition, the government sold the major steel firm USIMINAS in November 1991; and by late 1992, 14 state firms had been privatized, providing a reduction in government debt by $3 billion.

Debt Strategy

Brazilian debt strategy went through successive cycles of cooperation and alienation during the 1980s. Through 1986, the country's negotiations resembled those of Mexico within the evolving mainstream debt strategy. Thus, in 1983–84 Brazil rescheduled some $10 billion in long-term bank credits, rolled over $15 billion in short-term credits, and secured about $10 billion in new money. By mid-1986 Brazil had again reached agreement to reschedule $31 billion in long- and short-term debt, at a lower spread than before ($1\frac{1}{4}$ percent rather than $2\frac{1}{4}$ percent; World Bank 1992a, vol. 1).

The first swing to a confrontational stance occurred by early 1987. As noted in chapter 5, after the Cruzado Plan entered into crisis in late 1986, the Sarney government turned to a debt moratorium in part as a way to recoup lost domestic political popularity. In February 1987, Brazil suspended interest payments to the banks. In so doing, it triggered a major new phase in the international debt strategy, by inducing the leading foreign banks to begin to set aside reserves. With a reserve cushion, the stage was set for the possibility of eventual debt reduction, because of the greater ability of the international financial system to withstand the shock.

As discussed in Cline (1987, 68–78), a temporary decline in Brazilian exports in late 1986 was the proximate reason for the early 1987 suspension. Overheating of the economy during the Cruzado Plan, combined with the withholding of export supply by firms expecting a devaluation after the exchange rate had been held fixed for several months, caused exports to fall to half their normal level by late in the year. That Brazil could enter into trade difficulties at a time when it was the beneficiary of favorable external shocks (the collapse of oil prices in 1986) was evidence that the new problems stemmed primarily from domestic policy distortions.

After arranging a large bridge loan from the banks in late 1987, by November of 1988 Brazil negotiated a MYRA involving $61 billion in rescheduling, $5.2 billion in new money, and the rollover of $15 billion in short-term credits. The rescheduling was at 20-year maturities, with interest rates cut to a spread of 13/16ths percent above LIBOR. The agreement marked an important evolution toward a "menu" approach that contained elements of both new money and debt reduction. Formal exit bonds were expected to reduce debt by about $1 billion over 1989–90. Debt-equity auctions had already reduced debt by about $3 billion in 1988; informal cruzado-based buybacks, by at least another $4 billion in 1988 (prior to government restriction because of concern about impact on the parallel exchange market spread). Use of new money in debt-equity conversions was expected to reduce debt by about $2 billion (Cline and Roett 1988).

By July 1989, Brazil again entered into arrears on its long-term bank debt. The Summer Plan of early 1989 had collapsed and inflation was back to the range of 25 percent monthly. Because Brazil's program with the IMF had broken down, the country could not draw down the final tranche of its new money under the 1988 agreement with the banks. The reentry into payment arrears by mid-1989 was undertaken in a mode of lack of alternative rather than aggressive confrontation. Even so, the domestic economic disarray and foreign fears that a leftist would be elected drove the secondary market price below 25 cents on the dollar in December 1989.

The new regime of Fernando Collor in March 1990 sought rapprochement with the banks but continued to withhold interest payments until a comprehensive debt agreement could be reached (*Gazeta Mercantil*, 21 May 1993). Through the rest of the year there were unsuccessful attempts at negotiating an IMF adjustment program, along with increasing tension with the banks over mounting interest arrears. The basic dynamic in 1990, however, was that the new Collor government was not in a position politically to strike a deal with the banks that might seem to give them comfort when he had asked for such painful sacrifice from the

Brazilian public in the form of the Collor Plan asset freeze. By May 1991 the government agreed to begin partial payment of interest arrears, for consolidation in an eventual comprehensive debt agreement.

In July 1992 Brazil reached a Brady Plan agreement with the banks. The package contained numerous options affecting some $50 billion in long-term bank claims and arrears. As discussed in chapter 5, the alternatives included discount bonds with a 35 percent reduction in principal; par bonds with interest reduced initially to 4 percent, rising to 6 percent by the seventh year; new money tied to conversion bonds; and other variants.

By March 1993, 95 percent of banks had adhered to the agreement, although it remained necessary to rebalance between the amounts of "discount" and "par" bonds chosen. In addition, because Brazil had not yet reached agreement with the IMF to revise its standby program, it remained unclear whether Brazil could secure IMF and other official support for the $4 billion in collateral needed, or whether it might instead have to take the amount from its large reserves. In part because of the lingering difficulty in negotiating an IMF agreement, the Brady agreement was not finalized until April 1994, and then only with the help of a bank waiver of an IMF program and the use of Brazil's reserves rather than foreign official resources for the conversion bond enhancements.

The willingness of the banks to complete the package without an IMF program represented several influences. One was the appeal to the banks of closing the book on the Latin American debt crisis, and the corresponding unattractiveness of continuing to let the largest debtor linger in limbo. Another was simply that Brazil had a large cache of reserves in hand and could provide the enhancements on its own, thereby fulfilling the guarantor role if not the policy assurance role of IMF presence. Another was that Brazil had just announced a new stabilization plan and prospective adoption of currency reform, and collapse of the agreement would have done little to help either the plan or the electoral chances of the centrist finance minister who had designed the new plan before entering the presidential race. Moreover, with Brazil as the last major country facing a Brady-type deal, there was no longer a significant issue of precedent.

Issues in the 1990s

Despite a move toward structural reform and toward resolution of external debt, by 1993 the Brazilian economy remained in the grip of macroeconomic disarray, with inflation gradually rising to the rate of 30 percent per month. There were important structural imbalances that contributed to the problem of chronic inflation. In particular, the constitution of 1988 had imposed several unrealistic requirements with costly budgetary implications: inability to dismiss government workers, retirement at as early as 30 years of service (rather than at a specified age), and generous indexation of pensions. An inefficient social security system with high payroll taxes (37 percent) and widespread evasion was another structural problem.

Among the most important problems posed by the 1988 constitution was its shift of revenue sharing toward states and municipalities, without a corresponding shift in responsibilities (at least in actual implementation). The new constitution had provided that the federal government's share in total revenue, net of transfers, should decline from about two-thirds in 1980 to about two-fifths in 1993, whereas the net share of states should rise from about one-fifth percent in 1980 to two-fifths, and that of municipalities, from one-tenth percent to one-fourth. As the subnational governments used the windfall resources largely to raise public-sector employment rather than reduce deficits or take over responsibility for services provided at the federal level, the shift in revenue sharing meant increasing difficulty in achieving overall fiscal balance. This trend and the rigidities in civil service brought an increase in the share of overall government salaries in GDP from about 7 percent in the 1970s and early 1980s to about 10 percent in 1990–91.

By early 1993 the new government of Itamar Franco was developing its economic program, with considerable difficulty and rapid succession of economic teams. Much of the plan stemmed from the fiscal reform proposed in mid-1992. A transitional tax of 0.25 percent on bank check transactions was to raise some $5 billion yearly through 1994, and revised indexation of corporate taxes was to raise another $3.3 billion annually (*Gazeta Mercantil*, 25 January 1993; 15 February 1993). However, congressional opposition to a proposed value-added tax left unclear what would be the permanent alternative to the distortional tax on checking accounts.

Any successful stabilization plan for Brazil had to include the following elements. First, it needed to achieve fiscal adjustment, probably aiming for a primary surplus of at least 4 percent of GDP. Second, this adjustment had to be of a nature that was permanent and credible. Decisive transfer of responsibilities for public services to the subnational governments, consistent with the increased transfers from revenue sharing, would be an example; a tax on checking accounts is not. Third, it was imperative to bring down high real interest rates. Rates far in excess of real GDP growth had caused a reescalation of the burden of domestic government debt, after the Collor asset freeze with inadequate indexation cut it substantially.[37] Fourth, there had to be some mechanism for reducing inertial

---

37. Government debt held by the public rose from $12 billion to $35 billion during 1992. Through much of 1992–93, interest rates were on the order of 20 percent annually or higher in real terms.

inflation.[38] Elimination or at least moderation of wage and other indexation was likely to be necessary for this purpose.

In early 1994 the government began a phased adoption of a stabilization program, the Real Plan designed by Finance Minister Fernando Henrique Cardoso and his economic advisers. As the first step, in April the government began transformation of all indexing into the Unit of Real Value (URV), which adjusted daily on a basis intended to keep pace with the dollar. Then in July it adopted the new currency, the *real*, at a rate of parity between the URV and the dollar. However, unlike in Argentina's Convertibility Plan, there was no ironclad commitment to holding the rate fixed. The plan prohibited indexation contracts for periods of less than a year. A Social Solidarity Fund pried about 15 percent of the budget loose from its otherwise earmarked uses, and provided some basis for fiscal adjustment.

Analytically the plan resembled the ingenious "Larida" proposal of Brazilian economists Persio Arida and Andre Lara-Resende (1985). The idea was essentially to get the public accustomed to indexing all prices and wages in a common index; move to a daily rather than monthly or less frequent index in order to bring relative prices into line; and then, at an appropriate moment, carry out a currency reform that effectively transformed the index itself into the new currency. Inertial inflation from indexation would thereby disappear. The Larida approach had always seemed too good to be true and smacked of defining away inflation; even so, if implemented with the generally acknowledged prerequisite of fiscal balance, it offered a potential way to break out of indexation-imposed inertial inflation. It was especially appropriate for a country such as Brazil, where the public seemed to attach more real value to such instruments as indexed government bonds, as opposed to such countries as Argentina and Mexico, where the dollar was much more widely followed as the true gauge of value.

The initial results of the plan were highly favorable. Monthly inflation fell from 50 percent in June to 5 percent by August and 1.5 percent in September. Capital inflow was strong enough to cause the *real* to settle at a premium against the dollar. Public enthusiasm enabled presidential candidate Fernando Henrique Cardoso to move from a poor second place to a large lead in the polls, and Cardoso won the election in the first round in October.

Brazil's war chest of $40 billion in reserves provided an important source of credibility for the plan, which had important elements of

---

38. Some would advocate a fixed exchange rate "anchor" for this purpose, or even dollarization of the economy. Although these options have become more plausible in view of the large holdings of foreign reserves, they would be incompatible with anything but an absolute and decisive break with past fiscal drift.

exchange rate–anchored stabilization even if in disguise. Nonetheless, by late 1994 it remained to be seen whether the new plan would permit a definitive break with the past record of failed stabilization efforts. Because constitutional reform efforts in the spring of 1994 had been largely unsuccessful, much of the task of permanent fiscal reform remained unfinished business for the next administration. Still, the chances for stabilization seemed the best in many years.

Peru

For most of the past decade, Peru has stood at the unfavorable end of the spectrum of economic policy and performance among major Latin American countries. The sharp contrast between the trends in real per capita income and inflation for Peru on the one hand and Colombia and Chile on the other reveal that economic outcomes broadly reflected the differences along this spectrum of policy quality (figures 6.2 and 6.4).

Macroeconomic Policies

The populist policies of the Alan García regime (1985–89) brought a classical cycle of initial, unsustainable economic boom followed by accelerating inflation and severe recession. An announced policy of limiting debt service to 10 percent of export earnings constituted the closest thing to official default among the major Latin American debtors, but it failed to limit payments to this ceiling and had the effect of cutting off Peru even from trade credits. By the late 1980s the unorthodox and confrontational policies had led to a reduction of real per capita income by 28 percent (the cumulative total for 1988–90) and the outbreak of hyperinflation (with an annual rate of 7,650 percent in 1990, December/December; ECLAC 1992, 41–43). Only with the change to more orthodox adjustment policies under the regime of Alberto Fujimori in 1990 did the economy begin to stabilize.

Webb (1991) has stressed that since the mid-1970s Peru has experienced a dramatic, involuntary collapse in the role of the state. Real government spending per capita fell by 83 percent from 1975 to 1990. An implosion of the revenue base rather than intentional privatization accounted for most of the reduction.

The reformist military regime of Juan Velasco (1968–75) had pressed import-substituting industrialization and government intervention in the economy, including extensive land reform and formation of "industrial communities" with worker participation in management. By 1975 a fiscal and balance of payments crisis led to a regime change, and by 1978 General Francisco Morales Bermúdez had carried out a relatively successful, orthodox stabilization program (Cline 1981). Then the deceptive

Table 6.7 Economic indicators for Peru, 1982-93 (percentages and billions of dollars)

Indicator	1982	1983	1984	1985	1986	1987	1988	1989	1990	1991	1992	1993
GDP growth (%)	-0.2	-12.6	5.8	2.1	9.3	8.3	-8.2	-11.8	-4.3	2.6	-2.8	6.4
Inflation (%)	64.4	111.2	110.2	163.4	77.9	85.8	667.0	3,398.7	7,841.7	409.5	73.5	..
Gross investment/GDP (%)	38.7	25.1	21.6	18.9	22.6	26.3	26.1	20.3	21.9	25.5	27.5	..
Fiscal balance/GDP (%) Cent	-3.1	-7.3	-4.4	-3.0	-4.3	-6.9	-3.9	-6.3	-5.4	-1.9	-2.0	..
Fiscal balance/GDP (%) NFPS	-7.2	-9.8	-6.7	-3.4	-5.7	-7.9	-8.1	-8.5	-5.9	-2.2	-1.5	..
Real effective EXR (1985=100)	94.3	100.4	102.9	127.1	110.8	97.9	99.7	64.7	49.5	40.4	39.4	..
XGS (billions of dollars)	4.1	3.7	3.8	3.8	3.4	3.6	3.7	4.4	4.1	4.2	4.3	4.4
MGS (billions of dollars)	4.8	3.7	3.0	2.8	3.8	4.5	4.2	3.6	4.4	5.1	5.7	5.6
Current account balance (billions of dollars)	-1.6	-0.9	-0.2	0.1	-1.1	-1.6	-1.2	-0.1	-0.8	-1.3	-1.7	-1.8
External debt (billions of dollars)	10.7	10.6	11.6	12.9	14.9	17.5	18.0	18.3	19.4	20.7	20.3.	..
Reserves excl. gold (billions of dollars)	1.3	1.4	1.6	1.8	1.4	0.6	0.5	0.8	1.0	2.4	2.8	3.4

.. = data not available.

Inflation: consumer prices, year over year.
Fiscal balances: Cent = central government; NFPS = nonfinancial public sector.
XGS, MGS: exports and imports of goods and nonfactor services.

Sources: IMF 1992a, 1993h (growth, inflation, trade, current account, reserves); World Bank 1993b (debt); IDB 1991, 1993 (investment, fiscal balances, real exchange rate); ECLAC 1993 (fiscal balances).

luck of higher commodity prices and oil discovery removed the pressure for fundamental reform.

The returning civilian president, Fernando Belaúnde, sharply raised public-sector wages and government investment in 1979–82. By 1981–82, however, there was a collapse of export earnings and real tax revenue, associated with floods, drought, and El Niño damage to the anchovy beds. A cycle of orthodox adjustment (by Finance Minister Carlos Rodríguez Pastor) brought exceptionally high real interest rates and cuts in real spending, but plummeting GDP (falling $12^{1}/_{2}$ percent in 1983) eroded revenue and widened the fiscal deficit (IMF 1992a, 573). The Latin American debt crisis brought a cutoff of credit and forced rescheduling. Shining Path terrorism added political disorder to economic.

In 1985 the new government of Alan García increased government spending, reduced taxes, rapidly expanded the money base, froze prices and wages, held interest rates at artificially low levels, and substantially increased import protection (Webb 1991, 8–9; Lago 1991). García attempted to nationalize the banks but failed. Initially the heterodox program was funded by drawing down reserves and by forcing the conversion of a large nest egg of private domestic foreign exchange deposits into domestic currency. For a time, there was a mirage of resulting economic expansion (1985–87). Local theorists even published glowing accounts of the Peruvian miracle, suggesting its adoption elsewhere (Carbonetto, as discussed in Lago 1991, 270–71). Then, as foreign reserves disappeared, the inevitable collapse arrived. After rising by a cumulative 17 percent in 1986–87, in 1988–90 real GDP fell by 23 percent. Inflation escalated to approximately 1,700 percent in 1988, 2,800 percent in 1989, and 7,600 percent in 1990 (December/December; ECLAC 1992, 40, 43).

By mid-1990 Peru's tax revenues had fallen to 4 percent of GDP, its external reserves had disappeared, and its monthly inflation rate stood at 60 percent (Lago 1991). The new government of Alberto Fujimori imposed a shock-treatment stabilization program. It placed government spending on a cash basis: spending each month could not exceed receipts. One early result was the voluntary departure of some 30,000 government workers. The new government raised prices of state enterprises sharply, causing a one-time price increase of 400 percent in August 1990. The program set tight credit limits, removed interest rate ceilings, set the exchange rate free to float, eliminated import quotas, and set a uniform 15 percent tariff rate for most imports and 25 percent for the rest (IDB 1992, 159).

By 1991, the end of exchange rate subsidies and reduced lending to development banks practically eliminated the central bank's "quasi-fiscal deficit," which had exceeded 8 percent of GDP in the late 1980s. The deficit of the nonfinancial public sector fell from $5^{1}/_{2}$ percent of GDP to 2 percent, and inflation fell to 140 percent for the year (December/December) despite the absence of price controls (IDB 1992, 155). By mid-1993, Peru's inflation was running at only 40 percent per year and was on a declining path (IMF 1993a). Moreover, after a reduction of GDP by 2.8 percent in 1992, for 1993 the economy was showing renewed growth of over 6 percent.

In an early analysis of the Fujimori strategy, Paredes (1991) broadly approved of the move to realism but criticized aspects of the sequencing of reforms. Tight money and high real interest rates had led to further real appreciation of the exchange rate, which, combined with immediate trade liberalization, caused a rapid increase in imports. More questionably, Paredes criticized the regime's early move to resume servicing of debt to the IMF and World Bank on grounds that the resulting fiscal burden was excessive.

For their part, Kiguel and Liviatan (1992) have considered puzzles arising from the Peruvian experience with hyperinflation. The first is that for a period of some 18 months in 1989–90, Peru's monthly inflation held steady at the extremely high level of 30 to 40 percent, contrary to the usual experience whereby inflation this high quickly escalates into hyperinflation (50 percent per month and more). They cite Lago (1991) to the effect that this period was one of relatively tight money and conclude that tight money can be used to prevent an explosion in inflation even when the fiscal position is out of control. They also ask why the Fujimori stabilization program, designed along the Bolivian lines, did not achieve the same result of prompt stability. Their answer includes three considerations. First, by 1991 Peru's fiscal reform remained fragile, as tax revenue had still not regained its pre-Garcia level. Second, even though the real exchange rate appreciated, and even the nominal rate stabilized temporarily, there was no formal fixing of the exchange rate to provide an anti-inflationary anchor (unlike the Bolivian case). Third, the high degree of dollarization of the Peruvian economy meant that there was much less anti-inflationary benefit from the normal rebound in demand for domestic money than would normally have accompanied stabilization. Despite these difficulties, the further progress in reducing inflation by mid-1993 suggested that the contrast to classic ending of hyperinflations was primarily one of a more prolonged adjustment rather than failure of the orthodox remedies.

Debt Strategy

The Peruvian experience provides a useful (but costly) test case for the consequences of an aggressive confrontational policy of quasi-default that had been advocated by many for Latin America more generally early in the debt crisis (e.g., Kaletsky 1985). Indeed, the Peruvian experiment is not only a cross-section (same time-period comparison with other Latin American countries) but also a time series (García versus Fujimori).

The Belaúnde debt policy began with an attempt to secure rollover lending, but by March 1983 it transformed to the general Latin American pattern of rescheduling-cum–new money.[39] However, a second rescheduling agreement in February of 1984 was not implemented (World Bank 1989b, 1: 69) because the country fell out of compliance with its IMF program. Toward the end of the Belaúnde regime, Peru was falling into arrears but servicing debt on a best-efforts basis. In contrast, the García regime adopted a highly publicized confrontational approach that promised to limit debt service to 10 percent of export earnings. At the same time, the new regime tried to convince creditors that new loans would be fully serviced and implicitly senior in status. This official quasi-default soon caused Peru to be classified as "value impaired" by US regulators.

Lago (1991) has shown that the García policy was ineffective in achieving the supposed limit, as the servicing of debt from mid-1985 to the end of 1986 was actually 25 percent of export earnings. His account of the experiment is chilling:

> The assumption, later proven erroneous, that Peru could selectively default against some creditors while obtaining financing from others led progressively to defaults with initially nontargeted creditor groups. It was only in 1988 that total debt service descended to the 10 percent limit. In August 1986, Peru was declared ineligible for IMF lending, and one year later was placed on "nonaccrual" by the World Bank. In early 1989, the Inter-American Development Bank also took the step of classifying Peru as a nonaccrual country due to protracted default. . . . By late 1987, the . . . [García] experiment turned . . . openly confrontational, both abroad and at home. . . . Net international reserves had reached the "red," Central Bank external deposits had to be moved from one country to another to avoid potential seizure by creditors, letters of credit for imports had to be collateralized with cash, and the Central Bank had to start drawing down gold reserves. . . . Unlike the case of other debtors, Peru's default was deliberately confrontational beginning in 1985 and was later extended to the multilateral institutions. . . .[The] costs of default . . . [included] paralyzed development projects, reluctant new foreign investments, increased trade restrictions abroad, reduced aid flows, and, above all, a major macroeconomic failure. (Lago 1991, 283–84, 318)

It is of course difficult to separate out the adverse effects of García's other economic policies from those of his debt policy. It is conceivable, though improbable, that an optimizing regime could have similarly defaulted on debt but pursued a sophisticated domestic macroeconomic policy. The strong presumption, however, is that the confrontational

---

39. Ironically, it was the large foreign banks that convinced Peruvian authorities to reschedule. They argued that otherwise the small banks would cut and run, leaving the large banks with a disproportionate burden of new lending (Cline, Schydlowsky, and Roett 1983).

debt strategy contributed importantly to the economy's plunge into depression and hyperinflation.[40]

The Fujimori regime adopted a 180-degree turnaround on debt policy and explicitly sought to "reinsert" Peru into the international economy through rapprochement with official and, eventually, private international lenders. To do otherwise would have been inconsistent with the new government's opening of the economy through import liberalization, with the implied objective of a corresponding increase in export orientation. The government first cleared up its arrears to the International Monetary Fund and World Bank. It then reached an agreement rescheduling principal and interest owed to the Paris Club of official bilateral creditors. By late 1993, the government had initiated discussions with the foreign banks aiming toward a Brady Plan agreement.[41]

In short, whereas the García regime had attempted a confrontational approach of quasi-default with disastrous results, the Fujimori government pursued a course of rejoining the mainstream strategy in the region: renegotiation of the debt and its normalization under the Brady Plan. The secondary market price vividly reflected the turnaround in policy. From a level of 11 cents on the dollar in the second quarter of 1987, secondary market prices fell as low as 3 cents on the dollar in the first half of 1989. With the Fujimori regime, they rose to an average of 13 cents in 1991, 16 cents in 1992, 28 cents in the first half of 1993, and 43 cents by the fourth quarter of 1993 (World Bank 1989a, 1993a; Salomon Brothers 1993b).

It is important to stress that Peru's more radical debt policy was not predestined by a more desperate debt burden than that faced by other major Latin American countries. As shown in chapter 2 (table 2.5), Peru's ratio of net interest payments to exports of goods and nonfactor services in 1984–85 stood at about 29 percent, similar to the levels for Brazil (29 percent) and Mexico (31 percent) and far below the levels for Argentina (52 percent) and Chile (43 percent). The principal special consideration in the Peruvian case was the much lower level of per capita income. At international purchasing power prices, Peru's per capita

---

40. An external trade credit cutoff manifests itself in a reduction of import availability, with repercussions on domestic production. Although imports rose rapidly in 1986–87, thanks to the running down of reserves and the conversion of private domestic dollar deposits, in 1988–89 there was a reduction in imports by 28 percent. The decline in import availability seems likely to have contributed to the 19 percent reduction in real GDP in these two years, although causation no doubt also ran in the opposite direction.

41. Earlier the country's relations with the banks had been complicated by a number of lawsuits, initiated in part because the banks in question feared that inaction on long-overdue payments would amount to forgiveness after a six-year period because of statutes of limitation. Discussions with the banks required an initial understanding that these suits would not be allowed to disrupt more general negotiations.

income in 1990 stood at only $2,720, compared with $4,680 for Argentina, $4,780 for Brazil, $5,980 for Mexico, and $6,190 for Chile (World Bank 1992b, 276–77). However, more acute poverty meant that there was an even greater premium on judicious policy (and even greater vulnerability of the population to hyperinflation), and thus, at least with the benefit of hindsight, there was little justification for a high-risk and in the end counterproductive debt strategy.[42]

Lessons from the Latin American Experience

In these and most other Latin American countries, the economic base had been weakened prior to the debt crisis by pursuit of the development model of import-substituting industrialization. That strategy, which relied on high import protection, had led to inefficiency and a weak export base as the consequence of the bias toward production for the domestic rather than the world market. Another typical feature of the Latin American economies was chronic difficulty in achieving fiscal balance.

As there were similarities in the problems, there were patterns in the remedies. Economic adjustment of the late 1980s was typically built around what has been called the ''Washington consensus'' (Williamson 1990b). This adjustment program involved

- trade liberalization;

- fiscal adjustment;

- privatization of state enterprises to stop their fiscal losses and to mobilize private capital to carry out needed investments;

- deregulation; and

- price decontrol.

The principal differences in implementation of successful adjustment have concerned exchange rate strategy. The two underlying alternatives have been the use of a fixed exchange rate as an ''anchor'' in the fight against inflation, on the one hand, and the adoption of a ''crawling peg'' exchange rate designed to maintain export incentives in the face of domestic inflation on the other.

---

42. Note moreover that Peru's default should not be identified with the de facto buildup of arrears by Argentina and Brazil in the late 1980s. President García's explicit 10 percent ceiling and suspension of payments even to international financial institutions went well beyond the Argentine and Brazilian policies of informally accumulating ''unavoidable'' arrears on the servicing of long-term debt owed to banks.

Figure 6.8 Primary fiscal balances, 1981-91

percent of GDP

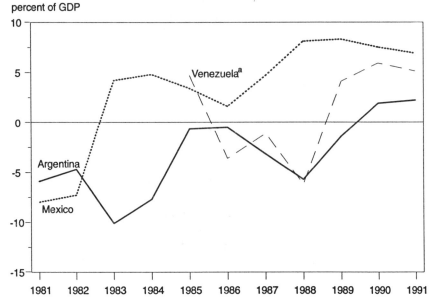

a. Data not available before 1985.

Sources: Banco de Mexico and IDB.

Fiscal Adjustment

Figure 6.8 shows the common element of fiscal adjustment in Mexico, Venezuela, and Argentina. As discussed above, fiscal balance had already been achieved much earlier in Colombia and Chile; in contrast, in Brazil and Peru fiscal performance has been weak through most of the past decade. In the three countries that achieved successful turn-arounds, the primary balance rose from a deficit of 8 percent of GDP in 1981 to a surplus of 8 percent in Mexico; from a deficit of 10 percent of GDP in 1983 to a surplus of 2 percent in Argentina; and from a deficit of 7 percent to a surplus of 5 percent of GDP in Venezuela.[43] Massive fiscal adjustment was the principal reason these three countries were able to reduce inflation. The reduction of inflation, in turn, was the precondition for a recovery of economic growth and investment.

43. Note, however, that by 1992 there had been fiscal slippage in Venezuela, in part because of weaker oil prices. Also note that the fiscal concepts reported in tables 6.4 and 6.7 differ from the primary balance considered here.

Table 6.8 Debt strategy and economic performance in Latin America

Country	Average per capita growth (%/yr)[a] A	Average inflation (%/yr)[b] B	Average logarithm, inflation C	Economic Performance Index (EPI) D = A–C	Ranking: EPI E	Ranking: Debt cooperativeness F
Chile	1.80	20.4	1.31	0.49	1	2
Colombia	1.40	24.0	1.38	0.02	2	1
Venezuela	–0.65	22.4	1.35	–2.00	3	4
Mexico	–0.40	50.1	1.70	–2.10	4	3
Brazil	–0.45	436.5	2.64	–3.09	5	6
Argentina	–1.00	338.8	2.53	–3.53	6	5
Peru	–3.00	302.0	2.48	–5.48	7	7

a. Average annual cumulative growth, 1979–81 to 1991–92.
b. Geometric average, consumer price inflation, 1983–92.

Sources: World Bank 1993c (growth); IMF 1993e (inflation).

Cooperative versus Confrontational Debt Strategy

It is possible to synthesize the patterns of economic performance and debt strategy outlined above for the seven major Latin American debtors to examine the question of whether a cooperative or a confrontational debt strategy was more favorable for the country in terms of GDP growth and inflation performance. As discussed in chapter 4, Eichengreen and Portes (1989) have argued that countries that defaulted more deeply during the 1930s achieved better results on economic growth than those that did not default or only did so "lightly." Similarly, Kaletsky (1985) argued early in the debt crisis of the 1980s that Latin American nations could default with impunity.

The experience reviewed above suggests the contrary, however: in general, countries with more cooperative debt strategies achieved better results for their domestic economies. It is possible to conduct a simple statistical test of this hypothesis by ranking the countries on debt cooperativeness and on economic performance, and then examining whether the two rankings are positive (as hypothesized here), random, or negative.

Table 6.8 shows the data for these two rankings. The annual average rate of per capita income growth for the cumulative change from the 1979–81 base to the 1991–92 terminal period is one element of the economic performance criterion. On this measure, Chile ranked first among the seven countries, and Peru last.[44]

---

44. Brazil's mid-1980s maintenance of output fails to place it high in the growth ranking here, because by the end of the period real per capita income had fallen to levels in the middle of the group (figure 6.1).

However, inflation has been the scourge of Latin America in the past decade, and it certainly must be taken into account in any overall measure of economic performance. The classic measure for doing so in industrial countries is the "misery index," which is the sum of the unemployment rate and the inflation rate. However, unemployment rates have little meaning in developing countries, where the lack of unemployment benefits typically means low open unemployment. Moreover, absolute inflation rates are often in three or four digits rather than low one-digit rates as in industrial countries, and would overwhelm the misery index.

Table 6.8 presents a new measure of economic performance, the "Economic Performance Index" (EPI). It is obtained by subtracting the average logarithm (base 10) of consumer price inflation from the average growth rate of per capita income. For example, if per capita income grows at 3 percent and inflation is only 10 percent, the EPI is 2 ($= 3 - \log_{10}10$). If per capita income grows at 2 percent and inflation is 10,000 percent, the EPI is -2 ($= 2 - \log_{10}10,000$). As shown in the table, the corresponding "geometric" average of inflation was typically on the order of 320 percent annually for the three high-inflation countries (Argentina, Brazil, and Peru), and on the order of 30 percent for the four low-inflation countries (Colombia, Chile, Mexico, and Venezuela).[45]

The difference in the inflation rate between the two groups of countries is in the range of 10-fold, and thus a difference of unity in the Economic Performance Index. As a result, economic growth was "worth" about one percentage point less than its observed rate for the high-inflation countries than for the low-inflation countries. There is of course no rigorous mapping between the two, but this order of magnitude seems appropriate.[46] Surely perceived economic welfare was substantially less in the countries with very high inflation, for a given real growth rate.[47]

The country rankings on the Economic Performance Index are broadly consistent with conventional perceptions. Chile and Colombia are at the top, and Peru is at the bottom. Somewhat surprisingly, Venezuela ranks higher than Mexico, showing the influence of incorporating inflation as well as growth (inflation reached 160 percent in Mexico in 1987, and never exceeded 80 percent in Venezuela). It is also somewhat surprising that Brazil ranks above Argentina, although more favorable results for Argentina only began in 1991–92.

---

45. The geometric average is the nth root of the product of n observations (on inflation, in this case). Equivalently, it is the antilog of the average logarithm of inflation.

46. For this reason, the logarithm to the base 10 is selected in preference to the natural logarithm, which would give a higher weight to inflation in the EPI.

47. The main reason is that there is much higher "risk" associated with an income stream in a high-inflation country, as witnessed by the violent swings in real wages in the face of hyperinflation.

The rankings do depend on the time period. For example, economic performance had deteriorated in Venezuela by 1994, whereas it had improved in Peru and seemed to be on the verge of doing so in Brazil. However, the analysis here seeks to identify the patterns associated with relatively continuous policy approaches, so the shifts from significant regime changes by 1993–94 are appropriately omitted.

As for the rankings on cooperativeness versus confrontation in debt strategy, they must necessarily be more subjective. Nonetheless, most analysts would probably agree with the ranking suggested in table 6.8. Colombia is placed first because it did not even reschedule debt. Chile is second, because it did not ask for Brady debt forgiveness. Mexico is third, because it never entered into arrears. Venezuela is fourth, because it only went into arrears briefly. The other three countries all had extended periods of interest arrears. Among them, Argentina places fifth, because it had already reached Brady Plan settlement by early 1993. Brazil is sixth, because it had not. Peru is seventh, because under Alan García it had the most explicitly confrontational debt policy in the region.

It is evident in table 6.8 that there is a close correlation between the two rankings. The Spearman rank correlation test shows a correlation coefficient of .89 between the two rankings.[48] This positive correlation is statistically significant at the 5 percent level.[49] These results strongly suggest that cooperation on external debt was more successful than confrontation in the debt crisis of the 1980s, in terms of the resulting impact on the economic welfare of the countries involved.

It is possible in principle but largely irrelevant in fact that the correlation could have worked the other way around: purely random factors might have generated the array of economic performance, and, given the outcome, countries with more favorable growth and price stability might have been more able to afford the luxury of being cooperative on debt. However, the review in this chapter makes it amply clear that the outcomes were not random.

A second alternative interpretation is that economic performance indeed was systematic and reflected the quality of domestic economic policy, but it was not a consequence of debt policy one way or the other. If this view is accepted, however, it essentially conveys the same message about debt policy in a different way. If there is a complete overlap

48. On a scale from −1 for perfect *inverse* correlation, to 0 for random association, to a maximum of +1 for perfect positive correlation. The Spearman rank correlation coefficient is computed as: $r = 1 - (n - 1)[\Sigma d_i^2/\{n(n^2 - 1)\}]$ where n is the number of observations, and d_i is the difference in ranks assigned to the same observation by the two ranking criteria. See Hogg and Craig (1978, 339).

49. The "t-statistic" of the debt cooperativeness ranking in a simple linear regression of EPI on this variable is 4.4.

between good domestic policies and cooperation on debt, then the implication is that the wisest and most responsible policymakers systematically choose to cooperate on debt as part of their policy strategy. That revealed preference is simply another way of documenting the superiority of the cooperative approach (unless the policymakers who were astute and effective on domestic economic performance were for some reason systematically mistaken on external debt).

A third view might be that the set of countries considered here is too narrow, and that cases can be found where good domestic policy achieves good economic results while at the same time the country successfully pursues an aggressive, confrontational strategy on external debt. Some would argue that this description fits Bolivia, where economic policy reforms after the 1985 hyperinflation brought favorable results. Bolivia pursued a policy of ongoing moratorium on bank debt, together with aid-financed buybacks. The secondary market price was still as low as 16 cents on the dollar in 1992 (World Bank 1994b). By 1993 the country had virtually eliminated bank debt by buybacks at that price financed by the World Bank, and by conversion of about $100 million of the remaining bank debt into bonds (World Bank 1993e).

However, the Bolivian case is unrepresentative of the mainstream Latin American debt problem. Bank debt was less than one-fifth of total external debt for Bolivia in 1985 (World Bank 1993b, vol. 2), far below the level for larger Latin American countries. As a small debtor dependent on and with access to official aid, the country was in a position to engage in moratorium on its bank debt with less adverse repercussions than the large debtors. The banks could afford to ignore actions by a small debtor that would have been too costly for them to tolerate in a larger debtor.

Moreover, by the early 1990s Bolivia was missing from the private capital markets, to an important degree because of the debt strategy it had chosen. Its official debt remained a heavy burden (World Bank 1993e, 55). The country is thus neither a likely example of what larger countries might have attempted nor a felicitous case with regard to the outcome on reintegration into the private capital market.

Overall, the close correlation in table 6.8 remains as evidence that the mainstream experience in Latin America tended to show that a cooperative debt policy was more beneficial for country economic performance than a confrontational policy.

Other Patterns

In addition to the centrality of fiscal adjustment, the pattern of structural adjustment following the "Washington consensus," and the benefits of cooperative debt strategy, other lessons from recent experience in the large Latin American economies and others in the region warrant attention.

Exchange Rate Policy

It is evident that the choice of the exchange rate strategy has played a central role in the outcome for these adjustment experiences. The basic choice has been between use of a fixed exchange rate as an anti-inflationary anchor or pursuit of a crawling-peg exchange rate that off-sets domestic inflation to maintain export incentives. At least four things may be said about this choice.

First, unless fiscal policy is under control it is fatuous to adopt a fixed exchange rate. Underlying inflationary pressure will sooner or later cause a run on the exchange rate.

Second, however, where fiscal adjustment is in place, a fixed exchange rate may help stabilize expectations and prices. This is especially true where there has been a recent history of high inflation and the public is highly accustomed to observing the exchange rate against the dollar. In Argentina and Mexico such "dollarization" had reached advanced levels, and fixing the exchange rate (or specifying a minimal "slide" in Mexico) made a major contribution to reduced inflationary expectations.

Third, special fiscal feedback can influence the choice between the two approaches. It makes much more sense for Venezuela to use the crawling-peg exchange rate than a fixed rate against the dollar. If domestic inflation exceeds the international rate, a fixed bolivar-dollar rate imposes a widening fiscal deficit—because the government gets most of its revenue from dollar oil export earnings and thus a fixed bolivar sum when the rate is fixed.

Fourth, the choice in the trade-off between monetary anchor and export stimulant requires balance and proper diagnosis of the dominant problem at the time. By 1992–93 there were growing signs in both Mexico and Argentina that the problem was shifting from inflation to external balance once again, with the implication that the fixed exchange rate could increasingly be a problem. Current account deficits were becoming uncomfortably large, placing a high priority on stimulating exports through productivity gains in view of the likely still high responsiveness of domestic inflationary expectations to devaluation.

Heterodox versus Orthodox Programs

In the mid-1980s the "heterodox shock" model was popular. In Argentina and Brazil, sophisticated economists had concluded that inflation was "inertial," locked in at high levels because of automatic "indexing" corrections in wages and prices. The 1985 Austral Plan in Argentina and the 1986 Cruzado Plan in Brazil adopted wage-price freezes, or "heterodox shocks" designed to break inertial inflation. Within a few years it was apparent that any heterodox program would require orthodox adjustment as its fundamental underpinning, or otherwise be worth very little. Both the Austral and Cruzado Plans broke down because permanent fiscal adjustment did not accompany the heterodox measures. In contrast, Mexico's Solidarity Pact amounted to a joint heterodox-orthodox plan that used a wage-price freeze to break inertial inflation but at the same time carried out massive fiscal adjustment. Mexico's program worked where its heterodox-only precursors had failed.[50]

Vicious and Virtuous Circles

Recent Latin American experience has once again reminded economists of the existence of vicious and virtuous circles in economic management. The "Tanzi-Oliveira Effect" is a major example of a vicious circle. It refers to the erosion of real tax revenue caused by accelerating inflation. Higher inflation shrinks the real value of taxes during the lag between when they are due and when they are in the treasury's hands. The Tanzi-Oliveira effect was frequently responsible for fiscal deterioration on the order of 2 to 3 percentage points of GDP or more in some of the episodes of accelerating inflation in the region. This circle reversed and turned virtuous once inflation started coming down.

The role of state firm pricing is closely related. Governments are understandably reluctant to raise the price of gasoline, electricity, telephones, and other basic services to the public. As inflation increases, these public prices tend to lag further behind. As a consequence, the state firms lose more money, widening the fiscal deficit and aggravating the inflationary pressure. One side benefit of privatization is to remove this potential source of a fiscal vicious circle, because private firms tend to keep their prices up with the general inflation rate.

Policy Mix and Domestic Debt

Another pattern is the importance of a balanced fiscal-monetary posture. When fiscal policy is weak and the government attempts to compensate with tight money policy, the interest rate typically reaches extremely high levels. High interest rates in turn mean that the government's domestic debt is growing rapidly from "inherited" interest on old debt in addition to the accumulation of new fiscal deficits.

Savings Freezes

The extreme instability in Latin America in the late 1980s generated some extreme policy experiments. In December 1989 the Argentine government adopted the "Bonex Plan," which converted short-term

---

50. The designers of the Austral and Cruzado Plans had of course been aware of the need for accompanying fiscal adjustment. However, they could not convince their political superiors to take the necessary unpopular measures.

interest-earning bank deposits to 10-year dollar-denominated bonds. In March of the next year, Brazil adopted the similar Collor Plan that froze a large portion of bank deposits for a period of 18 months. The intention was broadly to reduce the effective money supply in a monetarist approach to reducing inflation.[51] One wag observed that both plans were of the "Chicago school." Asked whether he was referring to the views of monetarist Milton Friedman, he replied that he instead had those of Al Capone in mind.

Like their Austral and Cruzado predecessors, the Bonex and Collor plans amounted to gimmicks that gave a temporary but false impression of stability and failed without more fundamental fiscal adjustment. They tended to undermine future confidence in the banking system.[52]

Teams and Traumas

A clear pattern of recent Latin American experience is that where there is a combination of a forceful president with a skilled economic team, there are good chances for economic adjustment and stabilization. The key economic advisers to Chile's Augusto Pinochet, Mexico's Carlos Salinas, Venezuela's Carlos Andrés Pérez, and Argentina's Carlos Menem were all economists with PhD training from top US universities, and Salinas held a PhD himself.

The contrast between Venezuela and Argentina suggests, unfortunately, that public trauma may also contribute to the political scope for adjustment. In Argentina, the experience of hyperinflation so completely traumatized the public that it was ready for a complete repudiation of the past economic model. In contrast, inflation never reached the shock level in Venezuela, and the public tended to persist in the belief that it was possible to return to the easy times of earlier days.

Conclusion

Colombia, Chile, Mexico, Venezuela, and Argentina are among the key Latin American countries that have made impressive recoveries from the debt crisis of the 1980s. By 1994 there were encouraging signs that Brazil and Peru could begin to achieve the same outcome. In most cases, the key to successful recovery was the correction of fiscal imbalance.

---

51. By the "quantity theory" of money, $MV = PQ$, where M is money supply, V is the velocity at which it turns over, P is the average price level, and Q is the level of real output. With stable velocity and output, we have the result that an increase in the money supply causes an increase in prices: $\uparrow M[V] \rightarrow \uparrow P[Q]$.

52. However, it is at least arguable that they were necessary because otherwise the governments would have had to pay such high interest rates on short-term debt that domestic debt would have spiraled to unmanageably high levels.

The challenge facing these countries and the region more generally by 1993–94 was, first, to sustain the economic reforms that had been put in place at such high cost and to resist understandable political pressures for relaxation and a drift toward populist measures. Second, there was a challenge to avoid repeating the mistakes of the 1970s when there was overreliance on external capital and to exercise restraint on external deficits even if foreign capital could easily be obtained to finance them.

7

Debt Problems in the 1990s: Russia, Eastern Europe, and Sub-Saharan Africa

Latin America was the primary locus of the debt crisis of the 1980s. By the early 1990s a new debt problem had emerged in the former Soviet Union (FSU). At the same time, the politics and economics of the transition from communism in Eastern Europe revived the external debt issue for this region, which had actually preceded Latin America in entering into debt problems at the beginning of the 1980s. For its part, much of Africa remained in debt difficulties by the early 1990s, just as in the previous decade.

For the economies in transition and for Africa, the question of external debt tends to be more political and less economic than in the case of Latin America. Most of the debt of such countries as Brazil and Mexico has been owed to the private sector, primarily foreign banks. In contrast, most of the debt of several of the economies in transition is owed to foreign governments, typically in the form of export credits at near-market rates. Sub-Saharan Africa owes the bulk of its debt to international agencies and bilateral donors, on much more concessional terms.

A greater government creditor role inherently makes creditor strategy in debt problems more politically oriented. It also somewhat changes the calculus of the debtors, reducing considerations of the commercial market (such as secondary market price or eventual return to access) and increasing those of special political ties to creditors. The principal issues are thus determining the severity of the debt problem, evaluating the merits of alternative creditor responses and their relationship to debtor country economic policies, and designing the proper approach to parallel resolution of debt problems for the (minority share) private-sector creditors.

Russia

The external debt of the former Soviet Union stood at about $60 billion in 1990 and almost $80 billion by 1992 (World Bank 1993b, vol. 2), corresponding to the third rank among troubled debtor countries (below the total for Brazil and Mexico, and above that for Argentina). The collapse of communist rule in the USSR and disintegration of the union into 15 republics transformed this debt from blue chip to questionable status. At least initially the fundamental problem was not high indebtedness, but instead an unraveling of the center's control over exports and fiscal revenue and the plunge of the economy into deep recession and near hyperinflation.

The slide into troubled debtor status had already begun in 1990–91 before dissolution of the USSR. Arrears to Paris Club (bilateral export credit) lenders reached $5 billion by the end of 1990 (World Bank 1993b, vol. 2). In 1991, US banks refused to provide Commodity Credit Corporation lending on the usual terms and insisted instead on complete guarantee. By September 1991, the publication *Euromoney* had reduced the country credit ranking of the Soviet Union from 17th (in 1988) to 111th (Schulmann 1991).

Allocating the Debt

In December 1991, immediately after the dissolution of the Soviet Union, eight of the new FSU states signed an agreement with the Group of Seven (G-7) industrial countries providing that the external debt of the former Soviet Union would be the "joint and several liability" of the new states.[1] The G-7 had made this arrangement a condition for rescheduling Paris Club payments due.

The objective of the creditors was to assure that Russia would be responsible for the full extent of the debt, in view of the prospect that the smaller and weaker states might be unable to service their share. Armendariz and Williamson (1993) sharply criticized the arrangement. They pointed out that in other historical examples (the breakups of Gran Colombia and the Central American Federation in the early 19th century and the Austro-Hungarian and Ottoman Empires after World War I), debt had been allocated according to population, revenue, or other measures of economic size. They argued that the arrangement effectively placed an unfair burden on Russia and moreover created distorted incentives whereby an individual state could discontinue debt servicing in the expectation that other FSU members would have to pick up the tab.

---

1. The three Baltic states rejected any responsibility for the debt on grounds of their past involuntary membership of the USSR.

Table 7.1 FSU exports to non-FSU markets (millions of dollars)

	1991	1992	Export share 1992 (percent)	Population 1992 (millions)	Population share (percent)
I. Country data					
Armenia	86	12	0.0	3.7	1.3
Azerbaijan	3	754	1.5	7.3	2.5
Belarus	1,661	1,061	2.1	10.3	3.5
Estonia	..	300	0.6	1.6	0.6
Georgia	..	161	0.3	5.4	1.9
Kazakhstan	776	1,489	2.9	16.9	5.8
Kyrgyz Republic	4	76	0.1	4.5	1.5
Latvia	..	429	0.8	2.6	0.9
Lithuania	345	557	1.1	3.8	1.3
Moldova	155	118	0.2	4.4	1.5
Russian Federation	50,911	39,967	77.5	148.7	51.1
Tadjikistan	..	..	0.0	5.1	1.8
Turkmenistan	1,187	1,145	2.2	3.8	1.3
Ukraine[a]	5,200	4,600	8.9	52.2	17.9
Uzbekistan	677	869	1.7	20.6	7.1
TOTAL FSU	61,005	51,538	100	290.9	100
II. DOT, Partner trade data					
FSU	45,660	49,300	100		

.. = data not available.

DOT= IMF Direction of Trade Statistics.

a. IMF *Economic Review*; average of balance of payments and customs declaration estimates.

Source: Country data from IMF, *International Financial Statistics*, supplement.

As shown in table 7.1, on the basis of population alone Russia accounted for only about half of the FSU. However, Russia's exports to the rest of the world comprised a much larger share, an estimated 78 percent in 1992. Moreover, the Asian republics tended to have low per capita income, so that their economic size was smaller than indicated by their population shares. Thus, allocation of the debt based on economic capacity might have yielded a share of some two-thirds for Russia.

Ironically, Russian authorities were willing to assume not only joint and several liability but outright responsibility for the entire debt, so long as they could correspondingly lay claim to the entire foreign assets of the USSR. These assets included gold and foreign exchange and embassies abroad as well as a portfolio of loans (to such countries as India, Libya, Cuba, and Vietnam) nominally worth more than hard-currency debt (Armendariz and Williamson 1993, 14). In reality, these loans had an effective value far below external debt. Russia's willingness nonetheless to take over the entire debt and assets reflected the following considerations: a single creditor would be in a better position to collect on loans to other countries, fragmentation of assets such as embassies would make little sense, and Russia had the strongest resource base for servicing debt. It is also likely that Russian authorities saw assumption of the debt as appropriate for the state's hegemonic role within the FSU. This last reason was presumably why Ukraine opposed Russian assumption of the debt.

As it turned out, joint and several liability proved unworkable, as neither Russia nor the other states serviced debt in 1991 and most of 1992. The breakdown in turn acted as an obstacle to Paris Club lending. By mid-1992 Russia began negotiations with the other FSU states on "zero-option" agreements whereby Russia assumed the other states' shares of both debt and foreign assets. By late 1993 Russia had concluded final or tentative zero-option agreements with 10 of the 14 states (importantly including Ukraine), excepting only the three Baltic states and Georgia (World Bank 1993b).

Russian Debt Capacity

The FSU debt problem thus became the Russian debt problem. The appropriate strategy for dealing with the problem accordingly depended on the prospects for Russia's capacity to service the debt.

As in the majority of problem debtor experiences, Russia began to build up arrears in the absence of agreed arrangements with creditors. Arrears reached $11.8 billion by the end of 1992 and continued to rise in 1993. In addition, scheduled payments on interest and arrears for 1993 amounted to $20 billion, reflecting how short maturities had become as the USSR entered its final crisis phase. Russian authorities announced that the country could pay only $2.5 billion in 1993. An agreement with Paris Club creditors in April of 1993 rescheduled $13 billion in interest and principal due for the year. In July the government reached an interim agreement with commercial banks for partial payment of arrears.

These arrangements were merely transitory. The central issues of debt renegotiation remained to be resolved. These issues included the following:

- Should Russian debt be merely rescheduled or partially forgiven?

- If debt forgiveness were appropriate, how would it be handled in view of the large share of official claims rather than bank claims as in the Brady Plan?

- What should be the economic policy conditions for either approach?

- How much additional debt could Russia safely take on as part of its process of investment for structural transformation and growth?

The usual point of departure in examining whether debt forgiveness is necessary is to consider debt-carrying capacity. The more traditional dimension of this capacity concerns the "external transfer" and thus the size of debt-servicing obligations relative to the present and prospective export base. However, as suggested in chapter 4, it has become increasingly recognized that the "internal transfer problem" between the public and the government can also be a relevant constraint.

The dominant view has been that from the standpoint of the external transfer, at least, neither the USSR nor its successor debtor Russia was in a particularly heavily indebted position. This view has been based on the fact that the debt-exports ratio was considerably below the levels usually associated with severe debt problems (Schulmann 1991; Armendariz and Williamson 1993).

However, there are major data problems as well as real economic issues that cloud analysis of the problem. The data problem is that the level and trend of Russia's exports are seriously in doubt. There are at least three economic problems, just with respect to the external transfer. First, the zero-option Russian assumption of debt meant that the relevant debtbase was for the entire FSU, whereas the relevant export base shrank to that of Russia. Second, debt has been rising rapidly so that debt ratios for the late 1980s are out of date. Third, the state enterprises have increasingly gained autonomy (especially after corporatization in preparation for privatization), and they have consequently been able to sequester foreign exchange abroad. In these circumstances, the Russian government does not really dispose of all of the foreign exchange that would normally be inferred from the export figures to be available.

The net effect of these statistical and economic considerations was to give Russian debt a much more questionable appearance by 1992 than had been the case for Soviet debt in the late 1980s. More fundamentally, the economic collapse of the Russian economy by 1992–93 undermined the country's debt-servicing capacity regardless of the specific debt indicators, much as economic depression had done for many Latin American countries in the 1980s. Indeed, the collapse was more severe in Russia, where net material product fell by a cumulative 35 percent during 1991–93 and inflation averaged some 25 percent per month in 1992–93 (IMF 1993f, 85, 89).

As recently as late 1991, the Institute of International Finance, comprising the leading international banks, estimated USSR hard-currency debt at $55 billion and hard-currency export earnings at $40 billion (Schulmann 1991, 3–4). The organization concluded that "the Soviet Union is not a highly indebted country." Armendariz and Williamson reached the same conclusion, estimating 1989 external debt at $54 billion and the debt/exports ratio at 112 percent (implying exports of $49 billion), well below the threshold of 200 percent usually associated with creditworthiness risk.

However, the World Bank (1993b) has recently estimated that FSU exports were much higher at $83 billion in 1990, and that *Russian* exports by 1992 had fallen to $40 billion. At the same time, it reported that FSU/ Russian debt rose from $59.4 billion in 1990 to $78.7 billion.[2] If these data were accurate, it would imply a remarkable rise in the debt/exports ratio: from 72 percent in 1990 to 197 percent in 1992.

Annex 7A shows that such a rise in the debt/exports ratio is overstated by statistical illusion. If trade data reported by partners are used instead of official Russian data, FSU exports to non-FSU countries never reached anywhere near $83 billion, but instead held relatively steady over the past few years in the vicinity of $45 billion to $50 billion. The problem is data pollution arising from the dollar translation of ruble-based trade with Eastern European countries. If the Russian valuation of this trade is used, its dollar value is high; if the Eastern European partner country data reported to the International Monetary Fund are used, the value is much lower.

As shown in table 7.1, the partner data (converted from CIF to FOB by deducting 8 percent) place FSU exports to the rest of the world at $49.3 billion in 1992. If we assume that Russia exported 77 percent of this total (applying the trade shares in the IMF balance of payments export data to the partner trade data), Russia's exports outside the FSU amounted to $38 billion in 1992. Its debt/exports ratio thus stood at 207 percent in 1992, right at the traditional threshold for concern but still well below the levels of 300 to 400 percent or even higher that characterized most Latin American countries in the 1980s. Calculated on the same basis, the debt/exports ratio for the FSU stood at 127 percent in 1990 and 160 percent in 1992. Thus, with proper correction of the export base, there was a substantial rise in the FSU debt/exports ratio, but not by nearly as much as indicated by the IMF–World Bank estimates based on official Russian data. The corresponding ratio of total FSU debt to Russian exports stood at 164 percent in 1990 and 207 percent in 1992.

In sum, using partner trade data as superior to official Russian data, there has been no massive collapse in Russian or FSU exports. However, there has nonetheless been a major increase in the relevant debt/exports ratio. This increase is composed of two approximately equal parts: a proportionate increase of 30 percent ($1 - 1/.77$) caused by the consolidation of FSU debt into the sole responsibility of Russia and an additional proportionate increase of 26 percent in the debt/exports ratio even for the FSU as a whole. The result was to turn more problematical the earlier diagnoses that the debt was at a comfortable level.

The external transfer problem is worse once it is considered that enterprise export earnings are not automatically available to the domestic foreign exchange market and thus the government. In contrast, in the

---

2. The figure does not include $2 billion in interest arrears.

1980s most Latin American countries required that export earnings be converted into local currency.

External Assets and Capital Flight

Russia's external assets could be an important offset to its debt, although the line between inaccessible flight capital and potentially available foreign assets of the state is difficult to draw. Dollars and other hard currency circulating within Russia reportedly amount to some $15 billion to $20 billion (Fedorov [1994] cites the latter figure). Also, the Russian banking system accepts dollar deposits and places most of the funds abroad where the banks can obtain money market returns. At the end of 1993, these assets and other legal foreign holdings of Russian enterprises amounted to an estimated $18 billion (*Financial Times*, 7 February 1994, 11). These assets are sometimes called legal capital flight.

In addition, some estimates place unauthorized foreign bank holdings of a new class of wealthy individuals on the order of $13 billion (*Washington Post*, 27 February 1994, H1). Other accounts further indicate that the Communist Party holds several billion dollars abroad. The sum of all these categories of hard-currency assets could thus be on the order of $50 billion or more.

Furthermore, the government holds direct claims on many developing countries, often as the result of arms loans. Usually these loans were extended in rubles, and the government has attempted to establish the dollar exchange rate before the collapse of the ruble as the basis for the claims, whereas the debtors understandably have sought instead to value the debt at current (sharply devalued) ruble-dollar rates. Based on the government's valuation method, these claims amount to $150 billion (*Izvestia*, 2 July 1994, 2). In practice they may be worth on the order of $10 billion to $15 billion.

Two salient points emerge from consideration of all of these foreign assets. First, the amount the government could potentially mobilize would seem to be conservatively on the order of $25 billion or more. Indeed, in mid-1994 the head of Russia's privatization program not only stated that there was some $25 billion in flight capital abroad, but noted that it was beginning to return to Russia because of the shift in policy to high real interest rates (*Financial Times*, 5 July 1994, 2). Russia's net debt burden is thus considerably lower than suggested by the debt ratios just reviewed. Second, the estimates underscore the importance of establishing conditions that could bring back tens of billions of flight capital dollars. As analyzed in chapter 8, repatriation seems to have played a major role in the surge of private capital flows to Latin America in the early 1990s. A similar virtuous circle would seem possible for Russia as well, under the right circumstances.

Internal Transfer Problem

In 1992 Russia's fiscal deficit reached 20 percent of GDP (IMF 1993f, 86). In addition, central bank credit (largely to other FSU central banks and to Russian state enterprises) amounted to 23 percent of GDP (89); and arguably the bulk of these credits amounted to quasi-deficit spending because of unlikely repayment. The effective deficit was thus on the order of 30 to 40 percent of GDP. Under these circumstances, there is a massive internal transfer problem: insufficient resources are being transferred from the public to the government. This internal transfer problem adds a further constraint to the government's ability to service external debt.

There is an additional structural reason why Russia could face an internal transfer problem. The country is in the process of turning over state firm assets to private citizens, primarily existing workers in the firms, with minimal payment into state coffers. If a nation divides its assets among private groups but does not correspondingly assign these groups pro rata shares of the nation's liabilities (including foreign liabilities), then the public sector is increasing its net liability position. The result is the analogue of the much-criticized "socialization of the debt" in Latin America. That is, privatization of assets but not liabilities creates the same net increase in the burden on the general public that results from socialization of the debt.

That an internal transfer problem existed in Russia in the early 1990s was beyond dispute, as witnessed by the deficit ratios and the near hyperinflation. What was less clear was how quickly fiscal balance could be restored to close the internal transfer gap, and whether it was appropriate for foreign creditors to incur any of the burden of closing this gap through debt forgiveness.

Lessons From Latin America

In considering the right debt strategy for Russia, it is useful to draw upon experience from the Latin American debt crisis. As discussed in chapters 5 and 6, the quality of domestic economic policies turned out to be the most important determinant of success in dealing with the debt problem. Those countries with the best policies (Colombia, Chile, and Mexico) tended to emerge the soonest and most decisively from the debt problem, even though in some instances they faced more difficult debt burdens (Chile had an initially high debt ratio, and Mexico suffered from the oil price collapse in 1986). Moreover, among the domestic economic policies, fiscal balance emerged as the single most important element.

The implication for Russia is clear. Until the domestic economy is stabilized, it is unlikely that any meaningful resolution of the external debt problem can be achieved. Stabilization will require closing the massive fiscal and quasi-fiscal gap. However, it does not follow that the best approach is an intensification of the shock treatment that arguably has been responsible for the collapse in domestic production. Similarly, too narrow a target for the fiscal deficit itself may simply mean that the quasi-fiscal deficit through the central bank is more out of control, as that entity lends to keep state firms afloat (Tanzi 1993).

Appropriate domestic economic policy in Russia seems likely to require a more innovative approach than the orthodox shock treatment that has so far been attempted (but not enforced). The great bulk of the labor force has been employed by state firms. It is unrealistic and inequitable to seek fiscal and quasi-fiscal balance by throwing a large portion of this workforce onto the street. That is why the central bank systematically lent heavily to state firms in the course of 1992–93, derailing monetary stabilization. Nor is privatization an automatic solution. The model chosen will essentially leave a social compact between the existing workers and managers whereby the former do not question actions of the latter (potentially including questionable use of enterprise resources) so long as the latter do not displace the former. Under these circumstances, many of the privatized firms will soon be back requesting central bank financing.

What would seem to be needed is what may be called a "triage" approach (Cline 1994). Support from the center would be cut off for those state firms that are egregious in excessive employment and production of goods with little value. Support would be focused on those firms that have good chances for achieving productivity (evaluated at appropriate "shadow prices" for foreign exchange) and quality close to world market standards. Support would be cut off for the most successful firms too prosperous to need it. To the extent possible, support from the center would be redirected to occur directly through the budget rather than in a disguised way through central bank credit. The central objective would be to revive the devastated level of production and move the system toward responsiveness to the price mechanism (through privatization), while at the same time avoiding massive labor displacement.

If the importance of coherent domestic policy is the foremost lesson from the Latin American debt crisis, the utility of a market-oriented, cooperative approach on external debt is a close second. As shown in Chapter 6, there is a close correlation between the degree of cooperativeness on external debt and the overall resulting economic performance of economies. Colombia and Chile stood at the top of the list in cooperation with foreign banks on external debt and also had the best overall economic performance over the course of the debt-crisis decade (measured by economic growth per capita and price stability). Peru, and to a lesser extent Brazil and Argentina, had confrontational debt strategies and ran arrears for long periods of time. Among the seven major countries of the region, Peru ranked worst on economic outcome over the decade, and Argentina and Brazil ranked well below the countries with more cooperative strategies (Colombia, Chile, Mexico, and Venezuela).

Debt Strategy Alternatives

By 1993–94 Russian authorities faced two basic alternative strategies on external debt. The first was to pursue debt reduction: forgiveness (although Russian sovereign pride was unlikely to be comfortable with that term) of some portion of both Paris Club and private bank debt. The case of Poland offered a precedent for a country in systemic transition. This second alternative was to seek a long-term rescheduling but not forgiveness of debt, and to work toward development of energy and other exports and pursue private capital inflow as key elements in a market-oriented recovery from the debt problem. The second alternative required the belief that the Russian economy was only temporarily in chaos, and that within a period of three to five years a much more stable and productive economy would be in place. Otherwise the inconsistency of accumulating further debt on a continued weak economic base would arise.

Through 1993 and early 1994 the official Russian position was that the country was not seeking debt forgiveness. However, in August 1994 Minister of Foreign Economic Relations Oleg Davydov stated that some of Russia's debt should be forgiven in recognition of the country's contribution to disarmament. Other key economic officials (including Deputy Prime Minister Alexander Shokin) promptly denied that a request for debt forgiveness was official policy (AP–Dow Jones and Reuters, 17 August 1994; Itar-Tass, 24 August 1994). Clearly the debate on debt forgiveness was underway.

As of 30 June 1993 Russia owed $39.2 billion in medium- and long-term (MLT) debt to official creditors (mainly Paris Club), $25.2 billion in MLT debt to commercial banks, $4.4 billion in short-term debt to commercial banks, $1.7 billion in bonds, and $11 billion in other debt (mainly short-term debt to official creditors; World Bank 1993b, vol. 2). Official sources thus accounted for about $50 billion out of a total external debt of about $80 billion. As noted, this structure meant that "Brady Plan" debt reduction focusing only on private long-term claims was not of the highest relevance to Russia. Instead, the main question was whether official creditors should be asked to forgive debt, as they had in the case of Poland where they reduced claims by half.

The experience of Latin America suggests that countries that can avoid debt forgiveness are able to obtain better lending terms in the future. As noted in chapter 6, by 1992–93 the spreads above US Treasury rates for bonds for Chile were less than 100 basis points, whereas for Argentina and Venezuela they were on the order of 300 to 400 basis points or more. Similarly, statistical tests in chapter 8 identify a spread premium of 75 basis points for countries that have resorted to Brady forgiveness. Moreover, it seems likely that the volume of capital available to Russia will be greater in an approach that does not seek debt forgiveness. If the domestic rate of return on foreign capital is high, access to greater capital volume can provide important gains.

Latin American experience also suggests the value of a contingent-staged approach. In the first stage, the strategy is based on the notion that the country can work its way out of the problem without forgiveness. Upon reexamination, in a second stage the strategy stays with relending if the country is doing well on exports and domestic economic performance but shifts to forgiveness if export growth and domestic stability are far below expectation (especially if external shock is a major reason).

Consider two alternative debt strategies for Russia, designated as DROL for debt rollover and DRED for debt reduction. Essentially, the two approaches correspond to the Baker and Brady Plans, respectively (but with "Brady" here being understood to encompass bilateral official as well as private forgiveness). Suppose that under DROL, the borrowing spread is a flat 100 basis points; under DRED, the spread begins at 500 basis points and falls over 7 years to 150 basis points. Suppose that new capital inflow under DROL amounts to $10 billion annually, rising to $16 billion annually by the seventh year (in constant prices). Under DRED, the new inflow is only $1 billion annually, rising to $7 billion by the seventh year. Under both cases, the domestic return on foreign capital is 20 percent in the first two years, falling to 15 percent in the next two, 12 percent in the next two, and 10 percent thereafter.

Assume that a debt reduction strategy eliminates 40 percent of Russia's debt. The Polish precedent of 50 percent was declared exceptional by the Paris Club, and the banks have insisted that Russia has not had a severe debt problem, so a 50 percent cut would seem unlikely. A cut of 40 percent against a debt base of some $80 billion would provide a gain of $32 billion in base-year constant dollars.

Now consider the alternative of debt rollover with new borrowing. As indicated in the illustrative table 7.2, the opportunity to invest a larger amount of capital inflow at the very high domestic rates of return initially characterizing the economy under acute foreign exchange and capital scarcity means that there are potentially large advantages of the DROL strategy that must be compared with the windfall gain of debt forgiveness under the DRED strategy. Not only are the volumes of capital inflow greater, but the unit borrowing costs are also lower under DROL, as the country remains more integrated with capital markets and sovereign risk is perceived as lower. Summing the cumulative net real earnings on each year's tranche of capital inflow, net gains over the seven years amount to $30 billion (at constant prices) under DROL and

Table 7.2 Russia: alternative debt strategies (billions of
                dollars and percentages)

Year:	1	2	3	4	5	6	7	Total
I. DROL								
Exports ($ bn nom.)	40	45.3	51.3	58.2	65.9	74.7	84.6	....
New Loans ($ bn real)	10	11	12	13	14	15	16	91
Real return (%)	20	20	15	15	12	12	10	...
Real cost (%)	4	4	4	4	4	4	4	...
Cumulative real net earnings	7.6	6.6	5.3	4.3	3.1	2.1	1.0	29.9
(7 yrs) ($ bn real)								
II. DRED								
Exports ($ bn nom.)	40	43.7	47.7	52.1	56.8	62.1	67.8	...
New Loans ($ bn real)	1	2	3	4	5	6	7	28
Real return (%)	20	20	15	15	12	12	10	...
Real cost (%)	8	8	7	7	6	6	4.5	...
Cumulative real net earnings	0.5	0.7	0.9	0.8	0.8	0.6	0.4	4.7
(7 yrs) ($ bn real)								

... = not applicable.

DROL = debt rollover ; DRED = Debt reduction.
World inflation: 3 percent;

Real international interest rate: 3 percent;
Real export growth: DROL = 10 percent DRED = 6 percent

only $5 billion under DRED. There is thus an advantage of $25 billion for
the DROL strategy.

This advantage is of comparable scale to the $32 billion windfall gain
from forgiveness under the DRED strategy. In this illustration, the country is approximately indifferent between the two strategies for the
seven-year period in question, at least on the basis of the direct gains.
However, the DROL strategy does build up more debt. Assuming that
real interest payments on preexisting debt are paid from trade surpluses, debt at the end of the period equals the initial stock plus cumulative real borrowing, all converted to end-period prices. Under DROL,
nominal debt by year 7 is $202 billion.[3] If, as in table 7.2, it is assumed
that this strategy is associated with an outward-oriented, high export
growth performance, at 10 percent real annual export growth, nominal
exports rise to $85 billion.[4] As a result, despite the rapid debt buildup,
the debt/exports ratio at the end of the period is 239 percent, not sharply
above either the initial level of 207 percent or the notional warning

3. That is: $79 billion initial debt plus $91 billion cumulative real new net borrowing,
inflated to year 7 prices.

4. On average, the following group of developing countries achieved real export growth
rate of 10 percent annually during 1980–90: South Korea, Malaysia, Singapore, Taiwan,
Hong Kong, Colombia, Thailand, and Turkey (World Bank 1992b).

threshold of 200 percent.[5] With GDP estimated by the IMF at $515 billion in 1990 on a purchasing-parity basis (or some $700 billion by year 7 allowing for world inflation and Russian growth), the terminal debt would stand at 28 percent of GDP, a substantial but not overwhelming level.[6] By comparison, in 1991 the average debt/GNP ratio stood at 41.3 percent for Latin America and the Caribbean and 28.2 percent for East Asia and the Pacific (World Bank 1993c, 285). Moreover, the estimates in the exercise here omit the potentially large external assets discussed above, and thus they exaggerate rather than understate the prospective debt burden.

In contrast to the DROL scenario, the table assumes that under the DRED strategy export growth is lower (6 percent real). Nominal debt by year 7 stands at $89 billion.[7] The terminal debt/exports ratio is thus 132 percent. There is thus less of a potential external transfer problem at the end of the period. Although lower external debt means a lower net *foreign* liability position, it does not mean a higher *total* net asset position for the country including domestic assets. If the new borrowing has been invested in domestic assets, the balance sheet shows both higher foreign debt and higher domestic assets under DROL than under DRED at the end of the period, but not lower total net assets. Instead, as shown above, the net real total asset difference is minimal, because the greater opportunity for investment at high domestic return under DROL approximately compensates for the windfall liability reduction under DRED.

An important implication of the exercise in table 7.2 is that if net borrowing were still larger than the range of $10 billion to $15 billion annually in the DROL scenario, Russia's external debt indicators might begin to be uncomfortably high, although again the analysis omits offsetting external assets. The entry of a large component of capital in non-debt-creating forms—direct investment flows or repatriation of capital (including that held by state enterprises)—could ameliorate any emerging external transfer overhang. However, this range of magnitudes is useful for placing some boundary on the plausible amount of foreign capital flows to Russia on the basis of lending at market rates. By implication, if Russian and G-7 authorities concluded that far larger flows were required, the incremental amounts beyond a threshold of perhaps

5. Note moreover that the usual rule of thumb includes service exports in the denominator, whereas the discussion here abstracts from any nonmerchandise exports.

6. The IMF's estimate for purchasing-parity per capita GDP for the FSU in 1990 is $3,430 (IMF 1993c, 85). Applying Russian population of 150 million (table 7.1), the result is GDP of $515 billion. This estimate is biased downward from the standpoint that Russian per capita income should exceed that of most other FSU republics.

7. That is: initial debt of $79 billion, less $32 billion forgiven, plus $28 billion borrowed, all in constant prices, and inflating to year 7 prices.

some $15 billion annually might have to come on a concessional basis in order to avoid excessive buildup of debt-servicing obligations.

In sum, under plausible assumptions a technical comparison shows that a debt rollover strategy can provide benefits to Russia comparable to a debt reduction strategy. The ultimate difference depends in part on how closely the economy is integrated into the world capital and goods markets at the end of the period. On this criterion, the debt rollover strategy is likely to be superior. Thus, the gap between the interest spread under DROL and DRED is unlikely to be eliminated by the seventh year, and the export base is likely to be considerably higher under DROL. Clearly the assumptions of the exercise in table 7.2 can be varied to make DROL more or less favorable compared to DRED. However, the main message of the calculations is that if Russian authorities choose to do so, they could leave the economy equally well or even better off at the end of a seven-year period through adopting essentially the Chilean strategy of debt rollover and export expansion rather than by pursuing the Polish strategy of debt forgiveness. This conclusion is reinforced if allowance is made for substantial foreign assets, as discussed above.

There are, of course, other fundamental considerations that would have to be addressed in determining whether Russia should be granted debt forgiveness along Polish lines. One concerns the relative levels of indebtedness. In 1991–92, Poland's ratio of net debt to exports of goods and services stood at 260–270 percent (chapter 2, table 2.3; table 7.3 below). The corresponding 1991 ratio of gross debt to merchandise exports (the concept used in the discussion here) was approximately 340 percent (calculated from IMF 1992a), or almost two-thirds larger than that of Russia.

A second issue is equity. Any forgiveness of Paris Club claims involves a grantlike transfer from the publics of industrial countries to that of the debtor country. Whereas such transfers are consistent with international equity considerations when the country is a low-income developing country (such as the countries eligible for concessional assistance from the International Development Association), they are less clearly so when the debtor is middle income. Despite the ludicrously low levels of estimated per capita income for Russia when evaluated at the (distressed) market exchange rate, on a purchasing-parity basis Russia's income level at over $3,000 per capita is squarely within the middle-income group (World Bank 1992b).

Adoption of a debt rollover strategy would require dealing with the problem of free-rider private banks, the classic problem of mobilizing "new" lending to roll over principal and the bulk of interest coming due. In the Russian case, a large portion of bank debt is owed to German banks. Given that in the 1980s debt crisis European banks were at least initially favorable to the idea of capitalization of interest as a vehicle for refinancing interest due (a proposal that caused severe regulatory difficulties for US banks), it is possible that this approach would warrant consideration. US and other banks that preferred to do so could refinance a large fraction of interest through new loans or new-money bonds. It seems likely, however, that the banks could mobilize capital by one means or another to refinance most interest due if they continued to adhere to the position that Russia was not overindebted. It would be unrealistic to expect them to finance more than that. As a result, the net capital inflows assumed in table 7.2 would have to come primarily from bilateral and multilateral sources, plus a growing share from bond and other portfolio finance from the private sector.

In terms of political economy, it is by no means clear that the government of Boris Yeltsin will have the room for maneuver to make debt decisions on technical grounds such as those considered here. The strong performance of extremist Vladimir Zhirinovsky in the parliamentary elections of December 1993 suggested that the political constraints on government economic policy could intensify. One possibility was that these constraints could press the government toward a position that would more actively seek Polish-style debt forgiveness. On the other hand, one of the chief critiques of the radical right was that the reformers had stripped the Soviet Union of its former grandeur. There could thus be a political stigma attached to formal forgiveness of debt, on grounds that a great nation does not ask for such largesse.

On the policy supply side, the specter of a future extreme rightist in charge of Russian ICBMs had the potential to shift the Western official community in the direction of debt forgiveness. The problem for the West was substantially complicated by the lack of a persuasive economic model for Russian transition. It was highly appropriate to make economic support and especially major debt forgiveness conditional on proper domestic policy. However, it was by no means clear that the proper policy was an orthodox austerity program of the type attempted (but not fully carried out) in 1992–93.

The discussion above suggests certain areas for policy conditions. One has to do with the somewhat bizarre evolution of a situation in which the state is the complete or majority shareholder of state firms but is unwilling or unable to lay claim to the firms' assets. As discussed, an appropriate reform in the privatization process would be to assign to each privatized firm a pro rata share of Russia's external debt.[8] The Russian government could still *guarantee* this debt, but the newly privatized enterprise would bear responsibility for it—much in the same way as the Chilean government guaranteed private external debt but made the private sector pay for it (chapter 6). An important related

---

8. For firms generating foreign exchange, this share of debt would be denominated in dollars. For other firms, it would be denominated in ruble equivalent, presumably with appropriate indexation against inflationary erosion.

reform would be for the government to press the state firms to repatriate their external assets. As a larger fraction of the economy becomes privatized, it could similarly become necessary to require even private firms to convert foreign exchange earnings into domestic currency, as was the general practice in Latin America in the 1980s. Without the first reform, the Russian state will be placing itself in jeopardy on the internal transfer problem; without the second reform, it will be doing so on the external transfer problem.[9]

On balance, by 1994 there were technical arguments for a Russian debt strategy modeled after the Baker Plan/Chilean approach, at least as a contingent strategy subject to review after evidence on export performance, response of capital inflows, and improving domestic economic conditions. This conclusion is reinforced if one takes into account Russia's external assets. However, there were political pressures that seemed capable of pushing the strategy to a Brady Plan/Polish approach emphasizing debt forgiveness at the possible expense of subsequent integration into world capital and trade markets.

Eastern Europe

Debt strategy in Eastern Europe may be divided into two models: the Polish and the Czech-Hungarian. The Polish model was characterized by excessive debt buildup, followed by chronic debt reschedulings and eventually extraordinary official relief, with strong influence of political considerations. The Czech-Hungarian model instead featured greater internal and external economic prudence and pursuit of a favorable creditworthiness record. Bulgaria followed the Polish model. In contrast, Romania followed an extreme and costly version of the Czech-Hungarian model. Civil war obscured which path Yugoslavia otherwise might have followed.

Eastern Europe experienced a debt crisis similar and prior to that of Latin America. Poland triggered the crisis in 1981, when acute foreign exchange shortage forced the country to negotiate large debt rescheduling agreements with official and commercial bank creditors. In the 1970s an ambitious program of industrial investment financed by external borrowing had failed to generate enough export capacity to service the resulting debt. The eventual need to curtail imports brought recession

---

9. The issue of Russian exchange rate convertibility for the capital account is a complicated one that the discussion here will not seek to resolve. Certainly such experiences as that of Venezuela in the 1980s suggest that assured convertibility when domestic policies are distorted can be a recipe for capital flight. However, to the extent that the exchange rate floats rather than being held at a preset official crawl, the capital flight problem is ameliorated. Moreover, capital controls require effective administration, a service in short supply in contemporary Russia.

that cut domestic product by more than one-fourth from 1978 to 1992 (Balcerowicz 1994, 154).

From the start, the Polish debt crisis of the 1980s was heavily influenced by geopolitics. Imposition of martial law in December 1981 and repression of the Solidarity movement induced trade sanctions by Western governments and a suspension of debt talks. US authorities came close to declaring Poland in default. Under these circumstances, there was a chill on private capital markets that extended to the region more generally. In 1982 and again in 1983, Poland negotiated the rollover of 95 percent of private bank claims coming due, with a tie-in clause that essentially refinanced half (and later two-thirds) of interest coming due through side commitments on increased trade credits (Cline 1984, 279–80). After the lifting of martial law in August 1983, Western governments resumed rescheduling negotiations on official debt.

From 1981 through 1990, Poland had five reschedulings of official debt and seven for commercial bank claims, with about one-third of the reschedulings involving as much as $10 billion in principal and interest due (World Bank 1993b, 1: 94–97). With this background, it was not surprising that when the communist military government ceded power to a democratically elected government led by Solidarity in late 1989, international political support through debt relief was on the agenda.

In early 1990 the new government adopted a radical program of macroeconomic stabilization (in the face of hyperinflation) combined with structural transformation. As the then finance minister has written:

> The Polish economic program had, since its earliest incarnation, devoted special attention to dealing with the foreign debt. The goal here was to achieve a radical debt reduction, in the first place from the official creditors (who hold about two-thirds of the total debt). We assumed that the pioneering role of Poland in the political transition of Eastern Europe and the radical nature of its economic transition made such a goal realistic. The debt reduction was viewed in turn as a factor that increased the chances for success of economic stabilization and transformation. (Balcerowicz 1994, 160)

Poland asked the Paris Club to forgive 80 percent of bilateral claims. In the spring of 1991, the Paris Club agreed effectively to forgive 50 percent (although primarily through interest rather than principal reduction), to be phased in over three years.[10] Shortly thereafter these industrial country creditors also forgave 50 percent of Egypt's bilateral debt, on similar

---

10. US officials led the campaign for deep reduction of Polish debt. The negotiations took place primarily in the G-7, where the United States called for a 55 percent reduction of bilateral claims but other members initially favored no forgiveness at all (David Mulford, interview, 19 November 1994). Despite the low share of the United States in claims in Poland on official and especially bank debt, in view of the country's pivotal political position (rightly perceived by Balcerowicz) the US position ultimately prevailed.

terms (*Financial Times*, 28 May 1991). Previously, Paris Club forgiveness had been limited to one-third and restricted to low-income countries ("Toronto terms," discussed below). The creditors called the two arrangements "exceptional" (World Bank 1992a, 1: 77). Even so, Japanese authorities in particular expressed concern about precedential effects and the possible adverse impact on new lending (*Japan Times*, 3 April 1991).

Officials of G-7 countries insisted that private banks forgive a comparable portion of their claims on Poland. However, the 50 percent forgiveness appeared rich to the banks, whose cuts for the principal Latin American debtors under the Brady Plan had not exceeded 35 percent (even though the Latin debtors had relatively heavier debt burdens, as discussed below). By late 1993, the banks still had not come to agreement with Poland, and interest and principal arrears amounting to about one-third of bank claims persisted (World Bank 1993b, vol. 2). However, by March 1994 the government had reached agreement with the banks that involved forgiveness equivalent to 45 cents on the dollar (Salomon Brothers 1994b).

In broad terms, Poland's way of dealing with the debt resembled what Fishlow has called the "revenue default," in reference to the politically oriented debt defaults and forgiveness earlier in the twentieth century (e.g., German default on the politically inspired loans under the Dawes and Young plans in the interwar period), as contrasted with "developmental defaults" in Latin American countries in the late 19th century (in which temporary terms-of-trade collapses interrupted growth financed by external capital; see chapter 4).

Bulgaria pursued the Polish model. In Bulgaria too, excessive foreign borrowing had been used to spur growth and sustain living standards in the 1970s (especially after the delayed increase in Soviet oil prices eventually arrived). In the late 1970s, the apparent willingness of the USSR to stand as lender of last resort gave the foreign banks sufficient comfort that they continued to lend relatively heavily through the 1980s.[11]

By the early 1990s, bad luck added to the consequences of questionable earlier policies. The Gulf War adversely affected Bulgaria's exports to, and claims on, Iraq. Bulgaria had an exceptionally high share of exports going to the Soviet Union, and thus it was affected more than most other countries by the collapse of the Council for Mutual Economic Assistance (COMECON) as the bloc's trade shifted to a hard-currency basis. The country was also geographically in the wrong place during this period, because civil war in former Yugoslavia disrupted export routes to Western Europe.

---

11. Long-term debt to banks rose from $2.6 billion in 1985 to $6.7 billion in 1990 (World Bank 1993b, vol. 2).

It is difficult to document the impact of these effects, because trade data for Bulgaria appear to be at least as chaotic as those for the FSU.[12] If the lowest of the export data series from the various sources is used (IMF 1993d), Bulgaria's debt/exports ratio by 1992 was closer to 500 percent than to the 200 percent range indicated by the World Bank (table 7.3).

Perhaps in part for this reason, by 1993 the International Monetary Fund judged that Bulgaria faced a "large inherited overhang" of debt from the previous regime in Bulgaria, and that "a lack of progress toward an agreement with its commercial creditors on a comprehensive debt and debt-service reduction deal has undermined its trade performance" (IMF 1993b, 59). Paris Club creditors agreed that relief was necessary and cut claims coming due over a two-year period by 50 percent in 1991 and again in 1993. For their part, the banks reached a London Club agreement with Bulgaria in November 1993 to reduce claims by 50 percent (*Financial Times*, 26 November 1993). Bank claims had represented the bulk of external debt, the reverse of the Polish profile.

In contrast to the Polish and Bulgarian cases, in Hungary, the former Czechoslovakia, and Romania there has been no attempt to secure political "revenue default" relief. One reason is that Czechoslovakia and Hungary never accumulated as much debt as Poland. At the same time, these two countries pursued borrowing strategies based more on market principles than on political considerations. In late 1991, the managing director of the banks' Institute of International Finance summarized the difference:

> As is well known, Poland's relations with its external creditors have been fairly stormy in the past ten years. Poland has totally lost market access. . . . The contrast with Hungary is striking. . . . Hungary has painstakingly serviced its external debt and maintained market access both before and after the revolution of 1989. Czechoslovakia is another success story. . . . Czechoslovakia will make a bond issue in Frankfurt this week—the first since the end of World War II. (Schulmann 1991)

There were, of course, similar pressures on all of these economies in the transition from communism. All of the Eastern European countries suffered a severe shock in 1991 from the collapse of COMECON trade,

---

12. The IIF (1990) reported that Bulgaria's exports in 1985 had amounted to $4.6 billion in hard currency and $8.8 billion in nonconvertible currency, with the corresponding levels at $3.1 billion and $11 billion by 1989. This level of $14 billion total exports is radically at odds with IMF (1992d) data, which show total exports at $2.5 billion in 1985, $2.8 billion in 1989, and $2.2 billion by 1991. Subsequent IMF (1993d) data show instead a constant plateau of exports at about $2.1 billion annually from 1986 through 1992. In contrast, as shown in table 7.3, the World Bank gives an intermediate export estimate of about $6 billion in 1992. However, the World Bank series showed that exports had been as high as $11.5 billion in 1985.

Table 7.3 Debt indicators for Eastern Europe, 1992 (billions of dollars and percentages)

	Bulgaria	Czechoslovakia	Hungary	Poland	Romania	Yugoslavia[a]
External debt	12.2	9.3	21.9	48.5	3.5	16.3
XGNFS	5.9	15.5	13.5	18.7	5.0	16.3
Interest (accrual)	1.1	0.5	1.8	4.7	0.1	0.9
Interest/XGNFS (percent)	18.2	3.4	13.2	25.4	2.5	5.7
Debt/XGNFS (percent)	207.7	60.2	162.7	259.4	70.1	100.2
Arrears						
Interest	1.54	0	0	3.28	0	0
Principal	5.02	0	0	2.86	0	0.91
Commercial bank debt	6.82	2.02	6.41	9.27	0	4.73
Export growth 1985–92 (percent/year)	–10.0	–1.5	1.9	3.0	–6.0	3.9

XGNFS = exports of goods and nonfactor services.

a. 1991.

Source: World Bank 1993a; IMF, 1993g.

primarily with the Soviet Union, and from the deterioration of terms of trade as the USSR eliminated subsidized oil exports. Macroeconomic restraint and the disruption associated with structural transition further aggravated recession, and for 1990–91 domestic output fell by nearly one-fourth in Eastern Europe as a whole (IMF 1992b). Nonetheless, Hungary and Czechoslovakia did not seek debt relief.

Nor did Romania. Indeed, after the chill on new commercial lending in the early 1980s demonstrated the financial vulnerability of Eastern Europe, Romania's President Nicolae Ceaușescu embarked on an extreme program to repay the debt. The country's long-term debt to commercial banks fell from $4.2 billion in 1980 to zero by 1989 (World Bank 1993b, vol. 2). The austerity required to purchase this complete financial independence was severe, and surely contributed to Ceaușescu's violent downfall in December 1989.

Table 7.3 reports World Bank debt indicators for Eastern Europe in 1992. Three countries in the region have light debt: Romania, Czechoslovakia, and Yugoslavia—all with debt/exports ratios of 100 percent or less, and interest/exports ratios in single digits. According to these estimates, Bulgaria and Hungary have intermediate debt burdens, with debt/exports ratios on the order of 160 to 200 percent and interest/exports ratios of 13 to 18 percent. However, as noted the debt/exports ratio for Bulgaria is on the order of 500 percent if IMF export data are used.[13]

Some observers suggest that Hungary's debt burden is extremely high.[14] If so, the difficulty would seem to stem primarily from an internal transfer problem. The debt/exports ratio is not particularly high, but the debt/GNP ratio of 65 percent in 1992 is higher than that of Latin America at its peak (51 percent in 1989; World Bank 1993b). Interest payments amounted to 5.5 percent of GNP. Under these circumstances, a nation might be able to extract sizeable short-term windfall gains by shifting to a strategy of requesting debt forgiveness, even if otherwise creditors would continue capital market access on grounds of a good past credit record.

However, longer-term consequences of such a shift could be less favorable. Moreover, although the debt/ and interest/GNP ratios are higher for Hungary than they were for the large, closed Latin American economies (Brazil and Mexico), they are considerably lower than these ratios reached for more open Chile, where in 1985 the debt/GNP ratio reached 141.7 percent and the interest/GNP ratio 13.5 percent (World Bank 1993b, vol. 2). Yet Chile successfully pursued a credit reputation-maximizing strategy and eschewed Brady forgiveness.

13. There is no substantial discrepancy between World Bank (table 7.3) and IMF (1994a) estimates of goods and services for Hungary.

14. Richard Portes, personal communication with author, 20 May 1994.

Poland is the largest Eastern European debtor, with nearly $50 billion in obligations. If the IMF balance of payments accrual data are used (as in table 7.3), Poland's interest/exports ratio in 1992 was approximately 25 percent. If instead interest actually paid is considered, the interest/exports ratio for 1992 stood at only 6 percent (calculated from World Bank 1993b, vol. 2). Although the debt/exports ratio remained at about 260 percent, this indicator did not yet reflect the alleviation provided through reduction of Paris Club interest in the 1991 agreement.

With the possible exceptions of Poland and Bulgaria, no country in the region has external transfer debt indicators of the severity typical of the Latin American countries that received Brady Plan debt reduction. Thus, in 1989 on the eve of the Brady Plan, the interest/exports ratio ranged from a low of 27 percent to a high of 51 percent for Venezuela, Mexico, Brazil, and Argentina (listed in ascending severity); the debt/exports ratio, from 257 percent to 538 percent (ECLAC 1993).

Whereas the Polish-Bulgarian strategy did achieve substantial forgiveness, the Czech-Hungarian strategy has secured greater market creditworthiness. The secondary market price for private debt stood at 35 cents on the dollar for Poland in the third quarter of 1993, versus 65 cents for Hungary. Czechoslovakia enjoyed an investment-grade rating of BBB (Standard and Poors), the same as that for Chile; Hungary, a rating of BB+. In contrast, Poland was not even rated. Similarly, in the period 1991–92, Hungary floated $2.47 billion in international bond issues and Czechoslovakia, $294 million; Poland floated none (World Bank 1993d).

The next steps for debt policy in Eastern Europe would appear to be as follows. For the Czech Republic and Slovakia, and for Hungary, adherence to the existing strategy of integration with the world credit market makes the most sense. The 13 percent interest/exports ratio in Hungary is too light to warrant jeopardizing the impressive credit record the country has built up, a result that could occur if the country shifted to a policy of seeking debt forgiveness. Three-fourths of Hungary's long-term debt is private; and the private debt is evenly divided between bonds (until now strictly exempt from forgiveness in the international debt strategy) and bank loans. Interest on Hungary's long-term bank debt is only about 2 percent of export earnings, so the savings from a Brady cut would be minimal. The same is even more true for the more lightly indebted Czechoslovakia (not to mention Romania).

For Poland, the tentative March 1994 Brady deal with the banks presumably closes the books on debt forgiveness. Yugoslav debt is something of an enigma. The nation repeatedly rescheduled its debt in the 1980s with both official and commercial creditors (World Bank 1993b, 1: 94–97). Private interest arrears stand at nearly $1 billion, as might be expected with the disruption of civil war. Yet the debt indicators do not show particularly heavy indebtedness. Conceivably, when and if a peace accord is reached, Polish-style official debt forgiveness might provide a contribution to postwar reconstruction. Such relief would nonetheless be modest: bilateral claims stand at only $3.6 billion, compared with an export base of $16 billion.

Two final considerations provide important nuances on these diagnoses. First, for several of the Eastern European countries, exports have fallen in nominal dollar terms since the mid-1980s (see the export growth rates in table 7.3). It is reasonable to expect some rebound of exports, as the countries shift their markets from the CMEA to the European Union and other countries, and as the transition from communism reaches a more stable phase. The "cyclically adjusted" debt ratios would thus be somewhat more favorable than shown in table 7.3, because their denominators would rise with more normal export levels.

Second, and pointing in the opposite policy direction, the debt burdens may be substantial in terms of "internal transfer" as opposed to external transfer (chapter 4). The economies in transition have experienced severe fiscal problems. Moreover, their exchange rates can be extremely undervalued, making the dollar debt-servicing obligation high as a percent of GDP. However, this distortion too should moderate as the transition enters a more normalized phase and higher exports begin to provide the underpinnings for a real appreciation in the exchange rate.

Sub-Saharan Africa[15]

The popular image of African debt depicts a subcontinent mired in hopeless overindebtedness that thwarts attempts to grow out of extreme poverty. The usual solution seen for this problem is politically courageous action on both sides: by creditor governments in the forgiveness of a large portion of their claims and by debtor governments in the adoption of serious economic reform, including in such "governance" spheres as anticorruption efforts.

At the same time, it is well known that the African debt problem did not arise from the same origins as that of Latin America. Most debt in Africa is from bilateral and multilateral official sources, not from syndicated lending by private commercial banks. This fundamental difference

---

15. The analysis here omits South Africa and Namibia, in part because they are excluded from the published data of the World Bank's debt reporting system (World Bank 1993b). South Africa did encounter payments difficulties and reached rescheduling agreements with commercial banks in 1986 and after. However, its external debt of about $20 billion (CIA 1991) is small compared to its exports of $24 billion (IMF 1994a). Thus, in 1992 the finance minister called the amounts coming due at the end of 1993 under the third in a series of interim arrangements with the banks "exceptionally modest" (Hughes, O'Malley, and Couldry 1992, 26).

should immediately suggest important distinctions in the proper design of the solution. Considerations of donor political will are more important, and those of private credit market "memory" less important, than was the case for Latin America.

The analysis that follows will show that the African debt problem is sharply differentiated by country type. There is indeed a group of highly indebted countries. However, there is another group of many countries that have low debt when measured in economically meaningful terms.

Even many of the lightly indebted countries can face what might more appropriately be called a problem of debt "management" rather than one of debt "burden" or "overhang." If their repayments coming due are not offset by disbursements on new loans, they can encounter cash-flow problems and run into arrears. This situation becomes more likely when the donors who would normally extend new development assistance hold up loans because they are at loggerheads with national authorities on domestic economic policies. Under these circumstances a somewhat artificial debt problem can arise even though the interest burden on the debt is light.

In such circumstances the key issue is policy reform, not debt forgiveness; indeed, forgiving the debt will not provide much real change in long-term resource flows. Correspondingly, the relevant policy judgment is whether a "short leash" approach to the debt serves as a positive vehicle for securing policy reform or is instead counterproductive in causing severe uncertainty.

Debt Burden Trends and Levels

The total external debt of sub-Saharan Africa (SSA) rose from $84 billion in 1980 to $138 billion by 1986 and $194 billion in 1992 (World Bank 1993b). During the same period, the nominal value of exports stagnated. Excluding Nigeria, the region's merchandise exports fell from $23 billion in 1980 to approximately $19 billion in 1986, remaining at $19 billion by 1990 (calculated from IMF 1992a). In large part because of volatile oil prices, Nigeria's export earnings fell from $26 billion in 1980 (or more than half of the region's total) to $5.2 billion in 1986, before rebounding to the range of $13 billion annually in 1990–92. Stagnant exports increased the pressure to borrow abroad and weakened the economic base for servicing the debt. As discussed below, falling commodity prices played an important role in the eroding export base.

Table 7.4 shows key debt indicators for the 45 sub-Saharan countries (excluding South Africa, not considered in the analysis below). The table indicates that 27 of the 45 countries are considered as "severely indebted" by the World Bank. These 27 countries account for 87 percent of the total debt value and 88 percent of the population of the subcontinent.[16] To the veteran debt practitioner, nonetheless, the immediately striking feature of these data is the surprisingly small number of countries that have a high level for the most meaningful indicator: the ratio of interest to exports of goods and nonfactor services (XGNFS). First, however, a word about the interest data is necessary.

The first three columns of table 7.4 report the ratio of interest to exports to XGNFS under three alternative measures of interest. All three measures seek to identify what interest was supposed to be paid rather than what was actually paid and are thus "accrual" concepts rather than "cash." Measure "A" is based on the interest payment figure reported in the World Bank's *World Debt Tables*. This is a cash concept, so the estimate adds any increase in interest arrears experienced during 1992 to obtain an estimate of the interest obligation on an accrual basis. Measure "B" imputes the accrual interest that should have been expected in 1992 on the basis of the end-1991 stock in each category of debt, multiplied by the estimated "typical" SSA interest rate applicable to each type of debt (based on statistical estimates discussed below). Measure "C" takes the sum of 1993 projected interest obligations on long-term debt as reported in the *World Debt Tables* and adds imputed interest on short-term debt (based on a rate of 7 percent applied to the end-1992 short-term debt stock).

For some countries, there are extremely large divergences among the three alternative estimates of the interest burden. In general, the (World Bank) cash-based estimates (A) are somewhat lower than the standard-rate imputed estimates (B), but closer to the estimates based on 1993 scheduled long-term interest plus imputed short-term interest (C). For SSA as a whole, the aggregate interest/exports ratio is 14.5 percent under concept A and 13.9 percent under concept C, but 17 percent using concept B. The lower interest burdens on the cash-based measure than on the standard-rate imputed measure—especially for Somalia and Uganda, but also for such countries as Cameroon, Tanzania, and Sierra Leone—suggest that there were important instances of interest forgiveness, and/or exceptional cases where "mixed credit" lending yielded abnormally low interest rates on nonconcessional debt.[17]

Subject to the caveat of ambiguity in the underlying data, the pattern is one of high interest burdens for a number of countries but also low interest obligations for many others. Thus, based on the measure "A" for interest, in 1992 only 13 countries out of the 45 had interest/exports

16. The debt total in table 7.4 is for the sum of individual countries included in the World Bank's Debt Reporting System (DRS). The regional aggregate given in the *World Debt Tables* include non-DRS countries South Africa and Namibia and is about 9 percent higher (World Bank 1993b).

17. Correspondingly, the debt projections developed below tend to err on the conservative rather than optimistic side, because they apply the method imputing interest obligations at standard rates.

Table 7.4 Debt indicators for sub-Saharan Africa

Country	INT/XGS A (%)	INT/XGS B (%)	NT/XGS C (%)	INT/GDP A (%)	DEBT92 ($ bn)	POPUL (mn)	GNP per cap	SILIC	SIMIC
Sudasombis									
Guinea-Bissau	230.8	230.8	179.4	6.9	0.6	1.0	218.9	1	
Sudan	97.0	77.9	47.2	5.0	16.1	25.9	276.6	1	
Somalia	76.5	134.7	44.3	6.2	2.4	7.7	108.6	1	
SUBTOTAL	95.8	127.4	48.8	5.2	19.2	34.6	237.7		
Mozagascaire									
Madagascar	30.0	30.6	25.0	5.3	4.4	11.5	248.0	1	
Mozambique	28.3	22.3	45.0	8.7	4.9	16.1	52.4	1	
Zaire	26.6	42.4	16.9	7.4	10.9	36.7	225.2	1	
SUBTOTAL	27.3	25.6	21.0	7.1	20.2	64.3	188.1		
Congethivoire									
Cote d'Ivoire	21.7	30.4	27.0	8.6	18.0	12.5	697.6		1
Sao Tome and Principe	19.2	28.8	27.0	4.8	0.2	0.1	302.4	1	
Congo	18.3	16.6	12.5	9.2	4.8	2.4	1,091.5		1
Burundi	17.3	16.3	14.1	1.5	1.0	5.8	187.4	1	
Rwanda	16.0	11.0	13.4	1.0	0.9	7.5	210.5	1	
Ethiopia	16.0	22.8	20.6	1.1	4.4	55.1	120.5	1	
SUBTOTAL	20.2	25.9	22.5	5.3	29.2	83.3	247.5		
Nigeria	18.4	18.3	15.9	7.9	31.0	112.2	249.6	1	
Kentzamgola									
Uganda	14.5	65.6	25.2	0.9	3.0	19.5	158.6	1	
Zambia	14.3	24.6	13.9	7.1	7.0	8.8	207.5	1	
Kenya	13.7	15.5	12.9	3.5	6.4	27.0	311.0	1	

Central African Republic	13.0	10.2	9.5	1.8	0.9	3.1	415.9	1
Tanzania	12.1	34.6	19.7	2.4	6.7	28.4	88.2	1
Niger	11.9	18.2	18.7	1.7	1.7	8.0	290.0	1
Gabon	11.8	9.7	8.9	5.6	3.8	1.2	4,426.4	
Malawi	11.4	12.3	10.2	1.9	1.7	8.6	206.1	1
Ghana	10.8	13.8	10.0	1.7	4.3	15.5	437.0	1
Mauritania	10.6	14.1	12.5	4.6	2.3	2.0	549.0	
Zimbabwe	10.5	9.5	11.3	3.6	4.0	10.0	539.9	
Cameroon	10.3	22.2	23.2	1.5	6.6	12.2	797.2	1
Angola	10.0	12.0	10.5	5.8	9.6	10.0	620.7	1
SUBTOTAL	11.5	15.4	12.8	3.3	58.0	154.3	376.2	
Senguinali								
Lesotho	9.9	7.3	8.8	1.3	0.5	1.8	622.8	
Equatorial Guinea	9.5	19.0	11.9	2.7	0.2	0.4	413.6	1
Chad	9.5	5.6	6.3	1.7	0.7	5.8	223.0	
Sierra Leone	9.0	24.8	19.7	3.0	1.3	4.3	146.7	1
Senegal	7.9	9.0	8.0	1.9	3.6	7.5	825.8	
Togo	7.3	10.2	8.5	2.1	1.4	3.6	430.5	
Burkina Faso	5.9	6.5	7.4	0.7	1.1	9.5	309.5	
Guinea	5.4	9.6	8.7	1.2	2.7	5.9	522.4	
Cape Verde	5.2	5.2	5.7	0.8	0.2	0.4	930.0	
Mali	4.3	8.5	7.0	0.6	2.6	9.5	293.0	1
Comoros	4.1	6.1	4.1	0.8	0.2	0.6	459.1	
Gambia, The	3.6	4.0	2.8	2.1	0.4	0.9	422.8	

(table continued next page)

Table 7.4 (continued)

Country	INT/XGS A (%)	INT/XGS B (%)	NT/XGS C (%)	INT/GDP A (%)	DEBT92 ($ bn)	POPUL (mn)	GNP per cap	SILIC	SIMIC
Mauritius	3.1	2.7	2.9	2.0	1.0	1.1	2,424.3		
Benin	2.3	5.9	5.3	0.6	1.4	1.6	1,366.5		
Liberia	1.9	17.3	6.3	0.8	2.0	2.6	412.0	1	
Djibouti	1.8	1.1	1.4	1.0	0.2	0.4	1,143.1		
Swaziland	1.3	1.3	1.2	0.9	0.2	0.8	1,170.7		
Botswana	0.1	1.5	1.7	0.1	0.5	1.4	2,602.9		
SUBTOTAL	3.9	5.8	5.0	1.2	20.2	58.0	558.9		
TOTAL	14.5	17.0	13.9	4.3	177.8	506.7	318.3	23	4
SILIC+SIMIC	17.8			5.1	154.1	445.6	270.2	23	4

INT/XGS = Accrual interest/exports of goods and services.
SILIC = Severely indebted low income country (1 = member).
SIMIC = Severely indebted middle income country (1 = member).
A: Based on cash payments plus buildup in interest arrears.
B: Calculated using debt stocks and interest rate estimates.
C: Calculated using 1993 interest payment obligations.

Sources: World Bank 1993a; IMF, International Financial Statistics.

ratios in excess of 15 percent, traditionally a relatively comfortable threshold.[18] These 13 countries account for 56 percent of the face value of SSA external debt. On this basis, only about one-third of the countries by number and one-half by debt are represented by cases with high debt burdens. In contrast, at an acute phase of the Latin American debt crisis, fully 17 out of 18 major countries in that region had interest/exports ratios higher than 15 percent (ECLAC 1988). The average interest/exports ratio for Latin America that year was 35.8 percent, compared with 14.5 percent for SSA in 1992 (table 7.4; ECLAC 1988).

For many countries the interest burden is also low relative to GDP (reported in table 7.4 for interest measure ''A''). For the countries with interest/exports below 15 percent, the ratio of interest to GDP is an average of 2.5 percent. Thus, despite a relatively high average ratio of exports to GDP (29 percent), the modest interest burden relative to exports also translates into a modest burden relative to income.[19]

The figures in table 7.4 thus suggest that the World Bank's definition of ''severely indebted'' is substantially misleading for many African countries. The Bank's new definition (used in the table) is that the ''present value of debt service to GDP ratio'' in 1989–91 exceeded 80 percent, or that the ''present value of debt service to exports of goods and all services'' exceeded 200 percent (World Bank 1992a, 1: appendix VI). However, the debt service ratio (whether or not taken in terms of present value) is not as meaningful a measure of debt burden as the interest/exports or interest/GDP ratio. The reason is that debt service includes amortization of principal.

Principal repayment is essentially no more than a reshuffling of the balance sheet. It reduces both the asset side (domestic reserves) and the liability side (foreign debt), but leaves the country's net worth unchanged. So long as new lending can be arranged to cover principal coming due, amortization is largely irrelevant to the true debt burden. So, accordingly, is the debt service ratio.[20]

Most African debt is from official sources, so it is typically not vulnerable to the same sudden cutoffs of principal rollover that can occur with private loans (and did, in the Latin American debt crisis). Of course,

---

18. Before the World Bank shifted its definition of ''highly indebted'' to a present value basis (as discussed below), one of its four criteria was an interest/exports ratio above 15 percent. The other three were debt/GNP > 50%; debt/XGS (exports of goods and services) > 275%; and debt service/XGS > 30%. Three of the four thresholds had to be exceeded to indicate heavy indebtedness (World Bank 1992a, 1: appendix VI).

19. The exception of Zambia appears to reflect an implausibly low estimate of 1992 GDP in the World Bank database.

20. Even (accrual) interest alone somewhat overstates the debt burden, insofar as the interest rate has an inflationary component, because inflationary erosion of the principal provides net worth gains.

suspensions of new principal from official sources can occur because of unacceptable domestic economic policies in the recipient country, but in that case the problem is not one of excessive debt burden but the need for domestic policy reform.

To sharpen the point that principal amortization should be excluded from the measure of debt burden, consider the following thought experiment. Suppose the author and the reader were jointly extended a $1 billion loan interest free. By the World Bank criterion, we would be hopelessly overindebted, because the ratio of our debt to our income would be close to infinity, for practical purposes. By the criterion suggested here, in contrast, we would have no real debt burden at all. Surely the latter is right, in this experiment. We can place the $1 billion in a vault and return it upon maturity with no more effort than a walk to the bank. So long as we can arrange for the principal to be rolled over, we do not even have to walk to the bank.

Latin American experience confirmed that it was interest, not principal, that mattered. Throughout the 1980s neither the banks nor even the bilateral creditors expected repayment of principal, as rescheduling of amortization was the norm. For their part, the multilateral lenders typically provided new loans that exceeded principal coming due. The real question, especially for the banks, was what fraction of interest coming due would be paid net as opposed to re-lent.

One suspects that in the African case, if there is concern about principal as well as interest, the reason is that much of the debt is owed to multilateral agencies or the IMF, and these entities have rigorously avoided rescheduling principal. Nonetheless, typically new loans from these sources at least keep pace with amortization due, unless there is a breakdown in the policy dialogue. Once again, then, principal typically poses a real burden only when the underlying problem is a policy distortion, not excessive debt.

In short, the interest/exports and interest/GDP ratios in table 7.4 would seem a more meaningful basis for judging the debt burden than debt service ratios including amortization, or than the World Bank's present-value variants of the debt service ratios.[21] The relatively low interest burden for a large number of African countries should come as no surprise. Many countries in the region have always been too poor to borrow on market terms. Moreover, much of the official debt is concessional. Thus, the World Bank reports that one-third of the region's debt stock in 1992 was owed to multilateral or bilateral donors in the form of concessional loans (World Bank 1993b, 1: 174–75).

At the same time, the table does reveal exceptionally high interest/exports ratios in a handful of countries. Once again using the 15 percent

---

21. Nor does a focus on the internal transfer problem change this judgment, given the low level of the interest/GDP ratio for the countries with relatively low interest/exports ratios.

interest/exports threshold, the four largest debtors in the region (Nigeria, Côte d'Ivoire, Sudan, and Zaire) are in the high-debt group. As a result, as noted, slightly more than half of the SSA total debt is owed by countries with the relatively higher debt burdens, even though this group includes fewer than one-third of the nations in the region. Measured by population, the corresponding share is slightly less than half for the more highly indebted group.

In contrast to the picture of a numerical majority of African nations with relatively light debt, Husain and Underwood (1991b) have portrayed the African debt problem as similar to that of Latin America by noting that in 1988 "scheduled debt service payments were about 50 percent of export earnings in both regions" (24). However, this statement again focuses on debt service rather than interest, and thereby on the wrong measure of debt burden.[22]

A more recent World Bank study (1994c) reaches a more schizophrenic position that reflects ambiguity about the burden of principal as opposed to interest.

> African countries are among the most indebted economies in the world, although so far external debt has not been a cash-flow problem (except for Congo and Nigeria) thanks to new loans and frequent reschedulings. But the high external debt has costs: long negotiations occupy much of the time of policymakers, and the access to trade credit is limited. . . . As countries move toward better policies, the debt burden will become an obstacle, deterring investment. . . . [I]f the debt is on the books, there is always some expectation that it will have to be serviced and that investors will be taxed to service it. (World Bank 1994c, 213)

The World Bank authors have taken eastward the argument of investment-suppressing debt overhang, even though that thesis has increasingly been discredited for Latin America (chapter 4). Their analysis begins with a finding that essentially confirms the diagnosis here of relatively light effective debt burden for many countries; but they then seem to fall into the trap of taking the principal of low-interest loans seriously. Moreover, it is curious indeed to hear from the World Bank that it is a dangerous principle that debt "on the books" might "have to be serviced"; presumably this potential vice becomes a virtue when it comes to World Bank claims. A more general view would instead be that it is always ideal for a nation fully to service its debt if possible, because only nations that do so are fully integrated into financial markets. Correspondingly, it is ideal that the interest burden of the debt be sufficiently light that its full service is not burdensome.

---

22. The statement also appears to include all of short-term debt as payable in the current year, whereas short-term debt is typically for trade credit and normally rolled over. The estimate developed below of SSA's debt service ratio, defined as interest (accrual basis) plus amortization on long-term debt, is 42 percent for 1992.

The authors do reach an important conclusion that concurs with the findings here: debt reduction should be reduced to a "viable level" depending on individual country circumstances, and this is likely to involve "different levels of debt reduction for different countries," contrary to the "across the board, fixed-percentage debt reductions" of uniform proposals (Toronto, Trinidad) considered so far (214–15).

In short, the conventional wisdom on African debt suffers from important misconceptions of the real burden of the debt because of the failure to recognize that the principal value of concessional debt is largely meaningless, with a consequential overstatement of the long-term economic burden (but not necessarily renegotiating hassle) of the debt. This message is deceptive for debtors as well, because the other side of the same coin of low interest/exports ratios is that, for many African countries, debt forgiveness would provide little boost to real resource flows and growth. Almost half of the nations listed in table 7.4 have interest/exports ratios of 10 percent or less. As a result, completely extinguishing their debt would have no more beneficial impact than a recovery of 10 percent or less in export prices—simply not enough of a change to spell the difference between economic disaster and prosperity. Focusing on face (or even present) value of debt principal can thus give debtors an exaggerated impression of their prospective gains from debt forgiveness.

Even from this initial consideration of the interest/exports ratios in table 7.4, a strategy for handling the debt problem of many African nations begins to suggest itself: multiyear rollover of principal. In the Latin American debt crisis, a relatively early phase of the policy response was to roll over principal and provide new lending in Multiyear Rescheduling Agreements (MYRAs) covering 5 years and more. As discussed below, the "Toronto terms" suggested for Africa would roll over amortization coming due on bilateral debt for several years and in addition would provide substantial forgiveness on this debt. Where the initial interest/exports ratio is relatively low, even an approach based solely on multiyear rescheduling could provide policy certainty without risking excessive debt buildup.

African Debt Dynamics

Low initial interest/exports ratios are by no means the whole story. An important distinction between Latin America and Africa has been that, in general, the Latin countries have tended to run trade surpluses to work their way out of the debt crisis, whereas the African nations tend to have trade deficits. The cumulative effect of a trade deficit can be to raise the interest/exports ratio, so that many countries in SSA that have relatively low ratios today might be on an unsustainable path of rising interest/exports ratios.

It can be shown (Cline 1985b, 1994) that the annual proportionate change in the debt/exports ratio may be approximated as

$$\dot{d} = i - \beta/d - k - g_x, \qquad (7.1)$$

where d is the debt/exports ratio, the overdot signifies proportionate change, β is the trade surplus (on goods and nonfactor services) as a fraction of exports, k is the ratio of annual direct investment inflow to the stock of debt, and g_x is the nominal growth rate of exports. Essentially this equation says that the debt/exports ratio tends to rise by "inheritance" from interest on past debt; that it can be reduced by a persistent trade surplus ($\beta > 0$) and moderated by the securing of capital in the form of non-debt-creating direct investment (k); and that it is negatively related to the growth of the denominator, exports. Compared with Latin America, Africa has in its favor that the term i tends to be lower; but working against SSA, the term β tends to be negative rather than positive, and the term k smaller.

Table 7.5 shows typical values for the parameters of equation 7.1 for Latin America in the depths of the debt crisis (1983–86) and in the recovery phase (1990–92), and for SSA as of 1992. For Africa, a variant (β') of the "trade balance" parameter (and more generally the "export base") is augmented to include grant receipts (primarily development assistance), on grounds that these are comparable to a relatively steady stream of export earnings.

As may be seen in the table, in the period 1983–86 Latin America faced high international interest rates and falling exports (primarily because of the collapse of oil prices in 1986). The region achieved a high surplus on trade in goods and nonfactor services (more than one-fourth of the export base). This surplus, together with moderate direct investment inflows, kept the debt/exports ratio from deteriorating very fast; even so, the period parameters meant a tendency toward a 1 percent annual rise in the ratio, beginning from an already high level of about 360 percent. By 1990–92, interest rates were much lower, direct investment was much higher, and export growth was once again positive (if less than stellar). The changes in these parameters meant that the debt/exports ratio was on a declining trajectory at about 6 percent (i.e., some 20 percentage points) annually, despite the sharp drop in the trade balance surplus parameter. Of course, with lower interest rates the interest/exports ratio already showed much more improvement than the debt/exports ratio.

As indicated in table 7.5, these stylized parameters for sub-Saharan Africa in 1992 showed major differences from the Latin American pattern. The interest rate at an average of 4.8 percent (calculated from the data developed below) was lower than in the second Latin American period, although by less than perhaps might have been expected. As

Table 7.5   Indicators of debt dynamics in Latin America and sub-Saharan Africa

		LA 1983-86	LA 1990-92	SSA 1992
i	interest rate	0.101[a]	0.068[a]	0.048
β	balance on trade in goods and nonfactor service (fraction of exports of goods, nfs)	0.256	0.033	–0.108
β′	balance including grants	..	..	0.075[b]
k	direct investment inflow as fraction of debt	0.047	0.103	0.009
gx	export growth rate (nominal)	–0.027	0.015	0.000
d	debt/exports ratio	3.590	3.480	3.110[b]
ḋ	predicted rate of change in debt/export ratio	0.010	–0.059	0.074
ḋ′	rate including grants	..	..	0.015[b]

.. = not available

i=LIBOR + 1.25%, 1983-86; LIBOR + 13/16, 1990–92
a. For 1990–92
b. Including grants as exports.

Source: IFS, BOP, and WDT.

noted, two-thirds of sub-Saharan Africa's debt is nonconcessional. The balance of trade on goods and nonfactor services was substantially in deficit, at about 11 percent of the export base. However, if grant receipts are added into exports, the parameter β becomes positive and relatively large, at 7½ percent. SSA received little direct investment (k was only 0.9 percent of debt). Based on 1990–92 trends, export growth was nil. Taking account of a "debt/exports" ratio of 311 percent (incorporating grants into the "exports" denominator for the purposes of this analysis), the predicted rate of change in the debt/exports ratio based on equation 7.1 was an annual rise of 1.5 percent. As indicated by the alternative measure, this predicted rate would have been an annual increase of about 7½ percent in the absence of grant income.

The analysis of table 7.5 suggests that if SSA exports remain stagnant, the debt/exports ratio would continue to rise slowly (at 1½ percent annually), despite the help of about $9 billion in annual grants.[23] However, it seems likely that real commodity prices should begin to reverse their decline of the 1980s, and that some rise in export volume should be feasible as well. Thus, the World Bank (1994a) predicts that for the rest of the 1990s, nonfuel commodity prices are likely to rise more than 2 percent annually in real terms (deflating by prices of manufactured exports of industrial countries). This rate is consistent with a 4 percent annual

23. On a cash basis (IMF 1993e). On a commitments basis, the figure amounts to $14 billion (calculated from World Bank 1993b, vol. 2).

rise in nominal export values (even with zero volume growth). If exports do grow at 4 percent nominal, then the calculation of table 7.5 turns into a growth rate for the debt/exports ratio ($\dot{d}$) of −2.5 percent annually. That would mean an *improving* baseline trend, though not as rapid as at the Latin American (1990–92) rate (table 7.5). However, as suggested above, it is crucial to conduct a more disaggregated analysis.

African Debt Simulations

Annex 7B develops a simple "accounting" debt projection model that can be applied to SSA as a whole and also to different subgroups within the region. The model simply postulates reasonable growth rates for exports of goods and nonfactor services (XGS), imports (MGS), new lending (by debt category), direct investment, and income from grants. It applies existing interest and amortization rates by class of debt. After taking account of profit remittances (based on a specified rate of return on cumulative foreign investment) and the buildup of reserves, the model "closes" the balance of payments by permitting the accumulation of arrears, if formal finance is insufficient, or the decumulation of arrears if formal net finance exceeds the capital account requirement.

The model assumes nominal (dollar) growth rates of 4 percent for trade (both exports and imports), grants, and new disbursements of all classes of lending, and 5 percent for direct investment.[24] As discussed in annex 7B, on the basis of statistical regression from data reported in the World Bank's *World Debt Tables*, the average (nominal) interest rates on major loan categories are as follows: multilateral concessional, 0.84 percent; bilateral concessional, 1 percent; multilateral nonconcessional, 8.7 percent; and bilateral nonconcessional, 6.8 percent.[25] An interest rate of 7 percent is assumed for private, IMF, and short-term debt, and 6 percent for interest on interest arrears. As noted above, this "imputed interest" approach tends to overstate interest obligations in the base year 1992, and so provides projections that err on the side of over- rather than understatement of the interest burden. Regression-based estimates are also used to determine average amortization rates on outstanding debt, which are a low 2.5 percent for multilateral concessional, 4.1 percent for bilateral concessional, 8.2 percent for multilateral nonconcessional, and 10.5 percent for bilateral nonconcessional.

The nominal growth rates and interest rates are broadly consistent with a world of 2 percent real growth and 2 percent international infla-

---

24. The absence of any change in the terms of trade makes these projections conservative, in view of the World Bank's projections of a partial recovery.

25. The seeming anomaly of higher rates on multilateral than bilateral nonconcessional debt may reflect the impact of dollar devaluation in the late 1980s on multilateral debt denominated in nondollar currencies.

tion in tradeable goods. Export growth is set at a rate that should be feasible once the European economy recovers.[26]

Export growth of 2 percent real and 2 percent nominal is considerably more modest than the region achieved in 1970–80. Excluding Nigeria, and deflating by the US wholesale price index, the real value of exports from SSA grew at a rate of 3.8 percent in that decade. However, this real value growth rate fell to a −4.5 percent annually in 1980–90 (calculated from IMF 1992a). The most important reason for this reversal was the shift of real commodity prices from a rising to a falling trend. Using the IMF index of nonfuel commodity prices as a proxy for African commodity export prices, and again deflating by the US wholesale price index, real commodity prices rose at 1.7 percent annually in 1970–80, then fell at 3.5 percent annually in 1980–90. Based on this approximation, the real volume of exports from SSA (excluding Nigeria) grew at 2.1 percent (= 3.8 − 1.7%) in 1970–80, but declined at 1 percent (= −4.5 − −3.5%) in 1980–90. The use of a notional 2 percent volume and 2 percent price increase in the 1990s presumes a return to more normal export conditions. However, a sensitivity test is included for a lower export growth rate, as discussed below.

Table 7.6 presents the baseline projections of the model for SSA as a whole. The debt indicators consider only exports of goods and nonfactor services in the denominator, and they are thus more conservative than might be warranted by including grant receipts in the denominator (as was done in table 7.5). The first column reports the best estimates for the base year, 1992. The rest of the table refers to projections using the parameters discussed in annex 7B as applied to the base year data.[27]

The projections show a small but steady decline in the interest/exports and debt/exports ratios over the period 1993–97. This gradual improvement is broadly consistent with the annual reduction of 2¹/₂ percent in

26. In 1992, 45 percent of Africa's exports went to the European Community (IMF 1993d).

27. Note that the aggregates in table 7.6 for 1992 differ from those in the summary regional table in World Bank (1993b). The figures on debt and arrears are the sums of the individual country estimates reported in that source. The principal elements of the current account flows are from IMF (1993e) for 1992 or the most recent year available. One reason is that the World Bank export and import data include factor services, whereas the nonfactor service concept is required here. More generally, however, the IMF balance of payments source is the more reliable. The accrual interest estimate for 1992 is calculated by applying the interest rates by debt category to 1991 debt stocks. The World Bank flows are used for profits remittances and direct investment. IMF balance of payments data are used for other factor services and grants.

The resulting SSA aggregate current account for 1992 is a deficit of $5.5 billion. This estimate is broadly consistent with the figure given in IMF (1993f, 177), where it is reported that the current account balance excluding official transfers was −$16.1 billion. After adjusting for inclusion here of Nigeria (current account surplus of $2.3 billion), and adding in official transfers ($7.9 billion), the IMF figure translates to a current account deficit of $5.9 billion for SSA, close to the estimate here.

Table 7.6 Baseline run: sub-Saharan Africa
(millions of dollars)

Year	1992	1993	1994	1995	1996	1997
Debt	177,779	182,676	187,751	193,016	198,484	204,167
Mult conc	28,376	30,907	33,505	36,172	38,913	41,732
Mult nonc	13,770	14,206	14,669	15,159	15,677	16,222
Bilat conc	34,993	35,112	35,227	35,336	35,442	35,542
Bilat nonc	36,288	36,021	35,747	35,478	35,222	34,987
IMF	6,344	6,439	6,569	6,730	6,918	7,129
Private	31,559	31,026	30,593	30,255	30,008	29,848
Short term	12,344	12,344	12,344	12,344	12,344	12,344
Interest arrears	14,105	16,621	19,097	21,542	23,961	26,363
Exports	48,322	50,255	52,265	54,356	56,530	58,791
Imports	53,528	55,669	57,896	60,212	62,620	65,125
Interest due	8,204	8,628	8,791	8,963	9,145	9,337
Profits	1,610	1,616	1,862	2,120	2,392	2,676
Other FSM	821	854	888	924	960	999
Interest received	510	310	323	336	349	363
Other FSX	874	909	945	983	1,022	1,063
Grants	8,817	9,170	9,536	9,918	10,315	10,727
Current account	−5,540	−6,123	−6,367	−6,626	−6,901	−7,193
Capital account	865	6,537	6,797	7,073	7,366	7,677
Reserve change	−3,540	414	430	447	465	484
Direct investment	1,562	1,640	1,722	1,808	1,899	1,994

(table continued next page)

the debt/exports ratio implied by the simpler analysis of table 7.5 when export growth is set at 4 percent rather than zero. Interest on an accrual basis falls from 17.2 percent in 1993 to 15.9 percent in 1997. The debt service ratio falls from 41.3 percent in 1993 to 37.0 percent by 1997.

Correspondingly, there is only modest buildup of debt. The stock of debt rises by about 15 percent in nominal terms over the period, and thus only about 5 percent in real terms. The debt/exports ratio falls from 363 percent to 347 percent. The limited debt buildup reflects the modest current account deficit (only about 12 percent of the export base, or 10 percent counting grants in exports).

The one indicator that shows deterioration in the baseline is the amount of arrears. Interest arrears rise from 9 percent of total debt in 1993 to 13 percent in 1997. Arrears on principal rise from 19 percent of formal debt (i.e., debt excluding interest arrears) to 29 percent. The accumulation of arrears reflects the fact that in the base year 1992, and thus throughout the period, amortization due exceeds new disburse-

Table 7.6 (continued)

Year	1992	1993	1994	1995	1996	1997
Loans	9,337	9,648	9,972	10,309	10,659	11,023
Mult conc	3,116	3,241	3,370	3,505	3,645	3,791
Mult nonc	1,505	1,565	1,628	1,693	1,761	1,831
Bilat conc	1,554	1,554	1,554	1,554	1,554	1,554
Bilat nonc	360	374	389	405	421	438
IMF	1,311	1,363	1,418	1,475	1,534	1,595
Private	1,491	1,551	1,613	1,677	1,744	1,814
Amortization	12,139	12,139	12,170	12,223	12,298	12,394
Mult conc	709	709	773	838	904	973
Mult nonc	1,129	1,129	1,165	1,203	1,243	1,285
Bilat conc	1,435	1,435	1,440	1,444	1,449	1,453
Bilat conc	3,810	3,810	3,782	3,753	3,725	3,698
IMF	1,269	1,269	1,288	1,314	1,346	1,384
Private	3,787	3,787	3,723	3,671	3,631	3,601
Arrears	41,426	48,814	56,087	63,267	70,374	77,428
Official interest	10,771	12,692	14,583	16,450	18,298	20,132
Private interest	3,334	3,929	4,514	5,092	5,664	6,231
Official principal	17,767	20,936	24,055	27,134	30,182	33,208
Private principal	9,554	11,258	12,935	14,591	16,230	17,857
Debt indicators						
Debt/XGS	368	363	359	355	351	347
Interest/XGS	17.0	17.2	16.8	16.5	16.2	15.9
Debt service/XGS	42.1	41.3	40.1	39.0	37.9	37.0

FSM = factor service imports; FSX = factor service exports; XGS = exports of goods and nonfactor services

ments. This adverse discrepancy is especially large for bilateral nonconcessional lending, primarily official export credits. The only category with a substantial surplus of disbursements over amortization is that of concessional multilateral lending, primarily through the International Development Association (IDA). This concessional window of the World Bank is providing net credit even as the nonconcessional window (International Bank for Reconstruction and Development) is receiving net repayments.[28]

The resulting reshuffling maintains a positive net flow of principal from the World Bank group and multilateral lending overall. The same is not true of bilateral lending. The excess of new concessional bilateral lending over repayments ($119 million in 1992) is small compared with

---

28. In 1992, for sub-Saharan Africa as a whole IDA disbursed $2.1 billion and received amortization of $74 million. The IBRD disbursed $540 million and received amortization of $862 million (World Bank 1993b, 1: 175). These flows are on a cash basis, so the negative principal flow for the IBRD is presumably larger on an accrual basis.

the excess of scheduled repayments over new disbursements in bilateral nonconcessional loans ($3.5 billion, table 7.6).[29] Of course, to the extent that bilateral donors are increasing their grants, the picture is more favorable. However, after a rapid increase from 1980 to 1990 (an annual nominal rate of 12 percent for commitments), grants expanded at a slower pace (6.4 percent annually, 1990–92; World Bank 1993b, 1: 174). Moreover, on a cash-flow basis, official transfers to SSA in 1992 amounted to only $7.9 billion. Accordingly, almost half of grants would have gone to pay off bilateral nonconcessional net repayments, if arrears had not been building up.

The result was that the subcontinent resorted to "self-help" finance through the accumulation of arrears. The persistence and intensification of arrears in the projection baseline reveals symptoms of serious debt stress not otherwise evident in the indicators for aggregate SSA data. This outcome is not inevitable, however. The simulation results stem from projection of the base-period conditions, in which new loans fell substantially short of amortization coming due (table 7.6). The normalization of many debt-impasse situations would tend to generate a higher level of new loans and, probably, reduce amortization rates as a consequence of MYRA stretch-outs. In addition, as discussed below, appropriately tailored debt reduction seems likely to be required for at least the more heavily indebted countries.

The discrepancy between a steady increase projected for SSA arrears, on the one hand, and the finding above that many countries in the region are relatively lightly indebted, on the other, reflects the crucial point already suggested by table 7.4: SSA aggregates are not particularly meaningful because of the wide disparities in debt profiles within the region. Accordingly, the analysis here divides the region into six composite "countries." These groupings, shown in table 7.4, are based on the rankings by the interest/exports ratio. The groups are named for the principal debtor countries contained in each set. Thus, the most highly indebted group, "Sudasombis," includes Sudan, Somalia, and Guinea-Bissau. The next highest debt group, "Mozagascaire," includes Mozambique, Madagascar, and Zaire. Next is "Congethivoire," which includes Côte d'Ivoire, Ethiopia, and Congo. Next is Nigeria, examined individually because of its large size. The next group, "Kentzamgola," contains the 14 countries with interest/exports ratios of 10 to 15 percent. The group includes Kenya, Tanzania, Zambia, and Angola. The final, and least indebted, grouping, "Senguinali," incorporates the 19 countries with interest/exports ratios below 10 percent, including Senegal, Guinea, and Mali.

---

29. This fact is not evident in the cash-based data of the *World Debt Tables*, which show *positive* net disbursements of $62 million in 1992 (World Bank 1993b, 1: 175). The difference is buildup in arrears.

Appendix tables 7B.2 through 7B.7 report the baseline projections for the six composite countries. Table 7.7 shows summary results from these projections, reporting the 1993 and 1997 estimates for total debt, arrears (interest plus principal), the ratio of interest to exports of goods and nonfactor services, and the debt service ratio. The "baseline" results refer to the projections shown in the annex.

The subregional projections in table 7.7 and tables 7B.2 through 7B.7 confirm the impression of a broad dichotomization of the African debt problem. At one extreme, clearly the most impossible debt burden is that for Sudan and Somalia (Sudasombis). Here 1993 interest is almost 200 percent of the export base, and the ratio rises further over the projection period. At the other end of the spectrum, Kentzamgola and especially Senguinali show relatively modest interest/exports ratios that hold steady over the period.

After Sudasombis, the heaviest debt burden is for Mozagascaire, which shows high interest/exports ratios of about 30 percent and high debt service ratios of over 70 percent, with no improvement over the period in the baseline. The grouping including Côte d'Ivoire and Congo shows a similar debt burden, with interest/exports ratios slightly below 30 percent. Trends for Nigeria are more favorable, as the interest/exports ratio falls from about 16 percent to 7 percent as the result of the persistent (and unusual) current account surplus.

The baseline results suggest that something radical needs to be done to address the debt problems of Sudan and Somalia, and that moreover there is considerable potential for benefits from debt reduction in Mozagascaire and Nigerivoire. However, the baseline suggests that for the 32 countries comprising Kentzangola and Senguinali, the prospective interest/exports ratios are too low to signify an oppressive debt burden. For these countries, the main content of debt reform could thus appropriately center on improved assurance of principal rollover, and the cleaning up of arrears, rather than on major forgiveness of existing debt.

To shed light on the sensitivity of the projections, baselines B and C calculated for SSA as a whole report the results of more pessimistic trade assumptions (table 7.7). Baseline B sets nominal export growth at 2 percent rather than 4 percent. Baseline C does the same, and in addition places nominal import growth at 5 percent rather than 4 percent. These two alternatives cause the 1997 ratio of interest to exports to rise from 15.9 percent to 18.9 percent (case B) or 19.7 percent (case C), so that in the more pessimistic scenarios the baseline shows a modest deterioration rather than a modest improvement as in the main case. A more dramatic manifestation of debt stress in the more pessimistic scenarios is the buildup of arrears to much higher levels (as high as nearly half of total debt rather than approximately one-third as in the main baseline).

Debt Reform Simulations

Table 7.7 reports the results of simulations that calculate the impact of administering alternative reforms to African debt. These include "enhanced Toronto terms" or alternatively "Trinidad terms" for bilateral claims, and "Brady Plan" reduction of private bank claims.

At the 1988 economic summit meeting of the Group of Seven industrial countries in Toronto, the Paris Club creditors adopted a format for concessional rescheduling of bilateral debt owed by low-income countries. There were three options (World Bank 1989b, 1: 57). First, creditors could cancel one-third of principal coming due during the "consolidation period," typically some 16 months. The remainder of principal due during this period would be rescheduled at 14-year maturities with 8 years' grace, at market interest rates. Second, the relevant debt could be rescheduled at 14-year maturities with 8 years' grace, at below-market interest rates. Third, and least concessional, the relevant principal could simply be rescheduled at 25-year maturities and 14 years' grace, but at market interest rates. In 1988–89, eight OECD creditors (including Canada, the United Kingdom, and Germany) chose the second option, and five (including the United States) chose the third. Only France chose the most concessional (first) option.

Analysts tended to conclude that this first formulation of the Toronto terms yielded little debt relief. Thus, Husain and Underwood (1991b) calculated that on the $5 billion in debt "consolidated" for 17 SSA countries under these terms in 1988–91, the resulting savings on debt service were only $100 million annually (compared with total SSA debt service on the order of $17 billion annually in that period). They cited three reasons for the limited impact: first, the consolidation period was short; second, "standard" Paris Club reschedulings had already provided 100 percent rollover of interest and principal; and third, some bilateral debt was excluded.[30]

In September 1990 England's then chancellor of the Exchequer, John Major, proposed at the meetings of the Commonwealth Secretariat in Trinidad that the concessionality of Toronto terms for low-income debtors be pushed much further. He suggested that Paris Club creditors forgive two-thirds of their bilateral official claims and reschedule the rest over 25 years with 5 years' grace (Husain and Underwood 1991b, 30; Lancaster 1991, 44).

Although the Paris Club did not adopt debt relief as deep as the Trinidad terms, in late 1991 it did move to "enhanced Toronto terms."

---

30. Note, however, that judging the program against the alternative of 100 percent debt-service rescheduling as "normal," and then calculating the impact measured by debt service, would seem to bias the impact estimate against the Toronto terms. A more meaningful calculation might have been the amount of principal and interest forgiven.

Table 7.7 Impact of alternative policies on African debt, 1993 and 1997 (billions of dollars and percentages)

	Debt (billions of dollars)		Arrears (billions of dollars)		INT/XGS (%)		DSVC/XGS(%)	
	1993	1997	1993	1997	1993	1997	1993	1997
Sub-Saharan Africa								
Baseline	183	204	49	77	17.2	15.9	41.3	37.0
Toronto	142	154	37	34	13.5	11.3	27.2	22.4
Trinidad	118	125	30	-1	11.5	8.9	25.3	19.1
Brady	174	193	47	70	16.1	14.7	38.8	34.4
Trinidad+Brady	109	114	27	-7	10.4	7.7	22.7	16.8
Baseline B	184	222	50	96	17.5	18.9	42.1	43.6
Baseline C	184	232	50	108	17.5	19.7	42.1	45.3
Sudasombis								
Baseline	20	27	15	24	191.5	233.7	414.9	470.2
Toronto	12	16	12	16	100.5	128.1	218.5	228.5
Trinidad	9	12	10	11	64.1	86.3	182.1	177.2
Brady	20	25	14	23	180.1	221.4	391.0	447.0
Trinidad+Brady	8	11	10	10	52.7	73.9	158.2	157.4
Mozagascaire								
Baseline	21	27	8	17	27.7	32.2	69.1	74.0
Toronto	15	19	6	10	18.0	20.4	32.7	33.7
Trinidad	11	15	5	3	12.8	14.3	27.5	25.3
Brady	21	27	8	17	26.6	31.1	66.8	71.7
Trinidad+Brady	11	14	5	3	11.7	13.2	25.1	23.3
Congethivoire								
Baseline	31	40	8	19	26.6	29.6	60.1	65.2
Toronto	26	34	7	14	23.4	25.2	44.9	46.5

Trinidad	23	31	6	8	21.6	22.8	43.1	41.3
Brady	27	35	7	16	22.2	24.9	50.1	55.1
Trinidad+Brady	19	26	5	5	17.2	17.8	33.1	32.3
Nigeria								
Baseline	28	10	2	-10	15.9	6.6	38.4	16.3
Toronto	20	1	0	-19	12.7	3.0	24.3	7.4
Trinidad	16	-5	-2	-25	10.6	0.8	22.3	4.3
Brady								
Trinidad+Brady								
Kentzamgola								
Baseline	61	73	13	21	15.4	15.7	38.3	38.5
Toronto	50	61	10	10	13.2	12.6	28.0	26.4
Trinidad	44	53	9	2	11.9	10.8	26.7	23.9
Brady	58	69	12	19	14.3	14.5	35.4	35.6
Trinidad+Brady	41	49	8	0	10.7	9.6	23.9	21.6
Senguinali								
Baseline	21	26	3	5	5.9	6.3	15.6	16.2
Toronto	17	22	2	2	4.8	4.6	10.5	10.3
Trinidad	15	19	2	0	4.3	3.8	9.9	9.3
Brady	21	26	3	5	5.7	6.0	15.1	15.7
Trinidad+Brady	15	19	2	0	4.1	3.6	9.5	8.9

INT: Interest due.
XGS: Exports of goods and non-factor services.
DSV: Debt service (all interest plus amortization on long-term debt)

These replaced the first option of the original Toronto terms with 50 percent forgiveness of debt service due in the consolidation period, with the added possibility of 50 percent reduction in the stock of debt after three years. The enhanced second option provided for rescheduling the debt coming due during the consolidation period at 23 years' maturity and at interest rates sufficiently low to reduce the present value of debt service by 50 percent. The third, essentially nonconcessional, option remained unchanged, and continued to be applied in particular by the United States. From December 1991 through September 1993, thirteen African countries received enhanced Toronto terms (World Bank 1993b, 1: 88).

The simulations here specify enhanced Toronto terms as follows. Because of the blend of 50 percent forgiveness by some countries and rescheduling at market interest rates by others, it is assumed that enhanced Toronto terms have the effect of a 40 percent reduction in bilateral claims. Moreover, it is assumed that these terms can be repeated in successive "consolidation" periods over the horizon examined here, and/or that the debtors can successfully negotiate the stock reduction at the end of three years. As a result, the effect of the enhanced terms is calculated by an effective reduction of bilateral debt stock by 40 percent at the outset of the period (1993). The effect of the grace period for the rescheduling of the remaining bilateral debt is to suppress principal repayments to zero during the five-year horizon considered. The simulations for the Trinidad terms are identical except that they place the initial stock forgiveness at two-thirds rather than 40 percent, and, in addition, they effectively capitalize the remaining bilateral interest due over the horizon by increasing new bilateral lending from baseline by corresponding amounts. In both cases, all official interest arrears are treated as subject to the forgiveness, under the assumption that they are largely owed to bilateral creditors.

It is also of interest to consider the impact of a Brady Plan reduction in long-term debt owed to private banks. In January 1992 Nigeria concluded a Brady deal with the banks (World Bank 1993b, 1: 111). There were two options: a cash buyback at 40 cents on the dollar and debt conversion to a 30–year par bond with no change in principal but with interest reduced to $5^1/2$ percent for three years and $6^1/4$ percent thereafter. Somewhat surprisingly, 62 percent of banks opted for the buyback, implying considerable skepticism that the bond alternative would be fully honored.

The simulations of a Brady cut thus exclude Nigeria, which already secured its deal, with benefits already incorporated in the baseline. For the other groupings, it is assumed that long-term bank claims are reduced by 50 percent. For Congethivoire, where these claims represent 80 percent of private debt, the effect is to cut the stock of private debt (and private interest arrears) by 40 percent. For the rest of SSA, where long-term bank claims are only 47 percent of private debt, the simulation cuts private debt (and private interest arrears) by 23.5 percent. The average cut for SSA as a whole excluding Nigeria amounts to 29 percent of private long-term debt.

Table 7.7 shows the simulated impact of each of these reforms on sub-Saharan Africa's debt indicators, by composite country groups. For SSA as a whole, enhanced Toronto terms reduce total interest payments by $2.24 billion in 1995 (the period midpoint), reducing the interest/exports ratio from 16.5 percent to 12.4 percent in that year, and from 15.9 percent to 11.3 percent in 1997. Again for the entire SSA, Trinidad terms reduce total interest in 1995 by $3.4 billion from the baseline, reducing the interest/exports ratio from 16.5 percent to 10.2 percent in that year, and from 15.9 percent to 8.9 percent by 1997).[31]

In contrast, the Brady Plan applied to all of SSA except Nigeria would save only about $620 million in annual interest (for 1995), or only about 7 percent of the baseline level. The limited impact of a Brady-type reduction reflects the relatively small share of commercial bank claims in Africa's total debt. In terms of the interest/exports ratio, Brady relief reduces the indicator for 1997 from 15.9 percent to 14.7 percent. Finally, the combination of both the Trinidad and Brady packages reduces total SSA interest in 1995 by $4.0 billion, or nearly half. As a result, by 1997 the interest/exports ratio falls from 15.9 percent to 7.7 percent, an impressive reduction.

In sum, debt relief is relatively small for Brady forgiveness, considerably more significant from enhanced Toronto terms, even larger for Trinidad terms, and amounts to an effective reduction of the overall debt burden by about half if the joint Trinidad-Brady package is applied. Moreover, to the extent that debt rollover is a source of uncertainty, there is additional benefit from the rescheduling of principal coming due. From this standpoint, enhanced Toronto terms have a relatively larger impact. They cut the total debt service/exports ratio from 37.0 percent in 1997 (baseline) to 22.4 percent. Indeed, by this measure the additional impact of deeper relief is moderate. Thus, even the combination of Trinidad and Brady terms only cuts the debt service ratio further to 16.8 percent by 1997. This suggests that if cash flow as opposed to underlying real burden of interest is the problem, enhanced Toronto terms can provide much of the potential alleviation (more than two-thirds).

Once again it is informative to consider the behavior of arrears, this time as evidence of the effectiveness of alternative reforms. Enhanced Toronto terms enable the region to avoid the further buildup of arrears over the five-year period, and Trinidad terms permit the elimination of

---

31. Note that Husain and Underwood (1991b, 30) estimate that Trinidad terms would reduce annual debt service by "$4 billion" for "low-income" African countries. The corresponding figure for SSA as a whole, based on the estimates here, would be $9.2 billion, comprised of $3.4 billion interest reduction and $5.8 billion in elimination of bilateral principal amortization (based on changes for 1995).

arrears at the aggregate level.[32] These results are encouraging, because the cleaning up of arrears is an important part of the psychological fresh start that debt relief seeks to accomplish.

The simulation results for the individual composite "countries" show sharply diverging patterns. The most extreme result is that for the Sudan, Somalia, and Guinea-Bissau (Sudasombis), even the most generous debt relief under discussion—Trinidad plus Brady—leaves debt indicators impossibly high (with an interest/exports ratio of 74 percent and debt service ratio of 157 percent in 1997). These results differ so radically from those for the rest of the region that there should be little doubt that these three countries pose a unique debt problem that will have to be dealt with specially.

For "Mozagascaire," in contrast, Trinidad terms are quite successful in reducing the prospective debt burden to manageable levels. By 1997 they cut the interest/exports ratio from approximately 32 percent to approximately 14 percent, and the debt service ratio from 74 percent to 25 percent. Enhanced Toronto terms leave the interest/exports ratio arguably too high at 20.4 percent in 1997; and Brady relief makes almost no difference because of the limited role of bank debt in these countries.

For the group including Côte d'Ivoire and Congo, the Brady Plan has a somewhat greater impact, reducing the interest/exports ratio from approximately 30 percent in 1997 to approximately 25 percent. For these countries, enhanced Toronto terms provide about the same impact as Brady relief: both plans cut the interest/exports ratio in 1997 by about 5 percentage points, or one-sixth. Trinidad terms are more powerful, reducing the ratio by 7 percentage points (to 22.8 percent in 1997). Reducing the ratio substantially below 20 percent requires the combined Trinidad-Brady package, which leaves the interest/exports ratio at 18 percent by 1997.

Because the baseline for Nigeria already shows a sharp improvement, it is unclear that any further relief beyond the 1992 Brady agreement is necessary. However, the baseline improvement relies on persistent current account surplus, and the country could well prefer to spend the surplus on faster growth. It is thus useful to consider the impact of alternative official debt reductions on the flows for 1993 (the first year of the simulations), before the baseline has had a chance to reduce the debt indicators. Enhanced Toronto terms cut the interest/exports ratio from 15.9 percent to 12.7 percent in 1993; Trinidad terms, to 10.6 percent. Even the 1993 baseline level of 15.9 percent is arguably manageable without further relief, however.

For the countries in the group "Kentzamgola," enhanced Toronto terms have a moderate impact, as they cut the 1997 interest/exports ratio

---

32. Thanks in part, however, to large negative arrears in Nigeria by 1997. These should be seen as an idiosyncracy of the model formulation and should be interpreted as amounts by which the country could theoretically prepay debt.

from 15.7 percent to 12.6 percent. The largest possible package, Trinidad plus Brady, reduces the 1997 interest/exports ratio further to 9.6 percent. This cut by 6.1 percentage points is much smaller than the corresponding reductions for Mozagascaire (19 percentage points) and Congethivoire (11.8 percentage points). Lighter initial debt burden means more modest scope for the effects of debt relief.

This same result applies with even more force for the final group, Senguinali. Here the 1997 baseline ratio of interest to exports remains at its low 1993 level of about 6 percent. Even the deepest debt relief provides quite modest benefits, reducing the ratio from 6.3 percent to 3.6 percent in 1997. If certainty of debt rollover is the problem, a simple MYRA could provide the bulk of the potential gains from debt reform for this group. Thus, complete rescheduling of bilateral and private principal would reduce the debt service ratio from 15.8 percent to 10.8 percent in 1995.

Policy Implications

The results of the debt reform policy simulations suggest the following approach. First, a special program will be required for Sudan and Somalia, as discussed below. Second, for Mozambique, Madagascar, and Zaire, debt forgiveness along the lines of Trinidad terms would appear to be appropriate. The additional relief from adding Brady treatment for private bank claims would be limited (interest reduction of only 1 percent of export earnings), and thus perhaps not worth the time-consuming negotiations that might be required.

Third, for the group including Côte d'Ivoire and Congo, the appropriate package would seem to be a combination of Trinidad terms and Brady relief. Brady reduction has more impact for these countries because of their relatively higher bank debt. Forgiveness to the depth of Brady plus Trinidad appears to be necessary to reach a relatively moderate debt burden. However, Trinidad terms would require increased flexibility on the part of donors, who in the past have ruled out the application of even Toronto terms to "middle-income" countries such as Côte d'Ivoire (Lancaster 1991, 51).

Fourth, Nigeria would at most appear to need enhanced Toronto relief, and then only if the sharp improvement in the baseline is discarded as unrealistic. Arguably, the nation could manage adequately with no further debt relief, following its 1992 Brady agreement.

Fifth, for the 13 countries included in Kentzamgola, the most appropriate debt reform would appear to be application of enhanced Toronto terms.[33] For this group of nations, accounting for about 30 percent of the subcontinent's population, these terms would suffice to hold down the

---

33. Once again, donors would have to redefine eligibility to include countries in this group classified as middle income, such as Cameroon.

interest/exports ratio to about 12^1/$_2$ percent and the debt service ratio to about 26 percent by 1997. For these countries, the depth of true debt relief would be modest: only about 3 percent of export earnings in outright forgiveness of interest. However, because their interest/exports ratios are not particularly high even without forgiveness, the chief problem is not one of oppressive debt burden. Insofar as the problem is lack of certainty about principal rollover, the enhanced Toronto terms make an important difference, reducing the debt service ratio from the range of 38.5 percent to 26.4 percent at the end of the period.

For the 19 countries in Senguinali, debt forgiveness seems unnecessary on economic grounds. Their average interest/exports ratio of 6 percent in the baseline is too low to pose a problem of underlying debt overhang. At the most, enhanced Toronto terms might be appropriate. These terms would cut the 1997 interest/exports ratio by only 1.7 percentage point, but would reduce the debt service ratio by 6.1 percentage points, providing some reduction in uncertainty about new money to cover amortization. As suggested above, on purely economic grounds the approach of MYRAs would seem sufficient. On political grounds, however, it could be difficult for donors to deny enhanced Toronto terms to the countries in Senguinali while extending these or even more concessional terms to the rest of sub-Saharan Africa.

At the opposite extreme, for Sudan and Somalia[34] a truly radical debt plan would appear necessary. Part of the problem is that exports of goods and nonfactor services have fallen sharply in the two countries, from a peak of $817 million in 1989 to $368 million in 1992 in Sudan, and from $94 million in 1987 to $68 million in 1989 (the last year with data available) in Somalia (IMF 1993e). Civil war and famine have afflicted both countries, and it is reasonable to suppose that under more normal circumstances exports could perhaps double from their 1992 levels (especially considering that Sudan has oil reserves).

However, even with twice the export base, the existing debt burden would be unsupportable. Reducing the interest/exports ratio from approximately 200 percent (table 7.7) to 100 percent by doubling exports would still leave the rate infeasibly high.

A radical plan for Sudan and Somalia might have the following shape. Claims of the international financial institutions would be maintained intact. Together with interest on short-term debt (excluding interest arrears), the resulting total interest would be approximately $160 million annually. This flow would correspond to about 20 percent of the approximately $900 million in annual exports after the two countries regain double their current exports. This level would be close to the 20 percent threshold traditionally assumed to be a ceiling for what can be managed.

---

34. And Guinea-Bissau, also in the Sudasombis group but with much smaller total debt.

That essentially implies a need to forgive the rest of the debt: $7 billion in bilateral concessional and nonconcessional debt, $5.4 billion in interest arrears (mostly official), and $2 billion in private debt (table 7B.2). Forgiving some $14 billion in debt for just two countries may seem extreme; but the central fact is that these claims should be considered nearly worthless in any event. To the reasonable question of how creditors could have lent so much in the first place, the answer is that the great bulk of the debt (two-thirds) is in interest and principal arrears, and so was not lent voluntarily. Even so, coming to grips with the reality of this debt is likely to be a shock. Thus, the $14 billion potential write-off is equivalent to one year's flow of grant commitments to the subcontinent as a whole. The main ameliorating consideration is that about $4 billion of the face amount to be forgiven is in bilateral concessional claims, which have practically zero real present value because interest rates are less than 1 percent.

The Sudan-Somalia package raises serious questions of moral hazard and policy performance. In 1990, the IMF declared Sudan to be a "noncooperating state"; and despite resumption of negotiations in 1992, in August 1993 the IMF formally suspended the country's voting rights because of accumulation of arrears (Banks 1993, 788). It would be appropriate to withhold formal forgiveness until the two countries have policy reforms that reinstate them into IMF Structural Adjustment Facility or other relevant programs. In the meantime, G-7 countries that have not already done so would seem well advised to begin a process of "reserving" against these claims: for example, taking whatever budgetary measures are necessary to successively remove the fiscal fiction that the two countries will pay. As was the case with private bank claims before the Brady Plan in Latin America, this process could also facilitate outright forgiveness when the two countries' economic policies are more in order.

As a whole, the package of debt reform suggested here for sub-Saharan Africa has a somewhat but not unjustifiably skewed allocation of relief benefits. The Sudan-Somalia package provides about $890 million in annual interest relief by 1995. Also based on 1995 flows, the Trinidad terms save approximately $570 million in annual interest for Mozambique, Madagascar, and Zaire. The Trinidad-Brady combination saves Côte d'Ivoire, Congo, and Ethiopia about $630 million per year.[35]

Nigeria's interest savings from the 1992 Brady deal amount to about $240 million annually.[36] An enhanced Toronto deal would save another

---

35. This figure includes the savings on the much smaller debts of Burundi and Rwanda, also in this group.

36. The arrangement converted or extinguished $5.6 billion in long-term bank claims (World Bank 1993b, 2: 335). The calculation here assumes 7 percent original interest and 60 percent effective forgiveness.

$495 million in 1995, for a total of $735 million in debt relief savings on annual interest. In comparison, enhanced Toronto terms applied to all of the 32 other countries in Kentzamgola and Senguinali would relieve them of a total of only about $650 million in annual interest.

As a result, just three nations (Sudasombis) accounting for only 7 percent of the region's population would receive 26 percent of the interest forgiven; another three (Mozagascaire) representing 13 percent of the population would receive 16 percent. Five countries (Congethivoire) accounting for 16 percent of the region's population would receive 18 percent of the interest relief. Nigeria, with 22 percent of SSA population, would receive 21 percent of interest relief if enhanced Toronto terms were added to the existing Brady deal, but only 9 percent otherwise. In contrast, the 32 counties of Kentzamgola and Senguinali, representing 42 percent of the population, would receive only 19 percent of the interest relief.

The disproportionately high share of Sudan and Somalia in interest relief might seem inequitable to other countries. However, in the case of these two countries, debt relief would essentially amount to simple accounting candor on the part of donor nations, not a meaningful forgiveness of payments that otherwise could be expected to be made. That leaves the principal disparity between share of benefits and share of population for the countries in Kentzamgola and Senguinali.

The fundamental point, however, is not that interest relief should be passed out equally among all parties, but that it is appropriate only where the interest burden is considerably higher than a sustainable level. Moreover, the two country groupings receiving only enhanced Toronto terms would receive considerable debt-service rollover and the benefits of associated improved certainty. Thus, measured by total debt-service alleviation, Kentzamgola and Senguinali receive about 1.7 times as much as Mozagascaire, compared with a population that is about three times as high for the first two groups as for the latter.[37] The disparity is thus considerably smaller than for interest forgiveness alone.[38]

Nor is there a problem of inequity with respect to income levels. Average per capita income stands at $559 for Senguinali and $376 for Kentzamgola, versus $250 for Nigeria, $248 for Congethivoire, $188 for Mozagascaire, and $238 for Sudasombis (table 7.4).[39] The groupings

---

37. Thus, in 1995 the reform package suggested here reduces the Mozagascaire debt service by about $1.6 billion, and that for Kentzamgola and Senguinali by about $2.7 billion.

38. The ratio of the benefits share to the population share is 2.8 times as high for Mozagascaire as for Kentzamgola and Senguinali, measured by interest savings alone, but 1.8 times as high measured by debt service.

39. All of these figures are much lower than purchasing-parity per capita income, typically some three times as high for countries this poor.

with higher per capita income thus receive relatively less relief, especially measured by interest, so the package is progressive rather than regressive.

There are several additional dimensions of policy issues raised by the approach suggested here, and more generally by the African debt problem.

First, there is the issue of opposition by some donors to any forgiveness of bilateral claims. The United States had traditionally opposed Paris Club forgiveness of nonconcessional bilateral debt, but under Toronto terms for the first time acquiesced in allowing other creditors to reschedule this debt on concessional terms (while providing only the principal rollover relief on US claims; Lancaster 1991, 44). Japan, too, had systematically opposed forgiveness of bilateral claims.

However, both countries effectively shifted their policies (though Japan grudgingly so) in the 1991 forgiveness of 50 percent of bilateral credits owed by Poland and Egypt. The United States subsequently provided for debt forgiveness on Export-Import Bank claims on low-income countries in Latin America under the Enterprise for the Americas Initiative. Then, before the Tokyo economic summit in July 1993, the United States announced that it would write off half of the debt owed by 18 of the poorest African countries (IMF 1993f, 27). The broad implication seemed to be that after forgiveness for Egypt and Poland, refusal to forgive claims on low-income countries seemed inequitable. In any event, if the United States, Japan, or any other donor continued to oppose any forgiveness under either Toronto or Trinidad terms, it could nonetheless participate in burden sharing by increasing the amount of new grants to the countries in question by amounts corresponding to the forgiveness that otherwise would have been provided.

Second, there is the related issue of additionality. To the extent that the obligations forgiven under either Toronto or Trinidad terms cause cutbacks in the levels of new grants and concessional lending, the net effect of the debt reduction package is curtailed. There is greater risk of this outcome where budgetary accounting procedures are such that the amount forgiven must be appropriated in donor government budgets. As suggested above, it is desirable that some procedure for the reserving of questionable claims be instituted (where this is not done already), so that when actual forgiveness takes place the budgetary "hit" is minimized. Whatever the accounting treatment, some leakage to induced reductions in new aid is likely, so from this standpoint the calculations here tend to overstate the scope for effective debt relief through forgiveness of official claims.

Third, there is the question of how to treat claims of the multilateral development banks and the IMF. These institutions have tended to receive preferred treatment. Thus, in 1989 multilateral institutions received 86 percent of the debt service scheduled to be paid by SSA countries, whereas bilateral creditors received only 20 percent of the amount due, and private creditors only about one-third (World Bank 1990, 1: 89).

The general official position is that the claims of the international financial institutions (IFIs) must be considered sacrosanct, on the pain of an increase in their borrowing costs on the international credit markets otherwise. For its part, the IMF often has negative cash flows to these (and other) developing countries, defended on grounds that IMF funds are specifically designed to be of a shorter-term, revolving nature.

There is an important element of truth to each of these propositions, although it is difficult to believe that the World Bank's borrowing spread would rise significantly if the organization forgave (for example) the $9 million it holds in IBRD claims on Sudan (World Bank 1993b, 2: 407). The Bank's concessional loans outstanding through the International Development Association are much larger ($1.1 billion for Sudan and $400 million for Somalia), but there is little interest relief to be gained by forgiving concessional claims.

The real reason to oppose forgiving IFI claims is that this approach simply shifts the forgiveness burden from Peter to Paul. The G-7 countries are essentially the shareholders of the IFIs, and any loss of the IFIs is indirectly a loss to the G-7 countries. Because there is at least some value in the preferred creditor IFI status, it makes sense to continue their insulation from forgiveness. However, the corresponding implication is that the G-7 shareholders of the IFIs should stand ready to implement de facto IFI forgiveness indirectly where that seems to be an unavoidable part of an overall package.

The simplest means to accomplish this result would be pro rata increases in G-7 grant aid in amounts sufficient to cover repayment of arrears to IFIs. Alternatively, there could be a G-7 buyback of claims held by the World Bank, IMF, or regional multilateral banks. The buyback would have to be at full face value to preserve the principle of preferred creditor status. It is conceivable that some of the debt relief packages suggested here (primarily for Sudan, Somalia, Madagascar, Mozambique, and Zaire) might require some degree of such relief. If so, the G-7 countries would appropriately purchase the IBRD claims (for example), presumably in proportion to each donor country's share in total G-7 capital subscriptions in the World Bank.

A fourth underlying issue is the nature of policy conditionality for debt relief. Virtually all observers of African development concur that policy reform is crucial, in areas ranging from the normal areas of fiscal balance and removal of price distortions to corruption and other problems of ''governance'' (World Bank 1989c; Husain and Underwood 1991a; Killick 1991; Lancaster 1991).

Some add hopefully that countries in the region have been moving generally toward better policies (World Bank 1990). Recent World Bank analysis shows that among 29 SSA countries that had adjustment programs at some time in the period 1987–92, six had a large improvement in macroeconomic policies, nine some improvement, and eleven a deterioration; two-thirds had improved agricultural taxation policies. The six countries that had improved policies experienced a median increase of about 2 percent in per capita growth rates from previous levels, whereas those that did not improve policies had a median decline of 2 percent (World Bank 1994c, 1–3).

Lancaster (1991) suggests that, because of the paramount importance of domestic policy reform, African countries should be given debt relief only on the installment plan. She suggests that an Adjustment Review Consortium of donors should meet every two years or so to evaluate country policy reform. Where past performance has been favorable,

> creditor governments would be expected to cancel or reschedule on highly concessional terms the debt owed them for the coming performance period. . . . In addition, developed-country governments and the IFIs would commit appropriate amounts of aid. . . . Should the participating African government fail to make satisfactory progress toward reform, creditors and aid donors might decide to terminate, delay, or scale down the amount of their relief or assistance.

Lancaster thus favors the "short leash" approach to debt forgiveness. Her approach would give more complete forgiveness than either enhanced Toronto or Trinidad, but for much shorter periods than Trinidad (and shorter principal rollover than in either plan). Indeed, a key difference between Toronto and Trinidad is not just the depth of the cut, but also the fact that Trinidad forgives ex ante whereas Toronto forgives only in successive installments as they come due in serial "consolidation" periods of approximately one and one-half years (although the enhanced Toronto terms do provide for possible debt stock reduction after three years). The simulations reported here do not capture this important qualitative difference.

The difficulty with too short a leash is that it discards much of the expectational effect that can be associated with longer-term certainty resulting from a debt relief agreement. As suggested in chapter 6, the sharp decline in real domestic interest rates in Mexico after the announcement of the Brady Plan agreement was to some extent disproportionately large in view of the amount of debt forgiven. An important part of the favorable impact of relief was thus the elimination of a high risk premium attributable to exchange rate and other uncertainty in lieu of an agreement, as opposed to the direct effect of the forgiven payments. If the reappraisal period is set as short as two years, considerably more uncertainty would remain. This effect would then have to be traded off against the extent to which revocability would be more likely to ensure country adherence to improved policy performance.

Where past policy departures have been frequent and egregious, prudence would recommend Lancaster's short leash. However, for those countries that have sustained participation in Structural Adjustment Facility (SAF), Enhanced Structural Adjustment Facility (ESAF), or other adjustment programs linked to policy reform, it could be more appropriate to seek the more "definitive" and permanent debt relief of enhanced Toronto, Trinidad, or Brady terms.

Fifth, there is an important linkage implicit between future nonconcessional lending and the extent of debt forgiveness as opposed to rollover. In broad terms, enhanced Toronto terms place a greater emphasis on rolling over bilateral claims (as in the Baker Plan, for private bank claims) whereas Trinidad terms place more emphasis on forgiving them (as in the Brady Plan). A logical implication of forgiveness is that the country is not a good candidate for new borrowing on a nonconcessional basis. If the debt burden were light enough to sustain accumulation of nonconcessional debt, it should have been light enough not to warrant forgiveness.

There is an economic literature from the 1960s that addresses this issue, called the "economics of charity" (Schmidt 1964). This literature considers the form of assistance that maximizes the benefit to recipients at a given cost to donors, or minimizes donor cost for a given benefit to recipients. The principle is that if the rate of return is higher in the recipient country, the most efficient form of assistance is a loan; otherwise, it is a grant. A nonconcessional loan has much less (if any) real cost to the donor, so a much larger volume can be extended at no increased cost to the donor.

The implication of this literature for debt forgiveness is that a country so indebted that it requires forgiveness has an implicit rate of return on additional foreign borrowing that is low or negative (e.g., because of the associated debt buildup), so that the country should be in the position of receiving only grants. If donor cost is to be held constant, the implication is a much lower volume of assistance but on a grant rather than nonconcessional loan basis.

The suggested configuration of debt packages above is consistent with this broad admonition. Of the total volume of new loans extended to Sudan and Somalia in 1992 (excluding IMF funds), only about 12 percent was nonconcessional. The corresponding figure for Mozagascaire was 7 percent (tables 7B.2 and 7B.3). These nonconcessional flows continue to be small in the Trinidad reform simulated for Mozagascaire and the special program suggested here for Sudan and Somalia. In contrast, in 1992 the countries in Kentzamgola and Senguinali had new loans on a nonconcessional basis that amounted to about one-fifth of the total volume of bilateral and multilateral lending (excluding IMF; tables 7B.6 and 7B.7). Cutting off these nonconcessional loans and replacing them with grants of much smaller face value but equal present discounted value to the donors would impose a substantial opportunity cost on these countries, if their domestic return (even after allowing for a risk premium associated with external debt) is considerably higher than the rates charged on the loans. Because African countries are capital scarce, the general presumption would be that, so long as their domestic economic policies are sound, their rates of return on capital should be higher than those in the donor countries.

Indeed, this broad consideration is another reason why it is not inequitable to withhold deep forgiveness from one block of African countries (Kentzamgola and Senguinali) while extending it to others (Sudasombis, Mozagascaire, and Congethivoire).[40] Those not receiving deep forgiveness avoid the concomitant implication of a cutoff in new flows of nonconcessional lending.

Sixth, another fundamental issue is whether African countries might need debt forgiveness even if their measured debt burdens are relatively low, because they are poor and because their economies are not diversified. Thus, the World Bank (1990, vol. 1) argues that "two factors make sub-Saharan Africa's debt a greater burden than the debt of other highly indebted regions: the greater poverty and the more serious structural weaknesses of African economies" (89). The same document suggests that "debt-servicing difficulties are pervasive across the continent. Of the 44 countries in the region, 30 have resorted to rescheduling of their debt with their creditors, most often bilateral official debt reschedulings at the Paris Club" (89).

It is not clear that the arguments of "poverty" and "structure" stand up to scrutiny. At the empirical level, the estimates of the "debt Laffer curve" (Sachs and Huizinga 1987; Claessens 1990; D. Cohen 1990; see chapter 4) typically do not include a term for per capita income, but presumably they would have done so had it been significant. The implication is that there is little further information about debt-carrying capacity from the level of per capita income once the influence of the primary variables (e.g., debt/GDP ratio) have been taken into account. However, at the theoretical level, the specification of a debt overhang suggested by Corden (1989; see chapter 4) could provide for an influence of per capita income, because it turns on the prospect that the country will be pushed below a subsistence income.

In practice, the analysis here makes some allowance for a "poverty" shift factor, by examining debt reform packages that essentially hold the interest/exports ratio to the vicinity of 12–14 percent or below.[41] This

---

40. This strategy would be even more sharply dichotomous if debt reform for Kentzamgola and Senguinali were limited to MYRAs. Enhanced Toronto terms do include significant forgiveness.

41. In the packages recommended, 1997 interest/exports ratios stand at 14.3 percent for Mozagascaire, 12.6 percent for Kentzamgola, only 3 to 6 percent for Nigeria, and only 4.6

range is lower than has been characteristic of postcrisis Latin America. Thus, in 1992 the interest/exports ratio stood at 14.5 percent for Colombia and 18.9 percent for Mexico. For Chile, the ratio was an average of 16.2 percent in 1990–91 (though lower by 1992–93), and for Argentina, the ratio stood at 21.8 percent in 1993 (ECLAC 1993). Yet, at least provisionally, all of these countries are successful graduates from the Latin American debt crisis.

Moreover, India is a low-income country, with per capita income of about $350; yet that nation has been able to sustain interest/exports ratios in the vicinity of 15 percent (the 1992 level; calculated from World Bank 1993b, and IMF 1992a). The implicit ceiling of 12 to 14 percent suggested here is modestly lower.

As for structure of the economy, greater vulnerability to commodity price swings implies a greater role for consumption smoothing through borrowing and repaying, but not necessarily a lower sustainable debt ratio to exports (or GDP). Indeed, the Eaton-Gersovitz framework (chapter 4) would argue that countries with wider export fluctuations can sustain higher commercial debt, because the cost of default is greater to them, and creditors know this and can safely lend them more accordingly.

Nonetheless, the characterization by the World Bank just cited does leave the empirical fact that nearly three-fourths of African countries have been involved in debt rescheduling in recent years. Yet even this fact is consistent with the view stated at the outset of this section: for many African countries, the debt problem is more one of management than underlying excessive debt burden or "overhang."

Seventh, and finally, the simulations here make no allowance for capital flight. As reviewed in chapter 3, the omission of allowance for future capital flight was a principal source of understatement of the debt crisis in the 1983–84 projections for Latin America presented in Cline (1984). The same could be true for the calculations here for Africa.

Capital flight has indeed affected sub-Saharan Africa. Claessens and Naude (1993) place Sudan, Gabon, and Uganda among the 10 countries with the highest ratio of the stock of flight capital to GDP. They estimate that in 1991 SSA had a ratio of flight capital stock to GDP of 90 percent, compared with 35 percent in Latin America. However, the much greater divergence between purchasing-parity GDP and GDP at market exchange rates for SSA than for Latin America (because of the higher

---

percent for Senguinali. Congethivoire is an exception, with a ratio of 17.8 percent in 1997 (table 7.7). A higher postreform interest/exports ratio than for Mozagascaire, despite application of both Brady and Trinidad to Congethivoire, stems from the higher share of untouchable multilateral nonconcessional debt (10.5 percent for Congethivoire versus 3.8 percent for Mozagascaire) and only partly touchable private debt (22.6 percent versus 7.5 percent; tables 7B.3 and 7B.4). Sudasombis also pierces the 12–14 percent interest/exports ceiling, but it is an extreme case.

per capita income levels of the latter region) suggests that the relative stocks of flight capital may not be as different as these ratios suggest.[42]

For policy purposes, it would be a severe case of moral hazard to design the amount of debt forgiveness "necessary" by including a substantial allowance for capital flight. Moreover, if a debt consolidation program is implemented (including some degree of forgiveness), there are good reasons to expect that some of the stock of flight capital abroad will start to return, as has occurred in large magnitudes in several Latin American countries. From this standpoint the calculations here might even overstate the amount of forgiveness required. For these reasons, whereas it is important to keep the role of capital flight in mind, it does not seem appropriate to include capital flight in the policy analysis simulations.

Africa Summary

The analysis here takes a much more differentiated approach to the African debt problem than is usually encountered. The simulations suggest that over 30 countries in the region do not need deep debt forgiveness (and some 20 may need none at all), because their debt burdens are relatively light. For them, the assurance of principal rollover is probably the most important need, and this could be provided by multiyear rescheduling agreements. Some parallel framework of presumptively assured rollover of principal through new loans from the IFIs would be an important part of the Africa-style MYRA (call it the AMYRA), because these institutions bulk large in the debt yet are exempt from rescheduling. Beyond the AMYRA, moderate forgiveness under enhanced Toronto terms should certainly be sufficient for these countries.

At the opposite extreme, Sudan and Somalia are hopelessly indebted, and billions of dollars in nominal claims on these countries will have to be written off, if only for the purpose of truth in accounting. In between are countries representing a sizeable share of the region's debt and population where the deeper forgiveness of official claims under Trinidad terms would seem appropriate (Madagascar, Mozambique, and Zaire), with the added help of a Brady plan for private debt where bank claims are substantial (Côte d'Ivoire and Congo).

It is important to recognize that the corollary of relatively light indebtedness for many African countries is that debt forgiveness would provide little help for economic development. For most of the countries in the lighter-debt groupings, the key to sustained growth lies in adoption of and adherence to sound domestic policies, rather than in debt relief.

---

42. Purchasing-parity GDP tends to diverge the most from market exchange rate GDP for the poorest countries, because they have the cheapest labor. Because nontradeables are primarily labor-intensive, this phenomenon makes their exchange rates (determined only by tradeable goods) tend to overstate their domestic prices for a full basket of goods and services (and correspondingly understate the real value of their GDP).

Annex 7A

Reestimating Russia's Exports

It is an emerging stylized fact that Russia's exports have fallen by as much as half since the breakup of the former Soviet Union and in association with the economic disruption during the transition to capitalism. Several important policy issues are driven by this perception, including the urgency of foreign support and the viability of external debt. However, an important set of official international data suggests that the export collapse is primarily a statistical illusion.

The Implosion Estimates

The main data behind the new stylized fact are those from the Russian government. As reported by Lipton and Sachs (1992, 221), these data indicate that Russia's exports to non-FSU countries amounted to $80.9 billion in 1990 and fell to $51.6 billion in 1991. Lipton and Sachs report that oil exports fell from $27.1 billion in 1990 to $11.8 billion in 1991, although natural gas exports held approximately constant at $10 billion. Apparently using the same source, the World Bank (1993b, 1: 139) reports that the exports of "the former Soviet Union/Russia" stood at $82.6 billion in 1990, fell to $50.9 billion in 1991, and declined further to $40 billion in 1992. A special supplement of the IMF's standard statistical series released in late 1993 (IMF 1993a) repeats the same figures for 1991 and 1992.

These authoritative sources thus say that Russia's exports have fallen by half. Other estimates might imply that the collapse has been even greater. Thus, Collins and Rodrik (1991, 9) estimate that exports of the Soviet Union in 1988 were as high as $110 billion. If exports have fallen by half or more, no wonder the economy is in chaos, the exchange rate has been ridiculously undervalued, and debt cannot be serviced.

The Contrary Evidence

Curiously, however, nobody except the Russian government seems to have noticed the decline in Russian exports. As shown in table 7A.1, the import data reported by all of the trading partners of the former Soviet Union show that *exports from the FSU to the rest of the world were actually higher in 1992 than in 1990*. These data are from the International Monetary Fund's *Direction of Trade Statistics* (IMF 1993d). They are reported on a standardized basis to the IMF. Although the Soviet Union itself did not report, all of its trading partners (including the Eastern European coun-

Table 7a.1 FSU exports according to IMF[a], 1986-92 (billion of dollars)

	1986	1987	1988	1989	1990	1991	1992
Industrial countries	20.08	22.64	23.25	25.10	31.39	30.58	31.16
Germany	4.28	4.05	3.91	4.47	7.35	8.82	8.29
US	0.61	0.47	0.65	0.79	1.17	0.92	0.92
Japan	1.99	2.37	2.77	2.99	3.37	3.32	2.51
Other	13.20	15.75	15.92	16.85	19.50	17.52	19.44
Developing countries	21.05	21.14	21.95	20.76	19.61	19.04	22.44
EE5	15.63	15.24	14.88	13.16	10.78	10.33	10.91
Czechoslovakia	4.74	5.07	4.56	4.24	2.86	3.17	3.08
Hungary	2.97	2.80	2.35	1.96	1.64	1.59	1.86
Poland	3.24	2.68	3.45	1.87	1.62	2.19	2.41
Romania	2.81	2.76	2.71	2.85	2.21	0.88	0.81
Yugoslavia	1.87	1.93	1.81	2.24	2.45	2.50	2.75
LDC4	2.91	3.31	4.24	4.35	5.66	4.69	6.56
Afghanistan	0.42	0.50	0.63	0.76	0.88	0.96	1.06
China	1.47	1.29	1.80	2.15	2.21	2.11	3.88
India	0.67	1.21	1.37	0.81	1.32	0.52	0.57
Turkey	0.35	0.31	0.44	0.63	1.25	1.10	1.05
Other	2.51	2.59	2.83	3.25	3.17	4.02	4.97
TOTAL	41.12	43.78	45.20	45.86	51.00	49.63	53.60

a. Partner country imports, CIF.

Source: IMF, Direction of Trade Statistics Yearbook, 1992, 1993.

tries) did so. The former Council for Mutual Economic Assistance (COMECON) partners reported relatively well-behaved series of the dollar value of imports from the Soviet Union (now the FSU states), as shown in table 7A.1. Presumably the dollar values they reported bore a much closer resemblance to reality than arbitrary ruble values at the old official ruble-dollar exchange rates.

Largely for this reason, the goods actually arriving at the borders of the rest of the world never reached anywhere near the $110 billion suggested by Collins and Rodrik (1991), or even the $80 billion suggested by the Russian government.[1] Instead, the FSU has been exporting about $45 to $50 billion annually rather steadily over the past several years, and by 1992 exports were at the high rather than the low end of this range. That is, if we accept the trading partners' data rather than the Russian data.

Russia versus the FSU

Of course, the trading partner data in the *Direction of Trade* database are for imports from the full FSU, not just the Russian state. In principle this

---

1. Collins and Rodrik (1991) did note that their estimates were "sensitive to the accuracy of prices used to value ruble exports" (9).

could be a source of the statistical illusion of the export collapse. Thus, "Russia's" exports for 1990 might have been reconstructed by the Russian government as including exports to other FSU states, and thus exports that never reached the rest of the world. However, the World Bank (1993b) explicitly notes that the $80 billion figure for Russian exports in 1990 "exclude intra-FSU trade." Moreover, it reports the data as applicable to "the former Soviet Union/Russia," implying that for 1990 the data are FSU and thereafter they are for Russia.

We are thus confronted with the problem that Russian authorities believe the FSU exported $80 billion in 1990 whereas the rest of the world believes the FSU exported only $51 billion (table 7A.1; actually about 10 percent less allowing for FOB/CIF conversion). The discrepancy almost certainly stems from the exchange rate applied to ruble trade with COMECON countries. As noted, these partners reported one set of dollar-equivalent data to the IMF. Apparently the Russian authorities apply a much higher exchange rate for the ruble-based trade, giving a larger figure.

Thus, from table 7A.1 it may be seen that imports of the five largest Eastern European countries from the FSU in 1990 amounted to $11 billion in 1990. If the ruble conversion were three times higher for this trade, the measured FSU exports for that year would have stood at about $70 billion instead of $50 billion, getting close to the $80 billion figure (but for the full FSU rather than Russia alone).

Nor is it at all plausible that there has in fact been a collapse of Russian exports to non-FSU countries but an unchanged level of total FSU exports. That would imply that suddenly the exports of Ukraine and other FSU states besides Russia had soared to high levels. Surely that is not the case. Although these other FSU (OFSU) states apparently did make a major effort by 1992 to redirect exports from Russia to the rest of the world, the magnitude of this effect was limited. As their total exports in 1992 were on the order of $15 billion,[2] even if OFSU exports to the rest of the world doubled from 1990 to 1992 the implication would have been only a decline of about $5 billion in Russian exports to non-FSU countries, given the increase of $2.6 billion for total FSU exports reported by non-FSU countries (table 7A.1).

It is probably true that Russian exports *including* (properly valued) exports to OFSU states have declined substantially. One reason is that in 1992 Russia began limiting acceptance of payment in rubles for OFSU purchases of Russian goods. Another is that, partly in response to IMF urging, Russia cut subsidies of exports to OFSU, just as it had done on exports to Eastern Europe in 1991.

---

2. Calculated from IMF (1993j). The estimate here imputes a figure of $5 billion for Ukrainian exports to non-FSU countries, as the IMF source provides no figure.

In contrast, it is far less apparent that Russian exports to the rest of the world have fallen. Indeed, one source that explicitly reports Russian rather than FSU exports indicates that Russia's exports to non-FSU countries stood at $30 billion in 1989, $26 billion in 1990, and $36.8 billion in 1991 (Vasiliev 1993, 331). Ironically, these data are also from an official Russian source (Goskmostat). Yet their $10 billion *increase* from 1990 to 1991 is in stark contradiction to the $30 billion *decline* reported by Lipton and Sachs and by the World Bank. Vasiliev also reports that at purchasing-parity exchange rates, Russia's exports to OFSU stood at about $50 billion in both 1990 and 1991. Intriguingly, their inclusion places the total at the mythical $80 billion figure for 1990; yet those (official) sources using that figure explicitly state that it excludes exports to OFSU states.

Underinvoicing?

Suppose we discard the figure of $80 billion for 1990 as meaningless and concentrate attention on the estimated decline of Russia's exports (to non-FSU states) from $50.9 billion in 1991 to $40 billion in 1992 (World Bank 1993b). Setting aside for the moment that the 1991 figure still looks too high (non-Russian FSU exports probably were on the order of $10 billion, meaning—from table 7A.1 here—that Russian exports to non-FSU should only have been about $40 billion in 1991), it might be the case that an increase in underinvoicing caused a reduction of some $10 billion in official data on Russian exports. Massive capital flight has been a problem, and underinvoicing is one means of achieving capital flight.

The problem with the explanation that underinvoicing has increased is that Russia's reported export figure for 1992 is too high. Suppose underinvoicing is 25 percent. The official figure for exports of $40 billion in 1992 (according to the Washington agencies) would imply true exports of $50 billion. Adding $15 billion for OFSU exports to non-FSU countries in 1992, total FSU exports would be $65 billion—much too high for consistency with partner trade data. So although a surge in underinvoicing is appealing as an explanation of why reported Russian exports dropped by $10 billion from 1991 to 1992, it is inconsistent with the still high level of officially recorded exports in 1992.

Conclusion

It is time to discard the new stylized fact that Russia's exports have plummeted by half or more. Until better data are provided by the official community, one should treat the Russian data as a statistical chaos. In these circumstances, partner trade data are the best source of measurement. On this basis, an appropriately revised stylized fact should be that

FSU exports meaningfully measured have not changed much, or have actually risen, from the late 1980s to 1992 (table 7A.1). Because even by generous estimation the increase in exports by the Ukraine and other OFSU countries has been modest, the same data strongly suggest that any decline in Russia's exports to non-FSU countries has been small, probably no more than 10 percent.

Annex 7B

A Debt Simulation Model for Africa

To evaluate the severity of the debt problem in sub-Saharan Africa, and to examine the impact of alternative debt relief proposals, a simple debt projection model may be specified as follows. The model is of an "accounting" rather than "behavioral" nature. Thus, growth of key variables such as exports, imports, lending by assistance category, and so forth may be specified at exogenously given and constant nominal rates. Debt stocks and interest flows then may be derived from the resulting financial gaps and the relevant interest burdens on them. The model provides for the accumulation of arrears. As discussed in the text, the model may be applied to SSA in the aggregate, and individually to subgroups within the region.

The Model

Nominal exports of goods and nonfactor services in year t' are projected as

$$XGS_t = XGS_0(1 + g_x)^t \tag{7B.1}$$

Imports of goods and nonfactor services are projected similarly:

$$MGS_t = MGS_0(1 + g_m)t \tag{7B.2}$$

The main estimates set both rates equal to nominal 4 percent growth, compatible with 2 percent annual international inflation for tradeable goods and 2 percent real growth, or combinations of higher inflation and lower growth or the converse.

Interest payable on an accrual basis is

$$IPAY_t = \Sigma_k D_{k,t-1} r_k + r_{AR} IAR_{t-1} \tag{7B.3}$$

where k is the category of debt, r_k is the corresponding interest rate, r_{AR} is the interest rate applicable to interest arrears, and IAR is interest arrears.

Interest earnings on reserves provide the income

$$IREC_t = r_R RES_{t-1} \tag{7B.4}$$

where RES is the level of reserves and r_R is the US Treasury bill rate.

Remittance of profits abroad is calculated as

$$PROF_t = \rho KDFI_{t-1} \tag{7B.5}$$

where *KDFI* is the estimated stock of direct foreign investment.

Net inward transfers are estimated as official development assistance in the form of grants and are assumed to grow at the nominal rate g_G, so that

$$GRANT_t = GRANT_0(1 + g_G)^t \tag{7B.6}$$

The current account balance is then obtained as

$$CA_t = XGS_t - MGS_t - IPAY_t + IREC_t - PROF_t + GRANT_t \tag{7B.7}$$

The capital account must cover the current account deficit and in addition provide for any buildup in reserves, so that

$$KA_t = \Delta R_t - CA_t \tag{7B.8}$$

Reserves are assumed to grow at the exogenous rate g_R, so that

$$\Delta R_t = g_R R_{t-1} \tag{7B.9}$$

New loan disbursements in each debt category are assumed to grow at constant individual rates, so that

$$L_{kt} = L_{k0}(1 + g_{Lk})^t \tag{7B.10}$$

Amortization due on each debt category, on an accrual basis, is estimated as

$$AZ_{k,t} = \alpha_k D_{k,t-1} \tag{7B.11}$$

Direct investment (net inflow) grows at the exogenous rate g_{DFI}, so that

$$DFI_t = DFI_0(1 + g_{DFI})^t \tag{7B.12}$$

The existing stock of foreign direct investment is estimated as

$$KDFI_t = KDFI_{t-1} + DFI_t \tag{7B.13}$$

This treatment ignores depreciation and reinvestment of domestic earnings, as they are of secondary importance and to some extent mutually offsetting.

The residual in the system is the accumulation of arrears. This source of ''financing'' must be just the right amount so that, together with formal new loans net of amortization, as well as direct investment, the resulting capital flow equals the capital account determined in equation 7B.7. Thus,

$$\Delta ARS_t = KA_t - \Sigma_k[L_{k,t} - AZ_{k,t}] - DFI_t \tag{7B.14}$$

It is assumed that new arrears are allocated into four categories: official interest, private interest, official principal, and private principal. All official arrears are considered bilateral nonconcessional. The division into these four categories is assumed proportional to their respective shares in the stock of arrears in the base period. As a result, interest arrears accumulate as

$$IAR_t = IAR_{t-1} + \Delta ARS_t(\phi_{IO} + \phi_{IP}) \tag{7B.15}$$

where ϕ is the category share in base period arrears, and IO and IP refer to official interest and private interest, respectively.

Similarly, the path of principal arrears is

$$PAR_{O,t} = PAR_{O,t-1} + \phi_{PO}(\Delta ARS_t) \tag{7B.16a}$$

$$PAR_{P,t} = PAR_{P,t-1} + \phi_{PP}(\Delta ARS_t) \tag{7B.16b}$$

where PAR refers to principal arrears and subscripts O and P refer to official and private, respectively.

The path of debt in each category is then traced as

$$D_{k,t} = D_{k,t-1} + L_{k,t} - AZ_{k,t} + \Delta ARS_t\phi_{Pk} \tag{7B.17}$$

where ϕ_{Pk} is the share of category k principal in total (i.e., interest plus principal) arrears in the base period. Note that ϕ_{Pk} is assumed to be zero except for bilateral nonconcessional loans and private loans.

The model then calculates alternative debt indicators: ratio of debt to exports (of goods and services), ratio of interest (accrual basis) to exports, and debt service (accrual) to exports. Note that the debt service ratio excludes short-term debt, as that debt is typically related to trade and is rolled over.

Parameters

Table 7B.1 reports the parameters used in the model. The World Bank's *World Debt Tables* are the source of most of the parameter estimates. Because this source reports interest and amortization on a cash rather than accrual basis, accrual interest and amortization rates must be estimated indirectly. For this purpose, statistical regressions across the 45 SSA countries are conducted relating total multilateral interest due in 1993 to two variables: the stock of multilateral concessional debt in 1992 and the stock of multilateral nonconcessional debt in 1992 (with the intercept forced to zero). The regression coefficients tell the best estimate of the typical interest rates on multilateral concessional and nonconcessional lending, respectively. The same approach is used to estimate the interest

Table 7b.1 Africa debt projection model parameters

Symbol	Concept	Value
	Growth rates (nominal):	
g_X	exports	.04
g_m	imports	.04
g_G	grants	.04
g_{DFI}	direct investment	.05
	Rates of interest or return (nominal):	
ρ	direct investment	.15
r_R	treasury bill	.03
r_{MC}	multilateral concessional debt	.0084
r_{MN}	multilateral nonconcessional debt	.087
r_{BC}	bilateral concessional debt	.01
r_{BN}	bilateral nonconcessional debt	.0683
r_P	private debt	.07
r_{IMF}	IMF obligations	.07
r_{ST}	short term debt	.07
r_{AR}	interest arrears debt	.06
	Growth rates of new loans (nominal):	
...	all except short term	.04
...	short term	0.00
	Amortization rates	
α_{MC}	multilateral concessional debt	.025
α_{MN}	multilateral nonconcessional debt	.082
α_{BC}	bilateral concessional debt	.041
α_{BN}	bilateral nonconcessional debt	.105
α_{IMF}	IMF obligations	.2
α_P	private debt	.12

rates on bilateral concessional and nonconcessional debt, as well as the amortization rates on all four categories of debt. All of the coefficients (rates) are statistically significant at the 1 percent level or better.

All growth rates are in nominal (dollar) terms and are simply postulated.

Policy Simulations

The model is shocked to simulate the impact of four alternative policies: (1) enhanced Toronto terms, (2) Trinidad terms, (3) Brady Plan, and (4) joint application of Trinidad terms and Brady Plan. The main text describes the policy assumptions for each of these cases.

Table 7b.2 Baseline run: Sudasombis, 1992-97
(millions of dollars)

	1992	1993	1994	1995	1996	1997
Debt	19,165	20,424	21,784	23,251	24,833	26,535
Mult conc	2,737	2,782	2,830	2,882	2,938	2,997
Mult nonc	189	190	192	194	197	200
Bilat conc	3,869	3,720	3,578	3,441	3,310	3,184
Bilat nonc	3,126	3,594	4,072	4,563	5,069	5,594
IMF	1,082	1,100	1,123	1,152	1,184	1,221
Private	2,036	2,094	2,168	2,257	2,361	2,479
Short term	667	667	667	667	667	667
Interest arrears	5,459	6,276	7,154	8,096	9,107	10,192
Exports	444	462	480	499	519	540
Imports	1,596	1,660	1,726	1,795	1,867	1,942
Interest due	565	884	969	1,061	1,158	1,262
Profits	0	0	0	1	1	2
Other FSM	−201	−209	−217	−226	−235	−245
Interest received	2	2	2	2	2	2
Other FSX	21	22	23	24	25	26
Grants	567	590	613	638	663	690
Current account	−926	−1,260	−1,361	−1,468	−1,582	−1,704
Capital account	839	1,262	1,363	1,471	1,585	1,707
Reserve change	16	2	3	3	3	3
Direct investment	3	3	3	3	4	4

(table continued on next page)

Table 7b.2 (continued)

	1992	1993	1994	1995	1996	1997
Loans	360	374	389	404	419	436
Mult conc	109	113	118	123	128	133
Mult nonc	16	17	17	18	19	19
Bilat conc	10	10	10	10	10	10
Bilat nonc	0	0	0	0	0	0
IMF	225	234	243	253	263	274
Private	0	0	0	0	0	0
Amortization	1,030	1,032	1,086	1,146	1,209	1,278
Mult conc	68	68	70	71	72	73
Mult nonc	15	15	16	16	16	16
Bilat conc	159	159	153	147	141	136
Bilat nonc	328	328	377	428	479	532
IMF	216	216	220	225	230	237
Private	244	244	251	260	271	283
Arrears	12,801	14,718	16,775	18,984	21,355	23,900
Official interest	4,834	5,558	6,335	7,169	8,064	9,025
Private interest	625	719	819	927	1,043	1,167
Official principal	5,320	6,117	6,972	7,890	8,875	9,933
Private principal	2,022	2,325	2,650	2,999	3,373	3,775
Debt indicators						
Debt/XGS	4,316	4,423	4,536	4,655	4,781	4,912
Interest/XGS	127.3	191.5	201.9	212.4	223.0	233.7
Debt service/XGS	359.2	414.9	428.1	441.7	455.8	470.2

Table 7b.3 Baseline run: Mozagascaire, 1992-97
(millions of dollars)

	1992	1993	1994	1995	1996	1997
Debt	20,224	21,470	22,807	24,240	25,777	27,424
Mult conc	3,393	3,597	3,808	4,026	4,250	4,482
Mult nonc	763	725	692	662	636	613
Bilat conc	4,910	4,816	4,725	4,639	4,555	4,476
Bilat nonc	6,276	6,532	6,818	7,135	7,486	7,871
IMF	734	748	766	787	811	838
Private	1,511	1,719	1,927	2,135	2,347	2,563
Short term	468	468	468	468	468	468
Interest arrears	2,169	2,864	3,603	4,388	5,224	6,115
Exports	3,099	3,223	3,352	3,486	3,625	3,770
Imports	4,224	4,393	4,569	4,751	4,941	5,139
Interest due	793	893	965	1,043	1,126	1,215
Profits	64	64	71	79	87	96
Other FSM	128	133	138	144	150	156
Interest received	17	14	15	15	16	17
Other FSX	61	63	66	69	71	74
Grants	871	906	942	980	1,019	1,060
Current account	−1,161	−1,276	−1,369	−1,467	−1,573	−1,685
Capital account	1,145	1,295	1,389	1,488	1,594	1,707
Reserve change	−13	19	20	21	21	22
Direct investment	47	49	52	54	57	60

(table continued on next page)

Table 7b.3 (continued)

	1992	1993	1994	1995	1996	1997
Loans	578	597	616	637	658	680
Mult conc	278	289	301	313	325	338
Mult nonc	24	25	26	27	28	29
Bilat conc	107	107	107	107	107	107
Bilat nonc	4	4	4	4	5	5
IMF	155	161	168	174	181	189
Private	10	10	11	11	12	12
Amortization	1,336	1,336	1,389	1,446	1,508	1,575
Mult conc	85	85	90	95	101	106
Mult nonc	63	63	59	57	54	52
Bilat conc	201	201	197	194	190	187
Bilat nonc	659	659	686	716	749	786
IMF	147	147	150	153	157	162
Private	181	181	206	231	256	282
Arrears	6,193	8,178	10,287	12,530	14,917	17,459
Official interest	1,863	2,460	3,095	3,769	4,487	5,252
Private interest	306	404	508	619	737	863
Official principal	2,841	3,752	4,719	5,748	6,843	8,009
Private principal	1,183	1,562	1,965	2,393	2,849	3,335
Debt indicators						
Debt/XGS	653	666	680	695	711	727
Interest/XGS	25.6	27.7	28.8	29.9	31.1	32.2
Debt service/XGS	68.7	69.1	70.2	71.4	72.6	74.0

Table 7b.4 Baseline run: Congethivoire, 1992-97
(millions of dollars)

	1992	1993	1994	1995	1996	1997
Debt	29,188	31,151	33,238	35,458	37,819	40,331
Mult conc	3,372	3,812	4,262	4,722	5,194	5,677
Mult nonc	3,070	3,053	3,047	3,052	3,066	3,089
Bilat conc	6,335	6,363	6,390	6,416	6,441	6,465
Bilat nonc	3,905	4,059	4,239	4,446	4,680	4,942
IMF	367	385	403	422	440	459
Private	6,586	7,184	7,802	8,447	9,120	9,826
Short term	3,758	3,758	3,758	3,758	3,758	3,758
Interest arrears	1,795	2,537	3,336	4,195	5,120	6,114
Exports	5,362	5,576	5,800	6,032	6,273	6,524
Imports	6,663	6,930	7,207	7,495	7,795	8,107
Interest due	1,388	1,483	1,584	1,692	1,809	1,934
Profits	114	114	123	132	142	153
Other FSM	192	200	208	216	225	234
Interest received	14	15	16	16	17	18
Other FSX	60	62	65	67	70	73
Grants	1,028	1,069	1,112	1,156	1,203	1,251
Current account	−1,895	−2,003	−2,129	−2,264	−2,408	−2,562
Capital account	1,677	2,023	2,150	2,285	2,430	2,585
Reserve change	31	20	21	22	22	23
Direct investment	57	60	63	66	69	73

(table continued on next page)

Table 7b.4 (continued)

	1992	1993	1994	1995	1996	1997
Loans	1,453	1,500	1,548	1,598	1,651	1,705
Mult conc	504	524	545	567	590	613
Mult nonc	226	235	244	254	264	275
Bilat conc	288	288	288	288	288	288
Bilat nonc	14	15	15	16	16	17
IMF	88	92	95	99	103	107
Private	333	346	360	375	390	405
Amortization	1,869	1,870	1,972	2,081	2,196	2,319
Mult conc	84	84	95	107	118	130
Mult nonc	252	252	250	250	250	251
Bilat conc	260	260	261	262	263	264
Bilat nonc	410	410	426	445	467	491
IMF	73	73	77	81	84	88
Private	790	790	862	936	1,014	1,094
Arrears	5,643	7,976	10,487	13,188	16,095	19,221
Official interest	668	944	1,241	1,561	1,905	2,275
Private interest	1,127	1,593	2,094	2,634	3,214	3,839
Official principal	1,329	1,879	2,470	3,106	3,790	4,527
Private principal	2,519	3,561	4,681	5,887	7,185	8,580
Debt indicators						
Debt/XGS	544	559	573	588	603	618
Interest/XGS	25.9	26.6	27.3	28.1	28.8	29.6
Debt service/XGS	60.7	60.1	61.3	62.5	63.8	65.2

Table 7b.5 Baseline run: Nigeria, 1992-97 (millions of dollars)

	1992	1993	1994	1995	1996	1997
Debt	30,999	27,544	23,752	19,599	15,060	10,108
Mult conc	175	209	244	279	316	353
Mult nonc	3,913	4,107	4,306	4,509	4,719	4,934
Bilat conc	1,038	1,165	1,288	1,405	1,517	1,625
Bilat nonc	13,373	11,520	9,586	7,569	5,461	3,258
IMF	0	0	0	0	0	0
Private	10,290	8,736	7,172	5,588	3,978	2,333
Short term	1,013	1,013	1,013	1,013	1,013	1,013
Interest arrears	1,197	794	144	−764	−1,943	−3,407
Exports	12,844	13,358	13,892	14,448	15,026	15,627
Imports	8,991	9,351	9,725	10,114	10,518	10,939
Interest due	2,352	2,129	1,888	1,626	1,342	1,034
Profits	116	116	257	406	561	725
Other FSM	26	27	28	29	30	32
Interest received	162	29	30	31	33	34
Other FSX	3	3	3	3	4	4
Grants	754	784	816	848	882	917
Current account	2,268	2,552	2,843	3,156	3,492	3,852
Capital account	−5,783	−2,513	−2,803	−3,115	−3,449	−3,807
Reserve change	−3,468	39	40	42	44	45
Direct investment	897	942	989	1,038	1,090	1,145

(table continued on next page)

Table 7b.5 (continued)

	1992	1993	1994	1995	1996	1997
Loans	706	727	750	773	797	822
Mult conc	37	38	40	42	43	45
Mult nonc	495	515	535	557	579	602
Bilat conc	170	170	170	170	170	170
Bilat nonc	0	0	0	0	0	0
IMF	0	0	0	0	0	0
Private	4	4	4	4	5	5
Amortization	3,007	3,007	2,648	2,279	1,900	1,508
Mult conc	4	4	5	6	7	8
Mult nonc	321	321	337	353	370	387
Bilat conc	43	43	48	53	58	62
Bilat nonc	1,404	1,404	1,210	1,007	795	573
IMF	0	0	0	0	0	0
Private	1,235	1,235	1,048	861	671	477
Arrears	3,489	2,313	419	−2,227	−5,664	−9,930
Official interest	1,021	677	123	−652	−1,657	−2,906
Private interest	176	117	21	−112	−286	−501
Official principal	1,333	884	160	−851	−2,164	−3,794
Private principal	959	636	115	−612	−1,557	−2,729
Debt indicators						
Debt/XGS	241	206	171	136	100	65
Interest/XGS	18.3	15.9	13.6	11.3	8.9	6.6
Debt service/XGS	41.7	38.4	32.6	27.0	21.6	16.3

Table 7b.6 Baseline run: Kentzamgola, 1992-97 (millions of dollars)

	1992	1993	1994	1995	1996	1997
Debt	58,010	60,779	63,684	66,737	69,945	73,321
Mult conc	11,651	12,778	13,934	15,120	16,338	17,589
Mult nonc	4,474	4,657	4,848	5,045	5,250	5,463
Bilat conc	12,872	13,040	13,202	13,356	13,505	13,647
Bilat nonc	7,839	8,290	8,767	9,276	9,821	10,407
IMF	3,145	3,169	3,215	3,278	3,357	3,450
Private	10,147	10,493	10,871	11,282	11,726	12,207
Short term	5,209	5,209	5,209	5,209	5,209	5,209
Interest arrears	2,673	3,141	3,639	4,171	4,739	5,349
Exports	16,244	16,894	17,570	18,272	19,003	19,763
Imports	17,905	18,621	19,366	20,141	20,946	21,784
Interest due	2,502	2,607	2,719	2,839	2,967	3,105
Profits	809	809	864	921	981	1,045
Other FSM	648	674	701	729	758	788
Interest received	85	48	50	52	54	56
Other FSX	80	83	87	90	94	97
Grants	2,516	2,617	2,721	2,830	2,943	3,061
Current account	−2,887	−3,070	−3,222	−3,385	−3,559	−3,744
Capital account	1,976	3,133	3,288	3,454	3,630	3,819
Reserve change	−309	64	66	69	71	74
Direct investment	347	364	383	402	422	443

(table continued on next page)

Table 7b.6 (continued)

	1992	1993	1994	1995	1996	1997
Loans	4,592	4,748	4,910	5,078	5,254	5,436
Mult conc	1,364	1,419	1,475	1,534	1,596	1,660
Mult nonc	529	550	572	595	619	644
Bilat conc	696	696	696	696	696	696
Bilat nonc	294	306	318	331	344	358
IMF	628	653	679	706	735	764
Private	1,081	1,124	1,169	1,216	1,265	1,315
Amortization	3,856	3,856	3,999	4,155	4,323	4,502
Mult conc	291	291	319	348	378	408
Mult nonc	367	367	382	397	414	431
Bilat conc	528	528	535	541	548	554
Bilat nonc	823	823	870	921	974	1,031
IMF	629	629	634	643	656	671
Private	1,218	1,218	1,259	1,305	1,354	1,407
Arrears	10,708	12,584	14,580	16,709	18,986	21,428
Official interest	1,771	2,081	2,411	2,763	3,140	3,544
Private interest	902	1,060	1,228	1,407	1,599	1,805
Official principal	5,525	6,493	7,523	8,621	9,796	11,056
Private principal	2,510	2,950	3,418	3,917	4,450	5,023
Debt indicators						
Debt/XGS	357	360	362	365	368	371
Interest/XGS	15.4	15.4	15.5	15.5	15.6	15.7
Debt service/XGS	39.1	38.3	38.2	38.3	38.4	38.5

Table 7b.7 Baseline Run: Senguinali, 1992-97 (millions of dollars)

	1992	1993	1994	1995	1996	1997
Debt	20,193	21,301	22,472	23,711	25,024	26,414
Mult conc	7,048	7,729	8,427	9,143	9,878	10,634
Mult nonc	1,361	1,473	1,585	1,697	1,809	1,922
Bilat conc	5,969	6,007	6,044	6,079	6,113	6,145
Bilat nonc	1,769	1,876	2,002	2,148	2,317	2,509
IMF	1,016	1,037	1,064	1,094	1,128	1,165
Private	989	998	1,016	1,042	1,077	1,121
Short term	1,229	1,229	1,229	1,229	1,229	1,229
Interest arrears	812	951	1,106	1,279	1,473	1,688
Exports	10,330	10,743	11,173	11,620	12,085	12,568
Imports	14,149	14,715	15,304	15,916	16,552	17,214
Interest due	605	633	667	704	744	788
Profits	507	507	540	575	612	650
Other FSM	28	29	30	31	33	34
Interest received	230	202	211	219	228	237
Other FSX	650	676	703	731	760	791
Grants	3,080	3,203	3,331	3,465	3,603	3,747
Current account	−938	−1,059	−1,123	−1,192	−1,265	−1,344
Capital account	1,012	1,329	1,404	1,484	1,569	1,660
Reserve change	203	270	281	292	304	316
Direct investment	211	222	233	244	256	269

(table continued on next page)

Table 7b.7 (continued)

	1992	1993	1994	1995	1996	1997
Loans	1,649	1,704	1,760	1,820	1,881	1,945
Mult conc	824	857	891	927	964	1,003
Mult nonc	215	224	233	242	252	262
Bilat conc	283	283	283	283	283	283
Bilat nonc	48	50	52	54	56	58
IMF	216	225	234	243	253	263
Private	63	66	68	71	74	77
Amortization	1,041	1,040	1,085	1,133	1,186	1,244
Mult conc	176	176	193	211	229	247
Mult nonc	112	112	121	130	139	148
Bilat conc	245	245	246	248	249	251
Bilat nonc	186	186	197	210	226	243
IMF	203	203	207	213	219	226
Private	119	119	120	122	125	129
Arrears	2,594	3,038	3,534	4,087	4,704	5,394
Official interest	614	719	836	967	1,113	1,277
Private interest	198	232	270	312	359	412
Official principal	1,419	1,662	1,933	2,236	2,573	2,951
Private principal	363	425	494	572	658	755
Debt indicators						
Debt/XGS	195	198	201	204	207	210
Interest/XGS	5.9	5.9	6.0	6.1	6.2	6.3
Debt service/XGS	15.9	15.6	15.7	15.8	16.0	16.2

8

Capital Markets in the 1990s

Introduction

After the Latin American defaults on bonds in the 1930s, the region was locked out of the international capital market for four decades. The debt crisis of the 1980s and the policy response to it have left a much more favorable legacy this time around. By 1990 and especially 1991 there had already been a rebound in capital flows to the debtor countries. One reason was that most major debtors had undertaken massive policy reforms prompted in part by the debt crisis itself. Another was that Brady Plan debt reduction agreements helped to remove uncertainty. A third reason was that with recession in the United States, dollar-based interest rates fell to lows that encouraged capital flows in pursuit of higher returns in the debtor countries. Repatriation of flight capital originally from these countries themselves played an important role in these flows.

This chapter examines the nature and sustainability of the resurgence in international capital flows to developing countries, especially the formerly troubled debtors. Several major questions stand out.

- Is the resurgence primarily the consequence of economic policy reforms in debtor countries and resolution of the debt crisis, or primarily the result of low interest rates abroad?

- Are the capital flows patient investments or hot money likely to turn around and exit if international interest rates rise?

- Is the shift in composition from bank lending to bonds and equity a sign of system strengthening? Is rapid increase in the new channels a transitory adjustment or a sustainable pattern?

- Can those countries that have chosen a fixed exchange rate "anchor" to fight inflation, and as a consequence have developed large current account deficits, sustain this policy and their large capital inflows?

- How much of the resurgence has been attributable to the reversal of capital flight, and how much scope is there for this phenomenon to provide ongoing reflows?

- What adverse side effects have there been from the new environment of ample capital inflows, and how have countries tried to deal with them?

- Has there been a lasting imprint of the debt crisis on perceived country credit risk? Has the capital market shown sensible discrimination among countries by past credit record and domestic economic policies, or has the new capital market environment been one of reckless money with no memory of the past decade?

- Does the resurgence of capital flows mean that Latin America and perhaps other regions are in the opening phases of another cycle of financial boom and bust leading eventually to another debt crisis?

- Is the international financial system any less vulnerable to another debt crisis than it was in the early 1980s?

- What international policy measures, if any, should be taken to enhance both systemic stability and improved growth prospects for developing countries in light of the new trends in the international capital market?

The Capital Market Resurgence

Table 8.1 shows a broad measure of net capital flows to developing countries. The measure is obtained by summing the negative of the current account balance and the change in official reserves. By balance of payments accounting, this sum equals the net inflow of capital plus errors and omissions, the latter themselves essentially a form of short-term capital as well.

By this measure, net inflows of capital to Latin America[1] had reached a peak of $41 billion in 1981, then fell to an average of only about $10 billion annually in 1983–89 in the wake of the debt crisis. The resurgence

---

1. Western Hemisphere developing countries.

Table 8.1 Current accounts and capital flows: developing countries, 1980–93

	1980	1981	1982	1983	1984	1985	1986	1987	1988	1989	1990	1991	1992	1993
Current account														
LDCs	30.1	-48.7	-87.3	-63.8	-34.2	-27.5	-48.4	-6.4	-24.9	-16.2	-12.1	-82.2	-62.4	-80.1
Africa	-1.9	-22.6	-21.7	-12.5	-7.4	-0.5	-9.4	-4.5	-9.7	-6.6	-2.4	-4.4	-7.6	-9.3
Latin America	-30.2	-42.7	-42.4	-10.9	-2.6	-4.1	-18.6	-11.1	-11.7	-8.6	-6.0	-18.8	-34.4	-37.9
Asia	-14.6	-19.2	-17.5	-15.4	-4.2	-13.8	4.0	21.1	9.4	0.9	-2.3	-1.4	-4.7	-20.5
Middle East and Europe	76.8	35.7	-5.7	-25.0	-19.9	-9.1	-24.3	-11.9	-12.9	-1.8	-1.4	-57.5	-15.8	-12.4
Change in reserves														
LDCs	42.7	5.1	-48	-5.8	12.4	9.8	6.2	51.9	-3.3	25.0	48.1	70.5	48.3	35.6
Africa	4.4	6.5	-8.0	-4.3	0.1	1.4	1.5	1.3	-0.1	2.8	5.2	4.5	-1.5	2.2
Latin America	3.7	-1.4	-19.1	2.0	11.4	1.0	-7.0	3.2	-7.9	2.3	15.7	18.2	23.1	4.5
Asia	7.6	13.4	0.0	4.0	6.3	2.9	23.5	41.3	11.6	9.6	23.5	41.5	21.9	21.0
Middle East and Europe	27.0	-13.4	-20.9	-7.5	-5.4	4.5	-8.5	6.1	-7.0	10.3	3.8	6.3	4.7	7.9
Implicit capital inflow														
LDCs	12.6	53.8	39.3	58	46.6	37.3	54.6	58.3	21.6	41.2	60.2	152.7	110.7	115.7
Africa	6.3	29.1	13.7	8.2	7.5	1.9	10.9	5.8	9.6	9.4	7.6	8.9	6.1	11.5
Latin America	33.9	41.3	23.3	12.9	14.0	5.1	11.6	14.3	3.8	10.9	21.7	37.0	57.5	42.4
Asia	22.2	32.6	17.5	19.4	10.5	16.7	19.5	20.2	2.2	8.7	25.8	42.9	26.6	41.5
Middle East and Europe	-49.8	-49.1	-15.2	17.5	14.5	13.6	15.8	18.0	5.9	12.1	5.2	63.8	20.5	20.3

Source: IMF, *World Economic Outlook* Oct. 1993, April 1987.

began in 1990, when net inflows doubled. They nearly doubled again in 1991 and reached a peak of approximately $58 billion by 1992. Although net inflows moderated to an estimated $42 billion in 1993, as a whole the first four years of the new decade marked a dramatic reentry of the region into the international capital markets.

As reviewed in chapter 6, macroeconomic and structural reform in the major Latin American economies in the late 1980s meant that the necessary conditions for economic fundamentals had been put in place for a return to capital market access (with Brazil as an important exception, although even there by 1990 fiscal deficits were far lower than before). Moreover, it is no accident that the year of the initial upsurge, 1990, was the first year after the shift in international debt strategy to the Brady Plan. Announced in March 1989, the plan set the stage for a new psychological environment of putting the debt crisis into the past.

Nonetheless, there were clearly more global elements at work as well, because the capital market resurgence was not limited to the recovery of troubled Latin American debtors. As shown in figure 8.1, there was an uncanny similarity between net capital inflows to Latin America and those to Asian developing countries throughout the 1980s and early 1990s. Net inflow peaked in both regions in 1981, fell to low levels in 1983-89, and experienced a simultaneous upsurge in the period 1990-93. Yet except for the Philippines, Asia had remained outside of the locus of the debt crisis of the 1980s.

Two factors would appear to account for the broad cycle in international capital flows to Latin America and Asia in the past 15 years. The first was a structural transformation from syndicated bank lending, which dominated flows in the early 1980s, to international bonds, direct investment, and portfolio equity flows in the early 1990s. The second was the shift in the international economic environment, from one of high growth and high interest rates in industrial countries in the late 1980s to one of industrial country recession and low interest rates (except in Europe) in the early 1990s. Thus, real GDP growth in the Group of Seven industrial countries fell from an average of 3.4 percent annually in 1985-89 to 1.5 percent annually in 1990-93 (IMF 1993a, 132). For the same two periods, US Treasury bill rates fell from an average of 6.8 percent to an average of 4.8 percent (IMF 1992a, 1994a). Lower US interest rates provided an outward push to the supply of capital for developing countries.

With respect to the first of these two phenomena, the Latin American debt crisis ruptured the new institutional mechanism of private resource transfer that had emerged in the 1970s: syndicated bank lending fueled by petrodollar deposits and facilitated by the advent of floating rate loans that removed interest rate risk to lenders. When the debt crisis exploded the myth that sovereign debt was safe because nations cannot go broke, flows through this financial vehicle came to an abrupt halt in

Figure 8.1   Capital inflows, Latin America and Asia

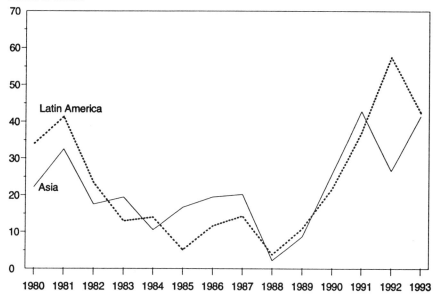

billions of dollars

Source: IMF, *World Economic Outlook.*

Latin America. Moreover, the chill on syndicated lending affected Asia as well, although more on the demand side than on the supply side. Thus, South Korea embarked on an aggressive program to repay debt in view of the revealed danger of being dependent on borrowing.

By 1990–91 the investment bankers were stepping in where the commercial bankers now feared to tread. The Brady Plan had securitized the debt problem (as debt-equity conversion had to a lesser degree begun to do earlier). With the Brady deal signed in early 1990, Mexico began to float bonds in the international market, initially at high junk-bond spreads as a way to reenter. Secondary market discounts on the Brady bonds narrowed sharply from those on preconversion debt, and these bonds became an attractive trading asset. Domestic stock markets rose briskly in 1990 in Chile, Mexico, and Venezuela, and in 1991 soared dramatically in Argentina, Brazil, and Mexico (figure 8.2), with a major contribution from external inflows.

In short, the moribund commercial bank financial market for lending to Latin America was being replaced by portfolio security financing. As analyzed below, nationals repatriating flight capital provided an important part of the demand for the new, securitized flows to Latin America. There was even a change in vocabulary that signaled the transforma-

Figure 8.2 Stock market nominal dollar index

1991 = 100

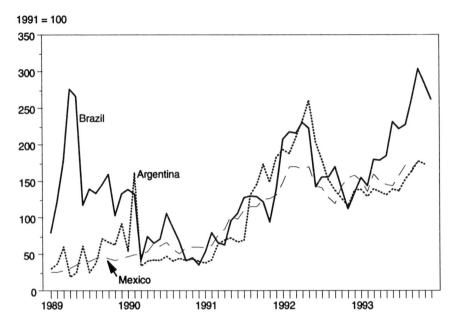

Source: International Finance Corporation.

tion: "emerging markets" became the Wall Street phrase to describe
Latin America and Asia, with psychological connotations far more buoyant than "LDC debt."

Whereas recovery from debt crisis and transformation of financial market structure played major roles in the resurgence of capital flows to Latin
America, the international macroeconomic environment was also important. Indeed, for the Asian countries it was more important. The slowdown in industrial country growth in the early 1990s intensified the
decoupling of Asian developing-country growth from that of the advanced nations. As Asian countries maintained high growth, their imports rose relative to exports. Country-specific factors such as large wage
increases in South Korea contributed to the erosion of trade surpluses, as
did the real appreciation of Asian currencies that occurred as part of the
correction following the overvaluation of the US dollar in the mid-1980s.

Figure 8.3 shows that whereas Asian developing countries had a relatively large current account surplus in 1987, the peak year of US external
trade deficit, by 1993 there had been a swing to sizable current account
deficit. The shift to softer world capital market conditions meant that
relatively cheap finance was available to cover rising external deficits. In
the Asian case, there was much more continuity in access to commercial

Figure 8.3 Current account, Latin America and Asia

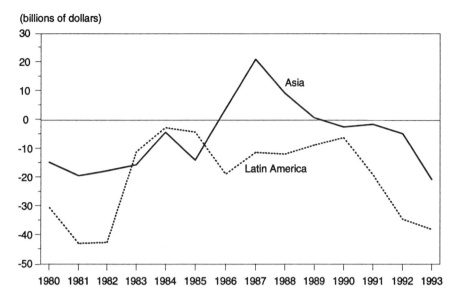

(billions of dollars)

Source: IMF, *World Economic Outlook.*

bank lending. However, even in Asia the new wave of securitization of the capital market meant that by 1992–93 bond issues had risen substantially, as discussed below.

The striking similarity of capital flows to Latin America and Asian developing countries shown in figure 8.1 raises the question of whether low US (and Japanese) interest rates in 1991–93 were the driving force of the resurgence of capital flows to emerging markets, rather than any special market judgment that Latin America had adopted policy reform. Calvo, Leiderman, and Reinhart (1993) have conducted statistical tests that support this hypothesis. To obtain quarterly data, they use changes in reserves and in real exchange rates as proxies for capital inflows. Regional indexes for Latin America show a sharply rising trend for both variables from early 1989 through late 1991. They then use principal components techniques to construct a composite measure of US financial market conditions (led by the Treasury bill rate). They find that for eight of the ten largest Latin American countries, there is a statistically significant influence of US financial conditions on reserves change and real exchange rate.[2]

---

2. For the period 1988–91, foreign factors explain the greatest share of real exchange rate variance in Bolivia, Colombia, Chile, and Ecuador, and the least in Argentina, Brazil, Mexico and Venezuela (137). The authors reason that in the first group, domestic stabiliza-

The authors also cite capital flows to Brazil as evidence that exogenous capital market shifts rather than internal policy improvement dominated the resurgence of the early 1990s. However, as shown below, Brazil had to pay high, junk-bond spreads for its capital, and moreover there was significant improvement in the fiscal situation of Brazil (if not the inflationary outcome) in the early 1990s (as described in chapter 6).

Calvo, Leiderman, and Reinhart (1993) cite three policy concerns raised by their findings. First, capital inflows driven by exogenous factors may adversely affect export performance by causing real exchange rate appreciation. Second, these inflows may not be properly intermediated and may cause resource misallocation (a rather vague critique). Third, "capital inflows—especially the 'hot money' variety—may be reversed on short notice, possibly leading to a domestic financial crisis" (145).

The discussion below returns to the issues of adverse side effects of capital inflow and vulnerability to reversal. The broad view on the issue of causality in the capital market resurgence in the early 1990s must surely be that both elements were present: improved domestic policy and exogenous outward shift in the capital supply curve in the international financial market. Both were necessary to the outcome; neither alone would have been sufficient.

Changing Composition of Capital Flows

Table 8.2 provides evidence on the impressive growth of bond, equity, and direct investment capital flows to Latin America in the early 1990s, and the contrasting continued stagnation of new long-term loans from the commercial banks. In Asian developing countries, where banks and borrowers largely avoided the debt crisis, new long-term bank loans have accounted for considerably larger flows. Even there, however, direct investment and securities have provided a rising share of capital inflows.

Figures 8.4 and 8.5 show the level and composition of gross long-term capital inflows to Latin America and Asian developing countries since the 1970s (real dollars of 1985 and annual averages). It is evident that real inflows rose more steadily in Asia than for Latin America, where the collapse in the mid-1980s is apparent (figure 8.4). As a result, whereas in 1971–81 real capital flows to Latin America were more than twice as large as those to Asia, by 1989–92 the flows to Asia were about 50 percent larger than those to Latin America.

It is also evident that the main reason for this reversal was the massive reduction in real flows to Latin America from banks. Only by the early

---

tion policies had already been adopted before the period, whereas in the second group there were important policy changes during the period, increasing the weight of domestic relative to foreign influences.

Table 8.2   Private capital flows to Latin America and Asia: selected categories, 1989–93 (billions of dollars)

	1989	1990	1991	1992	1993[a]
Latin America					
Bond issues	0.83	2.59	6.83	12.39	11.17
Equity issues	..	0.1	4.12	4.06	2.61
Bank commitments, long term	1.92	3.27	0.99	0.93	0.53
Direct investment[b]	5.29	5.66	9.9	13	..
TOTAL	..	11.62	21.84	30.38	..
Asia					
Bond issues	1.6	1.63	3.00	5.85	5.43
Equity issues	..	1.04	1.02	4.73	1.48
Bank commitments, long term	8.21	12.02	13.56	10.51	6.82
Direct investment[c]	9.03	12.19	13.77	19.17	..
TOTAL	..	26.88	31.35	40.26	..

.. = data not available.

a. First half.
b. Argentina, Brazil, Chile, Colombia, Mexico, Peru, Uruguay, Venezuela.
c. China, India, Indonesia, South Korea, Malaysia, Singapore, Thailand.

Source: Collyns et al. 1993, 18, 22, 67; IMF, *International Financial Statistics*.

1990s was the rise in inflows into the region from direct investment, equities, and bonds sufficient to compensate. There has been a similar rise in direct investment and equity inflows to Asia (although less of a rise in bonds), but bank inflows there had never been as large as in Latin America in the late 1970s. Bank flows to Asia rose relatively steadily, if modestly, from a low initial base.

Figure 8.4 does not convey the full extent of the drop in capital availability to Latin America during the debt crisis, because the International Monetary Fund estimates in the figure are for gross inflows of long-term capital. In contrast, table 8.3 examines the composition of net capital flows, including short-term capital. The difference between the two concepts is primarily capital flight (or repatriation), which makes net flows smaller (larger) than gross, and adds the influence of short-term capital. This difference can be large. Thus, the gross flow data show an annual average for Latin America of $36.7 billion (current dollars) in 1982–88 (IMF 1993f, 77). In contrast, the net flow estimate in table 8.3 here for this period averages only $8.4 billion.

It is surprisingly difficult to assemble data to answer the question of how the composition of net capital flows has evolved.[3] The data in

---

3. For its part, the IMF's *World Economic Outlook* only presents the broad categories of (a)

Figure 8.4 Capital flow decomposition, Western Hemisphere

billions of 1985 dollars, annual averages, gross

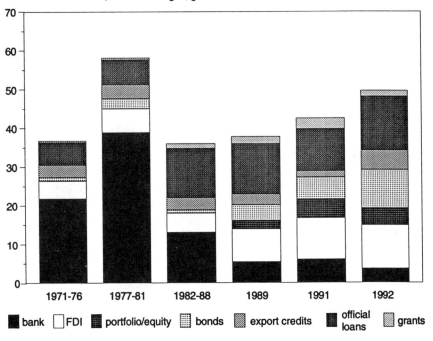

Source: IMF, *World Economic Outlook*.

table 8.3 use IMF balance of payments statistics for direct investment; World Bank *World Debt Tables* estimates for net flows of long-term capital

---

net external borrowing, (b) non-debt-creating flows, and (c) reserve-related liabilities—a minor item. Non-debt-creating flows are primarily direct investment plus official grants. Net external borrowing is too broad to provide much insight into the principal sources of capital. This source does provide a memorandum item reporting net borrowing from commercial banks. However, this data series is suspect. It is inconsistent with the net bank flows reported in the World Bank's *World Debt Tables* and compiled in table 8.3 here. The problem seems to be that whereas the World Bank considers disbursements and repayments directly, the IMF derives implicit flows from changes in stocks. Although the IMF data attempt to correct for debt reduction operations such as discounted buybacks, this correction appears to be incomplete. Thus, the IMF data show cumulative negative capital flows from banks amounting to $18.8 billion during 1985-88 (IMF 1993f, 175). In contrast, the corresponding figure for the seven major Latin American countries shown in table 8.3 here is +$3.6 billion. Nor is the difference between long-term (table 8.3) and total claims (IMF) likely to explain the difference. Such difficulties suggest the utility of a joint World Bank–IMF review of the adequacy of statistics on capital flows, given the new circumstances of the post–debt crisis period and the ascendancy of private nonbank flows.

Figure 8.5 Capital flow decomposition, Asia

billions of 1985 dollars, annual averages, gross

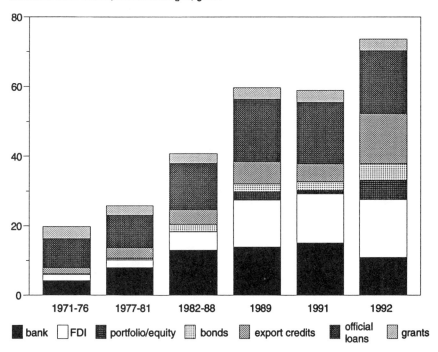

Source: IMF, *World Economic Outlook.*

from the IMF and official lenders (bilateral and multilateral), commercial banks, and through public and publicly guaranteed bonds, as well as for financing through the buildup of arrears; and Collyns et al. (1993) for private bond issues. Total capital flows are estimated as before (table 8.1) by the sum of (−) current account and buildup of reserves.

The resulting estimates are able to explain the bulk of capital flows, except in years when capital flight or repatriation is large. The residual not accounted for by the longer-term flows (and arrears) is large and negative in the period 1983–85, and large and positive by 1992. The behavior of capital flight is examined in detail below.

The estimates of figures 8.4 and 8.5 and table 8.3 confirm the proposition that capital flows to Latin America have experienced a historical shift from dominance by commercial bank lending before the debt crisis to direct investment and bonds (especially private) by the beginning of the 1990s. Thus, on the basis of table 8.3 the banks accounted for 69 percent of positive inflows in 1981–82, but only 10 percent in

Table 8.3 Composition of net capital flows to seven Latin American countries, 1981-92 (billions of dollars)

	1981	1982	1983	1984	1985	1986	1987	1988	1989	1990	1991	1992
Latin America seven countries												
Total	31.72	26.57	4.39	6.48	1.90	7.99	12.25	-1.10	3.94	16.19	29.44	54.37
Direct investment	4.99	4.81	3.08	2.85	3.91	2.88	3.60	5.21	5.98	6.53	11.08	13.28
IMF	-0.16	0.99	4.95	2.72	2.59	1.67	1.94	-1.36	-0.30	2.74	-0.98	-2.04
Official	2.36	3.33	2.54	3.44	3.34	3.93	2.47	2.66	1.56	5.22	1.40	-0.23
Banks, long term	29.78	18.03	9.61	7.95	2.34	-1.00	2.04	0.23	-6.38	1.80	2.80	10.10
Interest arrears	0.00	0.00	0.84	1.61	0.85	0.69	3.80	2.48	6.98	7.89	3.01	0.60
Bonds, public and p.g.	1.33	3.96	-0.81	-1.09	-0.91	-1.40	-2.05	-1.53	-1.27	0.10	2.66	-2.46
Bonds, private	0.00	0.00	0.00	0.00	0.00	0.00	0.00	0.00	0.15	0.61	2.01	7.68
Subtotal	38.30	31.13	20.22	17.47	12.13	6.78	11.80	7.69	6.71	24.89	21.98	26.93
Residual	-6.58	-4.56	-15.83	-11.00	-10.23	1.21	0.45	-8.78	-2.77	-8.70	7.46	27.44
Group A												
Total	18.28	10.05	-4.56	-3.51	-1.42	4.03	5.77	-1.64	4.67	9.45	21.66	28.99
Direct investment	2.46	2.19	1.30	1.07	1.65	1.97	2.37	1.07	3.62	3.75	7.68	7.52
IMF	-0.07	0.18	1.64	1.27	0.92	1.33	1.24	-0.50	1.23	3.36	0.25	-1.36
Official	1.26	2.05	0.41	1.69	2.10	2.51	1.61	2.05	1.62	5.49	2.16	1.05
Banks, long term	15.81	8.27	5.18	2.85	0.53	-0.99	1.35	-2.91	-2.18	3.93	2.57	3.96
Interest arrears	0.00	0.00	0.00	0.00	0.01	0.00	0.00	0.00	0.01	0.03	0.00	0.14
Bonds, public and p.g.	1.45	0.83	-0.52	-0.75	-0.54	-0.70	-0.87	-1.03	0.01	0.85	1.72	-3.01
Bonds, private	0.00	0.00	0.00	0.00	0.00	0.00	0.00	0.00	0.15	0.59	1.22	4.20
Subtotal	20.90	13.52	8.01	6.13	4.65	4.12	5.69	-1.33	4.46	17.99	15.59	12.51
Residual	-2.63	-3.48	-12.57	-9.64	-6.07	-0.09	0.08	-0.30	0.21	-8.54	6.06	16.48

Group B

Total	13.44	16.52	8.96	9.99	3.32	3.96	6.48	0.54	-0.73	6.75	7.78	25.38
Direct investment	2.53	2.62	1.78	1.78	2.27	0.92	1.24	4.14	2.35	2.78	3.40	5.76
IMF	-0.09	0.81	3.32	1.44	1.68	0.34	0.70	-0.86	-1.53	-0.62	-1.23	-0.68
Official	1.10	1.28	2.13	1.75	1.24	1.42	0.86	0.61	-0.06	-0.27	-0.76	-1.28
Banks, long term	13.97	9.76	4.44	5.10	1.82	-0.01	0.69	3.15	-4.21	-2.13	0.23	6.14
Interest arrears	0.00	0.00	0.84	1.61	0.84	0.69	3.79	2.48	6.97	7.87	3.01	0.45
Bonds, public and p.g.	-0.12	3.14	-0.29	-0.34	-0.37	-0.70	-1.17	-0.50	-1.28	-0.75	0.94	0.55
Bonds, private	0.00	0.00	0.00	0.00	0.00	0.00	0.00	0.00	0.00	0.02	0.79	3.48
Subtotal	17.40	17.61	12.21	11.35	7.48	2.65	6.12	9.02	2.26	6.90	6.38	14.42
Residual	-3.96	-1.09	-3.25	-1.36	-4.16	1.30	0.37	-8.48	-2.99	-0.15	1.40	10.96

Group A: Chile, Colombia, Mexico, Venezuela.
Group B: Argentina, Brazil, Peru.

Source: World Bank 1993a; IMF, *International Financial Statistics;* Collyns et al. 1993.

1990–91.[4] Data on gross flows similarly show a decline in the bank share from 66.7 percent in 1977–81 to 14.2 percent in 1989–92, and only 7.3 percent in 1992 (IMF 1993b, 77). Alternative gross flow estimates based on commitments (table 8.2) place the bank share even lower by 1991–92.

In contrast, direct investment provided only 14 percent of positive inflows in 1981–82 but rose to 32 percent in 1990–91, based on table 8.3. The gross flow data show a similar increase from 10.7 percent in 1977–81 to 22.6 percent in 1989–92 (IMF 1993b). The share of bonds in positive inflows rose from 7.6 percent in 1981–82 to 10 percent in 1990–91 (table 8.3).[5] The corresponding rise using the gross flow data was even larger, from only 4.5 percent in 1977–81 to 14.2 percent in 1989–92, and 20 percent in 1992 (IMF 1993b). Similarly, equity flows rose from negligible levels in 1977–81 to 10 percent of the total gross flows in 1991–92.

It is clear from table 8.3 that by 1991–92 the largest new source of capital inflow was in the residual category, primarily equities and short-term capital. An important component of these flows was flight capital, which reversed to repatriation by 1991 and after. Whether this category is hot or merely warm money, in the sense of how quickly it might turn around and exit, is not obvious. The equity component is to some extent locked in, as attempts to flee on short notice would be associated with stock market declines and their market-imposed tax on flight. Nonetheless, it gives pause that the residual category accounted for almost half of positive inflows by 1992.

As against the buoyant private inflows that characterized both 1981–82 and 1990–92, albeit in sharply different forms, the sluggish inflows during the debt crisis of the mid-1980s were dominated by official lending, involuntary concerted lending by banks in 1983–85, and even more involuntary lending in the form of interest arrears in 1987–90.[6] It is striking that for the three large debtors that went into arrears (Argentina, Brazil, and Peru), the average capital "inflow" provided by interest arrears amounted to $5.3 billion annually in the period 1987–90, and exceeded the total net inflow in this period by about 60 percent (table 8.3, group B).

It is useful to compare the pattern of the new capital flow resurgence with expectations during the years of managing the debt crisis. Bergsten, Cline, and Williamson (1985, 13) anticipated that "banks will be prepared to return to voluntary financing once debtor countries reestablish credit-

---

4. Note that the bank figure for 1992 is exaggerated, because it includes approximately $7 billion in rescheduled Brazilian interest arrears (World Bank 1993b, 2: 520).

5. Note that repayments of over $5 billion on existing public and publicly guaranteed bonds in 1992 made the net capital flow negative for this category. This and the lag from commitments to disbursements meant a smaller role for actual bond flows by 1992 than suggested in table 8.2.

6. The gross flows in figures 8.4 and 8.5 omit interest arrears.

worthiness." In 1985, however, the strategy did not yet envision debt reduction. It was clear even by 1987 that banks that chose the exit option of debt reduction on the menu of alternatives would not provide a source of future voluntary lending (Cline 1987). In the aggregate data for the seven large Latin American countries, there is little evidence of a return to bank lending. However, the country data reveal substantial positive long-term bank flows to Mexico in 1990–92 (totaling $9.3 billion) and Chile ($2.3 billion). The countries that had most successfully restored their credit-worthiness did indeed show signs of renewed bank lending.[7]

Through 1993 the verdict was nonetheless still more on the side of the skeptics who in the mid-1980s had assumed that the banks would not return to substantial voluntary lending. Thus, Fishlow (1985a, 97) judged that "reduced bank lending will leave a large void and rule out a return to anything like the buoyant conditions that prevailed in the 1970s." However, he and others turned out to be too skeptical about the prospects for the return of capital through other channels. Thus, Fishlow was doubtful about the contribution that could be made by direct investment, because of its burden of profits repatriation.[8] He anticipated incorrectly as it turns out, that repatriation of flight capital was unlikely to play much role in financing. He concluded that financing would have to be provided mainly by official sources—which turned out to be an important part of the small total flows in the mid-1980s but only a minor origin of the large flows that had revived by the early 1990s. Neither Fishlow nor most others anticipated in the mid-1980s that the bond market and equities would become major channels for inflows by the 1990s.[9]

The potential for a bond revival was hinted at but not fully recognized in the evolving proposals for mobilizing funds through mechanisms that had some degree of seniority. Cline (1987) recommended the use of bonds as the primary vehicle for mobilizing new money from banks. Noting that countries had largely honored bonds during the debt crisis, in part because holders were dispersed and in part because bonds were small relative to total debt, Cline argued that bonds could help confer a de facto seniority on new money that would be difficult to obtain de jure. New money bonds later did in fact feature importantly in the 1988 package for Brazil.

---

7. The flows for Colombia were minimal, but by country choice rather than bank reluctance.

8. His estimate of the nominal volume of direct investment by the 1990s, however, was in the right range.

9. Lessard and Williamson (1985) did anticipate rising investments in LDC stockmarkets by nonbank financial institutions. They did not expect much revival in direct investment (48), and considered long-term fixed-interest bonds unlikely to be of much importance (80). So far, the markets have made little use of their more innovative proposals, such as commodity-indexed bonds.

From the perspective of early 1994, it would appear that the private market has reached the same conclusion—that bonds effectively enjoy senior status. The mushrooming of new bond issues reported in table 8.2, and its contrast to sluggish performance of new long-term bank commitments reveal this perception.

It must be asked whether rapid bond expansion based on perceived seniority involves a fallacy of composition. The outstanding stock of Latin American bonds in 1986 was about $18 billion, whereas long-term debt to commercial banks stood at $238 billion (World Bank 1993b, vol. 1). By 1992 the stock of bonds amounted to $81 billion, and the stock of normal bank claims was down to $97 billion. The bulk of this reconfiguration had involved the switching of bank debt claims for Brady bonds. The Brady bonds presumably enjoy seniority at least as much as other bonds, and indeed are structured with enhancement guarantees (US Treasury zero coupons) to assure that senior status.

These data do not incorporate the effect of Brady bond conversion for Argentina and Brazil. These two countries accounted for $65 billion of long-term bank claims in the region in 1992. If it is assumed that, in rough terms, the Brady deals cut these claims by 30 percent and transfer what remains to the category of bonds, then these operations would reduce the stock of long-term bank claims in Latin America to $32 billion (97–65) and increase the stock of bonds to $126 billion (= 81 + [0.7 × 65]). Post-Brady Latin America would then have 80 percent of its combined long-term bank and bond obligations in the form of bonds, whereas the bond share of the total for these two categories was only 7 percent in 1986.

Skiles (1994) estimates new bond issues by the five large Latin American countries for the full year 1993 at a total of $22.4 billion. If we assume an average of $25 billion in annual issues over four years, and further assume that normal bank claims (excluding Brady and other bonds) grow at, say, 5 percent in nominal terms (holding about constant in real terms), then by 1997 the outstanding bond total would stand at $286 billion, and the share of bonds in the bank-debt and bond total would reach 87 percent.

In short, after the Brady deals it will already be the case that bonds are the majority rather than the minority form of debt, and if recent trends in bond market issues continue, this majority share will be even greater. On this basis, it will no longer be feasible to count on bond seniority by virtue of free-rider status of the marginal instrument. The possible implications for public policy toward the bond market are considered below.

Repatriation of Flight Capital

As suggested above, one of the most important components of the capital market resurgence for Latin America has been short-term portfolio capital. There is every reason to believe that the return of the flight capital of nationals is an important part of this inflow, although it also contains portfolio investment by foreigners as well.

An important consideration in judging the sustainability of the renewed buoyancy of capital inflows in the 1990s is the reliability of this repatriation of flight capital sent abroad during the years of the debt crisis and before. Capital inflow in the form of new borrowing raises the future debt-servicing burden. Direct investment inflows also impose a future burden in the form of profits remittances. In contrast, the repatriation of flight capital may be seen as a windfall that provides financing for the current account deficit without imposing an external liability, debt or equity. Whatever the sustainable amount of capital inflow might otherwise be thought to be, the amount shifts upwards by a tranche corresponding to the expected flow of capital repatriation.[10]

To estimate the magnitude of such inflows, it is first necessary to estimate the stock of outstanding flight capital accumulated from the past. Then it is necessary to consider what portion of this stock might be repatriated, and over what time period.

On the first question, researchers at the World Bank have compiled alternative estimates of annual capital flight for developing countries during the period 1971–91 (Claessens and Naude 1993). Their preferred estimate uses the "World Bank residuals" method. This approach estimates capital flight as the difference between sources and uses of foreign capital. Uses are for the current account deficit and the buildup of external reserves. Sources are borrowing, direct foreign investment, and other equity investment inflows. Borrowing is estimated based on the change in external debt, adjusted for valuation changes from exchange rate movements.

The estimates presented below make two adjustments to the World Bank preferred estimates. First, whenever the balance of payments for the country in question reports capital income earnings that exceed earnings that would be predicted by applying the US Treasury bill rate to the stock of country reserves at the end of the preceding year, the excess is deducted from the reported current account. This adjustment takes account of the fact that for certain countries (especially Mexico and Venezuela), the balance of payments data on an accrual basis give a false impression of the current account balance by treating private capital income earned abroad as if it entered the country when in fact it simply accumulates abroad. By overstating the current account that crosses the country's borders, the unadjusted data overstate capital flight. That is, the cash-basis current account has a larger deficit and can therefore

---

10. A second-order effect in the opposite direction is that repatriated capital no longer earns interest abroad. However, this interest is of little help to the country if it is typically reinvested abroad, as was the tendency in the 1980s.

explain a greater use of foreign capital than does the accrual-basis current account, which includes capital income earnings retained abroad.[11] The adjustment for private capital income accrued abroad can be substantial, averaging $2.5 billion annually in 1987–91 for Mexico and $1.6 billion annually for Venezuela in the same period.

Second, the estimates here use the World Bank variant including private nonguaranteed debt. Although the conventional treatment (as here) includes this category, Claessens and Naude (1993) prefer to exclude it, and for some purposes exclusion makes sense. Thus, the core policy problem of capital flight arises when the government borrows abroad, only to turn around and use the foreign exchange to finance private capital flight. If instead there is a buildup in private debt with no observed counterpart current account deficit or buildup in reserves, what is happening is essentially that some private firms are borrowing abroad while others are buying up the resulting foreign exchange from them and placing it abroad again. These intra-private-sector differences of views or needs do not carry any particular implication of misguided government policy. Nonetheless, the private-sector assets acquired abroad in these transactions constitute part of the external cache of capital potentially available for repatriation. For the purposes here of analyzing the scope for such reflows, then, it is appropriate to include rather than exclude private nonguaranteed debt buildup in the capital flight estimates.

The World Bank database provides only annual flows in nominal dollar terms. To translate these flows into a stock figure for outstanding capital flight, it is necessary to take into account reinvested earnings.[12] Suppose $1 billion in capital flight occurred in year k (e.g., 1983). This specific vintage will make a contribution to today's outstanding stock of flight capital equal to λ billion, where λ is an expansion factor that shows the factor by which one dollar in year k would have been expected to grow over the intervening period.

---

11. This adjustment is the principal consideration in the "Cline method" also estimated by Claessens and Naude (1993). Other adjustments in their version of my method include removal of tourism and reinvested earnings on direct investment domestically. Under some circumstances tourism earnings should be excluded in assessing the amount of capital flight financed by the government (see my comment in Lessard and Williamson 1987, 82–83). However, for purposes of estimating private foreign assets, the objective here, the tourism trade surplus should not be excluded. As for reinvestment on direct investment, the calculations here make no adjustment, in part because these amounts tend to be small and in part because it is often unclear whether the direct investment inflows use an accounting methodology that includes them in the first place.

12. Note that this operation could not be done without first making the adjustment just described. Otherwise, there would be double counting. The annual capital flight data would count income on foreign private assets once, and the expansion for reinvestment would count it a second time.

The estimates here assume that flight capital is cautious capital. Thus, it is assumed that three-fourths was placed in US Treasury bills and one-fourth in the US stock market. At the same time, however, allowance should be made for consumption of some portion of the earnings on flight capital. One reason to expect some consumption is that during periods of capital controls, nationals cannot easily obtain foreign exchange to take their accustomed vacations and conduct their shopping abroad (e.g., by Argentines traveling to Uruguay and Brazil), and so they are likely to draw on the earnings for such purposes.

The outstanding stock of flight capital is thus estimated as

$$S_t = \sum_{k=1}^{t} \lambda_{kt} F_k;$$

$$\lambda_{kt} = 0.75 \prod_{k=1}^{t-1} (1 + \alpha r_{k+1}) + 0.25 \left[1 + \alpha \left(\frac{p_t^s}{p_k^s} - 1 \right) \right], k < t; \tag{7.1}$$

$$= 1, k = t$$

where r_{k+1} is the treasury bill rate in year $k + 1$, p_t^s is the stock price index in year t, and α is the fraction of earnings that is reinvested rather than consumed. The estimates set α at two-thirds. Note that there is no reinvestment expansion factor for the most recent installment of capital flight (F_t), because it has just arrived abroad.

The calculation of outstanding stock begins in the first year in which capital flight becomes positive (i.e., capital outflow rather than inflow). Moreover, because the estimated capital flight turned negative again in the period 1989–91 for some countries, a judgment must be made as to what portion of the inflow is from the stock of private assets held abroad by nationals and what portion is from foreigners.

Table 8.4 reports the resulting estimates of the stock of flight capital held abroad by nationals of eight major countries that experienced debt problems in the 1980s. The first block of estimates assume that any negative capital flight in 1989 and beyond is from repatriation of nationals' holdings abroad. The estimates in alternative A assume that only half of this negative capital flight was accounted for by nationals. The other half is assumed to have been capital inflow from foreign investors.[13]

The principal estimate used below is alternative A. Under either measure, the estimated stock of capital flight abroad is somewhat larger than often estimated, especially for Argentina and Mexico. By 1991, citizens of each of these two countries held estimated levels of $75 billion and

---

13. Note that the negative capital flight was especially large for Mexico: $11.0 billion in 1989, $6.4 billion in 1990, and $20.6 billion in 1991; and for Argentina: $12.4 billion in 1991.

Table 8.4 Stock of flight capital abroad, 1977–91 (billion of dollars)

	ARG	BRZ	CHL	COL	MEX	PER	VEN	PHL	SUM8
1977	4.9	5.5	0.8	1.5	11.9	2.6	1.4	3.3	31.9
1978	6.7	7.5	0.6	1.3	13.2	2.9	2.0	3.7	37.9
1979	10.3	10.3	0.7	1.1	16.5	2.7	5.3	4.6	51.5
1980	15.8	13.1	0.4	1.1	22.3	2.3	10.5	5.4	70.9
1981	25.1	14.5	-0.6	1.2	29.5	1.0	15.8	7.4	93.9
1982	32.4	17.3	0.1	0.9	36.4	1.6	18.7	7.9	115.3
1983	37.9	20.4	0.3	1.5	49.5	1.7	30.0	6.6	147.8
1984	40.3	24.2	-0.2	1.7	54.4	2.0	31.6	4.7	158.8
1985	42.8	23.1	-0.7	2.4	60.3	1.8	32.2	5.1	166.9
1986	45.2	29.4	-0.2	3.1	67.6	3.0	34.2	5.8	188.0
1987	52.2	37.9	0.7	4.8	82.0	4.6	36.2	6.4	224.8
1988	55.3	48.7	0.9	6.3	86.3	5.4	34.2	7.9	245.0
1989	66.8	47.5	-0.7	6.2	82.5	5.2	35.9	5.5	249.0
1990	76.9	40.8	-3.8	6.5	80.1	4.7	43.0	3.4	251.6
1991	69.1	43.0	-6.3	8.2	64.6	4.3	44.5	0.0	227.3
Alternative A:									
1989	66.8	50.1	0.2	6.5	88.1	5.6	36.5	7.1	260.8
1990	76.9	48.0	-1.4	6.9	89.1	5.4	46.7	6.2	277.8
1991	75.3	50.7	-2.6	8.5	84.3	5.4	45.8	4.8	272.2

Note: Stock expansions based on 2/3 reinvestment of earnings.

Sources: Capital flight residuals from World Bank capital flight database. Adjustment for earnings from IMF, *Balance of Payments Yearbook*.

$84 billion in capital abroad, respectively. For the eight countries, the total was about $270 billion.[14]

The next step in the analysis is to calculate what might be the annual flows associated with repatriation of some portion of these outstanding stocks. For this purpose, it is necessary to form some idea of the desired distribution of portfolio holdings of private households in these countries as between domestic and foreign assets. During the debt crisis, households placed an abnormally high share of their assets abroad for safekeeping. After a return to more normal conditions, one would expect the desired share of foreign holdings in the portfolio to decline.

In addition to considering the change in desired portfolio shares, it is necessary to take account of the exogenous influences affecting portfolio composition. These include the real rate of foreign asset growth from reinvestment, the corresponding real rate on domestic assets, and the contribution to domestic assets from new saving out of annual household income.

Let ϕ_f^* be the desired share of portfolio held abroad when the country has shifted from debt crisis circumstances to a new regime of macroeconomic stability (perhaps more favorable than that even before the 1980s). Let S_{ft} be the stock of private assets held abroad in year t; D_t, the stock of private assets held domestically. The actual portfolio share held abroad is thus $\phi_{ft} = S_{ft}/(S_{ft} + D_t)$. Suppose that the coefficient of adjustment during the first year is β, so that of the excess of foreign assets above the desired amount, the fraction β is repatriated. Thus, if households wanted to shift to a new portfolio equilibrium over five years, they might set β at 0.2.[15] Suppose that the rate of return abroad in real terms is ρ_f, and the rate of return domestically is ρ_d. Suppose that saving out of current income, if fully placed into domestic assets, will constitute the fraction s_d of the initial domestic asset stock. Let the amount of capital repatriation by nationals in year t be R_t.

Under these assumptions, a simple recursive model of the time path of capital repatriation over a period of n years will be as follows:

$$R_t = \beta[\phi_{f,t-1} - \phi_f^*][S_{f,t-1} + D_{t-1}] \tag{7.2}$$

$$S_{ft} = S_{f,t-1}(1 + \rho_f) - R_t \tag{7.3}$$

---

14. Morgan Guaranty (1986) estimated that in the period 1976–85 cumulative capital flight amounted to $26 billion for Argentina, $53 billion for Mexico, $30 billion for Venezuela, and $10 billion for Brazil. The Morgan estimates are broadly consistent with the estimates of table 8.4, given that the Morgan calculations did not attempt to incorporate reinvested earnings.

15. Note, however, that if the adjustment coefficient β stays constant at 0.2, and there is no other change, at the end of five years only the fraction 0.67 (= $1 - 0.8^5$) of the initial excess foreign holdings will have been repatriated.

$$D_t = D_{t-1}(1 + \rho_d + s_d) + R_t \qquad (7.4)$$

$$\phi_{ft} = \frac{S_{ft}}{(S_{ft} + D_t)} \qquad (7.5)$$

To implement this model, it is necessary to have an idea of the magnitude of domestic private assets and to postulate the rates of return and savings contribution. Table 8.5 reports estimates of private assets in seven major debtor countries. The foreign private assets are the capital flight stock figures just described. Domestic assets include stock market capitalization, domestic government bonds and bills, and savings, time, and other semiliquid assets designated by the IMF as quasi-money.[16]

Because the domestic asset estimates are questionable, in part because of data weakness and in part because the categories may not be comprehensive, an alternative estimate is made that assumes total private assets in each economy are equal to GDP.[17] Deducting the estimated stock of flight capital from a hypothetical total private asset value of GDP gives the alternative estimate of domestic assets shown in the table.

Under the main estimate for domestic assets, table 8.5 shows remarkably high portfolio shares in assets held abroad for Argentina and Venezuela: approximately two-thirds for each. Colombia also shows a relatively high share, at 40.9 percent. In contrast, the share is in the range of one-fourth to one-third for Mexico and Brazil, and is only 10.6 percent for the Philippines. Chile is the clear outlier in these estimates. Its stock of flight capital abroad is estimated to have been minimal through the 1980s, and indeed to have turned negative by 1989–90—an idiosyncrasy of the calculation method implying essentially negligible amounts held abroad.

These estimates are consistent with stylized facts about these economies. Thus, Chile is considered to have a robust domestic capital market, in part because of its privatized social security pension system. The Mexican stock market is known to be large; domestic government debt is known to be large in Brazil, as is the stock market. In Argentina and Venezuela, past capital flight is believed to be relatively large, and at least in Argentina a thin domestic capital market is a plausible consequence of hyperinflation.

---

16. Government obligation estimates are for the most recent year available. Stock market capitalization is for the first quarter of 1993. For Mexico, the figures are from Banco de Mexico (1993) and deduct holdings of foreigners in the Mexican market. Note that the domestic government debt data tend to be seriously outdated. The most recent figures are for 1982 for Chile, 1985 for Colombia, 1986 for Brazil and Venezuela, 1988 for Argentina, and 1991 for the Philippines (IMF 1991d, 1993h).

17. At the end of 1992, the corresponding asset values for the United States were quasi-money, $2.3 trillion; public debt securities, $3.4 trillion; and stock market capitalization, $4.9 trillion, for a total of $10.6 trillion or 175 percent of GDP (IMF 1994a; Council of Economic Advisers 1994, 369; IFC 1993).

Table 8.5 Private foreign and domestic assets, 1992 (billions of dollars)

| | Domestic | | | | | | | Foreign Portfolio Share (%) | Alternative: Domestic Assets | Foreign Share (%) |
	Stocks	Government obligations	Quasi–money	Total	Foreign	GDP				
Argentina	19.1	1.9	20.1	41.1	75.3	228.8		64.7	153.5	32.9
Brazil	59.5	41.9	70.2	171.6	50.7	394.2		22.8	343.5	12.9
Chile	33.5	1.7	14.9	50.1	–2.6	41.2		–5.5	43.8	–6.3
Colombia	6.6	2.6	3.1	12.3	8.5	43.5		40.9	35.0	19.5
Mexico	116.0	28.6	54.7	199.3	84.3	333.8		29.7	249.5	25.3
Venezuela	6.2	4.7	13.2	24.1	45.8	58.7		65.5	12.9	78.0
Philippines	16.3	10.5	13.8	40.6	4.8	53.0		10.6	48.2	9.1

Notes: Foreign assets are for 1991.
Alternative domestic assets = GDP – foreign assets.

Source: Table 8.4; IMF, *International Financial Statistics*, Feb. 1994; World Bank 1994b; IMF 1991d; Goldstein and Folkerts-Landau 1993, Part 2; Banco de Mexico , 1993.

The parameters used to apply the repatriation model are as follows. Two alternative measures are used for the desired foreign portfolio share, ϕ_f^*. First, it is assumed that the regime shift from debt crisis to normalization causes this desired share to fall by half from its base at the beginning of the 1990s. Second, it is assumed that the desired foreign share in the private portfolio is 15 percent. For foreign real return, a rate of 2 percent is assumed. For domestic real return, the rate is set at 4 percent. For the contribution of new saving from income, the rate is set at 3 percent (i.e., saving out of income causes domestic assets to rise at 3 percent real annually). The adjustment coefficient β is set at 0.2, meaning that if the investor sees an excess of a given amount in his foreign holdings, he will reduce the excess by one-fifth in the first year.

Table 8.6 shows the resulting estimates of capital repatriation that could be expected over the period 1992–96. The results show a relatively large potential for repatriation in Argentina and Mexico, with reflows beginning at about $8 billion and falling to about one-third that amount over the five years in each case. As it turned out, total capital inflows in 1992–93 were $49.8 billion for Mexico and $22.9 billion for Argentina (ECLAC 1993). If the estimates of table 8.6 are valid, repatriation of flight capital may have accounted for about one-third of the total for Mexico and two-thirds of the total for Argentina.

Predicted repatriation is also relatively large for Venezuela. However, actual total capital inflows were only a total of $3.6 billion in 1992–93 (ECLAC 1993), or about two-fifths of the predicted repatriation in table 8.6.

The model predicts zero repatriation flows for Chile and similar figures for the Philippines, because the initial portfolio shares of foreign holdings are near or already below the postulated 15 percent desired level. For Colombia, the absolute size of repatriation is modest because of the scale of assets. However, the amount of reflow predicted for 1992–93 is almost the same as the actual level of total capital inflows ($1.7 billion; ECLAC 1993), suggesting that the calculations may be on the right order of magnitude but perhaps overstated.

For Brazil, capital repatriation begins at $3.5 billion in 1992 and is down to $0.7 billion by 1996. Here too the prediction is consistent with actual experience, as total capital inflows amounted to $12.2 billion in 1992–93 (versus $6.1 billion predicted over the two years for repatriation alone) (ECLAC 1993). The alternative estimates shown in the sensitivity tests tend to confirm the large flows for Argentina and Mexico, but suggest that the Brazilian repatriation may be overstated in the main estimate.[18] The sensitivity run further increases the Venezuelan estimates,

---

18. The absence of much change for Argentina when the database is changed to alternative B illustrates the fact that just changing the estimate of domestic assets tends to have little effect at the outset of the period. This change reduces the initial foreign portfolio

Table 8.6 Predicted repatriation of flight capital (billions of dollars at 1992 prices)

	1992	1993	1994	1995	1996	Share	Data
Central estimates:							
Argentina	7.5	6.0	4.8	3.7	2.8	A	A
Brazil	3.5	2.6	1.8	1.2	0.7	B	A
Chile	0.0	0.0	0.0	0.0	0.0	C	A
Colombia	0.9	0.7	0.5	0.4	0.3	A	A
Mexico	8.4	6.6	5.1	3.8	2.7	A	A
Venezuela	4.6	3.7	2.9	2.3	1.7	A	A
Philippines	0.0	0.0	0.0	0.0	0.0	C	A
Sensitivity estimates:							
Argentina	7.5	5.9	4.6	3.5	2.5	A	B
Argentina	11.6	9.4	7.6	6.2	4.9	B	A
Brazil	0.0	0.0	0.0	0.0	0.0	C	B
Mexico	8.4	6.5	5.0	3.8	2.7	B	A
Venezuela	7.1	5.8	4.7	3.8	3.0	B	A

Share: A = cut in initial foreign portfolio share in half; B = cut to 15%; C = no repatriation because initial share < 15%
Data: A = main estimate; B = alternative estimate of domestic assets, table 8.5.

suggesting that the shortfall of actual from predicted repatriation in 1992–93 may be due more to such influences as political instability than to an overestimation of the potential for repatriation.

Table 8.6 reveals a crucial feature of prospective capital repatriation: it should be expected to decline over time. Thus, the total predicted amount falls from $24.9 billion for 1992 to $15.1 billion in 1994 and $8.2 billion by 1996 (all in 1992 dollars). Two forces drive this result. First, the model is a stock-adjustment mechanism that is expected to reduce excess foreign holdings until a new equilibrium is reached, and by construction the excess to be reduced will tend to be falling over time. Second, the higher growth rates for domestic assets mean that at some point it is necessary to build up foreign assets just to keep the portfolio share from falling below the desired level.

That capital repatriation may fall from the order of $25 billion in 1992 to $8 billion by 1996 is extremely important for judging the sustainability of large current account deficits in Latin America. It should be emphasized that this decline may be understated rather than overstated, from

share and thus the annual change in this share in working down to half the initial share. However, it raises the total portfolio base against which the changing share is applied. For Brazil, the collapse of repatriation flows in the sensitivity test stems from the fact that the share change being applied is a terminal level of 15 percent for foreign holdings, combined with the fact that in data set B the foreign share starts out barely above this threshold.

the standpoint that the model makes no attempt to relate target portfolio shares to varying rates of return. If US interest rates rise substantially in the 1994–96 period relative to the 1991–93 period, the postulated reduction in the target foreign portfolio share may be overstated, as Latin American citizens no longer face as large an interest differential between home capital markets and the US market.

Nonetheless, the shift in desired portfolio shares associated with the watershed regime changes toward macroeconomic stability should be much larger than any shift associated with modest widenings or narrowings of the interest differential. Consider the case of Mexico. In 1987, the country was in the depths of the debt crisis. Oil prices had collapsed the year before. Inflation was running at 160 percent. Capital flight, measured by the World Bank residuals method with the interest accrual adjustment discussed above, amounted to an outflow of $8.6 billion. Then in 1990, after the Solidarity Pact had brought inflation down to 30 percent, and after the Brady deal had restored confidence in sustainability of the exchange rate, capital flight was a negative $6.4 billion, or an inflow rather than an outflow.[19] By 1991 the inflow had surged to $20.6 billion. Yet if all that mattered was the push or pull of external interest rates, there should have been no such swing. The nominal interest rate on US Treasury bills was 5.8 percent in 1987 and 5.4 percent in 1991 (IMF 1992a). The discussion below returns to the question of falling capital repatriation in examining sustainability of current account positions in the Argentine and Mexican cases in particular.

Institutional Investors

The analysis of portfolio readjustment by holders of flight capital dovetails nicely with the evidence on large capital inflows to debtor countries in the period 1991–93, especially for the cases of Mexico and Argentina. However, research at the International Monetary Fund based primarily on discussions with capital market participants suggests that whereas capital repatriation was the dominant influence through 1992, by 1993 there was a broad shift toward entry of a wider class of institutional investors (Goldstein and Folkerts-Landau 1994, 86).

Mutual funds, pension funds, and to a lesser extent insurance companies entered aggressively into the emerging markets in 1993, according to the IMF analysis. Two reasons drove this trend. First, by then it was clear that some of the major debtor countries were consolidating greatly improved economic policies. Second, "some institutional investors, who face short-term performance goals" were under pressure not

---

19. As noted, it is assumed here that half of this amount was capital repatriation of nationals and the rest was investment by foreigners.

to miss out on large gains, as the dollar return on equity investments in emerging markets reached 80 percent in 1993 (87). A possible additional reason for the increased interest was the recognition that emerging country assets provided a way to diversify risk, because of limited correlation of returns with those in industrial countries (17).

The IMF study estimates that by the end of 1993, US mutual funds held about 2 percent of their assets, or $30 billion, in emerging markets, mainly in equity. One survey indicated that institutional fund managers had increased the share of emerging markets in their international portfolios from 2.5 percent in 1989 to 10 percent in 1992 and 13 percent in 1993 (87). As discussed below, among institutional investors more broadly bonds were the leading vehicle of increased inflows. Bond placements by developing countries doubled each year after 1990, to reach $59 billion in 1993 (82). International equity placements by developing countries reached $12 billion in that year, largely through American Depository Receipts or similar instruments.[20]

Whereas the flight capital portfolio model tends to point toward a moderation in capital inflows to debtor countries after the initial readjustment, the "institutional investor" model would seem to hold the promise of more sustained flows. However, even in this model the recent and sudden rise in the emerging-country shares has some of the same characteristics of a once-for-all portfolio adjustment. Moreover, mutual fund peer pressure would seem vulnerable to herd dynamics, with corresponding potential volatility for flows to debtor countries. Indeed, new issues of developing country bonds fell from $24 billion in the fourth quarter of 1993 to $18 billion in the first quarter of 1994 when US monetary policy tightened (Goldstein and Folkerts-Landau 1994, 82). Nonetheless, the seeming watershed entry of the institutional investors by 1993 can only be good news for debtor country access to capital flows in the future.

International Bond Market

Most of the large troubled debtors of the 1980s have by now reentered the international capital market. The return to large capital inflows for

---

20. ADRs are denominated and receive interest or dividend payments in dollars. They also facilitate tax payments to host countries. Most of the nearly 1,000 depository receipts (on both developing and industrial countries) are "level I," with exemptions from Securities and Exchange Commission registration and reporting requirements but with trading limited to the over the counter market. Levels II and III have more stringent reporting requirements and are listed on exchanges. Another growing vehicle is the private placement. The SEC's Rule 144a adopted in 1990 spurred private placements by giving them liquidity through sale to Qualified Institutional Buyers during the initial two-year minimum holding period. (Goldstein and Folkerts-Landau 1994, 89).

the four largest debtors (Brazil, Mexico, Argentina, and Venezuela) is shown in table 8.7. A distinctive feature of this return has been the large role of bonds floated in the international market. Skiles (1994) points out that for these four countries plus Chile, private portfolio investment in both fixed-income securities and equities "have become an important source of external financing for the first time since the 1920s" (1).

Various questions about this lending warrant inquiry. Why was it possible for countries to reenter the bond market relatively soon, whereas syndicated bank lending has remained minimal (as discussed below)? What was the penalty, if any, paid by countries that required Brady Plan debt reductions, in terms of their subsequent costs of borrowing on bond markets? Has the new wave of bond lending been discriminating or indiscriminate? Does the surge in bond lending raise any policy questions for monetary authorities in creditor countries?

Table 8.8 reports international bond issues by developing countries with substantial external debt in the period 1989–93. During this period, some 25 countries have raised a total of approximately $80 billion on the international bond markets. Mexico alone accounts for one-fourth of the total.

The three groupings in the table reveal three distinct patterns. For major debtors in Asia and the Middle East that did not get caught in the debt crisis of the 1980s (including such major debtors as Indonesia, China, India, South Korea, and Turkey), bond issues were already significant in 1989 and grew at a brisk but not extreme pace to twice as large by 1992. In contrast, for 10 mainly Latin American countries that were intimately involved in the debt crisis but had for the most part obtained Brady Plan agreements and achieved macroeconomic stability by 1991–92, annual bond issues exploded from only $930 million in 1989 to well over $20 billion in 1993. At the same time, a smaller group of troubled debtor countries, typically with more severe macroeconomic instability persisting, remained outside of the market through 1993 (Nigeria, Peru, Poland, and Russia).

Why was reentry into the bond market by Brady graduates so successful? Three reasons come to mind. First, in the aftermath of the Brady cuts it was implausible for these countries to return soon to unsecured, syndicated bank lending of the 1970s style. They thus were interested in bonds on the demand side. On the supply side, second, there was the collapse of interest rates in the US market and the resulting search of US investors for higher yields abroad. Third, during the debt crisis bonds had generally been held harmless, in contrast to long-term bank claims. The implicit senior status of bonds provided a psychological umbrella that made creditors more willing to lend through this instrument, another supply-side consideration. As noted above, de facto seniority for bonds will be much less plausible in the future as they shift from minority to majority share in debt outstanding.

In short, with the benefit of hindsight, it is not difficult to answer the question of why bonds provided the vehicle for explosive renewed borrowing by the debtor countries. As for the question of bond market discrimination or promiscuity, superficially the record in table 8.8 might suggest the latter. Large bond borrowers by 1993 included Brazil, where inflation remained at extremely high levels, alongside such model policy countries as Chile.

A closer look suggests, however, that bond investors were discriminating. They charged high, junk-bond premiums for borrowers with the least secure outlooks. Thus, Brazil paid an average spread of 500 basis points above US Treasury bonds of comparable maturity in bond issues in 1991–93, whereas Chile only had to pay an average spread of 150 basis points (and South Korea only 100 basis points; Collyns et al. 1993, 64). Private firms in Brazil were willing to pay the premium because domestic interest rates were even higher.

It is possible to provide a more formal test of two separate questions raised above: was the bond market discriminating; and how large a premium if any did it levy for country credit risk revealed by resort to Brady Plan debt reduction? For the bond flows shown in table 8.8, the spreads above comparable-maturity bonds of governments of the countries in which bonds were issued may be explained by a statistical regression that incorporates relevant measures of country risk as well as a Brady Debt Reduction (BDR) variable.

Table 8.9 reports the results of a simple linear regression of this type. The dependent variable is the spread (basis points). Dummy variables (with value 1 if applicable, 0 otherwise) are included for countries that have asked for Brady debt reduction, and for bonds issued by private borrowers rather than governments or state enterprises. Thus, although Chile and Mexico both experienced the shock of the debt crisis (and both had model macroeconomic policies by at least the late 1980s), Chile has a "0" BDR variable and Mexico a "1." The regression includes four indicators of economic performance and status. The first is the natural logarithm of inflation (e.g., with value 1 for inflation of 2.7 percent and 7 for inflation of 1,100 percent). Inflation serves as a proxy for overall macroeconomic stability and especially fiscal balance. The second economic variable is per capita income, to capture the possibility that creditors are more willing to lend to higher-income countries (again the logarithm is used because of the wide range and the unlikelihood that creditworthiness improves linearly with income level). The third and fourth economic variables are average real growth rates of exports and GDP, respectively, over the period 1980–91 (World Bank 1993c).[21]

---

21. Note that alternative specifications including either the debt/exports or debt/GDP ratio found these two variables statistically insignificant.

Table 8.7 Capital inflows and fiscal deficits in Argentina, Brazil, Mexico, and Venezuela, 1980-92 (billions of dollars and percentage of GDP)

	1980	1981	1982	1983	1984	1985	1986	1987	1988	1989	1990	1991	1992
Capital Inflow													
Argentina	2.5	1.8	2.1	0.4	2.7	2.5	1.7	2.4	3.6	0.2	0.8	5.8	13.0
Brazil	9.7	12.8	11.5	5.5	4.9	0.3	2.0	4.4	-1.6	1.5	5.3	0.8	8.8
Mexico	11.6	26.7	9.5	-2.4	-1.1	-2.1	1.1	-1.0	-1.4	1.4	8.5	20.4	26.0
Venezuela	0.2	-1.9	-1.5	-3.8	-2.0	-1.0	-1.1	0.5	-1.0	-3.4	-3.6	3.1	3.2
TOTAL	23.9	39.4	21.5	-0.3	4.6	-0.3	3.7	6.4	-0.4	-0.4	11.0	30.1	50.9
GDP													
Argentina	154.3	124.3	56.9	64.8	78.1	65.8	78.8	82.6	89.7	60.3	141.2	189.7	228.8
Brazil	234.9	263.5	281.6	203.2	208.9	223.1	268.1	294.1	328.5	447.3	473.7	405.4	394.2
Mexico	185.9	239.8	167.0	142.7	175.6	184.5	129.3	140.4	174.2	200.7	244.0	286.6	333.8
Venezuela	59.2	66.4	67.9	67.6	57.8	59.9	60.9	46.9	60.4	42.8	48.6	53.4	58.7
TOTAL	634.3	694.0	573.3	478.4	520.5	533.2	537.1	564.0	652.7	751.2	907.6	935.2	1015.5

Fiscal Deficit (% GDP)

Argentina[a]	2.6	5.3	3.7	10.1	5.7	3.1	3.2	5.7	4.0	2.7	1.4	1.1	0.3
Brazil[b]	6.4	6.2	7.3	4.4	2.7	4.4	3.6	5.7	4.8	6.8	-1.3	1.3	1.5
Mexico[b]	3.6	10.0	5.5	-0.4	0.3	0.8	2.4	-1.8	3.6	1.7	-2.2	-3.3	-3.6
Venezuela[a]	0.0	-2.2	2.1	0.6	-2.8	-2.0	0.4	1.6	7.4	1.0	2.1	-2.8	3.4

Fiscal Deficit (billions of dollars)

Argentina	4.0	6.6	2.1	6.5	4.5	2.0	2.5	4.7	3.6	1.6	2.0	2.1	0.7
Brazil	15.0	16.3	20.6	8.9	5.6	9.8	9.7	16.8	15.8	30.4	-6.2	5.3	5.9
Mexico	6.7	24.0	9.2	-0.6	0.5	1.5	3.1	-2.5	6.3	3.4	-5.4	-9.5	-12.0
Venezuela	0.0	-1.5	1.4	0.4	-1.6	-1.2	0.2	0.7	4.5	0.4	1.0	-1.5	2.0
TOTAL	25.7	45.4	33.3	15.3	9.0	12.1	15.5	19.7	30.1	35.9	-8.5	-3.6	-3.4

a. Central government.
b. Real (operational).

Source: IDB 1991, 1993; IMF, *International Financial Statistics,* 1992 Yearbook, Feb. 1994; Banco de Mexico 1993.

Table 8.8 International bond issues by major debtor countries, 1989-93 (billions of dollars)

	1989	1990	1991	1992	1993[a]	Memorandum: 1992 debt
I. Troubled debtors						
A. With reentry						
Argentina	0.00	0.02	0.80	1.57	6.20	68
Brazil	0.00	0.00	1.84	3.66	6.30	121
Bulgaria	0.10	0.00	0.00	0.00	0.00	12
Chile	0.00	0.00	0.20	0.12	0.30	19
Colombia	0.00	0.00	0.00	0.00	0.33	17
Mexico	0.57	2.31	3.37	5.92	8.40	113
Panama	0.00	0.00	0.05	0.00	0.00	6
Philippines	0.00	0.00	0.00	0.00	0.35	33
Uruguay	0.00	0.00	0.00	0.10	0.14	5
Venezuela	0.26	0.26	0.58	0.93	1.20	37
SUBTOTAL	0.93	2.59	6.83	12.29	23.21	431
B. Without reentry						
Nigeria	0.00	0.00	0.00	0.00	0.00	31
Peru	0.00	0.00	0.00	0.00	0.00	20
Poland	0.00	0.00	0.00	0.00	0.00	49
Russia	0.00	0.00	0.00	0.00	0.00	79
SUBTOTAL	0.00	0.00	0.00	0.00	0.00	179

(table continued next page)

For a total of 92 observations on developing-country bond issues during 1989–93 (pooled cross-section and time series data), the regression equation achieves relatively high explanation (adjusted $\bar{R}^2$ of nearly three-fourths). The dummy variables for Brady debt reduction and private borrowers are almost always statistically significant at the 95 percent level or higher, as is the inflation variable. Either the export growth or GDP growth variable is statistically significant as well. All variables have the right signs. The equation achieves even higher overall explanation for the shorter, more recent period of 1992 and first half of 1993 (68 observations); however, the export and GDP growth variables turn insignificant.

The broad message of table 8.9 is that the bond market has indeed been discriminating. Thus, a country with inflation of 1,100 percent has paid a spread of some 300 basis points above a country with 3 percent inflation (regression coefficient of 50 times [7 − 1]). Private borrowers pay about 80 basis points more than public-sector borrowers, reflecting a greater degree of credit risk.[22]

---

22. Even after the Latin American experience in the 1980s. Thus, lenders to private firms lost more in Mexico's Fideicomiso Para la Cobertura de Riesgo Cambiarios mechanism than did lenders to the government. Before the debt crisis the view tended to be that firms

Table 8.8 (continued)

	1989	1990	1991	1992	1993	Memorandum: 1992 debt
II. Others						
Algeria	0.16	0.09	0.00	0.00	0.00	26
China	0.00	0.00	0.12	1.29	1.06	69
Czechoslovakia	0.00	0.38	0.28	0.13	0.38	9
Hong Kong	0.19	0.07	0.10	0.19	0.66	..
Hungary	0.88	0.89	1.19	1.24	1.64	22
India	0.45	0.27	0.23	0.00	0.00	77
Indonesia	0.18	0.08	0.37	0.49	0.03	84
Korea	0.26	1.11	2.01	3.21	2.01	43
Malaysia	0.43	0.00	0.00	0.00	0.50	20
Singapore	0.00	0.11	0.00	0.00	0.00	..
Taiwan	0.10	0.00	0.16	0.06	0.04	..
Thailand	0.00	0.00	0.02	0.61	0.79	39
Turkey	1.19	0.59	0.50	3.19	2.10	55
Others	0.72	0.00	0.64	0.83	1.00	..
SUBTOTAL	4.55	3.58	5.60	11.24	10.21	444
TOTAL	5.49	6.17	12.43	23.53	33.42	1054

.. = data not available

a. First half only, except for Argentina, Brazil, Chile, Mexico, and Venezuela.

Sources: Collyns et al. 1993; Skiles 1994; World Bank 1993b.

The regression coefficient on Brady debt reduction shows that a country that asked for debt forgiveness now pays about 75 basis points above what it would otherwise pay in the international bond market. If the normal real Treasury bond rate is 3 percent, this premium means that the cost of borrowing is about one-fourth higher for countries that have been involved in debt forgiveness. The penalty would probably be higher except for the (fallacy of composition) perception that bonds have shown themselves to be aloof from sovereign risk. Nor does the later period show a lower premium than the full period, although one may hope that over time the penalty could disappear as (and if) the debt crisis of the 1980s recedes further into the past.

It is intriguing to consider the implications of the estimated spread penalty for Brady graduates compared with countries that did not seek forgiveness. At a 75-basis-point differential, Mexico would have to contract $200 billion in new bonds before its extra interest burden would

posed both credit risk and transfer (foreign exchange risk), whereas sovereign borrowers posed only the latter. Experience showed otherwise, but a sovereign discount remains.

Table 8.9 Developing country bond spreads: regression estimates (basis points)

Case	Years	Constant	Debt reduction dummy	Private dummy	ln(Infl)	Regression coefficients (std errors): ln(per-capita income)	Export growth	GDP growth	Adjusted R²
1	89-93:2	25.8 (109)	110.2 (29)	76.2 (24)	48.9 (7)	...	...	...	.693
2	"	172.9 (109)	113.8 (29)	84.5 (25)	50.2 (7)	-20.4 (15)	...	...	.699
3	"	249.6 (106)	76.7 (33)	83.8 (24)	50.1 (7)	-22.6 (15)	-7.1 (3)	...	.714
4	"	255.8 (105)	57.3 (35)	82.5 (24)	47.5 (7)	-19.8 (15)	0.8 (6)	-14.1 (8)	.724
5	92-93:2	388.8 (76)	74.4 (31)	85.0 (20)	42.9 (6)	-36.7 (12)	-5.1 (5)	-5.0 (7)	.833

... = not applicable.

exceed the $1¹/₂ billion direct annual interest savings it secured in its Brady deal. The spread is thus not large enough to classify Mexico's debt forgiveness as a debtor policy mistake, even without adding the probably more important psychological factor of normalization in expectations. Would Chile have done better to seek forgiveness and pay only 75 basis points extra in the future? Probably not. In 1989, Chile's secondary market price was much higher than that of Mexico, so the depth of cut in a deal would have been smaller. Indeed, the banks likely would have said that Chile did not need forgiveness. For their part, Chilean authorities might well have judged any small net gain they could extract from the trade-off between forgiven debt and higher future spreads not worth the opprobrium associated with not honoring the full debt (if, as suggested in chapter 4, country pride—or self respect—is one element in debtor behavior). Even so, this thought experiment does suggest that the penalty spread identified in table 8.9 may be understated rather than overstated, if Chilean and Colombian policymakers had a more accurate appraisal than the statistical estimates here.

At a broader level, the principal message of tables 8.8 and 8.9 is that by 1992–93 the bulk of middle-income developing countries had meaningful access to the international bond market, albeit at some premium.[23] Virtually all of the major countries of Latin America and Asia were present in the market. Only the low-income countries of sub-Saharan Africa were systematically absent. The tantalizing implication is that unless and until a new debt crisis occurs in the bond market (following the pattern of the penultimate historical episode, of the 1930s, rather than that of the most recent), the international bond market could be a major and growing source of capital for developing countries. The contrary hypothesis, as noted above, is that most of this finance will disappear when and if international interest rates, and especially those in the United States, return to substantially higher levels.

Sustainability

As discussed below, Chile, Colombia, Brazil, and some other Latin American countries were seeking to moderate capital inflows in the period 1991–93. In contrast, Argentina and Mexico were not only welcoming large inflows but were relying on them as an integral part of their stabilization programs. By 1994 there were increasing questions

---

23. Note that the underlying "developing-country" spread was surprisingly low. Thus, from regression (1), the government of a country that had not received debt reduction and had inflation of only 10 percent annually could expect to borrow at a spread of only 140 basis points above the US Treasury, and with inflation of 3 percent the spread was only 75 basis points.

Figure 8.6 Current account/XGNFS, four Latin American countries

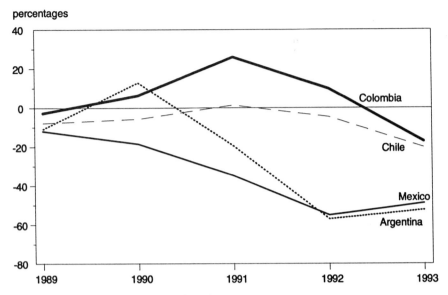

Source: IMF, International Financial Statistics.

about the sustainability of the large inflows and the current account deficits that were their counterpart. A widely publicized study by Morgan Guaranty Bank (Skiles 1994) argued that although debt/exports ratios had fallen and domestic policies (especially fiscal) had improved, "the external trade balances in many of the largest Latin American countries remain weak . . . [and] the countries may be vulnerable at some point in the future to a sudden shift in investor preferences" (5).

There is no denying the fact that the current account deficits of Argentina and Mexico have become large by any historical criterion. Mexico's deficit averaged $22 billion annually in 1992–93; Argentina's deficit, $8 billion (ECLAC 1993). As shown in figure 8.6, in both countries the current account deficit reached the range of 50 to 55 percent of exports of goods and nonfactor services in 1992 and 1993. In contrast, in Chile and Colombia the current account was near balance or in surplus in 1991–92 and in deficit by only about 20 percent of exports of goods and nonfactor services by 1993.[24]

The divergence between Chile and Colombia on the one hand and Argentina and Mexico on the other is a direct consequence of the different macroeconomic strategies adopted. As discussed in chapter 6, Chile and Colombia have employed the crawling-peg exchange rate, whereas

---

24. Note that in the face of domestic recession, Brazil had a sizeable current account surplus in 1992–93. For its part, Venezuela had a current account deficit in the vicinity of 15 percent of exports, associated with falling oil prices.

Argentina and in effect Mexico have adopted a fixed or quasi-fixed exchange rate "anchor" as a centerpiece to their anti-inflationary programs. The crawling peg tends to keep the real exchange rate constant, whereas the fixed-rate anchor tends to cause real appreciation of the exchange rate.[25] In addition, trade liberalization caused a structural increase in the level of imports.

Argentine and Mexican authorities vigorously defend their strategies. The central argument to their case is that the new episode of high current account deficits is not a macroeconomic problem because the deficits are driven by private borrowing, not by borrowing of a public sector that is experiencing fiscal deficits. As noted in chapter 6, this is what was formerly called the UK Treasury theory (of former chancellor of the exchequer Nigel Lawson, who applied the argument to UK external deficits in the late 1980s). It postulates that in the absence of a public fiscal deficit, there is no policy problem associated with an external deficit. The view suggests that it is largely private investment that is being financed by capital inflows, and that when and if private investors decide to stop sending capital, there will be an automatic reduction in the corresponding capital equipment imports associated with the investment projects.[26]

Table 8.7 and figure 8.7 confirm that there has been a historic break in the relationship between the fiscal deficit and capital inflows. Argentina and Mexico in particular were running tight fiscal policies by the early 1990s, in sharp contrast to their large fiscal deficits at the beginning of the 1980s. For the four largest Latin American economies as a group, there is a close correlation between the fiscal deficit and the capital inflow during the period 1980–84, a looser but still parallel relationship in 1984–87, and then a sharp divergence. As shown in figure 8.7, after 1987 higher fiscal deficits were instead associated with a cutoff in foreign capital access. One reason for this cutoff was that fiscal imbalance was associated with macroeconomic disarray that curtailed not only lending by official agencies but also the new-money packages that otherwise

---

25. As noted in chapter 6, however, in the Argentine case real appreciation is substantial if the consumer price deflator is used but absent if the wholesale price is used, and the wholesale price is arguably the more appropriate deflator.

26. For a more general statement of the view that the current account deficit does not matter unless it is a signal of excessive fiscal deficits, see Corden (1991). Corden's discussion primarily refers to industrial countries, but he cites the case of Chile in 1980–81 and argues that the Chilean external deficit would not have been a problem if the private sector had not induced the government to take over private external debt. As shown in chapter 6 in the present study, however, this popular view overstates the extent to which the government assumed the real burden of private external debt (as opposed to its external transfer dimension) and accordingly does not provide an adequate explanation of why Chilean external borrowing led to economic crisis even though it was private rather than public.

Figure 8.7 Fiscal deficit and capital inflow, four Latin American countries

billions of dollars

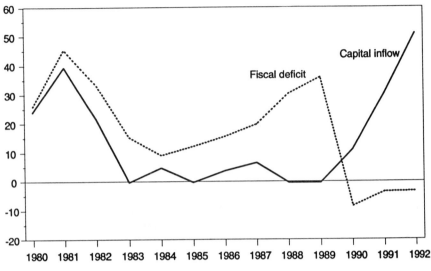

Sources: IDB 1991,1993; IFS; Banco de Mexico.

were being mobilized under the Baker Plan. Conversely, by 1990 and especially 1992, there were large capital inflows concomitantly with an aggregate fiscal surplus.[27]

The end to government fiscal deficits as the driving force in Latin America's external current account deficit is perhaps the single most important reason for optimism about the sustainability of capital inflows to the region in the 1990s. When fiscal imbalance is the source of external imbalance, there can eventually be an "internal transfer problem" of collapse of domestic government finances that adds to the external transfer problem in making debt unviable (chapter 4). Moreover, the viability of the external debt depends in part on how well the borrowing has been used. Often government borrowing has gone for government consumption, whereas private borrowing from abroad tends to be more associated with investment projects. For these reasons, there is an important element of truth in the Lawson thesis.

However, there are surely prudential limits to borrowing from abroad even when it is private rather than government. The eventual external transfer problem is still an issue. Importantly, the smoothness of external adjustment to a sudden drop in capital inflow is by no means

27. The fiscal surplus derives from the use of the "real" or operational definition. This is the appropriate concept for gauging real demand pressure and therefore the absorption gap associated with the current account deficit.

ensured by the presumed link of capital equipment imports to financial capital inflow. There could easily be wrenching adjustments required by a sudden decline in capital flows.

Historical experience is one guide to how large an external deficit is prudent. Figure 8.8 shows that among five high-borrowing developed countries during the past three decades, the largest current account deficits did not exceed 30 percent of exports of goods and nonfactor services (Australia in the mid-1980s, New Zealand briefly in the mid-1970s). Figure 8.9 shows that the same is true for three of the four high-borrowing Asian developing countries. Only South Korea reached current account deficits as high as 50 percent of exports of goods and services, and the country did so only for a brief period in the late 1960s. Moreover, South Korea's export growth rate was phenomenal.

The historical evidence in figures 8.8 and 8.9 strongly suggests that Argentina and Mexico are unlikely to be able to sustain current account deficits of 50 percent of exports of goods and services into the indefinite future. There is one crucial ameliorating consideration, however, that must be taken into account: the role of capital repatriation.

The current account deficit and capital inflows of a retirement community would appear strictly unsustainable by conventional standards. Retirees earn no current income. Following life-cycle savings plans, they are in the stage of running down their savings. Thus, there will be a constant capital inflow into the retirement village, and a correspondingly large "current account" deficit (excess of spending over current income). Yet there is no problem of viability. The reason is that the retirement village has large external assets that it is repatriating.

As analyzed above and reported in tables 8.4 and 8.6, Argentina and Mexico were precisely the two countries with the highest accumulation of flight capital assets, and correspondingly the largest volumes of repatriation that could be expected once the debt crisis was over. Like the retirement village, these economies have been in a phase in which the capital inflow and current account deficit was much larger than might normally be thought sustainable simply because they were in a period of drawing on external assets.

To sharpen the point, consider the concept of an adjusted current account deficit that simply subtracts the amount of capital repatriation. The analysis above calculated that capital repatriation by nationals could have been expected to amount to $13.5 billion for Argentina in 1992–93 and $15.0 billion in Mexico for these two years. The cumulative current account deficit in the period was about $16 billion for Argentina and $44 billion for Mexico. Subtracting, the "adjusted" current account deficit was only $2.5 billion for Argentina and $29 billion for Mexico. Thus, after removing the distorting influence of what is tantamount to the presence of a massive retirement community drawing on its external assets, it turns out that Argentina's adjusted current account deficit

Figure 8.8 CA/XGS five-year moving average, five OECD countries

percentages

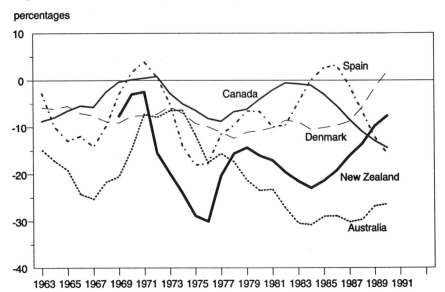

Source: IFS.

Figure 8.9 CA/XGS five-year moving average, four Asian countries

percentages

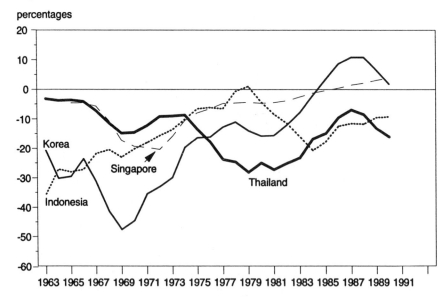

Source: IFS.

drops from 50 percent of exports to 8 percent; Mexico's, from 50 percent to 33 percent.

This exercise reveals why authorities in the two countries have been frustrated that foreign economic officials have not understood that the current account deficit does not necessarily have the conventional negative connotations for policy performance. Nonetheless, the exhaustion of the stock adjustment phase for capital repatriation means that at some point in the future Argentina and Mexico will largely have to return to other forms of financing current account deficits. Thus, the model above projects that by 1996 annual capital repatriation will be down to $2.8 billion for Argentina and $2.7 billion for Mexico. If so, by then even the "adjusted" current account deficits subtracting out capital repatriation would stand at about 30 percent of exports of goods and services for Argentina and 40 percent for Mexico, if nothing is done to increase exports by more than imports in the meantime.

In short, although the Argentine and Mexican external deficits in 1992–93 were abnormally large, the unique influence of stock adjustment in flight capital meant abnormally large repatriation of capital that made financing not difficult. Because of the predictable reduction of capital repatriation as the phase of stock adjustment is completed, if their current account deficits of recent magnitudes were to continue into the decade the countries could once again begin to face situations of unsustainability in external accounts.

Moreover, the well-behaved downward glidepath of capital repatriation predicted in table 8.6 assumes that the post-debt-crisis perception remains permanently in place, that there is a once-for-all downward shift in the desired portfolio share for holdings abroad. If instead domestic investors began to doubt the sustainability of the situation, the desired portfolio shares could shift again toward foreign assets. If this shift were sufficient, capital repatriation could once again reverse to capital flight.

In this regard, there is something of a "Triffin problem" in the model facing the region. In the 1960s, Yale University economist Robert Triffin identified an internal inconsistency in the dollar exchange standard whereby most countries held dollars as their reserve currency (Triffin 1960). If dollars were to be available for other countries to build up, the United States had to run chronic trade deficits. But these trade deficits themselves tended to erode confidence in the dollar, threatening a sudden attempt by foreign monetary authorities to unload their dollar holdings in exchange for gold. The system was thus unstable.

A similar dynamic is present in the Argentine-Mexican model of large current account deficits financed to an important degree by capital repatriation. The repatriation contributes to real exchange rate appreciation and the current account deficits that are the counterpart of capital inflow. But the large current account deficits may increasingly undermine investor confidence about sustainability. As a result, desired portfolio shares may shift once again toward foreign assets. If so, there is an internal inconsistency in this mechanism that leads to instability, as in the case of the Triffin problem.

It is difficult to escape the conclusion from this analysis that Argentina and Mexico would be well-advised to reduce their current account deficits from recent levels. Based on the historical experience reviewed in figures 8.8 and 8.9, more sustainable levels would be in the range of 25 percent of exports of goods and services. A reasonable rule of thumb would be to seek this level as a target, adding an additional tranche of permissible current account deficit equal to the amount of capital repatriation that can comfortably be anticipated for the year in question.

Narrowing the current account deficit need not mean reducing growth. As figure 8.9 shows, South Korea progressively reduced its large current account deficit of the 1960s and eventually reached significant current account surplus in the late 1980s, yet that country achieved high sustained growth. The investment-saving identity in the national accounts does of course require that investment for domestic growth be financed by domestic plus foreign saving, and a lower current account deficit means lower foreign saving. But there should be room to raise domestic saving in compensation. Indeed, the sharp drop in public-sector dissaving has meant a potential rise in the investment rate even without increased foreign saving. To some extent the rise of the current account deficit in the early 1990s was associated with a decline in domestic saving rather than a rise in the investment rate. The need, then, is for private saving to rise, just as government saving has done, so that excessive reliance on foreign saving is not required to achieve growth.

By far the best way to shrink the external deficit and reliance on foreign saving is to increase the export base, as South Korea did. Higher exports not only shrink the deficit but also raise the base against which the sustainable current account deficit may be gauged. From 1989 to 1993, nominal dollar exports rose by 19 percent for Latin America as a whole, compared with 61 percent for Asian developing countries (IMF 1993f, 168-9). However, exports grew by 29 percent over this period for Mexico and 36 percent for Argentina (ECLAC 1991, 1993). The problem for these two countries was thus not so much slow export growth as a surge in imports associated with trade liberalization, economic recovery, and real exchange rate appreciation. Imports rose by 280 percent in Argentina and 110 percent in Mexico over this period (ECLAC 1991, 1993). If the two countries can sustain relatively brisk export growth, the natural deceleration of import growth after this one-time trade regime change should permit a narrowing of the external deficit and a reduction in the ratio of the current account deficit to exports of goods and services.

An Embarrassment of Riches? Moderating Inflows

In the face of the outward shift in the international supply curve of capital in the early 1990s, several debtor countries deemed it advisable to moderate capital inflows rather than allowing their current account deficits to widen as much as in Argentina and Mexico. An emerging literature examines the rationale and degree of success in this effort. By early 1994, however, the environment for inflows was becoming less favorable, as long-term US interest rates had rebounded by 100 basis points from their 1993 low to reach over 7 percent, and in view of such factors as the assassination of a presidential candidate in Mexico and temporary declines in Latin American stock markets after 1992 (and again in early 1994). As a result, it was unclear whether the problem of an embarrassment of capital inflow riches would persist through the 1990s or was more likely to evaporate or even yield in turn to the more traditional problem of difficulty in mobilizing external capital. Whether merely as a historical footnote or alternatively as a guide to policy for the coming years, it is important to review the theory and practice of limiting capital inflows. At the outset, however, it should be emphasized that the need to consider this issue at all meant that for most practical purposes, and certainly with respect to the external transfer part of the problem, the Latin American debt crisis was over already by the early 1990s.

Countries concerned about excessive capital inflow typically face the following dilemma. There is a tendency for the increased inflow to appreciate the real exchange rate, sacrificing the country's trade competitiveness. This real appreciation is the proximate mechanism that prompts higher imports and discourages exports, so that the capital account surplus translates into a current account deficit. Alternatively, adherence to a fixed exchange rate tends to mean initial buildup in reserves, expansion of the money supply, increase in domestic inflation, and induced real appreciation through rising domestic prices rather than a rising nominal exchange rate.

At the same time, from the national accounts identity, the external current account deficit equals domestic investment minus domestic saving. Accordingly, if capital inflow and the current account deficit are larger than desired, increasing domestic saving or reducing domestic investment is likely to be required in response. The most certain way to achieve this outcome is to tighten fiscal policy so as to raise government saving.

At a relatively early stage in the capital flow resurgence, Calvo, Leiderman, and Reinhart (1993) considered experience with five alternative instruments: (a) a tax on capital inflows, (b) trade policy, (c) fiscal tightening, (d) sterilized and nonsterilized intervention by the central bank, and (e) increased marginal reserve requirements on bank deposits and increased regulation of equity and real estate investments. Noting that taxes on short-term borrowing abroad were tried by Israel in 1978 and Chile in 1991, they argued that after short-term effectiveness this policy soon faced circumvention through such measures as over- and underinvoicing of exports and imports (respectively) and use of the parallel foreign exchange market. In trade policy, an equal subsidy on exports and tariff on imports could offset real appreciation caused by excessive capital inflow without causing either price distortion between exportables and importables or excessive fiscal drain (the likely result with just an export subsidy). However, this package could face problems of countervailing duties on subsidized exports.[28]

Their third alternative is to tighten fiscal policy through higher taxes and lower government spending. They argue that this approach is unlikely to slow capital inflows but will reduce aggregate demand and thereby moderate inflationary consequences. However, presumably there should also be some reduction in capital inflow because of the tendency for the domestic real interest rate to fall as a consequence of a lower government claim on domestic credit markets (crowding in).

Calvo, Leiderman, and Reinhart note that sterilized intervention has been the most popular Latin American policy response to excessive capital inflow, as illustrated by the cases of Chile in 1990–91 and Colombia in 1991. By selling domestic government bonds to absorb liquidity and offset the increase in the money base that would otherwise result from capital inflow, this policy seeks to avoid inflationary consequences of these inflows. However, the sale of domestic bonds at an interest rate in excess of that earned on foreign exchange reserves raises the central bank's quasi-fiscal deficit. Moreover, sterilization prevents the interest differential between the domestic and foreign markets from falling, thereby perpetuating the incentive to capital inflow provided by this differential.

Comparing data for the cases of Chile and Colombia, which applied sterilization, with that of Argentina, which did not, the authors show a much smaller decline in interest rates in sterilizing countries. They conclude that sterilized intervention did not reduce inflows, but it did impose a fiscal burden that reached as high as 0.5 percent of GDP in Colombia. In contrast, unsterilized intervention tends to increase the money base and inflationary pressures, with upward pressure on the

---

28. Calvo, Leiderman, and Reinhart (1993) cite another reason for caution about this policy. They argue that with a credible commitment that the package is only temporary, "agents are likely to substitute future expenditure for present expenditure, thus cooling off the economy and attenuating the real exchange rate appreciation" (146). They see the problem as one of ensuring policy credibility. However, this reasoning would appear to have the stimulative effect backwards. A delay in import purchases and acceleration of export activity caused by a credibly temporary policy will raise the contribution of net exports to GDP, stimulating rather than cooling the economy.

real exchange rate. In this environment a floating rate can permit this appreciation to occur without an increase in the inflation rate.

Higher bank reserve requirements, for their part, can have a prudential benefit by providing a larger cushion against the risk of bank failures in the event of a sudden reversal of capital flows. Overall, Calvo, Leiderman, and Reinhart advocate a package of taxes on short-term capital inflows, increased flexibility of exchange rates, and higher marginal reserve requirements on short-term bank deposits (1993, 149). The recommendation of real appreciation through flexible exchange rate policy broadly accommodates rising capital inflow and widening current account deficits, thereby risking undermining investment in tradeables. Ironically, in practice the countries with crawling-peg exchange rates (Chile, Colombia, and Brazil) tended to use them to avoid rather than permit real appreciation, whereas the countries with effectively fixed exchange rates (Argentina and Mexico) experienced real appreciation.

A subsequent study by researchers at the International Monetary Fund (Schadler, Carkovic, Bennett, and Kahn 1993) highlights four adverse side effects of increased capital inflows: the possibility that higher consumption rather than investment is financed by the flows, loss of monetary control and resulting pressure on inflation, real appreciation of the exchange rate and thus the sacrifice of "hard-won improvements in competitiveness," and vulnerability to reversals and the possible need for severe and disruptive financial policies and exchange rate depreciation (2).

The authors stress that where the capital inflow results from improvements in domestic policy and institutions and resulting increases in potential productivity, the higher inflows and larger current account deficits are "equilibrating adjustments" rather than "signs of instability." If the inflow is caused by high domestic interest rates, it will tend to be self-correcting by reducing these rates in the absence of sterilized intervention. When increased inflows result from external influences, the result is downward pressure on interest rates but otherwise "the standard signs of overheating: an increase in demand[,] . . . higher output, a wider current account deficit, an acceleration in money and prices, and upward pressure on the real exchange rate" (3). A fourth cause may be "bandwagon effects" of fashion or overreaction to new information.

Schadler, Carcovic, Bennett, and Kahn lean toward the use of fiscal tightening as the proper response to external influences and bandwagon effects that raise capital inflows, because it is "the only means of containing inflation and avoiding a real appreciation" (1993, 16).[29] They judge that of the six country cases they study (Chile, Colombia, Egypt, Mexico, Spain, and Thailand) there was inadequate fiscal tightening in

---

29. Note that Calvo, Leiderman, and Reinhart (1993) omit fiscal tightening completely from their favored policy package.

all but one (Thailand). The authors reject sterilized intervention as "discredited . . . because it sustains the high domestic interest rates that attract inflows" (3). They favor nominal appreciation as a source of domestic monetary autonomy and lower inflation, arguing that without nominal appreciation the same real appreciation is likely to occur through higher inflation. At the microeconomic level, the authors are skeptical about most measures. They note, for example, that easing restrictions on capital outflows may stimulate inflows because of the increase in confidence about ease of future remittances and repatriation. They similarly suggest that controls or taxes on capital inflows are likely to be circumvented, even though a case might be made for them on grounds of existing distortions that cause excessive capital inflows.

The IMF authors survey the array of impediments to inflows imposed by the countries examined. These measures included a non-interest bearing 20 percent to 30 percent reserve requirement on new credits from abroad (Spain in 1989, Chile in 1991); a 3 percent withholding tax on foreign exchange receipts for personal service exports and transfers (Colombia, 1991); a 5 percent commission on all central bank purchases of foreign exchange (Colombia, 1991); a ceiling of 10 percent of loan portfolio for domestic bank holdings of foreign currency liabilities such as Euro CDs (Mexico, 1989); prior government authorization of foreign financial loans above a minimum threshold (Spain, 1989); and prohibition of payment of interest on large convertible currency bank deposits (Spain, 1987; Schadler, Carcovic, Bennett, and Kahn 1993, 18). The authors find that typically these measures had only a temporary effect and their coverage had to be successively widened to sustain restraint on capital inflows.

The broad thrust of the study by the IMF experts is that if the cause of capital inflows is successful internal reform, the country should sit back and enjoy the inflow because it is healthy; if the cause is external (e.g., low US interest rates), the government should tighten fiscal policy, with the 9 percentage points of GDP swing in Thailand cited favorably and the swings of only some 3 or 4 percent (Mexico and Spain) viewed as insufficient or merely part of a program already scheduled. In Latin America, Mexican authorities in particular adopted a mix of both policies: simply enjoying capital inflow (under the Lawson thesis), on the one hand, and applying some fiscal tightening on the other. As suggested above, however, the result has been a current account deficit of a size that would be excessive if maintained for a long period of time. At the same time, the relatively tight fiscal stance in Mexico contributed to a domestic growth rate that has been less than spectacular in view of the large capital inflows. Thus, from 1989 through 1993 the primary budget surplus averaged 6.3 percent of GDP (Banco de Mexico 1993, 175, 292). Although real growth averaged 3 percent over the same period, there was a declining trend after the peak of 4.4 percent in 1990, and growth had fallen to only 1 percent by 1993 (ECLAC 1993). The instrument of fiscal restraint had become exhausted by 1994, and selective tax cuts were adopted that election year.

Overall, the resurgence of capital market flows to Latin America in the early 1990s brought an unambiguous improvement in the economic opportunities open to the region in comparison with the period of capital market cutoff in the 1980s after the outbreak of the debt crisis. The new situation inevitably brought some adverse side effects in the form of pressure on domestic money expansion, real exchange rate appreciation, and widening of current account deficits to arguably excessive levels. Such instruments as nonremunerated reserve requirements on bank deposits of foreign inflows can play at least a temporary role in moderating inflows.

In the more important area of macroeconomic response, a case can be made that each of the major Latin American countries adopted a course that was most appropriate to its needs. Argentina and Mexico chose to hold the nominal exchange rate constant and tighten fiscal policy. The fixed rate contributed to real appreciation and widening external deficits, but switching to a crawl could have destabilized inflationary expectations in the context of past experience. In contrast, Chile and Colombia retained the crawl to limit real appreciation, thereby achieving relatively smaller widening of their current account deficits. Deflating by the average of consumer and wholesale prices, real appreciation from 1990 to 1993 was larger in Argentina and Mexico (simple average: 16.6 percent) than in Chile and Colombia (9.7 percent).[30] In exchange, Argentina and Mexico obtained greater inflation reduction, though not by as much in the case of Mexico where the rate was already moderate.[31] The choice in this trade-off implied higher weights on the benefits of stable prices in Argentina and Mexico, an understandable priority in view of the higher levels that inflation had reached after the debt crisis in these countries as compared to inflation in Chile and Colombia.

It seems likely that the problem of embarrassment of riches in capital inflow may moderate or disappear in what remains of 1994 and in the next few years. There was already some tightening of capital market access after mid-1992 (Goldstein and Folkerts-Landau 1993, 50), and as shown in figure 8.1, there was some decline in net capital inflow in 1993 from the high level of 1992. Political developments in Brazil and Ven-

---

30. ECLAC 1993. The individual changes in the real exchange rate over the period were Argentina, 10.7 percent (but 35 percent on the CPI alone); Mexico, 22.3 percent; Colombia, 12.0 percent; and Chile, 7.4 percent. In contrast, Brazil experienced a real depreciation of 24.4 percent, but from an abnormally overvalued base associated with the Collor Plan in 1989–90.

31. From 1990 to 1993, inflation fell from 1,344 percent to 7.7 percent in Argentina, from 29.9 percent to 8.7 percent in Mexico, from 27.3 percent to 12.2 percent in Chile, and from 32 percent to 21.2 percent in Colombia (ECLAC 1991, 1993).

ezuela, and concern over wide external deficits in Argentina and Mexico, contributed to a substantial reduction in stock prices from earlier highs in the second half of 1992 (Goldstein and Folkerts-Landau 1993, 60; figure 8.2). Concern in Mexico about the prospects of the NAFTA after US presidential candidate Ross Perot attacked the proposed agreement was another factor.

The real test of market conditions only came in early 1994, however, when the US Federal Reserve moved to a tighter monetary policy, with the associated correction in US and international stock markets and rise in long-term bond rates. By the third quarter of 1994 it remained unclear how severe any induced cooling of the capital market's interest in Latin America would be. However, one sensitive barometer of tightening capital market conditions for Latin America was a sharp decline in the secondary market price on Brady bonds.

From the end of 1993 to the end of March 1994, the prices of Brady discount bonds fell from 96 cents on the dollar to 83 cents for Mexico, 88 cents to 70 cents for Argentina, and 80 cents to 53 cents for Venezuela. Because the discount bonds were at fixed interest rates, some of this decline could have been attributed simply to the rise in US long-term rates. However, variable rate instruments should not have fallen on this account. Yet Brady par bonds, which have variable rates linked to the London interbank offer rate (LIBOR), also declined steeply: from 84 cents on the dollar to 69 cents for Mexico, 70 cents to 52 cents for Argentina, and from 73 cents to 50 cents for Venezuela (Salomon Brothers, 1994b).[32] The implication was that market access was tightening more broadly than could be attributed strictly to the rise in US long-term rates. Parallel retrenchment occurred in the stock markets, where share prices in Argentina, Brazil, and Mexico fell by about 10 percent in the last week of February 1994 following the first tightening by the Federal Reserve earlier in that month (*New York Times*, 1 March 1994).

Geographical Concentration

Whether or not tightening international credit conditions meant an end to any problem of excessive capital inflow for Latin America, the embarrassment of riches had not been a problem for Africa and Eastern Europe. On the contrary, as of late 1993 IMF researchers expressed disappointment that

---

32. The Brady bond index total rate of return, compiled by Salomon Brothers (1994c), had gained a cumulative 23 percent from June 1993 to January 1994, but it gave back all of this gain by April. After a 5 percent rise in May, the index was back to the April level by June 1994.

Notwithstanding the resurgence of flows to a number of countries, the availability of financing remains extremely limited for many developing countries, particularly where difficult economic situations are compounded by unresolved debt problems. For most low-income countries outside Asia and many of the countries in Eastern Europe and the former Soviet Union[,] . . . private financing is confined mainly to direct investment in export enclaves and to trade finance. (Collyns et al. 1993, 4)

It is no surprise that the private capital market resurgence of the early 1990s left out Africa. The only nations of the subcontinent that had participated significantly in the earlier episode of syndicated bank lending were Nigeria and to a lesser extent Côte d' Ivoire. Lower oil prices and serious policy distortions meant that Nigeria was not in a strong position to attract bond and equity finance even after a Brady deal. Moreover, European investors were perhaps the natural clientele for any bond market development in the stronger African economies, but they were reportedly "less willing than US investors to make a distinction between bank credit and securitized financing" after the traumatic experience with bank claims in the debt crisis (Goldstein and Folkerts-Landau 1993, 59).

In contrast, it was a big surprise to many, including many Latin American leaders, that the much-feared reallocation of capital away from Latin America toward Eastern Europe after the collapse of communist regimes not only failed to materialize but that capital flows to Latin America flourished much more than those to Eastern Europe.[33] The IMF staff had estimated in 1991 that annual "demands for external saving" in 1992–96 would amount to $55 billion for German unification, $12 billion for reconstruction in the Middle East, and $33 billion for Eastern Europe and the USSR (IMF 1991b, 47).

As indicated in table 8.1, there was a brief surge in capital flows to Europe and the Middle East associated with the aftermath of the Gulf War. However, by 1992–93, capital flows were back down to about $20 billion, less than two-thirds the amount indicated by the IMF as needed for Eastern Europe and the former Soviet Union alone. A direct estimate of capital inflows to Eastern Europe plus Russia and Ukraine for 1992 yields the meager figure of $2.6 billion; and if errors and omissions for Russia are included, the estimate turns into a net outflow of $5 billion.[34]

An IMF staff team notes that Eastern Europe and the former Soviet Union "face large and persistent external financing needs as they con-

---

33. Mexico's President Carlos Salinas is said to have decided to push for a free trade agreement with the United States after he returned from a trip to Europe in early 1990, where he had become convinced that European investors were fixated on Eastern Europe and would have little capital for Latin America.

34. Calculated from IMF 1994b; World Bank 1993b, vol. 2; IMF 1993c; IMF 1993g. Note that the estimates for the former Czechoslovakia and Yugoslavia are for 1991, and that no estimate is included for Bulgaria.

tinue with the difficult process of transition to market economies'' (Collyns et al. 1993, 5), but that except for Hungary and the Czech Republic these countries rely very little on private capital. They judge that ''over time it will be critical to increase recourse to private funding,'' ideally in the form of non-debt-creating flows (e.g., direct investment). One reason is that official credits are less flexible as they tend to be tied to specific uses and extended only to the public sector.

The authors cite Latin American experience as hopeful evidence on prompt response of financial markets once policy reforms are in place. However, they note that the formerly centrally planned economies lack much of the basic institutional infrastructure of a market economy. Moreover, equity investment in Eastern Europe has been limited (even in the cases of the Czech Republic and Hungary) because of the ''limited number of sizable private sector enterprises'' and the infant developmental stage of stock markets (6).

It should be added that the nature of privatization in most formerly centrally planned economies has been such that there has been much less opportunity or incentive for foreign equity participation than in the case of Latin American privatization. Frequently there has been spontaneous privatization amounting to asset stripping by managers. The formal programs typically redistribute shares to former workers or allocate vouchers to all citizens (IMF 1993f, 91–98). In contrast, the Latin American norm has been outright auction, often with the result of purchase by foreign firms or alliances of domestic and foreign investors.

If the international capital market does enter a new and tighter phase, as suggested by US financial market developments in early 1994, Eastern Europe and the former Soviet Union will have missed a chance to cash in on the easy capital market conditions that were associated with the sharp resurgence of capital flows to Asian and Latin American developing countries in 1991–93 (figure 8.1). Nonetheless, as suggested below, the size of the international capital market is so large compared with flows to developing countries that it should be possible to incorporate Eastern Europe and the FSU with little difficulty—albeit at perhaps higher interest rates than those available in the early 1990s—once domestic economic reforms are in place. In contrast, it seems likely that most African countries will remain more dependent on official sources of assistance for the foreseeable future (chapter 7).

A Future Debt Crisis?

The capital market resurgence of the early 1990s and the completion of Brady Plan debt reductions for all of the major debtors and most of those of intermediate size suggest that by 1994 (and for practical purposes earlier) the debt crisis was over.[35] At the same time, the large new capital inflows to some countries, and the possibility that these could reverse under tighter world capital market conditions, raise the question of whether a new debt crisis later in the 1990s is plausible. Corollary questions are whether the international financial system is any less vulnerable today than in 1982 to a debt crisis, and whether there are policy measures that should be taken at the international or national levels to minimize the danger of disruption from a new crisis.

Despite the revival of capital inflows to Latin America and Asian developing countries, the extent of borrowing and especially of its link to excessive domestic fiscal deficits was much more severe in the late 1970s and early 1980s than in 1991–93. As shown in figure 8.7, high borrowing in 1980–81 was closely associated with large fiscal deficits, but the large capital inflows of 1991–93 were not. As set forth in chapter 2, the various debt indicators, and especially the interest/exports ratio, are considerably more favorable for the major debtor countries today than in 1982. Moreover, domestic economic growth had recovered in the debtor countries by the early 1990s, and (with the important exception of Brazil) inflation had been brought under much better control.

If one considers the likely international economic environment over the next few years, there are both positive and negative prospective developments. On the positive side, economic growth in Europe and Japan seems likely to revive to more normal levels from the recessionary outcome of 1991–93. Export earnings of debtor countries should be more buoyant as a result. Similarly, the completion of the Uruguay Round of trade negotiations should provide additional export opportunities to developing countries, especially agricultural exporters.

On the negative side, interest rates seem likely to rise above their unusually low levels of 1992–93. LIBOR, the benchmark used for most variable-rate international lending, stood at a low average of only 3.5 percent in 1992–93, compared with an average of 7.5 percent in 1986–91, 9.6 percent in 1983–85, and 14 percent in 1979–82 (IMF 1994a; 1992a). There is practically no basis for expecting a return to the high interest rates and high inflation of the early 1980s. However, there are considerable chances that industrial country inflation will revert to the range of 4 to 5 percent rather than stay at the 3 percent range of 1992–93.[36] The combination of a revival of activity and moderate rise in inflation would be likely to generate monetary policies that yield positive real interest rates of, say, 2 to 3 percent. As a result, a rise of LIBOR to the range of 6 percent (for 4 percent inflation plus 2 percent real) to 8 percent (for 5

---

35. See chapter 5. Note that the debt reduction agreement for Brazil, the largest case still outstanding as of 1993, was finally concluded in April 1994.

36. Consumer prices in industrial countries rose by 5.0 percent in 1990 and 4.3 percent in 1991, compared with 3 percent in 1992 and 2.7 percent in 1993 (IMF 1994a).

Table 8.10 Exposure of debtor countries to interest fluctuation (billions of dollars)

	1982	1989	1992	1992 adj.
I. Variable interest long-term debt				
Argentina	18.0	34.0	27.4	18.3
Bolivia	1.0	1.0	0.8	0.8
Brazil	58.5	65.9	73.0	48.7
Chile	12.2	10.5	11.6	11.6
Colombia	3.8	7.7	7.6	7.6
Costa Rica	1.6	2.1	1.1	1.1
Côte d' Ivoire	3.6	6.8	8.2	8.2
Ecuador	3.7	6.2	6.1	4.0
Jamaica	0.4	1.0	0.9	0.9
Mexico	47.4	64.4	40.7	40.7
Morocco	3.0	8.5	10.6	10.6
Nigeria	5.8	10.9	5.1	5.1
Peru	4.0	4.6	7.1	4.7
Philippines	6.5	10.5	9.3	9.3
Uruguay	1.0	2.3	2.1	1.4
Venezuela	14.8	26.0	18.2	18.2
Yugoslavia	12.9	12.7	11.6	11.6
TOTAL	198.2	275.0	241.4	202.9
II. Short-term debt				
Argentina	16.5	8.5	16.2	16.2
Bolivia	0.2	0.3	0.2	0.2
Brazil	17.5	18.6	21.1	21.1
Chile	3.3	3.0	3.7	3.7
Colombia	3.1	1.6	2.8	2.8
Costa Rica	0.8	0.7	0.3	0.3
Côte d' Ivoire	1.1	2.9	4.4	4.4
Ecuador	2.2	1.4	2.2	2.2
Jamaica	0.1	0.4	0.3	0.3
Mexico	26.1	8.7	24.5	24.5

(table continued on next page)

percent inflation plus 3 percent real) is highly plausible, although the lower end of this range might be the more likely.

Table 8.10 reports estimates of the amount of variable interest debt owed by the 17 countries that were originally identified as priority countries under the Baker Plan of the mid-1980s (chapter 5), and relates this debt to the base of exports of goods and nonfactor services. These data provide a basis for examining the vulnerability of the major debtors to a rise in world interest rates.

Interest rates were variable on long-term syndicated bank loans linked to LIBOR, and on short-term debt. In 1982, short-term debt accounted

Table 8.10 (continued)

	1982	1989	1992	1992 adj.
Morocco	1.0	0.3	0.4	0.4
Nigeria	2.5	0.6	2.2	2.2
Peru	3.0	4.8	4.0	4.0
Philippines	11.5	4.0	4.5	4.5
Uruguay	0.6	0.9	1.8	1.8
Venezuela	14.7	2.3	5.3	5.3
Yugoslavia	1.8	0.8	1.0	1.0
TOTAL	106.2	59.7	95.0	95.0
III. Ratio: (I+II)/XGNFS (percent)				
Argentina	354	353	292	231
Bolivia	132	137	121	121
Brazil	324	218	241	179
Chile	301	136	118	118
Colombia	137	116	98	98
Costa Rica	209	146	55	55
Côte d' Ivoire	164	293	356	356
Ecuador	217	262	229	173
Jamaica	34	67	44	44
Mexico	266	194	140	140
Morocco	106	138	129	129
Nigeria	65	134	59	59
Peru	168	211	249	196
Philippines	218	113	78	78
Uruguay	96	146	145	119
Venezuela	146	181	139	139
Yugoslavia	73	53	74	74
TOTAL	201	173	155	137

a. Short-term debt plus variable long-term interest.
b. XGNFS = export goods and nonfactor services.
Note: 1992 variable interest adjusted is for countries with potential Brady deals (Argentina, Brazil, Ecuador, Peru, Uruguay).

Source: World Bank 1993b, vol. 2; 1989b, vol. 2.

for about one-third of total variable rate debt. After the debt crisis, short-term loans dried up and this component fell to only about 18 percent of the total. By 1992, however, there had been some normalization and a return to higher relative levels of short-term debt. By then, short-term claims were back up to 28 percent of total variable-interest debt for these countries.

The table reports actual 1992 levels and an "adjusted" concept for 1992. The adjusted measure arbitrarily cuts variable interest long-term debt by one-third for those countries that were close to Brady deals but had not yet received them as of 1992. This reduction reflects both a cut in the stock of debt and a reallocation of the converted claims into a higher portion bearing fixed interest (typically, so-called par bonds that kept full face value but had interest set at a moderate, fixed rate). A cut by one-third is approximately the outcome for Mexico and Venezuela (as shown in the table for 1992 compared with 1989).

Table 8.10 shows that for the Baker countries, the ratio of variable interest debt fell from about 200 percent of exports of goods and nonfactor services in 1982 to about 175 percent in 1989 and 155 percent in 1992. If the effect of completion of pending Brady deals is included (1992 adjusted), this ratio falls to only about 135 percent. On this basis, the major troubled debtor countries are now only about two-thirds as vulnerable to increased interest rates than they were in 1982, at the margin. Because the absolute level of interest rates was far higher in 1982, moreover, this lower marginal vulnerability applies to a much lower interest rate burden.

Using 137 percent of the export base as the stock of post-Brady variable debt for these countries, we have the result that a rise in LIBOR by one hundred basis points imposes increased interest payments equivalent to 1.4 percent of exports of goods and services. If, as suggested above, LIBOR could easily rise from 3.5 percent in 1992–93 to 6 percent in the medium term, and perhaps with somewhat less probability, to 8 percent, then the result is that a plausible range for interest rebound would mean an increase of 2.5 to 4.5 percentage points in LIBOR (250 to 450 basis points). Based on the marginal parameter just estimated, the result would be an increase in the debt servicing burden by 3.4 to 6.2 percent of export earnings.

As indicated in table 2.5 of chapter 2, the ratio of net interest payments (accrual basis) to exports of goods and services stood at 29.8 percent for these 17 countries in 1982, and had fallen to about 12.0 percent in 1991–92. On the basis of the figures just estimated, interest rate rebounds in the medium-term might add back some 3.5 to 6 percentage points to this level. After taking account of the reduction in the interest burden from the 1992 base as the result of completion of pending Brady deals, the growing export base, a boost in exports likely to be associated with any rebound in industrial country growth that is the main factor behind rising interest rates in the first place, and additional interest earnings on reserves, the range would be lower. For the moderate side of the range, the resulting interest-exports ratio might rise to some 17 percent; and for the higher range, perhaps 19 percent. The higher figure could begin to pose some difficulty. However, the more moderate increase is more likely to be the central case (and some would argue that interest increases will be even lower and inflation will stay closer to the 3 percent mark of 1992–94). Especially in the more moderate case, interest rebound should present little difficulty in financing for those countries that have improved domestic policies and have already reentered the bond market.

Dooley, Fernandez-Arias, and Kletzer (1994) have reached a much more pessimistic conclusion about future vulnerability of Brady graduates. On the basis of statistical regressions, they find that domestic fiscal policy reform and the Brady debt reductions explained relatively little of the increase in secondary market prices after 1989, and that the bulk of this increase was due to falling world dollar interest rates. They consider the secondary market price to be a barometer of capital market access. They argue that country creditworthiness varies inversely with world interest rates and find that there is a (negative) unitary elasticity of secondary market price with respect to the 10–year US bond rate. They thus conclude that with the prospect of rising US interest rates, debtor countries could face serious loss of capital market access despite having completed Brady deals and despite having adopted economic reforms. Essentially their study stands as a prime example of the increasingly popular view that the Greenspan plan mattered much more than the Brady Plan, and therefore the debt crisis might return as a consequence of higher US interest rates.

There would seem to be several problems with their analysis. First and foremost, it omits the most important factor identified in the political-economic model of chapter 5 in the present study: the shift from the political willingness-to-pay constraint to the debt capacity constraint following a Brady agreement. The benefits of this watershed shift for capital market access remain in hand regardless of the level of the international interest rate. Second, the identification of capital market access with secondary market price has been amply demonstrated to be at best loose. Thus, Brazil had massive capital inflows in 1992 despite a secondary market price of only 33 cents on the dollar. Third, at least some of the study's data are suspect. It places Mexico's stripped price after the Brady deal at 51 cents on the dollar, hardly a measure of the permanent post-Brady country risk that is consistent with Mexico's near-investment-grade ratings. Fourth, the most recent data belie the authors' fears. From July 1993 to June 1994, the price of Mexico's Brady discount bonds fell only from 85 cents to 83 cents. Yet the US 10–year bond rate rose from 4.4 percent to 6.3 percent. With a unitary elasticity, the Mexico Brady bond should have fallen to about 60 cents.[37] In sum, the new evidence in Dooley, Fernandez-Arias, and Kletzer (1994) would not seem to warrant reversal of the broad judgment here that major debtor countries that have adopted policy reforms and completed Brady deals should not be particularly vulnerable to increases in world interest rates.

Another source of vulnerability is that associated with lower oil prices. As examined in chapter 3, it has always been the case that the major debtor countries as a group experience debt-servicing difficulties when

---

37. $85 \times [4.4/6.3] = 0.6$.

the price of oil drops. By early 1994, it was doing just that. On 31 March 1994, Brent crude stood at $13 per barrel, compared with $24 in 1990 (a high associated with the Gulf War), $20 in 1991, $19 in 1992, and $17 in 1993 (IMF 1994a; *Wall Street Journal*, 1 April 1994). However, by late September 1994 the price was back up to $16 per barrel (*Wall Street Journal*, 26 September 1994).

The reductions in oil prices that already occurred from 1990 to 1993 contributed to a reduction in Venezuela's total exports from $17.3 billion to $13.9 billion (ECLAC 1991, 1993). In Mexico, where the share of non-oil exports is far higher now than in the early 1980s, total export earnings rose over the same period from $26.8 billion to $29.4 billion. For Latin America as a whole, oil exports in 1992 amounted to $16 billion.[38] On this basis, and in view of the trend in world prices, the region's oil exports probably fell to $14.3 billion in 1993 and could be as low as $11 billion in 1994. A reduction of about $3 billion in 1994 would represent a loss of 5 percent of total export earnings of the oil-exporting Latin American countries in 1993 (ECLAC 1993).[39] This erosion would be modest, even without taking account of increases in nonoil exports.

The World Bank (1994a) expects real oil prices to rise at an annual rate of 2.2 percent during the period 1994–2002. It anticipates increased oil demand in developing countries (including the FSU), but expects real oil price increases to be limited because of additions to capacity and resumption of Iraqi supply. Even so, the main scenario of moderately rising real prices means there is little anticipation of a further adverse shock to debt viability from this standpoint.[40]

In sum, debtor country vulnerability in the medium term would appear to be limited. Although some rebound in the interest rate can be anticipated, debtor countries are less vulnerable to rising interest rates today than they were on the eve of the debt crisis, both at the margin and, especially, in terms of the absolute level of interest/exports ratios. Their vulnerability to lower oil prices is also more limited, as nonoil exports have grown, and the likelihood of further oil price declines is more remote because of already low levels. At the same time, a likely

---

38. United Nations, UNCOMTRADE database.

39. Bolivia, Colombia, Ecuador, Mexico, Peru, and Venezuela.

40. Of course, the collapse of oil prices in 1986 was not anticipated either, but by early 1994 real oil prices were back down to levels close to those of 1973 before the first oil shock, suggesting there was little room left for further decline. US Energy Department estimates indicate that in 1993 dollars, the average price per barrel paid by refiners for crude oil rose from $14 in 1973 to $38 in 1974, eased to $32 by 1978, jumped to $62 in 1980–81, declined steadily to $38 by 1985, collapsed to $19 in 1986, and remained close to this low plateau thereafter (except for temporary increases to $22 in 1987 and $25 in 1990; *New York Times*, 3 April 1994).

recovery in industrial country economic activity in the mid-1990s should boost debtor country export earnings.

As discussed in chapter 2, for its part the international banking system is also much less vulnerable to a debt crisis today than it was in the early 1980s. For the nine largest US banks, debt owed by the Baker-17 countries plus three Eastern European countries (Hungary, Poland, and Romania) stood at 200 percent of capital in 1982 but had fallen to only 51 percent by 1992 (chapter 2, table 2.11). Ratios of exposure to capital are lower for other US banks and for banks of other industrial countries.

Another round of the debt crisis would thus be unlikely to pose anywhere near the same threat to viability of the banking system as the outbreak of the crisis in 1982. At the same time, it is illuminating to contemplate the implications of the sharp declines in Brady bond prices in the first quarter of 1994. As discussed above, these prices fell by some 15 percent for Mexico, 20 percent for Argentina, and 30 percent for Venezuela.

Goldstein and Folkerts-Landau (1993, 58) estimate that at the end of 1992 there were $58 billion outstanding in Brady bonds and $7 billion in bonds issued by Brazil to securitize interest arrears. They report that the total turnover in the secondary market for these and other bank claims on developing countries amounted to $450–$500 billion. The implication of a robust and relatively liquid market for Brady bonds is however difficult to square with the sharp drop in their prices in early 1994.

Because the Brady bonds are collateralized with US Treasury zero-coupon assets, a period of nervousness and low prices for these bonds would have little direct implication for banks' capital assets. Typically they would not need to raise loan-loss reserves. However, their potential for profit through trading off these bonds at prices higher than presently carried in their books would be considerably reduced. The broader implication is that the downside risk for the banks in the event of a renewal of debt-servicing difficulties later in the 1990s is primarily in the form of a profit squeeze rather than any major threat to bank solvency comparable to that in the early 1980s. Even this effect would be limited because many of the banks have sold off a significant fraction of their Brady bonds to investors.

Goldstein and Folkerts-Landau (1993) consider the systemic implications of the evolution of the capital market for developing countries in the early 1990s. They make the important point that the securitization of developing country debt after the Brady Plan, together with the increase in securitization of capital flows to developing countries with the rise of bond and equity finance, introduces important flexibility that was missing at the time of the debt crisis in the early 1980s. One reason is that the availability of market quotations for all of these instruments provides a mechanism for signaling the emergence of difficulties at an early stage. Another reason is that with a larger share of security claims on these countries held outside the banks, ''a drop in the price of securities [would] result in a decline in the financial wealth of investors, the global macroeconomic consequences of which would be limited, since most large investors hold only a small proportion of their assets in developing country securities'' (62).

A systemic issue related to the signaling provided by market prices is the possibility that the private capital market might provide a form of policy discipline to replace the earlier role of the IMF and other official agencies. Indeed, one account (*Wall Street Journal*, 14 June 1994) indicates that large US mutual funds forcefully pressed Mexican authorities on policy measures after the assassination of presidential candidate Luis Donaldo Colosio in March 1994, promising to raise billions of dollars in the coming year if the Mexican government defended the peso but threatening to cut off billions if it did not. If accurate, this account would suggest that such private-sector discipline may be too narrow in its objectives, excessively concentrated on the protection of short-term profits (e.g., earnings on large holdings of Mexican peso-denominated treasury obligations).[41] More generally, private-sector waves of pessimism and optimism in such experiences as international bond lending in the 1920s, syndicated bank loans in the 1970s, and purchases of US dollars in the early 1980s suggest that the markets are not always omniscient. The discussion below proposes a new private-public entity that might provide helpful additional policy discipline in one market area, that of international bonds.

The correction of Latin American stock prices in the second half of 1992 and the temporary tightening of the capital market at that time contributed to the moderation of capital inflows in 1993 shown in figure 8.1. This pattern suggests that there has already been some experience confirming the notion that the process of securitization of capital flows to the region has introduced pricing signals that help moderate excesses. It remains to be seen whether the same measured correction will follow the tightening of US financial markets in early 1994, or whether instead the modest reduction of capital flows in 1993 will turn into a rout.

Falling stock prices in the US market in 1994 and still relatively low interest rates could encourage rather than discourage continued capital repatriation to Latin America. Nor are direct investment flows likely to be influenced dramatically by shorter term market conditions. In contrast, the heady pace of bond flotations in 1993 could be difficult to replicate. By the third quarter of 1994, IMF (1994d) estimates showed little change for the current account for Latin America in 1994 compared with 1993, and a

---

41. As noted above, Mexico's already large current account deficit indicates that pursuing further real appreciation of the peso carries medium-term risk.

reserves buildup smaller by some $7 billion (165). The implication was that net capital inflows to the region did not fall off by more than about $10 billion from the 1993 level, despite the tightening of world capital market conditions. Net inflows of some $30 billion would still have stood in sharp contrast to the much lower levels of 1983–89 (figure 8.1).

The judgment here that another generalized debt crisis is unlikely in the 1990s should be qualified by the observation that if a new crisis does occur, it could be more difficult to deal with than that of the 1980s. The reason is that increasingly the bulk of debt will be held by individuals in the form of bonds rather than by banks in the form of syndicated loans. In the 1980s crisis, it was much easier to mobilize coordinated relending (in particular, with the help of the negotiating leadership of the bank advisory committees comprising the larger banks) than had been the case in the previous historic episode, bond defaults in the 1930s. At the same time, extended suspension of payments would not pose the same systemic threat as in the 1980s, precisely because the creditors would be numerous, small, and dispersed rather than concentrated at the fulcrum of the financial system. By implication, a new round of debt crisis might be harder on the debtors, on the one hand, and on the multilateral (and to a lesser extent bilateral) lenders who escaped largely without losses in the 1980s crisis, on the other hand.

Finally, although the analysis here suggests that a generalized debt crisis is unlikely in what remains of the 1990s, the probability is higher that individual countries with significant external debt could get into serious trouble again, including some that have received Brady deals. If this occurs, it will almost certainly be because a key premise of the debt resolution has broken down: that the country has achieved a permanent domestic economic reform. As emphasized throughout this study, the area where such a breakdown would be most likely to have serious effects would be that of fiscal reform.

In a scenario that includes a few backsliding Brady graduates, there would be no systemic threat, but the question would arise as to what to do next in these cases. Bank creditors (or the subsequent purchasers of their converted claims) would be likely to do nothing, as their interest payments on Brady bonds would begin to flow from escrow accounts rather than from the country directly. The escrow arrangements typically cover 18 months, so there would be a breathing space of that duration from this quarter. Beyond that horizon, there would begin to be the threat that individual Brady bond holders might attempt to call the country in default. If that occurred, as noted above the situation could be messier than when the claims were held by banks, because of the greater difficulty of coordinating widely dispersed bondholders.

A likely scenario for such individual cases of relapse would be entry into arrears, followed by one of two developments: either a renewal of domestic economic reform, or continued policy disarray and extended arrears. Where governments adopted intensified reforms, there might be a case for revisiting the extent of external debt forgiveness. This time, however, the candidate creditors would presumably be bilateral agencies (who largely escaped the Brady reductions), or even multilateral agencies (whose claims would presumably have to be effectively redeemed at par by industrial country governments, as discussed in chapter 7 with respect to some African countries). In the absence of a return to domestic policy reform, the appropriate international action would be to do nothing. The debtors in question would have an incentive to adopt reform, because although arrears provide automatic credit on a help-yourself basis, they carry their own penalties (as discussed in chapter 6 in the cases of Brazil and Peru).

New Institutions?

International Bondholders Insurance Corporation

The surge of capital flows to Latin America in 1991–93, combined with fears that these flows could be short-lived, raises the question of whether institutional change might help secure steadier and more reliable capital flows. As the bond market seems likely to be the principal vehicle to replace syndicated bank lending for financial flows other than direct investment, it would seem worthwhile to consider institutional innovation to strengthen the international bond market for developing countries.

There are two major areas in which strengthening might be desirable. The first is a widening of the sources of capital potentially participating. The second is an improvement in prudential discretion in the market. The two are interrelated, as the first could be risky to creditor country investors without the second. The first of the two goals would address the potential problem of a dearth of capital, the dominant problem in the 1980s. The second would address the issue of cycles of excessive, indiscriminate lending, the dominant problem of the 1970s.

It would seem useful to consider the creation of an International Bondholders Insurance Corporation (IBIC). This entity would provide insurance of international bonds issued by developing countries, in return for premiums paid by bond purchasers. The entity would seek to achieve the two objectives of market widening and improved prudential surveillance. Market widening could occur because with the availability of insurance, new classes of investors might be prepared to enter the LDC bond market. In particular, insurance companies might be more able to invest in this market. Currently the National Association of Insurance Companies issues country risk ratings that determine whether a nation's bonds are investment grade. In marginal cases, the presence of insurability might make the difference between conferring and not conferring this rating.

Prudential surveillance could be enhanced by the existence of an IBIC, because the agency's terms of access would send a powerful signal about the creditworthiness of a country. One approach would be simply to apply a binary criterion: the IBIC either would or would not stand ready to insure new bonds issued by a country in a given year. This approach could be too heavy-handed, however. If a country had enjoyed insured status for a period and then the IBIC cut it off, there could be a rush to the exit door by many creditors.

A better design would probably be to have the IBIC provide alternative levels of coinsurance for a standard premium, with the differing coinsurance rates reflecting greater or lesser risk. The top rate might be, for example, 80 percent. The IBIC would pay a claim of 80 percent of missed interest or principal payments on an insured bond issued in a country year judged to be in the highest creditworthiness category. The lowest rate might be, for example, only 20 percent (so low that investors might not bother to purchase the insurance). The premium might be 50 basis points in either case. A field of alternative coinsurance rates (with the norm perhaps 50 percent) would provide a vehicle for graded signals about the country's policy quality and creditworthiness. In a year of excellent domestic policy performance by a given country, the agency might set the coinsurance rate at 80 percent. If in a subsequent year domestic policies significantly deteriorated, the agency could reset the coinsurance rate at 50 percent or lower for new bonds, until such time as the policies improved again.

Annex 8A presents random-shock experiments to investigate the costs and profitability of an IBIC meant to insure bonds for the major developing country borrowers. The results indicate that such an entity might on average earn significant profits, although there would be major (but low-probability) risks as well. It might thus be appropriate for the structure of the IBIC to be mixed public-private. The entity could be housed in the World Bank family. It would be desirable to have both World Bank and IMF representatives participate in the agency's credit-rating decisions, as both have important institutional capacity for country analysis. The simulations in annex 8A suggest that initial capital of, say, $300 million would be sufficient. Perhaps half of this amount could be raised from stock issued to the private sector. The other half would be a modest investment for the official sector to make in what could be a useful instrument for strengthening country policies and the international capital market.

The IBIC would seek to do for bonds what the Multilateral Investment Guarantee Agency (MIGA) does for direct investment, but on a much larger scale. The IBIC would provide an alternative opinion to the private credit rating agencies. This function could be important, as there is always some risk that rating agencies become influenced by the rated countries that pay their fees. There is some risk that the IBIC could become politically influenced, for example if major creditor country governments did not wish to rock the boat for a borrowing country in an election year. Private-sector participation in the direction of the agency could be helpful in this regard as well, to minimize the risk of political capture.

An IBIC would also have the potential to play the role of orchestrating creditor response in the event of a future generalized debt crisis. It could thus help neutralize the potential problems in this dimension associated with the swing back from syndicated bank lending to bonds, as discussed above.

An International Bankruptcy Agency?

Williamson (1992) has proposed the creation of an entity that would adjudicate bankruptcy workouts for international lending. Earlier in the debt crisis, before the Brady Plan, he had proposed that such an entity might be able to act as arbiter on past loans (Williamson 1985). There, he suggested that criteria for determining whether and to what extent forgiveness was appropriate would incorporate some broad assessment of insolvency versus illiquidity, as well as other factors. The evaluation would consider whether exogenous shocks were responsible for the problem; the level of per capita income; whether forgiveness would threaten international financial stability; whether there were prospects that the debt could be serviced without unacceptable cost to domestic welfare; whether poor or good use had been made of the funds; whether banks had made proper assessments in their lending practices; and whether the debt had been contracted by a former, illegitimate government.

By the early 1990s the issue of a retrospective bankruptcy court for Latin American debt had been superseded by the Brady Plan. What is left is the idea of such an entity to address future loans. Williamson (1992) suggests that loan contracts in the future could include a clause committing the lender and debtor to accept the decision of the international bankruptcy agency.

Fukao (1992) has criticized this proposal on grounds that, unlike companies, countries cannot be subjected to a mandatory change in the board of directors, a typical measure in domestic bankruptcy. This critique is valid for any retroactive application of international bankruptcy proceedings. However, as formulated by Williamson the arrangement would be voluntary, and the critique by analogy would not seem compelling under conditions of ex ante voluntary undertaking. Lenders could either decide to enter into a contract containing the arbitration clause or could instead lend only without such a clause.

It is far from clear that the availability of an international bankruptcy arbitrator would lead to the coverage of a large portion of LDC lending by bankruptcy clauses. Creditors might have second thoughts, and indeed they might infer that if the IMF had been in this position in June 1989, its award of debt reduction for Mexico might have been 55 cents on the dollar rather than the 35 cents agreed between Mexico and the banks. At the same time, if a country pressed lenders to agree to a bankruptcy arbitration clause, creditors might interpret the position as a sign of less than full intent to honor the debt. It is unclear that countries such as South Korea, Chile, and Colombia would wish to cast doubt on their past credit records by beginning to insist on such a clause. However, the market would determine the popularity of this device, and there is no reason for public policy to oppose such arbitration if private creditors and borrowers find it useful to begin incorporating this feature into lending contracts.

Conclusion

The resurgence of capital flows to Latin America from a low plateau of $10 billion in the mid 1980s to a range of $40 billion to $55 billion in 1992–93 is the best evidence that the strategy of debt management has yielded successful reintegration of debtor countries into the world capital markets. This reintegration has involved much less new lending by banks, and much more capital repatriation by nationals and issuance of new bonds, than most analysts during the debt crisis had expected.

There has been a debate as to whether the resurgence reflected improved country economic policies and prospects or the exogenous impact of low interest rates in the US financial market. The nearly identical behavior of capital flows to Latin America, on the one hand, and Asian developing countries (where the debt crisis was never a major problem for most countries), on the other, suggests a strong role for exogenous capital market influences. However, it is highly unlikely that the renewed flows to Latin America would have paralleled those to Asia if policy reform had not occurred. Importantly, the tight link between public-sector deficits and capital inflows that existed in the early 1980s has been broken, and in the early 1990s the surge in capital flows went to the private sector rather than to finance government deficits. Nigel Lawson's thesis contains an important kernel of truth in that current account deficits are more sustainable if they are not driven by public-sector deficits (though the extreme form of the thesis seems to give inadequate weight to the risks of high costs of forced, rapid external adjustment).

Moreover, where reform was less far along, as in Brazil, the renewed flows of the early 1990s carried high, junk-bond interest rates. Indeed, a statistical test of bond rates suggests that countries that engaged in debt reduction through a Brady Plan had to pay a risk premium of about 75 basis points above other countries, after removing the influence of macroeconomic variables such as inflation.

The analysis here suggests that there is still considerable scope left for capital repatriation, based on a model of portfolio allocation, but that the magnitude of these reflows should be expected to decline. A special consideration of the cases of Argentina and Mexico suggests that although their large current account deficits may have made sense temporarily in view of unusually large flight capital stocks abroad and the critical role of restoring price stability through the use of an exchange rate anchor, historical experience suggests that more modest deficits should be sought in the future, primarily through expansion of the export base.

The large rise in the share of debt owed in the form of bonds rather than syndicated bank loans, caused by securitization in the Brady Plan as well as the actual and prospective flows of new bond debt, means that the market's implicit assumption that bonds hold senior status is already and will be increasingly at variance with the shift from minority to majority share in total debt. It is reasonable to ask whether in the new environment public policy ought to give some guidance, to lean against a repetition of excessive bond issuance that occurred in the leadup to the previous debt crisis—that of bond defaults in the 1930s.

The private rating agencies already impose rigorous quality tests and have not been hasty to award investment-grade ratings to countries recovering from the debt crisis. If the pace of bond placements nonetheless showed continued rapid growth similar to the expansion from 1991 to 1993, it could at some point become salutary for industrial country officials to state publicly that bondholders could expect to be on their own in the event of a new debt crisis. A formal position along these lines now would be premature and risky, because 1995 will already be a period of testing to determine whether the tightening of financial market conditions in the United States causes an implosion of the capital market flows that emerged in 1991–93.

The discussion of this chapter proposes the consideration of an International Bondholders Insurance Corporation, and annex 8A suggests that such an entity might widen the capital market for LDC bonds and send important signals to reinforce sound country policies without incurring enormous costs for the sponsors of the agency. Another institutional innovation, Williamson's international bankruptcy arbitrator, might warrant a try (but solely under Williamson's condition that it apply only to loans originally issued with relevant clauses entered into willingly by the lender and borrower).

As for the question of whether the 1990s will see a repeat of the debt crisis of the 1980s because of possibly excessive capital flows in the early 1990s, the analysis of this chapter concludes broadly in the negative. Debtor country vulnerability to variable-interest debt and oil price collapse has declined, and the rise of variable-price claims (especially equity) provides further cushioning against external shocks. Creditor bank vulnerability to developing-country exposure has also declined.

There remains the question of whether capital markets can accommodate robust borrowing by Latin America and Asia once industrial country recovery tightens credit markets and competition by Eastern Europe and the FSU for international capital intensifies. Past analyses of this issue (IMF 1991b) should be sufficient to dispel concerns in this regard. The central point is that the global capital market is simply too large for the incremental impact of Latin American and other formerly troubled debtor countries to make much difference. These countries should be able to secure capital if their domestic policies are sound.

Thus, the recent peak in capital flows to Latin America and Asian developing countries was an estimated total of about $85 billion in 1992 and again in 1993, and the total for all developing regions in that period was about $115 billion annually (table 8.1). As noted in the analysis of capital repatriation, the total of capital valuation for the US stock market, public debt, and quasi-money amounts to some $10 trillion. The total for all industrial countries is thus on the order of $20 trillion or more. Even if the total capital flow to developing countries were to double to the range of $200 billion, it would require a portfolio shift of only one half of one percent of industrial country capital holdings (excluding real estate) annually to raise the incremental capital.

There is every indication that such US institutions as pension funds are in fact engaged in raising the foreign shares in their assets.[42] The developing countries, including those that have passed successfully through the debt crisis, should be able to secure capital in amounts that easily bump up against prudential ceilings without making much of a dent in this market. The question of capital market access thus returns to the fundamental starting point emphasized throughout this study: sound domestic economic policy. Just as many Asian countries with sound policies were able to avoid the debt crisis altogether, and two major countries within Latin America with good policies (and adequate luck on external variables) managed to survive the regional capital market shutdown without the need to resort to debt forgiveness, so developing countries and countries in economic transition should be able to secure capital from the global markets over the coming decade if their domestic policies are in order. The price they will face for doing so will depend on market interest rates and thus world macroeconomic conditions, but their share of world capital supply is likely to be too modest to cause problems of capital scarcity.

---

42. One report indicates that within the past two years, US pension funds have increased their portfolio share held in foreign assets from less than 5 percent to about 8 percent (*Financial Times*, 5 April 1994).

Annex 8A

Costs of an International Bondholders Insurance Corporation

What would be the potential costs of the IBIC proposed in chapter 8 and the overview chapter? This annex provides simulations to obtain an approximate answer.

Suppose the IBIC sought to provide bond insurance for the 20 largest middle-income economies, measured by size of exports. In 1992, a large country sample comprising four countries in Africa, five in Asia, four in Eastern Europe, and seven in Latin America had total exports of $432 billion (IMF 1992a).[1] Assume nominal export growth is g percent annually (set at 6 percent: 2 percent for price increases and 4 percent for quantity growth). Suppose each country runs a current account deficit equal to 25 percent of its export base. Suppose that new bond issues cover one-fourth of the current account deficit. Suppose that half of bond purchasers (by value) decide to take out IBIC insurance. Then in year t over a 10-year horizon, new issues covered for country i will have the following current dollar value:

$$B_{i,t} = (.5)(.25)(.25)X_o(1 + g_x)^t \tag{8A.1}$$

Suppose IBIC charges a standard premium of 50 basis points on the principal of bonds covered and accomplishes its gradations reflecting creditworthiness by setting the coinsurance rate γ in a range from 20 percent up to 80 percent. A country with a high credit rating already, such as Chile, receives the maximum rate ($\gamma = 0.8$), whereas a country with a relatively poor credit record, such as Brazil, begins with the minimum ($\gamma = 0.2$) but is assumed to receive an increment of 10 percentage points ($\Delta\gamma = 0.1$) each year that it does not default, up to a maximum of 60 percent ($\gamma = 0.6$).

Now consider an IBIC scenario over 10 years in which M countries default (out of 20 countries in all). A defaulting country fails to pay the fraction α of interest due during a three-year period, and then resumes payment. This default proportion is set alternatively at $\alpha = 0.5$ and $\alpha = 1.0$. Once a country defaults, it has no new bond issues during the three-year default period; but it resumes bond issues at the value in the export-based time path by the fourth year after default. The first equation is thus altered to set $B_{it} = 0$ for default country years.

---

1. The countries considered are, respectively, Côte d'Ivoire, Nigeria, Morocco, and Tunisia; China, Indonesia, South Korea, the Philippines, and Thailand; Czechoslovakia, Hungary, Poland, and Yugoslavia; and Argentina, Brazil, Chile, Colombia, Mexico, Peru, and Venezuela.

In a given year, IBIC receives premiums equal to the premium rate ($\beta = .005$) times the outstanding bonds covered for the country in question. Note that the insured bondholder continues to pay the premium even if the country is in default (especially so, to retain the insurance claim). Thus, total premium income for all n countries in year t is

$$Y_t^p = \beta \sum_{i=1}^{n} K_{i,t}, \text{ where}$$

$$K_{i,t} = \sum_{j=1}^{t} B_{i,j} \tag{8A.2}$$

Note that the term $K_{i,t}$ is the cumulative sum of principal of bonds covered for country i by year t. Note also that there is no amortization, as the bonds are assumed to have the same life as the planning horizon (10 years).

Define the IBIC's sinking fund as its cumulative assets obtained from premium receipts plus investment earnings, less claim payments made to insured bondholders. In any given year, the corporation's earnings on its outstanding investments (sinking fund) amount to

$$Y_t^k = \rho S_{t-1} \tag{8A.3}$$

where S_t is the value of the sinking fund at the end of year t. The corporation's total revenue is thus $R_t = Y_t^p + Y_t^k$.

Now subject the IBIC to a set of random shocks that cause M countries to enter into default over the full horizon. Each randomly selected defaulting country first defaults in a randomly selected year and remains in default (making partial or no payments) during three years. Let $D_{i,t}$ be a dummy variable with value "1" if country i is in default in year t and value "0" otherwise. Assume that IBIC covers its coinsurance share of interest payments missed but provides no reimbursement of principal (because in the horizon considered the bonds have not reached maturity). Then the insurance claims on IBIC in year t will amount to

$$C_t = \alpha(i_w + s) \sum_{i=1}^{n} \gamma_{i,t} D_{i,t} K_{i,t}, \text{ where}$$

$$D_{i,t} = 1 \text{ if } (i \in \theta(M)) \cap (t \in \theta(M)); \tag{8A.4}$$

$$D_{i,t} = 0, \text{ otherwise}$$

Here, the function $\theta(M)$ refers to the outcome of generating M random numbers (set initially at three cases out of 20 countries) and carries an associated initial year of default, generated randomly out of the 10-year horizon.[2]

Thus, a country's normal interest payments on outstanding bonds of $K_{i,t}$ would amount to $(i_w + s)K_{i,t}$, where i_w is the interest rate for US Treasury bonds (10-year maturity) and s is the spread (assumed the same for all countries for simplicity). The country fails to pay fraction α. Of the shortfall in payments, IBIC must make good on the fraction $\gamma_{i,t}$.

In a given year, the agency's sinking fund will grow by the net amount of premium receipts and investment earnings less claims paid. Thus, sinking fund assets at the end of the year will stand at

$$S_t = S_{t-1} + R_t - C_t \qquad (8A.5)$$

Table 8A.1 reports the results of 100 random-shock simulations of the IBIC's sinking fund status over a 10-year horizon, for the 20 major developing countries considered. The table reports two alternative cases for incidence of default (either three or five countries, over the full period), and two alternative degrees of nonpayment of interest (50 percent or 100 percent). In addition, the fifth case superimposes a generalized debt crisis affecting seven countries simultaneously in a random year, but only occurring with a probability of 25 percent. For each year, the table reports the minimum, maximum, and 25th, 50th, and 75th percentile values of the sinking fund (S_t) out of the 100 random cases.[3] The estimates assume world interest rate of 7 percent and spread of 2.5 percent.

Before considering the specific results, it is useful to consider what one should expect from the exercise in general terms. Whether the IBIC makes or loses money basically depends on the rate of the insurance premium, on the one hand, and the loss rate, on the other. The premium rate is 50 basis points. Abstracting from reinvested earnings, the expected loss when 3 countries out of 20 at random default for three years and IBIC covers half of the missed interest (which in turn is at 9.5 percent) is as follows, relative to the entire base of debt covered: is $(3/20) \times (3/10) \times (.5 \times .095) = .0021$, or 21 basis points. That is, the first term is the fraction of countries that default; the second, the fraction of the whole horizon that each of those misses interest; and the third, the losses of IBIC as a rate of the average debt base for each defaulter during the default period. As the expected loss rate is less than half the premium rate, IBIC should make a profit on average. The more relevant question is, how large are its potential losses under adverse but less-than-average chances?

---

2. The symbols $\in$ and $\cap$ refer to "member of" and "jointly with," respectively.

3. The positional arrays are year rather than scenario specific. For example, the 75th percentile value for S in year 3 will typically refer to a different random-default scenario than the 75th percentile value in year 7.

Table 8a.1 Cumulative sinking fund value of an International Bondholders' Insurance Corporation (millions of dollars, current)

A:0.5 M:3

YEAR	1	2	3	4	5	6	7	8	9	10
min	-29.72	-3.30	86.10	243.51	125.40	-95.25	-66.12	428.10	943.28	1,772.86
10 pctl	56.76	147.97	254.55	361.64	591.31	962.77	1,234.65	1,736.98	2,263.10	2,841.06
25 pctl	65.85	189.53	357.56	598.23	924.39	1,312.18	1,743.70	2,248.67	2,973.64	3,645.33
50 pctl	67.42	210.36	410.89	707.44	1,080.22	1,547.18	2,099.71	2,775.56	3,516.28	4,371.77
75 pctl	67.42	210.36	437.62	749.90	1,137.54	1,649.43	2,279.99	3,003.08	3,784.14	4,775.76
max	67.42	210.36	437.62	758.82	1,184.42	1,725.77	2,395.25	3,206.27	4,115.40	5,180.55

A:1.0 M:3

YEAR	1	2	3	4	5	6	7	8	9	10
min	-126.85	-203.40	-223.14	-168.92	-812.79	-1,738.07	-2,232.44	-1,915.98	-1,834.05	-1,256.28
10 pctl	46.11	96.11	92.50	41.34	89.80	272.69	155.70	435.76	473.64	496.68
25 pctl	64.28	172.44	299.81	466.96	708.78	953.46	1,164.47	1,546.71	2,016.36	2,231.70
50 pctl	67.42	210.36	386.48	667.22	988.62	1,425.47	1,896.63	2,431.99	3,028.13	3,563.93
75 pctl	67.42	210.36	437.62	741.96	1,102.36	1,590.76	2,183.93	2,861.41	3,504.00	4,356.80
max	67.42	210.36	437.62	758.82	1,184.42	1,725.77	2,395.25	3,206.27	4,058.98	5,109.29

A:0.5 M:5

YEAR	1	2	3	4	5	6	7	8	9	10
min	-4.36	49.13	167.44	290.58	284.47	317.16	17.74	-93.57	-137.85	73.11
10 pctl	55.55	146.06	278.94	415.10	596.05	613.74	827.79	1,062.95	1,379.78	1,715.61
25 pctl	59.53	179.38	363.41	580.67	816.51	1,116.04	1,547.33	1,742.66	2,156.02	2,580.17
50 pctl	67.42	197.40	397.84	662.68	996.12	1,390.84	1,870.15	2,399.03	3,154.15	3,954.84
75 pctl	67.42	210.36	418.04	710.27	1,079.98	1,549.65	2,084.72	2,740.86	3,497.16	4,381.71
max	67.42	210.36	437.62	758.82	1,184.42	1,725.77	2,353.60	3,096.70	3,989.83	4,876.29

(table continued on next page)

491

Table 8a.1 (continued)

A:1.0 M:5

YEAR	1	2	3	4	5	6	7	8	9	10
min	-76.15	-98.74	-61.09	-97.98	-543.09	-947.57	-2,173.26	-3,082.78	-3,983.97	-4,740.74
10 pctl	43.67	91.94	152.65	137.36	162.26	-399.65	-557.33	-867.25	-1,069.56	-1,610.44
25 pctl	51.63	153.51	305.69	429.69	494.10	594.78	842.71	362.39	447.58	281.93
50 pctl	67.42	185.81	365.12	581.99	845.71	1,128.35	1,459.11	1,763.59	2,356.78	2,841.43
75 pctl	67.42	210.36	402.40	668.59	996.76	1,406.33	1,838.95	2,415.55	3,030.99	3,628.94
max	67.42	210.36	437.62	758.82	1,184.42	1,725.77	2,324.84	3,005.66	3,832.77	4,547.47

A:0.5 M:3 N:7
z:0.25

YEAR	1	2	3	4	5	6	7	8	9	10
min	-90.10	-161.19	-209.76	-110.38	90.43	-132.37	-675.89	-1,200.22	-957.34	-463.12
10 pctl	19.27	58.76	151.04	334.17	522.30	687.93	964.33	1,503.03	1,873.99	2,261.96
25 pctl	62.00	184.45	351.55	606.39	762.59	1,176.26	1,699.55	2,222.43	2,817.32	3,303.41
50 pctl	67.42	204.98	414.37	702.95	1,041.54	1,489.86	2,021.67	2,647.40	3,401.40	4,364.92
75 pctl	67.42	210.36	437.62	734.35	1,132.40	1,624.01	2,227.17	2,987.75	3,833.53	4,807.20
max	67.42	210.36	437.62	758.82	1,184.42	1,725.77	2,395.25	3,174.32	4,102.16	5,139.53

A: proportion of interest not paid.
M: number of specific default countries.
N: number of generalized default countries.
z: probability of generalized default.
pctl: percentile of distribution in 100 random scenarios.

The table shows that the worst possible outcome for each year out of the 100 random scenarios could leave the IBIC with large losses. The sinking fund would show cumulative losses of nearly $5 billion by the 10th year in the worst case (five default countries, 100 percent nonpayment of interest, shown in the fourth panel). However, for most cases the outcome is surprisingly favorable. Even if the 10th percentile is considered (so that 90 percent of outcomes would be expected to be more favorable), the time path of the sinking fund is strictly positive in four of the five cases.

Interestingly, the cases with complete nonpayment of interest but only individual country default show less favorable results than the case with generalized default but 50 percent interest payment. It should be kept in mind that during the worst years of the debt crisis, several major debtors such as Mexico, Venezuela, and Chile paid interest, so the 50 percent nonpayment formulation is perhaps more appropriate than that of 100 percent nonpayment.

The broad implication of the simulation results is that the IBIC might reasonably aspire to making a profit rather than expect to suffer large losses.

9

Epilogue: The Mexican Peso Crisis of December 1994

As this book went to press in late December 1994, the new administration of President Ernesto Zedillo Ponce de León devalued the Mexican peso. After first devaluing the limit of the currency band by about 14 percent, the government was almost immediately forced to set the peso free to float, and its cumulative decline widened to about 35 percent. By 3 January 1995 the government announced a new stabilization program that involved a labor union commitment to adhere to a 7 percent wage increase under the Solidarity Pact, budget-tightening measures, and further privatization. The package included an $18 billion program of international financial support for peso stabilization: $9 billion from the United States, $1 billion from Canada, $5 billion from the Bank for International Settlements, and $3 billion in a syndicated loan from large banks led by Citibank and Morgan Guaranty (*Wall Street Journal*, 3 January 1995). Then on 13 January the Clinton administration and congressional leaders announced a proposed program of up to $40 billion in loan guarantees for Mexico (*Financial Times*, 14 January 1995).

Causes and Policy Response

The underlying cause of the peso collapse was the market's growing conclusion that Mexico's large current account deficit was unsustainable (a risk highlighted in chapter 6). The proximate cause was the near exhaustion of reserves to defend the previous gently gliding official rate. Whereas buoyant capital inflows in 1991–93 had brought foreign exchange reserves to a high of about $29 billion in February 1994, tighter money in the United States and especially the increased uncertainty from the March assassination of presidential candidate Luis Donaldo Colosio and the lingering Chiapas rebellion (chapter 6) caused a shift to reserve losses. The net inflow of capital, which had been on the order of $30 billion in 1993, fell to some $9 billion in 1994, not enough to cover the current account deficit without a large drawdown of reserves. By June 1994, reserves were down to $16.4 billion (IMF, *International Financial Statistics*, December 1994). The past experience of devaluations at the end of *sexenio* presidential terms and an intensification of the Chiapas rebellion added to capital outflow in November and early December, and the one-day attempt to defend the devalued rate of 20 December cost several billions more. By 22 December, reserves were down to $6 billion (*Wall Street Journal*, 23 December 1994), less than the value of two months' imports. The government had no choice other than to float the peso.

Foreign investors who had placed funds in Mexican treasury obligations denominated in pesos (*cetes*) suffered losses corresponding to the depreciation of the currency, and losses on Mexican stocks were even greater because the peso index fell as well. Yet investors had little justification for anger, even though some spoke of betrayal by Mexican authorities who had reaffirmed there would be no change in the exchange rate regime. Investors in peso assets had engaged in high-risk, high-return investments, and until then they had been rewarded handsomely for doing so. Thus, funds placed in *cetes* at the beginning of 1991 would have earned a total of 55 percent in dollar terms through mid-December 1994, compared with a cumulative 18 percent on US treasury bills.

With its early January response, the government publicly recognized the policy error of not acting sooner to reduce the external deficit. After the new finance minister, Jaime Serra Puche, was forced by the crisis to resign, his replacement, Guillermo Ortiz, stated that the initial budget plan calling for a 1995 current account deficit once again at 8 percent of GDP ($31 billion) had been unrealistic and that investors had seen such a large external deficit as unsustainable (*Wall Street Journal*, 5 January 1994).

The policy package of early January first sought to assure that nominal devaluation would achieve real devaluation, as the ceiling on wage increases under the Pacto attempted to avoid a vicious circle of devaluation followed by induced wage and price increases. The package cut government spending by 1.3 percent of GDP, although the net reduction was likely to be about half that amount after taking into account higher interest rates on government debt. A key element of the package was to scale back credit from the national development banks, which had reached some 4 percent of GDP, to about half that level. The overall objective was to increase public-sector saving and, more substantially, reduce private-sector consumption and investment, by a combined amount of some 4 percent of GDP so that the current account deficit could be cut to half its 1994 level of $28 billion. The government expected to be able to finance a 1995 deficit of $14 billion through modest government borrowing abroad ($5 billion), projected inflows of direct investment ($8 billion), and moderate capital repatriation (*Wall Street Journal*, 5 January 1995).

At the same time, the package intensified the government's commitment to the market-oriented reforms of the 1980s by extending privatization to railroads and satellite communications, accelerating the timetable for entry of foreign competition in the banking sector, and increasing competition in telecommunications.

Prospects for Mexico

The peso crisis shifted Mexico back from the exchange rate anchor mode, in which a quasi-fixed exchange rate was maintained to reduce inflation, into the alternate mode in which the exchange rate was now to be used to achieve correction of an external imbalance. Mexico had oscillated between these two stances during the 1980s, depending on the primary problem at each phase (as discussed in chapter 6). A central question was whether domestic inflationary expectations could be held in check despite the abandonment of the anchor. Crucial to the answer was whether labor would adhere to the agreed limit on wage increases.

The new situation at the beginning of 1995 provided a painful test of the Lawson thesis (chapter 6) that external imbalances not caused by fiscal deficits could be readily redressed if private capital dried up. The peso shock already indicated that this view was incorrect in the monetary sphere; it seemed highly unlikely that the adjustment would occur painlessly in the real economy either.

Econometric models of the response of trade to the real exchange rate suggested that the government's adjustment goal was not unrealistic. The trade equation estimated in Cline (1991, 69) found that for the period 1980–90, the ratio of imports of goods and nonfactor services to nonoil exports of goods and nonfactor services responded to the real exchange rate (one-year lagged) with an elasticity of 1.5. A reasonable figure for the change in the real exchange rate was, say, 15 percent, composed of a nominal depreciation of about 27 percent offset by a 1995 excess of Mexican inflation over US inflation by 17 percent.[1]

---

1. The government's target for 1995 appeared to be 15 percent inflation. If this were achieved, differential inflation against the United States would be only 12 percent, and a 15 percent real depreciation could be achieved even with some recovery of the peso to 4.54 the dollar (against the early December level of 3.46 and early January 1995 level of 5.5). Even if domestic inflation reached, say, 30 percent, a 15 percent real depreciation would be consistent with the peso at 5.14 to the dollar by end-1995.

Experience in the 1980s sometimes showed the bulk of adjustment on the import side, and other times on the export side, typically with the import adjustment coming sooner. Applying a 15 percent real devaluation to the elasticity of 1.5, the ratio of imports to nonoil exports should fall by 22.5 percent. Dividing the adjustment evenly, at 12.5 percent import reduction and 12.5 percent export increase,[2] there would be a decline of imports of goods and nonfactor services (which amounted to $67 billion in 1994 based on the first half; *International Financial Statistics*, December 1994) by $8.4 billion and an increase in nonoil exports (about $40 billion in 1994) by $5 billion.

In addition, it seemed likely that growth for 1995 would be down to, say, 1 percent, or $1^{1}/_{2}$ percent below the average of the 1980s. The Cline (1991) model showed an elasticity of imports with respect to the domestic growth rate of 4.5, so deceleration by $1^{1}/_{2}$ percent would reduce imports by 6.7 percent, or an additional $4^{1}/_{2}$ billion.[3] On this basis, real depreciation of 15 percent and a 1995 growth slowdown would reduce the deficit on goods and nonfactor services by about $18 billion. Although the import component of this adjustment ($13.4 billion) would likely come largely within 1995, the export adjustment could stretch into 1996. These calculations suggest that the government's goal of cutting the current account deficit by $14 billion was not unrealistic.

Similar results are reached if the elasticities estimated by Dornbusch and Werner (1994, 293) are applied. They find a price elasticity of imports of −0.6, an income elasticity of imports of 2.5, and a price elasticity of exports of 1.8 (average between demand-side and supply-side approaches). Using these elasticities, a 15 percent real devaluation would reduce imports by 9 percent ($6 billion) and increase nonoil exports by well over 20 percent. If we limit the export response to, say, 15 percent (at least in the first year), and further add an import reduction of 3.8 percent (= 2.5 x 1.5%) or $2.5 billion for the cutback in domestic growth, the Dornbusch-Werner elasticities suggest an import reduction of $8.5 billion and export increase of $6 billion, giving a total adjustment very close to the government's target of $14 billion.

In short, the likely real exchange rate adjustment was consistent with the government's target for external adjustment. However, it was unclear that there would be enough net capital inflow to finance even a $14 billion current account deficit, even if the refinancing of Mexican treasury obligations went smoothly as a consequence of a US guarantee program (as discussed below). There was thus considerable possibility of a sharper downturn in growth in 1995, perhaps combined with a

---

2. That is: $(1 - .225) = .775 \approx (1 - .125)/(1 + .125)$.

3. The elasticity of much greater than unity for the growth rate is consistent with a lower long-term income elasticity combined with a high cyclical elasticity.

larger real devaluation than 15 percent (and correspondingly greater export expansion, especially by 1996).

The broader question was whether the 1994 peso crisis was a repeat of the 1982 debt crisis, somehow negating all of the progress made in responding to the debt crisis in the interim. The answer was almost certainly in the negative. As reviewed in chapter 2, all of the debt indicators for Mexico were much more favorable by 1992–94 than they had been on the eve of the debt crisis in 1981–82. This time Mexico had fiscal balance rather than double-digit fiscal deficits. This time Mexico's economic structure was much more flexibly attuned to market forces rather than hindered by regulation, import protection, and an excessive role of state firms. This time there was a NAFTA to provide longer-term direct investment interest.

Instead, the problem this time was one of cash flow and, in particular, the rollover of some $17 billion in dollar-indexed treasury bonds (*tesebonos*) held by foreigners. In the first week of January 1995, the Mexican government was working with US investment banks and brokerage houses to design attractive dollar-indexed securities with longer terms and higher yields to replace these bonds. Finance Minister Ortiz had sought to make clear to US investors at a meeting in New York that, with the war chest of $18 billion in special foreign credit lines and $6 billion in reserves, Mexico was in a position simply to pay off most of the bonds if necessary (*New York Times*, 6 January 1995). The US loan guarantee proposal redoubled the effort to show the markets that Mexico could meet any liquidity crisis on its domestic debt.

The rollover issue did highlight the reality that in the post-Brady world, the line between domestic and external debt had become blurred. By 1994 much of the internal peso debt (with or without indexation to the dollar) was held by foreigners. This consideration in turn reinforced the importance of taking into account the internal transfer (fiscal sustainability of the debt) in addition to the external transfer (foreign exchange availability). Argentina and Brazil had both sharply reduced the burden of their internal public debt through the Bonex Plan of 1989 and the Collor Plan of 1990, respectively, which had stretched out domestic public debt and reduced its interest rates to international levels instead of the much higher rates that had been paid before because of the high risk premium. Mexico had not carried out any forced conversion of this type, raising the question of whether its internal debt burden (and the risk premium in its interest charges) was sustainable.

Nonetheless, at a total of $28 billion in *tesebonos*, $8 billion in *cetes*, $6 billion in inflation-adjusted *ajustabonos*, and about $1½ billion in other bonds, for a total of some $43 billion, the domestic Mexican public debt was still only about 11 percent of 1994 GDP. Even adding the $72 billion in public debt owed abroad (World Bank 1993b), and even taking into account the lower dollar valuation of GDP after the devaluation, Mexico's public debt remained at only about 40 percent of GDP, well below the level of most OECD countries.[4]

Overall, the peso crisis amounted to a painful correction of an external account deficit that had become unsustainable and in retrospect exceeded benign levels, even though its origins were in the private sector and had stemmed initially from private capital inflows. This lancing of the overvaluation boil had the bright side of setting the stage for subsequent export growth, thereby eventually permitting greater flexibility for domestic economic growth, as the prospective adjustment would mean that subsequently it would no longer be necessary to attempt to limit the external deficit by clamping down on imports and domestic growth through fiscal restraint. Mexico's exchange rate crisis and the response to it represented the correction of a particular policy tactic (the anti-inflationary exchange rate anchor) adopted by a major country within the context of the broader international debt strategy rather than an important instance of collapse of that strategy. The peso problem was a currency crisis, not a debt crisis. It bore a closer resemblance to the problems of the Italian lira in 1992 than to the Mexican debt crisis a decade earlier.

Implications for the Debt Strategy

The peso crisis was thus first and foremost a currency crisis, not a debt crisis. With respect to debt itself, the crisis was almost certainly one of short-term liquidity rather than long-term insolvency. As argued in chapter 5, even the Mexican debt crisis of the 1980s might have eventually escaped insolvency and its counterpart, the need for partial debt forgiveness, if the price of oil had not collapsed in 1986. This time, the objective conditions for solvency were even stronger, as just reviewed. However, given the changes in the international capital market, the potential for herd behavior in this market, and the size of the Mexican case, the peso problem of 1994 posed a new challenge for international financial management.

The problem posed an early test of how financial crises could be handled now that myriad private investors holding bonds and equities were the main source of capital inflows rather than banks organized into syndicates. As noted in chapter 8, the option of concerted bank lending was no longer relevant under these new capital market circumstances.

Although the peso crisis was not a renewed debt crisis, it sent shock waves through the international capital market for emerging economies.

---

4. This estimate applies an exchange rate of 5 new pesos to the dollar and thus places nominal GDP for 1995 at about $300 billion, probably understating dollar GDP, and makes no downward adjustment for overstatement by Brady par bonds with low interest. However, the external public debt figure is for 1992 (the most recent with detailed World Bank data) and is probably somewhat understated.

Stock prices fell by about 7 percent in Argentina and Brazil within two days of the initial Mexican devaluation (*Wall Street Journal*, 22 December 1994). The $130 billion Brady bond market, already under pressure during 1994 (chapter 2, figure 2.2), fell further, bringing cumulative return for the year (including interest) to −29 percent for Mexican Brady bonds, −30 percent for Venezuelan, and −13 percent for Argentine (*Wall Street Journal*, 3 January 1995).

Superficially, the major country most vulnerable to the Mexican peso problem seemed to be Argentina, because only Argentina similarly had adopted the fixed exchange rate "anchor" and had entered into a large current account deficit (chapter 6). However, there were major differences that made the Argentine currency more durable. Argentina had a currency board system, with the money supply fully backed by dollar reserves (which stood much higher relative to GDP than in Mexico). The Argentine economy was already bimonetary, with about half of deposits and credit designated in dollars. The government was fully committed to maintenance of the fixed parity with the dollar and seemed more likely simply to allow more complete dollarization of the economy (further conversion of peso deposits into domestic dollar deposits) than to permit a major devaluation. Argentina's current account deficit was smaller relative to GDP (only about $2^{1}/_2$ percent compared with 8 percent in Mexico), even though the deficit was of nearly comparable size expressed against the export base (because Argentina had a much smaller share of trade in the economy). Moreover, Argentina's short-term domestic government debt was small, a legacy of the 1989 Bonex Plan, which had stretched out government debt. These differences from the Mexican case soon became apparent to the public, which, after initially queuing up at banks to shift from peso to dollar deposits (causing central bank sales of dollars of $350 million on 28 December alone) because of the Mexican "Tequila effect," once again began selling dollars for pesos in early 1995. Similarly, after surging from 10 percent to 26 percent in late December, short-term interest rates fell to 16 percent in the first few days of January, and the stock market regained 7 percent after falling 17 percent (*Financial Times*, 5 January 1995).

Otherwise there were few if any significant debtor countries vulnerable to the collapse of a fixed exchange rate anchor. Instead, the principal risk for the debt strategy more broadly was that there would be a further dampening of capital flows to the emerging markets because of the shift in perception: from a view that Mexico and similar countries were on the verge of investment-grade status to the view that these countries represented speculative risk (*Wall Street Journal*, 3 January 1995).[5] Ironically, considering that such countries as Chile and Colombia

---

5. Although there was also considerable opinion that the crisis represented a buying opportunity in emerging markets.

had been experiencing difficulties from excessive capital inflows rather than capital shortages in 1991–93 (chapter 8), for several countries such a further dampening from the deceleration already begun with the tightening of the US Federal Reserve in early 1994 may have been helpful rather than painful. At the same time, the Mexican object lesson was promptly seen as a warning for Brazil not to allow the shift from trade surplus to trade deficit under the Real Plan (chapter 6) to go too far.

Despite the lesser vulnerability of most other countries on objective criteria, the dynamics of market psychology nonetheless led quickly to an incipient contagion effect from the Mexican peso crisis. By the second week of January 1995, there was increasing and generalized pressure on emerging-market stock markets, as the shock of the Mexican crisis caused a "flight to quality" exodus from these markets, especially by mutual funds. At the same time, there was a wave of pressure on the financial markets of numerous countries perceived to be in relatively weak external sector positions, including not only Latin American countries but also Canada, Italy, Sweden, and Spain (*Wall Street Journal*, 12 January 1995).

US officials became increasingly concerned about a systemic spillover from the Mexico problem that could cause a growth slowdown in many developing countries and possibly affect the international financial system more broadly. On 13 January 1995, the Clinton administration announced discussions with US congressional leaders on a loan guarantee program for Mexico. Modeled on a 1992 program of $10 billion in guaranteed housing loans for the only other developing-country free trade partner of the United States—Israel—the proposal was to range up to $40 billion, far exceeding the earlier $18 billion arrangement (*Wall Street Journal*, 13 January 1995).

The program was designed to guarantee 5- to 10-year bonds issued by the Mexican government, permitting the country to stretch out the bunching of domestic debt coming due in 1995. Intended to be cost-free to the United States, the program was to set up-front fees calibrated on the basis of a country default risk spread of at least 200 basis points, a level Mexico had paid in the first half of 1993 (Collyns et al. 1993, 64) and somewhat higher than the low point of Mexico spreads. Thus, after taking account of present-value discounting, a five-year guarantee would bear an up-front fee of some 8 percent, and a 10-year guarantee, considerably more. As a result, the program would bring budgetary revenue to the United States rather than impose budgetary costs, so long as Mexico did not default. In essence, the program put the US government in the international financial insurance business, a function similar to that proposed in chapter 8 in the form of the International Bondholders Insurance Corporation.

The program included an "oil proceeds mechanism" designed to assure that if any US guarantee payments had to be made, the Mexican oil company PEMEX would channel oil revenue indirectly to the US

Federal Reserve to reimburse such payments.[6] The existence of this oil quasi-guarantee meant that the floor return of 200 basis points spread was all the more market-oriented rather than being a US subsidy, considering that private-market bonds had been floated by Mexico at such spreads or lower with no such additional assurance. Moreover, that fee basis was gauged to escalate with the volume of guarantees called upon, to provide considerable incentive to Mexico to use unsecured private finance rather than exhaust the full $40 billion arrangement.

In terms of potential for impact on market psychology, the total of $40 billion in the program compared favorably with Mexico's $43 billion in domestic debt (of which about 80 percent was due within one year), even if another $20 billion or so in Mexican bank certificates of deposit and credit lines were taken into account as adding to the prospective refinancing task. In addition, the other elements of the earlier $18 billion package (BIS, Canadian, and commercial bank) remained in place, presumably to deal with the shorter-term needs.

The fundamental stakes in, and motivation for, the large loan guarantee program included the following. First, Mexico's economic health had vital implications for that of the United States. Uncontained financial collapse—for example, including such possible phenomena as unilateral and unsecured stretchout of *tesebono* maturities and conceivably concommitant exchange controls and/or further rapid devaluation and inflation—would mean extreme pressure on illegal Mexican immigration to the United States and unnecessary overshooting in the decline of US exports to Mexico. Second, the change in the capital markets from bank intermediation to an atomized-investor basis posed the risk that psychological spillover from an unresolved Mexican crisis could severely limit capital flows to the emerging markets, even though in the 1990s most debtor countries had much stronger economic policies than in the early 1980s. If so, there would be corresponding adverse implications for growth in these countries and in industrial country exports to them. Third, because Mexico had been a model country in terms of adopting reforms of domestic economic policy and structure, failure in Mexico could call into question the validity of the overall reform strategy, even though the real problem was more attributable to one particular tactic—the exchange rate anchor—than to the reform strategy as a whole.

For their part, US policymakers were acting in a system-strengthening way through their ambitious loan guarantee proposal. In the 1982 debt

---

6. The arrangement provided that foreign customers of PEMEX would be instructed to make payments for oil to an intermediary bank, which in turn would make transfers to the Federal Reserve Bank of New York. This proceedure, which had been used in previous US-Mexico monetary swap arrangements, avoided infraction of the "negative pledge" clauses of other existing international loans to Mexico, which would have ruled out a direct escrow mechanism.

crisis, there had been crucial, decisive rescue packages at the outset that helped assure that there was no systemic rupture from a collapse in the international banking system. This time the systemic threat was less acute and more directly focused on the emerging-market countries than on industrial country economies. Even so, the policy calculus weighing the risks of inaction against the possible costs of insuring Mexican loans was correct in concluding that the benefits of action outweighed the costs (especially considering that in the base case, the mechanism should be profitable for US fiscal accounts).

There was a potential gap in the US initiative. The purpose was systemwide, but the instrument was Mexico-specific. It was conceivable that calming the financial markets for Mexico would suffice to calm the other emerging markets. However, it was also possible that the financial markets would instead draw the conclusion that other countries needed similar arrangements.

In this regard, in mid-1994 the managing director of the International Monetary Fund, Michel Camdessus, had proposed "a fast-disbursing, very short-term facility, which would help cushion the reserves of countries suddenly subjected to bursts of speculation in spite of policies that Fund surveillance had found to be appropriate."[7] Such a fund probably would not have achieved the stretchout of Mexico's domestic debt possible with the US guarantee program, but it would have been helpful to limit the ripple effects in other countries with smaller external deficits and less short-term government debt. The Mexican peso crisis seemed likely to provide a new impetus to consideration of the Camdessus proposal as well as other international arrangements for medium-term guarantee capacity.

By the third week in January, the loan guarantee proposal was poised for prompt consideration in the US Congress. Despite bipartisan leadership support, the proposal faced opposition from some of the former opponents of NAFTA. Some critics charged that the arrangement was a bailout of the banks, even though by now the commercial banks were minority rather than majority claimholders on Mexico (and their Brady bond holdings already had collateralized security). Nor were charges that the arrangement bailed out private investors particularly apt, considering that these investors had already experienced losses or sharp reversals of earlier profits as a consequence of the devaluation. There was also the risk of attempts to burden the program with conditions on Mexican labor and other institutional arrangements that the Mexican government could not accept politically.

Overall, assuming that it could clear the congressional political hurdles, the proposed US loan guarantee mechanism held major promise

---

7. "The IMF at Fifty," address presented at the Institute for International Economics, 7 June 1994.

for calming the financial markets and for ensuring that the peso crisis remained no more than a modest aftershock of the financial and economic earthquake that was the debt crisis of the 1980s. Nevertheless, a fundamental question as the second half of the final decade of the century began, was whether the Mexican peso crisis marked a sea change in the capital markets. There was some possibility that the event would cause a severe, generalized relapse in the emerging capital markets, reducing flows back to mid-1980s levels. There was a parallel possibility that the change could even cause a widespread retreat from the "Washington consensus" model of development policy that had swept Latin America by the late 1980s.

The more sanguine possibility was that the capital markets would be sophisticated and discriminating, rather than shift to a monolithic new mode of revulsion from emerging markets. Even under the more optimistic view, it seemed likely that for some time emerging-market borrowers would have to pay some additional risk premium in the international bond markets and that they would receive smaller inflows of capital for portfolio investments than in 1992–94. However, under the sophisticated investor (or stabilizing speculation) hypothesis, the likelihood was that eventually there would be a settling down in anxiety, and that countries with good policies (fiscal balance and, now especially, realistic exchange rates) would be able to borrow from the capital markets. In this more likely outcome, the reformed economic policies and structures that were a precious legacy of the adjustment to the debt crisis of the 1980s would be reinforced rather than reversed.

References

Aaron, Henry J. 1994. "Public Policy, Values, and Consciousness." *Journal of Economic Perspectives* 8, no. 2 (Spring): 3–22.

Ahmed, Masood, and Lawrence H. Summers. 1992. "Ten Lessons of the Debt Crisis." *International Economic Insights* 3, no. 4 (July–August): 15–19.

Aizenman, Joshua. 1989. "Investment, Openness, and Country Risk." In Frenkel, Dooley, and Wickham 1989.

Aizenman, Joshua, and Eduardo Borensztein. 1989. "Debt and Conditionality under Endogenous Terms of Trade Adjustment." In Frenkel, Dooley, and Wickham 1989.

Amex Bank Review. 1993. "LDC Flows: Liberalisation and Economic Growth." *Amex Bank Review* 20, no. 4 (26 April).

Ardeni, Pier Giorgio, and Brian Wright. 1992. "The Prebisch-Singer Hypothesis: A Reappraisal Independent of Stationarity." *Economic Journal* 102 (July): 803–12.

Arida, Persio. 1992. Remarks at the workshop "Brazil in a New World." InterAmerican Dialogue and Aspen Institute, Washington (14 December).

Arida, Persio, and Andre Lara-Resende. 1985. "Inertial Inflation and Monetary Reform: Brazil." In John Williamson, ed., *Inflation and Indexation: Argentina, Brazil, and Israel.* Washington: Institute for International Economics.

Argentine Economic Cabinet. 1993. *Argentina: A Growing Nation.* Buenos Aires: Ministerio de Economía.

Armendariz de Aghion, Beatriz, and John Williamson. 1993. *The G-7's Joint and Several Blunder.* Essays in International Finance 189. Princeton: Princeton University.

Arrieta, Carlos G., Luis J. Orjuela, Eduardo Sarmiento P., and Juan G. Tokatlian. 1990. *Narcotráfico en Colombia: Dimensiones Políticas, Económicas, Jurídicas e Internacionales.* Bogotá: Tercer Mundo.

Aspe, Pedro. 1993. *Economic Transformation the Mexican Way.* Cambridge, MA: MIT Press.

Bacha, Edmar. 1989a. "Latin America Debt Crisis and Structural Adjustment: The Role of the World Bank." Working Paper 198. Pontifícia Universidade Católica, São Paulo, Brazil.

Bacha, Edmar. 1989b. "A Three-Gap Model of Foreign Transfers and the GDP Growth Rate in Developing Countries." Pontifícia Universidade Católica, Rio de Janeiro. Photocopy (February).

Bacha, Edmar. 1993a. "O Fisco e a Inflacão: Uma Interpretação do Caso Brasileiro." Pontifícia Universidade Católica, Rio de Janeiro. Photocopy (28 June).

Bacha, Edmar. 1993b. "Selected International Policy Issues on Private Market Financing for Developing Countries." In UNCTAD 1993.

Bagehot, Walter. 1873. *Lombard Street*. 14th ed. John Murray. London: Kegan, Paul & Co. 1917.

Bailey, Norman J. 1990. "Another Perspective on the Economists and Third World Debt." *International Economy* 4, no. 3 (June/July) 22–23.

Balassa, Bela. 1964. "The Purchasing-Power Parity Doctrine: A Reappraisal." *Journal of Political Economy* 72, no. 6 (December): 584–96.

Balassa, Bela, Gerardo M. Bueno, Pedro-Pablo Kuczynski, and Mario Henrique Simonsen. 1986. *Toward Renewed Economic Growth in Latin America*. Washington: Institute for International Economics.

Balcerowicz, Leszek. 1994. "Poland." In Williamson 1994.

Banco de Mexico. 1993. *The Mexican Economy 1993*. Mexico City: Banco de Mexico.

Bank for International Settlements. 1984. *International Banking and Financial Market Developments*. BIS, Monetary and Economic Department, Basel, Switzerland (August).

Bank for International Settlements. 1987. *International Banking and Financial Market Developments*. BIS, Monetary and Economic Department, Basel, Switzerland (August).

Bank for International Settlements. 1990. *International Banking and Financial Market Developments*. BIS, Monetary and Economic Department, Basel, Switzerland (August).

Bank for International Settlements. 1994. *International Banking and Financial Market Developments*. BIS, Monetary and Economics Department, Basel, Switzerland (August).

Banks, Arthur S., ed. 1993. *Political Handbook of the World 1993*. Binghamton, NY: CSA Publications.

Basu, Kaushik. 1991. *The International Debt Problem, Credit Rationing and Loan Pushing: Theory and Experience*. Princeton Studies in International Finance 70. Princeton: Princeton University.

Berg, Andrew, and Jeffrey Sachs. 1988. "The Debt Crisis: Structural Explanations of Country Performance." *Journal of Development Economics* 29 (November): 271–309.

Bergsten, C. Fred, William R. Cline, and John Williamson. 1985. *Bank Lending to Developing Countries: the Policy Alternatives*. POLICY ANALYSES IN INTERNATIONAL ECONOMICS 10. Washington: Institute for International Economics.

Black, Stanley W. 1977. *Floating Exchange Rates and National Economic Policy*. New Haven: Yale University Press.

Blejer, Mario I., and Alain Ize. 1989. "Adjustment Uncertainty, Confidence, and Growth: Latin America after the Debt Crisis." IMF, Fiscal Affairs Department, Washington. Photocopy (October).

Borensztein, Eduardo. 1990. "Debt Overhang, Debt Reduction, and Investment: The Case of the Philippines." IMF Working Papers 90/77. International Monetary Fund, Washington.

Bottome, Robert, et al. 1992. *In the Shadow of Debt: Emerging Issues in Latin America*. New York: Twentieth Century Fund.

Bradley, Michael, and Michael Rosenzweig. 1992. "The Untenable Case for Chapter 11." *Yale Law Journal* 101.

"Brady Plan Progress Report." 1990. *International Economy* 4, no. 2 (April/May): 78–79.

Bresser Pereira, Luis Carlos. 1994. "Brazil." In Williamson 1994.

Bulow, Jeremy, and Kenneth Rogoff. 1988a. "The Buyback Boondoggle." *Brookings Papers on Economic Activity* 2: 675–704.

Bulow, Jeremy, and Kenneth Rogoff. 1988b. "Multilateral Negotiations for Rescheduling Developing Country Debt: A Bargaining-Theoretic Approach." *International Monetary Fund Staff Papers* 35 (December): 644–57.

Bulow, Jeremy, and Kenneth Rogoff. 1988c. *Sovereign Debt Restructurings: Panacea or Pangloss?* NBER Working Paper 2637. Cambridge, MA: National Bureau of Economic Research.

Bulow, Jeremy, and Kenneth Rogoff. 1989a. "A Constant Recontracting Model of Sovereign Debt." *Journal of Political Economy* 97, no. 1: 155–78.

Bulow, Jeremy, and Kenneth Rogoff. 1989b. *Sovereign Debt Repurchases: No Cure for Overhang.* NBER Working Paper 2850. Cambridge, MA: National Bureau of Economic Research.

Bulow, Jeremy, and Kenneth Rogoff. 1989c. "Sovereign Debt: Is to Forgive to Forget?" *American Economic Review* 79, no. 1 (March): 43–50.

Bulow, Jeremy, and Kenneth Rogoff. 1990. "Cleaning Up Third World Debt without Getting Taken to the Cleaners." *Journal of Economic Perspectives* 4, no. 1 (Winter): 31–42.

Bulow, Jeremy, Kenneth Rogoff, and Afonso S. Bevilaqua. 1992. "Official Creditor Seniority and Burden-Sharing in the Former Soviet Bloc." *Brookings Papers on Economic Activity* 1: 195–223.

Calvo, Guillermo. 1989. "A Delicate Equilibrium: Debt Relief and Default Penalties in an International Context." In Frenkel, Dooley, and Wickham 1989.

Calvo, Guillermo, Ronald Findlay, Pentii Kouri, and Jorge Braga de Macedo, eds. 1989. *Debt, Stabilization and Development: Essays in Honor of Carlos Díaz-Alejandro.* Oxford: Basil Blackwell.

Calvo, Guillermo A., Leonardo Leiderman, and Carmen M. Reinhart. 1993. "Capital Inflows and Real Exchange Rate Appreciation in Latin America." *International Monetary Fund Staff Papers* 40, no. 1 (March): 108–51.

Camdessus, M. 1989. "Strengthening the Debt Strategy: The Role of the IMF and the Banks." Remarks before L'Institut d'Etudes Financières et Bancaires, Paris (31 May).

Cardoso, Eliana, and Rudiger Dornbusch. 1989. "Brazilian Debt: A Requiem for Muddling Through." In Edwards and Larraín 1989.

CEA [Council of Economic Advisers]. 1984. *Economic Report of the President.* Washington: CEA.

CEA. 1994. *Economic Report of the President.* Washington: CEA.

CIA [Central Intelligence Agency]. 1991. *World Factbook, 1991.* Washington: CIA.

Claessens, Stijn. 1990. "The Debt Relief Laffer Curve: Some Estimates." *World Development* 18, no. 12 (December): 1671–77.

Claessens, Stijn, and Ishac Diwan. 1989. "Liquidity, Debt Relief, and Conditionality." In Husain and Diwan 1989.

Claessens, Stijn, and Ishac Diwan. 1990. "Investment Incentives: New Money, Debt Relief, and the Critical Role of Conditionality in the Debt Crisis." *World Bank Economic Review* 4, no. 1 (January): 21–42.

Claessens, Stijn, I. Diwan, K. Froot, and P. Krugman. 1990. *Market-Based Debt Reduction for Developing Countries.* World Bank Policy and Research Series 16. Washington: World Bank.

Claessens, Stijn, and David Naudé. 1993. "Recent Estimates of Capital Flight." Policy Research Papers. World Bank, Washington (September).

Claessens, Stijn, Daniel Oks, and Sweder van Wijnbergen. 1993. *Interest Rates, Growth, and External Debt: The Macroeconomic Impact of Mexico's Brady Deal.* World Bank Policy Research Working Papers 1147. Washington: World Bank.

Cline, William R. 1981. "Economic Stabilization in Peru, 1975–78." In William R. Cline and Sidney Weintraub, eds., *Economic Stabilization in Developing Countries.* Washington: Brookings Institution.

Cline, William R. 1983. *International Debt and the Stability of the World Economy.* POLICY ANALYSES IN INTERNATIONAL ECONOMICS 4. Washington: Institute for International Economics.

Cline, William R. 1984. *International Debt: Systemic Risk and Policy Response.* Washington: Institute for International Economics.

Cline, William R. 1985a. "International Debt: From Crisis to Recovery?" *American Economic Review* 75, no. 2 (May): 185–90.

Cline, William R. 1985b. "International Debt: Analysis, Experience, and Prospects." *Journal of Development Planning*, no. 16: 25–55.

Cline, William R. 1987. *Mobilizing Bank Lending to Debtor Countries*. POLICY ANALYSES IN INTERNATIONAL ECONOMICS 18. Washington: Institute for International Economics.

Cline, William R. 1988a. "International Debt: Progress and Strategy." *Finance and Development* 25, no. 2 (June): 9–11.

Cline, William R. 1988b. *Latin American Economic Outlook*. No. 88-1. Washington: Economics International.

Cline, William R. 1989a. "The Baker Plan and Brady Reformulation: An Evaluation." In Husain and Diwan 1989.

Cline, William R. 1989b. "Latin American Debt: Progress, Prospects, and Policy." In Edwards and Larraín 1989.

Cline, William R. 1989c. "The International Debt Problem: Status, Analytical Issues, and Policy." Paper prepared for Federal Reserve Board of Governors. Institute for International Economics, Washington. Photocopy (May).

Cline, William R. 1989d. "Estructura, Orígenes, y Administración de la Deuda Pública Externa de Venezuela." In Hector Valecillos T. and Omar Bello Rodriguez, eds., *La Economía Contemporanea de Venezuela*. Vol. 4. Caracas: Banco Central de Venezuela.

Cline, William R. 1990. "From Baker to Brady: Managing International Debt." In Richard O'Brien and Ingrid Iversen, eds., *Finance and the International Economy 3: The AMEX Bank Review Prize Essays*. Oxford: Oxford University Press.

Cline, William R. 1991. *Mexico: Economic Reform and Development Strategy. EXIM Review*, Special Issue. Tokyo: Export-Import Bank of Japan.

Cline, William R. 1992. "Argentina: Socio-Economic Report." Study prepared for the InterAmerican Development Bank, Washington. Photocopy (December).

Cline, William R. 1993. "Macroeconomic Convergence and the MERCOSUR." Paper prepared for the InterAmerican Development Bank, Washington. Photocopy (April).

Cline, William R. 1994. *International Economic Policy in the 1990s*. Cambridge, MA: MIT Press.

Cline, William R. 1995. *Argentina: Economic Reform and Growth in the 1990s*. Paper prepared for the Export-Import Bank of Japan, Washington. Photocopy.

Cline, William R., and Jonathan Conning. 1991. "Venezuela: Economic Strategy and Prospects." Study prepared for the InterAmerican Development Bank, Washington (November).

Cline, William R., and Riordan Roett. 1986. *Latin American Economic Outlook: Argentina, Brazil, Mexico*. No. 86-3. Washington: Economics International.

Cline, William R., and Riordan Roett. 1988. *Latin American Economic Outlook: Argentina, Brazil, Mexico*. No. 88-3. Washington: Economics International.

Cline, William R., Daniel M. Schydlowsky, and Riordan Roett. 1983. "Latin American Economic Outlook: Peru." Washington: International Economic Analysis.

Cohen, Benjamin J. 1992. "US Debt Policy in Latin America: The Melody Lingers On." In Bottome et al. 1992.

Cohen, Daniel. 1985. "Reassessing Third World Debt: How to Evaluate the Solvency of an Indebted Nation." *Economic Policy* (November): 140–67.

Cohen, Daniel. 1988. *Is the Discount on the Secondary Market a Case for LDC Debt Relief?* WPS 132. Washington: World Bank.

Cohen, Daniel. 1989. "How to Cope with a Debt Overhang: Cut Flows Rather than Stocks." In Husain and Diwan 1989.

Cohen, Daniel. 1990. "Debt Relief: Implications of Secondary Market Discounts and Debt Overhangs." *World Bank Economic Review* 4, no. 1 (January): 43–53.

Cohen, Daniel. 1993. "Low Investment and Large LDC Debt in the 1980s." *American Economic Review* 83, no. 3 (June): 437–49.

Cohen, Daniel, and Jeffrey D. Sachs. 1986. "Growth and External Debt under the Risk of Debt Repudiation." *European Economic Review* 30 (June): 529–60.

Collins, Susan M, and Dani Rodrik. 1991. *Eastern Europe and the Soviet Union in the World Economy*. POLICY ANALYSES IN INTERNATIONAL ECONOMICS 32. Washington: Institute for International Economics.

Collyns, Charles, et al. 1993. *Private Market Financing for Developing Countries.* World Economic and Financial Surveys. Washington: International Monetary Fund.

Conesa, Eduardo R. 1992. *La Crisis del 93: Una Agenda de los Riesgos que Enfrentará la Economía Argentina.* Buenos Aires: Planeta.

Cooper, Richard N. 1990. "Economic Stabilization and Debt in Developing Countries." Harvard University, Cambridge, MA. Photocopy (September).

Cooper, Richard N., and Jeffrey D. Sachs. 1985. "Borrowing Abroad: the Debtor's Perspective." In Smith and Cuddington 1985.

Corbo, Vittorio. 1990. "Comment." In Williamson 1990a.

Corden, W. Max. 1988a. "Debt Relief and Adjustment Incentives." *International Monetary Fund Staff Papers* 35, no. 4 (December): 628–43.

Corden, W. Max. 1988b. "An International Debt Facility?" *International Monetary Fund Staff Papers* 35: 401–21.

Corden, W. Max. 1989. "Debt Relief and Adjustment Incentives." In Frenkel, Dooley, and Wickham 1989.

Corden, W. Max. 1991. "Does the Current Account Matter? The Old View and the New." In Jacob Frenkel and Morris Goldstein, eds., *International Financial Policy: Essays in Honor of Jacques Polak.* Washington: International Monetary Fund.

Culagovski, Jorge, Victor Gabor, Maria Cristina Germany, and Charles P. Humphreys. 1991. "African Financing Needs in the 1990s." In Husain and Underwood 1991a.

Devlin, Robert. 1989. *Debt and Crisis in Latin America: The Supply Side of the Story.* Princeton: Princeton University Press.

Díaz-Alejandro, Carlos F. 1984. "Latin American Debt: I Don't Think We Are in Kansas Anymore." *Brookings Papers on Economic Activity* 2: 335–89.

Díaz-Alejandro, Carlos F. 1985. "Good-bye Financial Repression, Hello Financial Crash." *Journal of Development Economics* 19 (September/October): 1–24.

Dittus, Peter, and Paul S. O'Brien. 1991. "A Macroeconomic Model for Debt Analysis of the Latin America Region and Debt Accounting Models for the Highly Indebted Countries." OECD Department of Economics and Statistics Working Paper 93. Paris: OECD.

Dittus, Peter, Paul S. O'Brien, and Hans J. Blommestein. 1991. "International Economic Linkages and the International Debt Situation." *OECD Economic Studies* no. 16 (Spring): 133–68.

Diwan, Ishac, and Kenneth Kletzer. 1992. "Voluntary Choices in Concerted Deals: The Menu Approach to Debt Reduction in Developing Countries." *World Bank Economic Review* 6, no. 1 (January): 91–108.

Diwan, Ishac, and Dani Rodrik. 1992. *External Debt, Adjustment, and Burden Sharing: A Unified Framework.* Princeton Studies in International Finance 73. Princeton: Princeton University.

Dooley, Michael P. 1987a. "Market Discounts and the Valuation of Alternative Structures for External Debt." Research Department, International Monetary Fund, Washington. Processed.

Dooley, Michael P. 1987b. "Buybacks and Market Valuation of External Debt." *International Monetary Fund Staff Papers* 35, no. 2 (June): 215–29.

Dooley, Michael P. 1988. "Analysis of Self-financed Buy-backs and Asset Exchanges." *International Monetary Fund Staff Papers* 25, no. 4 (December): 714–22.

Dooley, Michael P. 1989a. "Buy-backs, Debt-equity Swaps, Asset Exchanges, and Market Prices of External Debt." In Frenkel, Dooley, and Wickham 1989.

Dooley, Michael P. 1989b. "Market Valuation of External Debt." In Frenkel, Dooley, and Wickham 1989.

Dooley, Michael P., Eduardo Fernandez-Arias, and Kenneth M. Kletzer. 1994. *Recent Private Capital Inflows to Developing Countries: Is the Debt Crisis History?* NBER Working Paper 4792. Cambridge, MA: National Bureau of Economic Research.

Dooley, Michael, William Helkie, Ralph Tryon, and John Underwood. 1986. "An Analysis of External Debt Positions of Eight Developing Countries through 1990." *Journal of Development Economics* 21: 283–318.

Dooley, Michael, and Mark R. Stone. 1992. *Endogenous Creditor Seniority and External Debt Values.* NBER Working Paper 4172. Cambridge, MA: National Bureau of Economic Research.

Dornbusch, Rudiger. 1984. "The Effect of OECD Macroeconomic Policies on Non-Oil LDCs: A Review." MIT, Cambridge, MA. Photocopy (October).

Dornbusch, Rudiger. 1985. "External Debt, Budget Deficits, and Disequilibrium Exchange Rates." In Smith and Cuddington 1985.

Dornbusch, Rudiger. 1988a. "Our LDC Debts." In Martin Feldstein, ed., *The United States in the World Economy.* Chicago: University of Chicago Press.

Dornbusch, Rudiger. 1988b. "Comments" on Bulow and Rogoff (1988a). *Brookings Papers on Economic Activity* 2: 699–703.

Dornbusch, Rudiger. 1989. "Debt Problems and the World Economy." In Sachs 1989, vol. 1.

Dornbusch, Rudiger, and Sebastian Edwards, eds. 1991. *The Macroeconomics of Populism in Latin America.* Chicago: University of Chicago Press.

Dornbusch, Rudiger, and Sebastian Edwards. 1993. "Chile: Exchange Rate Policy and Trade Strategy." MIT, Cambridge, MA. Photocopy (July).

Dornbusch, Rudiger, and Stanley Fischer. 1985. "The World Debt Problem: Origins and Prospects." *Journal of Development Planning,* no. 16: 87–82.

Dornbusch, Rudiger, Fedrico Sturtzenegger, and Holger Wolf. 1990. "Extreme Inflation: Dynamics and Stabilization." *Brookings Papers on Economic Activity* 2: 1–84.

Dornbusch, Rudiger, and Alejandro Werner. 1994. "Mexico: Stabilization, Reform, and No Growth." *Brookings Papers on Economic Activity* 1: 253–315.

Easterly, William R. 1989. "Fiscal Adjustment and Deficit Financing During the Debt Crisis." In Husain and Diwan 1989.

Easterly, William, and Paulo Vieira da Cunha. 1993. "Financing the Storm: Macroeconomic Crisis in Russia, 1992–93." World Bank, Washington. Photocopy (October).

Eaton, Jonathan. 1987. "Public Debt Guarantees and Private Capital Flight." *World Bank Economic Review* 1, no. 3 (May): 377–95.

Eaton, Jonathan. 1990. "Debt Relief and the International Enforcement of Loan Contracts." *Journal of Economic Perspectives* 4, no. 1 (Winter): 43–56.

Eaton, Jonathan, and Mark Gersovitz. 1981. "Debt with Potential Repudiation: Theoretical and Empirical Analysis." *Review of Economic Studies* 48 (April): 284–309.

Eaton, Jonathan, Mark Gersovitz, and Joseph E. Stiglitz. 1986. "The Pure Theory of Country Risk." *European Economic Review* 30 (June): 481–513.

Eaton, Jonathan, and Lance Taylor. 1986. "Developing Country Finance and Debt." *Journal of Development Economics* 22 (June): 209–65.

ECLAC [Economic Commission for Latin America and the Caribbean]. 1988. *Preliminary Overview of the Economy of Latin America and the Caribbean 1988.* Santiago: ECLAC.

ECLAC. 1991. *Preliminary Overview of the Economy of Latin America and the Caribbean 1991.* Santiago: ECLAC.

ECLAC. 1992. *Preliminary Overview of the Economy of Latin America and the Caribbean 1992.* Santiago: ECLAC.

ECLAC. 1993. *Preliminary Overview of the Economy of Latin America and the Caribbean 1993.* Santiago: ECLAC.

Edwards, Sebastian. 1988. *Exchange Rate Misalignment in Developing Countries.* Baltimore: Johns Hopkins University Press.

Edwards, Sebastian. 1989. "Structural Adjustment Policies in Highly Indebted Countries." In Sachs 1989–90, vol. 1.

Edwards, Sebastian. 1993. *Latin America and the Caribbean a Decade after the Debt Crisis.* Washington: World Bank.

Edwards, Sebastian, and Felipe Larraín, eds. 1989. *Debt, Adjustment, and Recovery: Latin America's Prospects for Growth and Development.* Oxford: Basil Blackwell.

Eichengreen, Barry. 1989a. "The U.S. Capital Market and Foreign Lending, 1920-1955." In Sachs 1989-90, vol. 1.

Eichengreen, Barry. 1989b. "Settling Defaults in the Era of Bond Finance." *World Bank Economic Review* 3, no. 2 (May): 211-39.

Eichengreen, Barry. 1991a. "After the Deluge: Default, Negotiation, and Readjustment of Foreign Loans during the Interwar Years." In Eichengreen and Lindert 1991.

Eichengreen, Barry. 1991b. "Historical Research on International Lending and Debt." *Journal of Economic Perspectives* 5, no. 2 (Spring): 149-69.

Eichengreen, Barry, and Peter Lindert, eds. 1989. *The International Debt Crisis in Historical Perspective*. Cambridge, MA: MIT Press.

Eichengreen, Barry, and Richard Portes. 1986. "Debt and Default in the 1930s: Causes and Consequences." *European Economic Review* 30 (June): 599-640.

Eichengreen, Barry, and Richard Portes. 1989. "Dealing with Debt: the 1930s and the 1980s." In Husain and Diwan 1989.

El-Erain, Mohamed. 1991a. "Mexico's External Debt and the Return to Voluntary Capital Market Financing." IMF Working Papers 91/83. International Monetary Fund, Washington.

El-Erain, Mohamed. 1991b. "The Restoration of Latin America's Access to Voluntary Capital Market Financing-Developments and Prospects." IMF Working Papers 91/74. International Monetary Fund, Washington.

Enders, Thomas O. 1994. "LDC Debt Policy." In Feldstein 1994.

Enders, Thomas O., and Richard P. Mattione. 1984. *Latin America: The Crisis of Debt and Growth*. Studies in International Economics. Washington: Brookings Institution.

Federov, Boris. 1994. Statement to the Bretton Woods Commission, Washington (22 July).

Feinberg, Richard E. 1991. "The Bretton Woods Agencies and Sub-Saharan Africa in the 1990s: Facing the Tough Questions." In Husain and Underwood 1991a.

Feinberg, Richard E., and Ricardo French-Davis, eds. 1988. *Development and External Debt in Latin America*. Notre Dame: University of Notre Dame Press.

Feldstein, Martin S. 1986. "International Debt Service and Economic Growth: Some Simple Analytics." NBER Working Paper 2138. Cambridge, MA: National Bureau of Economic Research (November).

Feldstein, Martin, Herve de Carmoy, Koei Narusawa, and Paul R. Krugman. 1987. *Restoring Growth in the Debt-Laden Third World*. New York: Trilateral Commission.

Feldstein, Martin, ed. 1994. *American Economic Policy in the 1980s*. Chicago: University of Chicago Press.

Fernandez, Raquel, and Jacob Glazer. 1989. *Why Haven't the Debtor Countries Formed a Cartel?* NBER Working Paper 2980. Cambridge, MA: National Bureau of Economic Research.

Fernandez, Raquel, and Robert W. Rosenthal. 1989. *Sovereign-Debt Renegotiations Revisited*. NBER Working Paper 2981. Cambridge, MA: National Bureau of Economic Research.

FFIEC [Federal Financial Institutions Examination Council]. 1982. *Country Exposure Lending Survey*. Washington: Federal Reserve Board of Governors.

FFIEC. 1993. *Country Exposure Lending Survey*. Washington: Federal Reserve Board of Governors.

FIEL [Fundación de Investigaciones Económicas Latinoamericanas]. 1993. *Indicadores de Coyuntura*. No. 327, Buenos Aires, Argentina.

Filatov, Victor S., and Richard P. Mattione. 1985. "Latin America's Recovery from Debt Problems: An Assessment of Model-based Projections." *Journal of Policy Modeling* 7, no. 3: 491-524.

Fischer, Stanley. 1987. "Sharing the Burden of the International Debt Crisis." *American Economic Review* 77 (May): 165-70.

Fischer, Stanley. 1989a. "Resolving the Debt Crisis." In Sachs, 1989-90, vol. 1.

Fischer, Stanley. 1989b. "Foreword." In Husain and Diwan 1989.

Fischer, Stanley, and Ishrat Husain. 1990. "Managing the Debt Crisis in the 1990s." *Finance and Development* 27, no. 2 (June): 24-27.

Fishlow, Albert. 1981. "Latin American External Debt: Problem or Solution?" Corporación de Investigaciones Económicas para Latinoamérica, Santiago, Chile. Photocopy (March).

Fishlow, Albert. 1984. "The Debt Crisis: Round Two Ahead?" In R. Feinberg, and V. Kallab, eds., *Adjustment Crisis in the Third World*. Washington: Overseas Development Council.

Fishlow, Albert. 1985a. "The Debt Crisis: A Longer Perspective." *Journal of Development Planning* no. 16: 83–104.

Fishlow, Albert. 1985b. "Coping with the Creeping Crisis of Debt." In M. Wionzcek, ed., *Politics and Economics of the External Debt Crisis: The Latin American Experience*. Boulder, CO: Westview Press.

Fishlow, Albert. 1986. "Lessons from the Past: Capital Markets During the 19th Century and the Interwar Period." In Miles Kahler, ed., *The Politics of International Debt*. Ithaca, NY: Cornell University Press.

Fontaine, Juan A. 1989. "The Chilean Economy in the Eighties: Adjustment and Recovery." In Edwards and Larraín 1989.

Franko, Lawrence G., and Marilyn J. Seiber. 1979. *Developing Country Debt*. Pergamon Policy Studies 36. Elmsford, NY: Pergamon Press.

Frenkel, Jacob, Michael Dooley, and P. Wickham, eds. 1989. *Analytical Issues in Debt*. Washington: International Monetary Fund.

Froot, Kenneth. 1989. "Buybacks, Exit Bonds, and the Optimality of Debt and Liquidity Relief." *International Economic Review* 30, no. 1 (February): 49–70.

Fukao, Mitsuhiro. 1992. Comment on Williamson. In Teunissen 1992.

Garay, Luis Jorge Salamanca. 1993. "Un Decenio de la Crisis de la Deuda Externa en América Latina: Una Nota Sobre Terapia y Efectos Distributivos." In A. Angulo, ed., *Conversión de la Deuda en Desarrollo*. Santafe de Bogotá: CINEP.

Gersovitz, Mark. 1986. Review of "International Debt: Systemic Risk and Policy Response." *Journal of Economic Literature* 24, no. 1 (March): 108–10.

Goldstein, Morris, and David Folkerts-Landau. 1993. *International Capital Markets*. Part 2, *Systemic Issues in International Finance*. World Economic and Financial Surveys. Washington: International Monetary Fund.

Goldstein, Morris, and Daivd Folkerts-Landau. 1994. *International Capital Markets: Developments, Prospects, and Policy Issues*. Washington: International Monetary Fund.

González Fraga, Javier. 1989. "Deuda Externa, Nuevo Financiamento, Inversión y Crecimiento." In Felipe de la Balze, ed., *El Financiamiento Externo Argentino durante la Década de 1990*. Buenos Aires: Sudamericano.

Guitian, Manuel. 1992. *Rules and Discretion in International Economic Policy*. Occasional Paper 97. Washington: International Monetary Fund.

Gurria, Angel. 1990. Remarks at "Forum on LDC Debt." Brookings Institution, Washington (6 April).

Gurria, Angel, and Sergio Fadl. 1991. "La Política de Deuda Externa de México Durante el Período 1982–90." Secretaria de Hacienda, Mexico City. Photocopy.

Harberger, Arnold C. 1986. "Economic Adjustment and the Real Exchange Rate." In Sebastian Edwards and Liaquat Ahamed, eds., *Economic Adjustment and Exchange Rates in Developing Countries*. Chicago: University of Chicago Press.

Helkie, William, and David Howard. 1991. "External Adjustment in Selected Developing Countries in the 1990s." International Finance Discussion Paper 417. Federal Reserve System, Washington.

Helpman, Elhanan. 1988. "The Simple Analytics of Debt Equity Swaps and Debt Forgiveness." IMF Working Paper 88/30. International Monetary Fund, Washington.

Helpman, Elhanan. 1989a. "Voluntary Debt Reduction: Incentives and Welfare." In Frenkel, Dooley, and Wickham 1989.

Helpman, Elhanan. 1989b. "The Simple Analytics of Debt Equity Swaps." *American Economic Review* 79, no. 3 (June): 440–51.

Herrhausen, Alfred. 1988. "Some Ideas on How to Solve the Debt Crisis." *Die Zeit* (Hamburg) September.

Hogg, Robert V., and Allen T. Craig. 1978. *Introduction to Mathematical Statistics*. New York: Macmillan.

Hommes, Rudolf. 1990. "Colombia." In Williamson 1990a.

Hughes, Martin, Susan O'Malley, and Nicholas Couldry. 1992. "Debt Restructuring on the African Continent." *International Financial Law Review* 11, no. 8 (August): 23–27.

Huizinga, Harry. 1989. "The Commercial Bank Claims on Developing Countries: How Have Banks Been Affected?" In Husain and Diwan 1989.

Husain, Ishrat, and Ishac Diwan, eds. 1989. *Dealing with the Debt Crisis*. World Bank Symposium. Washington: World Bank.

Husain, Ishrat, and John Underwood, eds. 1991a. *African External Finance in the 1990s*. Washington: World Bank.

Husain, Ishrat, and John Underwood. 1991b. "The Problem of Sub-Saharan Africa's Debt—and the Solutions." In Husain and Underwood 1991a.

IDB [InterAmerican Development Bank]. 1986. *Economic and Social Progress in Latin America: 1986*. Washington: IDB.

IDB. 1991. *Economic and Social Progress in Latin America: 1991*. Washington: IDB.

IDB. 1992. *Economic and Social Progress in Latin America: 1992*. Washington: IDB.

IDB. 1993. *Economic and Social Progress in Latin America: 1993*. Washington: IDB.

IFC [International Finance Corporation]. 1993. *Emerging Stock Markets Factbook, 1993*. Washington: International Finance Corporation.

IIF [Institute of International Finance]. 1989. *The Way Forward for Middle-Income Countries*. Washington: IIF.

IIF. 1990. *Building Free Market Economies in Central and Eastern Europe: Challenges and Realities*. Washington: IIF.

IMF [International Monetary Fund]. 1983. *World Economic Outlook* (April). Washington: IMF.

IMF. 1984. *World Economic Outlook*. Washington: IMF (April).

IMF. 1988. *Direction of Trade Statistics Yearbook*. Washington: IMF.

IMF. 1990a. *International Financial Statistics Yearbook 1990*. Washington: IMF.

IMF. 1990b. *World Economic Outlook*. Washington: IMF (October).

IMF. 1990c. *International Capital Markets: Developments and Prospects*. Washington: IMF.

IMF. 1991a. *World Economic Outlook*. Washington: IMF (May).

IMF. 1991b. *World Economic Outlook*. Washington: IMF (October).

IMF. 1991c. *International Financial Statistics Yearbook 1991*. Washington: IMF.

IMF. 1991d. *Government Finance Statistics Yearbook 1991*. Washington: IMF.

IMF. 1992a. *International Financial Statistics Yearbook 1992*. Washington: IMF.

IMF. 1992b. *World Economic Outlook*. Washington: IMF (May).

IMF. 1992c. *World Economic Outlook*. Washington: IMF (October).

IMF. 1992d. *Direction of Trade Statistics Yearbook*. Washington: IMF.

IMF. 1993a. *International Financial Statistics*. Washington: IMF (August).

IMF. 1993b. *World Economic Outlook*. Washington: IMF (May).

IMF. 1993c. *Russian Federation*. IMF Economic Reviews 8. Washington: IMF.

IMF. 1993d. *Direction of Trade Statistics Yearbook*. Washington: IMF.

IMF. 1993e. *International Financial Statistics*. Washington: IMF (December).

IMF. 1993f. *World Economic Outlook*. Washington: IMF (October).

IMF. 1993g. *Balance of Payments Statistics Yearbook*. Vol. 44, no. 1. Washington: IMF.

IMF. 1993h. *Government Finance Statistics Yearbook 1993*. Washington: IMF.

IMF. 1993i. *Ukraine*. IMF Economic Reviews 10. Washington: IMF.

IMF. 1993j. *International Financial Statistics: Supplement on Countries of the Former Soviet Union*. Washington: IMF.

IMF. 1993k. *International Financial Statistics Yearbook 1993*. Washington: IMF.

IMF. 1994a. *International Financial Statistics*. Washington: IMF (August).

IMF. 1994b. *World Economic Outlook*. Washington: IMF (May).

IMF. 1994c. *International Financial Statistics Yearbook 1994*. Washington: IMF.

IMF. 1994d. *World Economic Outlook*. Washington: IMF (October).

Islam, Shafiqul. 1988. *Breaking the International Debt Deadlock*. New York: Council on Foreign Relations.

Islam, Shafiqul. 1990. "Whither the Brady Plan?" *International Economy* 4, no. 5 (October/November): 80–81.

Ize, Alain, and Guillermo Ortiz. 1987. "Fiscal Rigidities, Public Debt, and Capital Flight." *International Monetary Fund Staff Papers* 34, no. 2 (June): 311–32.

Jorgensen, Erika, and Jeffrey Sachs. 1988. "The Costs of Default: The Settlement of Interwar Loans to Latin America." Paper presented at Conference on a Long-Run Perspective on the Debt Crisis. San Francisco (May).

Jorgensen, Erika, and Jeffrey Sachs. 1989. "Default and the Renegotiations of Latin American Foreign Bonds." In Eichengreen and Lindert 1989.

Kaletsky, Anatole. 1985. *The Costs of Default*. New York: Twentieth Century Fund.

Kaufman, Robert, and Barbara Stallings, eds. 1989. *Debt and Democracy in Latin America*. Boulder, CO: Westview Press.

Kenen, Peter. 1989. "Debt Buybacks and Forgiveness in a Model with Voluntary Repudiation." International Finance Section Working Paper 89-1. Princeton: Princeton University.

Kenen, Peter. 1990. "Organizing Debt Relief: The Need for a New Institution." *Journal of Economic Perspectives* 4, no. 1 (Winter): 7–18.

Keynes, John Maynard. 1930. *A Treatise on Money*. London: MacMillan.

Kiguel, Miguel A., and Nissan Liviatan. 1992. "Stopping Three Big Inflations: Argentina, Brazil, and Peru." Paper prepared for the National Bureau of Economic Research Conference on Stabilization, Economic Reform, and Growth. InterAmerican Development Bank, Washington (17–18 December).

Killick, Anthony. 1991. "The Development Effectiveness of Aid to Africa." In Husain and Underwood 1991a.

Klein, Lawrence. 1984. "World Recovery and Debt Prospects." University of Pennsylvania. Philadelphia. Photocopy.

Krueger, Anne O. 1985. "Prospects and Proposals." In Smith and Cuddington 1985.

Krugman, Paul. 1985. "International Debt Strategies in an Uncertain World." In Smith and Cuddington 1985.

Krugman, Paul. 1988. "Financing versus Forgiving a Debt Overhang." *Journal of Development Economics* 29 (November): 253–68.

Krugman, Paul. 1989a. "Market-Based Debt-Reduction Schemes." In Frenkel, Dooley, and Wickham 1989.

Krugman, Paul. 1989b. "Private Capital Flows to Problem Debtors." In Sachs 1989–90, vol. 1.

Krugman, Paul. 1990. "Reconsiderations." *International Economy* 4, no. 2 (April/May): 94–96.

Krugman, Paul. 1994. "LDC Debt Policy." In Feldstein 1994.

Kuczynski, Pedro-Pablo. 1988. *Latin American Debt*. Baltimore: Johns Hopkins University Press.

Lago, Ricardo. 1991. "The Illusion of Pursuing Redistribution through Macropolicy: Peru's Heterodox Experience, 1985–1990." In Dornbusch and Edwards 1991.

Lancaster, Carol. 1991. *African Economic Reform: The External Dimension*. POLICY ANALYSES IN INTERNATIONAL ECONOMICS 33. Washington: Institute for International Economics.

Larraín, Felipe, and Andrés Velasco. 1990. *Can Swaps Solve the Debt Crisis? Lessons from Chile*. Princeton Studies in International Finance 69. Princeton: Princeton University.

Lessard, Donald R., and John Williamson. 1985. *Financial Intermediation Beyond the Debt Crisis*. POLICY ANALYSES IN INTERNATIONAL ECONOMICS 12. Washington: Institute for International Economics.

Lessard, Donald R., and John Williamson. 1987. *Capital Flight and Third World Debt.* Washington: Institute for International Economics.

Lindert, Peter. 1991. "Response to the Debt Crisis: What is Different about the 1980s?" In Eichengreen and Lindert 1991.

Lindert, Peter, and Peter J. Morton. 1989. "How Sovereign Debt Has Worked." In Sachs 1989–90, vol. 1.

Lipton, David, and Jeffrey D. Sachs. 1992. "Prospects for Russia's Economic Reforms." *Brookings Papers on Economic Activity* 2: 213–283.

Lustig, Nora. 1990. "The Mexican Deal: No Margin for Error." *International Economy* 4, no. 2 (April/May): 80.

Lustig, Nora. 1992. *Mexico: the Remaking of an Economy.* Washington: Brookings Institution.

Macedo, Jorge de, and Ronald Findley, eds. 1989. *Essays in Memory of Carlos Díaz-Alejandro.* Oxford: Basil Blackwell.

Marquez, Jaime, and Caryl McNeilly. 1988. "Income and Price Elasticities for Exports of Developing Countries." *Review of Economics and Statistics* 70, no. 2: 306–11.

Meller, Patricio. 1990. "Chile." In Williamson 1990.

Miller, Morris. 1989. *Resolving the Global Debt Crisis.* New York: United Nations Development Programme.

Ministerio de Economía. República Argentina. 1993. *Informe Económico Año 1992.* Buenos Aires: Ministerio de Economía.

Miyazawa, Kiichi. 1988. "The Japanese Proposal on the Middle Income Debtor Nation Problem." Ministry of Finance, Tokyo. Photocopy (July).

Morales, Juan Antonio, and Jeffrey D. Sachs. 1990. "Bolivia's Economic Crisis." In Sachs 1989–90, vol. 2.

Morgan Guaranty. 1983. "Global Debt: Assessment and Long-term Strategy." *World Financial Markets* (June): 1–15.

Morgan Guaranty. 1986. "LDC Capital Flight." *World Financial Markets* (March): 13–15.

Morgan Guaranty. 1988. "LDC Debt Reduction: A Critical Appraisal." *World Financial Markets* (December): 1–12.

Morley, Samuel A. 1992. "Structural Adjustment and the Determinants of Poverty in Latin America." Paper presented at Conference on Poverty and Inequality in Latin America. Brookings Institution, Washington (July).

Naím, Moisés. 1993. *Paper Tigers and Minotaurs: The Politics of Venezuela's Economic Reforms.* Washington: Carnegie Endowment.

Nordhaus, William D. 1992. "Lethal Model 2: The Limits to Growth Revisited." *Brookings Papers on Economic Activity*: 1–59.

Ocampo, Antonio. 1989. "Colombia and the Latin American Debt Crisis." In Edwards and Larraín 1989.

O'Connell, Arturo. 1993. "A Report on Developing Countries' Finance and Debt with Commercial Banks." Centro de Economía Internacional, Buenos Aires. Photocopy (October).

Ozler, Sule. 1988. "Have Commercial Banks Ignored History?" Working Paper 498. Los Angeles: University of California, Department of Economics.

Paredes, Carlos E. 1991. "Epilogue: in the Aftermath of Hyperinflation." In Paredes and Sachs 1991.

Paredes, Carlos E., and Jeffrey D. Sachs, eds. 1991. *Peru's Path to Recovery: A Plan for Economic Stabilization and Growth.* Washington: Brookings Institution.

Pease, Don. 1988. "A Congressional Plan to Solve the Debt Crisis." *International Economy* 2, no. 2 (March/April): 98–105.

Perry, George L. 1989. "Comment." In Calvo et al. 1989.

Piñera, Jose. 1991. "Political Economy of Chilean Reform." *International Economic Insights* 2, no. 4 (July–August): 6–9.

Reed, John S. 1987. "Citicorp Adds $3 Billion to Reserve." Press release, Citibank, New York (19 May).

Reisen, Helmut, and Axel Van Trotsenburg. 1988. *Developing Country Debt: the Budgetary and Transfer Problem.* Development Centre Studies. Paris: OECD.

Rhodes, William R. 1994. "LDC Debt Policy: 3." In Feldstein 1994.

Rodriguez, Carlos A. 1989. "Argentina's Foreign Debt: Origins and Alternatives." In Edwards and Larraín 1989.

Rodriguez, Miguel A. 1987. "Consequences of Capital Flight for Latin American Debtor Countries." In Lessard and Williamson 1987.

Rogoff, Kenneth. 1990b. "Symposium on New Institutions for Developing Country Debt." *Journal of Economic Perspectives* 4, no. 1 (Winter): 3–6.

Rogoff, Kenneth. 1992. "Dealing with Developing Country Debt in the 1990s." *World Economy* 15, no. 4 (July): 475–86.

Rotemberg, Julio. 1988. *Sovereign Debt Buybacks Can Lower Bargaining Costs.* NBER Working Paper 2767. Cambridge, MA: National Bureau of Economic Research.

Rubio, Luis. 1992. "Mexico: Debt and Reform." In Bottome et al. 1992.

Sachs, Jeffrey. 1982. "LDC Debt in the 1980s: Risk and Reform." Harvard University, Cambridge, MA. Photocopy (January).

Sachs, Jeffrey. 1984. *Theoretical Issues in International Borrowing.* Princeton Studies in International Finance 54. Princeton: Princeton University.

Sachs, Jeffrey. 1985. "External Debt and Economic Performance in Latin America and East Asia." *Brookings Papers on Economic Activity* 2: 523–64.

Sachs, Jeffrey D. 1986. "Managing the LDC Debt Crisis." *Brookings Papers on Economic Activity* 2: 397–431.

Sachs, Jeffrey D. 1987. "Trade and Exchange Rate Policies in Growth-oriented Adjustment Policies." In Vittorio Corbo, Morris Goldstein, and Mohsin Khan, eds., *Growth-oriented Adjustment Programs.* Washington: International Monetary Fund and World Bank.

Sachs, Jeffrey D. 1988a. "Comprehensive Debt Retirement: The Bolivian Example." *Brookings Papers on Economic Activity* 2: 706–15.

Sachs, Jeffrey D. 1988b. "Recent Studies of the Latin American Debt Crisis." *Latin American Research Review* 23, no. 3: 170–79.

Sachs, Jeffrey D. 1989a. "New Approaches to the Latin American Debt Crisis." Princeton Essays in International Finance 174. Princeton: Princeton University.

Sachs, Jeffrey D. 1989b. "Making the Brady Plan Work." *Foreign Affairs* 68 (Summer): 87–104.

Sachs, Jeffrey D. 1989c. "Conditionality, Debt Relief, and the Developing Countries' Debt Crisis." In Sachs 1989–90, vol. 1.

Sachs, Jeffrey. 1989e. *Social Conflicts and Populist Policies in Latin America.* NBER Working Paper 2897. Cambridge, MA: National Bureau of Economic Research.

Sachs, Jeffrey, 1989f. "Efficient Debt Reduction." In Husain and Diwan 1989.

Sachs, Jeffrey. 1989g. "The Debt Overhang of Developing Countries." In Calvo et al. 1989.

Sachs, Jeffrey. 1989h. "Update on Making the Brady Plan Work." Paper presented at the Council on Foreign Relations, New York (28 September).

Sachs, Jeffrey, ed. 1989–90. *Developing Country Debt and Economic Performance:* Vol. 1, *The International Financial System* (1989); Vol. 2, *Country Studies: Argentina, Bolivia, Brazil, Mexico* (1990). Chicago: University of Chicago Press for NBER.

Sachs, Jeffrey D. 1990. "A Strategy for Efficient Debt Reduction." *Journal of Economic Perspectives* 4 , no. 1 (Winter): 19–30.

Sachs, Jeffrey, and Harry Huizinga. 1987. "U.S. Commercial Banks and the Developing Country Debt Crisis." *Brookings Papers on Economic Activity* 2: 555–606.

Salomon Brothers. 1993a. "Ratings of Sovereign, Sovereign-Supported, Local Government, and Supranational Issuers." Salomon Brothers, New York (29 July).

Salomon Brothers. 1993b. "Emerging Markets Biweekly." Salomon Brothers, New York (6 October).

Salomon Brothers. 1994a. "Emerging Markets Biweekly." Salomon Brothers, New York (14 March).

Salomon Brothers. 1994b. "Emerging Markets Biweekly." Salomon Brothers, New York (31 March).

Salomon Brothers. 1994c. "Emerging Markets Debt: Weekly Update." Salomon Brothers, New York (24 June, 19 August).

Schadler, Susan, Maria Carkovic, Adam Bennett, and Robert Kahn. 1993. *Recent Experiences with Surges in Capital Inflows.* IMF Occasional Paper 108. Washington: International Monetary Fund.

Schilling, John. 1989. "Comment." In Husain and Diwan 1989.

Schmidt, Wilson E. 1964. "The Economics of Charity: Loans versus Grants." *Journal of Political Economy* 72: 387-95.

Schuker, Stephen A. 1988. *American "Reparations" to Germany, 1919-33: Implications for the Third-World Debt Crisis.* Princeton Studies in International Finance 61. Princeton: Princeton University.

Schulmann, Horst. 1991. Statement before the Subcommittee on Economic Goals and Intergovernmental Policy of the Joint Economic Committee. US Congress, 102nd sess. (30 October).

Skiles, Marilyn. 1989. "Comment." In Husain and Diwan 1989.

Skiles, Marilyn E. 1994. "Sustainability of Latin America's Debts." Economic Research Note, J. P. Morgan. New York (4 February).

Smith, Gordon W., and John T. Cuddington. 1985. *International Debt and the Developing Countries.* World Bank Symposium. Washington: World Bank.

Solomon, Anthony M., et al. 1988. *Third World Debt: A Reexamination of Long-term Management.* New York: United Nations Association of the United States, Economic Policy Council.

Solomon, Robert. 1992. "The Status of the LDC Debt Problem." *International Economic Letter* 12, no. 4 (April).

Stallings, Barbara, and Robert Kaufman, eds. 1989. *Debt and Democracy in Latin America.* Boulder, CO: Westview Press.

Stiglitz, Joseph, and Andrew Weiss. 1981. "Credit Rationing in Markets with Imperfect Information." *American Economic Review* 71, no. 3 (June): 343-410.

Summit of the Arch. 1989. "Economic Declaration." G-7 Economic Summit, Paris (16 July).

Tanzi, Vito. 1993. *Fiscal Policy and the Economic Restructuring of Economies in Transition.* IMF Working Paper 93/22. Washington: International Monetary Fund.

Tavares, Maria Conceicao. 1992. "Las Políticas de Ajuste de Brasil: Los Límites de la Resistencia." InterAmerican Dialogue, Washington. Photocopy (December).

Terrell, Henry S. 1984. "Bank Lending to Developing Countries: Recent Developments and Some Considerations about the Future." *Federal Reserve Bulletin* 70, (October): 755-63.

Teunissen, Jan, ed. 1992. *Fragile Finance: Rethinking the International Monetary System.* The Hague: FONDAD.

"Third-World Debt: The Disaster That Didn't Happen." 1992. *Economist*, 12 September, 21-23.

Treasury [US Department of the Treasury]. 1989a. "Interim Report to the Congress Concerning International Discussions on and International Debt Management Authority." US Treasury Department, Washington. Photocopy (March).

Treasury. 1989b. "Final Report to Congress Concerning World Bank Strategy and Lending Programs in Debtor Countries." US Treasury Department, Washington. Photocopy (March).

Triffin, Robert. 1960. *Gold and the Dollar Crisis.* New Haven: Yale University Press.

Truman, Edwin M. 1989. "US Policy on the Problems of International Debt." *Federal Reserve Bulletin* 75, no. 11 (November): 727-35.

UNCTAD. 1993. *International Monetary and Financial Issues for the 1990s.* Vol. 3. Research Papers for the Group of Twenty Four. Geneva: United Nations Conference on Trade and Development.

Urrutia, Miguel. 1990. "Análisis Costo-beneficio del Tráfico de Drogas para la Economía Colombiana." *Coyuntura Económica* (October): 115–26.

Urrutia, Miguel. 1991. "On the Absence of Populism in Colombia." In Dornbusch and Edwards 1991.

Urrutia, Miguel. 1994. "The Political Economy of Colombian Economic Liberalism." In Williamson 1994.

van Wijnbergen, Sweder. 1989. "External Debt, Inflation, and the Public Sector: Toward a Fiscal Policy for Sustainable Growth." *World Bank Economic Review* 3, no. 3 (September): 297–320.

van Wijnbergen, Sweder. 1991. "The Mexican Debt Deal." *Economic Policy*, no. 2 (April): 13–56.

Vasiliev, Sergei A. 1993. "Russia." In John Williamson, ed., *Economic Consequences of Soviet Disintegration*. Washington: Institute for International Economics.

Vatnick, Silvina. 1988. "The Secondary Market for Debt: A Possible Explanation of How Developing Countries Debt Prices Are Determined." World Bank Latin America and Caribbean Country Department I, Washington. Processed.

Volcker, Paul, and Toyoo Gyohten. 1992. *Changing Fortunes: The World's Money and the Threat to American Leadership*. New York: Times Books.

Wallich, Henry C. 1983. "LDC Credit Risk and Bank Regulation." In Antonio Jorge Salazar-Carillo and Rene P. Higonnet, eds., *Foreign Debt and Latin American Economic Development*. New York: Pergamon Press.

Warner, Andrew M. 1991. *Did the Debt Crisis Cause the Investment Crisis?* International Financial Discussion Papers 40. Washington: Board of Governors of the Federal Reserve System.

Webb, Richard. 1991. "Prologue." In Paredes and Sachs 1991.

White, Michelle. 1984. "Bankruptcy Liquidation and Reorganization." In Dennis Logue, ed., *Handbook of Modern Finance*. Boston: Warren, Gorham and Lamont.

White, Michelle. 1989. "The Corporate Bankruptcy Decision." *Journal of Economic Perspectives* 3, no. 2 (Spring).

White, Weld. 1960. *International Bonds*. New York: White, Weld, and Co.

White, Weld. 1973. *International Bonds*. London: White Weld Securities.

Wiesner, Eduardo. 1985. "Latin American Debt: Lessons and Pending Issues." *American Economic Review* 75, no. 2 (May): 191–95.

Williamson, John. 1985. "On the Question of Debt Relief." In *Statement of the North-South Round Table on Money and Finance*. New York: Society for International Development. (13–14 December).

Williamson, John. 1988. *Voluntary Approaches to Debt Relief*. POLICY ANALYSES IN INTERNATIONAL ECONOMICS 25. Washington: Institute for International Economics.

Williamson, John. 1989. Revised ed. of Williamson 1988.

Williamson, John, ed. 1990a. *Latin American Adjustment: How Much Has Happened?* Washington: Institute for International Economics.

Williamson, John. 1990b. "The Progress of Policy Reform in Latin America." In Williamson 1990a.

Williamson, John. 1991. "Debt Crisis: Lessons of the 1980s." *Asian Development Review* 9: 1–13.

Williamson, John. 1992. "International Monetary Reform and the Prospects for Economic Development." In Teunissen 1992.

Williamson, John, ed. 1994. *The Political Economy of Policy Reform*. Washington: Institute for International Economics.

World Bank. 1974. *Annual Report, 1974*. Washington: World Bank.

World Bank. 1987. *World Debt Tables 1987–88*. Vol. 1, *Analysis and Summary Tables*; Vol. 2, *Country Tables*. Washington: World Bank.

World Bank. 1989a. *Financial Flows to Developing Countries*. Washington: World Bank.

World Bank. 1989b. *World Debt Tables 1989–90*, vol. 1, *Analysis and Summary Tables*; vol. 2, *Country Tables*. Washington: World Bank.

World Bank. 1989c. *Sub-Saharan Africa: From Crisis to Sustainable Growth*. Washington: World Bank.

World Bank. 1990. *World Debt Tables, 1990–91*, vol. 1, *Analysis and Summary Tables*; vol. 2, *Country Tables*. Washington: World Bank.

World Bank. 1991. *World Debt Tables, 1991–92*, vol. 1, *Analysis and Summary Tables*; vol. 2, *Country Tables*. Washington: World Bank.

World Bank. 1992a. *World Debt Tables, 1992–93*, vol. 1, *Analysis and Summary Tables*; vol. 2, *Country Tables*. Washington: World Bank.

World Bank. 1992b. *World Development Report, 1992*. Washington: World Bank.

World Bank. 1992c. *Trends in Developing Countries, 1992*. Washington: World Bank.

World Bank. 1993a. *Financial Flows to Developing Countries*. Washington: World Bank.

World Bank. 1993b. *World Debt Tables, 1993–94*. Vol. 1., *Analysis and Summary Tables*; vol. 2, *Country Tables*. Washington: World Bank.

World Bank. 1993c. *World Development Report, 1993*. Washington: World Bank.

World Bank. 1993d. *Financial Flows and the Developing Countries*. Washington: World Bank.

World Bank. 1993e. *Trends in Developing Countries, 1993*. Washington: World Bank.

World Bank. 1994a. *Global Economic Prospects and the Developing Countries*. Washington: World Bank.

World Bank. 1994b. *Financial Flows and the Developing Countries*. Washington: World Bank.

World Bank. 1994c. *Adjustment in Africa*. Washington: World Bank.

World Bank. 1995. *World Debt Tables, 1994–95*, vol. 1, *Analysis and Summary Tables*; vol. 2, *Country Tables*. Washington: World Bank (January).

Index

Aaron, Henry J., 141
Additionality, 395
Adjustment Review Consortia, 397
Advisory committees, bank, 34, 206
Africa. *See* Sub-Saharan Africa; *individual countries*
Agency for International Development, 266
Ahmed, Masood, 143, 161
Algeria, 69, 241, 243
Allende, Salvador, and regime of (Peru), 286
Allocated Transfer Risk Reserve (ATRR), 76
American Depository Receipts (ADRs), 449
Angola, 28, 383. *See also* Kentzamgola
Ardeni, Pier Giorgio, 115
Argentina
    arrears in, 317
    Austral Plan in, 23, 311, 341
    Bonex Plan in, 248, 342–43
    Brady Plan agreement for, 24, 248, 317–18
    capital flight from, 111, 315, 441, 442, 444, 446, 461–64
    capital flows to and from, 312
    commodity exports of, 64, 464
    Convertibility Plan in, 23, 311, 312, 314–15, 319
    currency board arrangement in, 311
    current account in, 31, 99, 310, 315, 458, 461, 464
    debt-equity conversions in, 317
    debt/exports ratios in, 64, 99, 318
    debt/GDP ratios in, 64–65, 318
    debt strategy of, 24, 316–18
    direct investment in, 319
    economic growth in, 57, 99, 101, 276, 309, 312
    exchange rate policy in, 24, 64, 310, 311–15, 458, 469
    fiscal balances in, 310, 311, 336
    foreign share of assets in, 445
    impact of 1994–95 Mexico crisis on, 500–01
    incidence of poverty in, 312, 318
    inflation in, 23, 57, 276, 280, 310, 311, 313, 469
    interest/exports ratios in, 64, 65, 99
    internal transfer problem in, 65, 317
    macroeconomic policies in, 23, 53, 311–12
    Menem administration in, 311, 319
    privatization in, 316
    return to international capital market of, 319
    secondary market prices for, 55
    social deficit in, 318
    socialization of debt in, 153, 316
    stock market in, 319, 428
    structural reform in, 23, 315–16
Arida, Persio, 328
Armendariz de Aghion, Beatriz, 346, 349
Arrears
    Brazil decision on, 260, 335
    in debt simulation for sub-Saharan Africa, 389, 408–09
    as contributing factor to Brady Plan, 215
    as contributing factor to loan-loss provisioning, 15
    as involuntary capital flow, 436
    lending into, 16, 219
    magnitude of, 436
Arrieta, Carlos G., 283–84
Asia, capital flows to, 426–31, 450
Aspe, Pedro, 222, 297
Austral Plan, 23, 311, 341
Australia, 194, 195, 462
Austria, 197
Aylwyn, Patricio, 289

Bacha, Edmar, 11, 156–57
Bagehot, Walter, 12, 92, 161, 203
Baker, James, 208
Baker Plan,
    banks and, 209–13
    conditionality under, 209
    description of, 14, 208–09
    and exit bonds, 215

and loan-loss provisioning, 15, 70, 213–14
as midcourse debt strategy correction, 209, 256
new money goal in, 208–10
perceived failure of, 209
as precursor to Brady Plan, 212
and privatization, 209
oil price decline and, 213
Baker 17. *See* HD17
Balance of payments. *See* Capital flows; Current account
Balassa, Bela, 309, 313
Balcerowicz, Leszek, 361
Baltic states, 346
Banco Latino, 308
Bank for International Settlements, 206, 495
Bankruptcy agency, international, proposed, 34, 272, 484–86
Banks. *See also* individual banks; Multilateral development banks; International financial system
advisory committees of, 34, 206
and Baker Plan, 209–13
burden sharing under Brady Plan within, 259–62
country concentration of claims of, 60
divergence of interests among, 15, 165, 176, 184–85, 186, 212–13, 215, 225, 233
European versus US, 76, 77, 212
exposure relative to capital of, 73–75, 78–83
lending during 1994–95 Mexico crisis by, 495
loan-loss provisioning by, 15, 70, 213–14, 259
overexposure and subsequent policies of, 70–77, 95, 209
role in 1980s crisis of, 206–07, 209–10, 261–62
public bailout of, 228–30
regulation of, 271, 467
trends in lending by, 42, 70–71, 430, 433
US, 72–77
Belaúnde, Fernando, administration of (Peru), 331, 333
Bennett, Adam, 32, 467–69
Bergsten, C. Fred, 185, 207, 297, 436
Bermúdez, Francisco Morales, administration of (Peru), 329
Black, Stanley W., 313
Blommestein, Hans J., 122–23, 147
Bolivia, 192, 224, 340
Bond insurance agency, proposed international, 35–36, 272, 482–84, 486, 488–93
Bonds
C-, 233
coinsurance for, 483
conversion, 15, 184, 219, 221, 427, 438, 470, 479
discount, 17, 158, 221–22, 232–33, 238, 306, 317, 326, 470, 477
exit, 15, 176, 191, 210, 225, 325
growing importance of, 34–35, 426–27, 436, 438, 449, 450

insurance agency proposed for, 35–36, 272, 482–84, 486, 488–93
moral hazard in, 270
new problems involving, 438
par, 17, 42–43, 54, 158, 199, 222, 232–33, 238–39, 306, 309, 317, 326, 388, 470, 476
risk premiums on, 248, 451–57, 501
seniority of, 30, 173, 437–38, 450, 486
versus syndicated bank lending, 450, 481, 486
Yankee, 199
zero-coupon, 184, 221, 232, 243, 479
Bonex Plan (Argentina), 248, 342–43
Bradley, Bill, 226, 263
Brady, Nicholas, 217
Brady bonds. *See* Conversion bonds; Discount bonds; Exit bonds; Par bonds
Brady Plan. *See also* Debt forgiveness; *individual countries*
amounts forgiven under, 17, 18, 232, 233, 243, 256
burden sharing in, 258–62
buybacks in, 232–33
capital flows following agreements under, 248
case-by-case approach of, 16–17, 262–63
description of typical agreement under, 232
early criticism of, 244–45
emergence of, 215–22
enhancements in, 219–21, 232, 238–40, 263–66
factors contributing to rise of, 214–15, 228–31
future candidates under, 240–42
initial estimates of relief under, 219
IMF evaluation of, 243
and international financial system, 20–21, 268–69
long-term success of, 17, 266
lower-middle-income countries and, 240
macroeconomic conditions following agreements under, 249
market orientation and voluntariness of, 16, 218, 220, 254–55
moral hazard under, 269
operational problems with, 238–40
policy lessons from, 268–73
proposed phaseout of, 36–37, 270–71
psychological impact of, 18–19, 43, 119, 205, 237, 245, 250, 298, 426
public cost of, 20, 228–30, 263–66
as risk-compensated debt reduction, 222
role of conditionality in, 15–17, 20, 239–40, 262–63
role of new money in, 17, 219, 222, 233, 238
role of World Bank in, 17, 221
secondary market response to agreements under, 248
SIMICs and, 241
similarities of Mexican debt strategy to, 297
timing of, 19–20, 77, 243, 258, 260
Brazil
asset and wage-price freezes in, 24, 319
actual versus projected performance of, 122

Baker Plan and, 212–13
Brady Plan agreement for, 25, 232, 239, 326
Bresser Plan in, 321
buybacks in, 76, 187, 213, 325
capital flight from, 111, 442, 444, 446
Collor de Mello administration in, 24, 321–25, 342
commodity exports in, 99, 320
confrontational stance in, 324
constitution of 1988 of, 322, 326–27
Cruzado Plan in, 319, 341
current account of, 99, 320, 458
debt/exports ratios in, 65, 99
debt/GNP ratios in, 65, 66
debt rescheduling for, 324–25
debt stock of, 99
debt strategy of, 15, 24–25, 213–14, 260, 324–26
economic growth in, 57, 99, 101, 276, 319, 320
exchange rate policy of, 66, 320, 323
fiscal balances in, 66, 319–21, 323
foreign share of assets in, 445
Franco administration in, 327
impact of 1994–95 Mexico crisis on, 501, 502
inflation in, 24, 57, 66, 276, 319–22, 324, 326, 328
interest/exports ratios in, 65, 99
interest rates in, 327
"Larida" proposal for, 328
macroeconomic policies of, 24, 87, 319–24
menu approach to debt reduction in, 325
political climate in, 267
Real Plan in, 24, 87, 328
renewed capital flows to, 430
revenue sharing in, 327
secondary market prices of debt of, 55
self-financing of enhancements by, 240
spread of 1982 crisis to, 206
stock market in, 428, 501
structural policies in, 24, 324
Summer Plan in, 321
US bank exposure in, 76
Bresser Pereira, Luiz Carlos, 321
Bueno, Gerardo M., 309
Bulgaria, 27, 360, 362–63
Bulow, Jeremy, 10, 13, 144–47, 187–93, 265
Burundi, 393
Bush, George, and administration of, 16, 216, 217
Buybacks. See also individual countries
in Brady Plan agreements, 232–33
critiques of, 13, 164, 175, 187–93
debt forgiveness and, 158, 192
effect on secondary market price of, 165, 190
and Extended Fund Facility loans, 238
free-rider problem and, 175
in 1930s crisis, 199–200
suitability for small, low-income countries of, 233
in Williamson model, 176

C-bonds, 233
Caldera, Rafael, 308
Calvo, Guillermo, 30, 301, 429–30, 465–67
Camdessus, Michel, 17, 220, 504
Cameroon, 369
Canada, 214, 462, 495, 502
Capital account. See Capital flows
Capital controls, 360, 468
Capital flight. See also individual countries
current account deficits and, 97, 439, 447
estimates of, 110–13, 439–48
implications for evaluation of debt strategy of, 113
importance of avoiding, 3
in OECD review of debt projections, 123
omission from Cline model of, 8–9, 109, 110–13, 125
repatriation of, 30–31, 423, 438–48, 461, 486
underinvoicing as means of, 405
Capital flows. See also individual countries
adverse side effects of, 465–69
arrears as, 436
in Asia, 426–31, 433, 450
and Brady Plan, 248, 423, 426
controls on, 360, 468
direct investment component of, 30, 426, 436
Eastern Europe and Africa crowded out from, 33, 471–72
economic reform as cause of renewed, 423, 426
equity, 436, 449
exchange rate policy and, 466–67
fiscal policy and, 452–53, 459–60, 466–68, 473
as hot money, 430, 436
IMF study of, 431, 467, 469
inflation and, 32
interest rate differentials and, 30, 423, 426, 429, 448, 450
and international economic environment, 426, 428, 473
and Latin America, 426–31, 433, 471
magnitude and trends in, 424–26, 430–38, 487
moderating inward, 457–59, 465–70
net versus gross, 431
portfolio diversification as reason for, 449
reasons for renewed capital market access, 423, 450
resurgence in early 1990s of, 18, 29–30, 424–30
and risk of future debt crisis, 472–82
role of institutional investors in, 448–49
secondary market debt prices and, 174
shift in composition of, 34–35, 426–27, 430–38, 449, 450
sustainability of, 32, 439, 457–64, 473
syndicated bank lending and, 426
systemic risk of, 268
Capitalization of interest, 176, 212, 233
Caracas, riots in, 16, 218, 306

Cardoso, Eliana, 94, 122
Cardoso, Fernando Henrique, 24, 267, 328
Carkovic, Maria, 32, 467–69
Cavallo, Domingo, 311
Ceauşescu, Nicolae, regime of (Romania), 365
Central banks, role in distinguishing illiquid
  borrowers of, 11, 92–93, 161, 203–04
Charity, economics of, 29, 398
Chemical Bank, 236
Chenery-Bruno model, 156
Chicago school, 286, 343
Chile
  Allende regime in, 286
  buybacks in, 291
  capital flight in, 444–46
  capital inflows in, 287
  commodity exports in, 285, 286
  costs and equity effects of adjustment in,
    288–89
  current account in, 287, 458
  debt-equity conversions in, 22, 291–92
  debt stock of, 285
  debt strategy in, 289–90, 457
  economic growth in, 276–77, 285
  eschewal of Brady Plan forgiveness by, 284
  exchange rate policy in, 20–21, 286–88, 458,
    466, 469
  fiscal balances in, 285
  foreign share of assets in, 445
  inflation in, 279, 285, 286, 287, 469
  internal transfer problem in, 290
  macroeconomic policy in, 286–89
  market-based debt reduction, 289–92
  Pinochet regime in, 286
  policymakers from Chicago school in, 286
  privatization in, 286
  socialization of private debt in, 152, 290
  structural reform in, 286–89
  wage indexation in, 287
Citibank, 76, 213–14, 495
Claessens, Stijn, 12, 17, 111, 163, 223, 246–48,
  250, 256, 400, 439, 440
Cline model
  backcasts using, 8, 101, 104–05, 114–19, 127–
    32
  central findings of, 7, 91–92
  choice of parameters in, 90–91, 93
  commodity prices in, 113–19, 126
  comparisons between other studies and, 7,
    95, 120, 149
  criticisms of, 7–8, 93–95, 122–23, 148
  description of, 7, 90–91
  diagnosis of illiquidity by, 92–93
  direct foreign investment in, 91
  error decomposition analysis of, 8, 101, 104–
    22, 127–32
  eschewal of Brady Plan forgiveness by, 284
  forecast versus actual outcomes of, 8, 96–
    101
  international environment in, 101–04

oil price decline and, 8, 92, 103
omission of variables from, 8, 94, 109, 110–
  13, 125
model error in, 8, 109–22
scenario error in, 8, 101, 104–09
sensitivity analysis of, 92
trade elasticities in, 93, 119–22
Cline, William R., 7–9, 11, 12, 70, 89–96, 101–
  23, 127–32, 143, 148–50, 159, 184–85, 203,
  206, 207, 209–10, 227, 246, 297, 313, 324,
  353, 377, 400, 436, 437
Cohen, Benjamin J., 244, 255
Cohen, Daniel, 12, 164, 182, 223
Coinsurance of developing-country bonds, 35,
  483
Collins, Susan M., 402
Collor de Mello, Fernando, and administration
  of (Brazil), 24, 321–25, 342
Collyns, Charles, 240, 433, 451, 471, 472
Colombia
  adjustment program of, 281
  capital flight from, 442, 444, 446
  clientelistic political system in, 279
  commodity exports of, 278
  current account of, 278, 458
  debt/exports ratios in, 280, 284
  debt stock of, 278
  debt strategy of, 280–82
  economic growth in, 276, 277, 278
  eschewal of Brady Plan agreement by, 281
  exchange rate policy of, 21, 278, 279, 458,
    466, 469
  fiscal balances in, 278, 279
  foreign share of assets in, 445
  inflation in, 279, 291, 469
  internal transfer problem in, 282
  "jumbo" loans to, 281
  Lopez administration in, 279
  macroeconomic policy in, 21, 279
  role of drug money in, 21, 282–84
  structural reform in, 21, 282–84
  trade policy in, 21
Commodity prices. See also Oil price decline
  in Cline model, 113–19, 126
  debt crisis as possible cause of falling, 230–31
  and exchange rates, 117
  impact on debt/exports ratios of changes in,
    119, 231
  industrial-country growth and, 116
  long-term declining trend in, 115
  procyclical behavior of, 116–17
  World Bank projections of rise in, 378
Concerted lending, 14, 205–08
Conditionality
  in Brady Plan, 15–17, 20, 239–40, 262–63
  in Diwan-Rodrik analysis, 13, 177–81
  market-based debt reduction and, 13
  for sub-Saharan Africa, 29, 396
Conesa, Eduardo R., 313
Congethivoire, 370, 383, 386, 388, 394, 415–16

Congo, 390, 391
Congress, US, 216, 226, 504
Conning, Jonathan, 307
"Consenting adults" view of current account
    deficits, 32, 287, 300, 459, 489, 497
Contagion (neighborhood) effect, 93, 280, 287,
    502
Contingent approach to debt strategy, 203, 223,
    256
Conversion bonds, 15, 184, 219, 221, 427, 438,
    470, 479
Convertibility Plan (Argentina), 24, 311, 314–
    15, 319
Cooper, Richard N., 10, 142–44, 223
Corbo, Vittorio, 287, 288
Corden, Max, 12, 167–71, 224, 399, 459
Corrigan, Gerald, 220
"Corset" clause, 242
Costa Rica, 208
Côte d'Ivoire, 241, 390, 391
Council for Mutual Economic Assistance, 362,
    403
Council of Economic Advisers, 11, 147, 148
Council on Foreign Relations, 225
Crawling-peg exchange rates, 458, 467
Credit ceilings, 140, 142, 145
Credit Suisse, 236
Creditor cartel fatigue, 122
Creditworthiness
    in Eaton-Gersovitz model, 139
    inflation and, 133–38
    trends in, 77–88
"Crowding-out" coefficient, 183
Cruzado Plan (Brazil), 319, 341
Cuddington, John T., 223
Currency boards, 311
Current account. See also individual countries
    actual versus projected, 96, 105
    capital flight and, 97, 439, 447, 462
    historical magnitudes of, 461
    importance of avoiding deficits in, 3
    Lawson thesis on, 32, 287, 300, 459, 489, 497
    and sustainability of capital flows, 458–64
    and Triffin problem, 463
Czechoslovakia and successor states, 27, 363,
    366

Darman, Richard, 208
Davydov, Oleg, 354
Dawes Plan, 195, 362
De la Madrid, Miguel, and administration of
    (Mexico), 292
De Larosière, Jacques, 205
Debt capacity projection models, 147–52
Debt crisis of the 1930s
    buybacks in, 199–200
    compared with 1980s crisis, 13, 19, 194–200,
        253–55, 481
    default as option in, 25, 139–47, 151, 177–78,
        197, 255, 337

"heavy" and "light" defaulters, 197–98, 253,
    254
Debt-equity conversions, 22, 42, 164, 213, 291–
    92, 317, 325. See also Debt reduction,
    market-based; individual countries
Debt/exports ratios. See also individual countries
    actual versus projected, 98
    Cline model projections of, 91–92
    IMF projections of, 95
    impact of commodity price changes on, 119,
        231
    inflation and, 134
    trends in, 43–50, 77–86
Debt forgiveness
    buybacks and, 158, 192
    and capital flow resurgence, 261
    Corden model of, 167–71
    creditors' interest in, 158–59
    Diwan-Rodrik analysis of, 177–82
    Dooley model of, 173–74
    Helpman model of, 171–73
    internal transfer problem and, 155, 157
    investment responses to, 172
    Kenen model of, 174–75
    Krugman model of, 159–65
    moral hazard problem in, 167, 260
    oil price decline and, 151–52, 256, 258
    to prevent consumption below minimum
        subsistence, 167
    rescheduling preferable to, 93
    Sachs model of, 165–67
    structure of economy and, 400
    versus "debt relief" and "debt reduction,"
        158–59
    Williamson model of, 175–77, 225
Debt indicators. See Debt/exports ratios;
    Interest/exports ratios; individual countries
Debt Laffer curve, 11–12, 162–64, 175, 399
Debt overhang
    critiques of concept of, 12–13, 17, 247
    and debt Laffer curve, 11–13, 162
    definitions of, 159, 161, 178
    and investment disincentives, 11–12, 158,
        173, 177, 224
Debt reduction. See also Buybacks; Debt-equity
        conversions; Debt forgiveness
    Bradley plan for, 226, 263
    ideal pattern of, 42
    impact of loan-loss provisions on, 214
    income effect of, 167
    intellectual transition from rescheduling to,
        222–31
    menu approach to, 15, 221, 232–33, 325
    proposed global program for, 262–63
    risk-compensated, 12, 176, 183–87
    simulation for sub-Saharan Africa, 28, 388–
        91, 407–22
Debt reduction, market-based. See also
        Buybacks; Debt-equity conversions
    advantages of, 3

during Baker Plan period, 15, 213
benefits to creditors of, 165
debt Laffer curve and, 162, 164
graphical treatment of, 184
IFI conditionality and, 13
in 1930s debt crisis, 200
reduction of bank exposure through, 210
Debt repurchases. See Buybacks
Debt rescheduling
IMF role in, 14, 206–07
menu approach to, 212
multiyear (MYRAs), 14, 17–18, 207, 232, 241, 247, 297, 324, 376, 391, 401
in 1982 Mexico crisis, 17, 206, 297
preferable to forgiveness, 93
Debt service. See also Interest/exports ratios
capacity versus willingness to pay, 250–52
political-economic model of, 18, 95, 250–52
ratios, 50, 373
Debt, socialization of, 3, 152–53, 269, 271–72, 290, 310, 352
Debt strategy of the 1980s. See also Baker Plan; Brady Plan; Concerted lending
adaptive policymaking in, 255–58
burden sharing in, 258–62
capital flight and, 113
contradictory critiques of, 42
cooperative versus confrontational, 336–40
debtor economic policies and, 337
evaluation of, 19, 87–88, 124–26, 253–68
goals of, 14
ideal pattern for, 42
impact of oil price decline on, 125
implications of 1994–95 Mexico crisis for, 500–05
intellectual evolution of, 222–28
new money in, 42
phases of, 14
political sustainability of, 125
Reagan administration and, 205
US Treasury review of, 16
Default
and access to credit markets, 140, 197–98, 253
and agency investment ratings, 147, 199, 282
and devaluation, 176
"developmental" versus "public revenue", 13, 195–96, 362
and economic growth, 255, 337
as policy option, 25, 139–47, 151, 177–78, 197, 255
Denmark, 462
Devaluation. See also Exchange rate policy
and budgetary problem, 11, 94, 155
and default, 176
and inflation, 57, 155, 296
"Developmental" default, 13, 195–96, 362
Díaz-Alejandro, Carlos F., 144
Direct foreign investment, 30, 91, 124, 319, 426, 436

Discount bonds, 17, 158, 221–22, 232–33, 238, 306, 317, 326, 470, 477
"Discovered" debt, 96, 98, 110
Disincentive effects of debt. See Debt Laffer curve; Debt overhang
Dittus, Peter, 120, 122–23, 147
Diwan, Ishac, 12, 13, 159, 167, 177–82, 223, 225, 247, 265
Dollarization, 332, 341
Dominican Republic, 242
Dooley, Michael, 11, 13, 120, 147, 150, 173–74, 223, 224, 477
Dornbusch, Rudiger, 11, 93–94, 122, 147, 149, 155, 203, 223, 287–88, 301, 498
Drug money in Colombia, 21, 282–84

Eastern Europe. See also individual countries
arrears in, 364
bank exposure to, 73, 75, 79, 81, 83, 364
Czech-Hungarian versus Polish-Bulgarian model for, 27, 360, 366
danger of capital market crowding out, 33, 471–72
debt/exports ratios in, 47, 69, 71, 364, 365
debt/GNP ratios in, 49, 69, 71
debt stock of, 41, 44
exports of, 364, 367
imports from former Soviet Union of, 404
interest/exports ratios in, 53, 69, 71, 364, 365
internal transfer problem in, 367
next steps for debt policy in, 366
privatization in, 472
secondary market debt prices in, 366
Eaton, Jonathan, 10–11, 139–42, 148, 151
Eaton-Gersovitz model, 139–42, 174, 400
Economic growth. See also individual countries
default and, 255, 337
high water mark in 1984 of, 207
impact of Brady Plan on, 249
paradox of ongoing debt difficulties and, 100
trends in, 57
Economic Performance Index, 288, 338–39
"Economics of charity," 29, 398
Economies in transition. See Eastern Europe; Russia
Ecuador, 57, 240
Edwards, Sebastian, 275, 276, 286, 287, 313
Egypt, 60, 69, 111, 361
Eichengreen, Barry, 13, 196–201, 253, 255, 337
"Emerging markets," 428
Enders, Thomas O., 11, 144, 147, 150, 260
Enhanced Toronto terms, 28–29, 237, 385–94, 397–98
Enhancements
cost of, 20, 232
IFI lending for, 17, 219, 221, 238, 263
need not shift loss to third party, 165
probability of nonrepayment of, 265
rigidities in, 238
as risk-compensated forgiveness, 183–85

size in relation to debt forgiveness of, 17
Enterprise for the Americas Initiative, 266, 395
Error decomposition analysis, 8, 101, 104–22, 127–32
Ethiopia, 383, 393
Exchange rate policy, 2, 458, 466–67. *See also* Devaluation; *individual countries*
Exchange rate valuation effects, 8–9, 110–13, 125
Exchange rates
  commodity prices and, 117
  crawling-peg mechanism of, 458, 467
  debt indicators and, 45
  reduced volatility due to Brady Plan of, 17, 246
Exit bonds, 15, 176, 191, 215, 225, 325
Export-Import Bank of Japan, 221
Exports
  actual versus model-predicted, 96, 105, 115
  in Cline model, 90, 126
  growth and capacity to pay, 147
  US to Latin America, 15, 216
Extended Fund Facility, 206, 238

Fadl, Sergio, 221
Federal Reserve
  debt capacity projections of, 95, 150–51
  reservations about Brady Plan of, 220
  response to 1982 Mexico crisis, 205
Feldstein, Martin, 147
Fernandez-Arias, Eduardo, 477
Filatov, Victor S., 147, 149–50
Finland, 141
Fiscal balances, 2, 55, 152, 294, 459–60. *See also individual countries*
Fiscal policy. *See also* Internal transfer problem
  and capital flows, 459–60, 466–68, 473
  and successful debt crisis resolution, 153
Fischer, Stanley, 11, 93, 94, 147, 149, 224
Fishlow, Albert, 13, 93, 94, 194–96, 199, 254, 362, 437
Flight capital. *See* Capital flight
Folkerts-Landau, David, 34, 449, 479
Fontaine, Juan A., 287–91
Foreign direct investment, 30, 91, 124, 319, 426, 436
Former Soviet Union. *See* Russia
France, 76, 82–83, 153
Franco, Itamar, and administration of (Brazil), 327
Free-rider problem, 161, 175, 181, 358
Frenkel, Jacob, 224
Froot, K., 13, 191–92
Fujimori, Alberto, and administration of (Peru), 329, 331, 334
Fukao, Mitsuhiro, 34, 484

Gabon, 400
Game theory, 141, 144
Garay, Luis Jorge Salamanca, 262, 282

García, Alan, and administration of (Peru), 25, 329, 331
General Agreement on Tariffs and Trade (GATT), 22, 194, 295
GDP. *See* Economic growth
Germany, 76, 80–81, 153
Gersovitz, Mark, 10–11, 94–95, 139–41, 151
Goldstein, Morris, 34, 449, 479
"Great Turnaround" in Venezuela, 23, 302, 305
Greece, 141
Group of Seven (G-7), 29, 217, 219, 361, 396
Guinea, 383. *See also* Senguinali
Guinea-Bissau, 392. *See also* Sudasombis
Gurria, Angel, 221, 222

Harberger, Arnold C., 314
Harrod-Domar model, 298
HD17
  bank exposure to, 74, 78, 80, 82
  commercial bank claims on, 61–63, 211, 229
  commodity exports of, 230
  debt/exports ratios of, 5, 43–46, 51
  debt/GNP ratios of, 5, 45–51
  debt stock of, 5, 40, 42, 44
  debt to official lenders of, 211, 229
  economic growth in, 57, 58
  fiscal balances in, 55, 56
  growth in exports in, 45
  growth in reserves in, 43
  high concentration of debt in, 60–64
  interest/exports ratios of, 5, 50–52
  real versus nominal debt growth in, 43
  secondary market prices for bank debt in, 5
  variable interest debt in, 474–76
Helkie, William, 11, 120, 147, 150, 151
Helpman, Elhanan, 12, 171–73
Herrhausen, Alfred, 15, 227
Highly indebted countries. *See* HD17
Historical lessons. *See also* Debt crisis of the 1930s
  of interwar period, 195–96
  of postwar period, 196
  of pre-1914 period, 194–95
  of 1980s debt crisis, 1–4
Howard, David, 120, 147, 151
Huizinga, Harry, 162
Hungary, 27, 69, 70, 363, 365–66
Husain, Ishrat, 223, 375, 385, 389
Hyperinflation. *See* Inflation; *individual countries*

Illiquidity versus insolvency
  in Cline model, 92–93
  in Cooper-Sachs analysis, 142–43
  as part of contingent strategy, 203–04, 223
  role of central bankers in distinguishing, 11, 92–93, 161, 203–04
Income effect of debt relief, 167
India, 60, 68, 400
Indonesia, 60, 68, 462
Inflation. *See also individual countries*

actual versus projected, 102
creditworthiness and, 133–38
debt/exports ratios and, 134
exchange rate anchor for combating, 22, 24,
  296, 312, 332, 341, 459
exchange rate overvaluation and, 57, 155, 296
impact on debt strategy of, 125
impact on oil exporters of, 108
inertial component of, 24, 287, 327–28, 341–
  42
interest/exports ratios and, 135–38
trends in, 57–60
world, 2, 102, 103, 57, 60, 108, 125, 133–38
and world interest rates, 103
Inflation tax, 154
Insolvency. *See* Illiquidity and insolvency
Institute for International Economics, 225
Institute of International Finance, 27, 229, 349,
  363
Intercreditor burden sharing, 266
Interest capitalization, 176, 212, 233
Interest/exports ratios. *See also individual*
  countries
  actual versus projected, 98
  as indicator of debt burden, 50, 98
  inflation and, 135–38
  interest rate changes and, 103
  trends in, 50–51, 86, 228
Interest rates
  actual versus projected, 102
  in Cardoso-Dornbusch critique, 122
  and exchange rate parity, 113
  growth of indebtedness and, 41, 42
  impact on debt strategy of, 125
  impact on debtors of rise in, 33, 149
  inflation, world, and, 103
  and interest/exports ratios, 103
  international differentials in, 30, 423, 426,
    429, 448, 450
  LIBOR, 50, 102, 103
  prospects for, 473
  risk premia on, 248, 451–57, 485
  trends in, 50
Internal transfer problem. *See also individual*
  countries
  absent in Cline model, 94, 125
  connection between fiscal crisis and, 2,
    54–55, 152–57
  in Cooper-Sachs analysis, 143
  and debt forgiveness, 155
  increasing analytical focus on, 11
  as principal impediment to recovery from
    debt crisis, 126
International banking system. *See* International
  financial system; Banks
International bankruptcy agency, proposed, 34,
  272, 484–86
International Bondholders Insurance
  Corporation, proposed, 35–36, 272, 482–84,
  486, 488–93, 502

International Debt Discount Corporation,
  proposed, 262
International Debt Management Authority,
  proposed, 226
International Development Association (IDA),
  232, 237, 382, 396
International financial institutions (IFIs). *See*
  also International Monetary Fund, World
  Bank
  and Baker Plan, 208–09
  conditionality imposed by, 13, 177–81
  and international financial system, 194, 205–
    06
  lending for enhancements by, 17, 219, 221,
    238, 263
  policy surveillance reviews by, proposed, 272
  proposed G-7 buyback of claims of, 396
  role in recovery from debt crisis of, 253
  senior creditor status of, 29, 181, 396
International financial system
  and Brady Plan, 20–21, 252–53, 255, 267–69
  stability of, 6, 34, 255, 268–69, 479, 482
International Monetary Fund
  analyses of debt problem by, 224, 231, 243
  data on former Soviet Union of, 402–03
  debt trends and projections by, 51, 95
  as enforcer of involuntary lending, 206
  Extended Fund Facility of, 206, 238
  future role of, 272
  role in Brady Plan implementation of, 17,
    219–21
  role in early phase of debt crisis of, 14, 206
  study of international capital flows by, 431,
    467, 469
Investment Laffer curve, 157
Islam, Shafiqul, 225, 244
Israel, 466, 502
Italy, 141, 502
Ize, Alain, 175

Jamaica, 208, 232, 241, 243
Japan, 217, 227, 314, 362, 395
Japanese Export-Import Bank, 17, 219, 263
Jorgensen, Erika, 198
"Jumbo" loans, 281
Junguito, Roberto, 281

Kahn, Robert, 32, 467–69
Kaletsky, Anatole, 25, 141, 337
Kenen, Peter B., 174–75, 216, 262
Kentzamgola, 28, 370, 383, 384, 387, 390, 391,
  394, 398, 419–420
Kenya, 383. *See also* Kentzamgola
Keynes, John Maynard, 19, 313
Kiguel, Miguel, 323, 332
Killick, Anthony, 396
Klein, Lawrence, 93
Kletzer, Kenneth M., 225, 477
Korea, South, 60, 69, 114, 141, 257, 427, 461
Krueger, Anne O., 223

Krugman, Paul R., 11–12, 148, 155, 159–65, 205, 209, 216, 220, 223, 228, 255
Kuczynski, Pedro-Pablo, 230, 309

LaFalce, John, 226
Laffer curve, 11–12, 157, 162, 164, 175, 399
Lago, Ricardo, 25, 332, 333
Lancaster, Carol, 29, 397
Lara-Resende, Andre, 328
"Larida" proposal for Brazil, 328
Larraín, Felipe, 291
Latin America. *See also individual countries*
  capital flows to, 426–31, 432, 434–35, 471
  concentration of developing-country debt in, 60, 275
  contagion effect in, 93, 280, 287
  cooperative versus confrontational debt strategy in, 336–40
  differences between sub-Saharan Africa and, 367, 377
  economic growth in, 6
  Economic Performance Index for, 338–39
  economic teams in, 343
  exchange rate policy in, 335, 341
  fiscal policy in, 336, 341
  heterodox versus orthodox reforms in, 341–43
  imports in, 207
  inflation in, 6, 57–60, 337
  indexation in, 341
  lessons from debt crisis for, 335–43
  portion of SIMIC debt owed by, 275
  role of debt crisis in policy reform in, 21–25, 259–60
  vicious and virtuous circles in economic management in, 342
"Law of one price," 314
Lawson, Nigel, 32, 287, 300, 459, 485, 497
Leiderman, Leonardo, 30, 429–30, 465–67
Lessard, Donald R., 437
LIBOR, 50, 102, 103. *See also* Interest rates
Lindert, Peter, 198
Lipton, David, 402
Liviatan, Nissan, 323, 332
Loan-loss provisioning, 15, 70, 213–14, 259
London Club, 241
Lopez, Alfonso, and administration of (Colombia), 279
Lusinchi, Jaime, and administration of (Venezuela), 306
Lustig, Nora, 244
Low-income countries
  bank exposure to, 73, 75, 79, 81, 83
  debt/exports ratios of, 47, 69
  debt/GNP ratios of, 48, 69
  debt stock of, 41, 44
  economic growth in, 59
  interest/exports ratios of, 53, 69
Macroeconomic policy. *See* Fiscal policy; *individual countries*

Madagascar, 28, 383. *See also* Mozagascaire
Major, John, 385
Malaysia, 69
Mali, 383. *See also* Senguinali
Marginal tax argument, 166
Market-based debt reduction. *See* Debt reduction, market-based
Marquez, Jaime, 120
Mattione, Richard P., 11, 144, 147, 149–50
McNeilly, Caryl, 120
Meller, Patricio, 286–88, 292
Menem, Carlos, and administration of (Argentina), 311, 319
Menu approach to debt rescheduling and reduction, 15, 212, 221, 232–33, 325
MERCOSUL, 315
Mexico
  Brady Plan agreement for, 22, 220–22, 245–48, 297
  buybacks by, 187
  capital flight from, 111, 300, 441, 442, 444, 446, 448, 461–64, 501–02
  commodity exports in, 100, 293
  current account in, 22, 31, 100, 267, 293, 299–300, 458, 461, 464
  debt/exports ratios for, 66, 100
  debt/GNP ratios for, 66, 499–500
  debt stock of, 293
  debt strategy of, 296–98, 457, 500
  de la Madrid administration in, 292
  early 1990s issuance of bonds by, 427
  economic growth in, 57, 100, 101, 276, 292, 293
  economic prospects for, 497–505
  exchange rate policy in, 22, 295–96, 299–302, 458, 469, 495–501
  fiscal balances in, 22, 293, 294, 336
  foreign share of assets in, 445
  impact of oil price decline on, 17–18, 66, 246, 294, 296, 478
  import growth in, 464
  incomes policy in, 295–96
  inflation in, 22, 276, 292, 293, 296, 299, 469
  interest/exports ratios in, 66, 100
  interest rates in, 299
  macroeconomic policies in, 294–95, 468
  and Morgan Guaranty, 215, 297
  multiyear rescheduling agreements for, 17, 207, 297
  NAFTA and, 22, 299
  National Solidarity Program (PRONASOL) in, 294
  1982 outbreak of debt crisis in, 205–08
  1994–95 currency crisis in, 495–505
  OECD review of debt projections for, 123
  privatization in, 22, 295
  reserves in, 300
  Salinas administration in, 216, 292, 295, 297, 471
  secondary market prices in, 55

Solidarity Pact in, 296, 342, 495
stock market indices in, 428
structural reform in, 22, 295
trade policy in, 22, 121, 295
Zedillo administration in, 495–505
Mexico City earthquake, 207, 297
Middle-income countries. *See also* Severely
    indebted middle-income countries
    (SIMICs)
  bank exposure to, 73, 75, 79, 81, 83
  debt/exports ratios of, 47, 70
  debt/GNP ratios of, 49, 70
  debt stock of, 41, 44
  economic growth in, 59
  interest/exports ratios in, 53, 70
Mitterrand, François, 15, 227
Miyazawa, Kiichi, 15, 227
Model error, 8–9, 101, 109–22, 127–32. *See also*
    Cline model
Moral hazard, 167, 260, 269–70, 393
Moreira, Marcilio Marques, 322
Morgan, J. P., 250
Morgan Guaranty Bank, 11, 144, 147, 149, 443,
    458, 495
Morocco, 241
Morrison, Bruce, 226
Morton, Peter J., 198
Mozagascaire, 370, 383–84, 386, 390–91, 394,
    398, 413–14
Mozambique. *See also* Mozagascaire
Mulford, David, 217–19, 245, 258, 361
Multilateral development banks, 112, 208–10,
    395. *See also* International financial
    institutions
Multilateral Investment Guarantee Agency
    (MIGA), 483
Multiyear rescheduling agreements (MYRAs),
    14, 17–18, 207, 232, 241, 247, 297, 325, 376,
    391, 401
Mutual funds, 448–49, 480

NAFTA (North American Free Trade
    Agreement), 23, 199, 299
Naím, Moisés, 308
Namibia, 367
National Association of Insurance Companies,
    482
National Solidarity Program (PRONASOL), 294
Naudé, David, 111, 400, 439, 440
Neighborhood (contagion) effect, 93, 280, 287
New money option
  in Baker Plan, 208–10
  in Brady Plan, 17, 219, 222, 233, 238
New Zealand, 462
Nicaragua, 164
Nigeria, 60, 370, 383–84, 387–91, 393–94, 417–
    18, 471
Nordhaus, William D., 115
North American Free Trade Agreement
    (NAFTA), 23, 199, 299

"Novation," 220

O'Brien, Paul S., 120, 122–23, 147
O'Connell, Arturo, 219
Ocampo, Antonio, 281
OECD (Organization for Economic Cooperation
    and Development), 122–23, 149
Oil-exporting countries
  actual versus projected outcomes of debt
    crisis for, 96–101, 105–08
  capital flight from, 110
  debt/exports ratios of, 45
  economic growth in, 100
  impact of inflation on, 108
  impact of oil price decline on, 45, 108, 126, 258
  model error for, 109, 121
  scenario error for, 109
  vulnerability to new debt crisis of, 477
Oil-importing countries
  actual versus projected outcomes of debt
    crisis for, 96–101, 105–08
  capital flight from, 110
  economic growth in, 100
  export prices of, 114
  impact of oil price decline on, 105–08, 258
  model error for, 109, 113–16, 120
  paradox of ongoing debt difficulties despite
    better indicators for, 98, 99
  scenario error for, 108–09
Oil price decline
  and Baker Plan, 213
  debt forgiveness and, 151–52, 256, 258
  impact on Cline projections of, 8, 92, 103
  impact on debt strategy of, 125
  impact on oil exporters of, 17–18, 66–67, 126,
    246, 294, 297, 307, 478
  impact on oil importers of, 105–08, 258
  in OECD review of debt projections, 123
  potential for further, 478
Oil proceeds mechanism, as a loan guarantee,
    502
Oks, Daniel, 17, 246–48, 250, 256
Optimizing deadbeat model, 10, 94–95, 175, 181
Organization for Economic Cooperation and
    Development (OECD), 122–23, 149
Ortiz, Guillermo, 175, 496, 499
Ozler, Sule, 198, 200

Pakistan, 68
Panama, 241, 242
Paraguay, 315
Par bonds, 17, 42–43, 54, 158, 199, 222, 232–33,
    238–39, 306, 309, 317, 326, 388, 470, 476
Paredes, Carlos E., 332
Paris Club, 27, 241, 334, 346, 348, 354–55, 358,
    361–62, 385
Pastor, Carlos Rodriguez, 331
Pension funds, 448, 487
Pérez, Carlos Andrés, and administration of
    (Venezuela), 23, 302, 307–08

Perry, George L., 167
Peru
  Belaúnde administration in, 331, 333
  Brady Plan negotiations with, 242, 334
  capital flight from, 442
  commodity exports of, 330
  confrontational approach of, 25, 329, 332, 333
  current account of, 330
  debt stock of, 330, 334
  debt strategy of, 332–35
  economic growth in, 57, 276, 277, 329, 330, 335
  exchange rates in, 330
  fiscal balances in, 330
  Fujimori administration in, 329, 331, 334
  García administration in, 25, 329, 331
  inflation in, 25, 57, 276, 280, 329–32, 330
  interest/exports ratios in, 334
  macroeconomic policies of, 329–32
  poverty in, 334
  secondary market price of debt of, 334
  sequencing of reforms in, 332
Philippines, 442, 444–46
Piñera, José, 286
Pinochet, Augusto, and regime of (Chile), 286
Poland
  debt/exports ratios in, 358, 366
  debt rescheduling and reduction in, 27, 266, 361–62
  interest/exports ratios in, 366
  macroeconomic stabilization in, 361
  1980s debt crisis in, 360–61, 69
  revenue default in, 362
Political discount rate, 251, 261
Political-economic model, 18, 95, 250–52
Populism, 153, 251, 252, 267
Portes, Richard, 13, 196–201, 253, 255, 337
"Poverty" shift factor, 399

Reagan, Ronald, and administration of, 205
Real Plan (Brazil), 24, 87, 328
Reed, John, 214
Reinhart, Carmen M., 30, 429–30, 465–67
Reisen, Helmut, 11, 153–55
Rescheduling. See Debt rescheduling
Revenue default, 195, 362
Rhodes, William R., 216, 218, 219, 236
Risk-compensated debt reduction, 12, 176, 183–87
Risk premia on interest rates, 248, 451–57, 485
Rodriguez, Miguel, 306
Rodrik, Dani, 12, 13, 159, 167, 177–82, 247, 265, 402
Roett, Riordan, 297, 317
Rogoff, Kenneth, 10, 13, 144–47, 187–93, 265
Romania, 69, 360, 363, 365
Rotemberg, Julio, 193
Rubio, Luis, 245

Russia
  assumption of entire former Soviet debt by, 26, 346–48
  buildup of arrears by, 26, 346, 348
  capital flight from, 351, 405
  conditionality for, 359
  debt/exports ratios in, 349, 350
  debt stock of, 346, 349
  debt strategy for, 26, 352–60
  external assets of, 26, 349, 351, 360
  external transfer situation of, 349–51
  fiscal balances in, 352
  free-rider problem in, 358
  G-7 agreement with, 346
  illusory collapse in export base of, 26, 350, 402–06
  interest capitalization for, 358
  internal transfer problem of, 352
  need for stabilization in, 26, 352
  political constraints in, 359
  privatization in, 352–53, 359
  relations between Paris Club and, 346, 348, 354
  "triage" approach to state enterprises of, 353
  zero-option agreements between other former Soviet republics and, 348–49
  exchange rate convertibility in, 360
Rwanda, 393

Sachs, Jeffrey D., 10, 94, 142–44, 155, 159, 162, 165–67, 198, 223–24, 244, 402
Salinas de Gortari, Carlos, 216, 292, 295, 297, 471
Salomon Brothers, 470
Scenario error, 8, 101, 104–09
Schadler, Susan, 32, 467–69
Schilling, John, 210
Schmidt, Wilson E., 29, 398
Schulmann, Horst, 27, 349, 363
Schumer, Charles, 226
Secondary market. See also Buybacks; individual countries
  capital flows and, 174
  empirical analysis of, 162
  impact of Brady Plan agreements on, 248
  impact of buybacks on, 165, 190
  impact of loan-loss provisioning on, 214
  prices as indicator of actual value, 224
  prices as measure of capital market access, 477
  trends in prices on, 5, 54, 249
Senegal, 383. See also Senguinali
Senguinali, 28, 370, 383–84, 387, 391, 392, 394, 398, 421–22
Seniority
  of bonds, 30, 173, 437–38, 450, 486
  of IFI claims, 29, 181, 396
Serra Puche, Jaime, 496
Severely indebted middle-income countries (SIMICs), 241, 275
Sierra Leone, 369
Simonsen, Mario Henrique, 309
Singapore, 462

Skiles, Marilyn E., 438, 450, 458
Slovakia, 366
Smith, Gordon W., 223
Socialization of private debt, 3, 152–53, 269, 271–72, 290, 316, 352
Solidarity Pact (Mexico), 296, 342, 495
Solomon, Anthony M., 225
Somalia, 28, 384, 392–93, 398, 401
South Africa, 367
South Atlantic war, 316
South Korea, 60, 69, 114, 141, 257, 427, 461
Sovereign lending
  capacity constraint on, 142, 147
  Bulow-Rogoff model of, 144–47
  Cooper-Sachs model of, 142–44
  Eaton-Gersovitz model, 139–42, 174, 400
  "optimizing deadbeat" model of, 10, 94–95, 141, 175, 181
  repudiation risk in, 142, 143, 146
  reputational considerations in, 139, 147
  rewards to nonrepudiation in, 141
Soviet Union. See Russia
Spain, 141, 462, 502
"Step-down" par bonds, 306
Sterilized intervention, 466–68
Stiglitz, Joseph E., 10, 140, 141, 151
Sub-Saharan Africa. See also individual countries
  arrears in, 381, 383
  bypassed by capital market resurgence, 471
  capital flight from, 400–01
  conditionality for, 29, 396
  debt forgiveness for, 28, 204, 376, 395, 398–99, 401
  debt indicators for, 28, 68, 368–76, 377, 380, 384, 389
  debt overhang in, 375
  debt simulation model for, 28, 379–91, 407–22
  differences between Latin America and, 367, 377
  enhanced Toronto terms for, 28–29, 237, 385–94, 397–98
  heterogeneity of countries in, 27, 369, 383
  IMF and, 395
  multilateral development banks and, 395
  multiyear rescheduling agreements for, 376, 391, 401
  potential effect of Brady relief on, 28
  poverty in, 394, 399
  predominance of official lending to, 27, 68, 345, 367, 373
  short-leash approach for, 29, 368, 397–98
  trade patterns of, 68, 368, 376
  World Bank debt classification of countries in, 374
Sudan, 28, 68, 164, 392–93, 398, 401. See also Sudasombis
Sudasombis, 370, 383, 384, 386, 390, 394, 411–12
Summer Plan (Brazil), 321
Summers, Lawrence H., 143, 161

Swaps, debt-equity. See Debt-equity conversions
Sweden, 502

Tanzania, 369, 383
Tanzi-Oliveira effect, 342
Tavares, Maria Conçeicão, 323
Taylor, Lance, 148
Thailand, 69, 462
"Three-gap" model, 156–57
Toronto terms. See Enhanced Toronto terms
Transition economies. See Eastern Europe; Russia
Treasury, US. See US Treasury
Triffin problem, 463
Trinidad terms, 28–29, 385–89
Truman, Edwin M., 112, 213
Tryon, Ralph, 11, 120, 147, 150
Turkey, 60, 69, 111

Uganda, 369, 400
Uncertainty, modeling of, 140, 145, 160
Underinvoicing, 405
Underwood, John, 11, 120, 147, 150, 375, 385, 389
United Kingdom, 76, 78–79, 199
United Nations Association of the United States, 225
United States. See also US Congress; US Treasury,
  active role in debt crisis of, 205–06, 254
  banks and bank regulation in, 72–77, 269
  Bush administration in, 16, 216, 217
  criticism of debt strategy in, 216
  exports to Latin America of, 15, 216
  forgiveness of bilateral debt by, 266
  loan guarantee program for Mexico in 1995, 502–05
  position on Paris Club forgiveness, 395
  Reagan administration in, 205
  response to 1994–95 Mexican crisis of, 495, 502–05
Urrutia, Miguel, 21, 279, 280, 283
Uruguay, 315
US Congress, 216, 226
US Treasury
  review of International Debt Management Authority proposal by, 226
  review of international debt strategy by, 16, 217
  zero-coupon bonds issued by, 184, 221, 232, 243, 479

Van Trotsenburg, Axel, 11, 153–55
van Wijnbergen, Sweder, 17, 246–48, 250, 256, 298
Velasco, Andres, 291
Velasco, Juan, regime of (Peru), 329
Velásquez, Ramón, 304
Venezuela
  antipoverty programs in, 305

Brady Plan agreement for, 306–07
capital flight from, 306, 308, 442, 444, 446
Caracas riots in, 16, 218, 306
causes of debt buildup in, 306
current account of, 100, 303, 458
debt/exports ratios in, 67, 100, 306
debt/GNP ratios in, 67
debt stock of, 303
debt strategy of, 305–07
economic growth in, 57, 100–01, 276, 304
exchange rates and exchange rate policy in,
    67, 155, 303, 305, 308
fiscal balances in, 67, 303, 336
"Great Turnaround" in, 23, 302, 305
impact of oil price decline on, 67, 307, 478
inflation in, 276, 279, 302–04
interest/exports ratios in, 67, 100
Lusinchi administration in, 306
macroeconomic policy in, 23, 302–05, 307
1994 financial crisis in, 308
Pérez administration in, 23, 302, 307–08
political discontent in, 23, 307
privatization in, 305
structural reform in, 305, 307
trade liberalization in, 305
Volcker, Paul, 204, 205, 260

Warner, Andrew M., 12, 182
Washington consensus, 286, 335, 505

Webb, Richard, 329
Werner, Alejandro, 301, 498
White, M., 204
Wickham, P., 224
Wiesner, Eduardo, 11, 152
Williamson, John, 34, 155, 175–77, 189–90, 193,
    207, 225, 227, 260, 282, 284, 297, 335, 346,
    349, 436–37, 484
World Bank
    conference volumes on debt crisis by, 223
    debt classification of, 373–74
    estimates of capital flight by, 111, 113, 439
    estimates of Russian exports by, 402
    oil market forecasts by, 478
    projections of commodity price rise by, 378
    role in Brady Plan of, 17, 219, 221
    secondary market prices of, 55
Wright, Brian, 115

Yankee bonds, 199
Young plan, 362
Yugoslavia, 206, 360, 366

Zaire, 28, 68, 375, 383. See also Mozagascaire
Zambia, 28, 68, 164, 373. See also
    Kentzamgola
Zedillo, Ernesto, 495
Zero-coupon bonds, 184, 221, 232, 243, 479
Zero-option agreements, 348–49

Other Publications from the
Institute for International Economics

POLICY ANALYSES IN INTERNATIONAL ECONOMICS Series

1 The Lending Policies of the International Monetary Fund
John Williamson/*August 1982*
                          ISBN paper 0-88132-000-5   72 pp.

2 "Reciprocity": A New Approach to World Trade Policy?
William R. Cline/*September 1982*
                          ISBN paper 0-88132-001-3   41 pp.

3 Trade Policy in the 1980s
C. Fred Bergsten and William R. Cline/*November 1982*
(out of print)   ISBN paper 0-88132-002-1   84 pp.
Partially reproduced in the book *Trade Policy in the 1980s.*

4 International Debt and the Stability of the World Economy
William R. Cline/*September 1983*
                          ISBN paper 0-88132-010-2   134 pp.

5 The Exchange Rate System, Second Edition
John Williamson/*September 1983, rev. June 1985*
(out of print)   ISBN paper 0-88132-034-X   61 pp.

6 Economic Sanctions in Support of Foreign Policy Goals
Gary Clyde Hufbauer and Jeffrey J. Schott/*October 1983*
                          ISBN paper 0-88132-014-5   109 pp.

7 A New SDR Allocation?
John Williamson/*March 1984*
                          ISBN paper 0-88132-028-5   61 pp.

8 An International Standard for Monetary Stabilization
Ronald I. McKinnon/*March 1984*
                          ISBN paper 0-88132-018-8   108 pp.

9 The Yen/Dollar Agreement: Liberalizing Japanese Capital Markets
Jeffrey A. Frankel/*December 1984*
                          ISBN paper 0-88132-035-8   86 pp.

10 Bank Lending to Developing Countries: The Policy Alternatives
C. Fred Bergsten, William R. Cline, and John Williamson/*April 1985*
                          ISBN paper 0-88132-032-3   221 pp.

11 Trading for Growth: The Next Round of Trade Negotiations
Gary Clyde Hufbauer and Jeffrey J. Schott/*September 1985*
                          ISBN paper 0-88132-033-1   109 pp.

12 Financial Intermediation Beyond the Debt Crisis
Donald R. Lessard and John Williamson/*September 1985*
                          ISBN paper 0-88132-021-8   130 pp.

13 The United States-Japan Economic Problem
C. Fred Bergsten and William R. Cline/*October 1985, 2d ed. January 1987*
(out of print)   ISBN paper 0-88132-060-9   180 pp.

14 Deficits and the Dollar: The World Economy at Risk
Stephen Marris/*December 1985, 2d ed. November 1987*
ISBN paper 0-88132-067-6   415 pp.

15 Trade Policy for Troubled Industries
Gary Clyde Hufbauer and Howard F. Rosen/*March 1986*
ISBN paper 0-88132-020-X   111 pp.

16 The United States and Canada: The Quest for Free Trade
Paul Wonnacott, with an Appendix by John Williamson/*March 1987*
ISBN paper 0-88132-056-0   188 pp.

17 Adjusting to Success: Balance of Payments Policy
in the East Asian NICs
Bela Balassa and John Williamson/*June 1987, rev. April 1990*
ISBN paper 0-88132-101-X   160 pp.

18 Mobilizing Bank Lending to Debtor Countries
William R. Cline/*June 1987*
ISBN paper 0-88132-062-5   100 pp.

19 Auction Quotas and United States Trade Policy
C. Fred Bergsten, Kimberly Ann Elliott, Jeffrey J. Schott,
and Wendy E. Takacs/*September 1987*
ISBN paper 0-88132-050-1   254 pp.

20 Agriculture and the GATT: Rewriting the Rules
Dale E. Hathaway/*September 1987*
ISBN paper 0-88132-052-8   169 pp.

21 Anti-Protection: Changing Forces in United States Trade Politics
I. M. Destler and John S. Odell/*September 1987*
ISBN paper 0-88132-043-9   220 pp.

22 Targets and Indicators: A Blueprint for the International
Coordination of Economic Policy
John Williamson and Marcus H. Miller/*September 1987*
ISBN paper 0-88132-051-X   118 pp.

23 Capital Flight: The Problem and Policy Responses
Donald R. Lessard and John Williamson/*December 1987*
ISBN paper 0-88132-059-5   80 pp.

24 United States-Canada Free Trade: An Evaluation of the Agreement
Jeffrey J. Schott/*April 1988*
ISBN paper 0-88132-072-2   48 pp.

25 Voluntary Approaches to Debt Relief
John Williamson/*September 1988, rev. May 1989*
ISBN paper 0-88132-098-6   80 pp.

26 American Trade Adjustment: The Global Impact
William R. Cline/*March 1989*
ISBN paper 0-88132-095-1   98 pp.

27 More Free Trade Areas?
Jeffrey J. Schott/*May 1989*
ISBN paper 0-88132-085-4   88 pp.

28 The Progress of Policy Reform in Latin America
John Williamson/*January 1990*
ISBN paper 0-88132-100-1   106 pp.

29 The Global Trade Negotiations: What Can Be Achieved?
Jeffrey J. Schott/*September 1990*
ISBN paper 0-88132-137-0   72 pp.

30 Economic Policy Coordination: Requiem or Prologue?
Wendy Dobson/*April 1991*
ISBN paper 0-88132-102-8   162 pp.

31 The Economic Opening of Eastern Europe
John Williamson/*May 1991*
ISBN paper 0-88132-186-9   92 pp.

32 Eastern Europe and the Soviet Union in the World Economy
Susan M. Collins and Dani Rodrik/*May 1991*
ISBN paper 0-88132-157-5   152 pp.

33 African Economic Reform: The External Dimension
Carol Lancaster/*June 1991*
ISBN paper 0-88132-096-X   82 pp.

34 Has the Adjustment Process Worked?
Paul R. Krugman/*October 1991*
ISBN paper 0-88132-116-8   80 pp.

35 From Soviet disUnion to Eastern Economic Community?
Oleh Havrylyshyn and John Williamson/*October 1991*
ISBN paper 0-88132-192-3   84 pp.

36 Global Warming: The Economic Stakes
William R. Cline/*May 1992*
ISBN paper 0-88132-172-9   128 pp.

37 Trade and Payments After Soviet Disintegration
John Williamson/*June 1992*
ISBN paper 0-88132-173-7   96 pp.

38 Trade and Migration: NAFTA and Agriculture
Philip L. Martin/*October 1993*
ISBN paper 0-88132-201-6   160 pp.

BOOKS

IMF Conditionality
John Williamson, editor/*1983*
ISBN cloth 0-88132-006-4   695 pp.

Trade Policy in the 1980s
William R. Cline, editor/*1983*
ISBN cloth 0-88132-008-1   810 pp.
ISBN paper 0-88132-031-5   810 pp.

Subsidies in International Trade
Gary Clyde Hufbauer and Joanna Shelton Erb/*1984*
ISBN cloth 0-88132-004-8   299 pp.

International Debt: Systemic Risk and Policy Response
William R. Cline/*1984*
ISBN cloth 0-88132-015-3   336 pp.

Trade Protection in the United States: 31 Case Studies
Gary Clyde Hufbauer, Diane E. Berliner, and Kimberly Ann Elliott/*1986*
ISBN paper 0-88132-040-4   371 pp.

Toward Renewed Economic Growth in Latin America
Bela Balassa, Gerardo M. Bueno, Pedro-Pablo Kuczynski,
and Mario Henrique Simonsen/*1986*
(out of stock)   ISBN paper 0-88132-045-5   205 pp.

Capital Flight and Third World Debt
Donald R. Lessard and John Williamson, editors/*1987*
(out of print)   ISBN paper 0-88132-053-6   270 pp.

The Canada-United States Free Trade Agreement:
The Global Impact
Jeffrey J. Schott and Murray G. Smith, editors/*1988*
ISBN paper 0-88132-073-0   211 pp.

World Agricultural Trade: Building a Consensus
William M. Miner and Dale E. Hathaway, editors/*1988*
ISBN paper 0-88132-071-3   226 pp.

Japan in the World Economy
Bela Balassa and Marcus Noland/*1988*
ISBN paper 0-88132-041-2   306 pp.

America in the World Economy: A Strategy for the 1990s
C. Fred Bergsten/*1988*
ISBN cloth 0-88132-089-7   235 pp.
ISBN paper 0-88132-082-X   235 pp.

Managing the Dollar: From the Plaza to the Louvre
Yoichi Funabashi/*1988, 2d ed. 1989*
ISBN paper 0-88132-097-8   307 pp.

United States External Adjustment and the World Economy
William R. Cline/*May 1989*
ISBN paper 0-88132-048-X   392 pp.

Free Trade Areas and U.S. Trade Policy
Jeffrey J. Schott, editor/*May 1989*
ISBN paper 0-88132-094-3   400 pp.

Dollar Politics: Exchange Rate Policymaking in the United States
I. M. Destler and C. Randall Henning/*September 1989*
ISBN paper 0-88132-079-X   192 pp.

Latin American Adjustment: How Much Has Happened?
John Williamson, editor/*April 1990*
ISBN paper 0-88132-125-7   480 pp.

The Future of World Trade in Textiles and Apparel
William R. Cline/*1987, 2d ed. June 1990*
ISBN paper 0-88132-110-9   344 pp.

Completing the Uruguay Round: A Results-Oriented Approach
to the GATT Trade Negotiations
Jeffrey J. Schott, editor/*September 1990*
ISBN paper 0-88132-130-3   256 pp.

Economic Sanctions Reconsidered (in two volumes)
  Economic Sanctions Reconsidered: Supplemental Case Histories
  Gary Clyde Hufbauer, Jeffrey J. Schott, and Kimberly Ann Elliott/1985, 2d ed.
    December 1990
                            ISBN cloth 0-88132-115-X   928 pp.
                            ISBN paper 0-88132-105-2   928 pp.

  Economic Sanctions Reconsidered: History and Current Policy
  Gary Clyde Hufbauer, Jeffrey J. Schott, and Kimberly Ann Elliott/December 1990
                            ISBN cloth 0-88132-136-2   288 pp.
                            ISBN paper 0-88132-140-0   288 pp.

Pacific Basin Developing Countries: Prospects for the Future
Marcus Noland/January 1991
                            ISBN cloth 0-88132-141-9   250 pp.
                            ISBN paper 0-88132-081-1   250 pp.

Currency Convertibility in Eastern Europe
John Williamson, editor/October 1991
                            ISBN cloth 0-88132-144-3   396 pp.
                            ISBN paper 0-88132-128-1   396 pp.

Foreign Direct Investment in the United States
Edward M. Graham and Paul R. Krugman/1989, 2d ed. October 1991
                            ISBN paper 0-88132-139-7   200 pp.

International Adjustment and Financing: The Lessons of 1985-1991
C. Fred Bergsten, editor/January 1992
                            ISBN paper 0-88132-112-5   336 pp.

North American Free Trade: Issues and Recommendations
Gary Clyde Hufbauer and Jeffrey J. Schott/April 1992
                            ISBN cloth 0-88132-145-1   392 pp.
                            ISBN paper 0-88132-120-6   392 pp.

American Trade Politics
I. M. Destler/1986, 2d ed. June 1992
                            ISBN cloth 0-88132-164-8   400 pp.
                            ISBN paper 0-88132-188-5   400 pp.

Narrowing the U.S. Current Account Deficit
Allen J. Lenz/June 1992
                            ISBN cloth 0-88132-148-6   640 pp.
                            ISBN paper 0-88132-103-6   640 pp.

The Economics of Global Warming
William R. Cline/June 1992
                            ISBN cloth 0-88132-150-8   416 pp.
                            ISBN paper 0-88132-132-X   416 pp.

U.S. Taxation of International Income: Blueprint for Reform
Gary Clyde Hufbauer, assisted by Joanna M. van Rooij/October 1992
                            ISBN cloth 0-88132-178-8   304 pp.
                            ISBN paper 0-88132-134-6   304 pp.

Who's Bashing Whom? Trade Conflict in High-Technology Industries
Laura D'Andrea Tyson/November 1992
                            ISBN cloth 0-88132-151-6   352 pp.
                            ISBN paper 0-88132-106-0   352 pp.

Korea in the World Economy
Il SaKong/*January 1993*
ISBN cloth 0-88132-184-2	328 pp.
ISBN paper 0-88132-106-0	328 pp.

Pacific Dynamism and the International Economic System
C. Fred Bergsten and Marcus Noland, editors/*May 1993*
ISBN paper 0-88132-196-6   424 pp.

Economic Consequences of Soviet Disintegration
John Williamson, editor/*May 1993*
ISBN paper 0-88132-190-7   664 pp.

Reconcilable Differences? United States-Japan Economic Conflict
C. Fred Bergsten and Marcus Noland/*June 1993*
ISBN paper 0-88132-129-X   296 pp.

Does Foreign Exchange Intervention Work?
Kathryn M. Dominguez and Jeffrey A. Frankel/*September 1993*
ISBN paper 0-88132-104-4   192 pp.

Sizing Up U.S. Export Disincentives
J. David Richardson/*September 1993*
ISBN paper 0-88132-107-9   192 pp.

NAFTA: An Assessment
Gary Clyde Hufbauer and Jeffrey J. Schott/*rev. ed. October 1993*
ISBN paper 0-88132-199-0   216 pp.

Adjusting to Volatile Energy Prices
Philip K. Verleger, Jr./*November 1993*
ISBN paper 0-88132-069-2   288 pp.

The Political Economy of Policy Reform
John Williamson, editor/*January 1994*
ISBN paper 0-88132-195-8   624 pp.

Measuring the Costs of Protection in the United States
Gary Clyde Hufbauer and Kimberly Ann Elliott/*January 1994*
ISBN paper 0-88132-108-7   144 pp.

The Dynamics of Korean Economic Development
Cho Soon/*March 1994*
ISBN paper 0-88132-162-1   272 pp.

Reviving the European Union
C. Randall Henning, Eduard Hochreiter and Gary Clyde Hufbauer, editors/*April 1994*
ISBN paper 0-88132-208-3   192 pp.

China in the World Economy
Nicholas R. Lardy/*April 1994*
ISBN paper 0-88132-200-8   176 pp.

Greening the GATT: Trade, Environment, and the Future
Daniel C. Esty/ *July 1994*
ISBN paper 0-88132-205-9   344 pp.

Western Hemisphere Economic Integration
Gary Clyde Hufbauer and Jeffrey J. Schott/*July 1994*
ISBN paper 0-88132-159-1   304 pp.

Currencies and Politics in the United States, Germany, and Japan
C. Randall Henning/*September 1994*
ISBN paper 0-88132-127-3   432 pp.

Estimating Equilibrium Exchange Rates
John Williamson, editor/*September 1994*
        ISBN paper 0-88132-076-5   320 pp.

Managing the World Economy: Fifty Years After Bretton Woods
Peter B. Kenen, editor/*September 1994*
        ISBN paper 0-88132-212-1   448 pp.

Reciprocity and Retaliation in U.S. Trade Policy
Thomas O. Bayard and Kimberly Ann Elliott/*September 1994*
        ISBN paper 0-88132-084-6   528 pp.

The Uruguay Round: An Assessment
Jeffrey J. Schott, assisted by Johanna W. Buurman/*November 1994*
        ISBN paper 0-88132-206-7   240 pp.

Measuring the Costs of Protection in Japan
Yoko Sazanami, Shujiro Urata, and Hiroki Kawai/*January 1995*
        ISBN paper 0-88132-211-3   96 pp.

Foreign Direct Investment in the United States, Third Edition
Edward M. Graham and Paul R. Krugman/*January 1995*
        ISBN paper 0-88132-204-0   232 pp.

The Political Economy of Korea-United States Cooperation
C. Fred Bergsten and Il SaKong, editors/*February 1995*
        ISBN paper 0-88132-213-X   128 pp.

International Debt Reexamined
William R. Cline/*February 1995*
        ISBN paper 0-88132-083-8   560 pp.

SPECIAL REPORTS

1 Promoting World Recovery: A Statement on Global Economic Strategy
   by Twenty-six Economists from Fourteen Countries/*December 1982*
   (out of print)   ISBN paper 0-88132-013-7   45 pp.
2 Prospects for Adjustment in Argentina, Brazil, and Mexico:
   Responding to the Debt Crisis
   John Williamson, editor/*June 1983*
   (out of print)   ISBN paper 0-88132-016-1   71 pp.
3 Inflation and Indexation: Argentina, Brazil, and Israel
   John Williamson, editor/*March 1985*
        ISBN paper 0-88132-037-4   191 pp.
4 Global Economic Imbalances
   C. Fred Bergsten, editor/*March 1986*
               ISBN cloth 0-88132-038-2   126 pp.
               ISBN paper 0-88132-042-0   126 pp.
5 African Debt and Financing
   Carol Lancaster and John Williamson, editors/*May 1986*
   (out of print)   ISBN paper 0-88132-044-7   229 pp.
6 Resolving the Global Economic Crisis: After Wall Street
   Thirty-three Economists from Thirteen Countries/*December 1987*
        ISBN paper 0-88132-070-6   30 pp.
7 World Economic Problems
   Kimberly Ann Elliott and John Williamson, editors/*April 1988*
        ISBN paper 0-88132-055-2   298 pp.
   Reforming World Agricultural Trade
   Twenty-nine Professionals from Seventeen Countries/*1988*
        ISBN paper 0-88132-088-9   42 pp.

8   Economic Relations Between the United States and Korea:
    Conflict or Cooperation?
    Thomas O. Bayard and Soo-Gil Young, editors/*January 1989*
                    ISBN paper 0-88132-068-4   192 pp.

FORTHCOMING

The Globalization of Industry and National Governments
C. Fred Bergsten and Edward M. Graham

Trade, Jobs, and Income Distribution
William R. Cline

American Trade Politics, Third Edition
I. M. Destler

Environment in the New World Order
Daniel C. Esty

Regionalism and Globalism in the World Economic System
Jeffrey A. Frankel

Overseeing Global Capital Markets
Morris Goldstein and Peter Garber

Global Competition Policy
Edward M. Graham and J. David Richardson

Toward a Pacific Economic Community?
Gary Clyde Hufbauer and Jeffrey J. Schott

The Economics of Korean Unification
Marcus Noland

The Case for Trade: A Modern Reconsideration
J. David Richardson

The Future of the World Trading System
John Whalley, in collaboration with Colleen Hamilton

For orders outside the US and Canada please contact:
    Longman Group UK Ltd.
    PO Box 88
    Fourth Avenue
    Harlow, Essex CM 19 5SR
    UK

    Telephone Orders: 0279 623923
    Fax: 0279 453450
    Telex: 81259

Canadian customers can order from the Institute or from either:
    RENOUF BOOKSTORE   LA LIBERTÉ
    1294 Algoma Road   3020 chemin Sainte-Foy
    Ottawa, Ontario K1B 3W8   Quebec G1X 3V6
    Telephone: (613) 741-4333   Telephone: (418) 658-3763
    Fax: (613) 741-5439   Fax: (800) 567-5449